Longest's Health Policymaking in the United States

SEVENTH EDITION

Longest's Health Policymaking in the United States

Michael R. Meacham

HAP

AUPHA

Health Administration Press, Chicago, Illinois

Association of University Programs in Health Administration, Washington, DC

Your board, staff, or clients may also benefit from this book's insight. For information on quantity discounts, contact the Health Administration Press Marketing Manager at (312) 424-9450.

25 24 23 22 21 5 4 3 2 1

Library of Congress Cataloging-in-Publication Data

Names: Meacham, Michael R., author. | Longest, Beaufort B., Jr. Health policymaking in the United States. 2016. | Association of University Programs in Health Administration, issuing body.
Title: Longest's health policymaking in the United States / Michael R. Meacham.
Other titles: Health policymaking in the United States
Description: Seventh edition. | Chicago, Illinois : Health Administration Press ; Washington, DC : Association of University Programs in Health Administration, [2021] | Preceded by Health policymaking in the United States / Beaufort B. Longest, Jr. Sixth edition. 2016. | Includes bibliographical references and index. | Summary: "This classic textbook links policy concepts to practical applications and real healthcare outcomes. It covers formulation, implementation, and modification of health policymaking at both the federal and state levels, while giving readers insight into real-life political results and details of on-the-ground policy decisions"— Provided by publisher.
Identifiers: LCCN 2020031577 (print) | LCCN 2020031578 (ebook) | ISBN 9781640552111 (hardcover ; alk. paper) | ISBN 9781640552135 (epub) | ISBN 9781640552142 (mobi)
Subjects: MESH: Health Policy | Health Planning—legislation & jurisprudence | Policy Making | United States
Classification: LCC RA445 (print) | LCC RA445 (ebook) | NLM WA 540 AA1 | DDC 362.10973—dc23
LC record available at https://lccn.loc.gov/2020031577
LC ebook record available at https://lccn.loc.gov/2020031578

The paper used in this publication meets the minimum requirements of American National Standard for Information Sciences—Permanence of Paper for Printed Library Materials, ANSI Z39.48-1984. ♾ ™

Acquisitions editor: Janet Davis; Manuscript editors: Theresa Rothschadl and Patricia Boyd; Project manager: Andrew Baumann; Cover designer: James Slate; Layout: Integra

Found an error or a typo? We want to know! Please e-mail it to hapbooks@ache.org, mentioning the book's title and putting "Book Error" in the subject line.

For photocopying and copyright information, please contact Copyright Clearance Center at www.copyright.com or at (978) 750-8400.

Health Administration Press
A division of the Foundation of the American College of Healthcare Executives
300 S. Riverside Plaza, Suite 1900
Chicago, IL 60606-6698
(312) 424-2800

Association of University Programs in Health Administration
1730 M Street, NW
Suite 407
Washington, DC 20036
(202) 763-7283

For "Dean Rhatigan" (Dr. James J. Rhatigan)

Lifelong friend and mentor who has shined the light of service to the common good throughout my life's journey and by whose example I offer to light the path for students in the abiding hope that they, too, will pass the torch

BRIEF CONTENTS

Appendixes

Appendixes

DETAILED CONTENTS

ACRONYMS AND ABBREVIATIONS

ACA	Affordable Care Act
ACO	accountable care organization
ACP	American College of Physicians
AHA	American Hospital Association
AHRQ	Agency for Healthcare Research and Quality
AIDS	acquired immunodeficiency syndrome
AMA	American Medical Association
AMDUCA	Animal Medicinal Drug Use Clarification Act
ANPRM	advance notice of proposed rulemaking
CBO	Congressional Budget Office
CDC	Centers for Disease Control and Prevention
CFR	Code of Federal Regulations
CHIP	Children's Health Insurance Program
CMS	Centers for Medicare & Medicaid Services
COGR	Council on Governmental Relations
CON	certificate of need
COPD	chronic obstructive pulmonary disease
CR	continuing resolution
CRS	Congressional Research Service
DME	durable medical equipment
DOJ	Department of Justice
EMTALA	Emergency Medical Treatment and Active Labor Act
EPA	Environmental Protection Agency
ERISA	Employee Retirement Income Security Act
ESRD	end-stage renal disease
FACA	Federal Advisory Committee Act
FCLAA	Federal Cigarette Labeling and Advertising Act
FDA	Food and Drug Administration
FDAMA	Food and Drug Administration Modernization Act
FDCA	Food, Drug, and Cosmetic Act

FEC	Federal Election Commission
FFS	fee-for-service
FPL	federal poverty level
FR	Federal Register
FY	fiscal year
GAO	Government Accountability Office
GDP	gross domestic product
HAP	Hospital and Healthsystem Association of Pennsylvania
HAPAC	Hospital and Healthsystem Association of Pennsylvania Political Action Committee
HCBS	home-care-based and community-based services
HELP	Health, Education, Labor and Pensions
HHS	Department of Health and Human Services
HIPAA	Health Insurance Portability and Accountability Act
HITECH	Health Information Technology for Economic and Clinical Health
HIV	human immunodeficiency virus
IMPACT	Improving Medicare Post-Acute Care Transformation Act
IOM	Institute of Medicine
IPAB	Independent Payment Advisory Board
IPPS	inpatient prospective payment system
IRS	Internal Revenue Service
KHN	Kaiser Health News
LTCH	long-term care hospitals
M&A	mergers, consolidations, acquisitions, and affiliations
MA	Medicare Advantage
MBHC	managed behavioral health care
MCO	managed care organization
MDUFMA	Medical Device User Fee and Modernization Act
MedPAC	Medicare Payment Advisory Commission
MHPA	Mental Health Parity Act
MHPAEA	Mental Health Parity and Addiction Equity Act
MMA	Medicare Modernization Act
MQSA	Mammography Quality Standards Act

NAACP	National Association for the Advancement of Colored People
NCSL	National Conference on State Legislatures
NFIB	National Federation of Independent Business
NHE	National Health Expenditures
NHSC	National Health Service Corps
NIH	National Institutes of Health
NOW	National Organization for Women
OAA	Older Americans Act
OECD	Organisation for Economic Co-operation and Development
OHRP	Office of Human Research Protections
OIG	Office of the Inspector General
OIRA	Office of Information and Regulatory Affairs
OMB	Office of Management and Budget
ONC	Office of National Coordinator
OSHA	Occupational Safety and Health Administration
PAMA	Protecting Access to Medicare Act
PCORI	Patient-Centered Outcomes Research Institute
PDUFA	Prescription Drug User Fee Act
PhRMA	Pharmaceutical Research and Manufacturers of America
PMTA	Premarket Tobacco Applications
PPRC	Physician Payment Review Commission
ProPAC	Prospective Payment Assessment Commission
R&D	research and development
RWJF	Robert Wood Johnson Foundation
SCHIP	State Children's Health Insurance Program
SRP	shared responsibility payment
SSA	Social Security Act
TCA	Tobacco Control Act
THC	tetrahydrocannabinol
WHO	World Health Organization

PREFACE

Health is an integral part of our lives, on a personal level especially, but also at the meta level. Many of us are concerned with the state of our personal health—weight, habits, chronic conditions, exposure to infectious disease, and the like. Health at the meta level, however, is a different matter. This concept aggregates personal health to the quantity of population health and the health status of communities or their subsets.

The beginning of this broader conversation invites a wide-ranging consideration of the factors that have an impact on health at the population level. Certainly, such health determinants as tobacco use, diet, and exercise have the greatest impact on an individual's health. Health policy, however, can alter those determinants and, sometimes, the behavior that affects an individual's health as well as the health status of larger populations. Health policy is composed of authoritative decisions made throughout all three branches of the federal government as well as the branches of state and local governments.

And therein, in part, is the reason to study health policy. If we see that our healthcare system is inefficient in delivering high-quality care, if we see that our healthcare system is inequitable because it perpetuates disparities in health among people living in the United States, and if we see that our healthcare system is ineffective because too many people live with chronic diseases that often become acute conditions, what are we to do? What will *you* do as a healthcare administrator? Because of your profession, do you have an obligation to the *common good* or to the *community* in which you live? If the answer to that ethical question is yes, then your understanding of health policy becomes your tool to serve others—to serve something beyond your own career and self-interest.

This book is intended to help the reader understand the *process* of health policy. Health policy is a key external factor that can threaten any healthcare organization. Or it can be an opportunity for a healthcare organization to extend its breadth and depth of care into the larger community. In short, it can limit our work or it can expand our reach. Understanding how policy decisions are made will provide background for healthcare leaders to turn threat into opportunity, to turn limits into expansions.

In summary, this book is intended to help emerging healthcare leaders develop competency in the domain of health policy. The well-rounded healthcare leader should be willing and able to become an effective advocate.

Understanding the process is a baseline requirement of that competency. In other words, the book seeks to help the reader understand what is important about the process of policymaking without editorializing on any particular policy position. The real-world examples included on these pages demonstrate the health policy process in both political and jurisprudential terms.

This seventh edition continues to rely on the policy process model originally developed by Professor Beaufort Longest in the first edition. Professor Longest developed the model for his students some 30 years ago and refined it multiple times through six editions of the book. This edition builds on Professor Longest's well-considered and time-honored theoretical foundations. It also, however, incorporates a few changes. While remaining true to Professor Longest's concepts, I have expanded the practical applications of the theory, including real-world examples of the major concepts, and have taken a slightly different approach to the structure presenting those concepts.

First, the book is divided into four parts to facilitate the focus on core aspects of the policy process model. Second, after each part's introduction, a policy snapshot captures the key elements addressed in that part of the book. Third, appendixes have been placed at the end of each part to help reinforce the model's framework with examples, many of them documents produced by government agencies or by parties interested in governmental policy, showing how that part's principles are being addressed. Finally, a new chapter, on federalism, has been added, delineating the dynamic nature of the relationship between federal and state governments and how that relationship affects health policy, health determinants, and, ultimately, our health.

Part 1, "Health and Its Policymaking Context" (chapters 1, 2, and 3), explores the meaning of health and health status. Material here compares the US health system with the rest of the industrialized world to provide a context for the cost and quality of the US healthcare system. This part also introduces the reader to the concept of federalism, which forms the basis of the frequently used federal and state "partnerships" that determine multiple aspects of health policy.

Part 2, "Legislative Policymaking" (chapters 4, 5, and 6), explores the introductory elements of the model—the beginnings of how health policy is made—with a focus on the legislative process. Here we begin to see the influence of politics and the political process on health policy. Indeed, the snapshot introducing part 2 speaks to the triumph of politics in one dramatic gambit resulting in a fundamental change in the US healthcare system: the creation of Medicare and Medicaid.

Part 3, "Policy Implementation and Judicial Review" (chapters 7 and 8), goes into further detail about how policy is made, as this part includes a discussion on the administrative implementation of legislative enactments. Policy is not fully a policy until it is implemented. While part 2 delves into the legislative process of policy pronouncements, part 3 is where the rubber hits the road, examining how those pronouncements are put into operation. Moreover, part 3 further elaborates on how American courts affect health policy.

Part 4, "Charting the Future" (chapters 9 and 10), wraps up all the other material pertaining to policy modification and discusses the competency of a healthcare executive as an advocate. This last part of the book takes an approach different from that of the first three parts, which focus on policymaking and emphasize the legislative process, administrative implementations, and court decisions. Unlike the other three policy snapshots, this part's snapshot does not address legislative actions or Supreme Court decisions. Rather, it invites the readers to consider their future role as advocates in the policymaking arena and encourages them to consider the right-versus-commodity question.

Throughout the book, the appendixes provide examples of legislation, executive orders, administrative rules, and regulations, along with congressional or administrative agency testimony. Although the appendixes are located in their respective parts of the book, readers are encouraged to jump between parts to find appendixes that may well reflect an issue in a different part of the book. For example, appendixes 1.1, 1.2, and 1.3 no doubt have application throughout the book but are placed with part 1 because they specifically relate to issues in the first three chapters.

As you study the health policymaking process and, indeed, as you move throughout your career, you will be confronted with the foundational question of whether healthcare is a fundamental right for all or a commodity available to those who can afford it. This is a question we have not fully answered as a society. History demonstrates that both sides of the coin seem to wax and wane over time. You will have the opportunity to consider this question in detail in the policy snapshot in part 4. You will, however, confront this question in a number of other ways throughout your career. The question as it is presented in this book invites you to consider the obligation a healthcare administrator has to the community at large. What is the role of the common good in your consideration of advocacy?

What are your personal and professional obligations to the common good as a part of your role as a healthcare professional and advocate?

Instructor Resources

This book's Instructor Resources include a test bank, presentation PowerPoint slides, and answer guides to the in-book discussion questions.

For the most up-to-date information about this book and its Instructor Resources, go to ache.org/HAP and search for the book's order code, 2429I.

This book's Instructor Resources are available to instructors who adopt this book for use in their course. For access information, please e-mail hapbooks@ache.org.

ACKNOWLEDGMENTS

Writing a textbook is not a solitary endeavor. Writing the seventh edition of a textbook that has enjoyed the success of six prior editions is even less so. In this case, I am tacitly standing on the shoulders of the author of the first six editions, Professor Beaufort Longest. It is an honor to have this opportunity, and I hope my contribution is worthy of this volume's history. The contribution of *Health Policymaking in the United States* over the decades of six editions is significant and substantial. This book has been utilized extensively across the span of time and throughout the country to help future healthcare leaders appreciate the health policymaking process. In those prior editions, Dr. Longest continued to develop and improve a model of the process and made the model more holistic. His theoretical foundation of the policymaking process has been validated many times over. I am deeply grateful to Professor Longest for his essential work in this field and am humbled by the responsibility to build on his work.

I am likewise grateful to my own personal "internal editor," my wife, Dr. Vicky L. Triponey. Every word of this volume has been vetted by this remarkable person before it went to the publisher. Her contribution to improving my work—not to mention my life—is immeasurable. I am grateful to her for this and for keeping me grounded—a challenging task at the least.

This work would also not be possible without the very capable help and leadership of Janet Davis, acquisitions manager at Health Administration Press. Janet's gentle nudges to move forward and her friendship have been indispensable, and I appreciate her excellent work and value her commitment to improving health services administration by providing support for those who teach it. I am especially grateful for the confidence she placed in me to add value and currency to the book.

I was very fortunate to have had two excellent editors for this book. Theresa Rothschadl has been an outstanding colleague. Her attention to consistency, style, and detail have been remarkable. She has made the hard work of editing easier through her excellent questions and gentle humor. Patricia Boyd of Steel Pencil Editorial played a critically important role in getting this project to the finish line. Her eye for detail is unparalleled, as is her exquisite sense of organization. Both Theresa and Patricia raised questions that were sometimes uncomfortable but always enlightening and thought-provoking. This volume is much better for both their efforts.

There are, of course, so many others who have contributed to my life experiences that ultimately prepared me for this capstone assignment. I learned many life lessons from colleagues during my service in the Kansas House of Representatives, which began on my 24th birthday. Those eight years provided me invaluable policymaking experiences and taught me that bringing possible solutions to policy challenges requires an intricate balance of logic, an understanding of human emotion, attention to detail, and appreciation for where one's efforts fit in the big picture of all things political. The men and women leading Community Care of Kansas, to which I served as legal counsel and administrator in the early 1990s, gave me a wonderful introduction to the world of healthcare, Medicaid, and managed care. Regrettably, the two-year experience resulted in a rejected proposal, but this effort, too, was a marvelous teacher about administrative policy decision-making and what influences it. The experience also inspired me to return to academia to earn my MPH. Subsequently, my time as director of Health System Development at the Office of Healthcare Access in Connecticut provided me with perspective as an implementer of legislative policy and taught me about the interaction between regulator and the regulated. I learned how to connect the dots between legislative decisions, administrative implementation, and the impact of those functions on a multiplicity of external stakeholders. It was also during this time that I first taught a course in health policy, using the second edition of this book, as an adjunct professor at the University of Connecticut. When I left state government to join Eastern Connecticut Health Network, I was privileged to serve on the executive team, discovering firsthand the challenges of leading an integrated health service organization and the impact of policy decisions on health services providers. The feeling of drinking from a firehose is an acquired taste, one I enjoyed immensely as a shared experience with clinicians and administrators alike. I gleaned important and priceless lessons from all of them.

My migration to the faculty at Pennsylvania State University and the Medical University of South Carolina taught me how to contextualize and share these accumulated experiences with future healthcare leaders without devolving into the proverbial teller of war stories. As a colleague once said, "You've done what we teach." And teaching it has made me a better student of health services delivery and the health policies that govern those services. For the past 17 years, students have been at the center of my thinking, always challenging me to learn more. Their questions, their ideas, and their careers have been sources of growth and inspiration. Likewise, my colleagues in the profession, particularly at the Association of University Programs in Health Administration (AUPHA), have also been a source of strength and countless innovative ideas about teaching. The conviviality I have enjoyed through them over the years has given me great comfort as, together, we confront ideas and concepts that are sometimes uncomfortable.

In short, the countless number of people whose lives have helped shape me through these experiences share in the credit for the production of this volume. I am grateful to each and every one of them. For me, this work is a culmination of my ongoing commitment to make a positive contribution for the benefit of the greater good. I have been fortunate enough to work in a variety of capacities where I had the opportunity to serve others: constituents, Medicaid beneficiaries, the general public, patients, students, and colleagues. In a world increasingly dominated by "me" in place of "we," it is deeply gratifying to contribute to the literature that strives to unite us—in academia and the healthcare profession—to improve the US healthcare delivery system for the benefit of us all. Over the years, the many people who believed in me, encouraged me, and supported me in my efforts to grow have strengthened my commitment to improve the lives of others through my ongoing work and public service. To the many master teachers of purposeful and priceless lessons throughout my life's journey, I say thank you.

PART

1

HEALTH AND ITS POLICYMAKING CONTEXT

Health. What does it mean? If a person feels good, are they enjoying good health? If they do not feel well, does that necessarily mean they are not healthy? In looking at populations, how does one define *health*? There are many ways to measure health status, but metrics without a meaningful application of them tell us little.

Part 1 does discuss metrics, however, comparing where the United States stands on the international stage. Do the outcomes of our healthcare system justify our costs relative to other developed countries? What drives the idea of being healthy, and how are those drivers affected by health policy?

Likewise, from where is health policy derived? Where does it begin? Why does a policymaker choose to focus on a health policy issue? What end does a policy seek to obtain?

Chapters 1 and 2 introduce the definition of *health* and the contexts—there are several—in which health policy is made. Bodies as diverse as US Congress and local health departments make policy. This part's policy snapshot, "The Affordable Care Act: A Cauldron of Controversy," demonstrates that the judicial branch also makes health policy. We will examine the background against which the policy process (detailed in the rest of the text) takes place, whether those processes be legislative, executive, or judicial.

Chapter 3 defines the concept of federalism and how it affects health policy. Recognizing that states and the federal government have dual responsibilities is key to understanding the past, present, and future of health policy. Taken together, the chapters in part 1 provide a foundation for discussing the legislative policy process in part 2.

THE AFFORDABLE CARE ACT: A CAULDRON OF CONTROVERSY

To say that passage of the Patient Protection and Affordable Care Act (P.L. 111-148), hereafter ACA, was acrimonious and highly partisan would be an understatement. In the eyes of the proponents, Republicans were seen as obstructionist. Opponents saw Democrats—who at the time held the majority in both houses and the White House—as overstepping and high-handed in the way they managed the legislation. Whether one believes one side or the other is immaterial for this discussion. It was a bitter, hard-fought battle that left substantial political ill will in its wake. Ultimately, the bill passed on the narrowest of party line votes: 219 to 212 (4 not voting) in the House and 60 to 39 (1 not voting) in the Senate, with the Democrat-controlled Senate using a seldom-employed procedural device to thwart a Republican filibuster. Despite the rancor, or perhaps because of it, the episode provides some interesting lessons about the policymaking process.

The bill was complicated; more than 900 pages long, it contained a multitude of provisions. Soon after its passage, a number of parties sued, claiming that the sweeping reform law was unconstitutional in several respects. *National Federation of Independent Business (NFIB) v. Sebelius*, 132 S. Ct. 2566, 567 US 519 (2012), was a landmark US Supreme Court decision that upheld Congress's power to enact most provisions of the ACA.

This policy snapshot will focus on only two issues decided by the court to illustrate the health policy interplay between the legislative branch, the executive branch, and the judicial branch as well as the relationships of the states to the federal government: (1) the individual mandate and (2) the expansion of Medicaid.

Parties to the Case and Its Origins

The hostility of the political process carried forward to the legal forum. The litigation fairly reflects the partisan and interest group divide that had dominated the political debate. Florida, joined by 12 other states (all led by Republican governors or Republican attorneys general), filed a complaint (the formal document to begin a lawsuit) in the US District Court for the Northern District of Florida the day the ACA was signed into law. Subsequently, 13 additional states (also represented by Republican governors or attorneys general, with two exceptions noted below), the NFIB, and several individuals joined in the action as plaintiffs. The district court ruled the individual mandate was unconstitutional and, therefore, struck down the entire act as unconstitutional. The defendant (referred to as *respondent* in the appeals process) was Kathleen Sebelius, the secretary of the Department of Health and Human Services (HHS), being sued in her official capacity. (It is common for cabinet secretaries to be defendants in litigation brought against the government.) After the district court rendered its decision, the federal government appealed to the 11th Circuit Court of Appeals. That court was divided, 2 to 1, in ruling that the individual mandate was unconstitutional but also held that the remainder of the ACA was "severable," meaning the rest of the act would survive as the law of the land. The Supreme Court agreed to hear the case on appeal from the 11th Circuit.

Multiple special interest groups on both sides filed amicus curiae ("friends of the court") briefs. (*Brief* is the term for the document making a legal argument to a court.) These groups included a diversity of organizations, including the American Public Health Association and the American Academy of Actuaries. Of course, the 26 states bringing the suit (referred to as *petitioners* in the appeals process) filed briefs attacking the constitutionality of the ACA, while 13 other states filed briefs in support of the ACA. (Underscoring the political controversy surrounding the issue, the states of Iowa and Washington filed briefs on both sides. In those two states, the respective attorneys general and governors, of opposite political parties, disagreed on the constitutionality of the ACA, such disagreement squarely reflecting the partisan divide regarding the act.)

Without delving too deeply into the processes of the Supreme Court, it is important to note there were four separate opinions composed by several of the justices. In some instances, a justice would join in *part* of a decision while dissenting from the rest. In order to cut through the thicket of those multiple decisions and dissents, suffice it to say there were majorities upholding the individual mandate and striking down the Medicaid expansion.

The Individual Mandate

The ACA requires every adult in the United States between the ages of 18 and 64 to obtain health insurance. Some groups were exempted from this requirement: undocumented immigrants, elderly, and those people who already had insurance. A few other exemptions for much smaller populations that need not be identified here were also included.

The requirement to obtain insurance could be satisfied in one of four ways: (1) employer-sponsored insurance, (2) individual insurance purchased through health exchanges created by the act, (3) an individual policy purchased on the open market, or (4) being enrolled in public insurance programs such as Medicare and Medicaid. An individual failing to obtain health insurance in compliance with the minimum benefit structure set forth in the act would be required to make a "shared responsibility payment" (SRP) to the federal government. Revenue from those payments was to be used in furtherance of the ACA's goals—expanding healthcare coverage.

The amount payable as an SRP was established as a percentage of the household income, subject to a flat dollar amount floor and a cap related to the insurance market. The SRP would be "assessed and collected by the IRS [Internal Revenue Service] and reported on federal income tax returns. The penalty is the greater of $95 or 1% of income in 2014, $325 or 2% of income in 2015, and $695 or 2.5% of income in 2016, up to a maximum amount equal to the national average premium for bronze level health plans in the exchanges for the respective year" (Musumeci 2012). (The coverage levels of health insurance policies sold through the exchanges established by the ACA are categorized by names of precious metals. From highest to lowest, those are platinum, gold, silver, and bronze.)

Arguments

The proponents of the act (respondents) relied on the power of the Congress to regulate interstate commerce as provided in Article I, Section 8, Clause 3 of the US Constitution to justify the imposition of the individual mandate. They argued that Congress had a right under what is called the *Commerce Clause* of the Constitution, which regulates activity in interstate commerce, to impose an individual mandate because the absence of insurance negatively affected interstate commerce. They further argued that the geographic diversity among purchasers and insurance companies in the transaction to purchase insurance constituted "interstate commerce" within the meaning of the Constitution. Simply stated, the proponents advanced the proposition that the failure of so many Americans to have insurance affected the economy across state lines, that this was "interstate commerce" as contemplated in the Constitution, and that, therefore, the individual mandate was constitutional.

Those seeking to overturn the ACA (petitioners) argued that Congress had no right to compel an individual to undertake a specific act, such as to obtain insurance, and that the ACA represented federal overreach encroaching on individuals' rights—each person should be able to decide for themselves if they needed to buy health insurance. They argued that the Commerce Clause was not applicable in this instance, because the concept existed to regulate activity. Here, opponents said, there was no activity but for the government compelling individuals to purchase insurance.

Decision and Rationale

The Court found that Congress did indeed have the right to regulate commerce; however, the ACA was *not* such a permissible regulation under the Commerce Clause. Chief Justice Roberts, writing for a majority of the Court, said:

> The power to regulate commerce presupposes the existence of commercial activity to be regulated. If the power to "regulate" something included the power to create it, many of the provisions in the Constitution would be superfluous. . . .
>
> Our precedent also reflects this understanding. As expansive as our cases construing the scope of the commerce power have been, they all have one thing in common: They uniformly describe the power as reaching "activity." . . .
>
> The individual mandate, however, does not regulate existing commercial activity. It instead compels individuals to become active in commerce by purchasing a product, on the ground that their failure to do so affects interstate commerce. Construing the Commerce Clause to permit Congress to regulate individuals precisely because they are doing nothing would open a new and potentially vast domain to congressional authority. (US Supreme Court 2012)

Having found the individual mandate impermissible under the Commerce Clause, the Court instead turned its attention to the SRP component of the individual mandate. The Court said even though Congress did not label the payment a "tax," it had the indicators of a tax. The SRP was to be collected by the IRS. Further, the payment was to be reported on an individual's federal tax returns; people whose incomes are so low that they are not required to file a tax return are exempt from the SRP; and the scheme structuring the payment is predicated on an individual's income, the number of dependents they have, and their tax filing status. In addition, the SRP produces revenue, the essential feature of any tax. Ergo, said the Court, the SRP is a tax. Further, Congress has broad power to levy taxes, even taxing a failure to act. It was on this basis that the Court found the individual mandate a permissible exercise of Congress's power—because the SRP is a "tax" within the penumbra of congressional power, the individual mandate is, indeed, constitutionally permissible.

Expansion of Medicaid

Federal law at the time of the ACA required Medicaid to provide insurance coverage for pregnant women and children younger than 6 years and whose household income was less than 133 percent of the federal poverty level (FPL), children aged 6 to 18 years whose household income was less than 100 percent of FPL, parents and caregivers otherwise eligible for the former Aid for Families with Dependent Children program, and elderly and disabled individuals eligible for Supplemental Security Income. At the time, federal law excluded from Medicaid nondisabled, nonelderly adults without dependent children. States were permitted to seek waivers to extend coverage if the states so chose. Likewise, states were permitted to fund (and receive federal matching funds for) benefit coverage to those whose incomes exceeded federal minimums, but states could not reduce the scope of coverage established by federal law. In other words, states could increase the scope of Medicaid benefits, could increase provider payments, and could expand the number of covered individuals, but no state could reduce the program to below federally prescribed minimums. It is important to note that Medicaid is a voluntary program for the states. If states chose to participate, they would be required to meet the minimum federal standards to receive federal matching funds. At the time of the ACA, all states participated in Medicaid. As will be discussed further in chapter 3, using federal funds as an inducement for states to engage in certain policies has long been recognized as constitutionally permissible.

The terms of the ACA changed the structure of Medicaid dramatically. It required that Medicaid provide coverage for *everyone* whose income was less than 133 percent of FPL. The inducements were both a carrot and a stick—the carrot was that the federal government would pay 100 percent of the cost of expansion from 2014 to 2016, at which time there would be a gradual reduction to 90 percent of the cost by 2020. Federal support would remain at 90 percent of cost thenceforth. The stick was that the ACA authorized the secretary of HHS to withhold *all* federal Medicaid funding for states that failed to expand coverage as provided in the ACA.

Arguments

The petitioners to the Court argued that the federal expansion of Medicaid, from a practical perspective, was a "new" program. They also stated that this provision of the ACA was again federal overreach, this time in violation of the states' Tenth Amendment purview of police power—that only the states, as separate sovereign entities from the federal government, had the right to determine the best course of action to be taken in protection of the public's health, safety, and welfare within their respective borders. The respondents, defending the ACA, argued that the Medicaid expansion, like Medicaid itself, was voluntary; that states could decide not to participate; and that, for this reason, the act did not violate the Tenth Amendment rights of the states.

Decision and Rationale

The Court compared Medicaid as it existed before the passage of the ACA to what the ACA created within the program. There are dramatic differences. Fundamentally, the ACA mandated that Medicaid cover *everyone* (not otherwise specifically exempt) with incomes of less than 133 percent of FPL. This provision went well beyond the pregnant women and children, caregivers, and elderly and disabled people covered by the then-existing Medicaid program. The Court found that this was basically a "new program."

The justices observed that it is permissible for Congress to attach conditions to the receipt of federal funds it provides to, in effect, do indirectly that which it could not do directly—regulate the public's health, safety, and welfare—because those matters remain the sole province of the states. In this case, however, the Court ruled that the structure of this initiative was constitutionally flawed. States did not have adequate notice to consent to this new program—which was a vastly more comprehensive coverage scheme than the existing Medicaid program. The Court reasoned that this provision was unduly "coercive" and amounted to a "gun to the head" because the penalty for noncompliance by the states was the potential loss of all federal Medicaid funds (US Supreme Court 2012). In other words, the ACA provided that states needed to expand their Medicaid programs or face the possible loss of *all* federal Medicaid funds. The Court concluded that this was not "voluntary" and that this particular structure did not conform to the precedents of the federal government's inducing the states to undertake certain activities.

The Court's remedy for this conundrum was to vitiate the HHS secretary's authority to enforce the expansion. The Court ruled that the secretary could not withhold any state's Medicaid funding for noncompliance. The enforcement mechanism was an "economic dragooning that leaves the States with no real option but to acquiesce." As a practical matter, the Court seized the "gun to the head," effectively making the Medicaid expansion provision voluntary for the states (US Supreme Court 2012).

The Interplay of Policy Preferences

This policy snapshot highlights the policy preferences (and outcomes) from a variety of sources, all of which are explored in more detail throughout the book. Here we see the will of Congress expressed in the passage of the ACA in its final form. We see the executive branch poised to collect a fee under one legal rationale, only to see that rationale completely changed by the Supreme Court. Similarly, the executive branch, as part of the implementation of the act, was empowered by Congress to withhold states' Medicaid funding. That particular matter never arose, however, because the Supreme Court stepped in to limit the executive branch's authority to enforce provisions relative to the expansion of Medicaid. Finally, we see the states making conflicting determinations regarding the value of expanded Medicaid as a matter of policy and in two instances—Iowa and Washington—coming down on both sides of the issue.

Thus are demonstrated the multiple contexts of health policy: federal legislative branch, federal executive branch (also as an advocate for the ACA and its defender in litigation), federal judicial branch, and states' executive branches. While it is not obvious here because this part of implementation would take place later, state legislatures likewise participated in this process when they voted to expand (or not) the Medicaid program, as structured in the ACA. As the readers engage further in this book, and this section particularly, they will find multiple contexts for health policy.

References

Musumeci, M. 2012. "A Guide to the Supreme Court's Decision on the ACA's Medicaid Expansion." Kaiser Family Foundation. Published August 1. www.kff.org/health-reform/issue-brief/a-guide-to-the-supreme-courts-decision.

US Supreme Court. 2012. "National Federation of Independent Business v. Sebelius." Cornell Law School Legal Information Institute. Published June 28. www.law.cornell.edu/supremecourt/text/11-393.

CHAPTER

1

HEALTH AND HEALTH POLICY

Learning Objectives

After reading this chapter, you should be able to

- define health and describe health determinants;
- define public policy and health policy;
- begin to appreciate the important historical roles of Medicare and Medicaid;
- begin to appreciate the significance of the Patient Protection and Affordable Care Act (ACA);
- identify some of the important challenges for health policy;
- understand and distinguish between the two fundamental forms of health policies, allocative and regulatory; and
- understand the impact of health policy on health determinants and health.

Health and its pursuit have long been woven tightly into the social and economic fabric of nations. Health is essential not only to the physical and mental well-being of people but also to nations' economies. The United States spent about $3.5 trillion in pursuit of health in 2017, representing about 17.9 percent of the nation's gross domestic product (GDP) and equaling about $10,739 per person (CMS 2020a). This aggregate spending for healthcare and health services is referred to as National Health Expenditures (NHE). Exhibit 1.1 provides a projection of NHE.

Because policymakers, particularly elected officials, often view this type of large abstract concept on an individual level, exhibit 1.2 brings the point a bit closer to home, as it displays the projected US healthcare expenditures per capita. Note the magnitude of the projected increase: approximately 60 percent over 10 years. Exhibit 1.2 also demonstrates NHE's continued growth as a percent of GDP. Over time, the growth rate in the cost of healthcare continues to exceed the growth rate in the national economy.

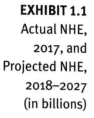

EXHIBIT 1.1
Actual NHE, 2017, and Projected NHE, 2018–2027 (in billions)

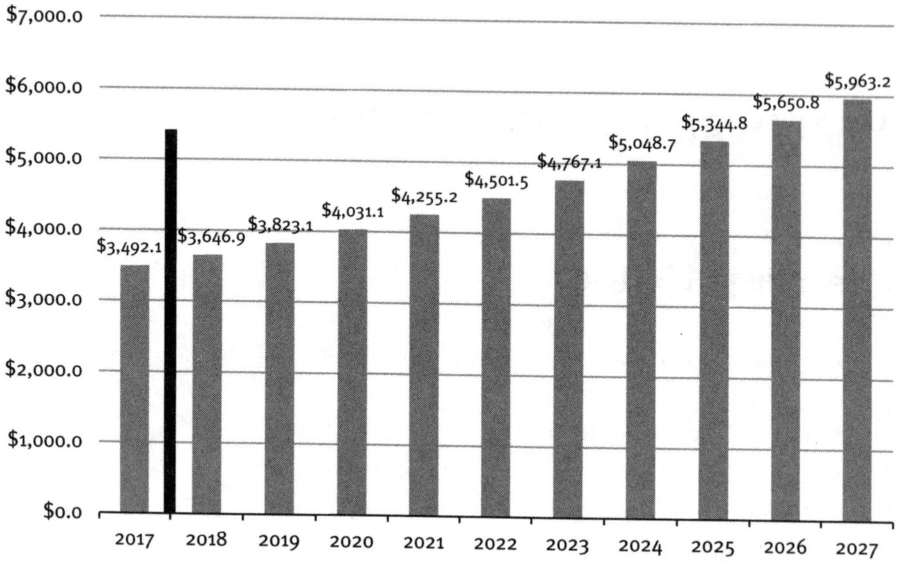

Source: Adapted from CMS (2020b).

Exhibit 1.3 provides an important comparison regarding the source of the money that pays for healthcare costs. The public insurance (Medicaid, Medicare, Veterans Administration, Department of Defense) portion continues to grow and will pay for an increasing share of the total NHE. This growth

EXHIBIT 1.2
Actual (2017) and Projected (2018–2027) NHE per Capita and as Percentage of GDP for 2017

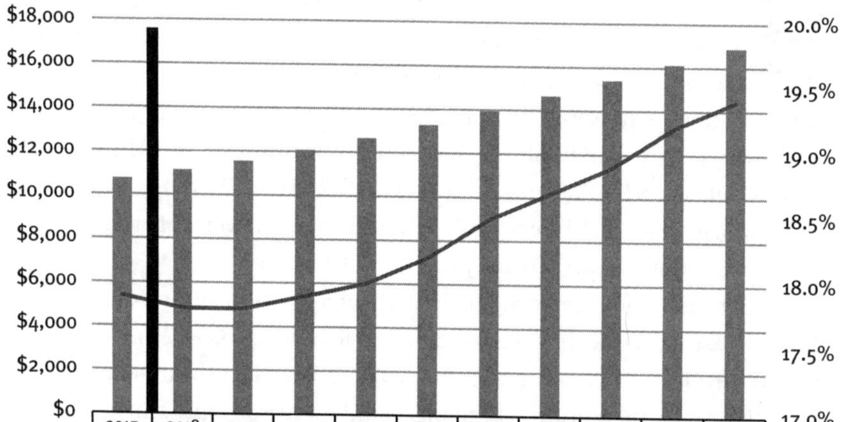

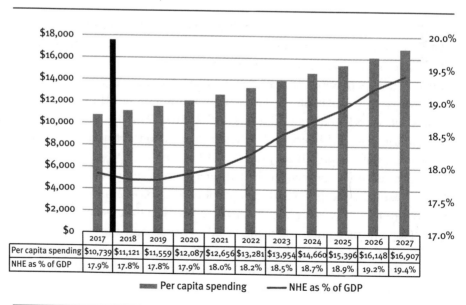

	2017	2018	2019	2020	2021	2022	2023	2024	2025	2026	2027
Per capita spending	$10,739	$11,121	$11,559	$12,087	$12,656	$13,281	$13,954	$14,660	$15,396	$16,148	$16,907
NHE as % of GDP	17.9%	17.8%	17.8%	17.9%	18.0%	18.2%	18.5%	18.7%	18.9%	19.2%	19.4%

Per capita spending — NHE as % of GDP

Source: Adapted from CMS (2020a).

EXHIBIT 1.3
NHE by Source: Actual 2017 and Projected 2027

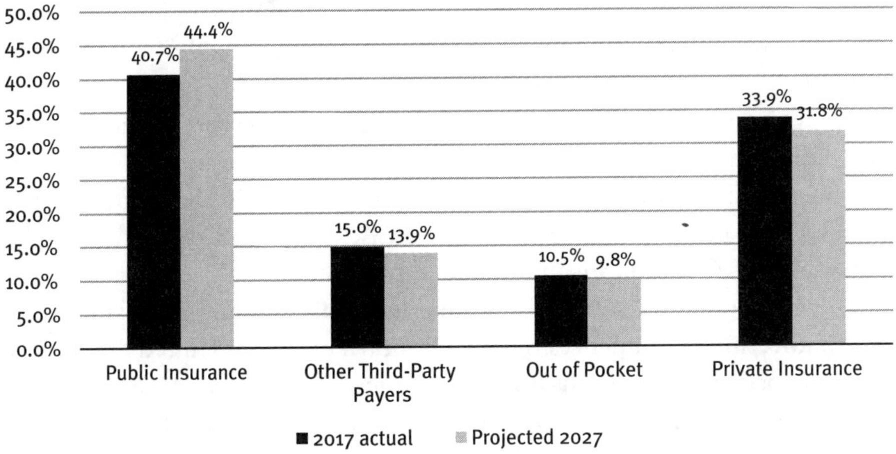

Source: Adapted from CMS (2020b).

is primarily attributable to the increase in Medicare expenditures, because of the growing percentage of elderly in the population and their greater use of healthcare resources, and Medicaid, because of the expansion funded in part by the Affordable Care Act. Thus, it is not surprising that governments at all levels are keenly interested in health and how it is pursued. As will be discussed throughout this book, government's interest is expressed largely through public policy.

The projections forecast that, in less than a decade, absent a significant event to change the course of events, nearly one-half of NHE will most likely come from public sources. The proportion of NHE provided by private insurance will decline slightly, as will out-of-pocket expenditures and funding from other third-party payers. (This category includes things such as workplace clinics, workers' compensation, vocational rehabilitation, and others, some of which are also publicly sourced [Sisko et al. 2019]).

Despite government's substantive role through health policy, most of the necessary clinical, diagnostic, and ancillary resources used in the pursuit of health in the United States are owned and controlled by the private sector. This unique public–private connection means that when government is involved in the pursuit of health for its citizens, it often seeks broader access to health services—for classes of people (Medicare: elderly and disabled people; Medicaid: the indigent) or to obtain broader access for everyone to address specific disease states (polio and flu vaccines)—that are provided predominantly through the private sector. While the private sector owns or controls the majority of the resources, government's role has expanded over time (as examined in detail in chapter 4).

The long-established Medicare and Medicaid programs provide clear examples of this public–private approach, which is continued in the more recent expansion of insurance coverage in the Patient Protection and Affordable Care Act (P.L. 111-148) of 2010. The ACA, as it is known, continues the pattern of using public dollars to purchase services in the private sector for beneficiaries, as is done under Medicare and Medicaid. These policies are critically important to understanding health policy and its effect on health in the United States. Appendix 1.1 provides an overview of the ACA, and appendix 1.2 offers similar summaries of the Medicare and Medicaid programs.

This book explores the intricate public policymaking process through which government influences the pursuit of health in the United States. The primary focus is on policymaking at the federal level, although much of the information also applies to state and local levels of government. This chapter discusses the basic definitions of health, health determinants, and health policy and their relationships to one another. Chapter 2 describes the context in which policymaking takes place. Chapter 3 discusses the dynamic nature of federalism and its impact on health policy, underscoring the different responsibilities between the federal and state governments. Chapter 4 presents a model of the public policymaking process and specifically applies this model to health policymaking. Building on the foundational material presented in the first four chapters, subsequent chapters cover in more detail the various interconnected components of the policymaking process. Chapter 10 concludes the book with attention to how health professionals, whether managers or clinicians, can build a more comprehensive and integrated, therefore more useful, level of policy competence. In this book, *policy competence* simply means that health professionals understand the policymaking process sufficiently to exert some influence and achieve their goals—improved healthcare services delivery. The path toward policy competence begins with some key definitions—of health, health determinants, public policy, and health policy.

Health Defined

A careful definition of health is important because it gives purpose to any consideration of health policy. Being precise about what causes or determines health is similarly important. As will be discussed more fully later, policy affects health through its impact on the determinants of health.

The World Health Organization (WHO; www.who.int) defines *health* as the "state of complete physical, mental, and social well-being and not merely the absence of disease or infirmity," a definition first appearing in the organization's constitution in 1946 and continuing unchanged through today (WHO 1946). Other definitions have embellished the original, including one that says health is "a dynamic state of well-being characterized by a physical and mental potential, which satisfies the demands of life commensurate with age, culture, and personal responsibility" (Bircher 2005). Another variation on the definition views health as a "state in which the biological and clinical indicators of organ function are maximized and in which physical, mental, and role functioning in everyday life are also maximized" (Brook and McGlynn 1991). Yet another definition adds the concept of health as a human right by saying health is "a condition of well-being, free of disease or infirmity, and a basic and universal human right" (Saracci 1997). The former European commissioner for health and consumer protection provides a definition with an important expansion by considering good health as "a state of physical and mental well-being necessary to live a meaningful, pleasant, and productive life" and further noting that "good health is also an integral part of thriving modern societies, a cornerstone of well performing economies, and a shared principle of . . . democracies" (Byrne 2004).

The WHO definition, especially as embellished with considerations of health as a right and a key principle of most democracies, not only permits consideration of the well-being of individuals and the health of the larger communities and societies they form, but also facilitates assessments of governmental performance in promoting health (Shi 2019). Throughout this book, health is defined as WHO defined it long ago, as its foundation has withstood the test of time:

> **Health is a state of complete physical, mental, and social well-being and not merely the absence of disease or infirmity.**

Health is important in all nations, although the resources available for its pursuit vary widely. Current international health expenditure comparisons for the member countries of the Organisation for Economic Co-operation and Development (OECD), all of which share a commitment to democratic government and market economies, reflect some of this variation and are available online at www.oecd.org.

The relative importance that leaders and citizens of nations place on the health of their populations is partially reflected in the proportions of available resources devoted to the pursuit of health. Exhibit 1.4 shows per capita health spending and percentage of GDP devoted to health in selected countries.

The other important lesson in exhibit 1.4 is the clear "most expensive in the world" position of the United States in spending for healthcare services. By whatever measure, the US spends more on healthcare services than any other nation: in total dollars, dollars per capita, or percentage of the GDP. But does that spending represent value? Are we getting a good return for our investment? More about this later in the chapter, but the short answer for

EXHIBIT 1.4
2017 NHE of Selected OECD Countries per Capita and as a Percentage of GDP (in dollars)

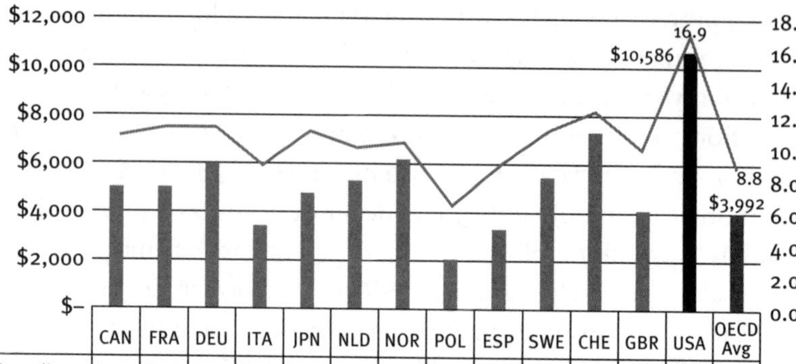

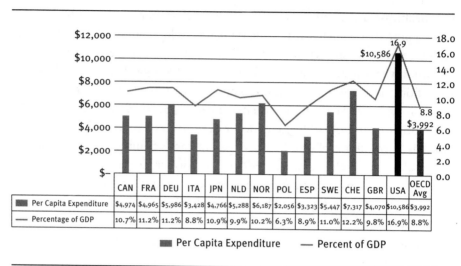

	CAN	FRA	DEU	ITA	JPN	NLD	NOR	POL	ESP	SWE	CHE	GBR	USA	OECD Avg
Per Capita Expenditure	$4,974	$4,965	$5,986	$3,428	$4,766	$5,288	$6,187	$2,056	$3,323	$5,447	$7,317	$4,070	$10,586	$3,992
Percentage of GDP	10.7%	11.2%	11.2%	8.8%	10.9%	9.9%	10.2%	6.3%	8.9%	11.0%	12.2%	9.8%	16.9%	8.8%

Per Capita Expenditure — Percent of GDP

Source: Adapted from OECD (2019).

the moment is no: the US does not obtain good results, especially in light of costs, in a number of metrics intended to elucidate the quality of a healthcare system.

Over time, the United States has opted for policies resulting in the most expensive healthcare system in the world. Although it is beyond the scope of this book to address how and why that came to be, you will see some interesting comparisons in the following sections. Important to appreciating the role health policy plays in the pursuit of health is the fact that health is a function of several variables, referred to as ***health determinants***. The existence of multiple determinants provides governments with a wide variety of ways to intervene in any society's pursuit of health.

Health determinants are defined as factors that affect health or, more formally, as a "range of personal, social, economic, and environmental factors that influence health" both at the individual and population levels (HHS 2020). The question of what determines health in humans has been of interest for a long time.

An important early theory about the determinants of health was the Force Field paradigm (Blum 1974). In this theory, four major influences, or force fields, determine health: environment, lifestyle, heredity, and medical care. In another conceptualization, the determinants are divided into two categories (Dahlgren and Whitehead 2006). One category, named ***fixed factors***, is unchangeable and includes such variables as age and gender. A second category, named ***modifiable factors***, includes lifestyles, social networks, community conditions, environments, and access to products and services such as education, healthcare, and nutritious food.

EXHIBIT 1.5
Determinants of Health

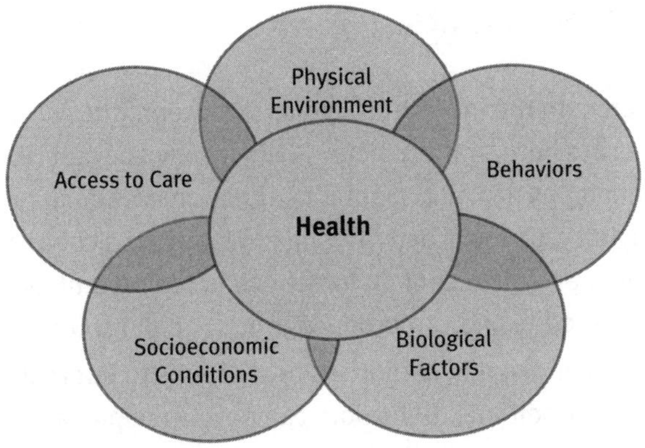

Source: Adapted from CDC (2019).

The research on determinants of health, which is now extensive, has led to a holistic approach to health determinants. The determinants are catalytic with one another. For individuals and populations, health determinants include the physical environments in which people live and work; people's behaviors; their biology (genetic makeup, family history, and acquired physical and mental health problems); social factors (including economic circumstances, socioeconomic position, and income distribution; discrimination based on such factors as race and ethnicity, gender, and sexual orientation; and the availability of social networks or social support); and their access to health services. Exhibit 1.5 provides a visual representation of how these variables interact with one another, contributing to overall health. Scientists generally use the five determinants of health shown in exhibit 1.5 (CDC 2019).

Another inclusive perspective on what factors determine health in humans is reflected in *Healthy People 2020* (www.healthypeople.gov), a comprehensive national agenda for improving health. Note that there are slight differences between the determinants advanced by the Centers for Disease Control and Prevention (CDC) and those that are part of a national health agenda. Why the differences? No one knows for certain, but consider the fact that the US health system has *two* components: public health and healthcare services. Note that *Healthy People 2020* is a function of the Office of Disease Prevention and Health Promotion in HHS. This agency is engaged in the public health function of advocacy and, therefore, would consider *policymaking* to be a health determinant. The following box provides a list of health determinants and brief definitions adapted from *Healthy People 2020* (HHS 2020).

Health Determinants

- *Biology* refers to the individual's genetic makeup (those factors with which they are born), family history (which may suggest risk for disease), and physical and mental health problems acquired during life. Aging, diet, physical activity, smoking, stress, alcohol or illicit drug abuse, injury or violence, or an infectious or toxic agent may result in illness or disability and can produce a "new" biology for the individual.
- *Behaviors* are individual responses or reactions to internal stimuli and external conditions. Behaviors can have a reciprocal relationship with biology; in other words, each can affect the other. For example, smoking (behavior) can alter the cells in the lung and result in shortness of breath, emphysema, or cancer (biology), which then may lead an individual to stop smoking (behavior). Similarly, a family history that includes heart disease (biology) may motivate an individual to develop good eating habits, avoid tobacco, and maintain an active lifestyle (behaviors), which may prevent their own development of heart disease (biology).
- An individual's choices and social and physical environments can shape their behaviors. The social and physical environments include all factors that affect the individual's life—positively or negatively—many of which may be out of their immediate or direct control.
- *Social environment* includes interactions with family, friends, coworkers, and others in the community. It encompasses social institutions, such as law enforcement, the workplace, places of worship, and schools. Housing, public transportation, and the presence or absence of violence in the community are components of the social environment. The social environment has a profound effect on individual and community health and is unique for each individual because of cultural customs; language; and personal, religious, or spiritual beliefs. At the same time, individuals and their behaviors contribute to the quality of the social environment.
- According to the CDC, *policymaking* at the local, state, and federal level affects individual and population health. An increase in taxes on tobacco sales, for example, can improve population health by reducing the number of people using tobacco products. Some policies affect entire populations over extended periods of time while simultaneously helping to change individual behavior. For example, the 1966 Highway Safety Act and the National Traffic and Motor Vehicle Safety Act authorized the federal government to set and regulate standards

for motor vehicles and highways. This led to an increase in safety standards for cars, including seat belts, which in turn reduced rates of injuries and deaths from motor vehicle accidents.

- *Public- and private-sector programs and interventions* can have a powerful and positive effect on individual and community health. Examples include health promotion campaigns to prevent smoking; public laws or regulations mandating child restraints and seat belt use in automobiles; disease prevention services, such as immunization of children, adolescents, and adults; and clinical services such as enhanced mental health care. Programs and interventions that promote individual and community health, such as fitness or exercise programs, may be implemented by public agencies, including those that oversee transportation, education, energy, housing, labor, and justice, or through such private-sector endeavors as places of worship, community-based organizations, civic groups, and businesses.
- *Quality health services* can be vital to the health of individuals and communities. Expanding access to services could eliminate health disparities and increase the quality of life and life expectancy of all people living in the United States. Health services in the broadest sense include not only those received from health services providers but also health information and services received from other venues in the community.

Source: Adapted from HHS (2020).

Nations differ in the relative importance they assign to addressing the various determinants of health. For example, among the OECD nations, the United States ranks first in health expenditures but twenty-fifth in spending on social services. This expenditure pattern reflects a particular prioritization among determinants and is not necessarily the most cost-effective pattern. For example, the 1.5 million people in the United States who experience homelessness in any given year use disproportionately more costly acute care services (Doran, Misa, and Shah 2013).

Not only do nations prioritize health determinants differently, but people, as individuals and populations, vary in their health and health-related needs. The population of the United States is remarkably diverse in age, gender, race and ethnicity, income, and other factors. Current census data put the US population at approximately 327 million people; 16 percent of them are older than 65. Persons of Hispanic or Latino origin make up about 18.3 percent of the population, and African Americans constitute approximately 13.4 percent of the population (US Census Bureau 2019). These demographics are important when considering health and its pursuit.

Older people consume relatively more health services, and their health-related needs differ from those of younger people. Older people are more likely to consume long-term care services and community-based services intended to help them cope with various limitations in the activities of daily living.

In discussing health and the healthcare system, we frequently encounter populations of people—minorities and the poor in particular—who do not enjoy the same level of health as others or who do not have the same kind of access to care as others. These differences are referred to as *disparities. Healthcare* disparities and *health* disparities, although related, are not the same. Healthcare disparities refer to differences in such variables as access to care, insurance coverage, and quality of services received. Health disparities occur when one population group experiences higher burdens of illness, injury, death, or disability than another group.

The healthcare system continues to confront the challenge of eliminating health and healthcare disparities. There is evidence that the ACA contributed to reducing disparities that existed for Hispanics and African Americans (Hayes et al. 2017). In recent years, policymakers have paid greater attention to racial and ethnic disparities in care, with notable, although unfinished, progress. Congress directed the Institute of Medicine (IOM; www.iom.edu) to study health disparities and established the National Center on Minority Health and Health Disparities at the National Institutes of Health (NIH; www.nih.gov). Congress also required the Department of Health and Human Services (HHS; www.hhs.gov) to report annually on the nation's progress in reducing healthcare disparities and health disparities (HHS 2014). There are some differences in how each agency sees "disparity" because one is dealing strictly with the science of health determination (NIH), while the other is also dealing with the disparities created in access to care (HHS).

The IOM (2002) report *Unequal Treatment: Confronting Racial and Ethnic Disparities in Health Care* called for a multilevel strategy to address potential causes of racial and ethnic healthcare disparities, including

- raising public and provider awareness of racial and ethnic disparities in healthcare,
- expanding health insurance coverage,
- improving the capacity and quantity of providers in underserved communities, and
- increasing understanding of the causes of and interventions to reduce disparities.

Progress in pursuing this multifaceted strategy continues, and it received a substantial boost from the passage of the ACA. Among the ACA's numerous goals, two of the most important are to reduce the number of uninsured people and to improve access to healthcare services for all citizens (Garfield, Orgera, and Damico 2019; Williams 2011).

In spite of progress, continued racial disparity is easily identified. For example, an African American woman is 22 percent more likely to die from heart disease than her white counterpart, 71 percent more likely to die from cervical cancer, and 243 percent more likely to die from pregnancy- and childbirth-related causes (Hostetter and Klein 2018). As a matter of equity, statistics like these are unacceptable.

Researchers are learning more about how health status is affected by income and other socioeconomic factors. Wealthier Americans tend to be in better health than their poorer counterparts primarily because of differences in education, behavior, and environment. Higher incomes permit people to buy healthier food; live in safer, cleaner neighborhoods; and exercise regularly (Luhby 2013). Exhibit 1.6 demonstrates this absence of equity in terms of access to care relative to income: the higher the income, the more likely one is to be able to access care, receive care, and be more satisfied with the care one receives.

However, low income does not necessarily mean poorer health. In part, the impact of income depends on what government does about supporting people with low incomes. A national survey has shown that the income variable interacts importantly with the extant health policy in the various states (Schoen et al. 2013). Using 30 indicators of access, outcomes, prevention, and quality, the survey documents sharp healthcare disparities among states, revealing up to a fourfold disparity in performance for low-income populations. The most important conclusion of this survey is that "if all states could reach the benchmarks set by leading states, an estimated 86,000 fewer people would die prematurely and tens of millions more adults and children would receive timely preventive care" (Schoen et al. 2013).

Although its population is diverse, several widely, though not universally, shared values directly affect the approach to healthcare in the United States.

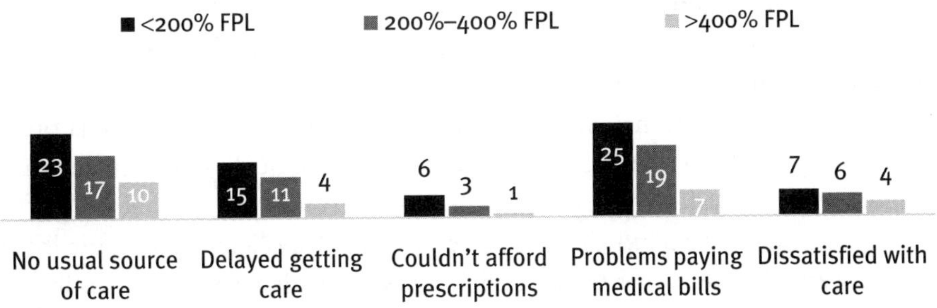

EXHIBIT 1.6
Access to Care by Income Level Relative to Federal Poverty Level (FPL)

Source: Commonwealth Fund (2018).

For example, many Americans place a high value on individual autonomy, self-determination, and personal privacy and maintain a widespread, although not universal, commitment to justice. Other societal characteristics that have influenced the pursuit of health in the United States include a common deep-seated belief in the potential of technological rescue and a cultural preference for the prolonging of individual life regardless of the monetary costs (although this attitude is changing). These values shape the private and public sectors' efforts related to health, including the elaboration of public policies germane to health and its pursuit. They also influence the prioritization of attention to the various determinants of health.

Defining Health Policy

A suitable context is necessary to understand the essence of health policy fully. First, it is important to realize that policy is made in both the private sector and the public, or governmental, sector. Policy is made in all sorts of organizations, including corporations such as Google, institutions such as the Mayo Clinic, health insurance companies, pharmaceutical companies, and governments at federal, state, and local levels. In all settings, *policies* are officially or authoritatively made decisions for guiding actions, decisions, and behaviors of others (Longest and Darr 2014). The decisions are official or authoritative because they are made by people who are entitled to make them based on their positions in their entities. Executives and other managers of corporations and institutions are entitled to establish policies for their organizations because they occupy certain positions. Similarly, in the public sector, certain people are positionally entitled to make policies. For example, members of Congress are entitled to make certain decisions, as are executives in government or members of the judiciary.

Policies made in the private sector can certainly affect health. Examples include authoritative decisions made in the private sector by executives of healthcare organizations about such issues as their product lines, pricing, and marketing strategies. Insurance companies also fall into this group, as they determine the breadth and depth of the coverage they provide. Official or authoritative decisions made by such organizations as The Joint Commission (www.jointcommission.org), a private accrediting body for health-related organizations, and the National Committee for Quality Assurance (www.ncqa.org), a private organization that assesses and reports on the quality of managed care plans, are also private-sector health policies. This book focuses on the *public* policymaking process and the public-sector health policies that result from this process. Private-sector health policies, however, also play vital roles in the ways societies pursue health.

Public Policy

There are many definitions of public policy but no universal agreement on which is best. For example, Peters (2013, 4) defines public policy as the "sum of government activities, whether acting directly or through agents, as those activities have an influence on the lives of citizens." Birkland (2001) defines it as "a statement by government of what it intends to do or not to do, such as a law, regulation, ruling, decision, or order, or a combination of these." Cochran and Malone (1999) propose yet another definition: "Political decisions for implementing programs to achieve societal goals." Drawing on these and many other definitions, we define *public policy* in this book as

> authoritative decisions made in the legislative, executive, or judicial branches of government that are intended to direct or influence the actions, behaviors, or decisions of others.

The phrase *authoritative decisions* is crucial in this definition. It specifies decisions made anywhere in the three branches of government—and at any level of government—that are within the legitimate, official purview of those making the decisions. The decision-makers can be legislators, executives of government (presidents, governors, cabinet officers, heads of agencies), or judges. Part of these roles is the legitimate right—indeed, the responsibility—to make certain decisions. Legislators are entitled (and expected) to decide on laws, executives to decide on rules to implement laws, and judges to review and interpret decisions made by others. Exhibit 1.7 illustrates these relationships in conceptual form, while the policy snapshot at the beginning of part 1 demonstrates how this looks in the real world.

In the United States, public policies—whether they pertain to health or to defense, education, transportation, or commerce—are made through a dynamic public policymaking process. This process, which is discussed in chapter 3, involves interaction among many participants in three interconnected phases: formulation, implementation, and modification.

Health Policy

Health policy is but a particular version of public policy. Public policies that pertain to health or influence the pursuit of health are health policies. Thus, we can define *public-sector health policy* as

> authoritative decisions regarding health or the pursuit of health made in the legislative, executive, or judicial branches of government that are intended to direct or influence the actions, behaviors, or decisions of others.

In the policy snapshot introducing part 1, "The Affordable Care Act: A Cauldron of Controversy," Congress and the executive branch sought to

EXHIBIT 1.7 Roles of Three Branches of Government in Policymaking

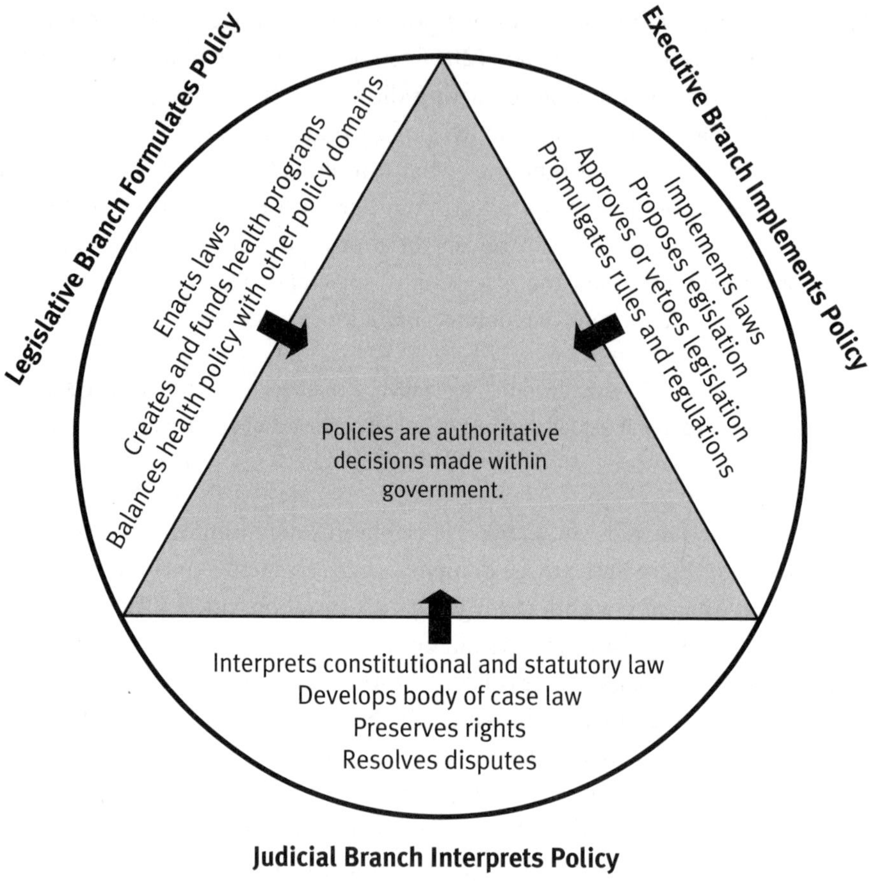

influence the behavior of (a) individuals with regard to the individual mandate and (b) the states with regard to the expansion of Medicaid. The Supreme Court altered the application (and resulting impact) of those initiatives by interpreting the law against the backdrop of the US Constitution.

Health policies are established at federal, state, and local levels of government, although usually for different purposes. Generally, a health policy affects or influences a group or class of individuals (e.g., physicians, the poor, the elderly, children), or a type or category of organization (e.g., medical schools, health plans, integrated delivery and financing [risk bearing or insurance] systems, freestanding healthcare organizations, pharmaceutical manufacturers, employers).

At any given time, the entire set of health-related policies made at any level of government constitutes that level's health policy. Thus, a government's health policy is a large set of authoritative decisions made through the public policymaking process. Throughout this book, we will say much more about health policy, its context, and the process by which these decisions are made. Much of what can be said about health policy in the United States is positive. People are healthier because of the impact of many health policies. However, the United States faces significant challenges in its efforts to improve the health of its people. The US healthcare system continues to be fractured, complex, often duplicative, and arguably both inefficient and ineffective. Although many health policies have had enormous benefit (e.g., Medicare for the elderly and those with disabilities, advances in science and technology fostered by public funding), many challenges remain, and the healthcare delivery system remains Kafkaesque with misaligned incentives. Policies, which are decisions made by humans, can be good (with positive consequences) or misguided (with negative or unintended consequences). As of this writing, government policy encourages new payment mechanisms, along with new clinical relationships, that are changing—improving—the way health services are delivered. Observers have noted a number of encouraging signs about modernizing the culture of healthcare services.

There is no shortage of thoughtful assessments of what health policy should achieve. One excellent set of measures regarding what it should do in the area of healthcare delivery and financing comes from the Partnership for Sustainable Health Care (2013), a diverse group of healthcare stakeholders including the hospital, business, consumer, and insurance sectors. Brought together under the auspices of the Robert Wood Johnson Foundation (RWJF; www.rwjf.org), this group envisions "a high-performing, accountable, coordinated health care system where patient experience and population health are improved, and where per-capita health care spending is reduced." The specific elements of their vision for healthcare in the United States are as follows:

- Health care that is affordable and financially sustainable for consumers, purchasers, and taxpayers
- Patients who are informed, empowered, and engaged in their care
- Patient care that is evidence based and safe
- A delivery system that is accountable for health outcomes and resource use
- An environment that fosters a culture of continuous improvement and learning
- Innovations that are evaluated for effectiveness before being widely and rapidly adopted
- Reliable information that can be used to monitor quality, cost, and population health (Partnership for Sustainable Health Care 2013)

The ACA held promise for achieving, at least in part, these and other goals through improved policy. However, implementation of many aspects of the ACA has proven difficult (Jost 2014; Thompson 2013). While it is unnecessary to complete a thorough review of the ACA's outcomes here, it bears mentioning that assessing its impact on the elements of healthcare's "iron triangle" of cost, quality, and access is important. Suffice it to say that the ACA has expanded the number of people with insurance coverage and appears to have made some progress in the quality domain by funding wellness visits, emphasizing vaccinations, and using payment mechanisms to encourage a higher degree of clinical integration and cooperation.

As with any new law or program, however, the effectiveness of achieving legislative goals relies on how the executive branch implements and administers the law. At its outset, the ACA, an initiative of the Obama administration, had the full support of the president and his executive team. That administration actively promoted the health insurance exchanges and enrollment in plans available through them. Between those efforts and the expansion of Medicaid, 21 million people not previously insured became beneficiaries. For them, at least one barrier to access had been removed. Subsequently, however, a new president was elected in 2016 who had a different idea about healthcare services, financing, and delivery. After entering office, President Donald Trump reduced or eliminated previous promotional efforts. Consequently, the number of newly insured Americans has declined (Jones et al. 2018; Kaiser Family Foundation 2018a; Rice et al. 2018).

Some countries, most notably Canada and Great Britain, have developed expansive, well-integrated policies to fundamentally shape their societies' pursuit of health (Ogden 2012). Instead, the traditional approach to health policy in the United States has been incremental. On occasion, there are significant events, such as the enactment of Medicare and Medicaid. But even those programs were built on legislative foundations already in place. As a result, the United States has only a few large health-related policies.

Even the ACA, for all of its complexity and breadth, makes mostly incremental changes in the healthcare delivery system: expansion of Medicaid, tax credits for individuals to buy insurance, extending private insurance availability through health insurance exchanges, among others. In essence, the ACA built on the existing Medicaid infrastructure, as well as the private insurance markets. The net result is a large number of policies, few of which have dealt with the pursuit of health in a broad, comprehensive, or integrated way until linked together in a single initiative such as the ACA. Legal and political challenges to the ACA have been frequent occurrences, as we saw in "A Cauldron of Controversy." To date, the various constitutional challenges to the ACA largely have been unsuccessful, and most legislative attacks on its component parts have been defeated—with notable exceptions, such the repeal of the "Cadillac tax" on high-value health insurance plans (Will 2019). The shared responsibility payment imposed on individuals for failing to comply with the individual mandate of insurance coverage has also been repealed following the election of 2016 (Jost 2017).

The fundamental challenge to the US healthcare services delivery system today is to increase value to the consumer by restraining cost increases—while becoming more effective in delivering care. In short, deliver a higher quality of care for smaller increases in costs. This necessity is intrinsic. In *Crossing the Quality Chasm*, the IOM ultimately defined six domains of healthcare quality, saying healthcare should be safe, effective, patient centered, timely, efficient, and equitable. Whether one uses the RWJF standards or the IOM's six domains, the goal remains the same: to improve the quality of healthcare services available to people in the United States.

A wide variety of stakeholders benefits from improved care, by either definition: payers, providers, patients, and others would all benefit from the kind of care described by IOM or RWJF. There remains, however, an extrinsic factor to consider as well. When we discussed costs earlier, we made some international comparisons. Here is the question: If we are spending more for healthcare services than anyone in the world by any measure, do we have the *best* healthcare system in the world? Regrettably, the answer is no. As shown in exhibit 1.8, the United States has relatively poor rankings in two of the most common standard measurements used to demonstrate the quality of a healthcare delivery system. Note that these are the same countries for which NHE comparisons were made in exhibit 1.4.

The point of this comparison is to invite you to think about how effective US policy is as it relates to health. If US policy supports the initiatives as

EXHIBIT 1.8
Selected OECD Countries: Life Expectancy at Birth (in Years) and Infant Mortality (Deaths per 1,000) in 2017

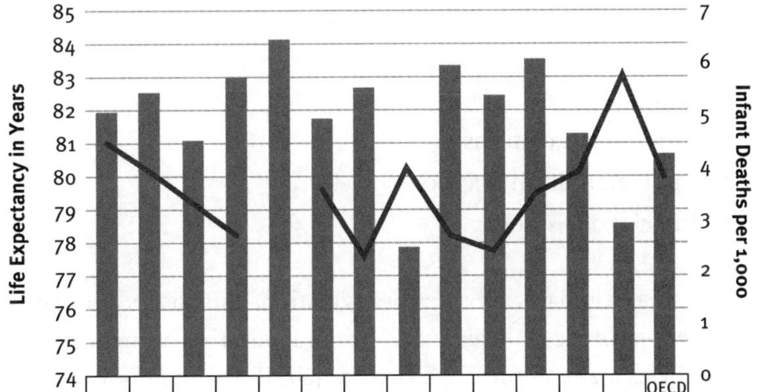

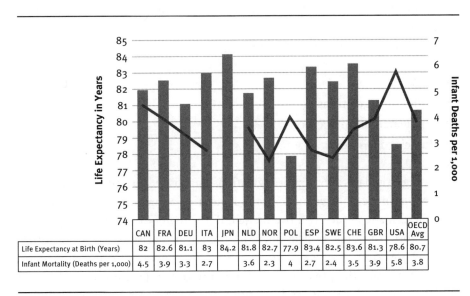

	CAN	FRA	DEU	ITA	JPN	NLD	NOR	POL	ESP	SWE	CHE	GBR	USA	OECD Avg
Life Expectancy at Birth (Years)	82	82.6	81.1	83	84.2	81.8	82.7	77.9	83.4	82.5	83.6	81.3	78.6	80.7
Infant Mortality (Deaths per 1,000)	4.5	3.9	3.3	2.7		3.6	2.3	4	2.7	2.4	3.5	3.9	5.8	3.8

Note: No data provided for Japanese infant mortality rate.

Source: Adapted from OECD (2019).

described by RWJF and the IOM, then indicators such as those shown here should improve over time. While this chapter has only presented two indicators to compare, students are invited to ruminate on this issue for themselves (for more information, see www.commonwealthfund.org).

With the enactment of the ACA, the United States entered a period of major national health reform. The healthcare system has been described accurately as "unsustainable" and "flawed" and is characterized by uncontrolled costs, variable quality, and millions of uninsured and underinsured people. Whether the ACA can solve all that there is to solve is unlikely. It has, however, moved the United States toward a greater degree of clinical integration, expanded insurance coverage, and a renewed focus on quality through the study of comparative effectiveness and payment mechanisms that reward good quality performance.

Forms of Health Policies

Health policies, which we defined earlier as authoritative decisions, take several basic forms (see exhibit 1.7). Some policies are decisions made by legislators that are codified in the statutory language of specific pieces of enacted legislation—in other words, laws. Federal public laws are given a number that designates the enacting Congress and the sequence in which the law was enacted. P.L. 89-97, for example, means that this law was enacted by the Eighty-Ninth Congress and was the ninety-seventh law passed by that Congress. A briefly annotated chronological list of important federal laws pertaining to health can be found in chapter 3.

Policies can take several forms:

- Laws
- Rules or regulations
- Implementation decisions
- Judicial decisions

Stemming from laws are rules or regulations established to implement the laws. Whereas laws are policies made in the legislative branch, rules or regulations are policies made in the executive branch. Both are important forms of policies. A third form of public policies includes numerous decisions made authoritatively by government officials, organizations, and agencies as they implement laws and operate the government and its programs. Policies in the form of implementation decisions are in addition to formal rules or regulations and are typically made by the same executive branch members who establish rules or regulations. Still other policies are the judicial branch's decisions.

Selective examples of health policies include

- the 2010 federal public law P.L. 111-148 (the ACA);
- an executive order regarding operation of federally funded health centers;
- a federal court's ruling that an integrated delivery system's acquisition of yet another hospital violates federal antitrust laws;
- a state government's procedures for licensing physicians;
- a county health department's procedures for inspecting restaurants; and
- a city government's ordinance banning smoking in public places within its borders.

Laws

Laws enacted at any level of government are policies. One example of a federal law is the Food and Drug Administration Amendments Act of 2007 (P.L. 110-85), which amended the federal Food, Drug, and Cosmetic Act to revise and extend the user-fee programs for prescription drugs and medical devices. Another example is the Breast and Cervical Cancer Prevention and Treatment Act of 2000 (P.L. 106-354), which created an optional Medicaid category for low-income women diagnosed with cancer through the Centers for Disease Control and Prevention's (www.cdc.gov) breast and cervical cancer early detection screening program. State examples include laws that govern the licensure of health-related practitioners and institutions. When laws trigger elaborate efforts and activities aimed at implementing the law, the whole endeavor is called a program. The Medicare program is a federal-level example. Many laws, most of which are amendments to prior laws, govern this vast program.

Policy, Law, and Technology: An Example

Policy objectives (e.g., improved women's health services) are achieved, in part, through the passage of legislation (law) intended to advance research for imaging and biomedical devices (technology) that, when used, will provide additional protection for women against cancer. The National Institute of Biomedical Imaging and Bioengineering Establishment Act of 2000 is an example of such a causal relationship. This law established the eponymously named institute to accelerate the development and application of biomedical technologies. Electronic versions of this and other federal laws dating back to 1973, the ninety-third Congress, can be found at www.congress.gov, a website maintained by the Library of Congress that provides access to official federal legislative information.

Rules or Regulations

Rules and regulations (the terms are used interchangeably in the policy context) are another form of public policy established by administrative agencies responsible for implementing laws. Administrative agencies, whether created by the US Constitution, Congress, or a state legislature, are official governmental bodies authorized and empowered to implement laws. These governmental bodies come in many forms, including agencies, departments, divisions, commissions, corporations, and boards. In this book, we will refer to them most often simply as *implementing organizations and agencies.* In chapter 8, which discusses the role of courts in policymaking, these bodies are referred to primarily as administrative agencies because that is the more widely used term in professional and legal fields. More information about implementing organizations or agencies, and more about rules and rulemaking, is provided in chapter 7.

The Administrative Procedure Act of 1946 defined *rule* as "the whole or part of an agency statement of general or particular applicability and future effect designed to implement, interpret, or prescribe law," a definition that still stands. Because such rules are authoritative decisions made in the executive branch of government by the organizations and agencies responsible for implementing laws, they fit the definition of public policies. The rules associated with the implementation of complex laws routinely fill hundreds and sometimes thousands of pages. Rulemaking, the processes through which executive branch agencies write the rules to guide law implementation, is an important activity in policymaking and is discussed in detail in chapter 7.

Rules, in proposed form (for review and comment by those who will be affected by them) and in final form, are published in the *Federal Register* (*FR*; www.federalregister.gov), the official daily publication for proposed and final rules, notices of federal agencies, and executive orders and other presidential documents. The *FR* is published by the Office of the Federal Register, National Archives and Records Administration.

Part 3 of this book will discuss rules and regulations in detail, including an example of a proposed rule.

Implementation Decisions

When organizations or agencies in the executive branch of any level of government implement laws, they must make numerous decisions about how to implement the rules and regulations that flow from the legislative authority. These are influential decisions that, although different from the formal rules that influence implementation, are policies as well. For example, effectively managing Medicare requires the federal government to undertake a complex and diverse set of management tasks, including the following:

- Implementing and evaluating Medicare policies and operations
- Identifying and proposing modifications to Medicare policies

- Managing and overseeing Medicare Advantage and prescription drug plans, Medicare fee-for-service providers, and contractors
- Collaborating with key stakeholders in Medicare (i.e., plans, providers, other government entities, advocacy groups, consortia)
- Developing and implementing a comprehensive strategic plan to carry out Medicare's mission and objectives
- Identifying program vulnerabilities and implementing strategies to eliminate fraud, waste, and abuse in Medicare

In carrying out these tasks, the Centers for Medicare & Medicaid Services (CMS; www.cms.gov), the agency responsible for implementing the Medicare and Medicaid programs as well as many aspects of the ACA, makes myriad decisions about implementation. Again, because they are authoritative, these decisions are policies.

Judicial Decisions

As noted in the policy snapshot, judicial decisions are another form of policy. Another example is the Supreme Court's 2008 *MetLife v. Glenn* decision regarding how federal courts reviewing claims denials by plan administrators under the Employee Retirement Income Security Act "should take into account the fact that plan administrators (insurers and self-insured plans) face a conflict of interest because they pay claims out of their own pockets and arguably stand to profit by denying claims" (Jost 2008, w430). These decisions are policies because they are authoritative and direct or influence the actions, behaviors, or decisions of others. Still another example is *King v. Burwell*, which upheld a section of the ACA providing tax credit subsidies to certain purchasers of insurance (Hickman 2015).

King v. Burwell, 536 S.Ct. 2480 (2015): Highlighting Three Types of Policies

The Patient Protection and Affordable Care Act, among other things, amended Section 36B of the Internal Revenue Code to provide tax credits for certain individuals purchasing health insurance through "an Exchange operated by the State." The Internal Revenue Service (IRS), following the process for adopting administrative rules and regulations in the Administrative Procedure Act of 1946 (discussed earlier in the chapter) interpreted Congress's language to include exchanges operated by the federal government. Several taxpayers sued, ultimately taking the case to the Supreme Court, which upheld the IRS interpretation (Gamage 2015). Thus, similar

(continued)

to the policy snapshot, we see policy as expressed legislatively in the statute, interpreted and enforced by the administrative agency, and further interpreted and upheld by the judicial branch. (*King v. Burwell* is a significant case and will be discussed further in part 4).

Although the judicial branch of government has played an important role in health policy for decades, its role is increasingly relevant. For example, as we saw in the policy snapshot, in *National Federation of Independent Business (NFIB) v. Sebelius*, the US Supreme Court ruled in 2012 that the ACA was indeed constitutional. This ruling was a crucial milestone for the law, permitting it to proceed (Liptak 2012). Its rationale and importance will be discussed in detail in chapter 8, which is devoted to the vital role played by the judiciary in health policy.

Categories of Health Policies

All policies, whether law, rule or regulation, implementation decision, or judicial decision, can be categorized in various ways. One approach divides policies into distributive, redistributive, and regulatory categories (Birkland 2001). Sometimes the distributive and redistributive categories are combined into an allocative category; sometimes the regulatory category is subdivided into competitive regulatory and protective regulatory categories. For our purposes, all of the various forms of health policies fit into two basic categories—*allocative* or *regulatory.*

In market economies, such as that of the United States, the presumption is that private markets best determine the production and consumption of goods and services, including health services. Of course, when markets fail and the economy slips into a recession, as they have several times in the last few decades, government intervention becomes essential. In market economies, government generally intrudes with policies only when private markets fail to achieve desired public objectives. The most credible arguments for policy intervention in the nation's domestic activities begin with the identification of situations in which markets are not functioning properly.

The health sector is especially prone to situations in which markets function poorly. Theoretically perfect (i.e., freely competitive) markets, which do not exist in reality but provide a standard against which real markets can be assessed, require that

- buyers and sellers have sufficient information to make informed decisions,
- a large number of buyers and sellers participate,
- additional sellers can easily enter the market,

- each seller's products or services are satisfactory substitutes for those of its competitors, and
- the quantity of products or services available in the market does not swing the balance of power toward either buyers or sellers.

The markets for health services in the United States violate these requirements in several ways. The complexity of health services reduces consumers' ability to make informed decisions without guidance from the sellers or other advisers. Entry of sellers into the markets for health services is heavily regulated, and widespread insurance coverage affects the decisions of buyers and sellers. These and other factors mean that markets for health services frequently do not function competitively, thus inviting policy intervention.

Furthermore, the potential for private markets on their own to fail to meet public objectives is not limited to production and consumption. For example, markets on their own might not stimulate sufficient socially desirable medical research or the education of enough physicians or nurses without policies that subsidize certain costs associated with these ends. These and similar situations provide the philosophical basis for the establishment of public policies to correct market-related problems or shortcomings.

The nature of the market problems or shortcomings directly shapes the health policies intended to overcome or ameliorate them. Based on their primary purposes, health policies fit broadly into allocative or regulatory categories, although the potential for overlap between the two categories is considerable.

Allocative Policies

Allocative policies *provide net benefits to some distinct group or class of individuals or organizations at the expense of others to meet public objectives.* Such policies are, in essence, subsidies through which policymakers seek to alter demand for or supply of particular products and services or to guarantee certain people access to them. For example, government has heavily subsidized the medical education system on the basis that without subsidies to medical schools, markets would undersupply physicians. Similarly, for many years, under the aegis of the Hill-Burton Act, the federal government subsidized the construction of hospitals on the basis that markets would undersupply hospitals in sparsely populated or low-income areas.

Other subsidies have been used to ensure that certain people have access to health services (see box on the Sheppard-Towner Act). A key feature of the ACA is its subsidization of health insurance coverage, in the form of tax credits, for millions of people. Preceding the ACA and continuing into the future, however, the Medicare and Medicaid programs have been massive allocative policies. Medicare expenditures will be more than $1 trillion in 2022, and Medicaid expenditures could surpass $732 billion by then (CMS 2020a).

Federal funding to support access to health services for Native Americans, veterans, and migrant farmworkers and state funding for mental institutions are other examples of allocative policies that are intended to help individuals gain access to needed services. Although some subsidies are reserved for the people who are most impoverished, subsidies such as those that support medical education, the Medicare program (the benefits of which are not based primarily on financial need), the expansive subsidies in the ACA, and the exclusion of employer-provided health insurance benefits from taxable income illustrate that poverty is not necessarily a requirement to be the beneficiary of an allocative policy.

Some of the provisions of the American Recovery and Reinvestment Act of 2009 (P.L. 111-5) provide examples of allocative policy. This law, enacted in response to the global financial crisis that emerged in 2008, contains many health-related subsidies. Exhibit 1.9 lists some examples.

EXHIBIT 1.9
Examples of Health-Related Subsidies Included in the American Recovery and Reinvestment Act of 2009

Program or Investment Area	Amount and Purpose of Funding
Continuation of health insurance coverage for unemployed workers	$24.7 billion to provide a 65% federal subsidy for up to 9 months of premiums under the Consolidated Omnibus Budget Reconciliation Act. The subsidy will help workers who lose their jobs to continue coverage for themselves and their families.
Health Resources and Services Administration	$2.5 billion, including $1.5 billion for construction, equipment, and health information technology at community health centers; $500 million for services at these centers; $300 million for the National Health Service Corps (NHSC); and $200 million for other health professions training programs.
Medicare	$338 million for payments to teaching hospitals, hospice programs, and long-term care hospitals.
Medicaid and other state health programs	$87 billion for additional federal matching payments for state Medicaid programs for a 27-month period that began October 1, 2008, and $3.2 billion for additional state fiscal relief related to Medicaid and other health programs.
Prevention and wellness	$1 billion, including $650 million for clinical and community-based prevention activities that will address rates of chronic diseases, as determined by the secretary of health and human services; $300 million to the Centers for Disease Control and Prevention for immunizations for low-income children and adults; and $50 million to states to reduce health care–associated infections.

Source: R. Steinbrook, 2009, "Health Care and the American Recovery and Reinvestment Act," *New England Journal of Medicine* 360 (11): 1057–60.

The Sheppard-Towner Act: An Important Policy and a Lasting Legacy

The first major legislation to pass in the aftermath of the women's suffrage movement was the Maternity and Infancy Act (P.L. 67-97), also known as Sheppard-Towner (for the two sponsors of the act). One of the novel features of this law was the use of federal tax revenue distributed on a formulaic basis as an incentive for the states. This act marked the first use of formulaic distribution of federal money in the healthcare arena. In this case, the federal government provided money for, among other things, development of state-level birth registries and aid for impoverished children. At the time of Sheppard-Towner's passage in 1922, 30 states, representing 76 percent of the births nationally, had birth registries. In 1929, when Congress opted not to renew the act, those statistics had risen to 46 states representing 95 percent of the births in the United States (Kotch 1997). Even in nonrenewal, however, Sheppard-Towner left a legacy.

The matching grant technique that the act debuted gets recycled in many domains, including healthcare. Examples include not only the expansion of Medicaid in the ACA, but Medicaid itself. Similarly, many of the other policy provisions of Sheppard-Towner have proven to be the historical antecedent or direct model for contemporary policy. Sheppard-Towner may have introduced many important innovations, but in the matching grant provision we see the power of an allocative policy to induce states to behave in certain ways intended to improve public health and, in particular, the health status of at-risk children.

Regulatory Policies

Regulatory policies are *designed to influence the actions, behaviors, and decisions of others by directive.* All levels of government establish regulatory policies. As with allocative policies, government establishes such policies to ensure that public objectives as established by the policy process are met. Following are the five basic categories of regulatory health policies:

1. *Market entry–restricting regulations* include licensing of health-related practitioners and organizations. Planning programs, through which preapproval for new capital projects by health services providers, such as certificate of need (CON), must be obtained, are also market entry–restricting regulations.

2. *Price or rate-setting regulations*, although generally out of favor, exert control over some aspects of the pursuit of health. The federal government's control of the rates at which it reimburses hospitals for care provided to Medicare patients and its establishment of a fee schedule for reimbursing physicians who care for Medicare patients are examples.
3. *Quality-control regulations* are those intended to ensure that health services providers adhere to acceptable levels of quality in the services they provide and that producers of health-related products, such as imaging equipment and pharmaceuticals, meet safety and efficacy standards. For example, the Food and Drug Administration (FDA) is charged with ensuring that new pharmaceuticals meet these standards. In addition, the Medical Devices Amendments (P.L. 94-295) to the Food, Drug, and Cosmetic Act (P.L. 75-717) placed all medical devices under a comprehensive regulatory framework administered by the FDA.
4. *Market-preserving controls* are necessary because the markets for health services do not behave in truly competitive ways. For that reason, government establishes and enforces rules of conduct for participants. Antitrust laws such as the Sherman Antitrust Act, the Clayton Act, and the Robinson-Patman Act—which are intended to maintain conditions that permit markets to work well and fairly—are good examples of this type of regulation.
5. *Social regulation*, the fifth category of healthcare policy, is a regulatory effort to achieve socially desirable outcomes such as workplace safety and fair employment practices and to reduce undesirable outcomes such as pollution or sexually transmitted disease. The first four classes of regulations are all variations of economic regulation. Social regulation usually has an economic effect, but this is not the primary purpose. Federal and state laws pertaining to environmental protection, disposal of medical wastes, childhood immunization, and the mandatory reporting of communicable diseases are examples of social regulations at work in the pursuit of health.

Sometimes polices are in conflict—differing objectives collide. When this happens, the conflict must be mediated in one way or another to facilitate the objectives of one policy or another. For example, Congress, through the ACA, created accountable care organizations (ACOs) to promote clinical integration. The idea is to promote quality of care (as well as restrain costs), so the ACA functions as both a quality-control regulation and a cost-limiting regulation. The nature of an ACO is to align a wide variety of providers: hospitals, primary care physicians, skilled nursing facilities, pharmacies, specialty physicians and surgeons, and others in the effort to manage the health of a population. In short, by aligning—and integrating—the services of all those providers, the ACO could amalgamate so much of the market share that it could run afoul of market-preserving regulations in the form of the Sherman Anti-Trust Act (absent some decisions by federal agencies to relax their interpretations of their own enforcement guidelines) (Kasper 2011).

The Impact of Health Policy on Health Determinants and Health

From government's perspective, the central purpose of health policy is to enhance health or facilitate its pursuit. Of course, there are multiple perspectives on how to accomplish these purposes, and other purposes may be served through specific health policies, including economic advantages for certain individuals and organizations. While improving the health status of the population is sometimes lost in the smoke of political war, the defining purpose of health policy, as far as government is concerned, is to support the people in their quest for health.

Health policies affect health through health determinants (see exhibit 1.10). Health determinants, in turn, directly affect health. Consider the role of health policy in the following health determinants and, ultimately, its impact on health through them:

- Physical environments in which people live and work
- Behavioral choices and biology
- Social factors, including economic circumstances; socioeconomic position; income distribution in the society; discrimination based on factors such as race or ethnicity, gender, or sexual orientation; and the availability of social networks or social support
- Availability of and access to health services

Political bodies monitor a population's health status and respond when it becomes a significant public—or political—issue. It is no coincidence that Sheppard-Towner passed immediately following women's suffrage. Motivation arising from constituents' concerns applies to legislative bodies and administrative agencies alike. Exhibit 1.10 not only displays the synergistic relationship between health determinants and health status but also a feedback loop from health status to health policy. Health status can come to be characterized as a possible problem in the agenda-setting component of our conceptual model of public policymaking, thereby becoming motivation for a policy response.

EXHIBIT 1.10
The Symbiotic Relationship Among Health Policy, Health Determinants, and Health Status

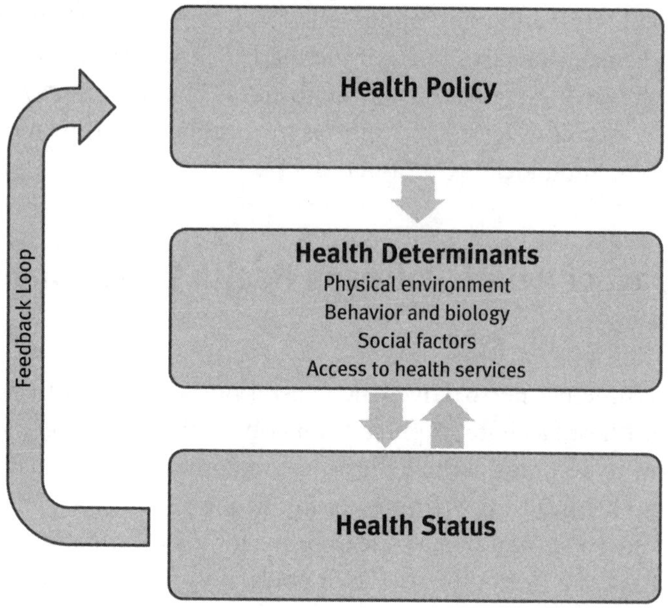

To summarize, health policies are intended to alter determinants of health to benefit the health status of a given population. Medicare, Medicaid, and the ACA demonstrate this principle. By providing or subsidizing the cost of health insurance, the federal government (and the states with regard to Medicaid) expects to improve access to health services for the elderly, disabled, and the indigent, and for working-class Americans—thereby improving the health status of those populations. Note also that health status and health determinants have a synergistic relationship. Not only do determinants affect one's health, but the reverse is also true. For example, good health may make it possible to attain a better education or a better job, perhaps one with employer-sponsored insurance. That insurance might improve access to needed care; the education could result in better health literacy. Some examples of how determinants may influence health policy include polluted water and air (physical environment); use and abuse of opioids (behavior); efforts to create safe public places (social factors); and Medicare, Medicaid, and the ACA (access to health services). Note, however, it is not the determinants that impact health policy: it is the resulting effect those determinants have on health status that motivates policymakers to act. While there is legislation intended to modify those determinants to benefit health status, the genesis of the legislation was the amalgamation of factors that provided a problem to be solved through public policy. Note that both regulatory and allocative policies are included in this example.

Health Policies and Physical Environments

When people are exposed to harmful agents, such as asbestos, dioxin, excessive noise, ionizing radiation, or toxic chemical and biological substances, their health is directly affected. Exposure risks pervade the physical environments of many people. Some of the exposure is through such agents as synthetic compounds that are by-products of technological growth and development. Some exposure is through wastes that result from the manufacture, use, and disposal of a vast range of products. Some of the exposure is through naturally occurring agents, such as carcinogenic ultraviolet radiation from the sun or naturally occurring radon gas in the soil.

The hazardous effects of naturally occurring agents are often exacerbated by combination with agents introduced through human activities. For example, before its ban, the widespread use of Freon in air-conditioning systems reduced the protective ozone layer in the earth's upper atmosphere. As a result, an increased level of ultraviolet radiation from the sun penetrated to the earth's surface. Similarly, exposure to naturally occurring radon appears to act synergistically with cigarette smoke as a carcinogen.

The health effects of exposure to hazardous agents, whether natural or human made, are well understood. We can examine the impact of health policy on physical environment in the air and in the water. Air, polluted by certain agents, has a direct, measurable effect on such diseases as asthma, emphysema, and lung cancer and aggravates cardiovascular disease. Asbestos, which can still be found in buildings constructed before it was banned, causes pulmonary disease. Lead-based paint, when ingested, causes permanent neurological damage in infants and young children. This paint is still found in older buildings and is especially concentrated in poorer urban communities.

Likewise, hazardous material has found its way into the nation's water supply. The story of the water supply in Flint, Michigan, provides a frightening reminder of what happens when toxins—in this case lead—leach into a community's water supply. The entire community, especially children, were at risk for damage to their brains and nervous systems (Ruckart et al. 2019).

Over many decades, government has made efforts to exorcise environmental health hazards through public policies. Examples of federal policies include:

- Clean Air Act (P.L. 88-206)
- Flammable Fabrics Act (P.L. 90-189)
- Occupational Safety and Health Act (P.L. 91-596)
- Consumer Product Safety Act (P.L. 92-573)
- Noise Control Act (P.L. 92-574)
- Safe Drinking Water Act (P.L. 93-523)

Note, however, the swinging political pendulum, which, as we shall see, is a part of the policymaking process; social and economic conditions change, which, in turn, drive political change. Most of the laws referenced here were enacted between 1987 and 1993, an era when protecting the environment had captured public and legislative attention. The winds of change, however, blow constant. The election of 2016 signaled a new era with different priorities, resulting in an administration that has taken several administrative steps to roll back some regulatory changes. One example includes the redefinition of the "Waters of the United States," which is central to protecting the water under Environmental Protection Agency jurisdiction. The Trump administration in effect narrowed the scope of the definition (Samet, Burke, and Goldstein 2017).

Health policies that mitigate environmental hazards or take advantage of positive environmental conditions are important aspects of any society's ability to help its members achieve better health. Others believe that the mitigation of environmental hazards has been too costly for businesses—the damage to the environment is minimal, making the trade-off of more robust economic activity beneficial—and that consumers do not share the sense of importance associated with protecting the environment evident in legislation from this domain.

Added to this milieu has been an increasing awareness on the part of the consuming public about both climate change and organic foods. The public has become increasingly aware of agriculture's impact on the environment. Consumers have organized around concerns about genetically modified organisms, as well as the use of insecticides, herbicides, and antibiotics in the production of food.

These two developments—the move toward less restrictive regulation and the countervailing awareness of climate change and organic, non-GMO foods—are a part of the ongoing political and social debate in the United States. Each side becomes a component part of the larger ebb and flow of social and economic factors that are always a part of life.

Health Policies and Human Behavior and Biology

As Rene Dubos (1959, 110) observed more than a half century ago, "To ward off disease or recover health, men [as well as women and children] as a rule find it easier to depend on the healers than to attempt the more difficult task of living wisely." The price of this attitude is partially reflected in the major causes of death in the United States. Ranked from highest to lowest, leading causes are heart disease, cancer, unintentional injuries, chronic lower respiratory diseases, stroke, Alzheimer's disease, diabetes, influenza and pneumonia, kidney disease, and suicide (Murphy, Kochanek, and Arias 2018). Many of these diseases are preventable through improved personal behavior.

Behaviors—including choices about the use of tobacco and alcohol, diet and exercise, illicit drug use, sexual behavior, and gun violence—and genetic predispositions influence many of these causes of death and help explain the pattern. Furthermore, underlying the behavioral factors are such root factors as stress, depression, and feelings of anger, hopelessness, and emptiness, which are exacerbated by economic and social conditions. In short, behaviors are heavily reflected in the diseases that kill and debilitate Americans.

Behavior modification can change the causes of death patterns. The death rate from heart disease, for example, has declined dramatically in recent decades. Although aggressive early treatment has played a role in reducing this rate, better control of several behavioral risk factors—including cigarette smoking, elevated blood pressure, elevated levels of cholesterol, poor diet, lack of exercise, and elevated stress—explains much of the decline. Even with this impressive improvement, however, heart disease remains the most common cause of death and will continue to be a significant cause for the foreseeable future.

Local Policy, Human Behavior, and Biology

Although cancer death rates have improved, they continue to be problematic, with much of the problem attributable to lung cancer. Of course, smoking is a leading cause of lung cancer, and therefore, a significant public health concern. Consequently, stakeholder groups mobilize at the state and local levels. Thus, there is a wide variety of city ordinances and state statutes limiting smoking in various ways. For a comprehensive list of state and local smoking laws, see American Nonsmokers' Rights Foundation, www.no-smoke.org.

Health Policies and Social Factors

A number of social factors can affect health. Chronic unemployment, the absence of a supportive family structure, poverty, homelessness, and discrimination, among other social factors, affect people's health as surely—and often as dramatically—as harmful viruses or carcinogens.

People who live in poverty experience measurably worse health status, meaning more frequent and more severe health problems, than those who are more affluent. Further, as income disparities continue to deepen, so do health disparities. African Americans and Hispanics feel the impact of this more acutely, as they are represented disproportionately below the poverty line. Finally, readers should note that income is difficult to isolate in this fashion, as it intersects with so many other social factors (Khullar and Chokshi 2018).

The poor also typically obtain their health services in a different manner. Instead of receiving care that is coordinated, continuing, and comprehensive, the poor are far more likely to receive a patchwork of services, often provided by public hospitals, clinics, and local health departments. In addition, poor people are more often treated episodically, with one provider intervening in one episode of illness and another provider handling the next episode. Part of the ACA's impact has been to alter this pattern, at least in part, by expanding insurance coverage. Approximately 20 million people in the United States now have health insurance who did not have it before 2010 (Garfield, Orgera, and Damico 2019).

The effect of economic conditions on the health of children is especially dramatic. Impoverished children, on average, have lower birth weights and more conditions that limit school activity compared with other children. These children are more likely to become ill and to have more serious illnesses than other children because of increased exposure to harmful environments, inadequate preventive services, and limited access to health services.

Economic circumstances are part of a larger set of social factors that unequally affect people in their quest for health. Living in an inner-city or rural setting often increases the challenge of finding health services because many such locations have too few providers. Lack of adequate information about health and health services is a significant disadvantage, one compounded by language barriers, functional illiteracy, or other factors specific to inner-city or rural life. Cultural backgrounds and ties, especially among many Native Americans, Latinos, and Asian immigrants, for all the support they can provide, can also create a formidable barrier between people and practitioners of traditional Western medicine.

An example of health policy intended to address social factors is the Balanced Budget Act of 1997 (P.L. 105-33). This policy provided for expanded health insurance coverage of children by establishing the State Children's Health Insurance Program. In 2009, President Obama signed a renewal of this program as the Children's Health Insurance Program (CHIP) Reauthorization Act of 2009 (P.L. 111-3). The CHIP reauthorization significantly expanded coverage to include an additional four million children and, for the first time, allowed the spending of federal money to cover children and pregnant women who are legal immigrants. As of January 1, 2019, 34 states use CHIP to cover pregnant women and children legally residing in the United States (Kaiser Family Foundation 2019). CHIP was again extended in 2018 for six years (Kaiser Family Foundation 2018b).

Health Policies and Health Services

As shown in exhibit 1.10, another important determinant of health is availability of and access to health services, which are any of a host of "specific activities undertaken to maintain or improve health or to prevent decrements of health" (Longest and Darr 2014, 253). Health services can be preventive (e.g., blood pressure screening, mammography), acute (e.g., surgical procedures, antibiotics to fight an infection), chronic (e.g., control of diabetes or hypertension), restorative (e.g., physical rehabilitation of a stroke or trauma patient), or palliative (e.g., pain relief or comfort in terminal stages of disease).

The production and distribution of health services require a vast set of resources, including money, workforce, and technology, all of which are heavily influenced by health policies. The organizations and networks that transform these resources into health services and distribute them to consumers are collectively known as the *health system*. The system itself is also influenced by health policies. Health policies determine the nature of health services through their effect on the resources required to produce the services and on the health system through which the services are organized, delivered, and paid for. Policies' effects on the resources used to provide health services and on the health system are examined in the next sections.

Money

As exhibits 1.1 and 1.2 demonstrate, the United States allocates enormous sums of money to health, and growth is expected to continue. NHE will approach $5 trillion by 2023, at which time the nation will be spending nearly 20 percent of its GDP on health. Nearly half of NHE will be by governments, in the form of allocative policies like Medicare and Medicaid, directed by their policy decisions. The United States spends more on health than does any other country (OECD 2019). Other countries have been far more likely to adopt policies such as global budgets for their healthcare systems or to impose restrictive limitations on the supplies of health services (Squires 2011).

Current health expenditures and projected future increases have significant implications. The increasing expenditures, in part, reflect higher prices. Higher prices reduce access to health services by making it more difficult for many people to purchase the services or the insurance needed to cover those services. Implementation of the ACA has helped address this problem for millions of people, but expenditure levels will remain problematic. They negatively affect the nation's competitiveness in the global economy (Vietor and Weinzierl 2012), and health expenditures have absorbed much of the growth of many workers' real compensation, meaning that as employers spend more to provide health insurance benefits, wages decrease.

Growing health expenditures are a continuing source of budgetary pressure for federal and state governments. As health expenditures consume an increasing portion of government resources, it is becoming more difficult for government to support other priorities, such as education or homeland security.

Workforce

The talents and abilities of a large and diverse workforce make up another basic resource used to provide health services. The healthcare workforce is directly affected by health policies, whether through public funding of educational programs or licensing of health professionals.

One in seven employed people work in healthcare services in the United States. Between 2006 and 2016, employment in this sector grew by 21 percent while other sectors grew 3 percent. Going forward from 2016 to 2026, projected growth is from 16.5 million to more than 19.5 million in 2026 (18 percent) (Martiniano and Moore 2018). While the healthcare workforce has grown, efforts to include more underrepresented populations in decision-making and strategic roles have been met with mixed success (Bouye, McCleary, and Williams 2016).

The nation's rapidly aging population, coupled with the large increase in insured people triggered by the ACA, will "strain a healthcare delivery system already struggling under the weight of its current load" (Association of Academic Health Centers 2013, 1). These pressures will require a new approach to national health workforce policy. The traditional approach focused on numbers of workers, producing health workforce policy that featured responses to projected shortages in the workforce, especially among physicians and nurses. For example, the number of physicians doubled from the mid-1960s to the mid-1990s, an accomplishment driven by federal policies intended to increase their supply, including the Health Professions Educational Assistance Act of 1963 (P.L. 88-129) and its amendments of 1965, 1968, and 1971. Similarly, the main federal response to a projected nurse shortage was the Nurse Reinvestment Act of 2002 (P.L. 107-205), which authorized the following provisions:

- Loan repayment programs and scholarships for nursing students
- Public service announcements to encourage more people to enter the nursing profession
- Career ladder programs for those who wish to advance in the profession
- Best-practice grants for nursing administration
- Long-term care training grants to develop and incorporate gerontology curriculum into nursing programs
- A fast-track faculty loan repayment program for nursing students who agree to teach at a school of nursing

Technology

A third type of resource that health policies significantly affect is health-related technology. Broadly defined, *technology* is the application of science to the pursuit of health. Technological advances result in better pharmaceuticals, devices, and procedures. A major influence on the pursuit of health in the United States, technology has helped eradicate some diseases and has greatly improved diagnoses and treatment for others. Diseases that once were not even diagnosed are now routinely and effectively treated. Advancing technology has brought medical science to the early stages of understanding disease at the molecular level and intervening to treat diseases at the genetic level.

The United States produces and consumes more health-related technology than does any other nation, and it spends far more on it. The nation has provided technology with a uniquely favorable economic and political environment resulting in its widespread availability.

Health policy provides funding for much of the research and development (R&D) that leads to new technology, although the private sector also pays for a great deal of R&D. The United States has a long history of support for the development of health-related technology through policies that support biomedical research and encourage private investment in such research. The NIH invests more than $39.2 billion annually in medical research. About 80 percent of the NIH's funding is awarded through almost 50,000 competitive grants to more than 300,000 researchers at more than 2,500 universities, medical schools, and other research institutions in every state and around the world. About 10 percent of the NIH's budget supports projects conducted by nearly 6,000 scientists in its own laboratories, most of which are on the NIH campus in Bethesda, Maryland (NIH 2020).

Encouraged by policies that permit firms to recoup their investments, private industry also spends heavily on biomedical R&D. In fact, the Pharmaceutical Research and Manufacturers of America (PhRMA; www.phrma.org), which represents the nation's leading biopharmaceutical research companies, reports that industry-wide research investment was nearly $90 billion in 2016 (PhRMA 2019).

Health policy also affects technology through the application of regulatory policies, such as those promulgated by the FDA to ensure technology's safety and efficacy. The FDA is responsible for protecting the public health by ensuring the safety, efficacy, and security of human and veterinary drugs, biological products, medical devices, the food supply, cosmetics, and products that emit radiation. The FDA also has responsibility for regulating the manufacture, marketing, and distribution of tobacco products to protect the public health and to reduce tobacco use by minors. Finally, the FDA plays a significant role in the nation's counterterrorism capability by ensuring the security of the food supply and by fostering the development of medical products to respond to deliberate and naturally emerging public health threats (FDA 2018).

The following are laws the FDA is responsible (or partially responsible) for implementing, including writing rules for implementation:

- Food, Drug, and Cosmetic Act of 1938 (P.L. 75-717)
- Infant Formula Act of 1980 (P.L. 96-359)

- Orphan Drug Act of 1983 (P.L. 97-414)
- Federal Anti-Tampering Act of 1983 (P.L. 98-127)
- Drug Price Competition and Patent Term Restoration Act of 1984 (P.L. 98-417)
- Prescription Drug Marketing Act of 1987 (P.L. 100-293)
- Generic Animal Drug and Patent Term Restoration Act of 1988 (P.L. 100-670)
- Sanitary Food Transportation Act of 1990 (P.L. 101-500)
- Nutrition Labeling and Education Act of 1990 (P.L. 101-535)
- Safe Medical Devices Act of 1990 (P.L. 101-629)
- Medical Device Amendments of 1992 (P.L. 102-300)
- Prescription Drug Amendments of 1992 (P.L. 102-353)
- Mammography Quality Standards Act (MQSA) of 1992 (P.L. 102-539)
- Prescription Drug User Fee Act (PDUFA) of 1992 (P.L. 102-571)
- Animal Medicinal Drug Use Clarification Act (AMDUCA) of 1994 (P.L. 103-396)
- Dietary Supplement Health and Education Act of 1994 (P.L. 103-417)
- FDA Export Reform and Enhancement Act of 1996 (P.L. 104-134)
- Food Quality Protection Act of 1996 (P.L. 104-170)
- Animal Drug Availability Act of 1996 (P.L. 104-250)
- Food and Drug Administration Modernization Act (FDAMA) of 1997 (P.L. 105-115)
- Best Pharmaceuticals for Children Act of 2002 (P.L. 107-109)
- Public Health Security and Bioterrorism Preparedness and Response Act of 2002 (P.L. 107-188)
- Medical Device User Fee and Modernization Act (MDUFMA) of 2002 (P.L. 107-250)
- Animal Drug User Fee Act of 2003 (P.L. 108-130)
- Pediatric Research Equity Act of 2003 (P.L. 108-155)
- Project BioShield Act of 2004 (P.L. 108-276)
- Food Allergen Labeling and Consumer Protection Act of 2004 (P.L. 108-282)
- Minor Use and Minor Species Animal Health Act of 2004 (P.L. 108-282)
- Dietary Supplement and Nonprescription Drug Consumer Protection Act of 2006 (P.L. 109-462)
- FDA Amendments Act of 2007 (P.L. 110-85)
- Family Smoking Prevention and Tobacco Control Act of 2009 (P.L. 111-31)

- FDA Food Safety Modernization Act of 2011 (P.L. 111-353)
- Drug Quality and Security Act of 2013 (P.L. 113-54)
- Sunscreen Innovation Act of 2014 (P.L. 113-195)
- 21st Century Cures Act of 2019 (P.L. 115-52)

Advances in technology drive up the costs of health services as the new technology is used and paid for. One paradox of advancing health-related technology is that as people live longer because of these advances, they then may need additional health services. The net effect drives up health expenditures for the new technology and for other services consumed over a longer life span. The costs associated with the use of technology generate policy issues of their own. For example, Medicare policies guide the determination of whether it will pay for new services, treatments, and technologies. Using an evidence-based process, with opportunities for public participation, CMS makes a national coverage determination based on whether an item or service is reasonable and necessary for the diagnosis or treatment of an illness or injury. This complex process can be reviewed at the CMS website (www.cms.gov/Medicare/Coverage/DeterminationProcess).

Health System

The health system in any country can be defined as the total national effort undertaken in the private and public sectors that is focused on pursuing health. In the United States, the health system is divided into two distinct components: (1) *public health*, and (2) *healthcare services delivery and financing organizations*. The distinctions between these two components are beginning to blur, but major differences remain. Each component is heavily influenced by policies.

The *public health* component of the health system produces services on a community-wide or population-wide basis, such as health promotion and prevention, communicable disease control, sanitation, food and water safety, the collection and analysis of health statistics, and air pollution control. The *healthcare services delivery and financing* component of the health system provides services primarily to individuals, including diagnosis, treatment, and rehabilitation.

Structurally, the public health component of the health system includes the following, and many more (CDC 2018):

- State and local public health agencies
- Community health centers
- Schools
- Drug rehabilitation facilities
- Doctors

- Home health agencies
- Faith organizations
- Elected officials

In addition to these public health infrastructure components, volunteer organizations such as the American Red Cross, American Diabetes Association, and American Cancer Society are widely considered part of the public health component. Reflecting the blurring of the lines between public health and healthcare components, some accounts also include hospitals and other providers of healthcare services. This trend reflects the increasing use of population health techniques and metrics. Structurally, however, the healthcare delivery and financing component of the health system in the United States remains largely distinct from the public health component. The healthcare services component is also much larger and more elaborate. One way to envision the variety and diversity of healthcare delivery organizations is to consider a continuum of health services that people might use over the course of their lives and to think of the organizational settings that provide them (Longest and Darr 2014).

The continuum could begin before birth with organizations that minimize negative environmental impact on human fetuses or that provide genetic counseling, family planning services, prenatal counseling, prenatal ambulatory care services, and birthing services. This stage would be followed early in life by pediatric ambulatory services; pediatric inpatient hospital services, including neonatal and pediatric intensive care units (ICUs); and ambulatory and inpatient psychiatric services for children.

Healthcare delivery organizations for adults include those providing adult ambulatory services, such as ambulatory surgery centers and emergency and trauma services; adult inpatient hospital services, including routine medical, surgical, and obstetrical services as well as specialized cardiac care units, medical ICUs, surgical ICUs, and monitored units; stand-alone cancer units with radiotherapy capability and short-stay recovery beds; ambulatory and inpatient rehabilitation services, including specific subprograms for orthopedic, neurological, cardiac, arthritis, speech, otologic, and other services; ambulatory and inpatient psychiatric services, including specific subprograms for psychotics, day programs, counseling services, and detoxification; and home health care services.

In their later years, people might add to the list of relevant healthcare delivery organizations those providing skilled and intermediate nursing services; adult day care services; respite services for caregivers of homebound patients, including services such as providing meals, visiting nurse and home health aides, electronic emergency call capability, cleaning, and simple home maintenance; and hospice care, palliative care, and associated family services, including bereavement, legal, and financial counseling.

Healthcare delivery traditionally took place in autonomous organizations with little attention paid to coordination of the continuum of services. In recent decades, however, most healthcare delivery organizations have significantly changed how they relate to one another. Mergers, consolidations, acquisitions, and affiliations (M&A) are now commonplace. This activity has led to vertical integration, in which multiple organizations unify in organizational arrangements or systems. Vertically integrated systems capable of providing a largely seamless continuum of health services—including primary, acute, rehabilitation, long-term, and hospice care—increasingly characterize healthcare in the United States. The ACA seems to have accelerated this activity: 2017 and 2018 were each record years for M&A activity, with the volume of activity reported in 2018 up 14.4 percent. While hospitals, physician practices, and ambulatory surgery centers have been at the center of this activity, current trends are also pointing to increased consolidation activity in the skilled nursing home field (Lagasse 2019). At the extreme end of this integrative activity are large integrated systems and networks in which providers, spanning the full continuum of health services, are integrated with financing mechanisms such as health plans or insurers (Longest and Darr 2014).

Each component of the health system is heavily influenced by policy. Public health policy concerns the government's power to protect and preserve the health of the citizenry while recognizing individual rights to autonomy, privacy, and other legally protected interests. Policy for healthcare delivery and financing includes licensing of institutions, regulation of health plans, reimbursement arrangements for services, and many other activities. Among its many provisions, the ACA includes some that clearly support the public health component of the health system (e.g., establishing the National Prevention, Health Promotion, and Public Health Council to coordinate federal prevention, wellness, and public health activities) and other provisions that support the healthcare delivery and financing component (e.g., improvements to and expansion of the Medicare and Medicaid programs, fostering accountable care organizations).

In terms of government's support, as expressed through policy, for the two components of the health system, it is fair to say that support for *public health* is inadequate and support for *healthcare delivery* has historically been generous but is now tightening under pressure for government at all levels to operate under budgetary constraints. Evidence of government's support for the healthcare delivery component includes enactment in 1946 of the Hospital Survey and Construction Act (P.L. 79-725), a policy that placed Congress squarely in support of expanded availability of health services and improved facilities. Called the Hill-Burton Act after its authors, this legislation provided funds for hospital construction and marked the beginning of a decades-long program of extensive federal developmental subsidies aimed at increasing the availability of health services. This law was another in the long line of federal allocative policies intended to induce certain behavior, in this case the construction of (or additions to) healthcare facilities.

Public policy has also supported and facilitated the expansion of health insurance coverage. During World War II, when wages were frozen for many workers, health insurance and other benefits in lieu of wages became attractive features of the American workplace. Encouraged by policies that excluded these fringe benefits from income taxes and by a US Supreme Court ruling that employee benefits, including health insurance, could be legitimately included in the collective bargaining process, employer-provided health insurance benefits grew rapidly in the mid-twentieth century (Murray 2007).

Summary

WHO (1946) defines health as the "state of complete physical, mental, and social well-being and not merely the absence of disease or infirmity," a definition first appearing in the organization's constitution in 1946 and continuing unchanged today. Health is a function of many health determinants: the physical environments in which people live and work; their behaviors and genetics; social factors (including economic circumstances, socioeconomic position, and income distribution); discrimination based on factors such as race and ethnicity, gender, or sexual orientation; and the availability of social networks or social support and the type, quality, and timing of health services that people receive. Examples of how health policy affects the various determinants of health are provided in the chapter.

A distinction is made between public- and private-sector policy. This book defines *public-sector health policy* as authoritative decisions regarding health or the pursuit of health made in the legislative, executive, or judicial branches of government that are intended to direct or influence the actions, behaviors, or decisions of others. In this definition, the phrase *authoritative decisions* is crucial. It specifies decisions made anywhere in the three branches of government—and at any level of government—that are within the legitimate purview (i.e., the official roles, responsibilities, and authorities) of those making the decisions.

Public-sector health policies are the principal means through which governments help shape the pursuit of health. In the United States, policies can take the form of laws, rules or regulations, implementation decisions, and judicial decisions. Health policies, like other public policies, can fit into broad allocative or regulatory categories.

As this chapter concludes, it will be useful to revisit exhibit 1.10 briefly. With the information provided in this chapter, the reader should be able to define health, health determinants, and health policy and understand the important interrelationships among them. Also important, health policy affects health by affecting one or more of the health determinants listed in exhibit 1.10.

Review Questions

1. Define health. What are the determinants of health?
2. Define public policies and health policies.
3. What forms do health policies take? Give an example of each.
4. Compare and contrast the two basic categories of health policies.
5. Discuss the connections among health policies, health determinants, and health.

References

Association of Academic Health Centers. 2013. *Out of Order, Out of Time: The State of the Nation's Health Workforce.* Accessed March 27, 2020. www.aahcdc.org/Portals/41/Publications-Resources/BooksAndReports/AAHC_OutofTime_4WEB.pdf?ver=2017-01-13-142428-477.

Bircher, J. 2005. "Towards a Dynamic Definition of Health and Disease." *Medicine, Health Care and Philosophy* 8 (3): 335–41.

Birkland, T. A. 2001. *An Introduction to the Policy Process: Theories, Concepts, and Models of Public Policy Making.* Armonk, NY: M. E. Sharpe.

Blum, H. 1974. *Planning for Health.* New York: Human Sciences Press.

Bouye, K., K. McCleary, and K. Williams. 2016. "Increasing Diversity in the Health Professions: Reflections on Student Pipeline Programs." *Journal of Healthcare Science and the Humanities* 6 (1): 67–97.

Brook, R. H., and E. A. McGlynn. 1991. "Maintaining Quality of Care." In *Health Services Research: Key to Health Policy,* edited by E. Ginzberg, 284–314. Cambridge, MA: Harvard University Press.

Byrne, D. 2004. *Enabling Good Health for All: A Reflection Process for a New EU Health Strategy.* European Commission. Accessed March 26, 2020. http://ec.europa.eu/health/ph_overview/Documents/pub_good_health_en.pdf.

Centers for Disease Control and Prevention (CDC). 2019. "NCHHSTP Determinants of Health." Reviewed December 19. www.cdc.gov/nchhstp/socialdeterminants.

———. 2018. "Introduction to Public Health Laboratories." Reviewed November 15. www.cdc.gov/publichealth101/laboratories.html.

Centers for Medicare & Medicaid Services (CMS). 2020a. "NHE Fact Sheet." Updated March 24. www.cms.gov/research-statistics-data-and-systems/statistics-trends-and-reports/nationalhealthexpenddata/nhe-fact-sheet.html.

———. 2020b. "Projected." Modified March 25. www.cms.gov/Research-Statistics-Data-and-Systems/Statistics-Trends-and-Reports/NationalHealthExpendData/NationalHealthAccountsProjected.html.

Cochran, C. L., and E. F. Malone. 1999. *Public Policy: Perspectives and Choices*, 2nd ed. New York: McGraw-Hill.

Commonwealth Fund. 2018. "Access to Care by Income." Published September 26. www.commonwealthfund.org/chart/2018/access-care-income.

Dahlgren, G., and M. Whitehead. 2006. *European Strategies for Tackling Social Inequities in Health: Levelling Up Part 2.* Accessed March 26, 2020. www.euro.who.int/__data/assets/pdf_file/0018/103824/E89384.pdf.

Doran, K. M., E. J. Misa, and N. R. Shah. 2013. "Housing as Health Care—New York's Boundary-Crossing Experiment." *New England Journal of Medicine* 369 (25): 2374–77.

Dubos, R. 1959. *The Mirage of Health.* New York: Harper.

Gamage, D. 2015. "Foreword—King v. Burwell Symposium: Comments on the Commentaries (and Some Elephants in the Room)." *Indiana Law Review.* Accessed September 17, 2019. www.repository.law.indiana.edu/facpub/2419.

Garfield, R., K. Orgera, and A. Damico. 2019. "The Uninsured and the ACA." Published January 25. www.kff.org/report-section/the-uninsured-and-the-aca-a-primer-key-facts-about-health-insurance-and-the-uninsured-amidst-changes-to-the-affordable-care-act-how-many-people-are-uninsured.

Hayes, S. L., P. Riley, D. C. Radley, and D. McCarthy. 2017. "Racial and Ethnic Disparities in Access to Care: Has the Affordable Care Act Made a Difference?" Commonwealth Fund. Published August 24. www.commonwealthfund.org/publications/issue-briefs/2017/aug/reducing-racial-and-ethnic-disparities-access-care-has.

Hickman, K. E. 2015. "The (Perhaps) Unintended Consequences of King v. Burwell." *Pepperdine Law Review* 56: 55–71.

Hostetter, M., and S. Klein. 2018. *In Focus: Reducing Racial Disparities in Health Care by Confronting Racism.* Commonwealth Fund. Published September 27. www.commonwealthfund.org/publications/newsletter-article/2018/sep/focus-reducing-racial-disparities-health-care-confronting.

Institute of Medicine (IOM). 2002. *Unequal Treatment: Confronting Racial and Ethnic Disparities in Health Care.* Washington, DC: National Academies Press.

Jones, D. K., M. K. Gusmano, P. Nadash, and E. A. Miller. 2018. "Undermining the ACA Through the Executive Branch and Federalism: What the Trump Administration's Approach to Health Reform Means for Older Americans." *Journal of Aging and Social Policy* 30 (3–4): 282–99.

Jost, T. 2017. "The Tax Bill and the Individual Mandate: What Happened, and What Does It Mean?" *Health Affairs Blog.* Published December 20. www.healthaffairs.org/do/10.1377/hblog20171220.323429/full.

———. 2014. "Implementing Health Reform: Four Years Later." *Health Affairs* 33 (1): 7–10.

———. 2008. "'MetLife v. Glenn': The Court Addresses a Conflict over Conflicts in ERISA Benefit Administration." *Health Affairs* 27 (5): w430–40.

Kaiser Family Foundation. 2019. "Medicaid/CHIP Coverage of Lawfully Residing Immigrant Children and Pregnant Women." Updated January 1. www.kff.org/health-reform/state-indicator/medicaid-chip-coverage-of-lawfully-residing-immigrant-children-and-pregnant-women/.

———. 2018a. "The Number of Uninsured People Rose in 2017, Reversing Some Coverage Gains Under the Affordable Care Act." Published December 10. www.kff.org/uninsured/press-release/the-number-of-uninsured-people-rose-in-2017-reversing-some-of-the-coverage-gains-under-the-affordable-care-act.

———. 2018b. "Summary of the 2018 CHIP Funding Extension." Published January 24. www.kff.org/medicaid/fact-sheet/summary-of-the-2018-chip-funding-extension.

Kasper, A. 2011. "Anti-Trust Review of Accountable Care Organizations: An Assessment of the FTC and DOJ's Relaxed Approach to Regulating Physician-Hospital Networks." *University of North Carolina Law Review.* Accessed September 19, 2019. http://scholarship.law.unc.edu/nclr/vol90/iss1/5.

Khullar, D., and D. A. Chokshi. 2018. "Health, Income, and Poverty: Where We Are and What Could Help." *Health Affairs.* Published October 4. www.healthaffairs.org/do/10.1377/hpb20180817.901935/full.

Kotch, J. B. (ed). 1997. *Maternal and Child Health: Programs, Problems and Policy in Public Health.* Gaithersburg, MD: Aspen Publishers.

Lagasse, J. 2019. "Healthcare Mergers and Acquisitions Had Record Year in 2018, Up 14.4 Percent." *Healthcare Finance.* Published January 24. www.healthcarefinancenews.com/news/healthcare-mergers-and-acquisitions-had-record-year-2018-144-percent.

Liptak, A. 2012. "Supreme Court Upholds Health Care Law, 5–4, in Victory for Obama." *New York Times.* Published June 28. www.nytimes.com/2012/06/29/us/supreme-court-lets-health-law-largely-stand.html.

Longest, B. B., Jr., and K. Darr. 2014. *Managing Health Services Organizations and Systems,* 6th ed. Baltimore, MD: Health Professions Press.

Luhby, T. 2013. "The New Inequality: Health Care." CNN Money. Published December 18. http://money.cnn.com/2013/12/18/news/economy/health-inequality/index.html.

Martiniano, R., and J. Moore. 2018. *Health Care Employment Projections, 2016–2026: An Analysis of Bureau of Labor Statistics Projections by Setting and by Occupation.* Center for Health Workforce Studies, School of Public Health, University at Albany, State University of New York. Published February. www.chwsny.org/wp-content/uploads/2018/02/BLS-Projections-2_26_18.pdf.

Murphy, S., J. Xu, K. Kochanek, and E. Arias. 2018. "Mortality in the US, 2017." National Center for Health Statistics. Published November. www.cdc.gov/nchs/data/databriefs/db328-h.pdf.

Murray, J. E. 2007. *Origins of American Health Insurance: A History of Industrial Sickness Funds.* New Haven, CT: Yale University Press.

National Institutes of Health (NIH). 2020. "What We Do: Budget." Reviewed March 3. www.nih.gov/about-nih/what-we-do/budget.

Ogden, L. 2012. "Financing and Organization of National Health Systems." In *World Health Systems: Challenges and Perspectives*, 2nd edition, edited by B. J. Fried and L. M. Gaydos, 49–70. Chicago: Health Administration Press.

Organisation for Economic Co-Operation and Development (OECD). 2019. "Healthcare Expenditure and Financing." Accessed August 13. https://stats.oecd.org/Index.aspx?DataSetCode=SHA.

Partnership for Sustainable Health Care. 2013. *Strengthening Affordability and Quality in America's Health Care System.* Published April. www.pcpcc.org/sites/default/files/resources/rwjf405432.pdf.

Peters, B. G. 2013. *American Public Policy: Promise and Performance*, 9th ed. Thousand Oaks, CA: CQ Press.

PhRMA. 2019. "Advocacy: Research and Development." Accessed August 13. www.phrma.org/advocacy/research-development.

Rice, T., L. Unruh, E. van Ginneken, P. Rosenau, and A. J. Barnes. 2018. "Universal Coverage in the USA: From Obama Through Trump." *Health Policy* 122 (7): 698–702.

Ruckart, P., A. Ettinger, M. Hanna-Attisha, N. Jones, S. Davis, and P. Breysse. 2019. "The Flint Water Crisis: A Coordinated Public Health Emergency Response and Recovery Initiative." *Journal of Public Health Management Practice* 25: S84–90.

Samet, J. M., T. A. Burke, and B. D. Goldstein. 2017. "The Trump Administration and the Environment: Heed the Science." *New England Journal of Medicine.* Published March 23. www.nejm.org/doi/full/10.1056/NEJMms1615242.

Saracci, R. 1997. "The World Health Organisation Needs to Reconsider Its Definition of Health." *British Medical Journal* 314 (7091): 1409–10.

Schoen, C., D. C. Radley, P. Riley, J. A. Lippa, J. Berenson, C. Dermody, and A. Shih. 2013. "Health Care in the Two Americas: Findings from the Scorecard on State Health System Performance for Low-Income Populations, 2013." Published September 18. www.commonwealthfund.org/publications/fund-reports/2013/sep/health-care-two-americas-findings-scorecard-state-health-system.

Shi, L. 2019. *Introduction to Health Policy*, 2nd ed. Chicago: Health Administration Press.

Sisko, A., S. Keehan, J. Poisal, G. Cuckler, S. Smith, A. Madison, K. E. Rennie, and J. Hardesty. 2019. "National Healthcare Expenditures, 2018–2027: Economic and Demographic Trends Drive Spending and Enrollment Growth."

Health Affairs. Published February 20. www.healthaffairs.org/doi/10.1377/hlthaff.2018.05499.

Squires, D. A. 2011. "The U.S. Health System in Perspective: A Comparison of Twelve Industrialized Nations." Commonwealth Fund. Published July 27. www.commonwealthfund.org/publications/issue-briefs/2011/jul/us-health-system-perspective-comparison-twelve-industrialized.

Steinbrook, R. 2009. "Health Care and the American Recovery and Reinvestment Act." *New England Journal of Medicine* 360 (11): 1057–60.

Thompson, F. J. 2013. "Health Reform, Polarization, and Public Administration." *Public Administration Review* 73 (S1): S3–12.

US Census Bureau. 2019. "QuickFacts United States: Population Estimates; Race and Hispanic Origin." Updated July 1. www.census.gov/quickfacts/fact/table/US/PST045219.

US Department of Health and Human Services (HHS). 2020. "Healthy People 2020." Accessed March 27. www.healthypeople.gov.

———. 2014. "National Healthcare Disparities Report, 2013." Published May. www.ahrq.gov/research/findings/nhqrdr/nhdr13/2013nhdr.pdf.

US Food and Drug Administration (FDA). 2018. "What We Do." Reviewed March 28. www.fda.gov/about-fda/what-we-do.

Vietor, R. H. K., and M. Weinzierl. 2012. "Macroeconomic Policy and U.S. Competitiveness." *Harvard Business Review* 90 (3): 113–16.

Will, G. 2019. "The Repeal of the 'Cadillac Care' Tax Showed a Hazard for Bipartisanship." *Washington Post.* Published July 24. www.washingtonpost.com/opinions/the-repeal-of-the-cadillac-tax-showed-a-hazard-of-bipartisanship/2019/07/24/28e169aa-ad76-11e9-a0c9-6d2d7818f3da_story.html.

Williams, R. A. 2011. *Healthcare Disparities at the Crossroads with Healthcare Reform.* New York: Springer.

World Health Organization. 1946. "Preamble to the Constitution of the World Health Organization." Accessed March 27, 2020. www.who.int/bulletin/archives/80(12)981.pdf.

CHAPTER

2

THE CONTEXT OF HEALTH POLICYMAKING

Learning Objectives

After reading this chapter, you should be able to

- describe the functions of the legislative, executive, and judicial branches of the federal government;
- describe the functions of the legislative, executive, and judicial branches of state governments;
- appreciate the roles of federal and state governments in health policy;
- understand the concept of a policy market and its operation;
- identify demanders and suppliers of health policy;
- identify and describe the role of interest groups;
- appreciate the role of interest groups in the health policy market; and
- distinguish between the pluralist and elitist perspectives on interest groups.

Whether health policies take the form of laws, rules or regulations, implementation decisions, or judicial decisions, all policies are authoritative decisions made in a context through a defined, often complicated, process. In this chapter, we consider the context. We will then examine the process of policymaking in chapter 3.

The most basic fact about the context of public-sector health policymaking is that the context includes government. The context is broader than government, but the various levels of government, and the branches in each, as well as the individuals and entities in each level and branch, provide a good starting point for understanding the context of public policymaking, including health policymaking. As Peters (2013, 3) has observed, government in the United States is "an immense network of organizations and institutions affecting the daily lives of all citizens in countless ways."

Encompassing all of government and more, the context of health policymaking is large and complex, and well beyond full description in this chapter. However, there is an abundance of literature on the structure of the US government, including the state and local levels. For example, see Edwards, Wattenberg, and Lineberry (2014). Brief descriptions of federal, state, and local governments in the United States follow.[1]

Federal Government

Since the Second Continental Congress declared America's independence from Great Britain on July 4, 1776, the federal government has sought to realize the fundamental principle on which the nation was founded: that all people have the right to life, liberty, and the pursuit of happiness. This principle was formalized in 1788 with the ratification of the Constitution. That document became the foundation of a federal government that brought the several states together to act as one while protecting the sovereignty of each individual state.

To ensure that no person or group would amass too much power, the founders established a government in which the powers to create, implement, and adjudicate laws were separated into legislative, executive, and judicial branches (see exhibit 2.1 for an organization chart of the federal government). Each branch of government is balanced by powers in the other two coequal branches: The president can veto the laws of the Congress; the Congress confirms or rejects many of the president's appointments and can remove the president from office in exceptional circumstances; and the justices of the Supreme Court, who can overturn unconstitutional laws, are appointed by the president and confirmed by the Senate.

Executive Branch

As head of the executive branch, the president is responsible for implementing and enforcing the laws written by Congress and, to that end, appoints the heads of the 15 federal executive departments, who must be confirmed by the Senate. These individuals comprise the president's cabinet. The cabinet departments and other independent federal agencies are responsible for the day-to-day implementation and enforcement of federal laws. These departments and agencies have missions and responsibilities as divergent as those of the Department of Defense, the Department of Health and Human Services (HHS), the Environmental Protection Agency, the Social Security Administration, and the Securities and Exchange Commission.

Among the 15 departments shown in exhibit 2.1, HHS (www.hhs.gov/about) is the federal government's principal agency for protecting the health of Americans and providing essential human services, especially for those who are

EXHIBIT 2.1
The Government of the United States

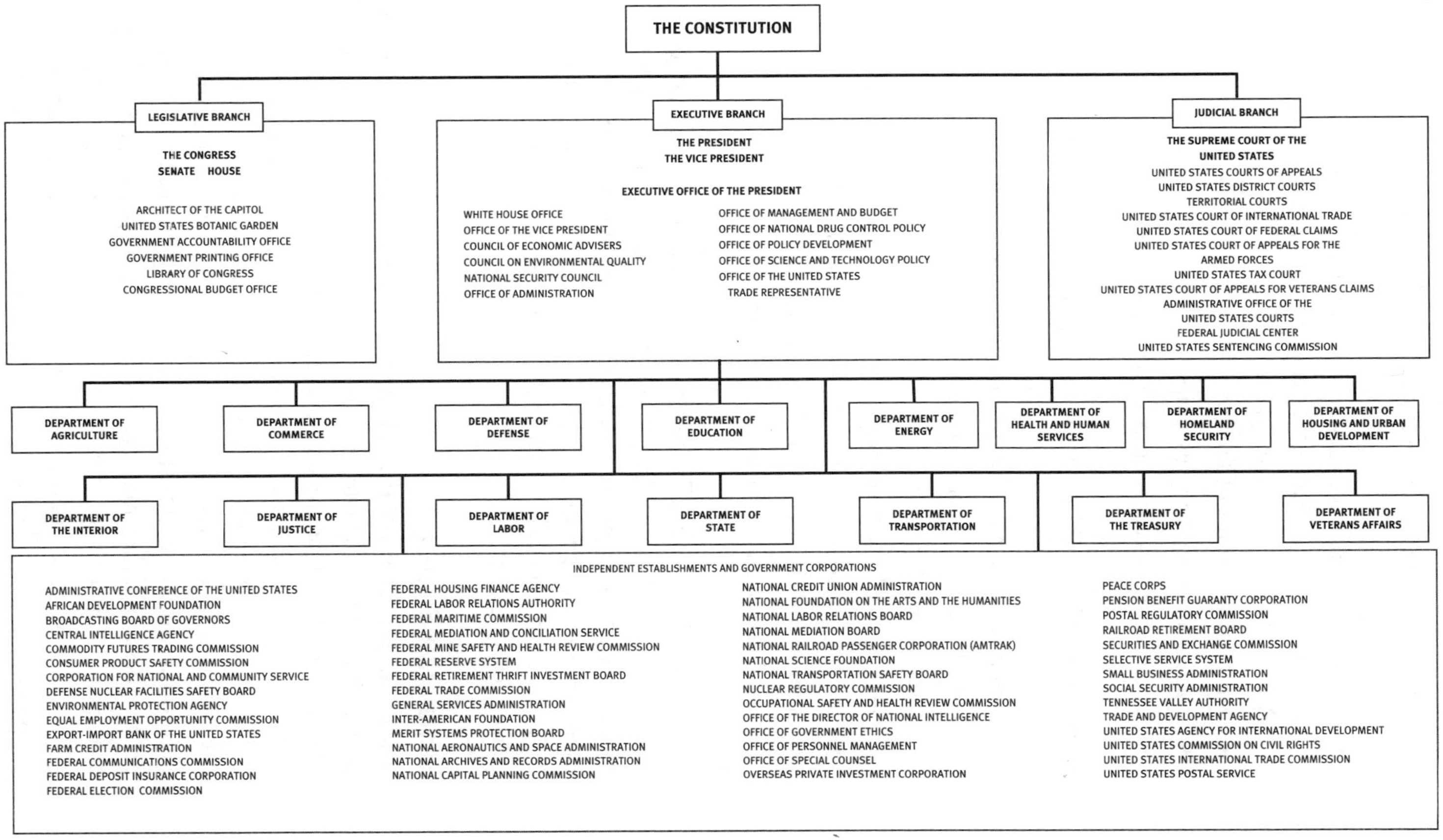

Source: US Government Printing Office (2020).

most vulnerable. Agencies of HHS conduct health and social science research, work to prevent disease outbreaks, ensure food and drug safety, and provide health insurance. Perhaps the most important agencies—certainly the most prominent in the public eye—include the following:

- Centers for Medicare & Medicaid Services (CMS), which administers the Medicare and Medicaid programs and many aspects of the Affordable Care Act (ACA)
- National Institutes of Health
- Food and Drug Administration
- Centers for Disease Control and Prevention

Other parts of the HHS portfolio of agencies include the following:

- Administration for Children and Families
- Health Resources and Services Administration
- Indian Health Service
- Substance Abuse and Mental Health Services Administration
- Agency for Toxic Substances and Disease Registry
- Agency for Health Research and Quality
- Administration for Community Living

HHS, employing 75,000 people, has an operating budget of approximately \$87.1 billion in discretionary funds and more than \$1.2 trillion in mandatory entitlement expenditures. The department's programs are administered by the 11 operating divisions listed earlier, which are all part of the US Public Health Service, as well as 3 human services agencies and 10 regional offices (HHS 2015).

Legislative Branch

The legislative branch of the federal government consists of the House of Representatives and the Senate, which together form the US Congress. (Extensive information about Congress is available at www.congress.gov.) The Constitution vests all legislative power at the federal level in Congress, meaning that it is the only part of the federal government that can make new laws or amend existing laws. To pass legislation and send it to the president for signature, both the House and the Senate must pass the same bill by majority vote. If the president vetoes a bill, they may override the veto by passing the bill again in each chamber with at least two-thirds of each body voting in favor (see exhibit 2.2).

Although the legislative process will be covered more fully in chapter 7, the process is outlined here. Additional information on this complex process is

EXHIBIT 2.2
Relationship of the Branches of the US Government

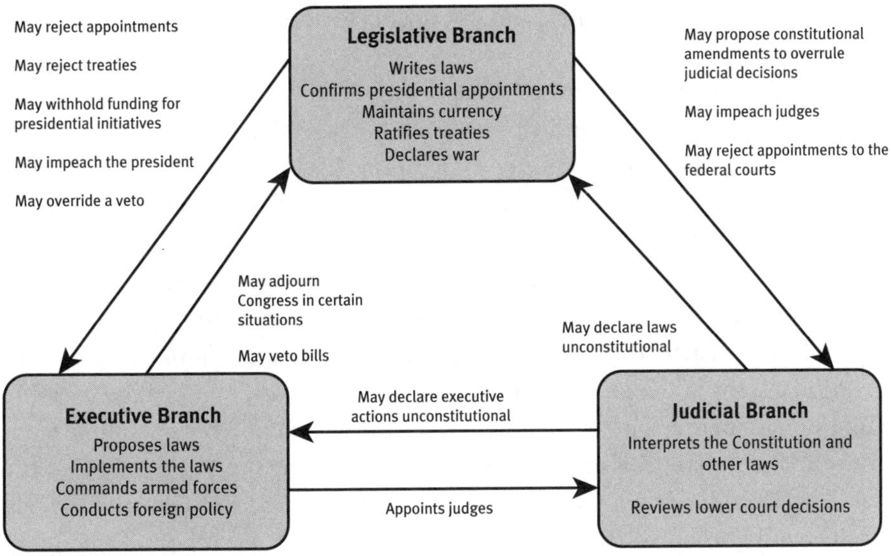

available at www.congress.gov/legislative-process. The first step in the legislative process is the introduction of a bill—which is a piece of proposed legislation—to Congress. Bills can be introduced in either chamber of Congress, and sometimes are introduced in both simultaneously. Anyone can draft a bill, but only representatives and senators can introduce bills.

After being introduced, whether in the House of Representatives, the Senate, or both, a bill is referred to the appropriate committee or committees for review. The role of the legislative committees in this process is critical. There are 20 Senate committees, with many subcommittees, and, coincidentally, 20 House committees, also with many subcommittees. There are four joint committees, composed of members from both houses. The committees are not set in stone, but change in number and form with each new Congress (every two years) as required for the meaningful consideration of legislation. Each committee oversees a specific policy area, and the subcommittees take on more specialized policy areas. For example, the House Committee on Ways and Means (http://waysandmeans.house.gov) includes subcommittees on health, Social Security, trade, and others. Its Senate analogue, the Senate Finance Committee, has a subcommittee on healthcare, among several others (http://finance.senate.gov).

A bill is first considered in a subcommittee, where it may be accepted, amended, or rejected entirely. If the members of the subcommittee agree to move a bill forward, it is reported to the full committee, where the process is repeated. Throughout this stage of the process, the committees and subcommittees call hearings to investigate the merits and flaws of the proposal. They invite experts, advocates, and opponents to appear before the committee and provide testimony.

If the full committee votes to approve the bill, it is reported to the floor of the House or Senate, and the majority party leadership decides when to place the bill on the calendar for consideration. If a bill is particularly pressing, it may be considered in short order. Others may wait for months or never be scheduled. When a bill is approved in one chamber, it is referred to the other for consideration. A bill must pass in both chambers of Congress before it goes to the president for consideration. Though the Constitution requires that the two bills have exactly the same wording, this rarely happens in practice without additional steps in the process. To bring the nonidentical bills dealing with the same subject matter into accord with one another, a conference committee is convened, consisting of members from both chambers. The members of the committee produce a conference report, intended as the final version of the bill. Each chamber then votes again to approve the conference report. Depending on where the bill originated (the house of origin has the final approval), the final text is then enrolled by either the clerk of the House or the secretary of the Senate, and presented to the Speaker of the House and the president of the Senate for their signatures. The bill is then sent to the president.

Upon receiving a bill from Congress, the president may substantially agree with it and sign it into law. If the president believes the law to be bad policy, he or she can veto the bill and send it back to Congress. Congress may override the veto with a two-thirds vote of each chamber, at which point the bill becomes law.

Part of Congress's exercise of legislative authority is the establishment of an annual federal budget. To this end, Congress levies taxes and tariffs to provide funding for essential government services. If enough money cannot be raised to fund the government, then Congress may also authorize borrowing to make up the difference. Regrettably, in recent decades, passing a budget has been observed in the breach more than in practice: "In the four decades since the current system for budgeting and spending tax dollars has been in effect, Congress has managed to pass all its required appropriations measures on time only four times: in fiscal 1977 (the first full fiscal year under the current system), 1989, 1995 and 1997" (Desilver 2018).

Oversight of the executive branch is an important congressional check on the president's power and a balance against the president's discretion in implementing laws and making rules and regulations. A major way that Congress conducts oversight is through hearings. The House Committee on Oversight and Government Reform and the Senate Committee on Homeland Security and Government Affairs are both devoted to overseeing government operations. Congress also maintains an investigative organization, the Government

Accountability Office (www.gao.gov), which audits and generates reports on every aspect of the government.

Structurally, the House of Representatives is made up of 435 elected members, divided among the 50 states in proportion to their total population. In addition, there are six nonvoting members, representing the District of Columbia, the Commonwealth of Puerto Rico, and four other territories of the United States. The presiding officer of the chamber is the Speaker of the House, elected by the representatives. Members or representatives are elected every two years and must be 25 years of age, a US citizen for at least seven years, and a resident of the state they represent. The House has several powers assigned exclusively to it, including the power to initiate revenue bills, impeach federal officials, and elect the president in the case of an electoral college tie.

Structurally, the Senate is composed of 100 senators, two for each state. Senators are elected to six-year terms by the people of each state. The vice president of the United States serves as president of the Senate and may cast the decisive vote in the event of a tie in the Senate. Senators' terms are staggered so that about one-third of the Senate is up for reelection every two years. Senators must be 30 years of age, a US citizen for at least nine years, and a resident of the state they represent. The Senate has the sole power to confirm those appointments of the president that require consent and to ratify treaties. The Senate also serves as a jury in the case of impeachment trials. To be "impeached" by the House is the equivalent of an indictment in a criminal proceeding: it is *not* a finding of guilt. As the court conducts the criminal case of an indicted defendant, the Senate conducts the trial of the impeached official and determines guilt or innocence. If the Senate concludes the official is guilty of an impeachable offense, that official is thereby removed from office. (For an excellent presentation of an impeachment case, see the case of Judge Alcee Hastings, at US Senate [2020].)

Judicial Branch

Although the role of the judicial branch in health policymaking is discussed much more extensively in chapter 8, the basic structure of the federal court system in the United States is outlined here as part of our discussion of the context of policymaking. Unlike the executive and legislative branches of the federal government, which are elected by the people, members of the judicial branch are nominated by the president and confirmed by the Senate. Federal judges hold their offices under life tenure and may remain in office until they resign, die, or are impeached and convicted by Congress. Because federal judges do not have to run or campaign for reelection, they have the opportunity to be insulated from political pressure when deciding cases.

The Constitution leaves Congress significant discretion to determine the shape and structure of the federal judiciary. Even the number of Supreme Court justices is left to Congress. The Constitution also grants Congress the power to establish courts inferior to the Supreme Court, and to that end, Congress has established the US district courts, which try most federal cases, and 13 US courts of appeals, also known as circuit courts, which review appealed district court cases in their respective circuits.

Federal courts enjoy the sole power to interpret the law, determine the constitutionality of the law, and apply it to individual cases. The courts, like Congress, can compel the production of evidence and testimony through a subpoena. The inferior courts are constrained by the decisions of the Supreme Court—once the Supreme Court interprets a law, inferior courts must apply the Supreme Court's interpretation to the facts of particular cases.

The Supreme Court of the United States is the highest court in the land and the only part of the federal judicial branch specifically required by the Constitution. The Court's caseload consists almost entirely of appeals from lower courts, and the Court's decisions cannot be appealed to any authority, as it is the final judicial arbiter in the United States on matters of federal law.

In almost all instances, the Supreme Court does not hear appeals as a matter of right; instead, parties must petition the Court for a writ of certiorari. A litigant who loses in a federal court of appeals, or in the highest court of a state, may file such a petition asking the Supreme Court to review the case. The Court typically will agree to hear a case only when it involves a new and important legal principle, or when two or more federal appellate courts have interpreted a law differently. Of the approximately 7,500 requests for certiorari filed each year, the Court usually responds positively to fewer than 150 (US Courts 2020). As noted in chapter 1, the Supreme Court's ruling in 2012 that the ACA was constitutional was a crucial milestone for the law, permitting it to proceed (Liptak 2012), and is an example of the type of cases the Court chooses to hear. In fact, the Supreme Court can also determine that one part of a law does not pass constitutional muster while upholding other sections as valid (see policy snapshot for part 1).

If the Supreme Court grants certiorari, justices accept legal briefs from the parties to the case, as well as from *amicus curiae*, or "friends of the court." These can include industry trade groups, academics, or even the US government itself. Before issuing a ruling, the Court usually hears oral arguments in which the various parties to the case present their arguments and the justices ask them questions. If the case involves the federal government, the solicitor general of the United States presents arguments on behalf of the United States. The justices then hold private conferences, make their decision, and issue the Court's opinion, along with any dissenting arguments that may have been written. In the case of *NFIB v. Sebelius* in the policy snapshot at the beginning of part 1, there were four separate opinions in which justices concurred in whole or in part, with multiple justices concurring with or dissenting from various elements of the opinions.

State Government

In the United States, each state is a sovereign government unto itself (Carruth and Goldstein 2014). Each state has a constitution and a bill of rights. These documents set forth the structure and function of the state government and of the local governments in their boundaries. State constitutions tend to be more elaborate than their federal counterpart. The Alabama Constitution, for example, contains 310,296 words—more than 40 times as many as the US Constitution has.

Each state has three branches of government, and the duties of each branch are essentially the same as those in the federal government. The legislative branch passes laws and oversees the executive branch, which implements the laws and the judicial branch, which determines the constitutionality of laws and adjudicates violations of them.

Executive Branch

In every state, the executive branch is headed by a governor who is directly elected by the people. In most states, the other leaders in the executive branch are also directly elected, including the lieutenant governor, the attorney general, the secretary of state, and auditors and commissioners. States reserve the right to organize in any way, so they often vary greatly in executive structure. No two state executive organizations are identical.

Legislative Branch

All 50 states have legislatures made up of elected representatives, who consider matters brought forth by the governor or introduced by its members to create legislation that can become law. The legislature also approves a state's budget and initiates tax legislation.

Except for Nebraska, all states have a bicameral legislature made up of two chambers: a smaller upper house and a larger lower house. Together the two chambers make state laws and fulfill other governing responsibilities. The smaller upper chamber is always called the *senate*, and its members generally serve longer terms, usually four years. The larger lower chamber is most often called the *house of representatives*, but some states call it the *assembly* or the *house of delegates*. Its members usually serve shorter terms, often two years.

Judicial Branch

State judicial branches are usually led by the state supreme court, which hears appeals from lower-level state courts. Court structures and judicial appointments or elections are determined either by legislation or the state constitution. Most states have a three-tiered judicial structure: trial courts, intermediate appellate courts, and a state supreme court. The supreme court of each state focuses on correcting errors made in lower courts and therefore holds no trials. Rulings made in state supreme courts are normally binding; however, when questions are raised regarding consistency with the US Constitution, matters may be appealed directly to the US Supreme Court.

Local Government

Local governments generally include two tiers: counties, also known as *boroughs* in Alaska and *parishes* in Louisiana, and municipalities, or cities and towns. In some states, counties are divided into townships. Counties are considered subdivisions of the state, while municipalities are a separate legal structure. Municipalities can be structured in many ways, as defined by state constitutions, and are called townships, villages, boroughs, cities, or towns. Various kinds of special districts also provide functions in local government outside county or municipal boundaries, such as school districts or fire protection districts.

Municipal governments—those defined as cities, townships, boroughs (except in Alaska), villages, and towns—are generally organized around a population center and in most cases correspond to the geographic designations used by the US Census Bureau for reporting housing and population statistics. Municipalities vary greatly in size, from the millions of residents of New York City and Los Angeles to the 322 people who live in Moscow, Kansas (City-Data.com 2020).

Municipalities generally take responsibility for parks and recreation services; police and fire departments; housing services; emergency medical services; municipal courts; public transportation; and public works such as streets, sewers, snow removal, and signage. Local governments often play important environmental protection roles through such activities as zoning, planning, and issuance of building permits.

Whereas the federal government and state governments are constitutionally based sovereign governments, which share power in countless ways, local governments must be granted power by the states in which they are located. In general, mayors, city councils, and other governing bodies are directly elected by the people, accountable to those who elected them.

Governments at All Three Levels Make Health Policy

In the United States, governments at the federal, state, and local levels make health policy. A debate over the appropriate distribution of health policy responsibilities between the levels of government dates from the nation's founding and remains unsettled. Government's responsibility for health rests primarily at the federal and state levels, but also to a more limited degree with local governments.

The term for the arrangement of shared responsibility among levels of government is *federalism*, especially pertaining to how responsibilities and powers are distributed between the states and the national government. (This concept will be explored in depth in chapter 3.) Federalism is any system of government with both a national, or central, authority and autonomous constituent jurisdictions such as states (Bovbjerg, Wiener, and Houseman 2003). In practical terms, federalism means that responsibility for health policy is shared between the federal government and the states, and to a limited degree with local governments, with each level playing important roles. Sometimes these roles overlap. For example, the federal government is largely responsible for the ACA and Medicare, but, as observed in the policy snapshot at the beginning of part 1, federal and state governments share responsibility for Medicaid and certain operational aspects of the ACA. All three levels of government are responsible for the health and well-being of their citizens, and all levels can use policy in the pursuit of health. Their policy tools include the ability to regulate, raise, and spend funds; confer benefits; and contract with private entities in pursuit of public purposes. Some of the key responsibilities at each level are described in the following sections.

An important source of state-level health policy information is available at this Kaiser Family Foundation website: http://kff.org/statedata. Interested readers may also wish to explore the Commonwealth Fund's website at www.commonwealthfund.org.

Federal Government's Role in Health Policy

Over the years since the enactment of Medicare and Medicaid and culminating with passage of the ACA, the federal government has played an increasingly dominant role in health policy. Other aspects of its role include maintenance of massive healthcare delivery programs for the Departments of Veterans Affairs, Defense, and HHS through which services are provided directly to veterans, the military and their dependents, and American Indians and Alaska Natives. In addition, the federal role in health policy includes regulation of food and drugs, support for medical research, prevention of diseases, and homeland security.

State Governments' Role in Health Policy

States play several important health policy roles (King 2005; Leichter 2008), which are summarized in the box on pages 68–69. Medicaid, in which the states play a critical role, is the largest health insurance program in the United States. States also play a major role in maintaining public health, in financing and providing services for individuals who are aged 65 and over or who have chronic mental illness, and in substance abuse prevention and treatment.

State Governments' Multifaceted Role in Health Policy

Guardians of the Public's Health

States have constitutional authority to establish laws that protect the public's health and welfare, including protecting against the consequences of natural and human-caused disasters, dealing with environmental challenges, ensuring safe practices in workplaces and food service establishments, mounting programs to prevent injuries and promote healthy behaviors, and providing health services such as public health nursing and communicable disease control.

Purchasers of Healthcare Services

In addition to their Medicaid funding roles, states also typically provide health insurance benefits to state employees and their dependents and, in many states, to other public-sector workers, such as teachers.

Regulators

States have legal authority to license and regulate health professionals and health-related organizations. States also establish and monitor compliance with environmental quality standards. A particularly important aspect of the role of states in health-related regulation is their responsibility for the health insurance industry as it operates within their boundaries. States control the content, marketing, and pricing of health insurance products and health plans, although the ACA established a larger federal role in regulation of the health insurance industry.

Safety Net Providers

States provide safety nets—although these are often porous—through their support for community-based providers, hospitals that provide charity care, local health departments and clinics that serve low-income people, and other programs that ensure access to appropriate healthcare services.

Educators

States subsidize medical education and graduate medical education through Medicaid payments to teaching hospitals, state appropriations, and scholarship and loan programs. More broadly, states provide funding and expertise for large-scale health education campaigns to improve population health through such educational programs as informing parents about immunization benefits and requirements or encouraging the general public to use seat belts and motorcycle helmets.

Laboratories

States are viewed as laboratories in which experimentation with new policy takes place. For example, Massachusetts enacted a health reform law, titled An Act Providing Access to Affordable, Quality, Accountable Health Care, in 2006. Many features of this state law presaged features of the federal ACA.

A salient feature of health policy in the United States is the wide variability from state to state in approaches to health policy and in the related health status of their populations. This variability across states can be seen in data reported in *The Commonwealth Fund's Scorecard on State Health System Performance, 2018* (Radley, McCarthy, and Hayes 2018). This study assesses performance in the states on 43 key indicators grouped into four categories as follows:

1. *Access and Affordability*, using seven indicators such as rates of insurance coverage and cost-related barriers to receiving care
2. *Prevention and Treatment*, using 16 indicators such as measures of receiving preventive care and the quality of care in various settings
3. *Potentially Avoidable Hospital Use and Cost*, using ten indicators such as hospital use that might have been reduced with timely and effective care and follow-up
4. *Healthy Lives*, using ten indicators such as measures of premature death and risky health behaviors

In addition, the study considers Disparity, which includes 19 factors that spread across the other four factors. Racial and ethnic disparities are the subject of a different report.

The Commonwealth Fund study found twofold to eightfold differences between the best-performing and worst-performing states on multiple indicators. Because the study was conducted as a time series, it also showed variation in rates of change in performance over time. Although this study does not show causation, at least some of the variation in performance across states' healthcare systems likely reflects policy differences among the states.

Local Government's Role in Health Policy

Local governments, especially in larger cities and urbanized counties, are major providers of services for the indigent through operation of public hospitals and clinics. They also play roles in wastewater management, local water supply, regulating smoking, and maintaining cleanliness standards for restaurants, among others.

Summary of Government Roles

Indeed, as noted at the outset of this discussion of the levels and branches of government, the context of public-sector health policymaking is large and complex because it encompasses all of government. Expanding and complicating the context even more is the fact that the context includes all those variables outside the policymaking process that affect or are affected by the authoritative decisions made in the policymaking process. These variables include the situations and preferences of individuals, organizations, and groups, as well as biological, biomedical, cultural, demographic, ecological, economic, ethical, psychological, science, social, and technological variables in the larger society. A useful way to consider the context of health policy is to view the context as a market.

The Health Policy Market

There is a market for health policies. In this market, some people provide the authoritative decisions that constitute health policy, and other people seek particular decisions. The market for health policies has characteristics in common with a traditional economic market. Many different products and services are bought and sold in the context of economic markets. In these markets, willing buyers and sellers enter into economic exchanges in which each party attains something of value. One party demands, and the other supplies. By dealing with one another through market transactions, individuals and organizations buy needed resources and sell their outputs. These relationships are summarized in exhibit 2.3. Because people are calculative regarding the relative costs and benefits of market exchanges, they negotiate. Negotiation is a key feature of economic markets and policy markets.

Negotiation in Markets

Negotiation, or bargaining, involves two or more parties attempting to settle what each will give and take (or perform and receive) in an economic transaction. In the negotiations that take place in an economic market, the parties seek a mutually acceptable outcome in a situation where their preferences are usually negatively related (e.g., buyers prefer lower prices, while sellers prefer

EXHIBIT 2.3
Relationships in Economic Markets

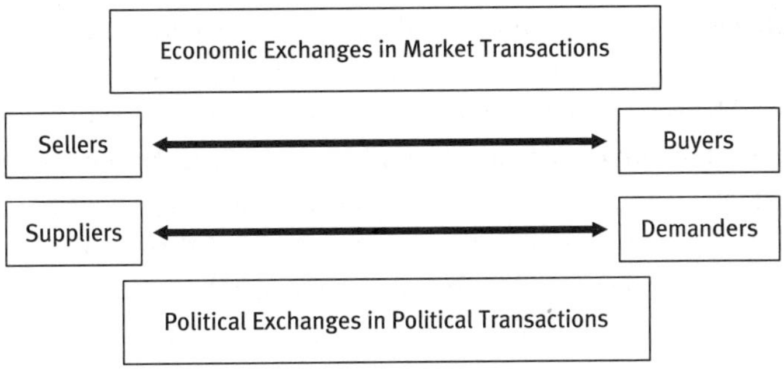

higher prices). Indeed, if the preferences for outcomes are positively related, an agreement can be reached almost automatically.

More typically, at least two types of issues must be resolved through the negotiations. One type involves the division of resources—the so-called tangibles of the negotiation, such as who will receive how much money and what products or services. Another type centers on the resolution of the psychological dynamics and the satisfaction of personal motivations of the negotiating parties. These issues are the intangibles of the negotiation and can include such notions as appearing to win or lose, to compete effectively, and to cooperate fairly.

Negotiations in economic exchanges usually follow one of two strategic approaches: cooperative (win–win) or competitive (win–lose) strategies. The better negotiating strategy in a particular situation is a function of the interaction of several variables (Wheeler 2013). For example, according to Greenberger and colleagues (1988), *cooperative* negotiating strategies work best when the factors in exhibit 2.4 are in play. The exhibit also includes circumstances that would give rise to *competitive* negotiating strategies.

EXHIBIT 2.4
Cooperative and Competitive Strategy Indicators

Cooperative Strategy Indicated	Competitive Strategy Indicated
Goal of both sides is fair and reasonable outcome	Tangible goal is to get as much as they can
Sufficient resources so both can achieve their goal (both can "win")	Insufficient resources to permit both to attain goals (only one can "win")
Each side believes in the negotiation process to attain their goals	Both sides believe mutual goal attainment is impossible
Intangible goal is to establish cooperative relationship, maximize joint outcomes	Intangible goal on each side is to "beat" the other

The Operation of Policy Markets

Health policies—indeed, all public policies—are made in the context of policy markets that, as noted earlier, operate like traditional economic markets in many ways. However, there are notable differences. The most fundamental difference is that buyers or demanders in economic markets express their preferences by spending their own money. That is, they reap the benefits of their choices, and they directly bear the costs of those choices. In policy markets, on the other hand, the link between who receives benefits and who bears costs is less direct. Often, this link is especially indirect in health policy markets.

Many decisions made by contemporary policymakers are influenced by the preferences of current voters, perhaps to the detriment of future generations of citizens. In the legislative context, and often in the administrative context, this consideration is inherently political. Feldstein (2006) observes that public policies that impose costs on future generations are routinely established. Allocative policies such as Medicare and Social Security are examples of this phenomenon. In the case of Social Security, outlays have begun to exceed tax revenues, and the trust funds supporting this program could be exhausted as early as 2026. Exhibit 2.5 displays the projected non–interest income and costs associated with Social Security.

EXHIBIT 2.5
Combined Annual Non–Interest Income, Cost, and Deficit (in billions of 2019 dollars) for Old-Age, Survivors, and Disability Insurance, Calendar Years 2020–2050

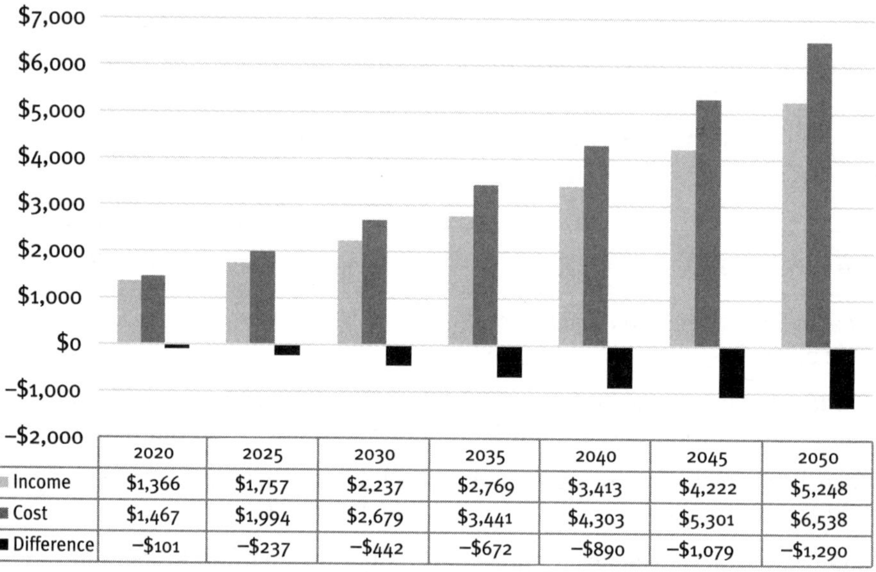

	2020	2025	2030	2035	2040	2045	2050
Income	$1,366	$1,757	$2,237	$2,769	$3,413	$4,222	$5,248
Cost	$1,467	$1,994	$2,679	$3,441	$4,303	$5,301	$6,538
Difference	–$101	–$237	–$442	–$672	–$890	–$1,079	–$1,290

Source: Social Security Administration (2019).

There are a limited number of ways to close Social Security's outlay–revenue gap, each of which has substantial drawbacks:

1. The benefits that are scheduled to be paid to future recipients under current law could be reduced.
2. The taxes that fund Social Security could be raised.
3. The resources consumed by other federal programs could be reduced to cover the gap.
4. The federal government's borrowing could be increased to cover the gap.

Of course, Social Security is not the only source of pressure on the federal budget. The aging of the US population—which is the main cause of the projected increase in Social Security spending—will raise costs for other entitlement programs. In particular, Medicare and Medicaid expenditures will grow dramatically because of rising healthcare costs, with National Health Expenditures (NHE) exceeding the growth rate of the gross domestic product (GDP) (CMS 2020). Whether that trend will continue into the future is an open question. Unless taxation reaches much higher levels in the United States, current spending policies are likely to prove financially unsustainable over the long term. The resulting burden of federal debt has the potential to constrict growth in the GDP.

Feldstein (2006) also points out that decision-makers in policy markets use different criteria from those used in traditional economic markets. In both markets, thoughtful decision-makers take benefits and costs into account. In policy markets, however, decision-makers may use different time frames. Because legislators often seek public approval to benefit their reelection, they typically favor policies that provide immediate benefits to their constituencies, and they tend to weigh only immediate costs, or at least consider them more carefully. Unlike most decision-makers in economic markets, who consider costs and benefits over the long run, decision-makers in policy markets are more likely to base decisions on immediate costs and benefits. An obvious consequence of such decisions is policies with immediate benefits but burdensome future costs. Exhibit 2.5, demonstrating the long-term projection for Social Security and disability insurance combined, is illustrative in this regard.

In policy markets, suppliers and demanders stand to reap benefits and incur costs because of the authoritative decisions called policies. Policies are therefore valued commodities in these markets. Given that demanders and suppliers will enter into exchanges involving policies, knowledge of whom the demanders and suppliers are and what motivates their decisions and actions in policy markets is helpful.

Demanders and Suppliers of Health Policies

As we noted earlier, policy markets operate much like typical economic markets. In both markets, something of value is exchanged between suppliers and demanders. Considering policy markets in this way permits us to view public policies as a means of satisfying certain demanders' wants and needs in much the same way that products and services produced and sold in economic markets serve to satisfy demanders (or, in an economic context, consumers). In commercial markets, demanders seek products and services that satisfy them. In policy markets, demanders seek public policies that satisfy their preferences, which, many times, are economic in nature. Policymakers are in a position to supply the public policies that demanders seek.

The Demanders of Health Policies

Broadly, the demanders of health policies can include (1) individuals who consider such policies relevant to the pursuit of their own health or that of others about whom they care and (2) individuals who consider such policies a means to some other desired end, such as economic advantage. These desires motivate participation in policy markets, just as desires motivate participation in economic markets.

For individuals, however, effective participation in a policy market presents certain problems and limitations. To participate effectively, individuals must acquire substantial policy-relevant information and, frequently, political resources, which can require considerable time and money. Beyond this, individual participants or demanders often must be prepared to expend additional time, money, and political capital in support of desired policies. Any particular health policy might have significant, or even noticeable, benefits for only a few individuals. Consequently, individual demander participation is limited in the markets for policies.

Organizations—such as large health systems, health plans, and technology suppliers—have a significant advantage over individuals in the health policy market. These large entities may have the necessary resources to garner needed policy-relevant information and to support their efforts to achieve desired policies. In addition, an organization's health policy interests may be concentrated. A change in Medicare policy that results in an increased deductible of $100 per year for certain individuals is one thing; a policy change that results in several million dollars of revenue for a health system is another. Organizations tend to be more effective demanders of health policies than individuals because they have more resources and the stakes for them tend to be higher.

The most effective demanders of policies, however, are well-organized interest groups. These are groups of people or organizations with similar policy goals that enter the policymaking process to try to achieve their goals. By combining and concentrating the resources of their members, interest groups can have a much greater impact than individuals or organizations alone.

In effect, interest groups provide their members—whether individuals or organizations—with greater opportunities to participate effectively in the policy market (Cigler and Loomis 2011). The American Nurses Association (www.nursingworld.org) provides such opportunities for individual nurses, AARP (www.aarp.org) does so for older individuals, and the Pharmaceutical Research and Manufacturers of America (www.PhRMA.org) does so for its member companies. Because of their power in policy markets, interest groups, as demanders of health policy, are described more fully in the next section.

Interest Groups in the Policy Market

Interest groups (also called advocacy groups, lobby groups, pressure groups, or special interest groups) arise in democratic societies because the opportunities to achieve particular outcomes are enhanced through collective action in the policy market, specifically through influencing the public policymaking process. They are ubiquitous in the United States, more in the health sector than any other sector of the economy. In 2018, lobbyists in the health sector spent almost $360 million seeking to influence health policy. The only other sector spending approximately as much was the finance/insurance/real estate sector, with the communications/electronics sector and the energy/natural resources sector spending $70 to $100 to $100 million less in their attempts to influence policy in their domains (Center for Responsive Politics 2019).

The First Amendment to the US Constitution guarantees the American people the right "peaceably to assemble, and to petition the Government for a redress of grievances." However, constitutional guarantees notwithstanding, political theorists from the nation's beginning to the present day have disagreed about whether interest groups play positive or negative roles in public policymaking (Cigler and Loomis 2011; Edwards, Wattenberg, and Lineberry 2014; Gray, Lowery, and Benz 2013; Peters 2013).

James Madison, writing in *The Federalist* in 1787, discusses the relationship of groups, which he called "factions," to democratic government. In *Federalist* Number 10, he defines a *faction* as "a number of citizens, whether amounting to a majority or a minority of the whole, who are united and actuated by some common impulse of passion, or of interest, adverse to the rights of citizens, or to the permanent and aggregate interests of the community." Madison felt strongly that factions, or interest groups, were inherently bad. He also believed, however, that the formation of such groups was a natural outgrowth of human nature (he writes in *Federalist* Number 10 that "the latent causes of faction are sown into the nature of man") and that government should not seek to check this activity. Madison felt that what he called the "mischiefs of faction" could and should be contained by setting the "ambition" of one faction against the selfish preferences and behaviors of others. So began the uncertainty about and ambiguity toward the role of interest groups in public policymaking in the United States.

One point about which there is neither uncertainty nor ambiguity, however, is that interest groups play an active role in the public policymaking process. Reflecting widely divergent views on the manner in which interest groups play their role in this process, two distinct perspectives have emerged: the *pluralist* and *elitist* models.

The Pluralist Perspective

People who hold the pluralist perspective on the role of interest groups in policymaking believe that because so many interest groups are operating, everyone's interests can be represented by one or more of them. Adherents to the pluralist model usually maintain that interest groups play an essentially positive role in public policymaking. They argue that various interest groups compete with and counterbalance each other in the policy marketplace. Pluralists do not question that some groups are stronger than others. However, they contend that as groups seek their preferred outcomes, power is widely dispersed among competing groups, with each group winning some of the time and losing some of the time.

Pluralist theory about how the policymaking process works includes several interconnected arguments that, taken together, constitute what has come to be called a group theory of politics (Edwards, Wattenberg, and Lineberry 2014). The central tenets of the group theory include the following:

- Interest groups provide essential links between people and their government.
- Interest groups compete among themselves for outcomes, with the interests of some groups counterbalanced by the interests of others.
- No group is likely to become too dominant in the competition; as groups become powerful, other countervailing interests organize or existing groups intensify their efforts. An important mechanism for maintaining balance among the groups is their ability to rely on various sources of power. Groups representing concentrated economic interests may have money, but consumer groups may have more members.
- The competition among interest groups is basically fair. Although there are exceptions, groups typically play by the rules of the game.

There are critics of the pluralist approach, claiming that it is dysfunctional and out of control. The pluralist critics make two key points:

1. Interest groups have become too influential in the policymaking process. Satisfying their multiple and often conflicting demands seems to drive government, rather than government being driven by a desire to base policy decisions on considerations of what is best for the nation as a whole—that is, on the public interest.
2. Seeking to satisfy the multiple and often conflicting demands of various interest groups leads to confusion, contradiction, and even paralysis in the policymaking process. Rather than making a difficult choice between satisfying X or Y, government seems frequently to pretend that there is no need to make the choice and seeks to satisfy both X and Y.

Some critics of pluralism believe that the perspective itself is misguided, even wrong. They believe that, instead of everyone having a chance to influence the policymaking process through one group or another, such influence actually resides only in the hands of an elite few. This belief gives rise to a second perspective on the ways groups influence policymaking.

The Elitist Perspective

Whereas pluralists point with pride to the large number of organized groups actively and aggressively participating in the American process of public policymaking, the elitist perspective holds that most groups are fairly powerless and ineffectual. The elitist perspective on the role of interest groups, which is the opposite of the pluralist viewpoint, grows out of a power elite model of American society.

This model is based on the idea that real political power in the United States is concentrated in the hands of the small proportion of the population that controls the nation's key institutions and organizations and much of its wealth. In the elitist perspective, these so-called big interests look out for themselves in part by disproportionately influencing, if not controlling, the public policymaking process. Whether this model accurately reflects American policy markets is debatable, but the model does represent the opinions of a growing majority of Americans concerning which members of the society have the most influence.

The elitist theory holds that a power elite, often referred to as "the establishment," acts as a gatekeeper to the public policymaking process. Unless the power elite considers an issue important, the issue does not get much attention in policymaking circles. Furthermore, the theory holds, once an issue is on the policy agenda, public policies made in response reflect the values, ideologies, and preferences of this governing elite (Dye 2012). Thus, the power elite dominates public policymaking through its superior position in society. Its powerful role in the nation's economic and social systems allows the elite to shape the formulation of policies and control their implementation. It has been argued that the nation's social and economic systems depend on the power elite's consensus regarding the system's fundamental values, and the only policy alternatives that receive serious consideration are those that fall within the shared consensus (Dye 2002).

The central tenets of the power elite theory stand in stark contrast to the pluralist perspective. These tenets are as follows (Dye, Zeigler, and Schubert 2012; Edwards, Wattenberg, and Lineberry 2014):

- Real political power resides in a small number of groups; the large number of interest groups is practically meaningless because the power differentials among them are so great. Other groups may win minor policy victories, but the power elite always prevails on significant policy issues.
- Members of the power elite share a consensus or near consensus on the basic values that should guide public policymaking: private property rights, the preeminence of markets and private enterprise as the best way to organize the economy, limited government, and the importance of individual liberty and individualism.
- Members of the power elite have a strong preference for incremental changes in public policies. Incrementalism in policymaking permits time for the economic and social systems to adjust to changes without feeling threatened, with minimal economic dislocation or disruption and with minimal alteration in the social system's status quo.
- Elites protect their power bases. Some limited movement of nonelites into elite positions is permitted to maintain social stability, but only after nonelites clearly accept the elites' consensus values.

Which Perspective Is Correct?

Those who hold the power elitist perspective challenge those who hold the pluralist perspective by pointing to the highly concentrated and interlocked power centers in American society. Studies of the concentration of power do find that many of the top leadership positions in the United States—on corporate, foundation, and university governing boards, for example—are held by people who occupy more than one such position (Domhoff 2013).

Those who prefer the pluralist perspective, however, are equally quick to cite numerous examples in which those who traditionally have been grossly underrepresented in the inner circles of the power elite have succeeded in their collective efforts to significantly influence the public policymaking process.

African Americans, women, and consumers in general provide examples of the ability of groups once ignored by policymakers to organize as effective interest groups and redirect the course of the public policymaking process.

Neither the pluralist nor the elitist perspective alone fully explains how the interests of individuals or organizations relate to the public policymaking process. The results of that process affect the interests of all individuals and all organizations to varying degrees. Many, if not all, individuals and organizations with interests can influence the policymaking process, although, again, not to equal degrees. The elitist and pluralist approaches each have something to contribute to an understanding of the roles interest groups play in the markets for public policies. Whether such groups work proactively, by seeking to stimulate new policies that serve the interests of their members, or reactively, by seeking to block policy changes that they do not believe serve their members' best interests, they are intrinsic to the public policymaking process. Interest groups provide their members with a way to link their policy preferences into a more powerful, collective voice that greatly increases the likelihood of significant influence on policymaking.

The Suppliers of Health Policies

Because policies are made in the executive, legislative, and judicial branches of government, the list of potential policymakers is lengthy. Members of each branch of government supply policies in the political market, although each branch plays its role differently.

Legislators as Suppliers

One important group of public policy suppliers is elected legislators, whether members of the US Congress, state legislatures, or city councils. Few aspects of the policy marketplace are as interesting, or as widely observed and studied, as the decision-making behaviors of legislators and the motives and incentives behind those behaviors. To a large extent, this intense interest in the motivations of policy suppliers reflects the desire of policy demanders to exert influence over the suppliers.

Although neither extreme fully reflects the motivations of legislators, the end points on a continuum of behaviors that policymakers might exhibit can be represented by those who seek to maximize the public interest on one end and by those who seek to maximize self-interest on the other end. A legislator at the public interest extreme would always seek policies—that is, would make authoritative decisions—that maximize the public interest, although the true public interest might not always be easy to identify. A legislator whose motivations lie at the self-interest extreme would always behave in a manner that maximizes self-interest, whether that interest is reelection, money, prestige, power, or whatever appeals to the self-serving person. There are some happy occasions, though increasingly rare, when the public's interest and the legislator's self-interest align.

In policy markets, legislators can be found all along the continuum between extreme public interest and extreme self-interest motivations. Although some people incorrectly ascribe dominant self-interest motives to all legislators, the actions and decisions of most legislators reflect a complex mixture of the two motivations, with exclusively self-interested or public-interested motives only rarely dominating decisions.

Motives aside, legislators at all levels of government are key policy suppliers, especially of policies in the form of laws. For example, only Congress can enact new or amend existing public laws. In policy markets, legislators constantly calculate the benefits and costs of their policymaking decisions and consider who will reap these benefits and bear these costs. Factoring in the interests they choose to serve, they make their decisions accordingly. Their calculations are complicated by the fact that the costs and benefits of a particular decision often affect many people in different ways.

In effect, policies typically create winners and losers. The gains some people enjoy come at the financial expense of others, or at least at the expense of having someone's problems ignored or someone's preferred solutions postponed. Indeed, politics has been called the art of who gets what, when, and how (Lasswell 1936). Most of the time, most legislators seek to maximize their own net political gains through their policy-related decisions, because reelection is an abiding objective.

In view of the reality of most policies creating winners and losers, legislators may find that their best strategy is to permit the winners their victory, but not by a huge margin, and in so doing cushion the impact on the losers. For example, suppose a legislator is considering a policy that would increase health services for an underserved population but at the expense of higher taxes on others. Options include various policies with the following outcomes: (1) few services at relatively low cost, (2) more services at higher cost, and (3) many services at high cost. Facing such a decision, and applying the concept of net political gain, policymakers might opt for the provision of a meaningful level of services, but one far below what could have been provided and at a cost below what would have been required for a higher level of services. This outcome is the kind produced by the political process: a mediated solution that is a balance—a compromise—between those who want many services at high cost and those who want few services at lower cost. As we shall see in subsequent chapters, much of US healthcare policy is a result of this kind of mediation. The winners receive more services, but the expense for the losers, who have to pay for the new services, is not as great as it might have been. Through such calculations and determinations, legislators routinely seek to maximize their net political gains.

Executives and Bureaucrats as Suppliers

At all levels of government, members of the executive branch are important policy suppliers, although their role differs from that of legislators (see exhibit 2.2). Presidents, governors, mayors, and other senior public-sector executives offer policies in the form of legislative proposals and seek to have legislators enact their preferred policies. Chief executives and those in charge of government departments and agencies are directly responsible for policies in the form of rules or regulations used to guide the implementation of laws and operational protocols and procedures for the policies they implement. Career bureaucrats who participate in these activities and thus become suppliers of policies in the policy markets join elected and appointed executives and managers in their rulemaking and other policy implementation duties.

Elected and appointed officials of the executive branch are often affected by the same self-interest versus public-interest dichotomy that affects legislators; reelection concerns, in particular, often influence their decisions. Like legislators, elected and appointed members of executive branches are apt to calculate the net political gains of their policy-related decisions and actions. As a result, their motivations and behaviors in policy markets can be similar to those of legislators, seeking the kind of compromises described earlier. However, the behaviors of members of the executive branch of a government and members of its legislative branch show some important differences.

The most fundamental difference derives from the fact that the executive branch generally bears greater responsibility than the legislative branch for the state of the economy, and it is widely perceived to bear even more responsibility than it actually does. Presidents, governors, and mayors, along with their top appointees, are held accountable for economic conditions much more explicitly than are Congress, state legislatures, or city councils. Although legislators do not escape this responsibility altogether, the public typically lays most of the responsibility at the feet of the executive branch. When people do blame the legislative branch, they tend to hold the entire Congress or the state or city legislature collectively responsible rather than to blame individual legislators.

The concentration of responsibility for the economy in the executive branch influences the decision-making that takes place there. Because of the close connection between the government's budget and the state of the economy, the budget implications of policy decisions are carefully weighed in the executive branch. Not infrequently, the legislative and executive branches will hold different positions on health policies because members in the two branches give different weight to the budget implications and other priorities of the policies they are considering.

Career bureaucrats, or civil servants, in the executive branch also participate in policymaking in the legislative branch when they collect, analyze, and transmit information about policy options and initiate policy proposals in their areas of expertise. However, the motivations and behaviors of career bureaucrats tend to differ from those of legislators and those of members of executive branches.

The behaviors and motivations of career bureaucrats in the public sector are often analogous to those of employees in the private sector. Workers in both settings typically seek to satisfy certain personal needs and desires through their work. Behaviors and motivations can obviously be categorized as self-serving in both cases. However, government employees are no more likely to be totally motivated by self-interest than are private-sector workers. Most workers in both sectors are motivated by blends of self-interest and interest in what is good for the larger society.

However, most career bureaucrats watch a constantly changing mix of elected and senior government officials—with an equally dynamic set of policy preferences—parade past, while they remain as the most permanent human feature of government. It should surprise no one that career bureaucrats develop a strong sense of identification with their home department or agency or that they become protective of it. This protectiveness is most visible in the relationships between government agencies or departments and those with legislative oversight of them, including authorization, appropriation, and performance review responsibilities. Many career bureaucrats equate the well-being of their agencies, in terms of their size, budgets, and prestige, with the public interest. Obviously, this is not always the case.

The Judiciary as Supplier

As we saw in the policy snapshot at the beginning of part 1, the judicial branch of government is also a supplier of policies. This role is discussed in more depth in chapter 8. For example, whenever a court interprets an ambiguous law, establishes judicial procedure, or interprets the US Constitution, it makes a policy. These activities are conceptually no different from those involved when legislators enact public laws or when members of the executive branch establish rules and regulations to guide implementation of laws or make operational decisions regarding their implementation. All of these activities are policymaking, because they lead to authoritative decisions made in government to influence or direct the actions, behaviors, and decisions of others.

Policymaking in the judicial branch, however, differs from that in the legislative and executive branches, not only in focus but in operation. The responsibilities of courts require them to focus narrowly on the issues involved in specific cases or situations. This narrow focus stands in stark contrast to the wide-open political arena in which most other public policymaking occurs.

The courts are involved in numerous and diverse aspects of health policy, reflecting the entire range of health determinants (e.g., physical environment, behavior and genetics, social factors, health services). For example, in a 1980 opinion in what is called the "Benzene Case," the US Supreme Court invalidated an Occupational Safety and Health Administration (OSHA; www.osha.gov) rule limiting benzene to no more than one part per million parts in the air in workplaces. In the Court's view, OSHA had not found a significant risk to workers' health before issuing the rule.

In a 1905 landmark ruling in *Jacobson v. Massachusetts* (197 US 11), the US Supreme Court upheld compulsory vaccination as an appropriate use of state police power to protect the health, welfare, and safety of a state's citizens. The states' police powers, as stipulated in the Tenth Amendment of the US Constitution, provide the legal basis for state authority in the field of public health. This case involved a compulsory vaccination regulation of the Cambridge (Massachusetts) Board of Health. Defendant Jacobson refused to be vaccinated and contended that the requirement invaded his liberty. The Court held, however, that "the liberty secured by the Constitution to every person . . . does not import an absolute right in each person to be at all times and in all circumstances wholly freed from restraint . . . It was the duty of the constituted authorities primarily to keep in view the welfare, comfort and safety of the many, and not permit the interests of the many to be subordinated to the wishes or convenience of the few." Furthermore, the Court stated that "it is equally true that in every well-ordered society charged with the duty of conserving the safety of its members the rights of the individual in respect of his liberty may at times, under the pressure of great dangers, be subjected to such restraint, to be enforced by reasonable regulations, as the safety of the general public may demand" (*Jacobson v. Massachusetts* 1905, 29).

The heart of the judiciary's ability to supply policies lies in its interpretative role. The courts can exercise the powers of nullification, interpretation, and application to the rules and regulations established by the executive branch in carrying out its implementation responsibilities. The courts also have the power to declare federal and state laws unconstitutional—that is, to declare laws enacted by the legislative branch to be null and void. This role of the courts is clearly illustrated in the NFIB policy snapshot, as well as the Ninth US Circuit Court of Appeals that overturned Arizona legislation requiring abortion clinics in that state to submit to warrantless searches and to make patient files available to state regulators. The court found that these were onerous regulations. The appeals court based its ruling on an interpretation that the regulations violated constitutional restrictions on searches and seizures and that requiring the clinics to submit patient files to state regulators on demand violated the patients' privacy rights, both concepts guaranteed by the Fourth Amendment of the Constitution (Kravets 2004).

Health policymaking in the judicial branch is far more prevalent in state courts and lower federal courts than in the US Supreme Court. A state-level example of courts making important health policy can be seen in a key

Pennsylvania Supreme Court case involving the tax-exempt status of healthcare organizations. In 1985, in *Hospital Utilization Project v. Commonwealth of Pennsylvania*, the court determined a five-part test to define a "purely public charity." Conforming with the court's test provides an organization a tax exemption under the Pennsylvania law. To summarize the court's ruling, such an organization must

1. Advance a charitable purpose;
2. donate or render gratuitously a substantial portion of its services;
3. benefit a substantial and indefinite class of persons who are legitimate objects of charity;
4. relieve the government of some of its burden, and;
5. operate entirely free from profit motive.

Variation in several Pennsylvania cases in the courts' interpretation of this test for tax-exempt status led to enactment in 1997 of clarifying legislation on this and other points regarding the determination of tax-exempt status. Late in that year, the governor of Pennsylvania signed into law House Bill 55, known as the Institutions of Purely Public Charity Act, or Act 55. This act permits an institution to meet the charitable purpose test and qualify for tax exemption if it has a charitable mission, is free of private profit motive, is designated as a 501(c)(3) entity by the federal government, and is organized for any of the following reasons:

- Relief of poverty
- Advancement and provision of education, including secondary education
- Advancement of religion
- Prevention and treatment of disease or injury, including developmental disability and mental illness
- Government or municipal purposes
- Accomplishment of a purpose that is recognized as important and beneficial to the public and that advances social, moral, or physical objectives

The act specifically clarified, quite liberally, how an institution could meet the requirement for donating or rendering gratuitously a substantial portion of its services. Act 55 established 3 percent of an institution's total operating expenses as the necessary contribution of charitable goods or services. In this instance, court decisions were policies themselves, and the impact of the decisions eventually led to a significant change in Pennsylvania's public laws.

Because the pursuit of health in the United States is so heavily influenced by laws and regulations, the courts are a major factor in the development and implementation of health policies (Gostin 2008; Jost 2014). The courts include not only the federal court system but also the court systems of the states and the territories. Each of these systems has developed in idiosyncratic ways, and each has a constitution to guide it, specific legislation to contend with, and its own history of judicial decisions. A great deal of information on the structure and operation of the US legal system can be found in the outline of the legal system provided by the Federal Judicial Center (2020).

Although the federal and state courts play significant roles as policy suppliers, their behaviors, motivations, and roles differ significantly from those of participants in the legislative and executive branches. In their wisdom, the drafters of the US Constitution created the three branches, and Article III ensured the judicial branch's independence, at least mostly so, from the other branches.

An independent judiciary facilitates adherence to the rules all participants in the policymaking process must follow. Federal judges are appointed rather than elected, and the appointments are for life. Consequently, federal judges are not subject to the same self-interest concerns related to reelection that many other policymakers face. This characteristic enhances their ability to act in the public interest, although judges, like all policymakers, vary in their personal commitments to this objective (Sunstein et al. 2006).

Interplay Among Demanders and Suppliers in Policy Markets

In the policy marketplace, demanders and suppliers of policies seek to further their objectives. These objectives can be based on self-interest or they can be based on what is best for the public, or at least some subset of society, such as individuals who are elderly, poor, or medically underserved. In either case, the outcome depends on the relative abilities of some participants in policy markets to influence the actions, behaviors, and decisions of other participants. As described in part 1's policy snapshot, those who feel their demands for desired policy outcomes are not met may carry the fight to the courts, where, ultimately, the court becomes a supplier of policy because the "normal" political bargaining between demanders and suppliers has been dysfunctional.

Influence in Policy Markets

Influence in policy markets is the power to shape or help determine policy. Such power can derive from several sources. The classic categories for sources of interpersonal power include legitimate, reward, coercive, expert, and referent

(French and Raven 1959). These bases of interpersonal power apply to individuals, organizations, and interest groups in policy markets.

Legitimate power, for example, derives from one's relative position in a social system, organization, or group; this form of power is also called *formal* position, power, or authority. It exists because assigning or ascribing certain powers to individuals, organizations, or groups better enables them to fulfill their duties or perform their work effectively. Elected officials, appointed executives, judges, health professionals, corporation executives, union leaders, and many other individual participants in policy markets possess certain legitimate power that accompanies their social or organizational positions. Suppliers and demanders of policies possess legitimate power. That is, they can exert influence in the policymaking process because they are recognized as legitimate in the process. As demonstrated in the case at the beginning of part 1, the Supreme Court possesses this power because of the authority assigned to it in the Constitution.

Reward power is based on the ability of one person, organization, or group to reward others for their decisions and actions. Reward power stems in part from legitimate power. It comes from many sources and takes many forms. In organizations, it includes the obvious: control over pay increases, promotions, work and vacation schedules, recognition of accomplishments, and such status symbols or perks as club memberships and office size and location. In economic markets, the buying power of consumers is a form of reward power. In policy markets, reward power is more likely to take the form of favors that can be provided or exchanged, specific influence with particular individuals or groups, and whatever influence can be stored for later use.

Coercive power is the opposite of reward power and is based on the capacity to withhold or to prevent someone from obtaining desired rewards. Coercive power flows from the ability to affirmatively inflict some form of (socially acceptable) punishment or the ability to withhold a favor or reward.

Expert power tends to reside in individuals but can also reside in a group or organization. It derives from possessing expertise valued in policy markets, such as expertise in solving problems or performing crucial tasks. People with expert power often occupy formal positions of authority, transferring some of the expert power to the organization or group. People who can exercise their expert power in the policymaking arena may also be trusted advisers or associates of other participants in policy markets.

Referent power derives from the influence resulting from the ability of some people, organizations, and interest groups to engender admiration, loyalty, and emulation from others. In the markets for policies, this form of power, when it pertains to individuals, is also called *charismatic power*. Charismatic power usually belongs to a select few people who typically have strong convictions about the correctness of their preferences, have great confidence in their own abilities, and are widely perceived to be legitimate agents of change. Rarely does a person, organization, or interest group gain sufficient power to heavily influence policymaking simply from referent or charismatic power, even in policy markets where charisma is highly valued. But it can certainly give the other sources of power in a policy market a boost.

The bases of power in policy markets are interdependent. They can and do complement and conflict with each other. For example, people, organizations, or groups in a position to use reward power and do so wisely can strengthen their referent power. Conversely, those who abuse coercive power might quickly weaken or lose their referent power. Effective participants in the marketplace for policies—those individuals, organizations, and groups that succeed at influencing policymaking—tend to be fully aware of the sources of their power and to act accordingly. They seem to understand intuitively the costs and benefits of using each kind of power and can draw on them appropriately in different situations and with various people they wish to influence.

Influence of Interest Groups: Breaking the Iron Triangles

Some interest groups, including several in the health domain, are extraordinarily influential in public policymaking. Yet these groups are not as influential as they once were. At the height of their influence, certain interest groups formed part of what were called *iron triangles*. The iron triangle was a model of the relationships that sometimes existed among participating individuals, organizations, and groups in policy markets.

Any policy domain attracts a set of participating individuals, organizations, and groups. Each participant has some stake in policies affecting the domain and thus seeks to influence policymaking. Some of the participants, or stakeholders, in a domain demand policies; others supply policies. Collectively, these stakeholders form a *policy community*.

Traditionally, the policy community formed around a particular policy domain (such as health) has included legislators with focused interest in a domain, usually serving on legislative committees with jurisdiction in the domain; the executive branch agencies responsible for implementing public laws in the domain; and the private-sector interest groups involved in the domain. The first two categories are suppliers of the policies demanded by the third category. This triad of organized interests has been called an *iron triangle* because when all three sides are in accord, the resulting stability allows the triad to withstand attempts to make undesired changes. Exhibit 2.6 illustrates these relationships.

A policy community that could be appropriately characterized as a strong and stable iron triangle dominated the health policy domain until the early 1960s, when battle lines began to be drawn over the eventual shape of the Medicare program. This triangle featured a few powerful interest groups with

EXHIBIT 2.6
The Policymaking Iron Triangle

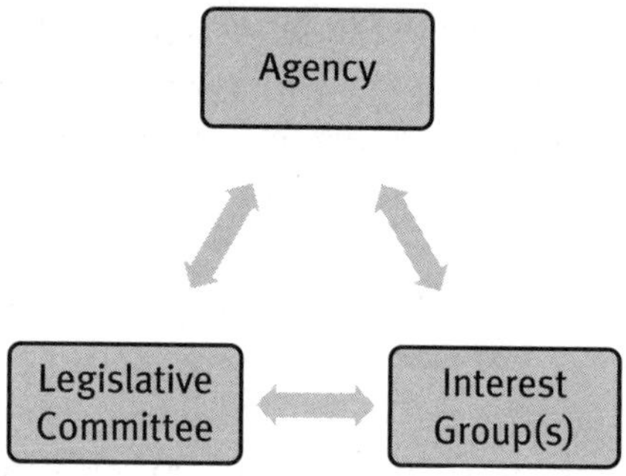

concordant views that, for the most part, found sympathetic partners among members of the legislative committees and in the relevant implementing agencies of government.

During this period, the private-sector interest group members of the iron triangle that dominated health policy, notably the American Medical Association (AMA; www.ama-assn.org) and the American Hospital Association (AHA; www.aha.org), joined later by the American College of Physicians (ACP; www.acponline.org) and the American College of Surgeons (www. facs.org), generally held a consistent view of the appropriate policies in this domain. Their shared view of optimal health policy was that government should protect the interests of health services providers and not intervene in the financing or delivery of health services (Peterson 1993). Under the conditions and expectations extant in these largely straightforward relationships, it was relatively simple for the suppliers and demanders of policies to satisfy each other. This triangle was unbreakable into the second half of the twentieth century.

As demonstrated in the policy snapshot at the beginning of part 2, the dynamics of this situation began to change dramatically with the policy battles over Medicare, and they worsened with the addition of Medicaid to the debate. Fundamental differences emerged among the participants in the health policy community in terms of their views of optimal health policy. Today, there is rarely a solid block of concordant private-sector interests driving health policy decisions. For example, differences over questions of optimal policy shattered the accord between the AMA and the AHA. Splintering within the memberships of these groups caused even more damage. Today, the medical profession no longer speaks through the single voice of the AMA; organizations such as the ACP and the American Academy of Family Physicians (www.aafp.org) can and sometimes do support different policy choices. Similarly, the AHA is now joined in policy debates by organizations with diverse preferences representing the specific interests of teaching hospitals, public hospitals, for-profit hospitals, and other hospital subsets. These changes have eroded the solidarity among private-sector interest groups and the public-sector members of the health policy community. This phenomenon has recently been seen clearly in the formulation and implementation of the ACA. A large number of active groups, with divergent views, are participating in policymaking and influencing policymaking in this area.

Rather than an iron triangle, the contemporary health policy community is far more heterogeneous in its membership and much more loosely structured. At most, this community can be thought of as a group of members whose commonality stems from the fact that they pay attention to issues in the health policy domain. There is an important difference, however, between shared attentiveness to health policy issues and shared positions on optimal health policy or related issues. The loss of concordance among the members of the old iron triangle has diminished the power of certain interest groups. Nevertheless, they remain highly influential, and other interest groups have also been able to assume influential roles in health policymaking.

Other, some newer, groups have entered the fray. "Big Pharma" was not so big when Medicare and Medicaid were enacted as it is today. The AARP was only seven years old in 1965. It has grown substantially since then and is a significant voice in issues affecting retirees, including health insurance. Other consumer groups such as Families USA also have emerged on the scene to have an active voice in health policy.

Having considered the context in which health policies are made, especially the structure and operations of policy markets, and having identified the demanders and suppliers who interact in these markets and the important operational aspects of these interactions, it is now possible to consider the intricate process through which public policies are made, which is the subject of the next chapter.

Summary

Health policies, like those in other domains, are made in the context of policy markets, where demanders for and suppliers of policies interact. The federal, state, and, to a lesser extent, local governments have important health policy roles. The federal role, in many ways, has been to influence states to address particular issues. This, and the establishment of multiple agencies with multiple responsibilities, has aggrandized the federal role, changing the dynamics of federalism on which the Constitution was premised.

The demanders of policies include those who view public policies as a mechanism for meeting their health-related objectives or other objectives, such as economic advantage. Although individuals alone can demand public policies, the far more effective demand emanates from organizations and especially from organized interest groups. The suppliers of health policy include elected and appointed members of all three branches of government and the civil servants who staff the government.

The interests of the various demanders and suppliers in this market cannot be completely coincident—often, they are in open conflict—and the decisions and activities of any participant always affect and are affected by the activities of other participants.

Review Questions

1. Discuss the roles of federal and state governments in health policy.
2. Compare and contrast the operation of traditional economic markets with that of policy markets.
3. Who are demanders and suppliers of health policies? What motivates each in the policy marketplace?
4. Compare and contrast the pluralist and elitist perspectives on interest groups in policy markets.
5. Define *power* and *influence*. What are the sources of power in policy markets?

Note

1. The sections describing the federal, state, and local levels of government in the United States are adapted from the White House website's "Our Government" pages, accessed April 1, 2020 (www.whitehouse.gov/our-government). Additional descriptive information about the federal judicial branch can be found at the United States Courts website (www.uscourts.gov/Home.aspx). Additional information about the federal legislative branch, including the legislative process, can be found at the US Congress website (www.congress.gov).

References

Bovbjerg, R. R., J. M. Wiener, and M. Houseman. 2003. "State and Federal Roles in Health Care: Rationales for Allocating Responsibilities." In *Federalism and Health Policy*, edited by J. Holahan, A. Weil, and J. M. Wiener, 25–57. Washington, DC: Urban Institute Press.

Carruth, R. S., and B. D. Goldstein. 2014. *Environmental Health Law*. San Francisco: Jossey-Bass.

Center for Responsive Politics. 2019. "Pharmaceuticals/Health Products: Lobby, 2019." Accessed August 30. www.opensecrets.org/industries/lobbying.php?ind=H04.

Centers for Medicare & Medicaid Services (CMS). 2020. "National Health Expenditure Projections 2019–2028." Accessed April 8. www.cms.gov/files/document/nhe-projections-2019-2028-forecast-summary.pdf.

Cigler, A. J., and B. A. Loomis (eds.). 2011. *Interest Group Politics*, 8th ed. Washington, DC: CQ Press.

City-Data.com. 2020. "Kansas Very Small Towns and Villages (Fewer Than 1,000 Residents)." Accessed April 1. www.city-data.com/city/Kansas3.html.

Desilver, D. 2018. "Congress Has Long Struggled to Pass Spending Bills on Time." Pew Research Center. Published January 16. www.pewresearch.org/fact-tank/2018/01/16/congress-has-long-struggled-to-pass-spending-bills-on-time.

Domhoff, G. W. 2013. *Who Rules America? The Triumph of the Corporate Rich*, 7th ed. Hightstown, NJ: McGraw-Hill.

Dye, T. R. 2012. *Understanding Public Policy*, 14th ed. New York: Pearson.

———. 2002. *Who's Running America? The Bush Restoration*, 7th ed. White Plains, NY: Pearson Longman.

Dye, T. R., H. Zeigler, and L. Schubert. 2012. *The Irony of Democracy: An Uncommon Introduction to American Politics*, 15th ed. Boston: Wadsworth Cengage Learning.

Edwards, G. C., M. P. Wattenberg, and R. L. Lineberry. 2014. *Government in America: People, Politics, and Policy*, 16th ed. Upper Saddle River, NJ: Pearson.

Federal Judicial Center. 2020. *The U.S. Legal System: A Short Description*. Accessed April 2. www.fjc.gov/sites/default/files/2015/US-Legal-System-A-Short-Description-2014-08-04.pdf.

Feldstein, P. J. 2006. *The Politics of Health Legislation: An Economic Perspective*, 3rd ed. Chicago: Health Administration Press.

French, J. R. P., and B. H. Raven. 1959. "The Basis of Social Power." In *Studies of Social Power*, edited by D. Cartwright, 150–67. Ann Arbor, MI: Institute for Social Research.

Gostin, L. O. 2008. *Public Health Law: Power, Duty, Restraint*, 2nd ed. Berkeley, CA: University of California Press.

Gray, V., D. Lowery, and J. K. Benz. 2013. *Interest Groups and Health Care Reform Across the United States*. Washington, DC: Georgetown University Press.

Greenberger, D., S. Strasser, R. J. Lewicki, and T. S. Bateman. 1988. "Perception, Motivation, and Negotiation." In *Health Care Management: A Text in Organization Theory and Behavior*, 2nd ed., edited by S. M. Shortell and A. D. Kaluzny, 81–141. New York: Wiley.

Jost, T. 2014. "The Courts." In *Health Politics and Policy*, 5th ed., edited by J. A. Morone and D. C. Ehlke, 76–93. Stamford, CT: Cengage Learning.

King, M. P. 2005. *State Roles in Health: A Snapshot for State Legislators*. Denver, CO: National Conference of State Legislatures.

Kravets, D. 2004. "Arizona Abortion Regulation Invades Privacy, Appeals Court Says." GUWS Medical. Published May 2. www.guwsmedical.info/health-policy/the-real-world-of-health-policy-qwo.html.

Lasswell, H. 1936. *Politics: Who Gets What, When, How.* New York: McGraw-Hill.

Leichter, H. M. 2008. "State Governments: E Pluribus Multa." In *Health Politics and Policy*, 4th ed., edited by J. A. Morone, T. J. Litman, and L. S. Robins, 173–95. Clifton Park, NY: Delmar Cengage Learning.

Liptak, A. 2012. "Supreme Court Upholds Health Care Law, 5–4, in Victory for Obama." *New York Times.* Published June 28. www.nytimes.com/2012/06/29/us/supreme-court-lets-health-law-largely-stand.html.

Madison, J. 1787. "The Same Subject Continued: The Union as a Safeguard Against Domestic Faction and Insurrection." *Federalist Papers* No. 10. Our-Documents.gov. Accessed April 1, 2020. www.ourdocuments.gov/doc.php?flash=true&doc=10.

Peters, B. G. 2013. *American Public Policy: Promise and Performance*, 9th ed. Thousand Oaks, CA: CQ Press.

Peterson, M. A. 1993. "Political Influence in the 1990s: From Iron Triangles to Policy Networks." *Journal of Health Politics, Policy and Law* 18 (2): 395–438.

Radley, D. C., D. McCarthy, and S. L. Hayes. 2018. "2018 Scorecard on State Health System Performance." Commonwealth Fund. Accessed April 1, 2020. https://interactives.commonwealthfund.org/2018/state-scorecard.

Social Security Administration. 2019. "The 2019 OASDI Trustees Report." Accessed August 29. www.ssa.gov/OACT/TR/2019/X1_trLOT.html.

Sunstein, C. R., D. Schkade, L. M. Ellman, and A. Sawicki. 2006. *Are Judges Political? An Empirical Analysis of the Federal Judiciary.* Washington, DC: Brookings Institution Press.

US Courts. 2020. "Supreme Court Procedures." Accessed April 1. www.uscourts.gov/about-federal-courts/educational-resources/about-educational-outreach/activity-resources/supreme-1.

US Department of Health and Human Services (HHS). 2015. "HHS Agencies and Offices." Reviewed October 27. www.hhs.gov/about/agencies/hhs-agencies-and-offices/index.html.

US Government Printing Office. 2020. "The United States Government Manual." Accessed April 1. www.usgovernmentmanual.gov.

US Senate. 2020. "The Impeachment Trial of Alcee L. Hastings (1989) U.S. District Judge, Florida." Accessed June 13. www.senate.gov/artandhistory/history/common/briefing/Impeachment_Hastings.htm#7.

Wheeler, M. 2013. *The Art of Negotiation: How to Improvise Agreement.* New York: Simon & Schuster.

CHAPTER

3

FEDERALISM: THE CHANGING CONTEXTS OF STATE AND FEDERAL HEALTH POLICY

Learning Objectives

After reading this chapter, you should be able to

- define and briefly describe *federalism*;
- articulate the differences in the kinds of policies states and the federal government make and why those differences are important;
- understand how the national federalism concept of today impacts health policy;
- describe how states may take similar or more individualized roles in the administration of Medicaid and elements of the Affordable Care Act (ACA);
- explain how differences in policy choices among the states impact national health goals;
- discuss and provide an example of each of the six predominant categories of federal health legislation:
  1. food and drug supply,
  2. disease research and protection,
  3. system infrastructure and training for health professionals,
  4. developmental and behavioral health,
  5. environmental health and pollution, and
  6. access to care; and
- discuss why understanding the interlocking nature of federal and state health policy is important.

A Brief History of Federalism in the United States

It is well beyond the scope of this text to examine the historical development and concept of federalism in detail. Nonetheless, a brief discussion of its history in the United States is pertinent here to explain the modern interpretation of federalism and what that means for health policy at both the state and national levels. Federalism is a system of government "in which sovereignty is shared [between two or more levels of government] so that on some matters the national government is supreme and on others the states, regions or provincial governments are supreme" (Wilson and DiIuilo 1995, A-49). The federalist system in the United States has transformed over time, progressing through somewhat distinctive eras.

When the founders replaced the Articles of Confederation with the Constitution, not only were the responsibilities—and the associated powers—of governing divided between three branches, but they were also allocated between the states, as sovereign entities, and the national government, a sovereign nation. As James Madison said in *The Federalist*, number 46, the states and the national government "are in fact different agents and trustees of the people constituted with different powers" (Madison 1788).

The Bill of Rights, part of which is a pillar of the federalism concept, was adopted on December 15, 1791, less than two years after the Constitution. The first eight amendments to the Constitution in the Bill of Rights address a variety of rights pertaining to individual liberty: freedom of speech, right to bear arms, freedom from unreasonable search and seizure, the right to a jury trial, the right to due process, and the like (Lawson and Schapiro 2020). It was the Tenth Amendment that specifically addressed limitations on the national government: "The powers not delegated to the United States by the Constitution, nor prohibited by it to the States, are reserved to the States respectively, or to the people."

The Tenth Amendment established a framework in which to further define the division of power between the federal government and the sovereign states. The Tenth Amendment is considered the "Police Power" clause of the Constitution because matters *not* delegated to the federal government include the inherent power of a state to protect the health and well-being of its people. It is from this language and interpretation that states have the authority to license healthcare providers of all types, regulate the type and nature of healthcare facility construction, inspect restaurants for cleanliness, and impose vaccination requirements, among a multitude of other things related to the health and safety of the states' populations.

Conversely, Article 1, Section 8 of the Constitution specifically enumerates those powers assigned to the national government, including the power to levy taxes and the power to regulate commerce between the states, among others. It likewise limits states' authority, banning states from making treaties and otherwise engaging in foreign affairs.

What states and the federal government can and cannot do is, of course, the product not only of the written words in Article l and the Tenth Amendment, but of interpretations provided by the Supreme Court and other authoritative decision-making bodies. Those definitions about governmental power have transformed the federal–state relationship throughout the years. Over time, federalism has become more interactive between the states and federal government, fostering a higher degree of cross-sovereign policymaking.

The relationship between the states and the federal government has been a question of debate since the birth of the republic. While the subject matter of any given political question may change—health, education, regulation of industry, and so forth—the core issue frequently is the determination of the appropriate roles of states and of the federal government. In general, more conservative voices advocate a stronger role for the states and a smaller federal government. More liberal voices suggest that the federal government should be stronger in order to address problems of national dimension that transcend individual state borders and variable state capacities. Therein lies one of the fundamental and transcending political and policy debates in the United States.

To Madison's point, the United States was a national government—a sovereign—borne of sovereign states and their people. From this germinated the concept of *separate spheres* for each of the states and the national government. The degree of separation, if you will, has narrowed over time, with each sphere becoming increasingly more engaged with the other. Exhibit 3.1 provides a shorthand reference tool representing the evolution of federalism in the United States.

Dual Federalism: The Nineteenth Century

The belief in the concept of duality between the states and national government—*dual federalism*—was prominent from late in the 1700s through the turn of the twentieth century. There was little discernible cooperation between the states and the federal government. States' rights advocates championed the notion that the states were equal to, or even superior to, the national government, advancing what was known as the "states' rights doctrine." During this time, the Supreme Court ruled the federal government had implied powers to do those things "necessary and proper" to carry out the functions delegated to it by the Constitution (*McCulloch v. Maryland* 1819). The *McCulloch* decision was prominent for upholding the Supremacy Clause in allowing the federal government to charter a national bank. Other debates during this time included whether the federal government could engage in internal improvements such as roads and bridges (yes) and whether states could effectively nullify federal law (no). Nonetheless, states' rights advocates continued to press the idea of states having the legal capacity to render federal law null and void within the boundaries of a state choosing to do so.

The concept of nullification was a transcending issue, arising in several different ways and forums even after *McCulloch*. South Carolina passed a nullification ordinance in an attempt to prevent implementation of tariffs

EXHIBIT 3.1
Evolution of Federalism Timeline

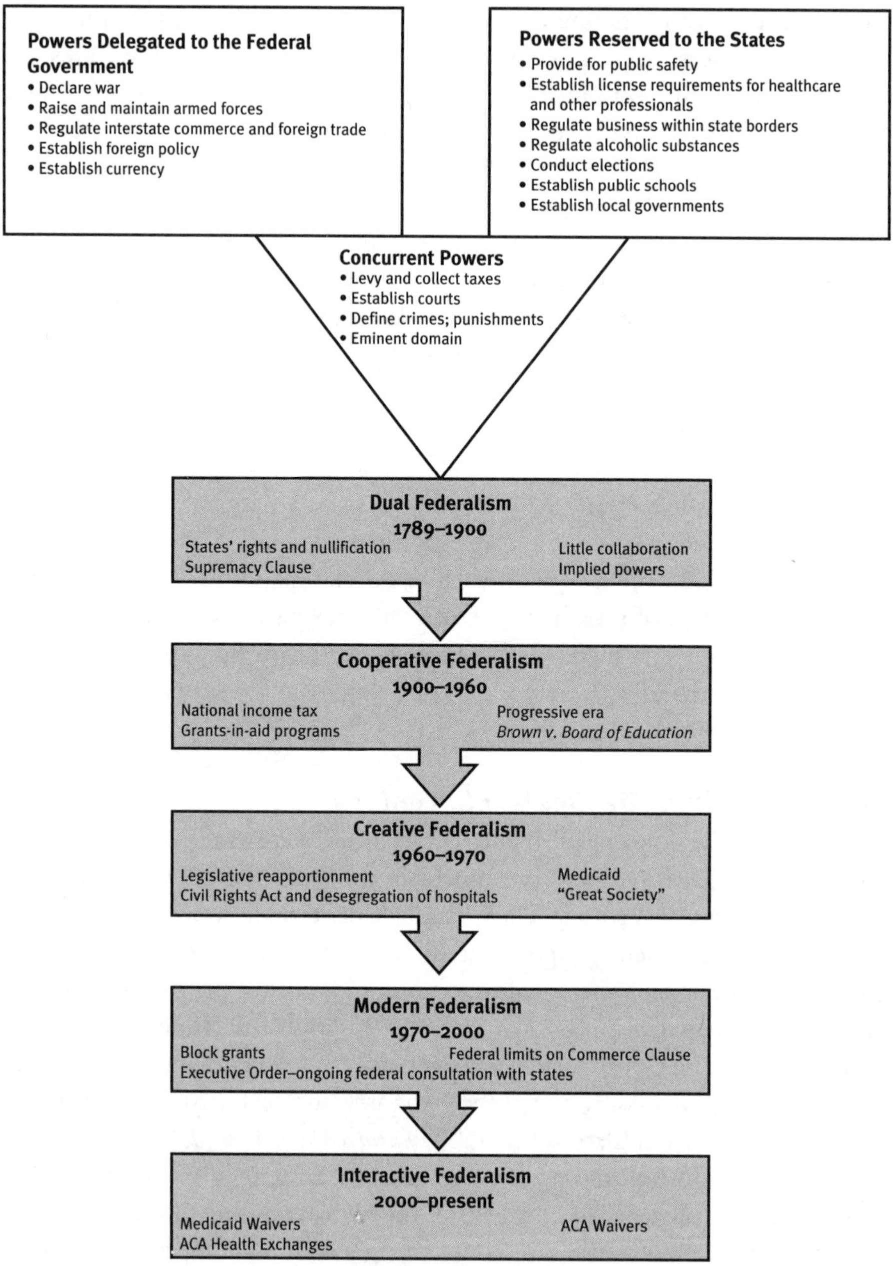

on raw goods. Pennsylvania (among other northern states), attempting to protect fugitive slaves, enacted "personal liberty" statutes that were found to be violative of the Supremacy Clause because of a federal act—the Fugitive Slave Act—enacted in 1793. The states' rights issue cut both ways in some instances. The view that the states had a right to nullify federal law was a part of the reason for the Civil War, in addition to eradicating slavery.

During and following the Civil War, federal power expanded. The national government regained control of currency; conscription into the national army replaced state militias. In the second half of the century, federal authority continued to grow with the enactment of the Fourteenth Amendment, which applied the Constitution's Due Process and Equal Protection clauses to the states. Also, during this period, federal power grew through enactment of the Sherman Anti-Trust Act and the Interstate Commerce Act, among others. Conversely, however, the Supreme Court upheld the rights of states to create a state-regulated monopoly and to ban people from accessing some public amenities and privileges on the basis of race or sex, upheld the "separate but equal" concept of public services, and upheld state literacy tests as mechanisms for determining who could have the right to vote. No longer was the federal government a "servant of the states" in a decentralized theory of governance, but states retained the power to control matters clearly within their own borders (Boyd and Fauntroy 2000).

Cooperative Federalism, 1901–1960

In the early 1900s, the fledgling idea of using federal resources to influence state behavior to achieve national health objectives was an idea whose time was about to come. This era saw the beginning of partnership programs or a grant-in-aid approach between the federal government and the states. During this time, Presidents Theodore Roosevelt and Woodrow Wilson pioneered an expansive definition of the national government's role.

The advent of the federal income tax ratified in the Sixteenth Amendment to the Constitution in 1913 was no doubt a significant factor in the capacity to experiment and begin to use the *grant-in-aid* approach: using federal government revenue to grant money to the states in pursuit of policy objectives. This aim was matched by the willingness of the states to accept federal funds to do things they otherwise could not afford to do.

The first seed of this concept sewn in health policy was with the Maternity and Infancy Act, also known as Sheppard-Towner for its two sponsors. Enacted in 1921, this was the first major legislation to follow women's suffrage and was on the books until 1929, when it was allowed to expire. (A form of this law reemerged as part of the Social Security Act [SSA] of 1935.) The thrust of the legislation was, in part, to encourage states to create birth registries and child hygiene bureaus. The "encouragement" was perhaps the most important feature of Sheppard-Towner: This legislation marked the first time in healthcare that funds were appropriated by the federal government to the states on a formulaic basis that required matching participation by the state. The act brought noteworthy success to the effort, as shown in exhibit 3.2.

The Great Depression in the early part of the 1930s brought widespread and profound poverty. The scope of the economic collapse was so deep and

EXHIBIT 3.2 Comparison of the Number of State Birth Registries and Child Hygiene Bureaus Before and After Sheppard-Towner

Activity	Before Sheppard-Towner	After Sheppard-Towner
Birth registries	30 states	46 states
Child hygiene bureaus	28 states	47 states

Source: Adapted from Kotch (1997).

so broad that it necessitated intervention on a national level. The nature of the contract between the federal government and the individual citizen was forever changed by the SSA: For the first time, individual citizens would receive cash payments directly from the federal government. Likewise, various new federal programs were created as shared ventures with the states, and exclusive federal initiatives sprang from the SSA as well. If the seeds of grants-in-aid or federal–state partnerships began to take hold in the early days of the century, the field was in full bloom from the Depression through the 1960s (Boyd and Fauntroy 2000).

In addition, the *Brown v. Board of Education* decision in 1954 brought federal civil rights principles to the states. As a matter of resistance, some states theorized a "doctrine of imposition" that suggested a state may interpose itself between an "improper" national act and the state's citizens, though this approach was not efficacious in the long run.

The formulaic funding approach worked. The legacy of Sheppard-Towner, beyond its impact on infant mortality and child health, is that is served as a prototype for federal grants-in-aid to the states to achieve national health policy objectives.

A representative sample of legislation employing this funding mechanism provides a picture of how the federal government, with the largesse of the federal purse, can achieve national policy objectives at the state level. The proliferation of this concept changed the dynamic of the federalist system from the "separate spheres" philosophy to interactive, collaborative exchanges between those spheres. A partial list of examples appears in exhibit 3.3.

To be clear, this federal–state "partnership" approach did not end with Medicaid in 1965. Subsequent examples, and there are many, include multiple amendments to Hill-Burton and the expansion of support for state efforts in developmental health, mental health, disease prevention, and, notably, the Children's Health Insurance Program of 1997, which many states folded into their Medicaid programs. Note that this list does *not* include legislation in which new federal agencies were created or new responsibilities were assigned to those agencies, a subject to be addressed later in this chapter, along with other partnership program legislation.

EXHIBIT 3.3
Selected Federal "Grant-in-Aid" Legislation

Year	Legislation	Key Issue(s) Addressed
1935	Social Security Act	Incentives for maternal and child health; child welfare services and increased assistance for state and local public health programs
1938	LaFollette-Bulwinkle Act	Funding for states to investigate and control venereal disease
1946	National Mental Health Act	Grants for states' mental health activities
1946	Hill-Burton Act	Grants to states in support of hospital planning and construction
1954	Medical Facilities and Construction Act	Expansion of Hill-Burton to include other kinds of health facilities
1955	Polio Vaccination Act	Support for state-administered polio vaccination programs
1956	Water Pollution Control Act Amendments	Technical and financial support to states and municipalities to prevent and control water pollution
1960	Kerr-Mills Act	Support for states to provide care for "medically indigent" elderly
1963	Health Professionals Educational Assistance Act	Construction grants for healthcare professional teaching facilities
1963	Maternal and Child Health and Mental Retardation Planning Amendments	Support for states' efforts to prevent developmental disability through prenatal, maternity, and infant care for at-risk individuals
1964	Hospital and Medical Facilities Amendments	Expansion of Hill-Burton to include modernization and replacement of existing facilities
1965	Medicaid	Support to states to insure medically indigent individuals

Creative Federalism, 1960–1970

The 1960s saw a plethora of significant developments in the dynamic of federal and state relationships. The Supreme Court ruled in 1962 that apportionment of legislative districts in every state but Oregon violated the Equal Protection Clause of the Fourteenth Amendment to the US Constitution. Migration of population to urban areas had caused rural areas to be, relatively speaking, overrepresented in state legislatures. Fundamentally, federal standards of "one man, one vote" were imposed on the states (*Baker v. Carr* 1962).

In addition, the "Great Society" advocated by President Lyndon Johnson empowered the federal government to pursue national policy objectives through state and local governments. This concept included initiatives such as Kerr-Mills, which ultimately became Medicaid; expansion of the Hill-Burton Act to provide more support for states to facilitate construction of medical facilities; and federal support for states to address developmental issues in their respective populations.

Moreover, the Civil Rights Act of 1964 provided a strong impetus to desegregate American hospitals. That drive to desegregate was accelerated with the passage of the Medicare program in 1965. Hospitals were not allowed to participate in the Medicare program—that is, would not be paid—if they did not first integrate patient care services (Hoffman 2012).

Modern Federalism, 1970–2000

In the 1970s and 1980s, the federal government took note of overlap and waste among multiple federal matching grant programs. During this time, the concept of block grants for a number of programs emerged in an effort to shift power from the federal government to the states by giving the states more latitude in using federal resources (Boyd and Fauntroy 2000).

In general, both court cases and legislative action pushed more activity to the state level. In *New York v. United States* (1992), the Supreme Court ruled that congressional imposition of liability on the states for failure to establish low-level radioactive waste–mitigation sites exceeded its authority under the Commerce Clause. The Workforce Investment Act of 1998 consolidated improvement in employment, literacy, and vocational rehabilitation training as a block grant to states. Finally, an executive order by President Clinton required federal agencies to have a consultation process in place with states prior to the release of regulations or publication of legislation (US President 1999).

Interactive Federalism, 2000–Present

The nature of the relationship between the federal and state governments continued to evolve. Having briefly examined the history of federalism's evolution, we now turn to how more contemporary national health policy objectives are served by state action incentivized by the federal government through a variety of "partnerships" leveraging federal revenue against the states' police powers. Some call this *national federalism* (Gluck 2014) or *interactive federalism* (Schapiro 2005). Regardless of the label, the key characteristic of this brand of federalism comes directly from federal statutes, says Gluck (2014):

> When Congress calls on states to implement federal law, states act in their sovereign capacities to do so: They pass new state laws and regulations, create new state

> institutions, appoint state officials, disburse state funds. . . . It is true that this state action is not wholly separate from federal law; *it is shaped by the federal statutes and states often need permission* from the federal government to begin a course of federal statutory implementation [emphasis added]. But that does not change the fact that, after such approval, the states' sovereign apparatus acts in ways that are often indistinguishable from the kind of autonomy we see in exclusively state-law domains.

As it relates to health policy, the observed trend is to engage states ever more deeply in national issues. The federal government is giving the states substantial flexibility with regard to federal programs addressing a national purpose—for example during this era, the expansion of Medicaid in the ACA. In short, Congress and the president wanted to expand healthcare coverage to include a significant population not included in the original Medicaid legislation as part of a national goal to achieve universal health insurance coverage. For that reason, state expansion of Medicaid was mandatory for the states in the legislation as it was enacted into law. In *NFIB v. Sebelius,* however, the Supreme Court decision made Medicaid expansion optional for the states. By dint of that decision, implementation of this important policy was handed to the states. As an incentive to encourage states to expand their Medicaid programs, the federal executive branch, as part of *its* implementation scheme, provided states significant latitude to implement that expansion of care in ways that met local needs. Those local needs varied from state to state, which directly—and at times adversely—affected the effectiveness of the national purpose that motivated program creation in the first place (Gluck and Huberfeld 2020).

While the federal government established the precedent for *cooperative federalism* by allocating resources to states conditioned on states' pursuit of broader national goals, it specifically also permitted and encouraged state innovation in the federal statutes establishing the program. This subtle transition to "interactive federalism" is most prominent in Medicaid, the Children's Health Insurance Program (CHIP), and the ACA. (For the purposes of this discussion, because many states have folded their CHIP programs into their Medicaid programs, those two will be considered together here.)

As we move to the discussion of state flexibility in administration of programs undertaken in partnership with the federal government, briefly take note of their relative expenditure levels for Medicaid. As seen in exhibit 3.4, the amount of a state's Medicaid expenditures paid by the federal government for federal fiscal year (FY) 2018 is, on average, 62.5 percent. The state portion is, on average, 37.5 percent. New Mexico had the greatest percentage of federal assistance with Medicaid at 79.7 percent, while Virginia had the smallest at 49.9 percent (Kaiser Family Foundation 2019). (For a complete list of states and their relative share of Medicaid expenditures, see Kaiser Family Foundation [2019].)

EXHIBIT 3.4
Percentage of Federal and State Share of Medicaid Expenditure (Federal FY 2018)

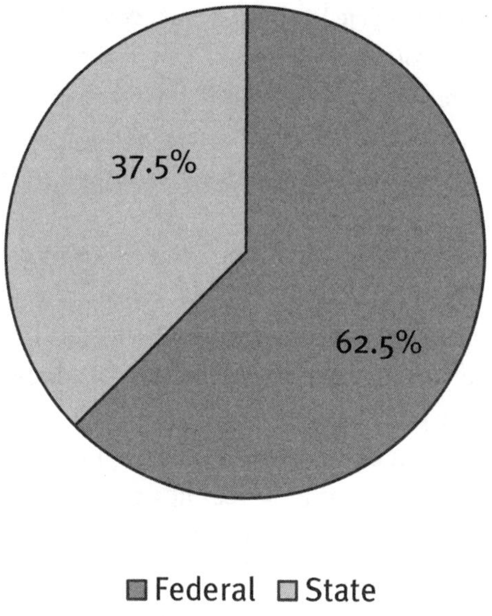

Source: Adapted from Kaiser Family Foundation (2019).

The Medicaid program permits states to innovate and experiment within the federal parameters of the program. States may apply to the secretary of the Department of Health and Human Services (HHS) for a waiver releasing them from some of the requirements of the program. There are three different kinds of Medicaid-program waivers, all of which are derived from sections of the SSA. (Remember, Medicaid—including CHIP—and Medicare are amendments to the original SSA.) References in the legislation to waivers, therefore, relate to those sections of the SSA that empower the secretary to grant the waivers.

Section 1115(b) Medicaid Waivers: Research and Demonstration Projects

Waivers under this section are for experimental or demonstration projects. The secretary of HHS can waive the mandate that the patient have freedom of provider choice and requirements that there be comparability of services, and HHS may also permit a program to be less than statewide. In other words, with the waiver, the federal government will continue to provide the usual matching funds to which the state would otherwise be entitled while the state experiments with nonconforming delivery models of innovations (Mitchell et al. 2019).

Consider an example: A state might want to contract with a managed care organization (MCO) that included a large group of providers—perhaps all the hospitals and the local medical society of a large urban area in an otherwise predominately rural state. The program might use a capitated model requiring Medicaid beneficiaries to use in-network providers. Further, the MCO might offer translation and transportation services to those patients who need them. This program would be markedly different from the Medicaid program in the rest of the state, as it would restrict provider choice, offer nonstandard services, and exist only in a subregion of the state. In this way, the program would speak to all of the conditions referenced previously.

The research or demonstration questions would be whether such an approach would be truly cost-effective compared to the standard Medicaid program. Does this approach save money? Does it improve the population's health status? Does it provide more overall value than the typical approach? By the terms of the waiver, the state and the organization with which it contracted would have an initial five years to answer such questions. The waiver is renewable (Mitchell et al. 2019).

Section 1915 Medicaid Waivers: Managed Care or Freedom of Choice Waivers and Home and Community-Based Services Waivers

There are additional waivers under Section 1915(b) of the SSA that allow states, subject to the approval of the secretary of the HHS, to restrict *freedom of provider choice* not for research or demonstration purposes, but for mandatory managed care programs as standard operating procedure.

Section 1915(c) permits the secretary to waive many requirements associated with home care–based and community-based services (HCBS) similar to those referenced in Section 1115 waivers in addition to income and financial resource requirements (Mitchell et al. 2019).

See exhibit 3.5 for a synopsis of how widespread this trend has become. Waivers are an important tool for states seeking to manage Medicaid programs in a way that each state perceives to be most effective. In this way, Medicaid is not a one-size-fits-all federal program but rather multiple individual federal–state partnerships that allow states flexibility in how to meet the needs of their populations. This demonstrates Gluck's point about national federalism. Yes, the state behaves like a separate sovereign, but it does so in the framework of law that has national requirements.

Exhibit 3.5 reflects how many states have participated in each of the three waiver programs and the number of waivers granted in those states. It further displays the characteristics included in some of those waivers. For example, of the 60 waivers in 44 states under Section 1115(b), at least some—but not necessarily all—included waivers related to the characteristics mentioned in the left-hand column of exhibit 3.5. Moreover, one state may have multiple waivers in each of the categories.

EXHIBIT 3.5 Comparison of Medicaid Waivers Usage (May 2019)

Key Characteristic	1115(b) R&D	1915(b) Managed Care	1915(c) HCBS
Number of waivers	60 waivers, 44 states	78 waivers, 38 states and District of Columbia	292 waivers, 47 states and District of Columbia
Statewide requirement waived	•	•	•
Comparable-service-to-Medicaid standard waived		•	•
Guaranteed freedom of provider choice waived	•	•	
Income and resource rules waived			•

Source: Adapted from Mitchell et al. (2019).

The Affordable Care Act and State Policy Innovation: Section 1332 Waivers

Waivers apply only to state Medicaid programs. The ACA also created a waiver process to permit states greater flexibility with respect to certain elements of the ACA that are not directly related to Medicaid. Keep in mind, however, that Medicaid expansion was a part of the original vision of ACA proponents, who planned to use it as a tool to help expand insurance coverage.

Before discussing requirements that a state can have waived under the provisions of the ACA, a brief examination of the allocation of responsibilities between the federal government and the states would be in order. In its most simplified form, the ACA delineates federal and state responsibilities in this way:

> The federal government provides:
>
> - Protections for people with preexisting health conditions
> - Uniform financial assistance for people with incomes below 400 percent of the federal poverty level [FPL]
> - Individual and employer mandates to ensure people gain and keep coverage.
>
> States have authority to:
>
> - Oversee their individual, small-, and large-group insurance markets
> - Manage their Medicaid program

- Run their own insurance marketplace
- Create a Basic Health Plan for people earning between 138 percent and 200 percent of FPL
- Set up risk adjustment and rate review programs
- Make significant changes to their individual markets (through a Section 1332 state innovation waiver) so long as the coverage offered is affordable, comprehensive, and available to the same number of people as under current law (Collins and Lambrew 2019).

Section 1332 of the ACA allows the secretary of the HHS to grant waivers to states relating to certain requirements of the ACA. Referred to as *state innovation waivers*, they are also called *state relief and empowerment waivers* (CMS 2020). Specifically, the secretary may grant waivers regarding the following:

- Benefits and subsidies
- Insurance markets
- The individual mandate
- Employer mandates

Fundamentally, this section permits states to do things necessary to ensure the stability of insurance markets—compensate for adverse selection, for example (Rosso and Mach 2019).

There are, of course, some federal "guardrails" that provide parameters beyond which a state may not go with its waiver. Any waiver under Section 1332 must do the following:

- Provide coverage at least as comprehensive as that available without the waiver.
- Be at least as affordable as the coverage would be without the waiver (out-of-pocket costs cannot be excessive).
- Provide the same breadth of coverage as the coverage would be without the waiver (in other words, the waiver plan must cover at least as many people as would be covered without the waiver).
- May not add to the federal deficit (i.e., must be cost neutral) (Rosso and Mach 2019).

There is more to this than the written word. Different interpretations can be applied that yield remarkably different decisions. Those operational decisions—policy decisions—can, in turn, produce dramatically different results. The following sections contain some striking examples.

Waivers in Detail

The Congressional Research Service has published two reports with significant detail about the waivers available under Medicaid and the ACA. For a complete table of waiver-related activity and more detailed discussion of Section 1115 and 1915 waivers, see Mitchell et al. (2019). For complete information regarding Section 1332 waivers under the ACA, see Rosso and Mach (2019).

The primary point of this discussion of federalism and the specifics of the waiver provisions is the enhanced flexibility the federal government provides the states with regard to administration of both Medicaid and ACA requirements. Not only may states undertake novel approaches to Medicaid, but they can also alter ACA terms. While it has not occurred yet, there is nothing that bars a state from seeking both Medicaid and ACA waivers to be used in concert with one another to help meet the mandate of reducing the number of uninsured individuals.

From a federal policy perspective, this flexibility enhances the role of the states in crafting health policy. This flexibility permits the local sovereign to shape the program in a way most beneficial to that state. This "new" version of federalism—which emanates from federal statutes, regulations, and operating decisions—is helping states to find new ways to manage both Medicaid and the healthcare reform brought forth by the ACA.

With respect to Medicaid in particular, however, the meaning of *reform*, as used during the tenure of one administration, is not necessarily the same as the next. The primary mandate of Medicaid is to provide insurance for the economically very poor among us—to expand health insurance coverage in order to improve access to care. Recall that Medicaid, prior to the ACA, was aimed primarily at parents (most frequently single mothers) and children whose income was below 100 percent of FPL. The ACA dramatically expanded eligibility to include essentially *everyone* with an income of 138 percent of FPL or less. This expansion was so significant that the Supreme Court considered it a new program and struck down the mandatory expansion in favor of making it an option for the states.

The mandate of Medicaid in its pre-ACA form, and certainly after, was to *expand* coverage and, thus, access to healthcare services. But in the eyes of some, the ACA expansion represented a fundamental change in the type of people covered. This example is one where the outcomes of elections matter. Those who hold this view—that this expansion of Medicaid goes beyond its original mandate and that the expansion was a "clear departure from the core, historical mission of the [Medicaid] program"—came to power in the election of 2016 (Price and Verma 2017). Thus began the modification of legislatively established policy through application of administrative regulation and operational decisions.

This view of the ACA resulted in a "shift in policy" with regard to how the HHS interprets applications for Section 1115 waivers (Rosenbaum 2017). The Trump administration announced it will consider state applications for waivers to permit the imposition of work requirements by states as a precondition to receive Medicaid benefits. Some have questioned whether this interpretation is, in fact, consistent with the program's mission (Huberfeld 2018).

Basically, the view of the political leadership of several states, and the interpretation of the Medicaid expansion by the federal government agency charged with its administration (CMS), have combined to give states a new way to manage Medicaid costs. Many people working part-time or poorly paid full-time jobs were previously denied Medicaid because their income exceeded the eligibility threshold. Now they may be eligible, thus Medicaid coverage was expanded irrespective of state-imposed work requirements for these individuals. Conversely, however, there are those who may not be able to find work or may not be able to work for reasons not accounted for in the program, and they will be disenrolled from the program. That feature of work requirements saves the states (and the federal government) money, but it comes at the cost of disenrolling people who would otherwise be eligible for Medicaid under the ACA.

The issue here is not whether one agrees with work requirements as a predicate for Medicaid eligibility. The point in this context is the level of flexibility afforded to the states by an administrative interpretation of a legislative action. State-by-state work requirements constitute a good example of how the federal government can and does permit state action that might yield dramatically different results from state to state. Work requirements imposed in one Medicaid expansion state may disqualify a person from Medicaid benefits, while a person of similar standing in another state may reap the benefits of the expanded Medicaid program. (As of this writing, the imposition of work requirements has been stayed by court order pending the outcome of litigation challenging the legality of such work requirements.) In another example, an individual who lives in a state that did not expand Medicaid, but close to the border of a state that did, may experience different health outcomes than their neighbor. Irrespective of work requirements in this instance, this schism has been referred to as the Medicaid "haves and have nots" (Ungar 2019).

The impact of the Supreme Court decision in *NFIB v. Sebelius* that vitiated the mandate to expand Medicaid certainly was a policy decision with profound consequences. Here, we see an administrative (operating) decision adding an additional policy layer, giving the states the opportunity to further alter ACA (as to the Medicaid expansion) rules, thereby also diminishing Medicaid's impact in expanding coverage. Again, the point is not whether one agrees—the point is that judicial and administrative decisions can alter the intended outcome of the legislative body. In the context of federalism, judicial and administrative decisions that mitigate the impact of legislatively established policy take place at both the federal and state levels of government. While the ACA happens to provide a rich example, this could occur in other fields as well.

History can recount how federalism in the United States has changed in ways that one might argue permits states, with the imprimatur of the federal government, to all but thwart the design of the federal government's intended program. While one administration might deny states the opportunity to apply the interpretation recounted earlier in the chapter, the next one might permit it (Huberfeld 2018). Thus, this chapter is not only an examination of federalism but also of policy modification (as described in chapter 4 and discussed in greater detail in chapter 10). Simply put, though it feels like the left hand doesn't know what the right hand is doing, that impression is not necessarily correct. The left hand is allowing the right hand to do things previously not permitted—this is a "modification" outcome.

If operational realities of the federalist system have changed throughout the history of the United States, so too has the role of the federal government. By the breadth and depth of Congressional and presidential policy decisions, the federal government has established an ever-increasing presence in health policy (see box).

Legal Marijuana: Federal Intransigence While States Move Forward

The legalization of marijuana is an issue for which the federal power to regulate interstate commerce and the police power of the states collide. Once highly controversial and universally illegal, marijuana has found a new place in society in recent years. As of early 2020, 34 states permit the medical use of marijuana in one fashion or another. Likewise, 11 states have made recreational use legal. While legalizing the possession and cultivation of marijuana, states have developed a variety of regulatory schemes limiting the amounts that may be dispensed or possessed, or the level of THC (tetrahydrocannabinol) permitted, but in a very real sense there is no legal consequence for possession of "weed" in these states. Conversely, however, "At the federal level, marijuana remains classified as a Schedule I substance under the Controlled

Substances Act, where Schedule I substances are considered to have a high potential for dependency and no accepted medical use, making distribution of marijuana a federal offense" (National Conference of State Legislatures 2020).

As is always the case—at federal, state, and local levels—prosecutors have a measure of discretion with regard to enforcement. In other words, prosecutors may consider mitigating circumstances in deciding whether to prosecute any criminal violation. In general terms, the less violent the crime, the greater the level of discretion that may be exercised. In this particular case, the federal government is slowly ceding to the states the prerogative to regulate marijuana. In October 2009, the Department of Justice (DOJ) under the Obama administration encouraged federal prosecutors to avoid prosecuting individuals who distributed marijuana for medical purposes under state law (National Conference of State Legislatures 2020).

In August 2013, the DOJ updated its policy, asserting that states such as Washington and Colorado (which had passed laws legalizing, but also regulating, the production and distribution of marijuana) were expected to have rigorous enforcement mechanisms, setting forth eight factors that should guide prosecution. Further, the DOJ said it was reserving the right to challenge state laws legalizing the use and distribution of marijuana (DOJ 2013).

Subsequently, under a new administration, in January 2018, Attorney General Jeff Sessions rescinded the previous memo and indicated the discretion would rest with local US attorneys. The memo "directs all U.S. Attorneys to use previously established prosecutorial principles that provide them all the necessary tools to disrupt criminal organizations, tackle the growing drug crisis and thwart violent crimes across our country" (DOJ 2018). As a practical matter, this change did not affect prosecutorial decisions materially.

In short, this conflict between the states' police power and the federal government's regulation of interstate commerce seems to be shifting the balance in favor of the states with regard to the legalization of marijuana. Of course, there are multiple variables in state decisions to legalize and regulate marijuana. First, state prisons are overcrowded. By reducing the number of imprisonments attributable to use and possession of marijuana, the states can save money and alleviate heavily burdened court dockets. At the same time, by legalizing and regulating the product, states can gain tax revenues much in the same way they tax tobacco and liquor. Finally, people of color are convicted of drug possession in disproportionate numbers, so legalization makes the justice system slightly less racially

(continued)

disparate in this respect (Langan 1995; Rosenberg, Groves, and Blankenship 2017).

It remains a crime to transport marijuana across state lines. Thus, in terms of growth, production, and consumption, the marijuana industry is legally constrained to function within the individual states.

By January 2020, the following states permitted medical or recreational marijuana.

Allow Medical Marijuana		Allow Recreational Marijuana
Alaska	Missouri	Alaska
Arizona	Montana	California
Arkansas	Nevada	Colorado
California	New Hampshire	Illinois
Colorado	New Jersey	Maine
Connecticut	New Mexico	Massachusetts
Delaware	New York	Michigan
District of Columbia	North Dakota	Nevada
Hawaii	Ohio	Oregon
Illinois	Oklahoma	Vermont
Louisiana	Oregon	Washington
Maine	Pennsylvania	
Maryland	Rhode Island	
Massachusetts	Utah	
Michigan	Vermont	
Minnesota		

Source: Governing.com (2019).

Growth in the Federal Government's Healthcare Role

The federal government's influence in healthcare has grown since the beginning days of the republic. The first federal law with respect to health was the Seaman's Sickness and Disability Act of 1798 that required

> the master or owner of every ship or vessel of the United States arriving from a foreign port into any port in the United States shall . . . render to the collector a true account of the number of seamen that shall have been employed on board such vessel . . . and shall pay to the said collector, at the rate of twenty cents per month, for every seaman so employed. . . . [The act stipulated in Section 2 that] the President of the

United States is hereby authorized, out of the same, to provide for the temporary relief and maintenance of sick or disabled seamen in the hospitals, or other proper institutions now established in the several ports.

Since that time, the federal role in health policy has grown. Consistent with changes in the concept of federalism as well as the US population and society, that growth has been significantly greater in the twentieth and twenty-first centuries than in the eighteenth or nineteenth. Indeed, federal growth in healthcare and health services has accelerated since the Great Depression. That event, leading to the SSA of 1935, brought a sea change in how individuals would relate to the federal government's new role in their lives. The SSA fundamentally changed the relationship of the federal government and US citizens—for the first time, individuals received a benefit directly from the federal government, not from the states. Likewise, the SSA amplified the "grant-in-aid" practice between the federal and state governments. Once enshrined into law, the SSA became the foundation for a multitude of federal interventions in both the lives of individuals and in the dynamic between the federal government and the states.

Expansion of the federal role in healthcare is, in many ways, predicated on the statutory base provided by the SSA. Keep in mind that Medicare, Medicaid, the Children's Health Insurance Program, and parts of the ACA are all amendments to the SSA. Likewise, a variety of grant programs to states and local communities for maternal and child health also spring from the SSA. Title V of the SSA can be portrayed as a Sheppard-Towner redux, along with similar matching grant programs embodied in Title V.

Likewise, as Congress saw threats to people's health from adulterated drugs and from communicable diseases, and as science learned more about terminal diseases, the federal government responded by establishing agencies such as the Food and Drug Administration (FDA), the Centers for Disease Control and Prevention (CDC), and the National Institutes of Health (NIH). In their infancy, those agencies had different names and relatively narrow missions. But as industry, agriculture, and science advanced, the health professions learned more about threats from drugs, pollutants, cancers, and the transmission of disease. Concomitantly, the missions of these agencies grew and, of course, new agencies were created. Sometimes agency names were changed to reflect an expanded mission. The FDA, the CDC, and the NIH are all good examples of this development.

Note, however, that in some policy subcategories, intervention is almost exclusively federal, with very little state interaction, while in other areas the federal program may be highly integrated with the states at multiple levels. Most of federal legislation that addresses health can be organized into six categories (see appendix 1.3). Many individual laws address more than one subject, but a law's primary purpose is the one used for this classification. Using this prism contributes to understanding the historical development of federal health policy. So, for discussion purposes, we will examine federal legislation using the following categories:

- Food and drug supply
- Disease research and protection
- System infrastructure and training health professionals
- Developmental and behavioral health
- Environmental health and pollution
- Access to care

These categories reflect healthcare issues that transcend state borders. Water quality assurance in one state, for example, may not mean much in terms of efficacious policy if a state upstream permits profligate polluting. Similarly, keeping food unadulterated in one state will not prevent illness in another that may not regulate food as closely. As we have seen previously, only the federal government can create policies that cross state lines to address issues affecting all states.

Food and Drug Supply

Public interest in food and drug safety began well before the first significant legislation on the subject. There were interest groups and several administrative appointments along with minor legislation concerning adulterated food. The federal Bureau of Chemistry evolved into FDA with the passage of the Pure Food and Drug Act of 1906.

Adulterated food and drugs have been—and remain— health concerns for many. As the incidence of events involving either began to accelerate, so too did Congressional response. Recall germ theory arose in 1864, when Louis Pasteur first purified wine by heating, then cooling, it. By the 1880s, pasteurization of milk was becoming common in Europe. It would be close to the turn of the century before the process became more widespread in the United States. With this advancement came new awareness of the impact of impurities in food and drugs. Congress acted to improve the purity of food and drugs in 1906 in response to studies of adulterated food and drug products done by the chief chemist of the United States, Dr. Harvey Wiley (FDA 2018).

Assurance of pure food and unadulterated pharmaceuticals is an area in which the federal government has taken the lead over states. The transmission of food and drugs flowing through interstate commerce puts the federal government in the superior position for this purpose. There are but a few "partnerships" between the federal government and the states in the category of food and drug purity. We see little evidence of interactive federalism, as discussed earlier in the chapter, in this body of legislation. The laws are all aimed at products that are trafficked across state lines. Further, it is a federal agency that is charged with administration and enforcement of US law and policy as it relates to food and drugs.

During the last part of the twentieth century and first part of the twenty-first, it was increasingly apparent that research and development of new pharmaceuticals and biologics was accelerating and exceeding the capability of the FDA to review such proposals thoroughly using contemporary analytical protocols. The 21st Century Cures Act (P.L. 114-255), signed into law in December 2016, made several changes to the drug and device approval pathways through the FDA to support innovation and accelerate development and review of certain medical products (e.g., combination products, antimicrobials, drugs for rare disease, regenerative therapies) (Dabrowska and Green 2019).

See appendix 1.3, section A, "Food and Drug Supply Legislation," for summaries of selected legislation related to food and drugs.

Disease Research and Protection

The NIH and the CDC have very different, but complementary, missions. Their respective mission statements and orientations highlight those differences. The NIH mission is focused on research: not just any research, but foundational research that will lead to knowledge of disease causes and, ultimately, cures. The NIH mission is to "seek fundamental knowledge about the nature and behavior of living systems and the application of that knowledge to enhance health, lengthen life, and reduce illness and disability" (NIH 2017).

In fulfilling that mission, the NIH is a collection of federal agencies dedicated to specific disease research. It has a mere handful of state partnerships related to selected data reporting and sharing. NIH funds research at universities and health science centers across the United States in addition to its own internal research. The volume of legislation directly impacting the NIH understates the importance of this agency and its mission; in this case, appropriation of budget is the more accurate reflection over time of the growth in, and importance of, the NIH's function. During the postwar era, America invested in science through its budget and expansion of research agencies. The first institute was created in 1945, and the number of institutes and agencies in the NIH purview grew to 24 by the end of the century. The budget underscored the value of science to the United States. As you can see in exhibit 3.6, America's interest in scientific research was increasingly robust from 1945 through approximately 2006. At that juncture, America's investment in science diminished and appropriations flattened or grew much more slowly until more recent times which have seen an uptick in this form of public investment. This increased funding for the NIH is a compromise that facilitated the 21st Century Cures Act, discussed in more detail in chapter 6.

EXHIBIT 3.6
NIH Appropriations, 1945–2019 (in billions)

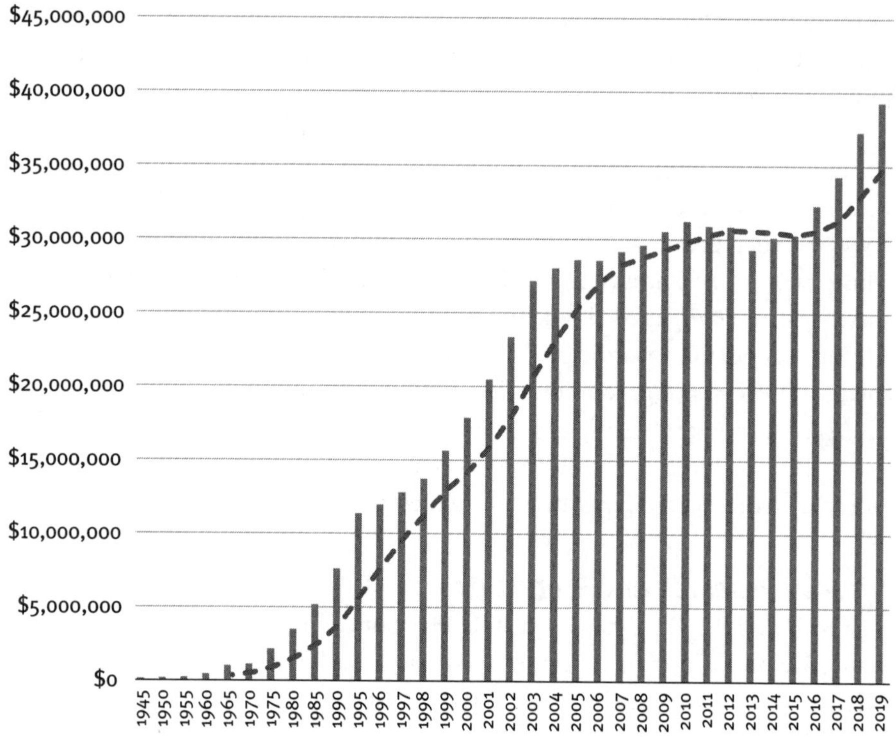

Note: The dotted line is a trend line using a five-year rolling average.
Source: Adapted from NIH (2019).

If the NIH represents the United States investment in foundational science, the CDC is the epitome of applied science in protecting against disease, as well as the quintessence of integration with state and local governments. The CDC's work represents the next step in science—applying what has been learned to benefit the population. In some ways, the CDC's work is an extension of federalism because of its deep state and local government engagement. Further, the CDC conducts its own research on a wide range of health-related topics. Its mission: "As the nation's health protection agency, CDC saves lives and protects people from health threats. To accomplish our mission, CDC conducts critical science and provides health information that protects our nation against expensive and dangerous health threats, and responds when these arise." In "provides health information," the mission statement looks past the breadth and depth of reporting information that is collected by the CDC. Disease outbreaks as well as routine prevalence data are collected at the local and state levels, then aggregated and analyzed by the CDC. When it provides its analysis and user-supplied information (from state and local units of government), the CDC provides a foundation for evidence-based policy. This output happens as a result of a remarkable degree of collaboration between all levels of government. The evidence-based nature of the CDC's work permits and facilitates integrated state and local policy, particularly in important areas such as national preparedness, travelers' health, and diseases and conditions, all representing the public health frontier in federalism. The CDC is leading in the core functions of public health: assessment, policy development, and assurance. Beyond that, the CDC facilitates the continuing improvement in communities' public health capabilities through its education and reporting (Kronstadt et al. 2016).

See appendix 1.3, section B, "Disease Research and Protection Legislation," for summaries of selected legislation related to disease research and protection.

System Infrastructure and Training Health Professionals

As foundational and translational research combined to provide new approaches to diagnoses and treatments, and as medicine became increasingly complex, the federal government intervened to support the advancement of science and to improve educational opportunities to provide further support for scholarships, fellowships, and other financial incentives for Americans to enter into one of the growing—and growing number of—health professions. Communicable disease knows no boundaries; as societal mobility increased, so did the spread of disease. As research revealed more to our society about the complexity of health, our need for more providers, including new kinds of specialist providers, also grew. The policy responses have included a plethora of legislation to address needs growing in both number and clinical scope.

Beyond addressing the supply of nurses, doctors, and (later) other kinds of providers, the federal government made a major contribution toward the growth in the number of hospitals and (ultimately) other forms of healthcare facilities. Known as *Hill-Burton*, the Hospital Survey and Construction Act provided support to states for building new hospitals and adding beds to address a wartime shortage in the aftermath of World War II. Later amendments expanded the scope of the act to include ambulatory care facilities as well as nursing homes.

In this context, federal engagement has relied heavily on the concept of collaboration with state governments and educational institutions. To be clear, this realm has included the creation of federal agencies such as the HHS, its predecessor agencies, and many subcabinet agencies. However, education in the United States is primarily the province of state and local governments. In order to increase the supply of health professionals and provide new or expanded medical facilities, the federal government's primary option has been to partner with states and local governments.

Digital infrastructure is a relatively new area of governmental engagement. As electronic health records gained market share in the 1990s, policymakers soon began to focus on the interoperability of such records. In 2004, the George W. Bush administration established the Office of National Coordinator (ONC) in the Department of HHS to begin the effort of fashioning the transfer of confidential health information among those providers who had legitimate need for it, while protecting the same from unnecessary disclosure. In 2009, the ONC was given official structure as part of the Health Information Technology for Economic and Clinical Health (HITECH) Act. In the same year, Congress enacted the American Recovery and Reinvestment Act, which allocated $150 billion in incentives to accompany requirements for providers to switch from paper to electronic health records. The effort to achieve a higher degree of interoperability continues, as demonstrated by the 2016 enactment of the 21st Century Cures Act.

See appendix 1.3, section C, "System Infrastructure and Training Health Professionals Legislation," for summaries of legislation related to system infrastructure and training of health professionals.

Developmental and Behavioral Health

Advocates have long complained that developmental and behavioral health have been given limited attention by federal (and state) policymakers. Part of this disinclination on the part of policymakers to advance the causes of developmental and mental health is the absence of a clear political constituency. Mental illness retains a stigma: patients are not inclined (generally) to make public their disease; some stakeholders misunderstand the nature of the illness; others simply prefer not to engage in this issue.

There is, within the penumbra of agencies that make up the NIH, a National Institute of Mental Health; it and other mental and developmental health–related agencies have become the foundation for programs related to people with mental health disorders. To the extent the policy process gives way to improvements in mental or developmental health services, it is usually done in a way consistent with the concept of interactive federalism. Developmental and behavioral health is an area in which the federal government initiatives nearly all take the form of federal assistance to state and local units of government to provide or improve services for people suffering these afflictions.

See appendix 1.3, section D, "Developmental and Behavioral Health Legislation," for summaries of legislation related to developmental and behavioral health.

Environmental Health and Pollution

Environmental issues have been particularly challenging for the federal government. The science behind the public health concerns is unrefuted—people living in environments of polluted air and water have poorer health status than those who do not. They are at increased risk for a variety of cancers and respiratory and cardiovascular diseases (Brunekreef and Holgate 2002). Children, especially those from lower-income zip codes, are more vulnerable to asthma-related hospitalizations (Neidell 2004). The crisis of lead in the water supply of Flint, Michigan, spurred additional studies that found water pollution to be associated with Legionnaires' disease in Flint as well (Schwake et al. 2016). Clearly a polluted environment leads to increased risk of adverse health status and outcomes.

Balanced against that, however, are the considerable economic interests of a variety of businesses and the people employed by them. While the Flint episode emanates from a governmental decision to change the source of community water, sources of air and water pollution are manifold: businesses associated with manufacturing and energy production, pesticides used in agribusiness, and the use of aerosol sprays, among other things, all contribute to depleted ozone layers, particulate matter in the air, and toxic substances in water. In addition, the use of internal combustion engines in cars, buses, and other modes of transportation contributes significantly to degrading the quality of air in particular. Millions of people are employed by entities that increase pollution, and millions more use aerosol sprays and automobiles. Thus, the question: Should we raise the cost of goods and services, or even prevent some from existing, in order to mitigate damage to the environment to protect the public at large and our overall health status?

In the late 1960s and early 1970s, there was heightened awareness of the environmental impact on human development and well-being. During this time, there were several notable legislative achievements promoting and ensuring clean water and air.

This conflict between environmentalists and business, most particularly energy and manufacturing interests, has reemerged in recent years in the debate over climate change. While many deny its existence, science points to a connection between a variety of adverse health effects, as well as increased severity in weather events, as a consequence of human impact on the earth's environment (Dessler and Parson 2019). Legislative response to this growing concern about (and evidence of) climate change's impact on our collective health has been mixed. This area also has seen the interpretations controlling administrative implementation change from administration to administration.

The posture of the federal government has changed over time. Early environmental legislation appeared to support state efforts to clean up polluted water. Over time, however, the concept of pollution has become one which transcends state borders, necessitating a more national response, as evidenced by federal legislation. Indeed, currently observers can point to ample evidence that this has become an international issue, which introduces a new dimension of policy.

See appendix 1.3, section E, "Environmental Health and Pollution Legislation," for summaries of legislation related to environmental health and pollution.

Access to Care

The most active area of federal legislation and federal government involvement in healthcare is in access to care. There are several issues associated with access to care by a prospective patient—the "Five As of Access"—access (physical), availability (of provider within a reasonable time), affordability (financial), acceptability (cultural), and accommodation (of patient needs). The federal government has addressed availability through its efforts to expand the number of providers, as we saw in the "System Infrastructure and Training Health Professionals" section earlier in this chapter.

Likewise, a number of those initiatives speak to improving quality of care. It is in the area of affordability that the federal government has acted most frequently. The issue of cost of healthcare services has been at the forefront of federal efforts. Sometimes this has taken the form of buying services for designated populations, such as programs like Medicare. Sometimes this takes the form of supporting states' efforts to prevent the spread of specific diseases, such as the federal initiatives in support of polio vaccination, or supporting states' attempts to limit the spread of sexually transmitted disease. As the legislative history suggests, the federal government has actively engaged the concept of interactive federalism in efforts to improve access to care. At the same time, the federal government has asserted its role singly in other cases. In short, the federal government, in pursuit of improved health for all Americans, has responded demographically on behalf of certain populations, geographically in assisting certain regions in the United States, and etiologically to stop the spread of specific diseases.

The great conundrum of federal intervention in healthcare is how the issue of cost is perspective dependent, resulting in vastly different interpretations. With passage of Medicare and Medicaid in 1965, the federal government was unequivocally saying that it would help defray the cost of healthcare for the nation's elderly and indigent: a recognition that for many people in these groups, the cost of healthcare was prohibitively high. More than 50 years later, that reality remains for many uninsured Americans—but of greater prominence in recent times is the growing belief that the escalating costs borne by the states and federal governments for healthcare simply are not sustainable. Thus, as noted earlier in the chapter, the federal government is now allowing states to modify Medicaid and ACA programs to reduce state (and federal) costs. Will this perspective adversely affect the underlying mission of the programs (to expand healthcare coverage)?

See appendix 1.3, section F, "Access to Care Legislation," for summaries of legislation related to access to care.

Summary

This chapter has focused on the historical underpinnings of *federalism*, with particular emphasis on health policy, and how that concept has evolved into the current relationships between the states and the federal government. The federal government's grant-in-aid legislation, which exists to a greater or lesser extent in all six categories of federal healthcare law, in many cases confers broad authority on the states to adapt national policy objectives to accommodate local needs. Can such accommodation lead to undermining national goals, particularly with regard to Medicaid and the ACA, however? Several states, with the support of CMS, recently adopted administrative policy modifications that may contravene the national purpose underlying the creation of either, or both, of those programs. Does national (or interactive) federalism mean subordinating the national agenda to needs of the states? Or is this an accommodation that strengthens the bond between the states and the federal government in furtherance of the national agenda? The chapter then provides an overview of the most significant federal legislation through the framework of six categories:

1. Food and drug supply
2. Disease research and protection
3. System infrastructure and training health professionals
4. Developmental and behavioral health
5. Environmental health and pollution
6. Access to care

One observation highlighted by the framework was that the "federalist" approach constitutes a more engaged and engaging relationship with the states (e.g., some CDC reporting requirements, some Medicaid programs) in some categories, while other categories reflect a largely "national" approach to their roles (e.g., NIH, FDA). Conflicting policies emanating from the interlinking of state and federal policy through national federalism are potentially sources of profoundly different outcomes among the states, in some ways thwarting the promotion of a universal health policy with regard to populations affected by Medicaid and the ACA. Finally, the growth of the federal role in health policy is undeniable, accelerating from the Great Depression into the beginning of the twenty-first century.

Review Questions

1. Describe what *federalism* means in the United States.
2. Discuss the pros and cons of requiring work or community service to be eligible for Medicaid.

3. Discuss how states and federal government work together to shape health policy. In what ways do they work at odds with one another?
4. Explain the source of differences between state health policy and federal health policy.
5. Describe briefly the six general categories of federal health legislation.

References

Boyd, E., and M. K. Fauntroy. 2000. "American Federalism, 1776 to 2000: Significant Events." Congressional Research Service. Updated November 30. https://crsreports.congress.gov/product/pdf/RL/RL30772.

Brunekreef, B., and S. T. Holgate. 2002. "Air Pollution and Health." *Lancet* (360) 9341: 1233–39.

Centers for Medicare & Medicaid Services (CMS). 2020. "The Center for Information and Insurance Oversight." Updated March 12. www.cms.gov/CCIIO/Programs-and-Initiatives/State-Innovation-Waivers/Section_1332_State_Innovation_Waivers-.html.

Collins, S. R., and J. M. Lambrew. 2019. "Federalism, the Affordable Care Act, and Health Reform in the 2020 Election." Commonwealth Fund. Published July 29. www.commonwealthfund.org/publications/fund-reports/2019/jul/federalism-affordable-care-act-health-reform-2020-election.

Dabrowska, A., and V. Green. 2019. "The Food and Drug Administration (FDA) Budget: Fact Sheet." Congressional Research Service. Updated May 8. https://fas.org/sgp/crs/misc/R44576.pdf.

Dessler, A. E., and E. A. Parson. 2019. *The Science and Politics of Global Climate Change*. Cambridge, UK: Cambridge University Press.

Gluck, A. R. 2014. "Our [National] Federalism." *Yale Law Review* 123 (6): 1626–2133.

Gluck, A. R., and N. Huberfeld. 2020. "Federalism Under the ACA." In *The Trillion Dollar Revolution*, edited by Ezekiel J. Emanuel and Abbe R. Gluck, 176–91. New York: Public Affairs.

Governing.com. 2019. "State Marijuana Laws in 2019 Map." Published June 25. www.governing.com/gov-data/safety-justice/state-marijuana-laws-map-medical-recreational.html.

Hoffman, B. 2012. *Health Care for Some: Rights and Rationing in the United States Since 1930*. Chicago: University of Chicago Press.

Huberfeld, N. 2018. "Can Work Be Required in the Medicaid Program?" *New England Journal of Medicine* 378: 788–91.

Kaiser Family Foundation. 2019. "Federal and State Share of Medicaid Spending." Accessed November 1. www.kff.org/medicaid/state-indicator/federalstate-share-of-spending.

Kotch, J. B. (ed.). 1997. *Maternal and Child Health: Programs, Problems and Policy in Public Health*. Gaithersburg, MD: Aspen Publishers.

Kronstadt, J., M. Meit, A. Siegfried, T. Nicolaus, K. Bender, and L. Corso. 2016. "Evaluating the Impact of National Public Health Accreditation—2016." *Morbidity and Mortality Weekly Report*. Centers for Disease Control and Prevention. Published August 12. www.cdc.gov/mmwr/volumes/65/wr/mm6531a3.htm.

Langan, P. A. 1995. "The Racial Disparity in U.S. Drug Arrests." US Department of Justice. Published October 1. www.bjs.gov/content/pub/pdf/rdusda.pdf.

Lawson, G., and R. Schapiro. 2020. "Common Intepretation: The Tenth Amendment." Accessed April 2. https://constitutioncenter.org/interactive-constitution/interpretation/amendment-x/interps/129.

Madison, J. 1788. "The Influence of the State and Federal Governments Compared." Congress.gov. Accessed April 2, 2020. www.congress.gov/resources/display/content/The+Federalist+Papers.

Mitchell, A., E. Baumrucker, K. Colello, A. Napili, and C. Binder. 2019. *Medicaid: An Overview*. Congressional Research Service. Updated June 24. https://fas.org/sgp/crs/misc/R43357.pdf.

National Conference of State Legislatures. 2020. "State Medical Marijuana Laws." Published March 10. www.ncsl.org/research/health/state-medical-marijuana-laws.aspx.

National Institutes of Health (NIH). 2019. "Budget Request by IC." Accessed October 23. https://officeofbudget.od.nih.gov/pdfs/FY21/br/5-SupplementaryTables.pdf.

———. 2017. "Mission and Goals." Reviewed July 27. www.nih.gov/about-nih/what-we-do/mission-goals.

Neidell, M. 2004. "Air Pollution, Health, and Socio-economic Status: The Effect of Outdoor Air Quality on Childhood Asthma." *Journal of Health Economics* 23 (6): 1209–36.

Price, T., and S. Verma. 2017. "Letter to Governors." US Department of Health and Human Services. Accessed April 2, 2020. www.hhs.gov/sites/default/files/sec-price-admin-verma-ltr.pdf.

Rosenbaum, S. 2017. "The Trump Administration Re-imagines Section 1115 Medicaid Demonstrations—and Medicaid." *Health Affairs Blog*. Published November 9. www.healthaffairs.org/do/10.1377/hblog20171109.297738/full.

Rosenberg, A., A. K. Groves, and K. M. Blankenship. 2017. "Comparing Black and White Drug Offenders: Implication for Racial Disparities in Criminal Justice and Reentry Policy and Programming." *Journal of Drug Issues* 47 (1): 132–42.

Rosso, R., and A. Mach. 2019. "State Innovation Waivers: Frequently Asked Questions." Congressional Research Service. Updated December 2. https://fas.org/sgp/crs/misc/R44760.pdf.

Schapiro, R. 2005. "Toward a Theory of Interactive Federalism." *Iowa Law Review* 91: 243–348.

Schwake, D. O., E. Garner, O. R. Strom, A. Pruden, and M. A. Edwards. 2016. "Legionella DNA Markers in Tap Water Coincident with a Spike in Legionnaires' Disease in Flint, MI." *Environmental Science Technology*. Published July 8. https://doi.org/10.1021/acs.estlett.6b00192.

Ungar, L. 2019. "The Deep Divide: State Borders Create Medicaid Haves and Have-Nots." *Kaiser Health News*. Published October 2. https://khn.org/news/the-deep-divide-state-borders-create-medicaid-haves-and-have-nots.

US Department of Justice (DOJ). 2018. "Justice Department Issues Memo on Marijuana Enforcement." Published January 4. www.justice.gov/opa/pr/justice-department-issues-memo-marijuana-enforcement.

———. 2013. "Justice Department Announces Update to Marijuana Enforcement Policy." Published August 29. www.justice.gov/opa/pr/justice-department-announces-update-marijuana-enforcement-policy.

US Food and Drug Administration (FDA). 2018. "Milestones in U.S. Food and Drug Law History." Published January 31. www.fda.gov/about-fda/fdas-evolving-regulatory-powers/milestones-us-food-and-drug-law-history.

US President. 1999. "Federalism." Exec. Order No. 13,132.64 FR 43255. www.govinfo.gov/content/pkg/FR-1999-08-10/pdf/99-20729.pdf.

Wilson, J. Q., and J. J. DiIuilo. 1995. *American Government Institutions and Policies*. Lexington, MA: D.C. Heath and Company.

APPENDIX

1.1

OVERVIEW OF THE AFFORDABLE CARE ACT

The following material is a concatenation of adaptations of several reports produced by the Congressional Research Service (CRS). The CRS is the professional research staff for Congress, known for its objective: the factual treatment of legislative matters. Each report is appropriately cited at the beginning of its respective section. In the interest of keeping the material from being completely overwhelming, footnotes, references, and some substantive material have been deleted. Language not deleted has been left intact throughout so that the reader is assured the material comes from CRS and is assiduous in its political neutrality. In several cases, lists in the form of text were changed to tables or numbered lists. Any explanatory notes are contained in brackets [ ]. In making deletions of material, priority was given to material that is (a) most current as of this writing, (b) most pertinent to graduate studies in health policy, and (c) evenhanded in its treatment of the subject. Students are advised to obtain the complete reports for more detailed information on any of the significant matters covered here.

Introduction of Health Reform Law

[Author's note: As we learned in the policy snapshot at the beginning of part 1, the 111th Congress passed major health reform legislation, the Patient Protection and Affordable Care Act (P.L. 111-148), which was amended by the Health Care and Education Reconciliation Act of 2010 (P.L. 111-152). This source refers to these laws jointly as PPACA.]

PPACA increases access to health insurance coverage, expands federal private health insurance market requirements, and requires the creation of health insurance exchanges to provide individuals and small employers with access to insurance. PPACA increases access to health insurance coverage by expanding Medicaid eligibility, extending funding for the Children's Health Insurance Program (CHIP), and subsidizing private insurance premiums and cost-sharing for certain lower-income individuals enrolled in exchange plans, among other provisions. These costs are projected to be offset by increased taxes and other revenues and reduced Medicare and Medicaid spending. The law also includes measures designed to enhance delivery and quality of care.

Coverage Expansions and Market Reforms: Pre-2014

Some private health insurance market reforms also took effect prior to 2014, such as extending coverage to children up to age 26 and not allowing children up to age 19 to be denied insurance and benefits based on a preexisting condition. Major medical plans can no longer impose any lifetime dollar limits on essential benefits, and plans may only restrict annual dollar limits to defined amounts. Plans must cover preventive care with no cost-sharing, and they cannot rescind coverage, except for fraud. They must also establish an appeals process for coverage and claims. Insurers must also limit the ratio of premiums spent on administrative costs compared to medical costs, referred to as medical loss ratios, or MLRs.

Coverage Expansions and Market Reforms: Beginning in 2014

The major expansion and reform provisions in PPACA took effect in 2014. State Medicaid programs that choose to participate in Medicaid expansion under the Act will be required to expand coverage to all eligible non-pregnant, non-elderly legal residents with incomes up to 133% of the federal poverty level (FPL). The federal government will initially cover all the costs for this group, with the federal matching percentage phased down to 90% of the costs by 2020. The law required states to maintain the existing CHIP structure through FY2019, and provided federal CHIP appropriations through FY2015 (thus providing a two-year extension on CHIP funding). CHIP was subsequently reauthorized for six years.

States are expected to establish health insurance exchanges that provide access to private health insurance plans with standardized benefit and cost-sharing packages for eligible individuals and small employers. The Secretary of Health and Human Services (HHS) will establish exchanges in states that do not create their own approved exchange. Premium credits and cost-sharing subsidies will be available to individuals who enroll in exchange plans, provided their income is generally above 100% and no more than 400% of the FPL and they meet other requirements.

The Act stipulated that beginning in 2014, and going forward after that time, most individuals will be required to have insurance or pay a penalty (an individual mandate) [see the discussion of *Texas v. United States* in chapter 9]. Certain employers with more than 50 employees who do not offer health insurance may be subject to penalties. While most of these employers who offer health insurance will meet the law's requirements, some may be required to also pay a penalty if any of their full-time workers enroll in exchange plans and receive premium subsidies.

PPACA's federal health insurance requirements are further expanded in 2014, with no annual dollar limits allowed on essential health benefits and no exclusions for preexisting conditions allowed regardless of age. Plans offered within the exchanges and certain other plans must also meet essential benefit standards, covering services such as emergency services, hospital care, physician services, preventive services, prescription drugs, and mental health and substance use disorder services, among others. Premiums may vary by limited amounts, but only based on age, family size, geographic area, and tobacco use. Additionally, plans must sell and renew policies to all individuals and may not discriminate based on health status.

Health Care Quality and Payment Incentives

PPACA contains a number of provisions to create and/or study payment incentives and service delivery models that are designed to improve quality of health and health care and to reduce expenditures. The law establishes pilot, demonstration, and grant programs to test integrated models of care, including accountable care organizations (ACOs), medical homes that provide coordinated care for high-need individuals, and bundling payments for acute-care episodes (including hospitalization and follow-up care). PPACA establishes the Center for Medicare and Medicaid Innovation [the CMS Innovation Center], to pilot payment and service delivery models, primarily for Medicare and Medicaid beneficiaries. The law also establishes new pay-for-reporting and pay-for-performance programs within Medicare that will pay providers based on the reporting of, or performance on, selected quality measures.

Additionally, PPACA creates incentives for promoting primary care and prevention, for example, by increasing primary care payment rates under Medicare and Medicaid; covering some preventive services without cost-sharing; and funding community-based prevention and employer wellness programs, among other things. In addition, the law increases funding for community health centers and the National Health Service Corps to expand access to primary care services in rural and medically underserved areas and reduce health disparities. PPACA also requires the Secretary of Health and Human Services (HHS) to develop a national strategy for health care quality to improve care delivery, patient outcomes, and population health.

Cost Containment and Financing of Health Reform

The Congressional Budget Office (CBO) and the staff of the Joint Committee on Taxation (JCT) estimated the direct spending and revenue effects of PPACA. CBO projects that PPACA will reduce federal deficits by $143 billion over the 10-year period of 2010–2019 and, by 2019, will insure 94% of the non-elderly, legally present U.S. population.

The costs of the coverage expansions under the law are offset by provisions designed to (1) slow the rate of growth of federal health care spending and (2) increase revenues through taxes and penalties. PPACA incorporates numerous Medicare payment provisions to slow the rate of growth in federal health care costs, including reductions in Medicare Advantage (MA) plan payments and a lowering of the annual payment update for hospitals and certain other providers. PPACA also establishes an Independent Payment Advisory Board (IPAB) to make recommendations for achieving specific Medicare spending reductions if costs exceed a target growth rate. IPAB's recommendations will take effect unless Congress overrides them, in which case Congress would be responsible for achieving the same level of savings. Finally, PPACA provides tools to help reduce fraud, waste, and abuse in both Medicare and Medicaid.

PPACA increases revenue using several mechanisms. Individuals who do not have health insurance, as well as large employers who do not comply with the law's requirements to provide such insurance, may be subject to penalties. PPACA raises a large share of its revenue from taxes on high-income households, such as an additional Medicare payroll tax on those with incomes over $200,000 (single) and $250,000 (married). PPACA also creates an excise tax on high-cost plans. The law limits the annual contribution to Flexible Spending Accounts (FSAs) to $2,500, and excludes over-the-counter medications (except insulin) from reimbursement by FSAs and other health tax savings accounts.

In calculating its estimates of the cost and savings of PPACA, CBO projected that the law will reduce the number of uninsured by 32 million people, leaving 23 million residents uninsured by 2019. Those without coverage will include those who choose not to purchase health insurance and are subject to the penalty for non-compliance and those who are exempt from the individual mandate for religious or other reasons, as well as about 7–8 million illegal immigrants.

The Essential Health Benefits (EHB)

The Patient Protection and Affordable Care Act (ACA; P.L. 111-148, as amended) requires all non-grandfathered health plans in the non-group and small-group private health insurance markets to offer a core package of health care services, known as the *essential health benefits* (EHB). The ACA does not specifically define this core package. Instead, it lists 10 categories from which benefits and services must be included and requires the Secretary of the Department of Health and Human Services (HHS) to further define the EHB. The categories are:

1. Ambulatory care
2. Emergency services
3. Hospitalization

4. Maternity and newborn care
5. Mental health and substance use disorder services and behavioral health treatment
6. Prescription drugs
7. Rehabilitative and habilitative services and devices
8. Laboratory services
9. Preventive and wellness services and chronic disease management
10. Pediatric services including oral and vision services.

EHB for 2014–2017

The HHS Secretary outlined a process in which each state identified a single plan to serve as a reference plan on which most non-group and small-group market plans must base their benefits packages in terms of the scope of benefits offered. These reference plans are known as *EHB-benchmark plans.*

A state selects a benchmark plan among (1) the state's small-group market health plans; (2) the state's state employee health benefit plans; (3) Federal Employees Health Benefits (FEHB) plans; or (4) the state's commercial non-Medicaid health maintenance organization (HMO). Generally, if an EHB-benchmark plan does not cover 1 or more of the 10 EHB categories, the state must supplement the EHB-benchmark plan by adding that particular category in its entirety from another benchmark plan option.

Inclusion of State Mandates

Prior to the passage of the ACA, many states had laws requiring health plans to cover certain health care services, health care providers, and/or dependents, known as *state benefit mandates.* A state may require non-group and small-group plans to cover these state benefit mandates in addition to the EHB. Moreover, any state benefit mandates enacted on or before December 31, 2011, are considered to be part of the EHB. States may choose to impose additional benefit mandates. If a state decides to impose additional benefits, the state itself must defray the cost of those benefits for plans offered in the *health insurance exchanges* (described below).

Variation in EHB Coverage

Because each state selects its own EHB-benchmark plan, there is considerable variation in EHB coverage from state to state. This variation occurs in terms of specific covered services as well as in terms of amount, duration, and scope. For example, some state EHB-benchmark plans may include bariatric surgery as a covered service whereas other state EHB-benchmark plans may not cover bariatric surgery.

In addition to EHB variation by state, benefit coverage among plans within a state may differ. States may allow non-group and small-group market plans that offer the EHB to substitute benefits. A benefit may be substituted if the substitution is equivalent to the benefit being replaced and is made within the same EHB category. For example, a plan could offer coverage of up to 10 physical therapy visits and up to 20 occupational therapy visits as a substitute for EHB-benchmark plan coverage of up to 20 physical therapy visits and 10 occupational therapy visits, assuming other criteria are met.

Applicability of EHB Requirements to Health Plans

Generally, non-group and small-group market health plans are required to offer the EHB. This requirement applies to non-group and small-group plans offered both inside and outside the exchanges. Additional plan types are subject to the EHB; examples of these plan types include qualified health plans (e.g., multistate plans or child-only plans) and catastrophic plans (see exhibit A1.1.1).

Certain health plans are not subject to the EHB requirements. For example, *grandfathered health plans* (health insurance plans that were in existence, and in which at least one person was enrolled, on the date of the ACA's enactment) are not subject to the EHB requirements as long as they maintain their grandfathered status. This exclusion includes non-group and small-group grandfathered health plans (see exhibit A1.1.1).

EHB and Other ACA Provisions

Cost Sharing

The ACA imposes an annual cap on consumer cost sharing for the EHB. The ACA specifies that the limits work in two ways: they prohibit (1) applying deductibles to preventive health services and (2) annual out-of-pocket limits that exceed existing limits in the tax code. The cost-sharing limits apply only to in-network benefits.

EXHIBIT A1.1.1 Applicability of EHB Requirements to Health Plans

Subject to EHB Requirements	
Yes	**No**
Non-group Market Plans	"Grandfathered" Plans
Fully-Insured Small Group Market Plans	Self-Insured Small Group Plans
Qualified Health Plans • Multistate Plans • Child-Only Plans	Large Group Market Plans • Fully Insured • Self-Insured
Catastrophic Plans	Dental-Only Plans

Lifetime and Annual Dollar Limits

Prior to the ACA, plans generally were able to set *lifetime* and *annual limits*—dollar limits on how much the plan would spend for covered health benefits either during the entire period an individual was enrolled in the plan (lifetime limits) or during a plan year (annual limits). The ACA prohibits both lifetime and annual limits on the EHB. Plans are permitted to place lifetime and annual limits on covered benefits that are not considered EHB, to the extent that such limits are permitted by federal and state law.

Minimum Essential Coverage

The EHB requirement differs from *minimum essential coverage*. Minimum essential coverage is a term defined in the ACA and its implementing regulations that refers to the *individual mandate*, or the ACA requirement that most individuals must have health insurance coverage for themselves and their dependents or potentially pay a penalty for noncompliance. The definition of minimum essential coverage does not refer to minimum benefits but rather includes most private and public coverage.

Health Insurance Exchanges

The Patient Protection and Affordable Care Act (ACA; P.L. 111-148, as amended) requires health insurance exchanges to be established in every state. Exchanges are marketplaces in which consumers and small businesses can shop for and purchase private health insurance coverage. In general, states must have two types of exchanges: an individual exchange and a small business health options program (SHOP) exchange.

Exchanges may be established either by the state itself as a state-based exchange (SBE) or by the Secretary of Health and Human Services (HHS) as a federally facilitated exchange (FFE). Some states have SBE-FPs: they have SBEs but use the federal information technology platform [FP], including the federal exchange website www.Healthcare.gov. In states with FFEs, the exchange may be operated by the federal government alone or in conjunction with the state. States may have different structures for their individual and SHOP exchanges. The ACA generally requires that health insurance plans offered through an exchange are qualified health plans (QHPs), which must comply with state and federal requirements.

Consumers who obtain coverage through the individual exchange may be eligible for financial assistance in one of two forms: premium tax credits and cost-sharing reductions. Small businesses that use the SHOP exchange may be eligible for small business health insurance tax credits. The tax credits assist small businesses with the cost of providing health insurance coverage to employees.

Types of Exchanges

Individual and SHOP Exchanges

The ACA required health insurance exchanges to be established in all states and the District of Columbia (DC). In general, the health insurance exchanges began operating in October 2013 to allow consumers to shop for health insurance plans that began as soon as January 1, 2014.

Most states have two types of exchanges—an *individual exchange* and a *small business health options program (SHOP) exchange*. In an individual exchange, eligible consumers can compare and purchase non-group insurance for themselves and their families and can apply for premium tax credits and cost-sharing reductions. In a SHOP exchange, small businesses can compare and purchase small-group insurance and can apply for small business health insurance tax credits; in addition, employees of small businesses can enroll in plans offered by their employers on a SHOP exchange. Besides facilitating consumers' and small businesses' purchase of coverage (by operating a web portal, making determinations of eligibility for coverage and any financial assistance, and offering different forms of enrollment assistance), the other major function of the exchanges is to certify, recertify, and otherwise monitor the plans that participate in those marketplaces. Individual and SHOP exchanges can be operated by either the state or the federal government, as described below.

State-Based and Federally Facilitated Exchanges

A state can choose to establish its own *state-based exchange* (SBE). If a state opts not to administer its own exchange, or if the Department of Health and Human Services (HHS) determines that the state is not in a position to do so, then HHS is required to establish and administer the exchange in the state as a *federally facilitated exchange* (FFE). States also may have a *state-based exchange using a federal platform* (SBE-FP), which means they have an SBE but use the federally facilitated information technology (IT) platform (i.e., HealthCare.gov).

For the 2018 plan year, 34 states have FFEs, 12 states have SBEs, and 5 states have SBE-FPs. In addition, state involvement in the FFEs may vary. In many states with FFEs, the exchange is wholly operated and administered by HHS. But in some cases, states partner with HHS to perform some functions, such as plan management or consumer assistance.

Individual Exchanges Eligibility and Enrollment Process

Consumers may purchase health insurance plans for themselves or their families in their state's individual exchange. Consumers may enroll as long as they (1) meet state residency requirements; (2) are not incarcerated, except individuals in custody pending the disposition of charges; and (3) are U.S. citizens, U.S. nationals, or "lawfully present" residents. Undocumented individuals are prohibited from purchasing coverage through the exchanges, even if they were to pay the entire premium without financial assistance.

Consumers can use their state's exchange website (Healthcare.gov or a state-run site) to compare and enroll in plans, and the exchange websites are required to display a calculator that estimates consumers' costs after any cost-sharing reductions or premium tax credits for which they are eligible (see "Premium Tax Credits and Cost-Sharing Reductions" in this report). Consumers may be linked to Medicaid or the State Children's Health Insurance Program (CHIP) enrollment pages if they are eligible.

In addition to using the exchange websites, consumers can enroll by phone, by mail, or in person—including through an agent, broker, or plan issuer—as available by state. Enrollment assistance is available for those who want it (see "Individual and SHOP Exchange Enrollment Assistance" in this report).

Consumers also may be allowed to enroll for coverage in an exchange if they qualify for a *special enrollment period* (SEP) due to a change in personal circumstances—for example, a change in marital status or number of dependents.

Premium Tax Credits and Cost-Sharing Reductions

The *premium tax credit* is generally available to consumers who do not have access to public coverage (e.g., Medicaid) or employment-based coverage that meets certain standards. The credit is designed to reduce an eligible individual's cost of purchasing health insurance coverage through the exchange. The amount of the premium tax credit is based on a statutory formula and varies from person to person. It is designed to provide larger credit amounts to individuals with lower incomes compared to those with higher incomes.

The premium credit is refundable, so individuals may claim the full credit amount when filing their taxes, even if they have little or no federal income tax liability. The credit also is advanceable, so instead of waiting until they file taxes, individuals may choose to receive the credit on a monthly basis to coincide with the payment of insurance premiums (technically, these advance payments go directly to issuers). Advance payments automatically reduce monthly premiums by the credit amount. Therefore, the direct cost of insurance to a consumer eligible for premium credits generally will be lower than the advertised cost for a given exchange plan.

In addition to premium tax credits, certain consumers also may be eligible to receive *cost-sharing reductions* that reduce out-of-pocket expenses. There are two forms of cost-sharing reductions, and individuals may receive both if they meet the applicable eligibility requirements.

- The first form of cost-sharing assistance reduces the annual out-of-pocket limit applicable to an individual's exchange plan. Annual out-of-pocket limits apply to all plans in the exchanges and to other plans under the ACA. In 2019, the annual out-of-pocket limits will be $7,900 and $15,800, respectively. This form of cost-sharing assistance further lowers the spending cap for eligible consumers.

- The second form reduces cost-sharing requirements applicable to an individual's exchange plan. All exchange plans must meet certain requirements related to the percentage of allowed health care expenses that issuers will cover. This form of cost-sharing assistance reduces the percentage of costs for which the individual will be responsible.

SHOP Exchanges Eligibility and Enrollment Process

Certain small businesses are eligible to use the SHOP exchanges. For the purposes of SHOP exchange participation, states may define *small employers* (or small businesses) as employers that have 50 or fewer full-time employees or employers that have 100 or fewer full-time employees. A majority of states define *small* as having 50 or fewer employees, and only four states employ the 100-or-fewer-employee definition for their SHOP exchanges. As of 2017, all states have the option to allow *large* businesses to use SHOP exchanges, as well, but no states have taken that option.

To participate in a SHOP exchange, a small business must offer coverage to all of its *full-time employees,* meaning those working 30 or more hours per week on average. Employees must meet the same citizenship and other eligibility requirements that apply in the individual exchanges.

For an employee to obtain coverage through a SHOP exchange, a SHOP-eligible employer must select one or more plan options on the SHOP exchange for its employees to choose from. Then, employees can visit the SHOP exchange website to compare their employer's plan options and to enroll. Employers and their employees also can work with a SHOP-registered broker or directly with a plan issuer. Small employers that want to offer more than one plan option to their employees generally are able to do so.

Small Business Health Care Tax Credit

Certain small businesses are eligible for small business health care tax credits. In general, these credits are available only to small businesses that purchase coverage through SHOP exchanges and subsidize their employees' premiums. The intent of the credit is to assist small employers with the cost of providing health insurance coverage to employees. The credits are available to eligible small businesses for two consecutive tax years (beginning with the first year, the small employer purchases coverage through a SHOP exchange).

The maximum credit is 50% of an employer's contribution toward premiums for for-profit employers and 35% of employer contributions for non-profit organizations. In general, the credit is phased out as the number of FTE employees increases from 10 to 25 and as average employee compensation increases to a maximum of two times the limit for the full credit.

Employees who enroll in a SHOP plan do not receive this tax credit, nor are they eligible for the premium tax credit or cost-sharing reductions available to certain consumers who purchase coverage on the individual market (discussed in this report in "Premium Tax Credits and Cost-Sharing Reductions").

Administering the Exchanges

In addition to carrying out their consumer-facing activities that facilitate the purchase of coverage, exchanges are responsible for several administrative functions, including certifying the plans that will participate in their marketplaces. SBEs, SBE-FPs, and state entities in some FFEs (where states have chosen to perform some plan management functions) are each responsible for annually certifying or recertifying plans to be sold in their exchanges as *qualified health plans* (QHPs, see "Qualified Health Plans," below). In FFEs in which HHS oversees all plan-related functions, CMS does this for each state.

QHP certification, to be completed each year in time for issuers to advertise their plans for annual enrollment, involves a review of various factors, including the benefits a plan will cover, the network of providers it will include, its premium rates, its marketing practices, and its adherence to quality-of-care standards.

Exchanges' other administrative activities include collecting enrollment and other data, reporting data to and otherwise interacting with the Departments of HHS and the Treasury, and working with state insurance departments and federal regulators to conduct ongoing oversight of plans.

Qualified Health Plans (QHP)

In general, health insurance plans offered through exchanges must be QHPs. A QHP is a plan that is offered by a state-licensed issuer that meets specified requirements, is certified by an exchange, and covers the *essential health benefits* (EHB) package. The EHB package requires plans to cover 10 broad categories of benefits and services, comply with limits on consumer cost sharing on the EHB, and meet certain generosity requirements.

QHPs must comply with the same state and federal requirements that apply to health plans offered outside of exchanges. A QHP offered through an individual exchange must comply with state and federal requirements applicable to individual market plans; a QHP offered through a SHOP exchange must comply with state and federal requirements applicable to plans offered in the small-group market. For example, QHPs offered through individual and SHOP exchanges must cover specified preventive services without imposing cost sharing, just like plans offered in the individual and small-group markets outside of exchanges.

A QHP is the only type of comprehensive health plan an exchange may offer, but QHPs may be offered outside of exchanges, as well.

Individual Mandate

Since January 1, 2014, most individuals have had to maintain health insurance coverage or pay a penalty for noncompliance implemented through the Internal Revenue Code (IRC). To comply with this individual mandate, individuals need to maintain minimum essential coverage, which includes most types of public and private health insurance coverage. Some individuals are exempt from the mandate and not subject to its associated penalty.

The individual mandate was established under the Patient Protection and Affordable Care Act (ACA; P.L. 111-148, as amended) and works in conjunction with other ACA provisions. Under the ACA, a number of federal requirements applicable to private health insurance issuers went into effect intending to improve access to private health insurance for sick individuals or those at high risk of becoming ill. The individual mandate works in tandem with the requirements by encouraging healthy individuals to participate in the market so that insurers' risk pools are not primarily composed of individuals who are at high risk of using health care services.

The individual mandate was modified under the 2017 tax revision, P.L. 115-97, which was enacted on December 22, 2017. The law effectively eliminates the penalty associated with the individual mandate beginning in 2019 (i.e., the penalty is in effect through 2018). However, the 2017 tax revision does not make any other substantive changes to the statutory language establishing the mandate and its associated penalty.

Most individuals are required to maintain *minimum essential coverage* for themselves and their dependents. The types of coverage that are considered minimum essential coverage are listed in Section 5000A of the IRC and its implementing regulations. Most types of comprehensive coverage are considered minimum essential coverage, including public coverage, such as coverage under programs sponsored by the federal government (e.g., Medicaid, Medicare), as well as private insurance (e.g., employer-sponsored insurance and nongroup, or individual, insurance).

The statute identifies types of coverage consisting of limited benefits, such as dental-only insurance, that are not considered minimum essential coverage.

Penalty and Calculating It

Individuals who do not comply with the mandate, or who have dependents who do not comply, may be required to pay a penalty annually for each month of noncompliance, to be implemented through the IRC. An individual's annual penalty is equal to one-twelfth of the annual penalty (described below) multiplied by the number of months in which the individual did not comply with the mandate.

The penalty for noncompliance (see exhibit A1.1.2) is calculated as the greater of either

- **a percentage of *applicable income*,** defined as the amount by which an individual's household income exceeds the applicable tax filing threshold for the tax year; or
- **a yearly flat dollar amount** assessed on each taxpayer and any dependents. The total dollar amount assessed on a taxpayer (for themselves and any dependents) is capped at 300% of the annual flat dollar amount. For example, in 2016, the annual dollar amount penalty for a taxpayer and three dependents (all of whom were without coverage for the entire year) was limited to three times $695, or $2,085.

An individual's annual penalty payment is equal to one-twelfth of either the percentage of income or the flat dollar amount, multiplied by the number of months not in compliance. Each total monthly penalty is also capped. The monthly penalty for a taxpayer and his or her dependents cannot be more than the cost of the national average premium for bronze-level health plans offered through health insurance exchanges (for the relevant family size).

Paying the Penalty

Any penalty that taxpayers are required to pay for themselves or their dependents must be included in their federal income tax return for the taxable year. Those individuals who file joint returns are jointly liable for the penalty.

Taxpayers who are required to pay a penalty but fail to do so will receive a notice from the Internal Revenue Service (IRS) stating that they owe the penalty. If the taxpayers still do not pay the penalty, the IRS can attempt to collect the funds by reducing the amount of their tax refund for that year or

EXHIBIT A1.1.2
Annual Individual Mandate Penalty

Year	Percentage of Annual Income	Flat Dollar Amount
2014	1.0%	$95
2015	2.0%	$325
2016	2.5%	$695
2017*	2.5%	$695 adjusted for inflation
2018*	2.5%	$695 adjusted for inflation
2019 and beyond*	0%	$0

* The flat dollar value was not adjusted for inflation in 2017 and 2018. The tax bill of 2017 repealed the penalty effective for the tax year 2019.

future years. However, individuals who fail to pay the penalty will not be subject to any criminal prosecution or penalty for such failure. The Secretary of the Treasury cannot file notice of lien or file a levy on any property for a taxpayer who does not pay the penalty.

Exemptions

Some individuals are exempt from the individual mandate or its associated penalty. An individual who obtains an exemption from the mandate is not required to make a penalty payment for any month in which he or she qualifies for the exemption. The exemptions are outlined in statute and in regulations (and are identified by category below).

The following *may* qualify for exemptions depending on relevant circumstances:

- Hardship
- Religious Conscience
- Healthcare Sharing Ministry
- Indian Tribe Membership
- Incarceration
- Affordability
- Unlawful Resident
- Coverage Gap
- Filing Threshold
- Living Abroad

In most cases, individuals must either apply for an exemption through a health insurance exchange or claim an exemption on their federal tax return, although individuals who can claim the living abroad exemption do not have to take any action for their exemption. Individuals whose exemption is granted by an exchange must report the exemption information to the IRS when they file their taxes. Most exemptions are applicable retrospectively and must be recertified annually, but some exemptions, including the religious conscience and Indian tribe exemptions, are eligible for prospective or retrospective applicability and continuous certification.

Medicaid Expansion

The primary goals of the Patient Protection and Affordable Care Act (ACA; P.L. 111-148, as amended) are to increase access to affordable health insurance for the uninsured and to make health insurance more affordable for those already covered. The ACA Medicaid expansion is one of the major insurance coverage provisions included in the law.

Supreme Court Decision

As enacted, the ACA Medicaid expansion was a mandatory expansion of Medicaid eligibility to non-elderly adults with incomes up to 133% of the federal poverty level (FPL). However, on June 28, 2012, in *National Federation of Independent Business v. Sebelius,* the U.S. Supreme Court found that the federal government could not withhold payment for a state's entire Medicaid program for failure to implement the ACA Medicaid expansion. Instead, the federal government could withhold only funding for the ACA Medicaid expansion if a state did not implement the expansion, which effectively made the expansion optional.

After the Supreme Court ruling, the Centers for Medicare & Medicaid Services (CMS) issued guidance specifying that states have no deadline for deciding when to implement the ACA Medicaid expansion. The guidance also stated that states opting to implement the ACA Medicaid expansion may end the expansion at any time.

States' Decisions

Since January 1, 2014, states have had the option to extend Medicaid coverage to most non-elderly, nonpregnant adults with income up to 133% of FPL. Twenty-four states and the District of Columbia implemented the ACA Medicaid expansion at that time. Since then, the following seven states have implemented the expansion: Michigan (April 1, 2014), New Hampshire (July 1, 2014), Pennsylvania (January 1, 2015), Indiana (February 1, 2015), Alaska (September 1, 2015), Montana (January 1, 2016), and Louisiana (July 1, 2016). Virginia began coverage of the ACA Medicaid expansion on January 1, 2019. Maine adopted the expansion through a ballot initiative in November 2017; however Maine's governor at the time refused to implement the expansion. The new governor has implemented the expansion.

The results of the November 2018 election could have implications for the ACA Medicaid expansion. In Idaho, Nebraska, and Utah, voters approved ballot initiatives to implement the expansion. Also, new governors and changes in the composition of state legislatures could change states' decisions regarding the expansion. Some non-expansion states might decide to adopt the expansion, and some expansion states could decide to end that coverage.

ACA Medicaid Expansion Waivers

Most states implementing the ACA Medicaid expansion have done so through an expansion of their existing Medicaid programs. However, seven states (Arizona, Arkansas, Indiana, Iowa, Michigan, Montana, and New Hampshire) operate their expansions through Section 1115 waivers. Under Section 1115 of the Social Security Act, the Secretary of the Department of Health and Human Services (HHS) may authorize a state to conduct experimental, pilot, or demonstration projects that, in the judgment of the Secretary, are likely to assist in promoting the objectives of Medicaid.

The waivers for these seven states vary significantly, but there are a few common provisions, such as: (1) premiums and/or monthly contributions on enrollees with income above 100% of FPL (Arizona, Arkansas, Indiana, Iowa, Michigan, and Montana); (2) healthy behavior incentives (Arizona, Indiana, Iowa, and Michigan); (3) waivers of the requirement to provide coverage of nonemergency medical transportation (Indiana and Iowa); and (4) disenrollment or lock-out provisions (Arizona, Arkansas, Indiana, Iowa, and Montana).

Private Option

Arkansas and Michigan have waivers that allow mandatory enrollment in the *private option*, which provides premium assistance for Medicaid enrollees to purchase private health insurance through the health insurance exchanges. Michigan is currently in the process of phasing out the private option.

Work and Community Engagement Requirements

State requests to include work requirements in Section 1115 waivers for the expansion population were denied under the Obama Administration. In January 2018, under the Trump Administration, CMS issued a State Medicaid Director Letter advising states that they could apply for Section 1115 waivers to implement work and community engagement requirements as a condition of eligibility for expansion adults [adults not covered previously by Medicaid, now eligible because the state expanded its Medicaid program] and other nonelderly, nonpregnant Medicaid enrollees.

To date, four states (Arkansas, Indiana, Kentucky, and New Hampshire) have received approval to implement work and community engagement requirements that affect expansion adults. Three states (Arizona, Ohio, and Michigan) have waiver requests pending that would affect expansion adults.

Financing of the Expansion

The federal government's share of most Medicaid expenditures is determined according to the federal medical assistance percentage (FMAP) rate, but exceptions to the regular FMAP rate have been made for certain states, situations, populations, providers, and services. The ACA adds a few FMAP exceptions for the ACA Medicaid expansion, including the *newly eligible* matching rate and the *expansion state* matching rate.

Newly Eligible Matching Rate

The *newly eligible* matching rate is used to reimburse states for Medicaid expenditures for newly eligible individuals who gained Medicaid eligibility due to the ACA Medicaid expansion. The newly eligible matching rate started at 100% in 2014 and phased down to 93% in 2019, and will decrease to 90% in 2020 and subsequent years. Federal statute specifies the newly eligible matching rate for each year, which means the newly eligible matching rates are available for these specific years regardless of when a state implements the ACA Medicaid expansion.

Enrollment

The ACA Medicaid expansion has significantly increased Medicaid enrollment and federal Medicaid expenditures. In FY2017, an estimated 12 million individuals were newly eligible for Medicaid through the ACA Medicaid expansion (i.e., expansion adults), and total Medicaid expenditures for the expansion adults were an estimated $71 billion. Enrollment for the expansion adults is projected to be 13 million in FY2026, and expenditures for the expansion adults are projected to be $120 billion in FY2026 (with the federal government paying $108 billion and states paying $12 billion).

Source: Drawn from C. S. Redhead, H. Chaikind, B. Fernandez, and J. Staman, 2012, "ACA: A Brief Overview of the Law, Implementation, and Legal Challenges," Congressional Research Service, published July 3, https://fas.org/sgp/crs/misc/R41664.pdf.

Drawn from V. C. Forsberg, 2016, "The Essential Benefits," Congressional Research Service, published July 6, https://crsreports.congress.gov/product/pdf/IF/IF10287.

Drawn from V. C. Forsberg, 2018, "Overview of Health Insurance Exchanges," Congressional Research Service, published June 20, https://fas.org/sgp/crs/misc/R44065.pdf.

Drawn from A. Mach, 2018, "The Individual Mandate for Health Insurance Coverage: In Brief," Congressional Research Service, published March 19, https://fas.org/sgp/crs/misc/R44438.pdf.

Drawn from A. Mitchell, 2018, "Overview of the ACA Medicaid Expansion," Congressional Research Service, published December 3, https://fas.org/sgp/crs/misc/IF10399.pdf.

APPENDIX

1.2

CENTERS FOR MEDICARE & MEDICAID SERVICES SUMMARIES OF ITS PROGRAMS

The following summaries of the Medicare and Medicaid programs were prepared by representatives of the Office of the Actuary, Centers for Medicare & Medicaid Services, Department of Health and Human Services. Material regarding national healthcare expenditures and projected healthcare expenditures has been deleted from the original Medicare summary because much of that information is covered elsewhere in the book.

Brief Summaries of Medicare and Medicaid: Title XVIII and Title XIX of the Social Security Act

As of October 15, 2018

Prepared by Barbara S. Klees, Eric T. Eckstein II, and Catherine A. Curtis
Office of the Actuary
Centers for Medicare & Medicaid Services
Department of Health and Human Services

Overview of Medicare

Title XVIII of the Social Security Act, designated "Health Insurance for the Aged and Disabled," is commonly known as Medicare. As part of the Social Security Amendments of 1965, the Medicare legislation established a health insurance program for aged persons to complement the retirement, survivors, and disability insurance benefits under Title II of the Social Security Act.

When first implemented in 1966, Medicare covered most persons aged 65 or older. In 1973, the following groups also became eligible for Medicare benefits: persons entitled to Social Security or Railroad Retirement disability cash benefits for at least 24 months, most persons with end-stage renal disease (ESRD), and certain otherwise non-covered aged persons who elect to pay a premium for Medicare coverage. Beginning in July 2001, persons with Amyotrophic Lateral Sclerosis (Lou Gehrig's Disease) are allowed to waive the

24-month waiting period. Beginning March 30, 2010, individuals in the vicinity of Libby, Montana who are diagnosed with an asbestos-related condition are Medicare-eligible. Medicare eligibility could also apply to individuals in other areas who are diagnosed with a medical condition caused by exposure to a public health hazard for which a future public health emergency declaration is made under the Comprehensive Environmental Response, Compensation, and Liability Act of 1980 (Public Law 96-510). This very broad description of Medicare eligibility is expanded in the next section.

Medicare originally consisted of two parts: Hospital Insurance (HI), also known as Part A, and Supplementary Medical Insurance (SMI), which in the past was also known simply as Part B. Part A helps pay for inpatient hospital, home health agency, skilled nursing facility, and hospice care. Part A is provided free of premiums to most eligible people; certain otherwise ineligible people may voluntarily pay a monthly premium for coverage. Part B helps pay for physician, outpatient hospital, home health agency, and other services. To be covered by Part B, all eligible people must pay a monthly premium (or have the premium paid on their behalf).

The Medicare Advantage program, sometimes known as Part C, is not a separate benefit but rather an optional program that allows most beneficiaries enrolled in both Part A and Part B to choose to receive their services through Medicare-approved private-sector health plans. Such plans have been available to some beneficiaries dating back to the 1970s, and, over time, numerous pieces of legislation have been enacted that have increased or decreased the attractiveness of, and enrollment in, the private plan option. The Balanced Budget Act of 1997 (BBA; Public Law 105-33) created Part C as the Medicare+Choice program; the Medicare Prescription Drug, Improvement, and Modernization Act of 2003 (MMA; Public Law 108-173) modified the program and renamed it as Medicare Advantage. (Most, but not all, Medicare Advantage plans also offer Part D prescription drug coverage, as discussed below.)

The MMA also established Medicare Part D to help pay for prescription drugs not otherwise covered by Part A or Part B. Part D initially provided access to prescription drug discount cards, on a voluntary basis and at limited cost, to all enrollees (except those entitled to Medicaid drug coverage) and, for low-income beneficiaries, transitional limited financial assistance for purchasing prescription drugs and a subsidized enrollment fee for the discount cards. This temporary plan began in mid-2004 and phased out during 2006. In 2006 and later, Part D provides subsidized access to prescription drug insurance coverage on a voluntary basis for all beneficiaries upon payment of a premium, with premium and cost-sharing subsidies for low-income enrollees. Beneficiaries may choose to enroll in either a Medicare-approved private-sector drug plan or a Medicare Advantage plan that offers Part D coverage (as most, but not all, do).

Part D activities are handled within the SMI trust fund, but in an account separate from Part B. It should thus be noted that the traditional treatment of "SMI" and "Part B" as synonymous is no longer accurate, since SMI now consists of both Parts B and D. The purpose of the two separate accounts within the SMI trust fund is to ensure that funds from one part are not used to finance the other.

When Medicare began on July 1, 1966, approximately 19 million people enrolled. In 2018, almost 60 million people are enrolled in one or both of Parts A and B of the Medicare program, and over 21 million of them have chosen to participate in a Medicare Advantage plan.

Entitlement and Coverage

Part A is generally provided automatically, and free of premiums, to persons aged 65 or older who are eligible for Social Security or Railroad Retirement benefits, whether they have claimed these monthly cash benefits or not. Also, workers and their spouses with a sufficient period of Medicare-only coverage in Federal, State, or local government employment are eligible beginning at age 65. Similarly, individuals who have been entitled to Social Security or Railroad Retirement disability benefits for at least 24 months, and government employees or spouses with Medicare-only coverage who have been disabled for more than 29 months, are entitled to Part A benefits. (As noted previously, the waiting period is waived for persons with Lou Gehrig's Disease, and certain persons in the Libby, Montana vicinity who are diagnosed with asbestos-related conditions are Medicare-eligible. It should also be noted that, over the years, there have been certain liberalizations made to both the waiting period requirement and the limit on earnings allowed for entitlement to Medicare coverage based on disability.) Part A coverage is also provided to insured workers with ESRD (and to insured workers' spouses and children with ESRD), as well as to some otherwise ineligible aged and disabled beneficiaries who voluntarily pay a monthly premium for their coverage. In 2017, Part A provided protection against the costs of hospital and specific other medical care to over 58 million people (over 49 million aged and almost 9 million disabled enrollees). Part A benefit payments totaled $293.3 billion in 2017.

The following health care services are covered under Part A:

- Inpatient hospital care. Coverage includes costs of a semi-private room, meals, regular nursing services, operating and recovery rooms, intensive care, inpatient prescription drugs, laboratory tests, X-rays, psychiatric hospitals, inpatient rehabilitation, and long-term care hospitalization when medically necessary, as well as all other medically necessary services and supplies provided in the hospital. An initial deductible payment is required of beneficiaries who are admitted to a hospital, plus copayments for all hospital days following day 60 within a benefit period (described later).

- Skilled nursing facility (SNF) care. Coverage is provided by Part A only if the care follows within 30 days (generally) of a hospitalization of 3 days or more and is certified as medically necessary. Covered services are similar to those for inpatient hospital but also include rehabilitation services and appliances. The number of SNF days provided under Medicare is limited to 100 days per benefit period (described later), with a copayment required for days 21 through 100. Part A does not cover nursing facility care if the patient does not require skilled nursing or skilled rehabilitation services.
- Home health agency (HHA) care (covered by both Parts A and B). The BBA transferred from Part A to Part B those home health services furnished on or after January 1, 1998 that are unassociated with a hospital or SNF stay. Part A will continue to cover the first 100 visits following a 3-day hospital stay or a SNF stay; Part B covers any visits thereafter. Home health care under Part A and Part B has no copayment and no deductible.

  HHA care, including care provided by a home health aide, may be furnished part-time by a HHA in the residence of a home-bound beneficiary if intermittent or part-time skilled nursing and/or certain other therapy or rehabilitation care is necessary. Certain medical supplies and durable medical equipment (DME) may also be provided, though beneficiaries must pay a 20-percent coinsurance for DME, as required under Part B of Medicare. There must be a plan of treatment and periodic review by a physician. Full-time nursing care, food, blood, and drugs are not provided as HHA services.
- Hospice care. Coverage is provided for services to terminally ill persons with life expectancies of 6 months or less who elect to forgo the standard Medicare benefits for treatment of their illness and to receive only hospice care for it. Such care includes pain relief, supportive medical and social services, physical therapy, nursing services, and symptom management. However, if a hospice patient requires treatment for a condition that is not related to the terminal illness, Medicare will pay for all covered services necessary for that condition. The Medicare beneficiary pays no deductible for the hospice program, but does pay small coinsurance amounts for drugs and inpatient respite care.

An important Part A component is the benefit period, which starts when the beneficiary first enters a hospital and ends when there has been a break of at least 60 consecutive days since inpatient hospital or skilled nursing care was provided. There is no limit to the number of benefit periods covered by Part A during a beneficiary's lifetime; however, inpatient hospital care is normally limited to 90 days during a benefit period, and copayment requirements (detailed later) apply for days 61 through 90. If a beneficiary exhausts the 90 days of inpatient hospital care available in a benefit period, he or she can elect to use days of Medicare coverage from a non-renewable lifetime reserve of up to 60 (total) additional days of inpatient hospital care. Copayments are also required for such additional days.

All citizens (and certain legal aliens) aged 65 or older, and all disabled persons entitled to coverage under Part A, are eligible to enroll in Part B on a voluntary basis by payment of a monthly premium. Almost all persons entitled to Part A choose to enroll in Part B. In 2017, Part B provided protection against the costs of physician and other medical services to over 53 million people (over 45 million aged and over 8 million disabled enrollees). Part B benefits totaled $308.6 billion in 2017.

Part B covers certain medical services and supplies, including the following:

- Physicians' and surgeons' services, including some covered services furnished by chiropractors, podiatrists, dentists, and optometrists.
- Services provided by Medicare-approved practitioners who are not physicians, including certified registered nurse anesthetists, clinical psychologists, clinical social workers (other than in a hospital or SNF), physician assistants, and nurse practitioners and clinical nurse specialists in collaboration with a physician.
- Services in an emergency room, outpatient clinic, or ambulatory surgical center, including same-day surgery.
- Home health care not covered under Part A.
- Laboratory tests, X-rays, and other diagnostic radiology services.
- Certain preventive care services and screening tests.
- Most physical and occupational therapy and speech pathology services.
- Comprehensive outpatient rehabilitation facility services, and mental health care in a partial hospitalization psychiatric program, if a physician certifies that inpatient treatment would be required without it.
- Radiation therapy; renal (kidney) dialysis and transplants; and heart, lung, heart-lung, liver, pancreas, bone marrow, and intestinal transplants.
- Approved DME for home use, such as oxygen equipment and wheelchairs, prosthetic devices, and surgical dressings, splints, casts, and braces.

- Drugs and biologicals that are not usually self-administered, such as hepatitis B vaccines and immunosuppressive drugs. (Certain self-administered anticancer drugs are covered.)
- Certain services specific to people with diabetes.
- Ambulance services, when other methods of transportation are contraindicated.

To be covered, all services must be either medically necessary or one of several prescribed preventive benefits. Part B services are generally subject to a deductible and coinsurance (see next section). Certain medical services and related care are subject to special payment rules, including deductibles (for blood), maximum approved amounts (for Medicare-approved physical, speech, or occupational therapy services performed in settings other than hospitals), and higher cost-sharing requirements (such as those for certain outpatient hospital services). The preceding description of Part B-covered services should be used only as a general guide, due to the wide range of services covered under Part B and the quite specific rules and regulations that apply.

Medicare Parts A and B, as described above, constitute the original fee-for-service Medicare program. Medicare Part C, also known as Medicare Advantage, is an alternative to traditional Medicare. While all Medicare beneficiaries can receive their benefits through the traditional fee-for-service program, most beneficiaries enrolled in both Part A and Part B can choose to participate in a Medicare Advantage plan instead. Medicare Advantage plans are offered by private companies and organizations and are required to provide at least those services covered by Parts A and B, except hospice services. These plans may (and in certain situations must) provide extra benefits (such as vision or hearing) or reduce cost sharing or premiums. Following are the primary Medicare Advantage plans:

- Local coordinated care plans (LCCPs), including health maintenance organizations (HMOs), local preferred provider organizations (PPOs), and other certified coordinated care plans and entities that meet standards set forth in the law. Generally, each plan has a network of participating providers. Enrollees may be required to use these providers or, alternatively, may be allowed to go outside the network but pay higher cost-sharing fees for doing so.
- Regional PPO (RPPO) plans, which began in 2006 and offer coverage to 1 of 26 defined regions. Like local PPOs, RPPOs have networks of participating providers, and enrollees must use these providers or pay higher cost-sharing fees. However, RPPOs are required to provide beneficiary financial protection in the form of limits on out-of-pocket cost sharing, and there are specific provisions to encourage RPPO plans to participate in Medicare.

- Private fee-for-service (PFFS) plans, which were not required to have networks of participating providers prior to 2011. Beginning in 2011, this is still the case for PFFS plans in areas (usually counties) in which there are fewer than two network-based LCCPs and/or RPPOs, and members may go to any Medicare provider willing to accept the plan's payment. However, for PFFS plans in network areas with two or more network-based LCCPs and/or RPPOs, provider networks are now mandatory, and members may be required to use these participating providers.
- Special Needs Plans (SNPs), which are restricted to beneficiaries who are dually eligible for Medicare and Medicaid, live in long-term care institutions, or have certain severe and disabling conditions.

For individuals entitled to Part A or enrolled in Part B (except those entitled to Medicaid drug coverage), the new Part D initially provided access to prescription drug discount cards, at a cost of no more than $30 annually, on a voluntary basis. For low-income beneficiaries, Part D initially provided transitional financial assistance of up to $600 per year for purchasing prescription drugs, plus a subsidized enrollment fee for the discount cards. This temporary plan began in mid-2004 and phased out in 2006.

Beginning in 2006, Part D provides subsidized access to prescription drug insurance coverage on a voluntary basis, upon payment of a premium, to individuals entitled to Part A or enrolled in Part B, with premium and cost-sharing subsidies for low-income enrollees. Beneficiaries may enroll in either a stand-alone prescription drug plan (PDP) or an integrated Medicare Advantage plan that offers Part D coverage. Enrollment began in late 2005. In 2017, Part D provided protection against the costs of prescription drugs to over 44 million people. Part D benefits totaled an estimated $100.1 billion in 2017. (This amount includes an estimated $10.5 billion in benefits that are financed by the portion of enrollee premiums that are paid directly to the Part D plans. These direct premium amounts are available only on an estimated basis.)

Part D coverage includes most FDA-approved prescription drugs and biologicals. (The specific drugs currently covered in Parts A and B remain covered there.) However, plans may set up formularies for their prescription drug coverage, subject to certain statutory standards. Part D coverage can consist of either standard coverage (defined later) or an alternative design that provides the same actuarial value. For an additional premium, plans may also offer supplemental coverage exceeding the value of basic coverage.

It should be noted that some health care services are not covered by any portion of Medicare. Non-covered services include long-term nursing care, custodial care, and certain other health care needs, such as dentures and dental care, eyeglasses, and hearing aids. These services are not a part of the

Medicare program unless they are a part of a private health plan under the Medicare Advantage program.

Program Financing, Beneficiary Liabilities, and Payments to Providers

All financial operations for Medicare are handled through two trust funds, one for HI (Part A) and one for SMI (Parts B and D). These trust funds, which are special accounts in the U.S. Treasury, are credited with all receipts and charged with all expenditures for benefits and administrative costs. The trust funds cannot be used for any other purpose. Assets not needed for the payment of costs are invested in special Treasury securities. The following sections describe Medicare's financing provisions, beneficiary cost-sharing requirements, and the basis for determining Medicare reimbursements to health care providers.

Program Financing

The HI trust fund is financed primarily through a mandatory payroll tax. Almost all employees and self-employed workers in the United States work in employment covered by Part A and pay taxes to support the cost of benefits for aged and disabled beneficiaries. Currently, employees and employers each pay 1.45 percent of a worker's wages, for a combined payroll tax rate of 2.9 percent, while self-employed workers pay 2.9 percent of their net earnings. Since 1994, this tax has been paid on all covered wages and self-employment income without limit. (Prior to 1994, the tax applied only up to a specified maximum amount of earnings.) Beginning in 2013, earned income in excess of $200,000 (for those filing income tax singly) and $250,000 (for those filing jointly) is subject to an additional Part A payroll tax of 0.9 percent. (The earnings thresholds are not indexed.) The Part A tax rate is specified in the Social Security Act and cannot be changed without legislation.

Part A also receives income from the following sources: (1) a portion of the income taxes levied on Social Security benefits paid to high-income beneficiaries; (2) premiums from certain persons who are not otherwise eligible and choose to enroll voluntarily; (3) reimbursements from the general fund of the U.S. Treasury for the cost of providing Part A coverage to certain aged persons (and spouses) who retired when Part A began and thus were unable to earn sufficient quarters of coverage, and those Federal retirees (and spouses) similarly unable to earn sufficient quarters of Medicare-qualified Federal employment (the former group of individuals is now deceased, and reimbursements for their costs are completed); (4) interest earnings on its invested assets; and (5) other small miscellaneous income sources. The taxes paid each year are used mainly to pay benefits for current beneficiaries.

The SMI trust fund differs fundamentally from the HI trust fund with regard to the nature of its financing. As previously noted, SMI is now composed of two parts, Part B and Part D, each with its own separate account within the SMI trust fund. The nature of the financing for both parts of SMI is similar, in that both parts are primarily financed by contributions from the general fund of the U.S. Treasury and (to a much lesser degree) by beneficiary premiums.

For Part B, the contributions from the general fund of the U.S. Treasury are the largest source of income, since beneficiary premiums are generally set at a level that covers 25 percent of the average expenditures for aged beneficiaries. The standard Part B premium rate will be $135.50 per beneficiary per month in 2019. There are, however, three provisions that can alter the premium rate for certain enrollees. First, penalties for late enrollment (that is, enrollment after an individual's initial enrollment period) may apply, subject to certain statutory criteria. Second, beginning in 2007, beneficiaries whose income is above certain thresholds are required to pay an income-related monthly adjustment amount, in addition to their standard monthly premium. Finally, a "hold-harmless" provision, which prohibits increases in the standard Part B premium from exceeding the dollar amount of an individual's Social Security cost-of-living adjustment, lowers the premium rate for certain individuals who have their premiums deducted from their Social Security benefits.

[Author's note: The standard monthly premium for 2019 of $135.50 includes a repayment amount of $3 (as did the 2016, 2017, and 2018 premium rates). This $3 amount is to be transferred to the general fund of the Treasury, as mandated by the Bipartisan Budget Act of 2015 (Public Law 114-74) and explained in detail in the 2015 and 2016 Summaries.]

Exhibit A1.2.1 displays the 2019 Part B income-related monthly adjustment amounts and total monthly premium amounts to be paid by beneficiaries who file either individual tax returns (and are single individuals, heads of households, qualifying widows or widowers with dependent children, or married individuals filing separately who lived apart from their spouses for the entire taxable year) or joint tax returns.

The Part B income-related monthly adjustment amounts and total monthly premium amounts to be paid by beneficiaries who are married and lived with their spouses at any time during the taxable year, but who file separate tax returns from their spouses, are shown in exhibit A1.2.2.

For Part D, as with Part B, general fund contributions account for the largest source of income, since Part D beneficiary premiums are to represent, on average, 25.5 percent of the cost of standard coverage. The Part D base beneficiary premium for 2019 will be $33.19. The actual Part D premiums paid by individual beneficiaries equal the base beneficiary premium adjusted by a number of factors. In practice, premiums vary significantly from one Part D plan to another and seldom equal the base beneficiary premium. As of this

EXHIBIT A1.2.1
2019 Part B Income-Related Monthly Adjustment Amounts and Total Monthly Premium Amounts

Beneficiaries who file individual tax returns with income	Beneficiaries who file joint tax returns with income	Income-related monthly adjustment amount	Total monthly premium amount
Less than or equal to $85,000	Less than or equal to $170,000	$0	$135.50
Greater than $85,000 and less than or equal to $107,000	Greater than $170,000 and less than or equal to $214,000	$54.10	$189.60
Greater than $107,000 and less than or equal to $133,500	Greater than $214,000 and less than or equal to $267,000	$135.40	$270.90
Greater than $133,500 and less than or equal to $160,000	Greater than $267,000 and less than or equal to $320,000	$216.70	$352.20
Greater than $160,000 and less than $500,000	Greater than $320,000 and less than $750,000	$297.00	$433.40
Greater than or equal to $500,000	Greater than or equal to $750,000	$325.00	$460.50

writing, it is estimated that the average monthly premium for basic Part D coverage, which reflects the specific plan-by-plan premiums and the estimated number of beneficiaries in each plan, will be about $32.50 in 2019.

The estimated $32.50 average premium does not account for three circumstances that can also alter premiums for individual beneficiaries. First, penalties for late enrollment may apply. (Late enrollment penalties do not apply to enrollees who have maintained creditable prescription drug coverage.)

EXHIBIT A1.2.2
Part B Income-Related Monthly Adjustment Amounts and Total Monthly Premium Amounts for Married Beneficiaries Who File Separate Tax Returns

Beneficiaries who are married and lived with their spouses at any time during the year, but who file separate tax returns from their spouses	Income-related monthly adjustment amount	Total monthly premium amount
Less than or equal to $85,000	$0.00	$135.50
Greater than $85,000 and less than $415,000	$297.90	$433.40
Greater than or equal to $415,000	$325.00	$460.50

Second, beneficiaries meeting certain low-income and limited-resources requirements pay substantially reduced premiums or no premiums at all (and are not subject to late enrollment penalties). Third, beginning in 2011, beneficiaries with income above certain thresholds are required to pay an income-related monthly adjustment amount, in addition to their monthly premium.

See exhibit A1.2.3 for the 2019 Part D income-related monthly adjustment amounts to be paid by beneficiaries who file either individual tax returns (and are single individuals, heads of households, qualifying widows or widowers with dependent children, or married individuals filing separately who lived apart from their spouses for the entire taxable year) or joint tax returns. A beneficiary pays his or her plan premium plus the amounts shown below.

The Part D income-related monthly adjustment amounts to be paid by beneficiaries who are married and lived with their spouses at any time during the taxable year, but who file separate tax returns from their spouses, are shown in exhibit A1.2.4.

In addition to contributions from the general fund of the U.S. Treasury and beneficiary premiums, Part D also receives payments from the States. With the availability of prescription drug coverage and low-income subsidies under Part D, Medicaid is no longer the primary payer for prescription drugs for Medicaid beneficiaries who also have Medicare, and States are required to defray a portion of Part D expenditures for those beneficiaries.

EXHIBIT A1.2.3
2019 Part D Income-Related Monthly Adjustment Amounts to Be Paid by Beneficiaries Who File Either Individual Tax Returns or Joint Tax Returns

Beneficiaries who file individual tax returns with income	Beneficiaries who file joint tax returns with income	Part D income-related monthly adjustment amount
Less than or equal to $85,000	Less than or equal to $170,000	$0.00
Greater than $85,000 and less than or equal to $107,000	Greater than $170,000 and less than or equal to $214,000	$12.40
Greater than $107,000 and less than or equal to $133,500	Greater than $214,000 and less than or equal to $267,000	$31.90
Greater than $133,500 and less than or equal to $160,000	Greater than $267,000 and less than or equal to $320,000	$51.40
Greater than $160,000 and less than $500,000	Greater than $320,000 and less than $750,000	$70.90
Greater than or equal to $500,000	Greater than or equal to $750,000	$77.40

EXHIBIT A1.2.4
Part D Income-Related Monthly Adjustment Amounts to Be Paid by Beneficiaries Who Are Married but File Separate Tax Returns from Their Spouses

Beneficiaries who are married and lived with their spouses at any time during the year, but who file separate tax returns from their spouses	Part D income-related monthly adjustment amount
Less than or equal to $85,000	$0.00
Greater than $85,000 and less than $415,000	$70.90
Greater than or equal to $415,000	$77.40

During the Part D transitional period that began in mid-2004 and phased out during 2006, the general fund of the U.S. Treasury financed the transitional assistance benefit for low-income beneficiaries. Funds were transferred to, and paid from, a Transitional Assistance account within the SMI trust fund.

The SMI trust fund also receives income from interest earnings on its invested assets, as well as a small amount of miscellaneous income. It is important to note that beneficiary premiums and general fund payments for Parts B and D are redetermined annually and separately.

Payments to Medicare Advantage plans are financed from both the HI trust fund and the Part B account within the SMI trust fund in proportion to the relative weights of Part A and Part B benefits to the total benefits paid by the Medicare program.

Beneficiary Payment Liabilities

Fee-for-service beneficiaries are responsible for charges not covered by the Medicare program and for various cost-sharing aspects of both Part A and Part B. These liabilities may be paid (1) by the Medicare beneficiary; (2) by a third party, such as an employer-sponsored retiree health plan or private "Medigap" insurance; or (3) by Medicaid, if the person is eligible. The term "Medigap" is used to mean private health insurance that pays, within limits, most of the health care service charges not covered by Parts A or B of Medicare. These policies, which must meet federally imposed standards, are offered by Blue Cross and Blue Shield and various commercial health insurance companies.

In Medicare Advantage plans, the beneficiary's payment share is based on the cost-sharing structure of the specific plan selected by the beneficiary, since each plan has its own requirements. Most plans have lower deductibles and coinsurance than are required of fee-for-service beneficiaries. Such beneficiaries, in general, pay the monthly Part B premium. However, some Medicare Advantage plans may pay part or all of the Part B premium for their enrollees as an added benefit. Depending on the plan, enrollees may also pay an additional plan premium for certain extra benefits provided (or, in a small number of cases, for certain Medicare-covered services).

For hospital care covered under Part A, a fee-for-service beneficiary's payment share includes a one-time deductible amount at the beginning of each benefit period ($1,364 in 2019). This deductible covers the beneficiary's part of the first 60 days of each spell of inpatient hospital care. If continued inpatient care is needed beyond the 60 days, additional coinsurance payments ($341 per day in 2019) are required through the 90th day of a benefit period. Each Part A beneficiary also has a lifetime reserve of 60 additional hospital days that may be used when the covered days within a benefit period have been exhausted. Lifetime reserve days may be used only once, and coinsurance payments ($682 per day in 2019) are required.

For skilled nursing care covered under Part A, Medicare fully covers the first 20 days in a benefit period. But for days 21 through 100, a copayment ($170.50 per day in 2019) is required from the beneficiary. After 100 days per benefit period, Medicare pays nothing for SNF care. Home health care has no deductible or coinsurance payment by the beneficiary. In any Part A service, the beneficiary is responsible for fees to cover the first 3 pints or units of non-replaced blood per calendar year. The beneficiary has the option of paying the fee or of having the blood replaced.

There are no premiums for most people covered by Part A. Eligibility is generally earned through the work experience of the beneficiary or of his or her spouse. However, most aged people who are otherwise ineligible for premium-free Part A coverage can enroll voluntarily by paying a monthly premium, if they also enroll in Part B. For people with fewer than 30 quarters of coverage as defined by the Social Security Administration (SSA), the 2019 Part A monthly premium rate will be $437; for those with 30 to 39 quarters of coverage, the rate will be reduced to $240. Penalties for late enrollment may apply. Voluntary coverage upon payment of the Part A premium, with or without enrolling in Part B, is also available to disabled individuals for whom coverage has ceased due to earnings in excess of those allowed.

The Part B beneficiary's payment share includes the following: one annual deductible ($185 in 2019); the monthly premiums; the coinsurance payments for Part B services (usually 20 percent of the remaining allowed charges, with certain exceptions noted below); a deductible for blood; certain charges above the Medicare-allowed charge (for claims not on assignment); and payment for any services not covered by Medicare. For outpatient mental health services, the beneficiary is liable for 20 percent of the approved charges for 2014 and later; this percentage had been 50 percent through 2009, phasing down to 20 percent during the period 2010–2014. For services reimbursed under the outpatient hospital prospective payment system, coinsurance percentages vary by service and currently fall in the range of 20 percent to 50 percent. There are currently no deductibles or coinsurance for certain services, such as laboratory tests paid under the clinical laboratory fee schedule, home health agency services, and some preventive care services (including an initial, "Welcome to Medicare" preventive physical examination and, beginning in 2011, an annual wellness visit to develop or update a prevention plan).

For the standard Part D benefit design, there is an initial deductible ($415 in 2019). After meeting the deductible, the beneficiary pays 25 percent of the remaining costs, up to an initial coverage limit ($3,820 in 2019). A coverage gap starts after an individual's drug costs reach the initial coverage limit and stops when the beneficiary incurs a certain threshold of out-of-pocket costs ($5,100 in 2019). Previously, the beneficiary had to pay the full cost of prescription drugs while in this coverage gap. However, provisions of the Patient Protection and Affordable Care Act (Public Law 111-148) as amended by the Health Care and Education Reconciliation Act of 2010 (Public Law 111-152)—collectively referred to as the Affordable Care Act—lower the out-of-pocket costs in the coverage gap gradually between 2010 and 2020. In 2019, beneficiaries who enter the coverage gap (excluding low-income enrollees eligible for cost-sharing subsidies) will receive a 70-percent manufacturer discount and a 5-percent benefit from their Part D plans for applicable prescription drugs and a 63-percent benefit from their plans for non-applicable drugs. "Applicable" drugs are generally covered brand-name Part D drugs (including insulin and Part D vaccines); "non-applicable" drugs are generally covered non-brand-name (that is, generic) Part D drugs (including supplies associated with the delivery of insulin). Reductions to beneficiary cost sharing in the coverage gap continue to increase such that, by 2020, the coverage gap will be fully phased out, with the beneficiary responsible for 25 percent of all prescription drug costs.

The 2019 out-of-pocket threshold of $5,100 is equivalent to estimated average total covered drug spending of $8,139.54 under the defined standard benefit design, during the initial coverage period and the coverage gap, for enrollees not eligible for low-income cost-sharing subsidies. This estimated amount is based on an average blend of usage of applicable and non-applicable drugs by enrollees while in the coverage gap. In determining out-of-pocket costs, the dollar value of the 70-percent manufacturer discount for applicable drugs is included, even though the beneficiary does not pay it. The dollar values of the 63-percent drug plan benefit on non-applicable drugs and the 5-percent drug plan benefit on applicable drugs do not count toward out-of-pocket spending. Under the defined standard benefit design, the out-of-pocket threshold of $5,100 for 2019 is equivalent to $7,653.75 in total covered drug costs for enrollees eligible for low-income cost-sharing subsidies.

For costs incurred after the out-of-pocket threshold is reached, catastrophic coverage is provided, which requires the enrollee to pay the greater of 5-percent coinsurance or a small defined copayment amount ($3.40 in 2019 for generic or preferred multi-source drugs and $8.50 in 2019 for other drugs). The benefit parameters are indexed annually to the growth in average per capita Part D costs. Beneficiaries meeting certain low-income and limited-resources requirements pay substantially reduced cost-sharing amounts. In determining out-of-pocket costs, only those amounts actually paid by the enrollee or another individual (and not reimbursed through insurance) are counted; the exceptions to this "true out-of-pocket" provision are cost-sharing assistance from the low-income subsidies provided under Part D and from State Pharmacy Assistance programs and the manufacturer discount (50 percent in 2011–2018 and 70 percent in 2019 and later) on applicable brand-name drugs purchased by enrollees in the Part D coverage gap.

Many Part D plans offer alternative coverage that differs from the standard coverage described above. In fact, the majority of beneficiaries are not enrolled in the standard benefit design but rather in plans with low or no deductibles, flat payments for covered drugs, and, in some cases, additional partial coverage in the coverage gap. The monthly premiums required for Part D coverage are described in the previous section.

Payments to Providers

Before 1983, Part A payments to providers were made on a reasonable cost basis. Medicare payments for most inpatient hospital services are now made under a reimbursement mechanism known as the prospective payment system (PPS). Under the PPS for acute inpatient hospitals, each stay is categorized into a diagnosis-related group (DRG). Each DRG has a specific predetermined amount associated with it, which serves as the basis for payment. A number of adjustments are applied to the DRG's specific predetermined amount to calculate the payment for each stay. In some cases the payment the hospital receives is less than the hospital's actual cost for providing the Part A-covered inpatient hospital services for the stay; in other cases it is more. The hospital absorbs the loss or makes a profit. Certain payment adjustments exist for extraordinarily costly inpatient hospital stays and other situations. Payments for skilled nursing care, home health care, inpatient rehabilitation hospital care, long-term care hospitals, inpatient psychiatric hospitals, and hospice are made under separate prospective payment systems.

For non-physician Part B services, home health care is reimbursed under the same prospective payment system as Part A; most hospital outpatient services are reimbursed on a separate prospective payment system; and most (although not all) payments for clinical laboratory and ambulance services are based on fee schedules. A fee schedule is a comprehensive listing of maximum fees used to pay providers. Most DME payments have also been based on a fee schedule, but a transition to a competitive bidding process for certain DME began on January 1, 2011, with implementation in nine metropolitan statistical areas

(MSAs). On July 1, 2013, competitive bidding was expanded to cover about 100 MSAs in all, and a national mail-order program for diabetic testing supplies was also implemented. As of July 1, 2016, the transition was completed for included DME, and all areas of the country are now subject to competitive bidding (or to payments based on the competitively bid rates).

In general, the prospective payment systems and fee schedules used for Part A and non-physician Part B services are increased each year either by indices related to the "market basket" of goods and services that the provider must purchase or by indices related to the Consumer Price Index (CPI). These indices vary by type of provider. The Affordable Care Act mandates that these payment updates be decreased, in most cases, from what they would have been, by stipulated amounts during 2010–2019, with starting dates and amounts varying by type of provider. In addition, payment updates are further reduced, on a permanent basis, by the growth in economy-wide productivity, with starting dates varying by type of provider, with some having started as early as October 2011. (There is a strong likelihood that the lower payment increases will not be viable in the long range. The best available evidence indicates that most health care providers cannot improve their productivity to this degree due to the labor-intensive nature of most of these services.)

For Part B, before 1992, physicians were paid on the basis of reasonable charge. This amount was initially defined as the lowest of (1) the physician's actual charge; (2) the physician's customary charge; or (3) the prevailing charge for similar services in that locality. Beginning January 1992, allowed charges have been defined as the lesser of (1) the submitted charges, or (2) the amount determined by a fee schedule based on a relative value scale (RVS). In practice, most allowed charges are based on the fee schedule. Under 1997 legislation, this fee schedule was supposed to be updated each year by a sustainable growth rate (SGR) system prescribed in the law, which set limits on how much doctor payments could change based on how quickly the rest of the economy was growing. For 2003 through June 2015, however, significant physician fee reductions scheduled under the SGR system were postponed by legislative action that was taken at least annually.

Effective April 1, 2015, the SGR system was permanently repealed and replaced by a new annual payment update system. Payment updates for all future years were prescribed, and incentive payments for 2019–2024—based on participation by individual physicians in an alternative payment model (APM) program or performance under the merit-based incentive payment system (MIPS)—were set forth in the law. (While the scheduled updates provided relief in the short term from significant reductions to physician payments scheduled under the SGR system, the specified rate updates are not expected to keep up with underlying physician costs over the long range and would provide lower physician payments than under the SGR system in the long run.)

If a doctor or supplier agrees to accept the Medicare-approved rate as payment in full ("takes assignment"), then payments provided must be considered as payments in full for that service. The provider may not request any added payments (beyond the initial annual deductible and coinsurance) from the beneficiary or insurer. If the provider does not take assignment, the beneficiary will be charged for the excess (which may be paid by Medigap insurance). Limits now exist on the excess that doctors or suppliers can charge. Physicians are "participating physicians" if they agree before the beginning of the year to accept assignment for all Medicare services they furnish during the year. Since beneficiaries in the original Medicare fee-for-service program may select their doctors, they have the option to choose those who participate.

Medicare Advantage plans and their precursors have generally been paid on a capitation basis, meaning that a fixed, predetermined amount per month per member is paid to the plan, without regard to the actual number and nature of services used by the members. The specific mechanisms to determine the payment amounts have changed over the years. In 2006, Medicare began paying to plans capitated payment rates based on a competitive bidding process.

For Part D, each month for each plan member, Medicare pays Part D drug plans (stand-alone PDPs and the prescription drug portions of Medicare Advantage plans) their risk-adjusted bid, minus the enrollee premium. Plans also receive Medicare payments representing premiums and cost-sharing amounts for certain low-income beneficiaries for whom these items are reduced or waived. In addition, under the reinsurance provision, Medicare pays plans for 80 percent of costs in the catastrophic coverage category (less corresponding rebates that the plans receive from drug manufacturers).

To help them gain experience with the Medicare population, Part D plans are protected by a system of "risk corridors" that allow Medicare to assist with unexpected costs and share in unexpected savings. The risk corridors became less protective after 2007.

Under Part D, Medicare provides certain subsidies to employer and union prescription drug plans that continue to offer coverage to Medicare retirees and meet specific criteria in doing so. These retiree drug subsidy (RDS) payments were previously tax-exempt but became taxable under the Affordable Care Act beginning in 2013.

Medicare Claims Processing

Since the inception of Medicare, fee-for-service claims have been processed by non-government organizations or agencies that contract to serve as the fiscal agent between providers and the Federal government. These entities apply the Medicare coverage rules to determine appropriate reimbursement amounts and make payments to the providers and suppliers. Their responsibilities also include maintaining records, establishing controls, safeguarding against fraud and abuse, and assisting both providers and beneficiaries as needed.

Before the enactment of the MMA in 2003, contractors known as fiscal intermediaries processed Part A claims for institutional services, including claims for inpatient hospital, SNF, HHA, and hospice services. They also processed outpatient hospital claims for Part B. Similarly, contractors known as carriers handled Part B claims for services by physicians and medical suppliers. By law, the Centers for Medicare & Medicaid Services (CMS) was required to select fiscal intermediaries from among companies that were nominated by health care provider associations and to select carriers from among health insurers or similar companies.

The MMA mandated that this system of intermediaries and carriers be replaced with a new system of contract entities known as Medicare Administrative Contractors (MACs). Each MAC processes and pays fee-for-service claims, for both Part A and Part B services, to all providers and suppliers within the MAC's defined geographical jurisdiction. MACs are selected through a competitive procedure. This new system is intended to improve Medicare services to beneficiaries, providers, and suppliers, who now have a single point of contact for all claims-related business. CMS evaluates MACs based in part on customer satisfaction with their services. The new system enables the Medicare fee-for-service program to benefit from economies of scale and competitive performance contracting.

The transition from fiscal intermediaries and carriers to MACs began in 2005, and the last intermediary and carrier contracts ended in September 2013. Under the initial implementation of the MAC system, Part A and Part B claims were processed by 15 "A/B MACs," with the exception of (1) durable medical equipment claims, which were processed by 4 specialty "DME MACs," and (2) home health and hospice claims, which were processed by 4 specialty "HH+H MACs." CMS has since consolidated the number of A/B MACs from 15 to 12, and the processing of home health and hospice claims has been assumed by 4 of the A/B MACs (although it should be noted that, for these 4 A/B MACs, their HH+H geographical areas do not coincide with their A/B geographical areas). DME claims continue to be processed by the 4 specialty DME MACs.

Claims for services provided by Medicare Advantage plans (that is, claims under Part C) are processed by the plans themselves.

Part D plans are responsible for processing their claims, akin to Part C. However, because of the "true out-of-pocket" provision discussed previously, CMS has contracted the services of a facilitator, who works with CMS, Part D drug plans (stand-alone PDPs and the prescription drug portions of Medicare Advantage plans), and carriers of supplemental drug coverage, to coordinate benefit payments and track the sources of cost-sharing payments. Claims under Part D also have to be submitted by the plans to CMS, so that certain payments based on actual experience (such as payments for low-income cost-sharing and premium subsidies, reinsurance, and risk corridors) can be determined.

Because of its size and complexity, Medicare is vulnerable to improper payments, ranging from inadvertent errors to outright fraud and abuse. While providers are responsible for submitting accurate claims, and intermediaries and carriers are responsible for ensuring that only such claims are paid, there are additional groups whose duties include the prevention, reduction, and recovery of improper payments.

Quality improvement organizations (QIOs, formerly called peer review organizations or PROs) are groups of practicing health care professionals who are paid by the Federal government to improve the effectiveness, efficiency, economy, and quality of services delivered to Medicare beneficiaries. One function of QIOs is to ensure that Medicare pays only for services and goods that are reasonable and necessary and that are provided in the most appropriate setting.

The ongoing effort to address improper payments intensified after enactment of the Health Insurance Portability and Accountability Act of 1996 (HIPAA; Public Law 104-191), which created the Medicare Integrity Program (MIP). The MIP provides CMS with dedicated funds to identify and combat improper payments, including those caused by fraud and abuse, and, for the first time, allows CMS to competitively contract with entities other than carriers and intermediaries to conduct these activities. MIP funds are used for (1) audits of cost reports, which are financial documents that hospitals and other institutions are required to submit annually to CMS; (2) medical reviews of claims to determine whether services provided are medically reasonable and necessary; (3) determinations of whether Medicare or other insurance sources have primary responsibility for payment; (4) identification and investigation of potential fraud cases; and (5) education to inform providers about appropriate billing procedures. In addition to creating the MIP, HIPAA established a fund to provide resources for the Department of Justice—including the Federal Bureau of Investigation—and the Office of Inspector General (OIG) within the Department of Health and Human Services (DHHS) to investigate and prosecute health care fraud and abuse.

The Deficit Reduction Act of 2005 (DRA; Public Law 109-171) established and funded an additional activity called the Medicare-Medicaid Data Match Program, which is designed to identify improper billing and utilization patterns by matching Medicare and Medicaid claims information. As is the case under the MIP, CMS can contract with third parties. The funds also can be used (1) to coordinate actions by CMS, the States, the Attorney General, and the DHHS OIG to prevent improper Medicaid and Medicare expenditures, and (2) to increase the effectiveness and efficiency of both Medicare and Medicaid through cost avoidance, savings, and the recoupment of fraudulent, wasteful, or abusive expenditures.

The Affordable Care Act included many provisions intended to improve the accuracy of payments and to link those payments to quality and efficiency in the Medicare program. Because these provisions are so numerous and broad in scope and cannot be described in detail in this brief summary, reputable documents that provide such detail should be consulted if more information is desired. One of the most important of these provisions is the establishment of the Center for Medicare and Medicaid Innovation (CMMI) within CMS. [Author's note: the CMMI is named the CMS Innovation Center throughout this book.] The purpose of the CMMI is to test innovative payment and service delivery models, with the goal of reducing program expenditures under Medicare, Medicaid, and the Children's Health Insurance Program (CHIP, known from its inception until March 2009 as the State Children's Health Insurance Program or SCHIP) while preserving or enhancing quality of care.

Administration

DHHS has the overall responsibility for administration of the Medicare program. Within DHHS, responsibility for administering Medicare rests with CMS. SSA assists, however, by initially determining an individual's Medicare entitlement, by withholding Part B premiums from the Social Security benefits of most beneficiaries, and by maintaining Medicare data on the master beneficiary record, which is SSA's primary record of beneficiaries. The MMA requires SSA to undertake a number of additional Medicare-related responsibilities, including making low-income subsidy determinations under Part D, notifying individuals of the availability of Part D subsidies, withholding Part D premiums from monthly Social Security cash benefits for those beneficiaries who request such an arrangement, and, for 2007 and later, determining the individual's Part B premium if the Part B income-related monthly adjustment applies. For 2011 and later, the Affordable Care Act requires SSA to determine the individual's Part D premium if the Part D income-related monthly adjustment applies. The Internal Revenue Service (IRS) in the Department of the Treasury collects the Part A payroll taxes from workers and their employers. IRS data, in the form of income tax returns, play a role in determining which Part D enrollees are eligible for low-income subsidies (and to what degree) and which Part B and Part D enrollees are subject to the income-related monthly adjustment amounts in their premiums (and to what degree).

A Medicare Board of Trustees, composed of two appointed members of the public and four members who serve by virtue of their positions in the Federal government, oversees the financial operations of the HI and SMI trust funds. The Secretary of the Treasury is the managing trustee. The Board of Trustees reports to Congress on the financial and actuarial status of the Medicare trust funds on or about the first day of April each year.

State agencies (usually State Health Departments under agreements with CMS) identify, survey, and inspect provider and supplier facilities and institutions wishing to participate in the Medicare program. In consultation with CMS, these agencies then certify the facilities that are qualified.

Medicare Financial Status

As measured by expenditures, Medicare is the largest health care insurance program—and the second-largest social insurance program—in the United States. Medicare is also complex, and it faces a number of financial challenges in both the short term and the long term. These challenges include the following:

- The solvency of the HI trust fund, which fails the Medicare Board of Trustees' test of short-range financial adequacy. (Trust fund assets are currently below 100 percent of projected annual expenditures and are not expected to attain the 100-percent level under the Trustees' intermediate assumptions.)
- The long-range health of the HI trust fund, as the trust fund fails the Trustees' test of long-range close actuarial balance.
- The rapid growth projected for SMI costs as a percent of Gross Domestic Product. (Although the Part B and Part D accounts in the SMI trust fund are automatically in financial balance—in both the short range and the long range—since premiums and general revenue financing rates are reset each year to match estimated costs, the rapid growth of SMI expenditures nevertheless places steadily increasing demands on beneficiaries and taxpayers.)
- The likelihood that the lower payment rate updates to most categories of Medicare providers for 2011 and later, as mandated by the Affordable Care Act, will not be viable in the long range (as discussed previously).
- The likelihood that the specified rate updates under the new Part B physician payment update system will not keep up with underlying physician costs over the long range (as discussed previously), possibly leading to decreased access to, or quality of, physician services for beneficiaries or to the overriding of the specified updates (as repeatedly occurred when the SGR system was in place), which would in turn lead to higher costs.

Though a detailed description of these issues is beyond the scope of this summary, more information can be found in the most recent Medicare Trustees Report, available on the Internet at www.cms.gov/Research-Statistics-Data-and-Systems/Statistics-Trends-and-Reports/ReportsTrustFunds/index.html.

The Medicare program covers most of our nation's aged population, as well as many people who receive Social Security disability benefits. In 2017, Part A covered over 58 million enrollees with benefit payments of $293.3 billion, Part B covered over 53 million enrollees with benefit payments of $308.6 billion, and Part D covered over 44 million enrollees with benefit payments of $100.1 billion. Administrative costs in 2017 were about 1.1 percent, 1.6 percent, and −0.1 percent of expenditures for Part A, Part B, and Part D, respectively. (Negative Part D administrative costs reflect transfers made to the Part D account from the other parts of Medicare; Part D had previously overpaid administrative costs and was reimbursed in 2017.) Total expenditures for Medicare in 2017 were $710.2 billion.

Overview of Medicaid

Title XIX of the Social Security Act is a Federal/State entitlement program that pays for medical assistance for certain individuals and families with low incomes and resources. This program, known as Medicaid, became law in 1965 as a cooperative venture jointly funded by the Federal and State governments (including the District of Columbia and the Territories) to assist States in furnishing medical assistance to eligible needy persons. Medicaid is the largest source of funding for medical and health-related services for America's low-income population.

Within broad national guidelines established by Federal statutes, regulations, and policies, each State establishes its own eligibility standards; determines the type, amount, duration, and scope of services; sets the rate of payment for services; and administers its own program. Medicaid policies for eligibility, services, and payment are complex and vary considerably, even among States of similar size or geographic proximity. Thus, a person who is eligible for Medicaid in one State may not be eligible in another State, and the services provided by one State may differ considerably in amount, duration, or scope from services provided in a similar or neighboring State. In addition, State legislatures may change Medicaid eligibility, services, and/or reimbursement at any time.

Title XXI of the Social Security Act, the Children's Health Insurance Program (CHIP, known from its inception until March 2009 as the State Children's Health Insurance Program or SCHIP), is a program initiated by the Balanced Budget Act of 1997 (BBA; Public Law 105-33). The BBA provided $40 billion in Federal funding through fiscal year (FY) 2007 to be used to provide health care coverage for low-income children—generally those in families with income below 200 percent of the Federal poverty level (FPL)—who do not qualify for Medicaid and would otherwise be uninsured. CHIP funding was extended through FY 2027 by subsequent legislation, including the

Children's Health Insurance Program Reauthorization Act of 2009 (CHIPRA; Public Law 111-3); the Patient Protection and Affordable Care Act (Public Law 111-148) as amended by the Health Care and Education Reconciliation Act of 2010 (Public Law 111-152)—collectively referred to as the Affordable Care Act; the Medicare Access and CHIP Reauthorization Act of 2015 (MACRA; Public Law 114-10); the Federal Register Printing Savings Act of 2017 (Public Law 115-120); and the Bipartisan Budget Act of 2018 (Public Law 115-123). Under CHIP, States may elect to provide coverage to qualifying children by expanding their Medicaid programs or through a State program separate from Medicaid. A number of States have also been granted waivers to cover parents of children enrolled in CHIP.

Medicaid Eligibility

Prior to 2014, Medicaid did not offer health care services for all poor persons. To qualify for the program, an individual needed not only to have low income but also to meet one of several eligibility criteria, such as being a child, a parent or caretaker adult of an eligible child, a disabled child or adult, or an aged adult. Other criteria also applied; for example, in many cases eligibility might have depended on an "asset test," which measured a person's assets against certain threshold levels.

In 2014 and later, the Affordable Care Act expands eligibility to all individuals under the age of 65 in households with income up to 138 percent of the FPL, as explained in more detail below. As a result of this legislation, most persons no longer need to meet the previously applied criteria, such as being in a designated group or undergoing an asset test, to qualify for Medicaid. However, due to a 2012 Supreme Court ruling that made the eligibility expansion effectively optional for each State's Medicaid program, some States have chosen not to implement it, but many have elected to do so.

States generally have broad discretion in determining which groups their Medicaid programs will cover and the financial criteria for Medicaid eligibility. To be eligible for Federal funds, however, States are required to provide Medicaid coverage for certain individuals who receive federally assisted income-maintenance payments, as well as for related groups not receiving cash payments. In addition to their Medicaid programs, most States have additional "State-only" programs to provide medical assistance for specified poor persons who do not qualify for Medicaid. Federal funds are not provided for State-only programs. The following enumerates the mandatory Medicaid "categorically needy" eligibility groups for which Federal matching funds are provided:

- Limited-income families with children, as described in Section 1931 of the Social Security Act, are generally eligible for Medicaid if they meet the requirements for the Aid to Families with Dependent Children (AFDC) program that were in effect in their State on July 16, 1996.

- Children under age 6 whose family income is at or below 133 percent of the FPL. (As of January 2018, the FPL has been set at $25,100 for a family of four in the continental U.S.; Alaska and Hawaii's FPLs are $31,380 and $28,870, respectively.)
- Pregnant women whose family income is below 133 percent of the FPL. (Services to these women are limited to those related to pregnancy, complications of pregnancy, delivery, and postpartum care.)
- Infants born to Medicaid-eligible women, for the first year of life with certain restrictions.
- Supplemental Security Income (SSI) recipients in most States (or aged, blind, and disabled individuals in States using more restrictive Medicaid eligibility requirements that pre-date SSI).
- Recipients of adoption or foster care assistance under Title IV-E of the Social Security Act.
- Special protected groups (typically individuals who lose their cash assistance under Title IV-A or SSI due to earnings from work or from increased Social Security benefits, but who may keep Medicaid for a period of time).
- All children under age 19, in families with incomes at or below the FPL.
- Certain Medicare beneficiaries (described later).

States also have the option of providing Medicaid coverage for other "categorically related" groups. These optional groups share characteristics of the mandatory groups (that is, they fall within defined categories), but the eligibility criteria are somewhat more liberally defined. The broadest optional groups for which States can receive Federal matching funds for coverage under the Medicaid program include the following:

- Infants up to age 1 and pregnant women not covered under the mandatory rules whose family income is no more than 185 percent of the FPL. (The percentage amount is set by each State.)
- Children under age 21 who meet criteria more liberal than the AFDC income and resources requirements that were in effect in their State on July 16, 1996.
- Institutionalized individuals, and individuals in home and community-based waiver programs, who are eligible under a "special income level." (The amount is set by each State—up to 300 percent of the SSI Federal benefit rate.)
- Individuals who would be eligible if institutionalized, but who are receiving care under home and community-based services (HCBS) waivers.

- Certain aged, blind, or disabled adults who have incomes above those requiring mandatory coverage, but below the FPL.
- Aged, blind, or disabled recipients of State supplementary income payments.
- Certain working-and-disabled persons with family income less than 250 percent of the FPL who would qualify for SSI if they did not work.
- Tuberculosis-infected persons who would be financially eligible for Medicaid at the SSI income level if they were in a Medicaid-covered category. (Coverage is limited to tuberculosis-related ambulatory services and tuberculosis drugs.)
- Certain uninsured or low-income women who are screened for breast or cervical cancer through a program administered by the Centers for Disease Control and Prevention. The Breast and Cervical Cancer Prevention and Treatment Act of 2000 (Public Law 106-354) provides these women with medical assistance and follow-up diagnostic services through Medicaid.
- "Optional targeted low-income children" included in the CHIP (formerly SCHIP) program established by the BBA.
- "Medically needy" persons (described below).

The medically needy (MN) option allows States to extend Medicaid eligibility to additional persons. These persons would be eligible for Medicaid under one of the mandatory or optional groups, except that their income and/or resources are above the eligibility level set by their State for those groups. Persons may qualify immediately or may "spend down" by incurring medical expenses that reduce their income to or below their State's MN income level.

Medicaid eligibility and benefit provisions for the medically needy do not have to be as extensive as for the categorically needy, and may be quite restrictive. Federal matching funds are available for MN programs. However, if a State elects to have a MN program, there are Federal requirements that certain groups must be covered (including children under age 19 and pregnant women) and certain services must be provided (including prenatal and delivery care for pregnant women and ambulatory care for children). A State may elect to provide MN eligibility to certain additional groups and may elect to provide certain additional services as part of its MN program. Data from 2013 indicate that 34 States plus the District of Columbia have elected to have a MN program and are providing services to at least some MN beneficiaries. All remaining States utilize the "special income level" option to extend Medicaid to the "near poor" in medical institutional settings.

Transitional Medical Assistance (TMA) is a Medicaid program that offers up to 1 year of additional Medicaid health insurance benefits for certain low-income families who would otherwise lose coverage. Specifically, under TMA provisions, families who would otherwise lose Medicaid eligibility because of earned income or hours of employment, or the loss of a time-limited earnings disregard, receive at least 6 months and as many as 12 months of Medicaid coverage. TMA provisions were subject to periodic reauthorization from the time of their enactment in 1988 but were made a permanent part of Medicaid by MACRA in April 2015.

The Personal Responsibility and Work Opportunity Reconciliation Act of 1996 (Public Law 104-193)—known as the Welfare Reform Act—made restrictive changes regarding eligibility for SSI coverage that affected the Medicaid program. For example, legal resident aliens and other qualified aliens who entered the United States on or after August 22, 1996 are ineligible for Medicaid for 5 years. Medicaid coverage for most aliens entering before that date and coverage for those eligible after the 5-year ban are State options; emergency services, however, are mandatory for both of these alien coverage groups. For aliens who lose SSI benefits because of these restrictions regarding SSI coverage, Medicaid benefits can continue only if these persons can be covered under some other eligibility status (again with the exception of emergency services, which are mandatory). Public Law 104-193 also affected a number of disabled children, who lost SSI as a result of the restrictive changes; however, their eligibility for Medicaid was reinstituted by Public Law 105-33, the BBA.

In addition, welfare reform repealed the open-ended Federal entitlement program known as Aid to Families with Dependent Children (AFDC) and replaced it with Temporary Assistance for Needy Families (TANF), which provides States with grants to be spent on time-limited cash assistance. TANF generally limits a family's lifetime cash welfare benefits to a maximum of 5 years and permits States to impose a wide range of other requirements as well—in particular, those related to employment. However, the impact on Medicaid eligibility has not been significant. Under welfare reform, persons who would have been eligible for AFDC under the AFDC requirements in effect on July 16, 1996 are generally still eligible for Medicaid. Although most persons covered by TANF receive Medicaid, it is not required by law.

Medicaid coverage may begin as early as the third month prior to application—if the person would have been eligible for Medicaid had he or she applied during that time. Medicaid coverage generally stops at the end of the month in which a person no longer meets the criteria of any Medicaid eligibility group. The BBA allows States to provide 12 months of continuous Medicaid coverage (without reevaluation) for eligible children under the age of 19.

The Ticket to Work and Work Incentives Improvement Act of 1999 (Public Law 106-170) provides or continues Medicaid coverage to certain disabled beneficiaries who work despite their disability. Those with higher incomes may pay a sliding scale premium based on income.

The Deficit Reduction Act of 2005 (DRA; Public Law 109-171) refined eligibility requirements for Medicaid beneficiaries by tightening standards for citizenship and immigration documentation and by changing the rules concerning long-term care eligibility—specifically, the look-back period for determining community spouse income and assets was lengthened from 36 months to 60 months, individuals whose homes exceed $500,000 in value are disqualified, and the States are required to impose partial months of ineligibility.

Beginning in 2014, the Affordable Care Act expands Medicaid eligibility to all individuals under age 65 in families with income below 138 percent of the FPL. (Technically, the income limit is 133 percent of the FPL, but the Act also provides for a 5-percent income disregard.) In addition to the higher level of allowable income, the legislation expands eligibility to people under age 65 who have no other qualifying factors that would have made them eligible for Medicaid under prior law, such as being under age 18, disabled, pregnant, or parents of eligible children. Since individuals are no longer required to be parents of eligible children, the category of non-disabled non-aged adults has experienced the greatest increase in Medicaid enrollment. However, in *National Federation of Independent Business et al. v. Sebelius, Secretary of Health and Human Services,* the Supreme Court ruled that states could not be required to implement this expansion as a condition of continuing to operate their existing Medicaid programs and receiving Federal financial participation. This ruling has made the eligibility expansion effectively optional for each State's Medicaid program. As of August 1, 2019, 36 states and the District of Columbia have adopted the Medicaid expansion (Kaiser Family Foundation 2019).

Scope of Medicaid Services

Title XIX of the Social Security Act allows considerable flexibility within the States' Medicaid plans. However, some Federal requirements are mandatory if Federal matching funds are to be received. A State's Medicaid program must offer medical assistance for certain basic services to most categorically needy populations. These services generally include the following:

- Inpatient hospital services.
- Outpatient hospital services.
- Pregnancy-related services, including prenatal care and 60 days postpartum pregnancy-related services.
- Vaccines for children.
- Physician services.
- Nursing facility services for persons aged 21 or older.
- Family planning services and supplies.

- Rural health clinic services.
- Home health care for persons eligible for skilled nursing services.
- Laboratory and X-ray services.
- Pediatric and family nurse practitioner services.
- Nurse-midwife services.
- Federally qualified health-center (FQHC) services, and ambulatory services of an FQHC that would be available in other settings.
- Early and periodic screening, diagnostic, and treatment (EPSDT) services for children under age 21.

States may also receive Federal matching funds to provide certain optional services. Following are some of the most common, currently approved optional Medicaid services:

- Diagnostic services.
- Clinic services.
- Intermediate care facility services.
- Prescribed drugs and prosthetic devices.
- Optometrist services and eyeglasses.
- Nursing facility services for children under age 21.
- Transportation services.
- Rehabilitation and physical therapy services.
- Hospice care.
- Home and community-based care to certain persons with chronic impairments.
- Targeted case management services.

The BBA included a State option known as Programs of All-Inclusive Care for the Elderly (PACE). PACE provides an alternative to institutional care for persons aged 55 or older who require a nursing facility level of care. The PACE team offers and manages all health, medical, and social services and mobilizes other services as needed to provide preventive, rehabilitative, curative, and supportive care. This care, provided in day health centers, homes, hospitals, and nursing homes, helps the person maintain independence, dignity, and quality of life. PACE functions within the Medicare program as well. Regardless of source of payment, PACE providers receive payment only through the PACE agreement and must make available all items and services covered under both Titles XVIII and XIX, without amount, duration, or scope limitations and without application of any deductibles, copayments, or other cost sharing. The individuals enrolled in PACE receive benefits solely through the PACE program.

Amount and Duration of Medicaid Services

Within broad Federal guidelines and certain limitations, States determine the amount and duration of services offered under their Medicaid programs. States may limit, for example, the number of days of hospital care or the number of physician visits covered. Two restrictions apply: (1) limits must result in a sufficient level of services to reasonably achieve the purpose of the benefits; and (2) limits on benefits may not discriminate among beneficiaries based on medical diagnosis or condition.

In general, States are required to provide comparable amounts, duration, and scope of services to all categorically needy and categorically related eligible persons. There are two important exceptions: (1) Medically necessary health care services that are identified under the EPSDT program for eligible children, and that are within the scope of mandatory or optional services under Federal law, must be covered even if those services are not included as part of the covered services in that State's Plan; and (2) States may request waivers to pay for otherwise uncovered home and community-based services (HCBS) for Medicaid-eligible persons who might otherwise be institutionalized. As long as the services are cost effective, States have few limitations on the services that may be covered under these waivers (except that, other than as a part of respite care, States may not provide room and board for the beneficiaries). With certain exceptions, a State's Medicaid program must allow beneficiaries to have some informed choices among participating providers of health care and to receive quality care that is appropriate and timely.

Payment for Medicaid Services

Medicaid operates as a vendor payment program. States may pay health care providers directly on a fee-for-service basis, or States may pay for Medicaid services through various prepayment arrangements, such as health maintenance organizations (HMOs). Within federally imposed upper limits and specific restrictions, each State for the most part has broad discretion in determining the payment methodology and payment rate for services. Generally, payment rates must be sufficient to enlist enough providers so that covered services are available at least to the extent that comparable care and services are available to the general population within that geographic area. Providers participating in Medicaid must accept Medicaid payment rates as payment in full. States must make additional payments to qualified hospitals that provide inpatient services to a disproportionate number of Medicaid beneficiaries and/or to other low-income or uninsured persons under what is known as the disproportionate share hospital (DSH) adjustment. During 1988–1991, excessive and inappropriate use of the DSH adjustment resulted in rapidly increasing Federal expenditures for Medicaid. Legislation that was passed in 1991 and 1993, and amended in the BBA of 1997 and later legislation, capped the Federal share of payments to DSH hospitals.

States may impose nominal deductibles, coinsurance, or copayments on some Medicaid beneficiaries for certain services. The following Medicaid beneficiaries, however, must be excluded from cost sharing: pregnant women, children under age 18, and hospital or nursing home patients who are expected to contribute most of their income to institutional care. In addition, all Medicaid beneficiaries must be exempt from copayments for emergency services and family planning services. Under the DRA, new cost-sharing and benefit rules provided States the option of imposing new premiums and increased cost sharing on all Medicaid beneficiaries except for those mentioned above and terminally ill patients in hospice care. The DRA also established special rules for cost sharing for prescription drugs and for non-emergency services furnished in emergency rooms.

The Federal government pays a share of the medical assistance expenditures under each State's Medicaid program. That share, known as the Federal Medical Assistance Percentage (FMAP), is determined annually by a formula that compares the State's average per capita income level with the national income average. States with a higher per capita income level are reimbursed a smaller share of their costs. By law, the FMAP cannot be lower than 50 percent or higher than 83 percent. In FY 2018, the FMAPs varied from 50 percent in 14 States to 75.65 percent in Mississippi, and averaged 59.3 percent overall.

The BBA permanently raised the FMAP for the District of Columbia from 50 percent to 70 percent. The American Recovery and Reinvestment Act of 2009 (ARRA; Public Law 111-5) provided States with an increase in their Medicaid FMAPs of up to 14 percentage points, depending on State unemployment rates, for the first quarter of FY 2009 through the first quarter of FY 2011. Section 201 of Public Law 111-226 (referred to as the Education, Jobs, and Medicaid Assistance Act of 2010) extended these increases for the second and third quarters of FY 2011, but at lower levels than had been the case under ARRA.

For children covered through the CHIP (formerly SCHIP) program, the Federal government pays States a higher share, or enhanced FMAP, which averaged 88 percent in FY 2018. An Affordable Care Act provision raises the enhanced FMAP for CHIP by 23 percentage points, to a maximum of 100 percent, through FY 2019; for FY 2020, the Federal Register Printing Savings Act of 2017 raises it by a lower amount—11.5 percentage points—to a maximum of 100 percent. Without these increases, the average enhanced FMAP would be about 71 percent.

The Federal government also reimburses States for 100 percent of the cost of services provided to American Indians and Alaskan natives through facilities of the Indian Health Service, for 100 percent of the cost of the Qualifying Individuals (QI) program (described later), and for 90 percent of the cost of family planning services, and shares in each State's expenditures for the administration of the Medicaid program. Most administrative costs are matched at 50 percent, although higher percentages are paid for certain activities and functions, such as development of mechanized claims processing systems.

Except for the CHIP program, the QI program, DSH payments, and payments to Territories, Federal payments to States for medical assistance have no set limit (cap). Rather, the Federal government matches (at FMAP rates) State expenditures for the mandatory services, as well as for the optional services that the individual State decides to cover for eligible beneficiaries, and matches (at the appropriate administrative rate) all necessary and proper administrative costs.

Medicaid Summary and Trends

Medicaid was initially formulated as a medical care extension of federally funded programs providing cash income assistance for the poor, with an emphasis on dependent children and their mothers, the disabled, and the elderly. Over the years, however, Medicaid eligibility has been incrementally expanded beyond its original ties with eligibility for cash programs. Legislation in the late 1980s extended Medicaid coverage to a larger number of low-income pregnant women and poor children and to some Medicare beneficiaries who are not eligible for any cash assistance program. Legislative changes also focused on increased access, better quality of care, specific benefits, enhanced outreach programs, and fewer limits on services.

In most years since its inception, Medicaid has had very rapid growth in expenditures. This rapid growth has been due primarily to the following factors:

- The increase in size of the Medicaid-covered populations as a result of Federal mandates, increased State coverage of optional groups, general population growth, and economic recessions.
- The expansion of coverage and utilization of services.
- The DSH payment program, coupled with its inappropriate use to increase Federal payments to States.
- The increase in the number of very old and disabled persons requiring extensive acute and/or long-term health care and various related services.
- The results of technological advances to keep a greater number of very-low-birth-weight babies and other critically ill or severely injured persons alive and in need of continued extensive and very costly care.
- The increase in drug costs and the availability of new expensive drugs.
- The increase in payment rates to providers of health care services, when compared to general inflation.
- The impact of Medicaid eligibility expansion and enhanced Federal matching under the Affordable Care Act.

As with all health insurance programs, most Medicaid beneficiaries incur relatively small average expenditures per person each year, and a relatively small proportion incurs very large costs. Moreover, the average cost varies substantially by type of beneficiary. Estimates for 2017, for example, show that Medicaid payments for services for 28.2 million children, who constituted 39.8 percent of all Medicaid beneficiaries, averaged $3,917 per child; for 27.7 million non-disabled non-aged adults, who represented 39.1 percent of beneficiaries, payments averaged $5,858 per person. Of these adults, 12.2 million were newly eligible under the Medicaid expansion, with average per enrollee costs of $6,152. Still, other groups had much larger per-person expenditures. Medicaid payments for services for 5.8 million aged, who constituted 8.2 percent of all Medicaid beneficiaries, averaged $15,703 per person; for 10.6 million disabled, who represented 15 percent of beneficiaries, payments averaged $20,999 per person. When expenditures for these high- and lower-cost beneficiaries are combined, the 2017 payments to health care vendors for 72.3 million Medicaid beneficiaries averaged $8,119 per person.

Long-term care is an important provision of Medicaid that will be increasingly utilized as our nation's population ages. According to the most recent projections (2017–2026) from the national health expenditure accounts, the Medicaid program paid $43.3 billion for nursing facility services, or over 25 percent of the national cost of nursing facility care, in 2017. Similarly, Medicaid paid $55.2 billion for home health agency services, or over 56 percent of the national cost of home health care, in 2017. With the percentage of our population who are elderly or disabled increasing faster than that of the younger groups, the need for long-term care is expected to increase.

Another significant development in Medicaid is the growth in managed care as an alternative service delivery concept different from the traditional fee-for-service system. Under managed care systems, HMOs, prepaid health plans (PHPs), or comparable entities agree to provide a specific set of services to Medicaid enrollees, usually in return for a predetermined periodic payment per enrollee. Managed care programs seek to enhance access to quality care in a cost-effective manner. Waivers may provide the States with greater flexibility in the design and implementation of their Medicaid managed care programs. Waiver authority under Sections 1915(b) and 1115 of the Social Security Act is an important part of the Medicaid program. Section 1915(b) waivers allow States to develop innovative health care delivery or reimbursement systems. Section 1115 waivers allow statewide health care reform experimental demonstrations to cover uninsured populations and to test new delivery systems without increasing costs. Finally, the BBA provided States a new option to use managed care without a waiver. According to expenditure data reported by the States to the Centers for Medicare & Medicaid Services (CMS), managed care and capitated payments to providers constituted 49.6 percent of total Medicaid expenditures in 2017.

In FY 2017, net outlays for the Medicaid program (Federal and State) were an estimated $584.9 billion, including direct payment to providers of $266.1 billion, payments for various premiums (for HMOs, Medicare, etc.) of $272.8 billion, payments to disproportionate share hospitals of $19.7 billion, and administrative costs of $26.3 billion. In addition, there were $4.4 billion in expenditures for the Vaccines for Children Program under Title XIX. With no other changes to the Medicaid program except for those already prescribed by current law, total Medicaid outlays are projected to reach $814.7 billion by FY 2023.

Expenditures under the CHIP program in FY 2017 were $17.5 billion. CHIP is funded by appropriations through FY 2027.

Reference

Kaiser Family Foundation. 2019. "Federal and State Share of Medicaid Spending." Accessed November 1. www.kff.org/medicaid/state-indicator/federalstate-share-of-spending.

Source: Adapted from B. S. Klees, E. T. Eckstein II, and C. A. Cursis. 2018. "Brief Summaries of Medicare & Medicaid Title XVIII and Title XIX of the Social Security Act." Centers for Medicare & Medicaid Services. Published October 15. www.cms.gov/Research-Statistics-Data-and-Systems/Statistics-Trends-and-Reports/MedicareProgramRatesStats/Downloads/MedicareMedicaidSummaries2018.pdf.

APPENDIX

1.3

SUMMARIES OF SELECTED FEDERAL LEGISLATION BY CATEGORY

Material for the summaries of the legislation in this appendix was taken from the US Congress website (www.congress.gov) and adapted for brevity.

A. Food and Drug Supply Legislation

1902

P.L. 57-244, *Biologics Control Act:* First federal law regulating interstate and foreign sale of biologics (viruses, serums, toxins, analogous products); established a national board and gave it authority to establish regulations for licensing producers of biologics.

1906

P.L. 59-384, *Pure Food and Drug Act* (also known as the Wiley Act): Defined adulterated and mislabeled foods and drugs and prohibited their transport in interstate commerce. Created the Food and Drug Administration (FDA).

1938

P.L. 75-717, *Food, Drug, and Cosmetic Act (FDCA):* Extended federal authority to ban new drugs from the market until they were approved by the FDA; gave the federal government more extensive power in dealing with adulterated or mislabeled food, drugs, and cosmetic products.

1958

P.L. 85-929, *Food Additive Amendment:* Amended the FDCA, stating that "no additive shall be deemed to be safe if it is found to induce cancer when ingested by man or animal."

1970

P.L. 91-601, *Poison Prevention Packaging Act:* Required that most drugs be dispensed in containers designed to be difficult for children to open.

1976

P.L. 94-295, *Medical Devices Amendments:* Amended the FDCA to strengthen regulation of medical devices. (Enacted amid growing public concern with the adverse effects of such medical devices as the Dalkon Shield intrauterine device).

P.L. 94-469, *Toxic Substances Control Act (TSCA):* Regulated chemical substances used in various production processes; defined chemical substances broadly. Intended to identify potentially harmful chemical substances before they were produced and entered the marketplace and, subsequently, the environment.

1984

P.L. 98-417, *Drug Price Competition and Patent Term Restoration Act:* Provided brand-name pharmaceutical manufacturers with patent term extensions; significantly increased manufacturers' opportunities for earning profits during the longer effective patent life.

1990

P.L. 101-629, *Safe Medical Devices Act:* Further amended the FDCA and the subsequent Medical Devices Amendments of 1976 requiring institutions that use medical devices to report device-related problems (death, illness, serious injury) to the manufacturers or to FDA.

1997

P.L. 105-115, *Food and Drug Administration Modernization and Accountability Act:* Directed the secretary of the Department of Health and Human Services (HHS) to fast-track certain products and to facilitate development and expedite review; also mandated development of guidance on the inclusion of women and minorities in clinical trials. Numerous other provisions.

2002

P.L. 107-250, *Medical Device User Fee and Modernization Act:* Amended the FDCA to impose on each medical device manufacturer a medical device fee for certain applications, reports, application supplements, and submissions sent to the FDA for evaluation.

2003

P.L. 108-155, *Pediatric Research Equity Act:* Amended the FDCA to require license applications for new drugs and biological products to assess such drugs' or products' safety and effectiveness, including dosage, for relevant pediatric subpopulations.

2007

P.L. 110-85, *Food and Drug Administration Amendments Act of 2007:* Amended the FDCA to revise and extend the user-fee programs for prescription drugs and for medical devices including postmarket safety activities.

2009

P.L. 111-31, *Family Smoking Prevention and Tobacco Control Act:* Amended the FDCA to provide for the regulation of tobacco products by the secretary of the HHS through the FDA.

2010

P.L. 111-353, *FDA Food Safety Modernization Act:* Amended the FDCA to expand the food safety activities of the HHS, including authorizing the inspection of records related to food.

2011

P.L. 112-144, *Food and Drug Administration Safety and Innovation Act:* Amended the FDCA to reauthorize and establish new FDA prescription drug user–fee programs and to revise and impose new requirements relating to (1) prescription, pediatric, and generic drugs; (2) medical devices; (3) biosimilar biological products; (4) new infectious disease drugs; and (5) drug manufacturer reporting.

2016

P.L. 114-255, *21st Century Cures Act:* Major legislative undertaking that included three significant, independent acts that affected a wide variety of areas, not just food and drug supply legislation. They were presented in divisions.

- *Division A:* Included funding for biomedical research, opioid crisis response, and support of new FDA (and National Institutes of Health [NIH]) initiatives; provided pathways for accelerated drug and device approval; streamlined the approval process for patented pharmaceuticals, rare disease drugs, antimicrobials, and vaccine development (Sarata 2016).
- *Division B* is discussed in the section titled Behavioral and Developmental Health.
- *Division C* is discussed in Access to Care.

B. Disease Research and Protection Legislation

1936

P.L. 74-846, *Walsh-Healy Act:* Authorized federal regulation of industrial safety in companies doing business with the US government.

1937

P.L. 75-244, *National Cancer Institute Act:* Established first categorical institute in the NIH (1930) to serve as administrative home for the research conducted by the US Public Health Service.

1944

P.L. 78-410, *Public Health Service Act (PHSA):* Revised and consolidated in one place all existing legislation pertaining to the US Public Health Service; provided for organization, staffing, and functions and activities of the Public Health Service; subsequently amended as a legislative foundation for a number of important federal grant-in-aid programs.

1948

P.L. 80-655, *National Health Act:* Pluralized NIH by establishing a second categorical institute, the National Heart Institute. Hereafter, NIH became the National Institutes of Health.

1956

P.L. 84-652, *National Health Survey Act:* Provided for the first system of regularly collected health-related data by the Public Health Service. Called the Health Interview Survey, it provides a national US household interview study of illness, disability, and health services utilization.

P.L. 89-92, *Federal Cigarette Labeling and Advertising Act:* Required that all cigarette packages sold in the United States bear the label "Caution: Cigarette Smoking May Be Hazardous to Your Health."

1966

P.L. 89-642, *Child Nutrition Act:* Established a federal program of support, including research, for child nutrition; a key component authorized the school breakfast program.

1967

P.L. 90-174, *Clinical Laboratory Improvement Act:* Amended the PHSA to provide regulation of laboratories in interstate commerce by the Center for Disease Control (CDC) through processes of licensure, standards setting, and proficiency testing.

1970

P.L. 91-464, *Communicable Disease Control Amendments:* Amended the PHSA by renaming the CDC the Centers for Disease Control *and Prevention*; broadened the CDC's functions beyond its traditional focus on communicable or infectious diseases to include other preventable conditions, including malnutrition.

P.L. 91-596, *Occupational Safety and Health Act:* Established an extensive federal program of standard setting and enforcement activities that were intended to ensure healthful and safe workplaces.

1974

P.L. 93-247, *Child Abuse Prevention and Treatment Act:* Created the National Center on Child Abuse and Neglect; authorized grants for research and demonstrations related to child abuse and neglect.

P.L. 93-296, *Research in Aging Act:* Established the National Institute on Aging in the NIH.

P.L. 93-270, *Sudden Infant Death Syndrome Act:* Provided for the development of informational programs related to this syndrome for both public and professional audiences.

1976

P.L. 94-317, *National Consumer Health Information and Health Promotion Act:* Amended the PHSA to add Title XVII, Health Information and Promotion; authorized grants and contracts for research and community programs related to health information, health promotion, preventive health services, and education of the public in the appropriate use of healthcare services.

1993

P.L. 103-43, *National Institutes of Health Revitalization Act:* Contained provisions for a number of structural and budgetary changes in the operation of NIH; established guidelines for the conduct of research on transplantation of human fetal tissue.

2000

P.L. 106-525, *Minority Health and Health Disparities Research and Education Act:* Amended the PHSA to establish in the NIH the National Center on Minority and Health Disparities to conduct and support research, training, dissemination of information, and other programs with respect to minority health conditions and other populations with health disparities.

P.L. 106-580, *National Institute of Biomedical Imaging and Bioengineering Establishment Act:* Amends the PHSA to provide for the establishment of the National Institute of Biomedical Imaging and Bioengineering.

2001

P.L. 107-9, *Animal Disease Risk Assessment, Prevention, and Control Act:* Directs the secretary of Agriculture to submit a preliminary report to Congress concerning (1) interagency measures to assess, prevent, and control the spread of foot and mouth disease and bovine spongiform encephalopathy ("mad cow disease") in the United States; (2) related federal information sources available to the public; and (3) the need for any additional legislative authority or product bans.

2002

P.L. 107-280, *Rare Diseases Act:* Amended the PHSA to (1) establish the Office of Rare Diseases at the NIH and (2) provide for rare disease regional centers of excellence; defines *rare disease* as any disease or condition affecting fewer than 200,000 persons in the United States.

2003

P.L. 108-276, *Project BioShield Act:* Amended the PHSA to provide protections and countermeasures against chemical, radiological, or nuclear agents that may be used in a terrorist attack against the United States by giving the NIH contracting flexibility to make infrastructure improvements and expedite the scientific peer review process and by streamlining the FDA approval process of countermeasures. This was enacted as a response to the terrorist attacks of September 11, 2001, on the New York World Trade Center and the Pentagon.

2008

P.L. 110-354, *Breast Cancer and Environmental Research Act of 2008:* Amended the PHSA to require HHS to establish the Interagency Breast Cancer and Environmental Research Coordinating Committee to (1) coordinate information on existing research, (2) develop a comprehensive strategy and advise the NIH, (3) develop a summary of advances in federal breast cancer research, and (4) make recommendations regarding changes to research activities.

2010

P.L. 111-264, *Stem Cell Therapeutic and Research Reauthorization Act of 2010:* Amends the Stem Cell Therapeutic and Research Act of 2005 to revise provisions related to the National Cord Blood Inventory, including to establish an inventory goal of at least 150,000 new units of cord blood to be made available.

2013

P.L. 113-55, *Prematurity Research Expansion and Education for Mothers Who Deliver Infants Early Reauthorization Act* (or the PREEMIE Reauthorization Act): Amends PREEMIE Act to revise and reauthorize requirements for research on prematurity and preterm births.

C. System Infrastructure and Training Health Professionals Legislation

1921

P.L. 67-97, *Maternity and Infancy Act* (also known as the Sheppard-Towner Act): Provided grants to states to help develop health services for mothers and their children. The law was allowed to lapse in 1929, although it has served as a prototype for federal grants-in-aid to the states.

1941

P.L. 77-146, *Nurse Training Act:* Provided schools of nursing with support to permit them to increase enrollments and improve their physical facilities.

1946

P.L. 79-725, *Hospital Survey and Construction Act* (also known as the Hill-Burton Act): "An Act to amend the Public Health Service to authorize grants to the States for surveying their hospital and public health centers and for planning construction of additional facilities, and to authorize grants to assist in such construction."

1954

P.L. 83-482, *Medical Facilities Survey and Construction Act:* Amended Hill-Burton to expand the program's scope greatly; authorized grants for surveys and construction of diagnostic and treatment centers (including hospital outpatient departments), chronic disease hospitals, rehabilitation facilities, and nursing homes.

1956

P.L. 84-911, *Health Amendments Act:* Amended the PHSA by initiating federal assistance for the education and training of health personnel.

1958

P.L. 85-544, *Grants-in-Aid to Schools of Public Health Act:* Established formulaic grants to the nation's schools of public health.

1963

P.L. 88-129, *Health Professions Educational Assistance Act:* Inaugurated construction grants for teaching facilities that trained physicians, dentists, pharmacists, podiatrists, nurses, or professional public health personnel; also provided for student loans and scholarships.

1964

P.L. 88-443, *Hospital and Medical Facilities Amendments:* Amended the Hill-Burton Act to specifically earmark grants for modernizing or replacing existing hospitals.

P.L. 88-581, *Nurse Training Act:* Added a new title, Title VIII, to the PHSA; authorized separate funding for construction grants to schools of nursing, including associate degree and diploma schools.

1965

P.L. 89-290, *Health Professions Educational Assistance Amendments:* Amended the original act to provide further support to "improve the quality of schools of medicine, dentistry, osteopathy, optometry, and podiatry"; expanded the availability of student loans and introduced loan forgiveness for practicing in an underserved area.

1966

P.L. 89-749, *Comprehensive Health Planning Act* (also known as the Partnership for Health Act): Amended the PHSA to "promote and assist in the extension and improvement of comprehensive health planning and public health services, [and] to provide for a more effective use of available Federal funds for such planning and services."

P.L. 89-751, *Allied Health Professions Personnel Training Act:* Provided grant support for the training of allied health professionals; patterned after the 1963 Health Professions Educational Assistance Act (see P.L. 88-129).

1968

P.L. 90-490, *Health Manpower Act:* Extended previous programs of support, authorizing formula institutional grants for training all health professionals.

1970

P.L. 91-296, *Medical Facilities Construction and Modernization Amendments:* Amended the Hill-Burton Act by extending the program and by initiating a new program of project grants for emergency rooms, communications networks, and medical transportation systems.

P.L. 91-623, *Emergency Health Personnel Act:* Amended the PHSA to permit HHS (formerly the Department of Health, Education, and Welfare) to assign commissioned officers and other health personnel of the US Public Health Service to areas of the country experiencing critical shortages of health personnel; established the National Health Service Corps (NHSC).

1971

P.L. 92-157, *Comprehensive Health Manpower Training Act:* Replaced institutional formula grants with a new system of capitation grants through which health professions schools received fixed sums of money for each student; loan provisions were broadened to cancel up to 85 percent of education loans for professionals who practiced in designated personnel shortage areas.

1972

P.L. 92-426, *Uniformed Services Health Professions Revitalization Act:* Established the Uniformed Services University of the Health Sciences; provided this educational institution to be operated under the auspices of the US Department of Defense in Bethesda, Maryland. The legislation also created the Armed Forces Health Professions Scholarship Program.

1973

P.L. 92-222, *Health Maintenance Organization Act:* Amended the PHSA to provide assistance and encouragement for the establishment and expansion of health maintenance organizations.

1974

P.L. 93-641, *National Health Planning and Resources Development Act:* Amended the PHSA in an attempt to ensure "the development of a national health policy and of effective state and area health planning and resource development programs, and for other purposes."

1976

P.L. 94-484, *Health Professions Educational Assistance Act:* Extended the program of capitation grants to professional schools that had been established under the Comprehensive Health Manpower Training Act.

1978

P.L. 95-559, *Health Maintenance Organization Amendments:* Further amended the Health Maintenance Organization Act to add a new program of loans and loan guarantees to support the acquisition of ambulatory care facilities and related equipment; also provided support for training for health maintenance organization (HMO) administrators and medical directors and for providing technical assistance to HMOs in their developmental efforts.

1979

P.L. 96-79, *Health Planning and Resources Development Amendments:* Amended the National Health Planning and Resources Development to add provisions intended to foster competition in the health sector, address the need to integrate mental health and alcoholism and drug abuse resources into health system plans, and make several revisions to certificate-of-need requirements.

1987

P.L. 100-177, *National Health Service Corps Amendments:* Reauthorized the NHSC, which had been created under a provision of the Emergency Health Personnel Act of 1970.

2001

P.L. 107-205, *Nurse Reinvestment Act:* Amended the PHSA to promote the nursing profession through public service announcements and to make grants to support state and local advertising campaigns; expanded eligibility for nursing loan repayment program; included contracts or grants to schools or healthcare facilities to expand nursing opportunities.

2006

P.L. 109-307, *Children's Hospital GME Support Reauthorization Act of 2006:* Amended the PHSA to (1) require HHS to make payments for FY (fiscal year) 2007–11 to children's hospitals for expenses associated with operating approved graduate medical residency training programs and (2) decrease from 26 to 12 the number of interim payments to hospitals per FY.

2007

P.L. 110-23, *Trauma Care Systems Planning and Development Act of 2007:* Amended the PHSA to (1) collect, compile, and disseminate information on achievements and problems in providing trauma care and emergency medical services and (2) promote the collection and categorization of trauma data in a consistent and standardized manner; enhanced development of trauma care systems, including telemedicine.

2009

P.L. 111-5, *American Recovery and Reinvestment Act of 2009:* Enacted in response to the global financial crisis that emerged in 2008, this massive economic stimulus package ($787 billion) directed about $150 billion in new funds to healthcare; included the HITECH Act, which established incentives for providers demonstrating "meaningful use" of electronic health records.

2016

P.L. 114-255, *21st Century Cures Act:* Major, wide-ranging legislative undertaking that included three significant, independent acts. They were presented in divisions.

- *Division A:* Included provisions that together addressed the federal policies to promote the adoption and use of electronic health record (EHR) technology (Sarata 2016). Division A also appears in the section titled Food and Drug Safety.
- *Division B:* See section titled Behavioral and Developmental Health.
- *Division C:* Discussed in the section titled Access to Care.

D. Developmental and Behavioral Health Legislation

1946

P.L. 79-487, *National Mental Health Act:* Authorized extensive federal support for mental health research and treatment programs and established grants-in-aid to the states for their mental health activities; transformed the Public Health Service's Division of Mental Health into the National Institute of Mental Health.

1963

P.L. 88-156, *Maternal and Child Health and Mental Retardation Planning Amendments:* Amended the Social Security Act (SSA) to "assist states and communities in preventing and combating mental retardation through expansion and improvement of the maternal and child health and crippled children's programs, through provision of prenatal, maternity, and infant care for individuals with conditions associated with childbearing that may lead to mental retardation, and through planning for comprehensive action to combat mental retardation."

P.L. 88-164, *Mental Retardation Facilities and Community Mental Health Centers Construction Act:* Provided "assistance in combating mental retardation through grants for construction of research centers and grants for facilities for the mentally retarded and assistance in improving mental health through grants for construction of community mental health centers, and for other purposes."

1967

P.L. 90-31, *Mental Health Amendments:* Amended the Mental Retardation Facilities and Community Mental Health Centers Construction Act to extend the program of construction grants for community mental health centers; also amended the term *construction* to cover acquisition of existing buildings.

P.L. 90-170, *Mental Retardation Amendments:* Amended the Mental Retardation Facilities and Community Mental Health Centers Construction Act to extend the program of construction grants and for university-affiliated and community-based facilities for individuals with mental retardation and for training educators working with this population.

1980

P.L. 96-398, *Mental Health Systems Act:* Extensively amended the Community Mental Health Centers program by including provisions for the development and support of comprehensive state mental health systems.

1996

P.L. 104-204, *Mental Health Parity Act of 1996:* Prohibited large employer-sponsored group health plans from imposing higher annual or lifetime dollar limits on mental health benefits than those applicable to medical or surgical benefits; applied to self-insured health plans and to purchased insurance plans, and only those that offered mental health benefits.

2002

P.L. 107-313, *Mental Health Parity Reauthorization Act:* Amended the Employee Retirement Income Security Act of 1974 (ERISA) and the PHSA to extend the mental health benefits parity provisions through 2003.

2008

P.L. 110-343, *Mental Health Parity and Addiction Equity Act of 2008:* Expanded coverage previously mandated under the Mental Health Parity Act of 1996 by extending the parity requirements to substance use disorders; ensures financial equivalence of deductibles and copayments for mental health and substance use disorders (MH/SUD) benefits to medical/surgical benefits; prohibits separate cost-sharing requirements for MH/SUD benefits; extends out-of-network parity to MH/SUD benefits.

2016

P.L. 114-255, *21st Century Cures Act:* Major, wide-ranging legislative undertaking that included three significant, independent acts. They were presented in divisions.

- *Division A:* See sections titled Food and Drug Safety and System Infrastructure and Training Health Professionals.
- *Division B:* Reorganized the structure of the HHS's Substance Abuse and Mental Health Services Administration (SAMHSA); created new planning and evaluation requirements; increased oversight of the agency's programming; codified the National Registry of Evidence-based Programs and Practice.
- *Division C:* See Access to Care.

2018

P.L. 115-271, *Substance Abuse-Disorder Prevention that Promotes Opioid Recovery and Treatment for Patients and Communities Act (SUPPORT for Patients and Communities Act):* Provided support in Medicaid and Medicare programs to identify at-risk individuals and facilitate their treatment; funded educational programs for mothers; strengthened regulation of controlled substances.

E. Environmental Health and Pollution Legislation

1948

P.L. 80-845, *Water Pollution Control Act:* Enacted in part "in consequence of the benefits to the public health and welfare by the abatement of stream pollution." The act left the primary responsibility for water pollution control with the states.

1955

P.L. 84-159, *Air Pollution Control Act:* Provided for research and technical assistance related to air pollution control. The law was enacted in part "in recognition of the dangers to the public health and welfare . . . from air pollution."

1956

P.L. 84-660, *Water Pollution Control Act Amendments of 1956:* Amended the Water Pollution Control Act and provided for federal technical services and financial aid to the states and to municipalities in their efforts to prevent and control water pollution.

1963

P.L. 88-206, *Clean Air Act:* Authorized direct grants to states and local governments to assist in their air pollution control efforts; established federal enforcement of interstate air pollution restrictions.

1965

P.L. 89-272, *Clean Air Act Amendments:* Amended the original Clean Air Act to provide for federal regulation of motor vehicle exhaust and to establish a program of federal research support and grants-in-aid in the area of solid waste disposal.

1967

P.L. 90-148, *Air Quality Act:* Amended the Clean Air Act to "authorize planning grants to air pollution control agencies; expand research provisions relating to fuels and vehicles; provide for interstate air pollution control agencies or commissions; authorize the establishment of air quality standards; and for other purposes."

1969

P.L. 91-190, *National Environmental Policy Act:* Enacted to "declare a national policy which will encourage productive and enjoyable harmony between man and his environment; to promote efforts which will prevent or eliminate damage to the environment and biosphere and stimulate the health and welfare of man."

1970

P.L. 91-604, *Clean Air Amendments:* Enacted because Congress became dissatisfied with progress toward control and abatement of air pollution under the Air Quality Act of 1967; took away the power of the states to establish different air quality standards in different air quality control regions.

1972

P.L. 92-574, *Noise Control Act:* Continued government's efforts to rid the environment of harmful influences on human health.

1974

P.L. 93-523, *Safe Drinking Water Act:* Required the Environmental Protection Agency (EPA) to establish national drinking water standards and to aid states and localities in the enforcement of these standards.

1980

P.L. 96-510, *Comprehensive Environmental Response, Compensation and Liability Act:* Established the Superfund program intended to provide resources for the cleanup of inactive hazardous waste dumps.

P.L. 111-380, *Reduction of Lead in Drinking Water Act:* Amended the Safe Drinking Water Act to permit the use or sale of lead pipes, solder, and plumbing fittings or fixtures, including backflow preventers, used exclusively for nonpotable services such as manufacturing, industrial processing, irrigation, outdoor watering, or any other uses for which the water is not anticipated to be used for human consumption.

2015

P.L. 114-45 *Amendments to the Safe Water Drinking Act:* Required the EPA to evaluate risk of, understand the adverse effects of, and plan for algae toxins in the water supply; determined the circumstances under which there would be a need for a health advisory.

P.L. 114-182, *The Frank R. Lautenberg Chemical Safety for the 21st Century Act:* Revised process and requirements for evaluating and determining whether regulatory control of a chemical is warranted.

F. Access to Care Legislation

1920

P.L. 66-141, *Snyder Act:* First federal legislation pertaining to healthcare for Native Americans; provided for general assistance, directing "the Bureau of Indian Affairs . . . to direct, supervise, and expend such monies as Congress may from time to time appropriate, for the benefit, care, and assistance of the Indians throughout the United States."

1938

P.L. 75-540, *LaFollette-Bulwinkle Act:* Provided grants-in-aid to the states to support their investigation and control of venereal disease.

1955

P.L. 84-377, *Polio Vaccination Assistance Act:* Provided for federal assistance to states for the operation of their polio vaccination programs.

1956

P.L. 84-569, *Dependents Medical Care Act:* Established the Civilian Health and Medical Program of the Uniformed Services for the dependents of military personnel.

1959

P.L. 86-121, *Indian Sanitation Facilities Act:* Provided for the surgeon general to "construct, improve, extend, or otherwise provide and maintain, by contract or otherwise, essential sanitation facilities for Indian homes, communities, and lands."

P.L. 86-352, *Federal Employees Health Benefits Act:* Permitted Blue Cross to negotiate a contract with the Civil Service Commission to provide health insurance coverage for federal employees.

The contract served as a prototype for Blue Cross's subsequent involvement in the Medicare and Medicaid programs as a fiscal intermediary.

1960

P.L. 86-778, *Social Security Amendments* (also known as the Kerr-Mills Act): Amended the SSA to provide aid to the states for payments for medical care for "medically indigent" persons who were 65 years of age or older.

1962

P.L. 87-692, *Health Services for Agricultural Migratory Workers Act:* Authorized federal grants to clinics serving migrant farmworkers and their families.

1965

P.L. 89-4, *Appalachian Redevelopment Act:* Promoted the economic, physical, and social development of the Appalachian region; facilitated steps to achieve this purpose, including the establishment of community health centers and training programs for health personnel.

P.L. 89-73, *Older Americans Act:* Established an Administration on Aging to administer programs for elderly individuals through state agencies on aging.

P.L. 89-97, *Medicare* and *Medicaid:* The Social Security Amendments, a landmark in the nation's health policy, established two new titles to the SSA: (1) Title XVIII, Health Insurance for the Aged, or Medicare, and (2) Title XIX, Grants to the States for Medical Assistance Programs, or Medicaid. In addition to establishing Titles XVIII and XIX, the SSA Amendments of 1965 also amended Title V to authorize grant funds for maternal and child health and services for children with disabilities and also authorized grants for training professional personnel for the care of children with disabilities.

1972

P.L. 92-603, *Social Security Amendments:* Established professional standards review organizations (PSROs) to monitor both the quality of services provided to Medicare beneficiaries and the medical necessity for the services; limited payments for capital expenditures by hospitals that had been disapproved by state or local planning agencies.

P.L. 92-303, *Federal Coal Mine Health and Safety Amendments:* Amended the earlier Federal Coal Mine Health and Safety Act to provide financial benefits and other assistance to coal miners who were afflicted with black lung disease.

1976

P.L. 94-437, *Indian Health Care Improvement Act:* Extensive piece of legislation intended to fill existing gaps in the delivery of healthcare services to Native Americans.

1977

P.L. 95-142, *Medicare-Medicaid Antifraud and Abuse Amendments:* Amended Medicare and Medicaid programs to reduce fraud and abuse in the programs to help contain their costs; specific changes included strengthening criminal and civil penalties for fraud and abuse affecting the programs.

P.L. 95-210, *Rural Health Clinic Services Amendments:* Amended Medicare and Medicaid programs to modify the categories of practitioners who could provide reimbursable services to Medicare and Medicaid beneficiaries, at least in rural settings.

1978

P.L. 95-292, *Medicare End-Stage Renal Disease Amendments:* Amended the Medicare program in an attempt to help control costs resulting from end-stage renal disease.

1980

P.L. 96-499, *Omnibus Budget Reconciliation Act (OBRA '80):* Contained in Title IX of the Medicare and Medicaid Amendments of 1980; made extensive modifications in the Medicare and Medicaid programs to address concerns with costs.

1981

P.L. 97-35, *Omnibus Budget Reconciliation Act (OBRA '81):* Amended Medicare and Medicaid programs; included extensive changes intended to reduce the federal budget.

1982

P.L. 97-248, *Tax Equity and Fiscal Responsibility Act (TEFRA):* Made a number of important policy changes in the Medicare program; added coverage for hospice services; set limits on hospital reimbursement on a per-case basis; limited the annual rate of increase for Medicare's reasonable costs per discharge. Another provision of TEFRA replaced PSROs.

P.L. 97-414, *Orphan Drug Act:* Provided financial incentives for the development and marketing of orphan drugs, defined by the legislation to be drugs for the treatment of diseases or conditions affecting so few people that revenues from sales of the drugs would not cover their development costs.

1983

P.L. 98-21, *Social Security Amendments:* Amended Medicare program to initiate prospective payment system (PPS); included provisions to pay hospitals predetermined rates per discharge for diagnosis-related groups (DRGs). PPS was a major departure from the cost-based system of reimbursement that had been used since Medicare's inception in 1965.

1984

P.L. 98-369, *Deficit Reduction Act:* Temporarily froze increases in physicians' fees paid under the Medicare program; placed a specific limitation on the rate of increase in the DRG payment rates.

1985

P.L. 99-177, *Emergency Deficit Reduction and Balanced Budget Act* (also known as the Gramm-Rudman-Hollings Act): Established mandatory deficit reduction targets for the five subsequent fiscal years and had significant impact on the Medicare program throughout the last half of the 1980s, as well as on other health programs and the NIH.

P.L. 99-272, *Consolidated Omnibus Budget Reconciliation Act (COBRA '85):* Contained a number of provisions that affected Medicare. Hospitals that served a disproportionate share of poor patients received an adjustment in their PPS payments; hospice care was made a permanent part of the Medicare program, and states were given the ability to provide hospice services under the

Medicaid program; the Physician Payment Review Commission was established to advise Congress on physician payment policies for the Medicare program.

Another important COBRA provision required employers to continue health insurance for employees and their dependents who would otherwise lose their eligibility for the coverage because of reduced hours of work or termination of their employment.

1986

P.L. 99-509, *Omnibus Budget Reconciliation Act (OBRA '86):* Altered the PPS payment rate for hospitals again and reduced payment amounts for capital-related costs by 3.5 percent for part of FY1987, by 7 percent for FY1988, and by 10 percent for FY1989.

P.L. 99-660, *Omnibus Health Act:* Significantly liberalized coverage under the Medicaid program, using family income up to the federal poverty line as a criterion; permitted states to offer coverage to all pregnant women and to infants up to one year of age; created the National Childhood Vaccine Injury Act, which established a federal vaccine injury compensation system.

1987

P.L. 100-203, *Omnibus Budget Reconciliation Act (OBRA '87):* Contained a number of provisions that directly affected Medicare; required HHS to update the wage index used in calculating hospital PPS payments and to do so at least every three years.

1988

P.L. 100-360, *Medicare Catastrophic Coverage Act:* Provided largest expansion of benefits covered by Medicare since its establishment in 1965; added coverage for outpatient prescription drugs and respite care; placed a cap on out-of-pocket spending by elderly individuals for copayment costs.

1990

P.L. 101-336, *Americans with Disabilities Act:* Provided a broad range of protections for people with disabilities, combining protections contained in the Civil Rights Act of 1964, the Rehabilitation Act of 1973, and the Civil Rights Restoration Act of 1988.

P.L. 101-381, *Ryan White Comprehensive AIDS Resources Emergency Act:* Provided resources to 16 epicenters, including San Francisco and New York City, and to states hardest hit by acquired immunodeficiency syndrome (AIDS) to assist them with the skyrocketing cost of care.

P.L. 101-508, *Omnibus Budget Reconciliation Act (OBRA '90):* Contained the Patient Self-Determination Act, which required healthcare institutions participating in Medicare and Medicaid to provide all patients with written information on policies regarding self-determination and living wills; institutions were also required to inquire and document whether patients had advance medical directives.

1993

P.L. 103-66, *Omnibus Budget Reconciliation Act (OBRA '93):* Established five-year cut in Medicare funding; included provisions to end return-on-equity payments for capital to proprietary skilled nursing facilities; reduced previously established payment rate increases for hospice care; also contained the Comprehensive Childhood Immunization Act, which provided $585 million to vaccinate children eligible for Medicaid, children with no health insurance, and Native American children.

1996

P.L. 104-191, *Health Insurance Portability and Accountability Act* (also known as the Kassebaum-Kennedy Act): Provided employees with employer-sponsored insurance guaranteed access to health insurance if they changed jobs or became unemployed; guaranteed renewability of health insurance coverage so long as premiums are paid; provided for increased tax deductions for self-employed purchase of health insurance and allowed tax deductions for medical expenses related to long-term care insurance coverage; limited distribution of "patient-specific information."

P.L. 104-193, *Personal Responsibility and Work Opportunity Reconciliation Act* (also known as the Welfare Reform Act): Significantly changed nation's welfare policy, with implications for social and economic environments faced by affected people; changed eligibility for Medicaid by decoupling eligibility for Medicaid with eligibility for Aid to Families with Dependent Children (AFDC); replaced AFDC with the Temporary Assistance to Needy Families (TANF) block grant, which gave states broad flexibility to design income support and work programs; required state imposition of federally mandated restrictions, such as time limits.

1997

P.L. 105-33, *Balanced Budget Act of 1997 (BBA):* Significant changes to Medicare; required a five-year reduction of $115 billion in expenditure growth and $13 billion reduction in Medicaid spending growth; created new "Medicare+Choice" program giving Medicare beneficiaries more plan choices; reduced hospital annual inflation updates; established cap on number of medical residents supported by Medicare graduate medical education payments; established the Children's Health Insurance Program (CHIP) and provided states with $24 billion in federal funds for 1998 until 2002 to increase health insurance coverage for children.

1999

P.L. 106-113, *Medicare, Medicaid and SCHIP Balanced Budget Refinement Act of 1999 (BBRA):* Changed provisions in the BBA of 1997 pertaining to payment mechanisms for hospitals treating a disproportionate share (DSHs) of low-income Medicare and Medicaid patients; adjusted reimbursement for graduate medical education (GME).

P.L. 106-117, *Veterans Millennium Health Care and Benefits Act:* Directed the secretary of Veterans Affairs to provide nursing home care to any veteran in need of such care through December 31, 2003, (1) for a service-connected disability or (2) who has a service-connected disability rated at 70 percent or more.

2000

P.L. 106-354, *Breast and Cervical Cancer Prevention and Treatment Act:* Amended Title XIX (Medicaid) of the SSA to give states the option of making medical assistance for breast and cervical cancer–related treatment services available during a presumptive eligibility period to certain low-income women.

P.L. 106-554, *Medicare, Medicaid, and SCHIP Benefits Improvement and Protection Act of 2000:* Changed numerous provisions previously enacted in BBA and BBRA; made a series of wide-ranging changes in payments from Medicare for inpatient and outpatient therapies, DSH, and GME.

2002

P.L. 107-251, *Health Care Safety Net Amendments of 2002:* Amended the PHSA to reauthorize and strengthen the health centers program and the NHSC; established Healthy Communities Access Program to coordinate services for the uninsured and underinsured.

2003

P.L. 108-74, *State Children's Health Insurance Program Allotments Extension:* Amends Title XXI (CHIP) of the SSA to revise the special rule for the redistribution and availability of unexpended FY1998 and FY1999 SCHIP allotments.

P.L. 108-173, *Medicare Prescription Drug, Improvement, and Modernization Act:* Created a new drug benefit as Part D of Medicare (2006); provided an interim Medicare-endorsed drug discount card for beneficiaries. Made Part B premium adjusted by income.

2005

P.L. 109-18, *Patient Navigator Outreach and Chronic Disease Prevention Act:* Amended the PHSA to authorize a demonstration grant program for patient navigator services to reduce barriers and improve healthcare outcomes.

2006

P.L. 109-415, *Ryan White HIV/AIDS Treatment Modernization Act of 2006:* Amended provisions of Title XXVI of the PHSA (popularly known as the Ryan White Care Act [RWCA]) concerning emergency relief grants for metropolitan areas to assist in delivering and enhancing HIV-related services.

P.L. 109-417, *Pandemic and All-Hazards Preparedness Act:* Amended the PHSA with respect to public health security and all-hazards preparedness and response; improved the public health, medical preparedness, and response capabilities for emergencies, whether deliberate, accidental, or natural.

2008

P.L. 110-233, *Genetic Information Nondiscrimination Act of 2008:* Amended ERISA, the PHSA, and the Internal Revenue Code to prohibit a group health plan from adjusting premium or contribution amounts for a group on the basis of genetic information.

P.L. 110-335, *Health Care Safety Net Act of 2008:* Amended the PHSA to reauthorize appropriations for FY2008–12 for health centers to meet the healthcare needs of medically underserved populations; required study of economic costs and benefits of school-based health centers and their impact on the health of students.

2009

P.L. 111-3, *Children's Health Insurance Program Reauthorization Act of 2009:* Amended Title XXI of the SSA to extend CHIP; reauthorized CHIP through 2013 and increased funding by an additional $35 billion over five years.

P.L. 111-87, *Ryan White HIV/AIDS Treatment Extension Act of 2009:* Amended provisions of Title XXVI of the PHSA to extend the RWCA and revive any expired programs retroactively to September 30, 2009.

2010

P.L. 111-148, *Patient Protection and Affordable Care Act of 2010 (ACA):* A major health reform law, culminating a century-long effort to expand health insurance coverage to nearly all Americans. It is a massive law, more fully described in appendix 1.2.

P.L. 111-152, *Health Care and Education Reconciliation Act of 2010:* Amended a number of aspects of the ACA and other laws necessary to implement the ACA; revised the formula for calculating the refundable tax credit for premium assistance for coverage for individuals and families with household incomes up to 400 percent of the federal poverty line; revises penalties to be imposed on individuals who decline to purchase healthcare coverage.

P.L. 111-309, *Medicare and Medicaid Extenders Act of 2010:* Amended Title XVIII (Medicare) of the SSA to set the 2011 update to the single conversion factor in the formula for the physicians' fee schedule at zero (thus freezing the physician payment update for 2011).

2014

P.L. 113-77, *Poison Center Network Act:* Amended the PHSA to reauthorize through FY2019 (1) a poison control nationwide toll-free phone number and (2) a national media campaign to educate the public and healthcare providers about poison prevention and the availability of poison control center resources in local communities and to conduct advertising campaigns about the nationwide toll-free number.

P.L. 113-146, *Veterans' Access to Care through Choice, Accountability, and Transparency Act:* Response to unreasonably long wait times for veterans to see physicians and other healthcare providers in Veterans Health Administration (VHA) facilities; requires hospital care and medical services for veterans through contracts with specified non-VHA facilities if the veterans (1) have been unable to schedule an appointment at a VHA medical facility within certain time-frames, and (2) opt for non-VHA care or services.

2015

P.L. 114-10, *The Medicare Access and CHIP Reauthorization* Act *(MACRA):* Ended the nearly annual Congressional practice of forestalling reductions in physician reimbursement; created alternative set of annual updates; introduced a new merit-based incentive payment system based on evaluation models. Also extended funding for CHIP and made certain increases in funding along with several technical changes and premium adjustments in several of the Medicare programs (Hahn and Blom 2015).

P.L. 114-60, *Protecting Affordable Coverage for Employees Act:* Redefined "large" employer to include employers with 51–100 employees for the purposes of the ACA; provided states the option to continue to treat this class of employers as "small." Large employers are not required to cover essential health benefits set forth in the ACA.

P.L. 114-115, *Patient Access and Medicare Protection Act:* Allowed for exemption by category of provider from some meaningful use requirements, expanding on the exemption for individual providers. Adjusts schedule of payments for certain radiation procedures.

2016

P.L. 114-145, *Ensuring Patient Access and Drug Enforcement Act of 2016:* Changed registration requirements for manufacturers, distributors, and dispensers of controlled substances; directed the Drug Enforcement Administration, Health Resources and Services Administration (HRSA), and SAMHSA to report to Congress on improving enforcement mechanisms regarding opioids while ensuring those who need them have adequate access.

P.L. 114-255, *21st Century Cures Act:* Major, wide-ranging legislative undertaking that included three significant, independent acts. They were presented in divisions.

- *Division A:* See section titled Food and Drug Safety.
- *Division B:* See section titled Behavioral and Developmental Health.
- *Division C:* Deals largely with Medicare—readmissions reduction program, inpatient payment rates, technical changes.

P.L. 114-270, *Expanding Health Outcome Act:* Requires HHS to analyze, report on, and facilitate linkages between primary care providers and specialists through videoconferencing.

2018

P.L. 115-113, *Law Enforcement Mental Health and Wellness Act of 2017:* Directed the Department of Justice to report on Department of Defense and Department of Veterans Affairs mental health practices and services that could be adopted by law enforcement agencies; streamlines reporting requirements while expanding the allowable use of grant funds under the Community Oriented Policing Services program.

P.L. 115-263, *The Patient Right to Know Drug Prices Act:* Prohibits the use of "gag clauses" by pharmaceutical companies and distributors that bar pharmacists from informing patients of lower-cost alternatives.

P.L. 115-320, *Improving Access to Maternity Care Act:* Amended PHSA to require the HRSA to identify maternity care target areas (geographical areas of shortages in maternity care health professionals) for purposes of assigning maternity care health professionals to those areas.

P.L. 115-398, *Stop, Observe, Ask, and Respond to Health and Wellness Act of 2018:* Provided statutory authority to expand the HHS program known as the Stop, Observe, Ask, and Respond to Health and Wellness Training Program; provided legal standards for training and assessment.

References

Hahn, J., and K. B. Blom. 2015. "The Medicare Access and CHIP Reauthorization Act of 2015 (MACRA; P.L. 114-10)." Congressional Research Service. Published November 10. https://fas.org/sgp/crs/misc/R43962.pdf.

Sarata, A. K. 2016. "The 21st Century CURES Act (Division A of P.L. 114-255)." Congressional Research Service. Published December 23. https://fas.org/sgp/crs/misc/R44720.pdf.

PART

2

LEGISLATIVE POLICYMAKING

Part 1 was about the context in which health policy is made. Part 2 introduces the policymaking process. From agenda setting to implementation to modification, one policy or another is always before us. There is an old saying: "Watching law being made is a bit like watching sausage being made. The outcome may be good, but the process is messy." Part 2 begins with a policy snapshot describing how two of the more colorful political actors in the twentieth century quietly collaborated to create Medicare and Medicaid. It brings to life the model that was the focus of chapter 3.

Chapter 4 puts to rest at least part of the "sausage-making" analogy by introducing a policymaking process model. The model defines the process by introducing its elements from agenda setting to implementation to modification using healthcare as a prism through which to examine these elements. Chapter 5 delves into the agenda setting, examining how problems get defined, the confluence of political circumstances, the roles played by lobbyists, and how these factors and potential solutions represent the potential opening of a window of opportunity to produce a policy result. Chapter 6 peers through that window and discusses the development of legislation, including several examples. Of course, the window facilitates multiple perspectives, leading perhaps to multiple possible solutions, which produces the (hopefully) creative tension of ideas resulting in policy solutions.

To be certain, the policy process can be, and often is, messy. The interactions of human desires, perspectives, and emotions all but dictate that it will be thus. The process does, however, have an underlying rationale supporting why policymaking in the United States is organized the way it is, and part 2 introduces the beginnings of that understanding.

POLICY SNAPSHOT

LEGISLATIVE CUNNING: THE BIRTH OF MEDICARE AND MEDICAID

The birth of Medicare and Medicaid in 1965 was a feat of legislative mastery. Before Medicare and Medicaid, the federal government had no direct involvement in healthcare other than for members of the armed services and veterans. An invisible political and policy wall had prevented federal participation in providing healthcare for individual US citizens. If one admires bold legislative achievement, overcoming that barrier was it. The enactment of Medicare was a significant attainment because it breached the wall that had existed between the federal government and the medical care system. But consistent with the process of health policymaking discussed in this text, the birth of Medicare and Medicaid also was built on some elements of health policy already in place.

There were two main actors in this legislative and political triumph. The first is the thirty-sixth president of the United States, Lyndon B. Johnson. President Johnson had been majority leader of the US Senate earlier in his career. He was elevated to the presidency upon the assassination of President John F. Kennedy, for whom Johnson was vice president. Johnson had an outsized personality and an uncanny ability to foresee others' political interests and ambitions. Those characteristics gave him a remarkable ability to bend others to his will. He knew the details of the legislative process and was unabashed about pushing it to the limit to get what he wanted. The other major player in this drama was Congressman Wilbur Mills (D-Ark.). Mills was an innately conservative man from a conservative state. Legend has it that the Harvard Law School graduate spent many evenings at home reading the tax code. Not only was he an expert in the legislative process, but he had a unique and broad understanding of the Internal Revenue Code. As chairman of the Ways and Means Committee, Mills stood as a titan in the legislative process. At the time, Congress was dominated by Democrats from Southern states. In this respect, Mills was not only in the mainstream but a leader.

When Mills and Johnson began their alliance, which would ultimately produce Medicare and Medicaid, the debate about governmental involvement in healthcare was not new. The concept went back as far as President *Theodore* Roosevelt's era in the first part of the twentieth century, as he advocated for a number of health-related initiatives during his career. President *Franklin* Roosevelt had decided against including healthcare in the original Social Security Act in 1935 because he thought it would be too controversial. When President Harry S. Truman proposed national healthcare in 1949, the proposal was blasted as "un-American" by conservative opponents.

Throughout most of the 1950s, employer-sponsored insurance grew because of (1) favorable tax treatment in the Internal Revenue Act of 1954 for companies that provided insurance, and (2) demands for better healthcare coverage from organized labor in negotiations with employers. The combination of these events had a chilling effect on the idea of national health insurance. But as some members of Congress in the second half of the decade observed, people over 65 required nearly twice the amount of hospital care than younger people. They became proponents of an idea to provide hospital care for Americans over the age of 65. That population—then and now—mostly lived on a fixed income, and many could not afford the high cost of hospitalization. Further, the liberal proponents at that time put their proposal under the Social Security Administration so they could argue they were merely expanding an existing program using the Social Security payroll tax. Thus, the concept of "Medicare" became part of the lexicon in the debate.

In 1960, responding to political pressure to provide healthcare coverage for elderly Americans and in an effort to forestall the drive for Medicare, Congress enacted the Medical Assistance for the Aged Act, a plan named for its two sponsors, Mills and Senator Robert Kerr (R-Okla.). Kerr-Mills was a fairly modest program: it provided insurance for elderly Americans who were also poor. The program's benefits were administered by the states to avoid direct federal engagement in medical services. The federal government provided modest matching funds to supplement state funding and support state management, thereby enabling the states to provide care for the indigent elderly. Indeed, the program was so very modest that some considered it ineffectual. Only 28 states adopted it and only a small fraction of the nation's elderly actually received any benefits (Fine 1998).

The larger Medicare proposal languished for several years during the late 1950s and into the early 1960s, despite the fact that President Kennedy campaigned in support of it as part of his campaign in 1960. When he proposed it, however, even with his energetic support, conservative southern Democrats in Congress led by Mills defeated it. Mills was steadfast in refusing to allow various Medicare proposals to come up for a vote in his committee. The demise of the Kennedy administration proposal was facilitated by the American Medical Association (AMA), which hyped that Medicare would come between patients and hospitals. The alliance between the AMA and Mills was strengthened by the chairman's innate fiscal conservatism. He was concerned about potential runaway costs of the program.

Even when Johnson became president in November 1963, despite his determination to pass Medicare, Mills and the conservative Democrats in Congress remained intransigent. The election of 1964, however, changed everything. The Democrats enjoyed a sweeping landslide victory that resulted in more Democrats in Congress, and those new members of Congress were more liberal—amenable to things like Medicare. So large was the new majority that the leadership changed the ratio of party membership on committees, including Ways and Means. With 295 seats in the house (of 435) and 68 (of 100) seats in the Senate, the balance of power had shifted significantly. This changed the political circumstances in which the Medicare debate would take place. Mills, ever the reader of political tea leaves, saw he would need to change his position or be left on the sidelines. He knew his own party would be able to pass Medicare without him.

Doubts as to whether Mills was really on board persisted because he had previously opposed expansive proposals. He had a long, very clear, record of opposing any form of Medicare. His previous position had been that Kerr-Mills helped states address the needs of the indigent elderly, which was sufficient. Thus, for a time, there was discussion about how to pass the Johnson administration bill over the objections of the Republican minority and even over the objection of Mills himself. The speaker of the House, Carl Albert, told the president he had the votes to simply pass the bill on a party line vote.

Fresh from the glow of that sweeping victory, President Johnson was certain this was the time for Medicare—with or without Mills. He would put the issue on the national agenda. The "with or without Mills" predicate was Johnson's public position. As it turns out, the president and Mills had been engaged in private conversation about how to pass Medicare. Out of public view, the two longtime masters of the legislative process were plotting the "what" of Medicare and how to get it passed. In 1965, the Johnson administration proposed Medicare to the Congress as a program that would provide for hospital coverage for all of the nation's elderly. It was one of the first items of business following the inaugural. Pointedly, that proposal was limited to hospital coverage. But the proposal brought several forces into play.

The AMA, fearful that Johnson's Medicare proposal would create a web of "socialized medicine," sought to temper the proponents' ardor by proposing a voluntary system of insurance that would provide coverage for physician services. The scheme would be financed through insurance premiums subsidized by appropriations from the federal government. This proposal was sponsored by a Republican congressman from Wisconsin named James Byrnes, the ranking minority member on Ways and Means. This fact was critically important. The idea of a voluntary system was attractive to the more conservative members of Congress, who wanted to prevent, or at least limit, the federal government's involvement in healthcare.

Second, some of the more liberal voices in Congress were concerned about the Johnson administration's proposal: It provided only hospital coverage, and some were afraid of a political backlash from the elderly when they realized how limited the benefits were.

The administration's proposal would displace the existing Kerr-Mills. There would be no need for a state-administered health insurance program that covered indigent elderly residents of those participating states, since hospital coverage would be provided to everyone over 65 in the Medicare proposal.

This was the foundation, in part, for the enactment of legislation creating Medicare Parts A and B and Medicaid. All of these initiatives represent elements of the Longest model described in chapter 4; they are the products of masterful legislative bargaining between Johnson and Mills. The steps taken by these two men represent agenda setting in the changed political circumstances presented by the 1964 election and a solution to the problem of providing healthcare for the nation's elderly population. It was, indeed, a window of opportunity.

As the longtime chairman of the House Ways and Means Committee, Wilbur Mills understood the legislative process as well as anyone. Likewise, President Johnson understood the ways of Congress and knew how motivate others to come to his side. The two of them made for a powerful alliance; both knowledgeable about the issue, both experts in the legislative process, and both committed to producing a major legislative win for the new Democratic majority. As history would later reveal, the two of them had prearranged much of what was to take place. Johnson was assiduous in giving credit to Mills, and the process moved ahead as Mills moved his previous position to the affirmative (Blumenthal and Marone 2010).

Various permutations of Medicare had been wafting through the halls of Congress since 1957. While Mills never allowed a vote on any of those proposals, his committee had held extensive hearings. Indeed, by the time the Ways and Means Committee concluded hearings on the Johnson administration proposal, the committee had heard from more than 640 witnesses (Blumenthal and Marone 2010). The concept was pretty well understood: as part of the Social Security Administration, the federal government would finance hospital care for the elderly using a payroll tax.

After the last hearing on the Johnson administration proposal, Mills turned to the Republican Byrnes and said he liked the voluntary approach. Supplementing the voluntary physician practice coverage with the mandatory hospitalization insurance would result in nearly comprehensive health insurance coverage. As if that was not surprising enough, Mills went on to explain that he wanted to marry the two bills and amend the existing Kerr-Mills program. Of course, such a linkage would result in massive new spending. Mills's concerns were partly assuaged by the fact that the physician portion would be paid for by premiums and general tax revenue, thereby partly dampening the prospects of costs spinning out of control. (Remember, this was 1965; Mills could not have foreseen the runaway costs we experience today.) The cost was not a concern to Johnson, who was committed to finishing the work begun by President Roosevelt's New Deal.

Conjoining the two pieces of legislation and the existing, amended Kerr-Mills program created Medicare Part A (hospitalization coverage taken from the Johnson administration bill), Medicare Part B (voluntary insurance coverage of physician services taken from the AMA/Republican bill), and Medicaid, drawing from the existing Kerr-Mills, to finance health coverage for the poor on a state-by-state basis.

Even if the plan was expensive, it was a brilliant legislative strategy. Combined into one legislative package, the federal government was committing to providing healthcare coverage for America's elderly as well as for much of the nation's indigent population. Seldom are legislative victories so dramatic or so sweeping. Importantly, the inclusion of the Byrnes bill brought a large number of Republicans on board, so the entire package passed with a substantial bipartisan majority, 313 to 115 (five not voting). The Senate passed the bill with several amendments (68–21, 11 not voting) that were dispatched subsequently by Mills in the House–Senate Conference Committee.

President Johnson now gleefully led the implementation process. He had been uncharacteristically quiet publicly during the groundbreaking Medicare debate but active behind the scenes. Now he would lead in establishing these new programs. While Medicare certainly was not universally popular, the broad bipartisan support had endowed both Medicare and Medicaid with a strong air of political legitimacy. The Republican opponents had been prevented from attacking the plan because their ideas were coopted into it, and, consequently, many of them voted for it. Opposition interest groups such as the AMA were cowed into acceptance if not support.

The debate at the time was every bit as acrimonious as the debate over the Affordable Care Act that would occur some 55 years later. The ACA also was a product of a Congress and White House controlled by the Democrats. However, while the views of each side in the Medicare debate were as intensely held then as they were for the later ACA debate, there was a greater sense of comity and a willingness to find some measure of common ground around which a larger consensus would yield a far stronger degree of political legitimacy, thereby establishing a positive legacy. Mills's ability to incorporate the Republican proposal was shrewd politics to be sure. Because of that, it also resulted in a policy—and a program—that has become a part of the fabric of American healthcare.

Consistent with the process of policymaking described in this section and throughout the text, Medicare and Medicaid will be amended and expanded many times over the decades. For what was intended at the time, both programs can be considered successful. In our current era of seemingly out-of-control costs, however, policymakers, as discussed in the chapters that follow, will once again revisit both of these programs, as well as the ACA.

References

Blumenthal, D., and J. Marone. 2010. *The Heart of Power: Health and Politics in the Oval Office*, 2nd ed. Los Angeles: University of California Press.

Fine, S. 1998. "The Kerr-Mills Act: Medical Care for the Indigent in Michigan, 1960–1965." *Journal of the History of Medicine and Allied Sciences* 53 (3): 285–316.

CHAPTER

4

THE OVERVIEW OF HEALTH POLICYMAKING

Learning Objectives

After reading this chapter, you should be able to

- appreciate some of the important frameworks and theories about policymaking;
- define the *stages heuristic* policymaking framework;
- explain how the phases of the policymaking process fit together;
- understand the relationship between the policymaking process and its external environment;
- discuss the agenda setting and development of legislation activities of policy formulation;
- discuss the designing, rulemaking, operating, and evaluating activities of policy implementation;
- discuss the modification phase of policymaking;
- discuss how the phases of policymaking interact with one another; and
- appreciate the political nature of policymaking.

Whether health policies take the form of laws, rules or regulations, implementation decisions, or judicial decisions, all policies are authoritative decisions typically made through a complex process. The most important thing to understand about policymaking is that it is a decision-making process. This chapter describes the process. Policies at the federal, state, and local levels of government are made through similar decision-making processes, though there are some variations (Bovbjerg, Wiener, and Houseman 2003).

Having considered the context in which health policies are made in chapter 2 (in particular the structure and operations of policy markets), having identified the demanders and suppliers who interact in these markets, and having reviewed the important operational aspects of these interactions, consideration of the intricate process through which public policies are made is now possible.

The discussion begins in this chapter at the conceptual level and includes a schematic model of the core policymaking process; applied discussions of the component parts of the policymaking process follow in subsequent chapters. This section's opening policy snapshot is representative of the real-world application of the conceptual model's formulation and legislative stages.

Conceptual Frameworks and Theories of Policymaking

As a precursor to discussing any model of the public policymaking process, consideration of some of the important frameworks and theories that have guided inquiry about how the process works will be useful. Theories, which are more specific than frameworks, postulate testable relationships between variables (Walt et al. 2008).

Both frameworks and theories are useful devices, but it must be admitted at the outset that there is no universally agreed-on framework or theory about how the public policymaking process works. Instead, there are many frameworks and theories about public policymaking (Sabatier and Weible 2014), each offering only a partial explanation of the process. We will review some of the most important and enduring ones and select relevant and workable frameworks and theories around which to structure a useful model.

Stages Heuristic

The best known of the policymaking frameworks is the stages heuristic, which is attributable to early work by Lasswell (1956). The policymaking process model presented later in this chapter is heavily influenced by this framework. The framework essentially views policymaking as occurring in four stages: agenda setting, formulation, implementation, and evaluation. The framework has been legitimately criticized for oversimplifying reality but remains useful for thinking about the policymaking process.

Among alternatives to the stages heuristic, Walt and Gilson (1994) developed the policy triangle framework, which considers how actors, context, and processes interact to produce policy. Another framework, networks, evolved to help explain the way growing numbers of actors interact around policy issues (Sabatier and Weible 2014). Policy communities, described in chapter 2, are simply tightly knit networks.

Multiple-Streams and Punctuated-Equilibrium Theories

Theories, which as noted earlier are more focused than frameworks, have been developed to explain certain aspects of the policymaking process. Among the most important policymaking theories are Kingdon's (2010) *multiple-streams theory* and Baumgartner and Jones's (1993) *punctuated-equilibrium theory*. The multiple-streams theory, which focuses on agenda setting, postulates that problems, possible solutions, and politics flow along in separate streams in our society. Sometimes the streams merge and the confluence creates a window of opportunity for government to engage in policymaking. The punctuated-equilibrium theory postulates that policy-making typically proceeds in small incremental steps that can be disrupted by bursts of rapid transformation.

The enactment of Medicare and Medicaid demonstrates a bit of each theory. The identification of the problem of healthcare costs—particularly hospitalization—for the elderly as a problem, combined with the possible solution through the Johnson administration's Medicare proposal, augmented by (a) the sweeping Democratic victory of 1964 and (b) the extraordinary legislative talent of Congressman Wilbur Mills and President Lyndon Johnson, represent the multiple-streams theory. Medicaid, building on the Kerr-Mills program, can be considered an example of the punctuated-equilibrium theory. One could also view this outcome through the prism of the policy triangle theory (actors, context, processes). As a practical matter, one theory alone cannot capture the policymaking process; it is far too complex and subject to literally countless variables for a single explanatory theory. This observation is not to suggest that one theory or the other is "wrong" but rather demonstrates the complexity of human behavior in an ever-changing environment. Multiple theories can—and do—apply concurrently. Human behavior defies the inherent simplicity of a single model.

A Core Model of the Public Policymaking Process

Incorporating some of the frameworks and theories noted previously and adding other components, we can diagram the complex and intricate process through which public policymaking occurs. Remember, the most important attribute of this process is that it is a decision-making process. Although such schematic models tend to be oversimplifications, they can accurately reflect the component parts of the process and their interrelationships. Exhibit 4.1 is a model, developed by Beaufort B. Longest, Jr., of the public policymaking process in the United States. This model depicts the policymaking process as it occurs at federal, state, and local levels of government. We discuss the component parts of the model in the remainder of the chapter and then in greater detail in subsequent chapters. As can be seen in the model, policymaking occurs in three interrelated and cyclical phases: formulation, implementation, and modification. Each of these phases of policymaking at the federal level is described in the following sections.

EXHIBIT 4.1
Three Phases of the Policymaking Process

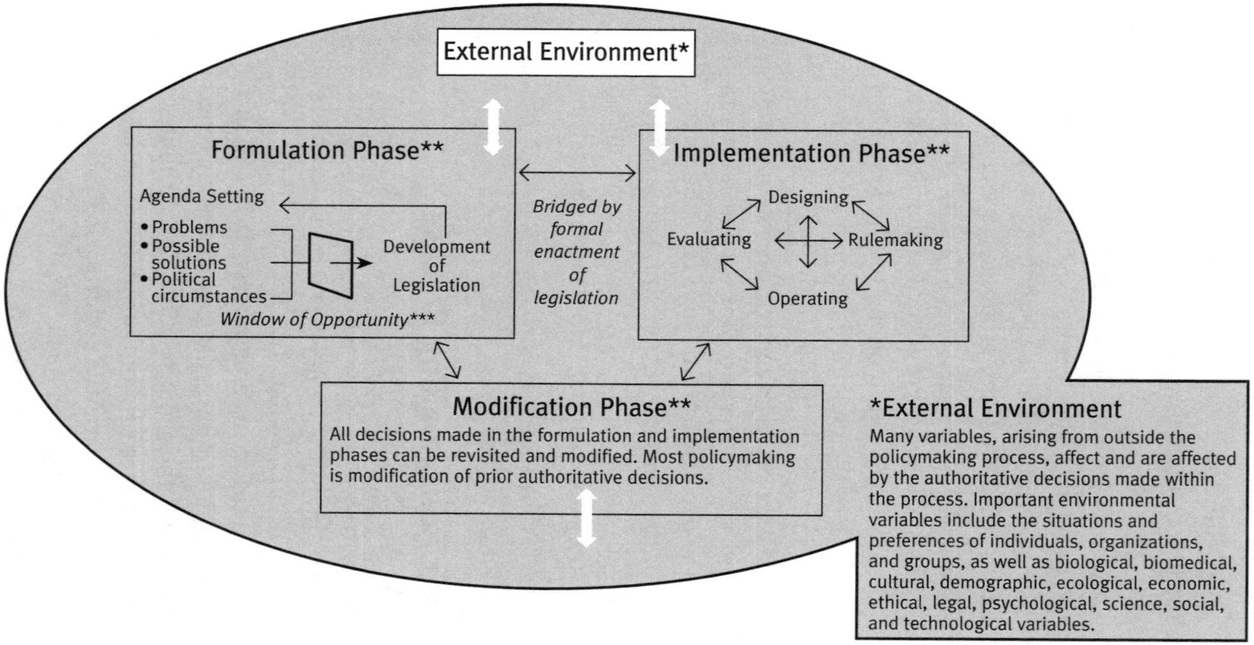
External Environment*
Formulation Phase**
Agenda Setting
• Problems
• Possible solutions
• Political circumstances
Development of Legislation
Window of Opportunity***
Bridged by formal enactment of legislation
Implementation Phase**
Designing
Evaluating
Rulemaking
Operating
Modification Phase**
All decisions made in the formulation and implementation phases can be revisited and modified. Most policymaking is modification of prior authoritative decisions.
*External Environment
Many variables, arising from outside the policymaking process, affect and are affected by the authoritative decisions made within the process. Important environmental variables include the situations and preferences of individuals, organizations, and groups, as well as biological, biomedical, cultural, demographic, ecological, economic, ethical, legal, psychological, science, social, and technological variables.

Policymakers in all three branches of government make policy in the form of position-appropriate, or authoritative, decisions. Their decisions differ in that the **legislative branch is primarily involved in formulation, the **executive branch** is primarily involved in implementation, and both are involved in modification of prior decisions or policies. The **judicial branch** interprets and assesses the legality of decisions made within all three phases of the policymaking process.

***A window of opportunity opens for possible progression of issues through formulation, enactment, implementation, and modification when there is a favorable confluence of problems, possible solutions, and political circumstances.

Note: The author gratefully acknowledges the work of Beaufort B. Longest, Jr., for this model, which Professor Longest developed for earlier editions of this book.

Formulation Phase

The formulation phase of health policymaking is made up of two distinct and sequential parts: agenda setting and development of legislation. Each part involves a set of activities in which policymakers and those who would influence their decisions and actions engage. The formulation phase results in policy in the specific form of new public laws or the far more likely result of amendments to existing laws. In other phases of the process, policies emerge in the forms of rules and regulations and other implementation decisions; policies in the form of judicial decisions can emerge throughout the entire process.

Agenda Setting

The public laws or amendments pertaining to health are initiated by the interactions of diverse health-related problems, possible solutions, and dynamic political circumstances that relate to the problems and to their potential solutions. Before the policymaking process can progress, some political actor must initiate the emergence of certain problem–solution combinations and their subsequent movement through the development-of-legislation process. In essence, this step is deciding what to prioritize in the policymaking process. In short, what will the institution making the policy consider to be more important relative to other policy demands? In addition to Medicare and Medicaid serving as examples of the problem–solution combination, a more recent example is the Affordable Care Act (ACA). Recognizing that lack of insurance is a barrier to access medical care, President Barack Obama and the Democratic majorities in both houses of Congress committed to using their mandate to push forward with expansion of healthcare coverage: they *made* the agenda, setting healthcare reform as the number one priority.

At any given time, there are many problems or issues related to health. Many of them have possible solutions that are apparent to policymakers. Often these problems have alternative solutions, each of which has its supporters and detractors. Diverse political circumstances surround the actual problems and potential solutions. Agenda setting, a crucial initial step in the policymaking process, describes the ways in which particular combinations of problems, possible solutions, and political circumstances emerge and advance to the next stage. Agenda setting is discussed in depth in chapter 5.

Development of Legislation

Once a problem or issue that might be addressed through public policy rises to a prominent, possibly actionable, place on the policy agenda—through the confluence of the problem's identification, the existence of possible policy solutions, and the political circumstances surrounding the problem and its potential solutions—it can, but does not necessarily, proceed to the next point in the policy formulation phase, the development of legislation. Kingdon (2010) describes the point at which problems, potential solutions to them, and political circumstances converge to stimulate legislation development as a window of opportunity (see exhibit 4.1).

At this second step in policy formulation, policymakers propose specific legislation. One can think of these proposals, or *bills* as they are technically called, as hypothetical or unproven solutions to the problems they are intended to address. The proposals then go through carefully prescribed steps that can, but do not always, lead to policies in the form of new public laws or, more often, amendments to previously enacted laws. The steps in the development of legislation, also called the *legislative process*, are listed in the box below.

Consider, however, the two very different methods employed by Presidents Johnson and Obama in advancing Medicare and the ACA, respectively. The Johnson administration proposed a very specific piece of legislation—hospitalization benefits for the nation's elderly. The Obama administration did not propose a specific piece of legislation for the ACA but, rather, communicated to Congress a set of principles the president was seeking in healthcare reform, leaving to Congress the task of drafting the legislation.

Legislative Process of the US Congress

Anyone may draft a bill; however, only members of Congress can introduce legislation, and by doing so become the sponsor or sponsors. There are four basic types of legislation: bills, joint resolutions, concurrent resolutions, and simple resolutions. The official legislative process begins when a bill or resolution is numbered (*H.R.* signifies a House bill and *S.* a Senate bill), referred to a committee, and printed by the Government Printing Office.

Step 1: Referral to Committee

With few exceptions, bills are referred to standing committees in the House or Senate according to carefully delineated rules of procedure.

Step 2: Committee Action

When a bill reaches a committee, it is placed on the committee's calendar. A bill can be referred to a subcommittee or considered by the committee as a whole. At this point, a bill is examined carefully and its chances for passage are determined. The committee not acting on the bill is the equivalent of killing it.

Step 3: Subcommittee Review

Often, bills are referred to a subcommittee for study and hearings. Hearings provide the opportunity to express formally the views of the executive branch, experts, other public officials, and supporters and opponents of the legislation on the record. Testimony can be given in person or submitted as a written statement.

Step 4: Mark Up

When the hearings are completed, the subcommittee may meet to "mark up" the bill, that is, make changes and amendments prior to recommending the bill to the full committee. If a subcommittee votes not to report legislation to the full committee, the bill dies.

Step 5: Committee Action to Report a Bill

After receiving a subcommittee's report on a bill, the full committee can conduct further study and hearings, or it can vote on the subcommittee's recommendations and any proposed amendments. The full committee then votes on its recommendation to the House or Senate. This procedure is called "ordering a bill reported."

Step 6: Publication of a Written Report

After a committee votes to have a bill reported, the committee chairman instructs staff to prepare a written report on the bill. This report describes the intent and scope of the legislation, impact on existing laws and programs, position of the executive branch, and views of dissenting members of the committee.

Step 7: Scheduling Floor Action

After a bill is reported back to the chamber where it originated, it is placed in chronological order on the calendar. In the House there are several different legislative calendars, and the Speaker and majority leader largely determine if, when, and in what order bills come up. In the Senate there is only one legislative calendar.

Step 8: Debate

When a bill reaches the floor of the House or Senate, there are rules or procedures governing the debate on legislation. These rules determine the conditions and amount of time allocated for general debate.

(continued)

Step 9: Voting

After the debate and the approval of any amendments, the bill is passed or defeated by the members voting.

Step 10: Referral to Other Chamber

When a bill is passed by the House or the Senate, it is referred to the other chamber, where it usually follows the same route through committee and floor action. This chamber may approve the bill as received, reject it, ignore it, or change it.

Step 11: Conference Committee Action

If only minor changes are made to a bill by the other chamber, the legislation commonly goes back to the first chamber for concurrence. However, when the actions of the other chamber significantly alter the bill, a conference committee is formed to reconcile the differences between the House and Senate versions. If the conferees are unable to reach agreement, the legislation dies. If agreement is reached, a conference report is prepared describing the committee members' recommendations for changes. Both the House and the Senate must approve of the conference report.

Step 12: Final Actions

After a bill has been approved by the House and Senate in identical form, it is sent to the president. The president signifies approval of the legislation by signature. Or, the president can take no action for ten days, while Congress is in session, and the bill automatically becomes law. If opposed to the bill, the president can veto it by sending a veto message to the Congress, or if the executive takes no action after the Congress has adjourned its second session, the bill has been "pocket vetoed" and the legislation dies.

Step 13: Overriding a Veto

If the president vetoes a bill, Congress may attempt to override the veto. To override the veto requires a two-thirds roll call vote of the members who are present in sufficient numbers for a quorum. See more at congress.org/advocacy-101/the-legislative-process.

Source: Congress.org (2019). Reprinted with permission.

EXHIBIT 4.2
Summary of Legislative Activity: Selected Congresses

Congress	Years (January to January)	Legislation Introduced*	Number Signed into Law	Percentage of Enacted Legislation
111th	2009–2011	11,192	385	2.8
112th	2011–2013	10,865	284	2.3
113th	2013–2015	9,184	296	2.8
114th	2015–2017	10,334	329	2.7
115th	2017–2019	11,474	443	3.3

*Includes House and Senate resolutions that do not become law.

Source: Adapted from GovTrack.us (2019).

Only a small fraction of the problems, health related or otherwise, that might be addressed through public policy ever emerge from agenda setting with sufficient impetus to advance them to legislation development. Even when they do, only some of the attempts to enact legislation are successful. The path of legislation—that is, of policy in the form of new public laws or amendments to existing laws—can be long and arduous (Hacker 1997). See exhibit 4.2 for the percentage of legislation that actually became law from January 2009 through January 2019. The details of this path that pertain to agenda setting are described more fully in chapter 5, and those that pertain to the development of legislation are discussed more fully in chapter 6.

Implementation Phase

When the formulation phase of policymaking yields a new or amended public law, enactment of legislation marks a transition from formulation to implementation, although the boundary between the two phases is porous. The bridge connecting formulation and implementation in the center of exhibit 4.1 is intentionally shown as a two-way connector.

The implementation phase of policymaking, including a discussion of the responsibility for implementation, is described in more depth in chapter 7. As can be seen in exhibit 4.1, policy implementation unfolds in a series of interrelated steps: designing, rulemaking, operating, and evaluating. These steps are briefly described in this section. First, however, a few words about responsibility for implementation.

Implementing organizations, primarily the departments and agencies in the executive branch of federal and state governments, are established and maintained and the people within them employed to carry out the intent of public laws as enacted by the legislative branch. Legislators rely on implementers to bring their legislation to life. Thus, the relationship between those who formulate policies and those who implement them is symbiotic.

In short, health policies must be implemented effectively if they are to affect the determinants of health. Otherwise, policies are only paper and rhetoric. An implemented law can change the physical or social environment in which people live and work, affect their behavior and, indirectly, even their biology, and an implemented law can certainly influence the availability and accessibility of health services.

The implementation phase of public policymaking involves managing human, financial, and other resources in ways that facilitate achievement of the goals and objectives embodied in enacted legislation. Policy implementation is primarily a management undertaking. That is, policy implementation in its essence is the use of resources to pursue the objectives inherent in public laws. This type of management is typically called public administration (Abramson and Lawrence 2014).

Depending on the scope of policies being implemented, the managerial tasks involved can be simple and straightforward, or they can require massive effort. For example, President Johnson, who played a major role in both formulation and implementation of Medicare, observed that implementing the Medicare program represented "the largest managerial effort the nation [had] undertaken since the Normandy invasion" (Iglehart 1992, 1468). More recently, implementation of the ACA was a monumental management undertaking (Jacobs and Skocpol 2012; Thompson 2013). No matter the scale, however, the implementation of public laws always involves the set of interrelated activities shown in exhibit 4.1: designing, rulemaking, operating, and evaluating.

For the ACA, in addition to significant information technologies difficulties establishing portals through which health insurance exchanges could function (since resolved), implementation was particularly challenging because of the need to bargain with the states to craft an exchange in each state. Some were to be federally operated, some state operated, and some hybrid, depending on whether the state chose to establish its own exchange. States have been able "to leverage their administrative capacity and policy expertise as well as their power to decline participation in federal programs in order to influence implementation of a federal initiative" (Dinan 2014, 399). Many states chose—and still choose—not to create the exchanges contemplated in the act. Challenges associated with implementing the ACA will be covered in greater detail in chapters 7 and 8. The implementation of the ACA involved multiple agencies. The US Department of Health and Human Services (HHS) is clearly involved through the expansion of Medicaid, the granting of waivers to the states, and multiple operational decisions. The Internal Revenue Service is engaged through the reporting and collection of the shared responsibility payment. In addition, the ACA established new agencies such as the Center for Medicare and Medicaid Innovation (the CMS Innovation Center) and the Independent Payment Advisory Board. It also created accountable care organizations (ACOs), which, because of their nature, invited the review of the Federal Trade Commission and the Department of Justice (DOJ), in addition to determinations by the Centers for Medicaid & Medicaid Services regarding the qualification and classification of an ACO.

Designing

The relationship among the activities in the implementation phase is essentially cyclical and interactive. As shown in exhibit 4.1, implementation begins with designing, which entails establishing the working agenda of an implementing organization (e.g., the Food and Drug Administration), planning how to accomplish the work, and organizing the agency to perform the work. This activity is rather straightforward management, which is defined as "the process, composed of interrelated social and technical functions and activities, occurring within a formal organizational setting for the purpose of helping establish objectives and accomplishing the predetermined objectives through the use of human and other resources" (Longest and Darr 2014, 255).

This implementation activity entails the traditional management functions: planning, organizing, staffing, directing (motivating, leading, and communicating), controlling, and decision-making (Daft 2016). Chapter 7 will address this topic in more detail. These interrelated functions, including how decision-making intertwines with all the other functions, are shown and briefly described in exhibit 4.3.

Rulemaking

Again, following exhibit 4.1, the next step in the implementation phase of policymaking is rulemaking. Rules, which may also be called regulations, are specific detailed directives developed by implementing organizations in the executive branch. Rules are themselves policies because they are authoritative decisions made in the executive branch to implement laws and amendments. Recall from chapter 1 that authoritative decisions refer to those made anywhere in the three branches of government that are under the legitimate purview (i.e., within the official roles, responsibilities, and authorities) of those making the decisions. For example, rules promulgated to implement a law are as much policies as are the laws they support. Similarly, operational decisions made by implementing organizations, to the extent that they require or influence particular behaviors,

EXHIBIT 4.3
The Management Functions in an Implementing Organization

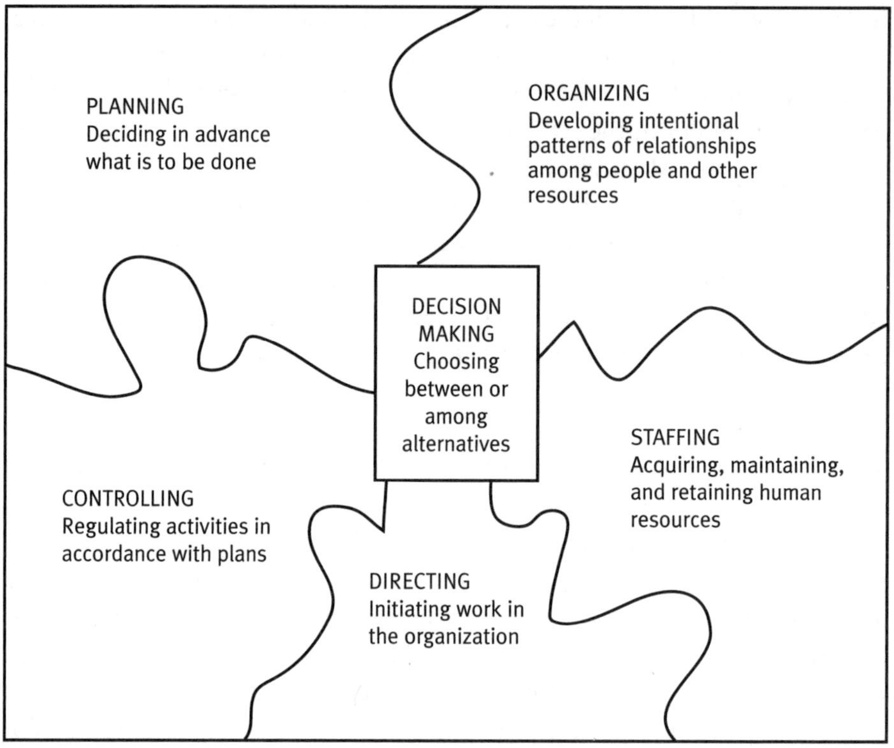

Source: B. B. Longest, Jr., and K. Darr, 2014, *Managing Health Services Organizations and Systems*, 6th ed., Baltimore: Health Professions Press, 259. © 2014 by Beaufort B. Longest, Jr., and Kurt Darr. Reprinted by permission of Health Professions Press, Inc.

actions, or decisions by others, are policies. Furthermore, decisions made in the judicial branch regarding the applicability of laws to specific situations or the appropriateness of the actions of implementing organizations are policies. By definition, policies are established in both the formulation and implementation phases of the policymaking process.

The Clean Air Act, the Food and Drug Act, the Civil Rights Act, and, more recently, the ACA are all examples of landmark legislation requiring extensive rulemaking to guide their implementation. The rules promulgated to implement laws and amendments can undergo revision—sometimes extensive and continual revision—and new rules can be adopted as experience with how existing rules are functioning dictates. This characteristic of policymaking tends to make the process more dynamic than it would be otherwise. Furthermore, when new administrations take office, policy modifications could include reversal of prior policy or new administrative approaches that render the prior policy ineffectual or more robust, depending on the choice made by the electorate.

The promulgation of rules is itself guided by certain rules and protocols set forth in legislation. Key among the rules of rulemaking is the requirement that implementing agencies publish *proposed* rules, which gives those with interests in the issue an opportunity to participate in the rulemaking prior to the adoption of a final rule. Proposed and final rules are published in the *Federal Register*, a daily publication of important official documents. The rulemaking process is discussed in more detail in chapter 9.

Operating

As demonstrated in exhibit 4.1, the responsible administrative agency must implement the policy to bring it to operational life. If a policy in the form of a public law or an amendment to a public law is intended to protect people from exposure to toxic substances in their environments, for example, its operation entails the activities involved in actually providing such protection. Such activities would include measuring and assessing dangers from substances in the environment and imposing sanctions (e.g., against polluters). If the intent of legislation is to expand Medicaid enrollment, as is the case with the ACA, successful operation of this policy requires enrolling new people in the program.

The essence of the implementation phase of policymaking is that one or more organizations or agencies undertake the operation of enacted legislation in accord with the design of how to do so and the rules established to guide operating the policy. As will be discussed more fully in chapter 7, the operation of policies is affected by a number of variables, including the fit between implementing organizations and a policy's objectives as well as the capabilities of the managers in the implementing organizations.

Evaluating

The fourth core activity in implementing policy is evaluating (again, see exhibit 4.1). This activity brings the other elements of implementation full circle and can lead to new rounds of designing, rulemaking, and operating policy. Evaluating, and using the results of evaluation, is an important activity in effective policy implementation.

Fundamentally, evaluating something means determining "its merit, worth, value, or significance" (Patton 2012, 2). Managers of implementing organizations approach this determination by asking questions such as, How effective is the policy, or some component of it? Were the policy's objectives achieved? Do the benefits of the policy justify its costs?

Policy evaluation is defined as systematically collecting, analyzing, and using information to answer basic questions about a policy. There are numerous types of evaluations, including process and outcome evaluations, formative and summative evaluations, and cost–benefit and cost-effectiveness evaluations.

Each of these types of evaluations has specific characteristics and uses, which are described more fully in chapter 7.

The legislative and executive branches of government are involved in policy evaluation and other forms of analysis because they are interested in the performance of the policies they enact and implement. A number of agencies support the evaluation activity at the federal level, including the Agency for Healthcare Research and Quality, which is currently involved in evaluating the ACA's coverage expansions, and the CMS Innovation Center, which was established by the ACA to test innovative payment and service delivery models for Medicare, Medicaid, and the Children's Health Insurance Program.

Modification Phase

As we have noted, policymaking is an intricate process. It is not a perfect process. Mistakes of omission and commission are routinely made in the formulation and implementation phases. The policymaking process model presented in exhibit 4.1 is brought full circle by the third phase of the process, modification. This phase is necessary because no policy is perfectly drawn in the formulation and implementation phases. Even policy decisions that seem to be correct when they are made must be adjusted to accommodate changing circumstances. In a hypothetical policymaking process without a modification phase, policies would be formulated in their original version and then implemented, and that would be the end of the process—except, of course, for the policies' consequences. In practice, however, policymaking does not work this way. The consequences of policies—including consequences for those who formulate and implement the policies and for the individuals, organizations, and interest groups outside the process but affected by policies—cause people to seek modification. They do so continually throughout the life of many policies. An example of a policy modification in the light of changed circumstances is Part D of Medicare. In 1965, at the time of Medicare's inception, drug costs for seniors were not known to policymakers as a significant concern. Over the ensuing 40 years, however, as pharmaceuticals became more prominent in the process of care (and increasingly expensive), the inability of seniors to pay for necessary medication became a problem that demanded a political solution. Thus, Congress and the George W. Bush administration amended the Medicare program to include prescription drugs in its penumbra in 2006.

At a minimum, individuals, organizations, or interest groups that benefit from a particular policy may seek modifications that increase or maintain these benefits over time. Similarly, those who are negatively affected by a policy will seek to modify it to minimize the negative consequences. In addition, when the policymakers who formulate and implement a public policy observe it in operation, they will evaluate it against their objectives for that policy. Finally, when a legislative body, or elected executive, becomes loyal to a new political party, new policy preferences may arise that will motivate efforts to modify, undermine, or eliminate policy. In short, when preferences and reality do not match, stakeholders usually begin efforts to modify the policy.

Policies have histories. An initial version is formulated and then evolves as it is implemented, either through amendments to the original legislation or through new or revised rules and other implementation decisions. Some policies eventually die—they are repealed by the legislative branch—but most have long and dynamic lives during which they are continually modified in various ways. Chapter 9 addresses the policy modification phase of public policymaking in more detail.

Key Features of the Policymaking Process

Having brought the policymaking process full circle, we can now turn our attention to several key features of the policymaking process that are especially helpful in understanding this complicated process. The first of these features is the fact that policymaking does not take place in a vacuum. It occurs in the context of a dynamic external environment with which the process interacts in many ways.

Policymaking Occurs in the Context of a Dynamic External Environment

An important feature of the public policymaking process is the synergistic nature of the relationship between the policymaking process and the external environment in which the process functions. The impact of external factors is depicted in exhibit 4.1 by the large double-headed arrows connecting each phase of the process to the external environment. The impact of external factors means the policymaking process is an *open system*, one in which the process interacts with—affects and is affected by—factors in its external environment.

The external environment in exhibit 4.1 is shown to contain a number of important variables, including the situations and preferences of individuals, organizations, and groups, as well as biological, biomedical, cultural, demographic, ecological, economic, ethical, legal, psychological, science, social, and technological variables. These environmental variables affect the policymaking process and are affected by the policies produced by the process. Technology provides an example of an environmental variable that illustrates the two-way relationship between policymaking and the processes' external environment.

The United States is the world's major producer and consumer of health-related technology. As exhibit 4.1 shows, technology variables flow into and out of the policymaking process. Technology is produced in part through public funding and the policies that determine funding levels and priorities, and once in place, various technologies must be factored into public and private insurance programs, including Medicare and Medicaid. Medical technologies can be cost increasing, neutral, or cost saving but must be taken into account in establishing funding for publicly financed health services (Congressional Budget Office 2014; Sorenson, Drummond, and Bhuiyan Khan 2013).

Legal variables provide another example of the two-way relationship between policymaking and its external environment. As we discussed briefly in chapter 1 and will discuss more fully in chapter 8, authoritative decisions made in judicial branches of governments, as the part 2 policy snapshot illustrates, are themselves policies. In addition, however, decisions made in the legal system influence other decisions made in the larger policymaking process. Legal variables may help shape all other policy decisions, including by reversing them when they are unconstitutional.

The Phases of the Policymaking Process Are Interactive and Interdependent

While the policymaking model shown in exhibit 4.1 emphasizes the phases of the policymaking process, it also shows that they are highly interactive and interdependent. Exhibit 4.4 illustrates the nature of the three phases of policymaking in a different way.

Furthermore, within the phases, much of the activity is also interactive and interdependent. Designing for implementation—planning, organizing, staffing, directing (motivating, leading, and communicating), controlling, and

EXHIBIT 4.4
The Interactive and Interdependent Relationships Among the Policy Formulation, Implementation, and Modification Phases of Policymaking

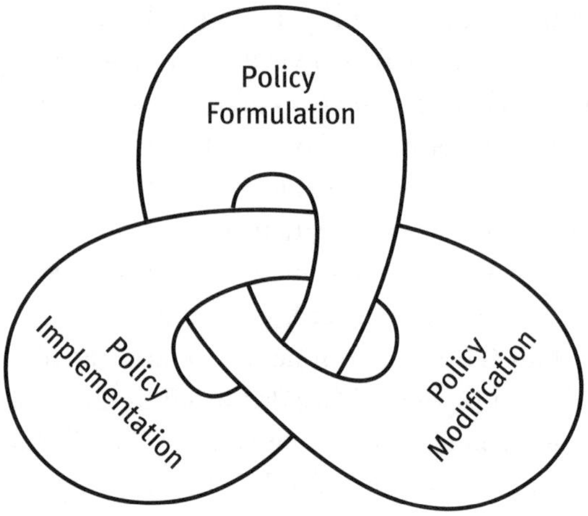

decision-making—leads to rulemaking, which in turn guides the operation of policies, which can be evaluated and may lead to new rounds of designing, rulemaking, and operating.

The public policymaking process modeled in exhibit 4.1 includes the following three interconnected phases:

1. *Policy formulation*, which incorporates activities associated with setting the policy agenda and, subsequently, with the development of legislation
2. *Policy implementation*, which incorporates activities associated with designing for implementation, rulemaking that helps guide the implementation of policies, the actual operationalization of policies, and evaluation, which may lead to subsequent rounds of these activities
3. *Policy modification*, which allows for all prior decisions made in the process to be revisited and perhaps changed

Once enacted as laws, policies remain to be implemented. The formulation phase (making the decisions that lead to or amend public laws) and the implementation phase (taking actions and making additional decisions necessary to implement public laws) are bridged by the formal enactment of legislation, which shifts the cycle from the formulation to the implementation phase.

Implementation responsibility rests mostly with the executive branch, which includes the HHS (www.hhs.gov) and the Department of Justice (www.usdoj.gov), and independent federal agencies such as the Environmental Protection Agency (EPA; www.epa.gov) and the Consumer Product Safety Commission (www.cpsc.gov). These and many other departments and agencies in the executive branch exist primarily to implement the policies formulated in the legislative branch. Authoritative decisions made in the course of policy implementation become policies themselves. Rules and regulations promulgated to implement a law and operational protocols and procedures developed to support a law's implementation are just as surely policies as is the law itself. Similarly, judicial decisions regarding the applicability of laws to specific situations or regarding the appropriateness of the actions of implementing organizations are public policies. Policies are routinely established during the formulation and the implementation phases of the overall process.

The policy modification phase exists because perfection cannot be achieved in the other phases and because policies are established and exist in a dynamic world. Suitable policies made today may become inadequate with future biological, biomedical, cultural, demographic, ecological, economic, ethical, legal, political, psychological, scientific, social, and technological changes. Pressure to change established policies may come from new priorities or the perceived needs of individuals, organizations, and interest groups affected by the policies. The enforcement mechanism for the ACA's individual mandate, the shared responsibility payment (SRP) referenced in the policy snapshot at the beginning of the first section, is a good example of this phenomenon. Forces opposing the ACA generally, and the individual mandate in particular, prevailed in modifying the ACA. This success represented a significant shift in policy with regard to a key pillar of the ACA. Rather than attack the mandate directly, policymakers chose to undermine it by repealing the SRP. With no enforcement mechanism—the tax for noncompliance—the individual mandate became a toothless tiger. Thus, as part of a larger tax reduction package, the SRP was repealed in 2017. In the space of six short years—between the enactment of the ACA in 2010 and the election of 2016—the political landscape had shifted: what was suitable in 2010 to the majority of policymakers was no longer acceptable by 2016. And as we shall see, the elimination of the SRP would draw additional legal challenges to the ACA.

Policy modification, which is shown as two-direction arrows in exhibit 4.1, may entail only minor adjustments in the implementation phase or modest amendments to existing public laws. In some instances, however, the consequences of implementing certain policies can feed all the way back to the agenda-setting stage. For example, formulating policies to contain the costs of providing health services—a continuing challenge facing policymakers today—is to a large extent an outgrowth of previous policies that expanded access and increased the supply of human resources and advanced technologies to be used in providing health services.

Policymaking Is a Cyclical Process

As exhibit 4.1 illustrates, the policymaking process is a continuous cycle in which all decisions are subject to modification. Public policymaking is a process in which numerous decisions are reached and then revisited as circumstances change. The continually cyclical nature of health policymaking can be seen in the pattern of Medicare policy presented in chapter 9, which demonstrates that Medicare policy is revisited and modified on a regular basis. Policymaking occurs in each of the three phases of interconnected activity. In reality, of course, all three phases are active simultaneously. At any point in time, in all levels of governments, it is possible to find multiple policies in the form of authoritative decisions being made in each of the three phases. The essence of the flow of these decisions, however, is cyclical: Policy in the form of laws and amendments is formulated, then implemented (which involves more policymaking, in the form of designing, rulemaking, operating, and evaluating decisions), after which all decisions made in the formulation and implementation phases can be revisited and possibly modified. It helps all involved in the process or affected by the decisions resulting from policymaking to know of the cyclical nature of the process. Observers may find comfort in the fact that the decisions made in the policymaking process are not final. The potential to change unsatisfactory policies always exists.

Policymaking Is a Highly Political Process

One feature of the public policymaking process that the model presented in exhibit 4.1 cannot adequately represent—but one that is crucial to understanding the policymaking process—is the political nature of the process in operation (Weissert and Weissert 2012). In this process, all decisions are made by humans. Thus, various mixes of altruism and egoism influence what takes place. Human control of the public policymaking process means that its operation, outcomes, and consequences are directly affected by the ethics of those who participate in the process. Ethical considerations help shape and guide the development of new policies by contributing to definitions of problems and the structure of policy solutions.

While many people naively believe—and still others hope—that public policymaking is a predominantly rational decision-making process, this is not the case. The process would no doubt be simpler and better if it were driven exclusively by fully informed consideration of the best ways for policy to support the nation's pursuit of health, by open and comprehensive debate about potential policies, and by rational selection from among policy choices strictly on the basis of ability to contribute to the pursuit of health, and all done by ethical decision makers. Therein lies at least part of the problem: people, including political actors, disagree on the best ways for policy to improve the nation's health. Policymakers may have honest philosophical disagreement about a problem that transcends the concept of self-interest versus altruism. Regrettably, however, survival instincts and self-aggrandizement remain prominent in the political, and thus policymaking, equation.

Those who are familiar with the policymaking process, however, know that a wide range of other factors and considerations influence the process. The preferences and influence of interest groups, political bargaining and vote trading, and ideological biases are among the most important of these factors. This is not to say that rationality plays no part in health policymaking. However, it is, at best, only one of many considerations involved in the complex decision-making that leads to policy.

The political nature of the policymaking process in the United States accounts for competing theories about how this process plays out. At the opposite ends of a continuum sit strictly public-interest and strictly self-interest theories of how policymakers behave. Policies made entirely in the public interest would be the result of all participants acting according to what they believe to be the public's interest. Here, however, we encounter a question: What is the *public* interest? No single answer to that question can be found with which all can agree. Alternatively, policies made entirely through a process driven by self-interests would reflect the interplay of the various self-interests of the diverse participants. Policies resulting from these two hypothetical extremes would indeed be different.

In reality, however, health policies always reflect a mix of public-interest and self-interest influences. The balance between public and self-interests being served is important to the ultimate shape of health policies. For example, the present coexistence of the extremes of excess (the exorbitant incomes of some physicians and health plan managers, esoteric technologies, various overcapacities in the healthcare system) and deprivation (lack of insurance for millions of people, inadequate access to basic health services for millions more) resulting from or permitted by some of the nation's existing health policies suggests that the balance has been tipped too often toward the service of self-interests. As the ACA is more fully implemented, some of the disparities and gaps in access may be diminished. However, that is unlikely to take place on a large scale for years to come. Recent evidence suggests the ACA has had a positive impact on the disparity of uninsured: The gaps between Hispanics and African Americans having insurance compared to the white population have narrowed (McMorrow et al. 2015). Concomitantly, socioeconomic disparities have been reduced (Griffith, Evans, and Bor 2017).

Public and self-interest aside, public policymaking in the US health domain is a remarkably complex process, though clearly an imperfect one. The intricacies of the process are explored more thoroughly in subsequent chapters. In general, policymaking is a highly political process, it is continual and cyclical in its operation, it is heavily influenced by factors external to the process, and the component phases and the activities within the phases of the process are highly interactive and interdependent.

Summary

Health policies, like those in other domains, are made in the context of policy markets, where demanders for and suppliers of policies interact, as was described in chapter 2. The federal, state, and to a lesser extent, local governments have important health policy roles, and their policymaking processes are similar.

Public policymaking, including in the health domain, is a human process, a fact with great significance for the outcomes and consequences of the process and one that argues for informed decision-making and good judgment by all involved in the process.

The policymaking process itself, as depicted in exhibit 4.1, is a highly complex, interactive, and cyclical process that incorporates formulation, implementation, and modification phases. These phases are outlined in this chapter and discussed in greater detail in subsequent chapters.

Review Questions

1. Draw a schematic model of the three phases of the public policymaking process.
2. Describe the general features of the model drawn in question 1.
3. Discuss the formulation phase of policymaking.
4. Discuss the implementation phase of policymaking.
5. Discuss the modification phase of policymaking.
6. Discuss how the phases of policymaking interact with one another.
7. How does passage of the ACA represent both the multiple streams and punctual equilibrium theories of public policymaking?

References

Abramson, M. A., and P. Lawrence. 2014. *What Government Does: How Political Executives Manage*. Lanham, MD: Rowman and Littlefield.

Baumgartner, F. R., and B. D. Jones. 1993. *Agendas and Instability in American Politics*. Chicago: University of Chicago Press.

Bovbjerg, R. R., J. M. Wiener, and M. Houseman. 2003. "State and Federal Roles in Health Care: Rationales for Allocating Responsibilities." In *Federalism and Health Policy*, edited by J. Holahan, A. Weil, and J. M. Wiener, 25–57. Washington, DC: Urban Institute Press.

Congress.org. 2019. "The Legislative Process." Accessed September 25. http://congress.org/advocacy-101/the-legislative-process.

Congressional Budget Office. 2014. "The Budget and Economic Outlook: 2014 to 2024." Published February 4. www.cbo.gov/publication/45010.

Daft, R. L. 2016. *Management*, 12th ed. Mason, OH: South-Western Cengage Learning.

Dinan, J. 2014. "Implementing Health Reform: Intergovernmental Bargaining and the Affordable Care Act." *Publius: The Journal of Federalism* 44 (3): 399–425.

GovTrack.us. 2019."Statistical and Historical Comparisons." Accessed October 8. www.govtrack.us/congress/bills/statistics.

Griffith, K., L. Evans, and J. Bor. 2017. "The Affordable Care Act Reduced Socioeconomic Disparities in Health Care Access." *Health Affairs* 36 (8): 1503–10.

Hacker, J. S. 1997. *The Road to Nowhere*. Princeton, NJ: Princeton University Press.

Iglehart, J. K. 1992. "The American Health Care System: Medicare." *New England Journal of Medicine* 327 (20): 1467–72.

Jacobs, L. R., and T. Skocpol. 2012. *Health Care Reform and American Politics*, 2nd ed. New York: Oxford University Press.

Kingdon, J. W. 2010. *Agendas, Alternatives, and Public Policies*, 2nd ed. Upper Saddle River, NJ: Longman.

Lasswell, H. 1956. *The Decision Process.* College Park, MD: University of Maryland Press.

Longest, B. B., Jr., and K. Darr. 2014. *Managing Health Services Organizations and Systems*, 6th ed. Baltimore, MD: Health Professions Press.

McMorrow, S., S. K. Long, G. M. Kenny, and N. Anderson. 2015. "Uninsurance Disparities Have Narrowed for Black and Hispanic Adults Under the Affordable Care Act." *Health Affairs* 34 (10): 1774–78.

Patton, M. Q. 2012. *Essentials of Utilization-Focused Evaluation.* Thousand Oaks, CA: Sage.

Sabatier, P. A., and C. Weible (eds.). 2014. *Theories of the Policy Process*, 3rd ed. Boulder, CO: Westview Press.

Sorenson, C., M. Drummond, and B. Bhuiyan Khan. 2013. "Medical Technology as a Key Driver of Rising Health Expenditure: Disentangling the Relationship." *ClinicoEconomics and Outcomes Research* 5: 223–34.

Thompson, F. J. 2013. "Health Reform, Polarization, and Public Administration." *Public Administration Review* 73 (S1): S3–S12.

Walt, G., and L. Gilson. 1994. "Reforming the Health Sector in Developing Countries: The Central Role of Policy Analysis." *Health Policy and Planning* 9 (4): 353–70.

Walt, G., J. Shiffman, H. Schneider, S. F. Murray, R. Brugha, and L. Gilson. 2008. "'Doing' Health Policy Analysis: Methodological and Conceptual Reflections and Challenges." *Health Policy and Planning* 23 (5): 308–17.

Weissert, C. S., and W. G. Weissert. 2012. *Governing Health: The Politics of Health Policy*, 4th ed. Baltimore, MD: Johns Hopkins University Press.

CHAPTER

5

POLICY FORMULATION: AGENDA SETTING

Learning Objectives

After reading this chapter, you should be able to

- define agenda setting,
- understand what opens a window of opportunity in agenda setting,
- describe how problems emerge for consideration in policymaking,
- appreciate the role of research in selecting possible solutions to problems,
- describe the role of political circumstances in agenda setting,
- understand the role of interest groups in agenda setting,
- describe the tactics used by interest groups to influence the policy agenda,
- understand the role of governors or the president in agenda setting, and
- describe and explain the evolving nature of the health policy agenda.

This chapter and the next examine in greater detail the formulation phase of the health policymaking process described and modeled in chapter 4. This chapter focuses on agenda setting. Chapter 6 focuses on the development of legislation. These chapters apply the model to health policymaking almost exclusively at the national level of government and emphasize the legislative process. However, as is true of previous chapters, much of what is said here about the process of public policymaking also applies at the state and local levels. The contexts, participants, and specific mechanisms and procedures obviously differ among the three levels, but the core process typically is similar. Remember from the discussion in chapter 4 that the formulation phase of health policymaking is made up of two distinct and sequential parts: agenda setting and legislation development (see the darkly shaded portion of exhibit 5.1). Each part involves a complex set of activities in which policymakers engage with those who seek to influence their decisions and actions, but policy formulation begins with agenda setting.

EXHIBIT 5.1

Policymaking Process: Agenda Setting in the Formulation Phase

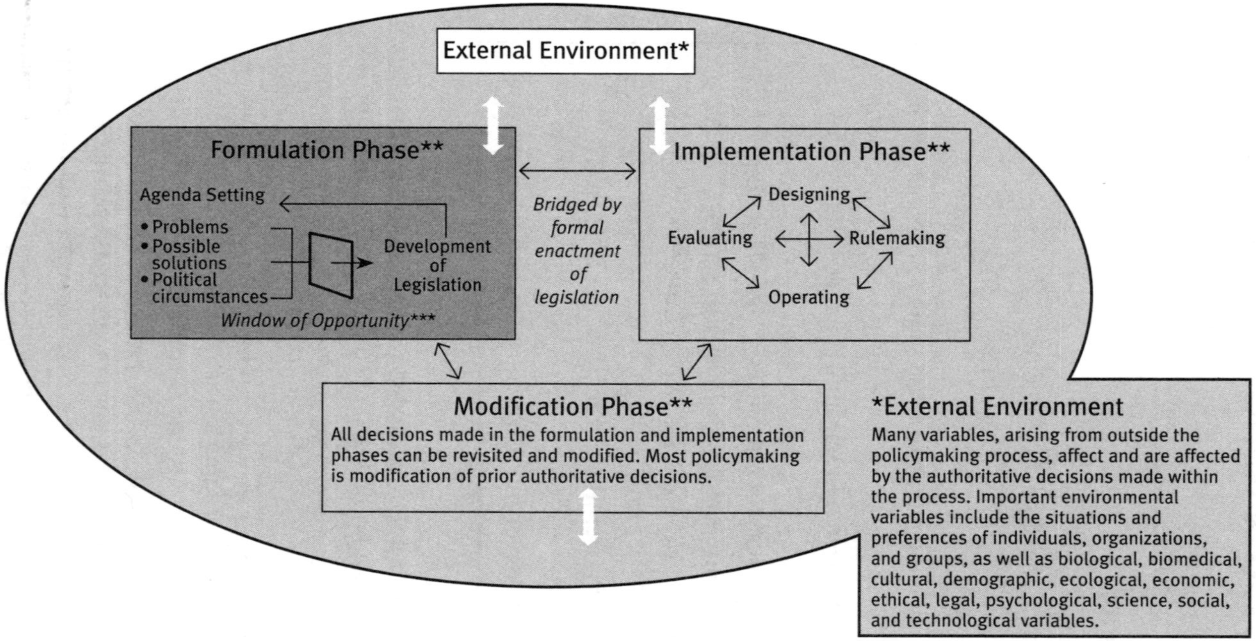
External Environment*
Formulation Phase**
Agenda Setting
• Problems
• Possible solutions
• Political circumstances
Development of Legislation
Window of Opportunity***
Bridged by formal enactment of legislation
Implementation Phase**
Designing
Evaluating
Rulemaking
Operating
Modification Phase**
All decisions made in the formulation and implementation phases can be revisited and modified. Most policymaking is modification of prior authoritative decisions.
*External Environment
Many variables, arising from outside the policymaking process, affect and are affected by the authoritative decisions made within the process. Important environmental variables include the situations and preferences of individuals, organizations, and groups, as well as biological, biomedical, cultural, demographic, ecological, economic, ethical, legal, psychological, science, social, and technological variables.

Policymakers in all three branches of government make policy in the form of position-appropriate, or authoritative, decisions. Their decisions differ in that the **legislative branch is primarily involved in formulation, the **executive branch** is primarily involved in implementation, and both are involved in modification of prior decisions or policies. The **judicial branch** interprets and assesses the legality of decisions made within all three phases of the policymaking process.

***A window of opportunity opens for possible progression of issues through formulation, enactment, implementation, and modification when there is a favorable confluence of problems, possible solutions, and political circumstances.

Agenda Setting

As noted in chapter 4, agenda setting is deciding what to make decisions about in the policy formulation phase of policymaking. It is a crucial initial step in the process. Kingdon (2010) describes agenda setting in public policymaking as a function of the confluence of three streams of activity: problems, possible solutions to the problems, and political circumstances. According to Kingdon's conceptualization, when problems, possible solutions, and political circumstances flow together in a favorable alignment, a "policy window" or "window of opportunity" opens. When a policy window opens, a problem–potential solution combination that might lead to a new public law or an amendment to an existing one emerges from the set of competing problem–possible solution combinations and moves forward in the policymaking process (see exhibit 5.2).

Current health policies in the form of public laws—such as those pertaining to environmental protection, licensure of health-related practitioners and organizations, expansion of the Medicaid program, cost containment of the Medicare program, funding for acquired immunodeficiency syndrome (AIDS) research or women's health, and regulation of pharmaceuticals pricing—exist because problems or issues emerged from agenda setting and triggered changes in policy. However, the existence of these problems alone was not sufficient to trigger the development of legislation intended to address them.

The existence of health-related problems, even serious ones such as inadequate health insurance coverage for millions of people or the continuing widespread use of tobacco products, does not always lead to policies intended to solve or ameliorate them. There also must be potential solutions to the problems and the political will to enact specific legislation to implement one or more of those solutions. Agenda setting is best understood in the context of its three key variables: problems, possible solutions, and political circumstances. Policymakers and interest groups may—and often do—disagree on elements of the policymaking process. Certainly, disagreement affects the level of political will a policymaker might have regarding an issue. A member of Congress who

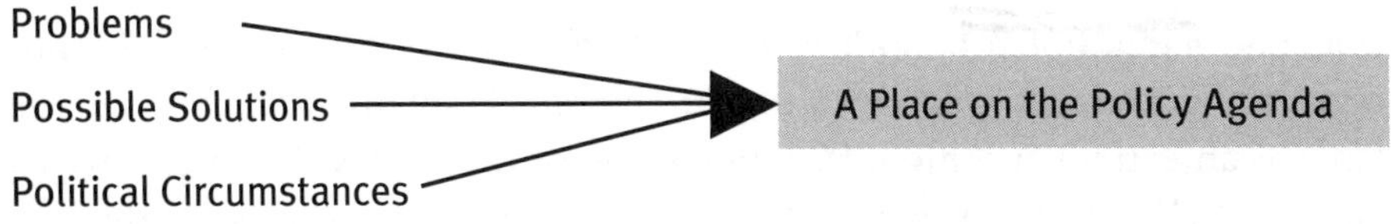

EXHIBIT 5.2 Agenda Setting as the Confluence of Problems, Possible Solutions, and Political Circumstances

wants to be reelected will consider carefully any involvement in a contentious debate. Likewise, an interest group could believe its best strategy may be minimizing or maximizing the scope of the problem of interest.

Problems

The breadth of problems that can initiate agenda setting is reflected in the broad range of health policies. Chapter 1 discussed how health is affected by several determinants: the physical environments in which people live and work; their behaviors and biology; social factors; and the type, quality, and timing of health services they receive.

Beyond these determinants, as shown in the external environment component of exhibit 5.1, the situations and preferences of individuals, organizations, and groups as well as biological, biomedical, cultural, demographic, ecological, economic, ethical, legal, psychological, science, social, and technological variables affect policymaking throughout the process. These inputs join with the results and consequences of the policies produced through the ongoing policymaking process to supply agenda setters continuously with a massive pool of contenders for a place on that agenda. From among the multiple contenders, certain problems find a place on the agenda while others do not.

The problems that eventually lead to the development of legislation are generally those that some policymakers broadly identify as important and urgent. (Keep in mind that this is a political process; not all policymakers are equally powerful. A senior member in the majority party of Congress can more easily get something on the policy agenda in a meaningful place than a freshman member in the minority party.) Problems that do not meet these criteria languish at the bottom of the list or never find a place on the agenda.

Price (1978), in a classic article, argues that whether a problem receives aggressive congressional intervention in the form of policymaking depends on its public salience and the degree of group conflict surrounding it. He defines a publicly salient problem or issue as one with a high actual or potential level of public interest. Conflictive problems or issues are those that stimulate intense disagreements among interest groups or those that pit the interests of groups against the larger public interest. Price contends that the incentives for legislators to intervene in problems or issues are greatest when salience is high and conflict is low. Conversely, incentives are least when salience is low and conflict is high.

An example of profound salience and equally profound conflict is the epidemic of gun violence. Both advocates of gun control measures and defenders of the gun rights hold views that are extremely intense (which is *not* the same as an extreme position; there are some of those in each camp as well). *Gun control* has a wide variety of meanings. The term can mean something as anodyne as (1) more rigorous background checks for buyers to something a bit more restrictive such as (2) denying access to semiautomatic weapons and any devices that can be used to convert them to fully automatic weapons, or even to (3) completely banning all firearms, and a host of positions in between. Proponents believe that making it harder to get guns to the public will result in a decrease of gun violence. Some opponents would accept more rigorous background checks, and some would accept restrictions on access to certain kinds of weapons. Other opponents, however, look to the Second Amendment in the Bill of Rights to assert an unfettered right to bear arms, objecting to any form of firearm regulation. Each side of the debate has an extreme position—complete ban versus no regulation—and a broad spectrum of more nuanced positions. The overall picture, however, is an issue with very high conflict and mixed salience. When the issue gets thrown into the same cauldron as taxes, healthcare, national security, and all the problems that make up everyday light, consensus is elusive. A political (and policy) standoff is the result.

Conversely, the opioid addiction problem that began to surface in 2017 and 2018 is salient to public policy because of the large number of overdose deaths and the loss of productivity from those who are addicted. Controversy over the need for action is minimal; it is one of the few mental health–related initiatives on which there is broad agreement. As a result, the Congress has acted by providing grant funding to comprehensive recovery centers and facilitating access to medication-assisted treatment programs (Itkowitz 2018). Problems that lead to attempts at policy solutions find their place on the agenda along one of several paths. Some problems emerge because trends in certain variables eventually reach unacceptable levels—at least, levels unacceptable to some policymakers. Growth in the number of uninsured and cost escalation in the Medicare program are examples of trends that eventually reached levels at which policymakers felt compelled to address the underlying problems through legislation. Both problems are addressed in the Affordable Care Act (ACA).

Problems also can be spotlighted by their widespread applicability (e.g., the high cost of prescription medications to millions of Americans) or by their sharply focused impact on a small but powerful group whose members are directly affected (e.g., the high cost of medical education). Another example of a widespread problem that led to specific legislation was that a large number of people felt locked into their jobs because they feared that preexisting health conditions might prevent them from obtaining health insurance if they found new positions. In response to this problem, the Health Insurance Portability and Accountability Act of 1996 (P.L. 104-191) significantly enhanced the portability of health insurance coverage. Other provisions in this law guarantee availability and renewability of health insurance coverage for certain employees and individuals and an increase in the tax deduction for health insurance purchased by the self-employed.

Moreover, just because policymakers find consensus in recognition that a problem is widespread and perhaps little conflict that it should be solved, the presence of conflicts over the possible solutions generally result in inaction. That seems to be the case with regard to ever-increasing prices for prescription medications. There is general agreement that increasing prices are challenging to a growing number of Americans. However, participants experience a high degree of conflict over the possible solutions, which include permitting importation from Canada, allowing Medicare to negotiate prices directly, and legally regulating pharmaceutical prices, among others. Failure to achieve a meaningful consensus around any of these solutions means no meaningful action will take place so long as that fractured perspective continues to exist. Some problems gain their place on the agenda or strengthen their hold on a place because they are closely linked to other problems that already occupy secure places. The coronavirus pandemic of 2020 provides a good example. Congress and the executive branch were committed to finding ways to both slow the spread of the disease as well as provide financial assistance for people and businesses suffering adverse impacts from the disease. Thus, the Payroll Protection Plan emerged to help small businesses retain employees in spite of disease mitigation efforts that caused losses in business revenue. Providing such payroll assistance—and thus keeping employees covered by their employers' health insurance—would not have been on the agenda without the crisis brought on by the pandemic.

Some problems emerge more or less simultaneously along several paths. Typically, problems that emerge this way become prominent on the policy agenda. For example, the problem of the high cost of health services for the private and public sectors has long received attention from policymakers. Though the rate of growth in health costs has slowed in the past few years, these costs remain high and problematic (Kamal, McDermott, and Cox 2019). This problem emerged along a number of mutually reinforcing paths. In part, the cost problem has been prominent because the cost trend data disturb many people. The data contribute to and reinforce a widespread acknowledgment of the problem of health costs in public poll after public poll and have attracted the attention of some of those who pay directly for health services through the provision of health insurance benefits, especially the politically powerful business community. Finally, the health cost problem as it relates to public expenditures—for the Medicare and Medicaid programs especially—has also been linked at times to the need to control the federal budget.

The variables of healthcare costs and the escalating federal budget form a combination of interacting circumstances, which is largely why this problem remains perennially prominent in the minds of many policymakers. The persistence of this problem, and many others, is also related to the difficulty of finding and pursuing potential solutions.

Possible Solutions

The second variable in agenda setting (see exhibit 5.2) is the existence of possible solutions to problems. Problems themselves—even serious, fully acknowledged ones with widespread implications such as the high cost of healthcare, poor quality, and uneven access to needed health services—do not invariably lead to remedial policies. Potential solutions must accompany them. The availability of possible solutions depends on the generation of ideas and, usually, a period of idea testing and refinement. As the following box, reprinted from the Centers for Medicare & Medicaid Services (CMS), illustrates, numerous ideas might serve as solutions to problems, either in single application or in various combinations.

Innovation Models

The [CMS] Innovation Center develops new payment and service delivery models in accordance with the requirements of Section 1115(a) of the Social Security Act. Additionally, Congress has defined—both through the ACA and previous legislation—a number of specific demonstrations to be conducted by CMS. These research and demonstration projects are exempt from the Common Rule under 45 CFR 46.104(d)(5). For additional guidance, refer to the OHRP [Office of Human Research Protections] Revised Common Rule Q&As on Exemptions.

The Innovation Center also plays a critical role in implementing the Quality Payment Program, which Congress created as part of the Medicare Access and CHIP Reauthorization Act of 2015 (MACRA) to replace Medicare's Sustainable Growth Rate formula to pay for physicians' and other providers' services. In this new program, clinicians may earn incentive payments by participating to a sufficient extent in Advanced Alternative Payment Models (APMs). In Advanced APMs clinicians accept some risk for their patients' quality and cost outcomes and meet other specified criteria.

The Innovation Center is working in consultation with clinicians to increase the number and variety of models available to ensure that a wide range of clinicians, including those in small practices and rural areas, have the option to participate. [Author's note: For more details, see CMS (2019)].

Our Innovation Models are organized into seven categories.

Accountable Care

Accountable Care Organizations and similar care models are designed to incentivize health care providers to become accountable for a patient

(continued)

population and to invest in infrastructure and redesigned care processes that provide for coordinated care, high quality and efficient service delivery.

Episode-Based Payment Initiatives

Under these models, health care providers are held accountable for the cost and quality of care beneficiaries receive during an episode of care, which usually begins with a triggering health care event (such as a hospitalization or chemotherapy administration) and extends for a limited period of time thereafter.

Primary Care Transformation

Primary care providers are a key point of contact for patients' health care needs. Strengthening and increasing access to primary care is critical to promoting health and reducing overall health care costs. Advanced primary care practices—also called "medical homes"—utilize a team-based approach, while emphasizing prevention, health information technology, care coordination, and shared decision making among patients and their providers.

Initiatives Focused on the Medicaid and CHIP Population

Medicaid and the Children's Health Insurance Program (CHIP) are administered by the states but are jointly funded by the federal government and states. Initiatives in this category are administered by the participating states.

Initiatives Focused on the Medicare-Medicaid Enrollees

The Medicare and Medicaid programs were designed with distinct purposes. Individuals enrolled in both Medicare and Medicaid (the "dual eligibles") account for a disproportionate share of the programs' expenditures. A fully integrated, person-centered system of care that ensures that all their needs are met could better serve this population in a high quality, cost effective manner.

Initiatives to Accelerate the Development and Testing of New Payment and Service Delivery Models

Many innovations necessary to improve the health care system will come from local communities and health care leaders from across the entire country. By partnering with these local and regional stakeholders, CMS can help accelerate the testing of models today that may be the next breakthrough tomorrow.

Initiatives to Speed the Adoption of Best Practices

Recent studies indicate that it takes nearly 17 years on average before best practices—backed by research—are incorporated into widespread clinical practice—and even then the application of the knowledge is very uneven. The Innovation Center is partnering with a broad range of health care providers, federal agencies, professional societies and other experts and stakeholders to test new models for disseminating evidence-based best practices and significantly increasing the speed of adoption.

Source: CMS (2020).

Although varying in size and quality, alternative solutions almost always exist. An excessive number of alternatives can slow the problem's advancement through the policymaking process as the relative merits of the competing alternatives are considered. Without at least one solution believed to have the potential to solve it, however, a problem does not advance, except perhaps in some spurious effort to create the illusion that it is being addressed.

When alternative solutions do exist, policymakers must decide whether the potential solutions are worth developing into legislative proposals. Frequently, multiple solutions to a particular problem will be considered worthy of such action, resulting in the simultaneous development of several competing legislative proposals. Competing proposals tend to make agenda setting rather chaotic, although rigorous research and analysis can sometimes provide more clarity.

Research and Analysis in Defining Problems and Assessing Alternatives

Health services research "is the science of study that determines what works, for whom, at what cost, and under what circumstances. It studies how our health system works, how to support patients and providers in choosing the right care, and how to improve health through care delivery" (AcademyHealth 2020). It has been defined more succinctly as "scientific inquiry into the ways in which health services are delivered to various constituents" (Forrest et al. 2008). Health services researchers seek to understand how people obtain access to healthcare services, the costs of the services, and the results for patients using this care. The main goals of this type of research include identifying the most effective ways to organize, manage, finance, and deliver high-quality care and services and, more recently, how to reduce medical errors and improve patient safety. Health services research, along with much biomedical research, contributes to problem identification and specification and the development of possible solutions. Thus, research can help establish the health policy agenda by clarifying problems and potential solutions. Well-conducted health services research provides policymakers with facts that might affect their decisions.

Policymakers generally value the input of the research community sufficiently to fund much of its work through the National Institutes of Health (NIH), the Agency for Healthcare Research and Quality (AHRQ), and other agencies. AHRQ, the health services research arm of the US Department of Health and Human Services (HHS), complements the biomedical research mission of its sister agency, NIH. AHRQ is the federal government's focal point for research to enhance the quality, appropriateness, and effectiveness of health services and access to those services.

Readers should note, however, that political support for scientific research waxes and wanes over time. In some eras, the predominant political ideology suggests a greater degree of ambivalence toward research than at other times. At the time of the ACA's enactment, there was a greater degree of appreciation for the potential of scientific research and accomplishment than in the decade that followed.

Center for Medicare and Medicaid Innovation. In addition to these traditional research and analysis agencies, the ACA significantly improved the government's ability to use analysis and research in guiding agenda setting. For example, the ACA created the CMS Center for Medicare and Medicaid Innovation (the CMS Innovation Center), appropriating $10 billion for the fiscal year (FY) 2011–2019 period, along with $10 billion for each subsequent ten-year period. The purpose of the CMS Innovation Center is to test and implement innovative payment and service delivery models. These models are intended to reduce program expenditures under Medicare, Medicaid, and the Children's Health Insurance Program (CHIP) while preserving or enhancing the quality of care furnished under these programs (Redhead 2017).

Independent Payment Advisory Board. The ACA also established and funded an Independent Payment Advisory Board (IPAB) to make recommendations to Congress for achieving specific Medicare spending reductions if costs exceed a target growth rate. IPAB's recommendations are to take effect unless Congress overrides them, in which case Congress would be responsible for achieving the same level of savings.

Patient-Centered Outcomes Research Institute (PCORI). Further supporting the research and analysis basis for policymaking, the ACA established a trust fund to finance the Patient-Centered Outcomes Research Institute (PCORI). The main purpose of PCORI is to support the conduct of comparative clinical effectiveness research (PCORI 2017). Appropriations to this trust fund totaled $210 million for FY 2010–2012. In FY 2013–2019, the fund received $150 million annually for a total of $1.26 billion over that ten-year period. The agency describes its funding (PCORI 2017):

> The PCOR Trust Fund receives income from three funding streams: appropriations from the general fund of the Treasury, transfers from the Centers for Medicare & Medicaid trust funds, and a fee assessed on private insurance and self-insured health plans (the PCOR fee).
>
> PCORI receives 80 percent of the monies collected by the PCOR Trust Fund to support its research funding and operations. The Department of Health and Human Services (HHS) receives the other 20 percent of trust fund monies to support dissemination and research capacity-building efforts (the majority of HHS's share goes to the Agency for Healthcare Research and Quality).

Research and analysis play two especially important roles in agenda setting. First, an important documentation role is played through the gathering, cataloging, and correlating of facts related to health problems and issues. For example, researchers documented the dangers of tobacco smoke; the presence of HIV; the numbers of people living with AIDS, a variety of cancers, heart disease, and other diseases; the effect of poverty on health; the number of people who lack health insurance coverage; the existence of health disparities among population segments; and the dangers imposed by exposure to various toxins in people's physical environments. Quantification and documentation of health-related problems give the problems a better chance of finding a place on the policy agenda.

The second way research informs, and thus influences, the health policy agenda is through analyses to determine which policy solutions may work or to compare alternative solutions. Health services research provides valuable information to policymakers as they propose, consider, and prioritize alternative solutions to problems. Often taking the form of demonstration projects intended to provide a basis for determining the feasibility, efficacy, or basic workability of a possible policy intervention, research-based recommendations to policymakers can play an important role in policy agenda setting. Potential solutions that might lead to public policies—even if the policies themselves are formulated mainly on political grounds—must stand the test of plausibility. Research that supports a particular course of action or attests to its likelihood of success—or at least to the probability that the course of action will not embarrass proponents—can make a significant contribution to policymaking by helping shape the policy agenda. What research cannot do for policymakers, however, is make decisions for them. Every difficult decision regarding the health policy agenda ultimately rests with policymakers.

It should also be noted, however, that political influence can sideline research that might be useful in addressing social issues that become public health issues. In 1996, Congress adopted the Dickey Amendment as part of an omnibus appropriations bill that specified that "none of the funds made available in this title may be used, in whole or in part, to advocate or promote gun control" (US Congress 1996). The amendment became an annual tradition in the appropriations process. While no agency took a position regarding gun control, scientists erred on the side of caution, understanding that *any* research on gun violence might reach a conclusion that appeared to favor limiting availability of firearms. For that reason, neither the Centers for Disease Control and Prevention (CDC) nor the NIH engaged in any research of the underlying causes of gun violence for 20 years (Rostron 2018). In response to a wave of mass shootings in 2018 and 2019, however, Congress appropriated $25 million for the NIH and CDC for gun violence research as part of an appropriations bill to avoid a government shutdown and did not include the Dickey Amendment (Stracqualursi 2019). This shift represents a policy modification arising from changed cultural circumstances. Further, it demonstrates the value of research in public health. By ending the prohibition and specifically funding this kind of research, Congress has demonstrated the value that research can have in setting the public policy agenda.

Making Decisions About Alternative Possible Solutions

Problems that require decisions and alternative possible solutions are two prerequisites for using the classical, rational model of decision-making outlined in exhibit 5.3. This model shares the basic pattern of the organizational decision-making process typically followed in the private and public sectors.

EXHIBIT 5.3
The Rational Model of Decision-Making

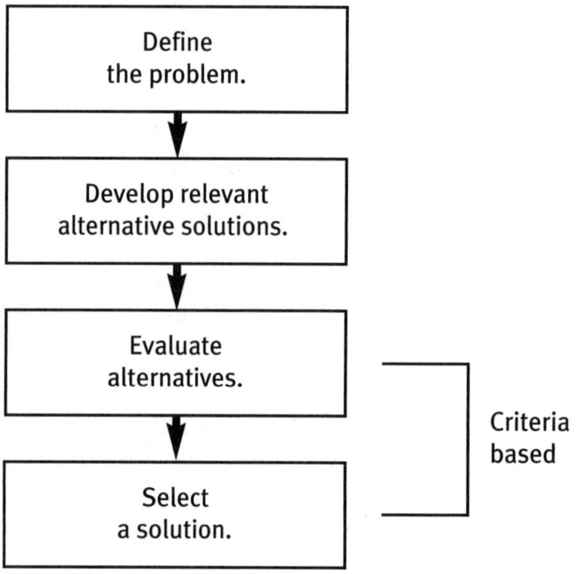

However, differences between the two sectors in the use of this model typically arise with the introduction of the criteria used to evaluate alternative solutions.

Some of the criteria used to evaluate and compare alternative solutions in the private and public sectors are the same or similar. For example, the criteria set in both sectors usually include consideration of whether a particular solution will actually solve the problem, whether it can be implemented using available resources and technologies, its costs and benefits relative to other possible solutions, and the results of an advantage-to-disadvantage analysis of the alternatives.

In both sectors, high-level decisions have scientific or technical, political, and economic dimensions. The scientific or technical aspects can be more difficult to factor into decisions when the evidence is in dispute, as it often is (Atkins, Siegel, and Slutsky 2005; Steinberg and Luce 2005). The most pervasive difference between the criteria sets used in the two sectors, however, is in the roles political concerns and considerations play. Decisions made by public-sector policymakers must reflect greater political sensitivity to the public at large and to the preferences of relevant individuals, organizations, and interest groups. The greater political sensitivity required helps explain the importance of the third variable in agenda setting, political circumstances.

Political Circumstances

A problem that might be solved or ameliorated through policy, even in combination with a possible solution to that problem, is not sufficient to move the problem–solution combination forward in the policymaking process. A political force, or what is sometimes called *political will*, is also necessary.

Thus, the political circumstances surrounding each problem–potential solution form the crucial third variable in creating a window of opportunity through which problems and potential solutions move toward development of legislation. This variable is generally as important as the other two variables in this complex equation (see exhibit 5.2), and in times of crisis such as the global financial crisis that emerged in 2008, political circumstances can be by far the most significant factor in stimulating policy changes. The American Recovery and Reinvestment Act of 2009 (P.L. 111-5) is an example of this phenomenon.

The establishment of a political thrust forceful enough to move policymakers to act on a health-related problem is often the most challenging variable in the problem's emergence on the policy agenda and progression to legislation development. This variable can be seen clearly in the passage of the ACA in 2010. Following decades of failed attempts to reform healthcare in the United States fundamentally, why did major health reform occur in 2010? The answer to this question is complex, but it certainly involves the political circumstances surrounding the issue. As Hacker suggests (2010), the election of a Democratic president and strengthening of the Democratic majority in Congress in 2008 were essential. Further, in this particular case, President Barack Obama was resolute in his determination to pass major healthcare reform legislation early in his tenure. Hacker further points out that the political circumstances in which the ACA occurred included not only a Democratic majority in Congress but a more homogeneously liberal composition of members of Congress.

Whether the political circumstances attendant on any problem–potential solution combination are sufficient to actually open a window of opportunity depends on the competing entries on the policy agenda. The array of problems is an important variable in agenda setting. When the nation is involved in serious threats to its national security or its civil order, for example, or when a state is in the midst of a sustained recession, health policy will be treated differently. In fact, health policy, which is often a high priority for the American people, can be pushed to a secondary position at times.

The political circumstances surrounding any problem–potential solution combination include such factors as the relevant public attitudes, concerns, and opinions; the preferences and relative ability of various interest groups to influence political decisions regarding the problem or the way it is addressed; and the positions of involved key policymakers in the executive and legislative branches of government. Each of these factors can influence whether a problem is addressed through policy and the shape and scope of any policy developed to address the problem. Two factors in particular exert great influence in establishing the policy agenda. These are interest groups and the chief executive (president, governor, mayor). The role of each in agenda setting is discussed in the next two sections.

Interest Group Involvement

As we discussed in chapter 2, interest groups are ubiquitous in the policy marketplace. The agenda setting activities and legislation development in the policy formulation phase are no exception (see exhibit 5.1). Interest groups and their representatives are omnipresent throughout the policy process.

To appreciate fully the role of interest groups in setting the policy agenda, consider the role of individual Americans. In a representative form of government, such as that of the United States, individual members of society, unless they are among the elected representatives, usually do not vote directly on policies. They can, however, vote on policymakers. Thus, policymakers are interested in what individuals, especially voters, want, even when that is not easy to discern.

However, one of the great myths about democratic societies is that their members, when confronted with tough problems such as the high cost of healthcare for everyone, the lack of health insurance for many, or the existence of widespread disparities in health among segments of the society, ponder the problems carefully and express their preferences to their elected officials, who then factor these opinions into their decisions about how to address the problems through policy. Sometimes these steps take place, but even when the public expresses its opinions about an issue, the result is clouded by the fact that the American people are heterogeneous in their views. Opinions are mixed on health-related problems and their solutions. Public opinion polls can help sort out conflicting opinions, but polls are not always straightforward undertakings. In addition, individuals' opinions on many issues are subject to change.

The public's thinking on difficult problems that might be addressed through public policies evolves through predictable stages, beginning with awareness of the problem and ending with judgments about its solution (Yankelovich and Friedman 2010). In between, people explore the problem and alternative solutions with varying degrees of success. The journey between awareness and judgment can be more of a short, emotive process than an intellectual inquiry. The progress of individuals through these stages is related to their views on the problems and solutions. Those views are most likely a product of self-interest: for example, a pharmaceutical sales representative whose compensation is based on commissions is less likely to be supportive of legislation that would regulate the price of prescription medications than a senior citizen on a fixed income whose health requires that they take several prescriptions a day.

The diversity among members of society, and hence organizations and interest groups, and the fact that individual views on problems and potential solutions evolve over time, explain in large part the greater influence of organizations and interest groups in shaping the policy agenda. Interest groups in particular can exert extraordinary influence in policy markets, as we discussed in chapter 2.

Whether made up of individuals or organizations, interest groups are often able to present a unified position to policymakers on their preferences regarding a particular problem or its solution. A unified position is far easier for policymakers to assess and respond to than the diverse opinions and preferences of many individuals acting alone. Although individuals tend to be keenly interested in their own health and the health of those they care about, their interests in specific health policies tend to be diffuse. These diffused interests stand in contrast to the highly concentrated interests of those who earn their livelihood in the health domain or who stand to gain other benefits there. This phenomenon is not unique to health. In general, the interests of those who earn their livelihood in any industry or economic sector are more concentrated than the interests of those who merely use its outputs.

One result of the concentration of interests is the formation of organized interest groups that seek to influence the formulation, implementation, and modification of policies to some advantage for the group's members. Because all interest groups seek policies that favor their members, their own agendas, behaviors, and preferences regarding the larger public policy agenda are often predictable.

Feldstein (2019) argues, for example, that all interest groups representing health services providers seek through legislation to increase the demand for members' services, limit competitors, permit members to charge the highest possible prices for their services, and lower their members' operating costs as much as possible. Likewise, an interest group representing health services consumers logically seeks policies that minimize the costs of the services to its members, ease their access to the services, increase the availability of the services, and so on. Essentially, interest groups are human nature at work.

As we noted earlier, interest groups frequently play influential roles in setting the nation's health policy agenda, as they subsequently do in the development of legislation and the implementation and modification of health policies. These groups sometimes proactively seek to stimulate new policies that serve the interests of their members. Alternatively, they sometimes reactively seek to block policy changes that they believe do not serve their members' best interests.

Interest Groups Are Ubiquitous in Health Policymaking

A significant feature of the policymaking process in the United States is the presence of interest groups that exist to serve the collective interests of their members. These groups analyze the policymaking process to discern policy changes that might affect their members and inform them about such changes. They also seek to influence the process to provide the group's members with some advantage. The interests of their constituent members define the health policy interests of these groups.

Health services providers rely heavily on interest groups to influence policymaking to their advantage, as do other types of health-related organizations. Some interest groups are consumer based. Without being exhaustive, some of the important health-related interest groups are noted next.

Hospitals can join the American Hospital Association (www.aha.org), long-term care organizations can join the American Health Care Association (www.ahca.org) or the American Association of Homes and Services for the Aging, now known as LeadingAge (www.leadingage.org), and health insurers and health plans can join America's Health Insurance Plans (www.ahip.org).

Other interest groups represent individual health practitioners. Physicians can join the American Medical Association (AMA; www.ama-assn.org). African American physicians may choose to join the National Medical Association (www.nmanet.org), and female physicians may choose to join the American

Medical Women's Association (www.amwa-doc.org). In addition, physicians have the opportunity to affiliate with groups, usually termed *colleges* or *academies,* where membership is based on medical specialty. Prominent examples are the American College of Surgeons (www.facs.org) and the American Academy of Pediatrics (www.aap.org). Other personal membership groups include the American College of Healthcare Executives (www.ache.org), the American Nurses Association (www.ana.org), and the American Dental Association (www.ada.org), to name a few.

Often, in addition to national interest groups, health services provider organizations and individual practitioners can join state and local groups—usually affiliates or chapters of national groups—that also represent their interests. For example, states have state hospital associations and state medical societies. Many urban centers and densely populated areas even have groups at the regional, county, or city level.

There are numerous other health-related interest groups in addition to those whose members provide health services directly. Examples include the following:

- America's Health Insurance Plans (www.ahip.org)
- Association of American Medical Colleges (www.aamc.org)
- Association of University Programs in Health Administration (www.aupha.org)
- Biotechnology Industry Organization (www.bio.org)
- Blue Cross and Blue Shield Association (www.bcbs.com)
- Pharmaceutical Research and Manufacturers of America (www.phrma.org)

Like groups whose members are health services providers, these groups focus particularly on policies that affect their members directly.

Moreover, a large number of patient advocacy groups highlight the need for specific disease remedies. An unknown number of these groups may have relationships with the pharmaceutical industry—indeed, with companies that provide drugs for the specific disease highlighted by the organization. In other words, the positions taken by the group may more nearly reflect those of the financial sponsor than of the patients or their caregivers. As many as 83 percent of such organizations receive financial support from the industry, while as many as 39 percent include industry representatives on their boards. Publicly available data are limited, so observing this trend in detail is impossible (McCoy et al. 2017).

There are also interest groups that serve consumers. Reflecting the populations from which their members are drawn, groups with individual member constituencies are diverse. Some are based in part on a shared characteristic such as race, gender, age, or connection to a specific disease or condition. Examples include the following:

- Alliance for Retired Americans (www.retiredamericans.org)
- AARP (www.aarp.org)
- American Heart Association (www.heart.org)
- Consortium for Citizens with Disabilities (www.c-c-d.org)
- Families USA (www.familiesusa.org)
- National Association for the Advancement of Colored People (NAACP; www.naacp.org)
- National Organization for Women (NOW; www.now.org)

Interest groups such as NAACP and NOW serve the health interests of their members as part of agendas focused broadly on racial and gender equality. Although the Fourteenth Amendment to the US Constitution guarantees equal protection under the law, American history clearly shows how difficult this equality has been to achieve. Interest groups such as NAACP and NOW have made equality their central public policy goal at the polls; in the workplace; and in education, housing, health services, and other facets of life in the United States. Income inequality in the United States is the newest of these variables.

The specific health policy interests of groups representing African Americans include adequately addressing this population segment's unique health problems: widespread disparities in health status and access to health services, higher infant mortality, higher exposure to violence among adolescents, higher levels of substance abuse among adults, and, compared to other segments of the population, earlier deaths from cardiovascular disease and other causes. Similarly, groups representing the interests of women seek to address their unique health problems. In particular, they focus on such interests as breast cancer, childbearing, osteoporosis, domestic violence, family health, and funding for biomedical research on women's health problems.

A growing proportion of the American population is older than 65. Older adults have specific health interests related to their stage of life; as people age, they consume relatively more healthcare services, and their healthcare needs differ from those of younger people. They also become more likely to consume long-term care services and community-based services intended to help them cope with limitations in the activities of daily living.

In addition to their health needs, older citizens have a unique health policy history and, therefore, a unique set of expectations and preferences regarding the nation's health policy. The Medicare program, a key feature of this history, includes extensive provisions for health benefits for older citizens. Building on the specific interests of older people and their preferences to preserve and extend their healthcare benefits through public policies, organizations such as AARP and the Alliance for Retired Americans (www.retiredamericans.org) play an important role in addressing the health policy interests of their members.

Other interest groups with individual constituencies reflect member interests based primarily on specific diseases or conditions, such as the American Cancer Society (www.cancer.org) or the Consortium for Citizens with Disabilities (www.c-c-d.org). The American Heart Association, for example, has 22.5 million volunteers and supporters pursuing the organization's mission of building healthier lives free of cardiovascular diseases and stroke. The association pursues its mission through such avenues as direct funding of research, public and professional education programs, and community programs designed to prevent heart disease. It also seeks to serve its members' interests through influencing public policy related to heart disease.

As the American Hospital Association (2019) notes on its web page, its federal policy agenda is organized into the following categories:

- Sustain the gains in health coverage
- Protect patient access to care
- Advance health system transformation
- Enhance quality and patient safety
- Promote regulatory relief
- Strengthen the workforce

Interest Group Tactics

As influential participants in public policymaking, interest groups are integral to the process. They are especially ubiquitous in the health domain. But how do they exert their influence? Interest groups rely heavily on four tactics: lobbying, electioneering, litigation, and (especially recently) shaping public opinion so that it might in turn influence the policymaking process to the groups' advantage (Edwards, Wattenberg, and Lineberry 2012). Each of these tactics is described in the following sections.

Lobbying

This widely used influencing tactic has deep roots in public policymaking in the United States, and it involves large sums of money. Lobbying expenditures on health issues at the federal level were nearly $568 million in 2018 (Center for Responsive Politics 2019d). In the minds of many people, lobbying conjures a negative image of backroom deals and money exchanging hands for political favors. Ideally, however, it is nothing more than communicating with public policymakers to influence their decisions to be more favorable to, or at least consistent with, the preferences of the lobbyist and the organization they represent (Andres 2009; Herrnson, Shaiko, and Wilcox 2005).

Lobbying, the word for these influencing activities, and *lobbyists*, the word for people who do this work, arose in reference to the place where such activities first took place. "The term is believed to have originated in British Parliament, and referred to the lobbies outside the chambers where wheeling and dealing took place. 'Lobbyist' was in common usage in Britain in the 1840's. Jesse Sheidlower, editor-at-large for the *Oxford English Dictionary,* believes the term was used as early as 1640 in England to describe the lobbies that were open to constituents to interact with their representatives" (Shannon 2009).

See exhibit 5.4 for a visual presentation of the number of lobbyists registered with the federal government. As you examine the graph, consider that the US House of Representatives has 435 members and the US Senate has 100. Granted, lobbyists also work with executive branch agencies, but the graph suggests that there are nearly 23 lobbyists for each member of Congress.

The vast majority of lobbyists operate in an ethical and professional manner, effectively representing the legitimate interests of the groups they serve. However, the few who behave in a heavy-handed, even illegal manner have, to some extent, tarnished the reputations of all who do this work. Their image is further affected by the fact that their work, properly done, is essentially selfish in nature. Lobbyists seek to persuade others that the position of the interests they represent is the correct one. Lobbyists' whole professional purpose is to

EXHIBIT 5.4
Number of Registered Lobbyists and Amount of Lobbying Expenditures (in billions)

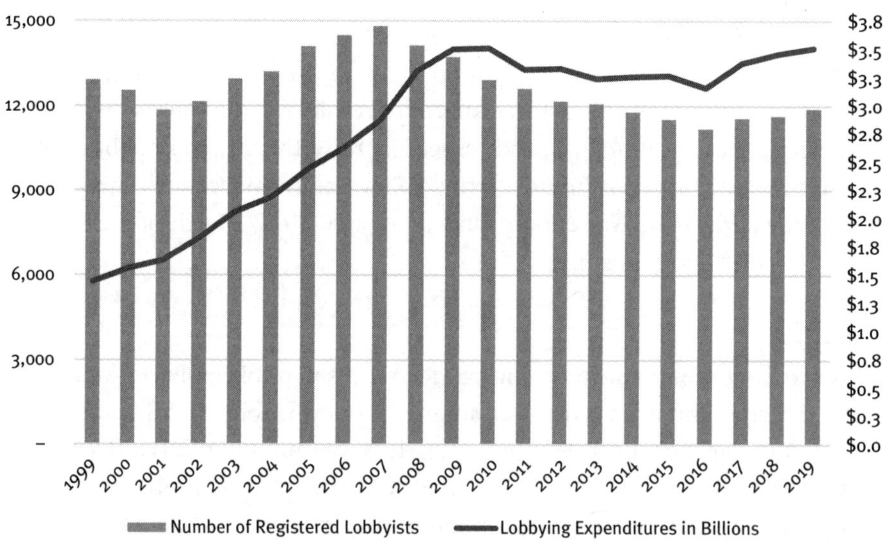

Source: Adapted from Center for Responsive Politics (2019b).

persuade others to make decisions that are in the best interests of those who employ or retain them.

Opinions and results of studies on the effectiveness of lobbying are mixed at best (Bergan 2009). Some ambivalence over the role of lobbying derives from the inherent difficulty in isolating its effect from the other influencing tactics discussed later. There is no doubt that lobbying affects the policymaking process, but it seems to work best when applied to policymakers who are already committed, or at least sympathetic, to the lobbyist's position on a public policy issue (Edwards, Wattenberg, and Lineberry 2012). Lobbyists certainly played a prominent role in the enactment of the Medicare Prescription Drug, Improvement, and Modernization Act of 2003 (P.L. 108173); the ACA; and, as discussed in the next chapter, the 21st Century Cures Act, along with other health policies (Kersh 2014; Weissert and Weissert 2019). The influence lobbyists exert on policymaking is facilitated by several well-recognized sources (Godwin, Ainsworth, and Godwin 2013; Herrnson, Shaiko, and Wilcox 2005). Lobbyists can do the following:

- Be an important source of information for policymakers. Although most policymakers must be concerned with many policy issues simultaneously, most lobbyists can focus and specialize. They can become expert and can draw on the insight of other experts in the areas they represent.
- Assist policymakers with the development and execution of political strategy. Lobbyists typically are politically savvy and can provide what amounts to free consulting to the policymakers they choose to assist.
- Assist elected policymakers in their reelection efforts. (See the next section on electioneering.) This assistance can take several forms, including campaign contributions, votes, and workers for campaigns.
- Be important sources of innovative ideas for policymakers. Policymakers are judged on the quality of their ideas as well as their abilities to have those ideas translated into effective policies. For most policymakers, few gifts are as valued as a really good idea, especially when they can turn that idea into a bill that bears their name.
- Be friends with policymakers. Lobbyists are often gregarious and interesting people in their own right. They entertain, sometimes lavishly, and they are socially engaging. Many of them have social and educational backgrounds similar to those of policymakers. In fact, many lobbyists have been policymakers earlier in their careers. Friendships between lobbyists and policymakers are neither unusual nor surprising.

Not only is there an astounding number of lobbyists, but the amount of money spent by interest groups seeking to influence the process is likewise considerable (see exhibit 5.4). Again, considering that there are 535 members of Congress, $3.45 billion divided by 535 suggests that lobbyists spent about $6.5 million on each member of Congress. Keep in mind that these expenditures include efforts to shape public opinion beyond just direct communication with policymakers.

Electioneering

Electioneering, or using the resources at groups' disposal to aid candidates for political office, is a common means through which interest groups seek to influence the policymaking process. Many groups have considerable resources to devote to this tactic. The effectiveness of electioneering in influencing the policymaking process is based on the simple fact that policymakers who are sympathetic to a group's interests are far more likely to be influenced than are policymakers who are not sympathetic. Thus, interest groups seek to elect and keep in office policymakers whom they view as sympathetic to the interests of the group's members.

Interest groups have, to varying degrees, a set of resources that involve electoral advantages or disadvantages for political candidates. For example, some groups—whose members are widely dispersed across congressional districts throughout the country, that can mobilize their members, and whose members have status or wealth—can affect election outcomes (Kingdon 2010).

One of the most visible aspects of electioneering is the channeling of money into campaign finances. Exhibit 5.5 shows the extent of this activity in the 2016 elections. Health-related interest groups participate heavily in this form of electioneering. Appendix 2.1 describes the types of groups permitted to be involved in financing political campaigns.

In 1975, Congress created the Federal Election Commission (FEC; www.fec.gov) to administer and enforce the Federal Election Campaign Act—the law that governs the financing of federal elections. The duties of the FEC, which is an independent regulatory agency, are to disclose campaign finance information; enforce the provisions of the law, such as the limits and prohibitions on contributions; and oversee the public funding of presidential elections.

The Center for Responsive Politics, a nonpartisan, not-for-profit research group based in Washington, DC, is a rich source of information on the use of money in politics and its effect on elections and public policymaking. The center's website (www.opensecrets.org) provides extensive, detailed information on the flow of money in the political process.

Although participation in campaign financing is an important source of influence for interest groups, the most influential groups are those who exert their influence through lobbying and electioneering activities. The hospital field is a notable example. The American Hospital Association is a leading

EXHIBIT 5.5

Money Raised in the 2016 Election Cycle

President

Financial activity for all presidential candidates, 2015–2016
Democrats: **$800,059,726**
Republicans: **$647,632,718**

Party	No. of Candidates	Total Raised	Total Spent	Total Cash on Hand	Total from PACs	Total from Individuals
All	26	$1,465,024,416	$1,449,708,126	$16,442,476	$4,124,295	$1,086,206,949
Dems	6	$800,059,726	$794,114,757	$5,962,742	$1,904,888	$638,007,713
Repubs	17	$647,632,718	$638,417,137	$10,112,799	$2,214,407	$432,203,093

House

Financial activity for all House candidates, 2015–2016
Democrats: **$469,245,791**
Republicans: **$558,520,332**

Party	No. of Candidates	Total Raised	Total Spent	Total Cash on Hand	Total from PACs	Total from Individuals
All	2086	$1,033,545,524	$971,524,520	$293,559,022	$362,619,038	$552,484,657
Dems	908	$469,245,791	$422,817,279	$143,811,790	$151,287,745	$275,105,343
Repubs	1074	$558,520,332	$542,951,592	$149,601,662	$211,319,899	$276,463,148

Senate

Financial activity for all Senate candidates, 2015–2016
Democrats: **$363,396,637**
Republicans: **$302,100,403**

Party	No. of Candidates	Total Raised	Total Spent	Total Cash on Hand	Total from PACs	Total from Individuals
All	460	$667,687,881	$674,985,540	$162,458,097	$115,868,475	$481,118,962
Dems	170	$363,396,637	$350,184,257	$85,928,423	$45,139,886	$286,750,451
Repubs	230	$302,100,403	$322,714,240	$76,373,059	$70,597,456	$193,036,593

Source: Center for Responsive Politics (2019a). Reprinted with permission.

campaign contributor through its political action committee. Furthermore, it has many additional resources at its disposal. As Kingdon (2010) points out, every congressional district has hospitals whose trustees are community leaders and whose managers and physicians are typically articulate and respected in their community. These spokespersons can be mobilized to support sympathetic candidates or to contact their representatives directly regarding any policy decision.

As Ornstein and Elder (1978, 74) observed decades ago, "The ability of a group to mobilize its membership strength for political action is a highly valuable resource; a small group that is politically active and cohesive can have more political impact than a large, politically apathetic, and unorganized group." The ability to mobilize people and other resources at the grassroots level helps explain the capabilities of various groups to influence the policymaking process. The most influential health interest groups, including those representing hospitals, physicians, and nurses, have particularly strong grassroots organizations to call into play in their lobbying and electioneering tactics. While the ability to organize at the grass roots continues to be a source of enormous influence in the policymaking process, the ability of any particular organization to be active in a grassroots campaign changes, and perhaps degrades, over time. The AMA, for example, was extremely vocal in its opposition to Medicare and was effective for many years in forestalling its enactment. In recent times, however, the AMA's ability to speak with a single voice on behalf of all physicians has diminished owing to the development of subgroups in the medical profession that develop different, perhaps more nuanced positions than can be articulated in the larger group (Girgis 2015).

Litigation

A third tactic interest groups can use to influence the policymaking process is litigation. Interest groups, acting on behalf of their members, seek to influence the policy agenda and the larger policymaking process through litigation in which they challenge existing policies, seek to stimulate new policies, or try to alter certain aspects of policy implementation. Use of the litigation tactic in state and federal courts is widespread, and interest groups increasingly employ it in their efforts to influence policymaking in the health domain. An excellent example is the policy snapshot at the beginning of part 1, in which the National Federation of Independent Business brought suit in federal court to challenge the constitutionality of the ACA. Other examples are noted in chapter 8.

Although interest groups are more likely to seek to influence legislative and executive branch decisions, they can and do pursue their policy goals in the courts. This tactic is especially attractive when interest groups believe there is a bona fide legal or constitutional question regarding the impact of legislative or executive branch action on their members. In these circumstances, groups may find the judicial branch a more fertile ground for their efforts. When interest groups turn to the courts, they are likely to use one of two strategies: test cases and amicus curiae ("friend of the court") briefs.

Because the judiciary engages in policymaking primarily by rendering decisions in specific cases, interest groups may attempt to ensure that cases pertaining to their interests are brought before the courts, which is known as using the *test-case strategy*. A particular interest group can initiate and sponsor a case, or it can participate in a case initiated by another group that is pertinent to its interests. The latter strategy involves filing amicus curiae briefs and is the easiest way for interest groups to become involved in cases. This strategy, which is used in federal and state appellate courts rather than trial courts, permits groups to get their interests before the courts even when they do not control the cases in which they participate by filing the briefs. To file a brief, a private group must obtain permission from the parties to the case or from the court. This requirement does not apply to government interests. In fact, the solicitor general of the United States is especially important in this regard, and in some situations the US Supreme Court invites the solicitor general to present an amicus brief.

Friend-of-the-court briefs are often intended not to strengthen the arguments of one of the parties but to assert to the court the filing group's preferences as to how a case should be resolved. Amicus curiae briefs are often filed to persuade an appellate court to either grant or deny review of a lower court decision (US Department of State 2004). For example, in one case, a group of commercial insurers and health maintenance organizations in New York City challenged the state of New York's practice of adding a surcharge to certain hospital bills to raise money to help fund health services for indigent people (Green 1995). The US Supreme Court heard this case. Because the outcome was important to their members, a number of health interest groups filed amicus briefs in an effort to influence the court's decision. Through such written depositions, groups state their collective position on issues and describe how the decision will affect their members. This practice is widely used by interest groups in health and other domains. It has made the Supreme Court accessible to these groups, who, in expressing their views, have helped determine which cases the court will hear and how it will rule on them (Collins 2008). This practice is also frequently and effectively used by interest groups in lower courts to help shape the health policy agenda.

The use of litigation is not limited to attempts to shape the policy agenda, however. One particularly effective use of this tactic is seeking clarification from the courts on vague pieces of legislation. This practice provides opportunities for interest groups to exert enormous influence on policymaking overall by influencing the rules, regulations, and administrative practices that guide the implementation of public statutes or laws. We will say more about the role of interest groups in chapter 9 in the discussion about rulemaking as part of the overall public policymaking process. For now, recall from chapter 1 that the rules and regulations established to implement laws and programs are themselves authoritative decisions that fit the definition of public policies.

Shaping Public Opinion

Because policymakers are influenced by the electorate's opinions, many interest groups seek to influence the policymaking process by shaping public opinion (Blendon et al. 2010; Schlesinger 2014). A good example of this influence is seen in some of the activities of the Coalition to Protect America's Health Care. On its Facebook page, the coalition describes itself as "an organization of hospitals and national, state, regional and metropolitan hospital associations . . . united to achieve one goal: to protect high quality patient care by preserving the financial viability of America's hospitals" (Coalition to Protect America's Health Care 2020). It pursues this goal in part by shaping public opinion through ads supporting hospitals.

This tactic, of course, is not new. It was used extensively in the congressional debate over national health reform in the 1990s. Interest groups spent more than $50 million seeking to shape public opinion on the issues involved. For example, many thought the health insurance industry's ubiquitous "Harry and Louise" ads were effective during the debate (Hacker 1997). These ads were not the first use of this public opinion tactic by healthcare interest groups, however.

Intense opposition in some quarters to the legislation, especially by the AMA, fueled the congressional debate over the Medicare legislation in the 1960s. The American public had rarely, if ever, been exposed to so feverish a campaign to shape opinions as it experienced in the period leading up to its enactment in 1965.

Among the many activities undertaken in that campaign to influence public opinion (and through it, policymakers), perhaps none is more entertaining in hindsight—and certainly few better represent the campaign's tone and intensity—than one action taken by the AMA. As part of its campaign to influence public opinion on Medicare, the AMA sent every physician's spouse a recording and advised them to host friends and neighbors and play the recording for their edification. The idea was to encourage the listeners to write letters to their representatives in Congress in opposition to the legislation. Near the end of the recording, narrated by Ronald Reagan, the following words can be heard (as quoted in Skidmore 1970, 138):

> Write those letters now; call your friends and tell them to write them. If you don't, this program, I promise you, will pass just as surely as the sun will come up tomorrow. And behind it will come other federal programs that will invade every area of freedom as we have known it in this country. Until one day . . . [we] will awake to find that we have socialism. And if you don't do this, and I don't do it, one of these days

you and I are going to spend our sunset years telling our children and our children's children what it was like in America when men were free.

Attempts to shape public opinion about government's role in health continue today. While it is difficult to discern precisely expenditures designed to affect public opinion, observers can say with certainty that the healthcare sector continues to spend enormous sums of money to influence public policy. For the year 2019, the pharmaceutical manufacturing industry, for example, spent nearly $131 million to employ 809 lobbyists on behalf of 145 clients. Likewise, the hospital and nursing home subsectors spent more than $78 million on behalf of 350 clients using 775 lobbyists (Center for Responsive Politics 2019c).

Although the effect of the appeals to public opinion made by interest groups on policymaking is debatable, the extent and persistence of the practice suggests that interest groups believe that it does make a difference. One factor clearly mitigates the usefulness of this tactic and makes difficult its use by interest groups: the heterogeneity of the American population's perceptions of problems and preferred solutions to them. For example, in the congressional debate over major health reform in the 1990s, the majority viewpoint at the beginning of the debate was that health reform was needed. However, at no time during the debate was a public consensus achieved on the nature of that reform. No feasible alternative for reform ever received majority support in any public opinion poll. During most of the debate, in fact, public opinion was about evenly divided among the possible reform options (Brodie and Blendon 1995). Similarly, public opinion was split during development of the ACA legislation and has continued to be split throughout its implementation (Kaiser Family Foundation 2013). The split was largely partisan in the early debate about reform in 2009, with Democrats (70 percent) supporting reform and Republicans (60 percent) opposing it (Kaiser Family Foundation 2009).

Interest Group Resources

Using lobbying, electioneering, litigation, and efforts to shape public opinion, interest groups seek to influence the policy agenda and the larger public policymaking process to the strategic advantage of their members. The degree of success they achieve depends on the resources at their disposal. In a classic book on the subject, Ornstein and Elder (1978) categorize the resources of interest groups as follows:

- Physical resources, especially money and the number of members
- Organizational resources, such as the quality of a group's leadership, the degree of unity or cohesion among its members, and the group's ability to mobilize its membership for political purposes

- Political resources, such as expertise in the intricacies of the public policymaking process and a reputation for influencing the process ethically and effectively
- Motivational resources, such as the strength of ideological conviction among the membership
- Intangible resources, such as the overall status or prestige of a group

An especially important physical resource is the size of a group's membership. Large groups, especially when a group can convince policymakers that it speaks with one united voice representing the preferences of its members, can influence all phases of the policymaking process from agenda setting through modification (Kingdon 2010). Larger groups can obviously have more financial resources, but perhaps even more important, size might provide an advantage simply because the group's membership is spread through every legislative district. However, the costs of organizing a large group can be high, especially if their interests are not concordant and focused.

The mix of physical, organizational, political, motivational, and intangible resources available to an interest group, and how effectively the group uses them, helps determine the group's influence on the policy agenda and other aspects of the policymaking process. A particular group's performance is also affected by its access to resources compared with groups that may be pursuing competing or conflicting policy outcomes (Edwards, Wattenberg, and Lineberry 2012; Feldstein 2019; Kingdon 2010). The policy marketplace, as we discussed in chapter 2, is a place where many people and groups promote their policy preferences.

The Influential Role of the President (or Governor or Mayor)

Chief executives—presidents, governors, or mayors—also influence the policy agenda, including the agenda for policy in the health domain. Popular chief executives can influence the policy agenda easily (Aberbach and Peterson 2006). Kingdon (2010) attributes the influence of presidents (his point also applies to other chief executives) to certain institutional resources inherent in the executive office. Morone (2014) notes that presidents can energize healthcare policy by setting the agenda and proposing solutions to problems. He also observes that bold federal health policies invariably require presidential leadership.

Political advantages available to chief executives include the ability to present a unified administration position on issues—which contrasts with the legislative branch, where opinions and views tend to be heterogeneous—and the ability to command public attention. Properly managed, the latter ability can stimulate substantial public pressure on legislators. Chief executives can even rival powerful interest groups in their ability to shape public opinion around the public policy agenda.

Chief executives can emphasize problems and preferred solutions in a number of ways, including press conferences, speeches, and addresses. Emphasizing problems and preferred solutions may be an especially potent tactic in such highly visible contexts as a president's state of the union address or a governor's state of the state address.

Candidates for the presidency are often specific in their campaigns on various health policy issues, sometimes even to the point of endorsing specific legislative proposals. Examples include the emphasis Presidents John F. Kennedy and Lyndon B. Johnson gave to enactment of the Medicare program in their campaigns and President Bill Clinton's highly visible commitment to fundamental health reform as a central theme of his 1992 campaign. President George W. Bush made enactment of the Medicare Prescription Drug, Improvement, and Modernization Act of 2003 a priority as he entered the campaign for his second term in 2004. In his 2008 campaign, and again in his 2012 reelection campaign, President Obama made health reform one of the highest priorities for his administration.

Another issue-raising mechanism some chief executives favor is the appointment of special commissions or task forces. President Clinton used this tactic in the 1993 appointment of the President's Task Force on Health Care Reform (Johnson and Broder 1996), as did President Obama in the creation of the National Commission on Fiscal Responsibility and Reform in 2010.

Governors can also use commissions and task forces to elevate issues on the policy agenda. For example, Massachusetts made history when that state's Gay and Lesbian Student Rights Law was signed by Governor William Weld in 1993. He established the nation's first Governor's Commission on Gay and Lesbian Youth, which helped lead the state legislature to enact the law. This law prohibits discrimination in public schools on the basis of sexual orientation. Gay students are guaranteed redress if they suffer name-calling, threats of violence, and unfair treatment in school. In another example, Governor Terry McAuliffe of Virginia established the Governor's Task Force on Mental Health Services and Crisis Response in 2013 and charged it to seek and recommend solutions to improve the state's mental health crisis services.

Governors (and certainly presidents) play key roles in shaping their parties' platforms. When others run as members of that party, they implicitly endorse the party platform (at the least). Some candidates are more explicit than others; some may have points of emphasis in the platform that they articulate more than others. A few may overtly contradict a portion of the platform from time to time. On the whole, however, an elected chief executive holds considerable sway over the positions taken by their party, which in turn affects the attitudes of others.

Chief executives occupy a position that permits them to influence each phase of the policymaking process. In addition to their issue-raising role in agenda setting, they are well positioned to focus the legislative branch on the development of legislation and to prod legislators to continue their work on favored issues even when other demands compete for their time and attention. In addition, chief executives are central to the implementation of policies by virtue of their position atop the executive (or implementing) branch of government, as we discuss in chapter 7, and they play a crucial role in modifying previously established policies, as we discuss in chapter 9.

The Nature of the Health Policy Agenda

The confluence of problems and potential solutions and the political circumstances that surround them invariably shapes the health policy agenda. This agenda, however, is extraordinarily dynamic, literally changing from day to day. In addition, the nation's health policy agenda coexists with policy agendas in other domains, such as defense, welfare, education, and homeland security. The situation is further complicated by the fact that in a pluralistic society where difficult problems exist and clear-cut solutions are rare, every problem and potential solution has different sides, each with its supporters and detractors. The number, ratio, and intensity of these supporters and detractors are determined by the perceived effect on them of a problem and its possible solution. One consequence of this phenomenon is severe crowding and confounding of the health policy agenda. This agenda is impossible to describe in its full form at any point in time; it is enormous and in constant flux.

As policymakers seek to accommodate the needs and preferences of different interests in problem–potential solution combinations, the inevitable result is a large and diverse set of policies that are riddled with incompatibilities and inconsistencies. The subset of US policies on the production and consumption of tobacco products—a mix that simultaneously facilitates and discourages tobacco use—provides a good example of the coexistence of public policies at cross-purposes.

Another example can be seen in the health policy agenda, and in the eventual pattern of public policies, related to medical technology. Policymakers have sought to spread the benefits of new medical technology and at the same time to protect the public from unsafe technologies and slow the growth in overall health costs through controlling the explosive growth of new technologies. The result is a large group of technology-related policies that seek to foster (e.g., NIH, National Science Foundation, other biomedical funding, tax credits for biomedical research in the private sector), to inhibit (e.g., state-run certificate-of-need programs that restrain the diffusion of technology), and to control (e.g., Food and Drug Administration regulation and product liability laws) the development and use of medical technology in the United States.

Its complexity and inconsistency aside, the most important aspect of the health policy agenda is that when a problem is widely acknowledged, when possible solutions have been identified and refined, and when political circumstances are favorable, a window of opportunity opens, albeit sometimes only briefly. Through this window, problem–potential solution combinations move forward to a new stage: development of legislation (see exhibit 5.1). As we describe in chapter 6, through the development of legislation, policymakers seek to convert some of their ideas, hopes, and hypotheses about addressing problems into concrete policies in the form of new public laws or amendments to existing ones.

Summary

The policy formulation phase involves agenda setting and the development of legislation, as exhibit 5.1 shows. Agenda setting is the central topic of this chapter. We discuss the development of legislation in chapter 6.

Following Kingdon's (2010) conceptualization, agenda setting in public policymaking is a function of the confluence of three streams of activity: problems, possible solutions to those problems, and political circumstances. When all three streams flow together in a favorable alignment, a window of opportunity opens (see exhibit 5.1), allowing a problem–potential solution combination, which might be developed into a new public law or an amendment to an existing one, to advance to the next point in the policymaking process: development of legislation.

Review Questions

1. Discuss the formulation phase of policymaking in general terms.
2. Discuss agenda setting as the confluence of three streams of activities. Include the concept of a window of opportunity for legislation development in your answer.
3. Describe the nature of problems that drive policy formulation.
4. Discuss the role of research and analysis in defining problems and assessing alternatives.
5. Contrast decision-making in the public and private sectors as it relates to selecting from among alternative solutions to problems.

6. Discuss the involvement of interest groups in the political circumstances that affect agenda setting. Incorporate the specific ways they influence agenda setting in your response.
7. Discuss the role of presidents or governors in agenda setting at the federal level.
8. Discuss the nature of the health policy agenda that results from agenda setting at the federal level.

References

Aberbach, J. D., and M. A. Peterson. 2006. *The Executive Branch.* New York: Oxford University Press.

AcademyHealth. 2020. "About AcademyHealth." Accessed April 24. https://academyhealth.org/about.

American Hospital Association. 2019. "2019 AHA Advocacy Agenda." Accessed December 26. www.aha.org/advocacy/2019-04-05-aha-2019-advocacy-agenda.

Andres, G. J. 2009. *Lobbying Reconsidered: Politics Under the Influence.* White Plains, NY: Pearson Longman.

Atkins, D., J. Siegel, and J. Slutsky. 2005. "Making Policy When the Evidence Is in Dispute." *Health Affairs* 24 (1): 102–13.

Bergan, D. E. 2009. "Does Grassroots Lobbying Work?" *American Politics Research* 37 (2): 327–52.

Blendon, R., M. Brodie, D. E. Altman, and J. Benson. 2010. *American Public Opinion and Health Care.* Washington, DC: CQ Press.

Brodie, M., and R. J. Blendon. 1995. "The Public's Contribution to Congressional Gridlock on Health Care Reform." *Journal of Health Politics, Policy and Law* 20 (2): 403–10.

Center for Responsive Politics. 2019a. "Election Overview." Accessed December 27. www.opensecrets.org/bigpicture.

———. 2019b. "Lobbying Data Summary." Accessed June 20, 2020. www.opensecrets.org/federal-lobbying.

———. 2019c. "Pharmaceutical Manufacturing." Accessed December 27. www.opensecrets.org/industries/lobbying.php?ind=H4300.

———. 2019d. "Ranked Sectors." Accessed December 27. www.opensecrets.org/federal-lobbying/ranked-sectors?cycle=2018.

Centers for Medicare & Medicaid Services (CMS). 2020. "Innovation Models." Accessed April 21. https://innovation.cms.gov/initiatives/#views=models.

———. 2019. *Alternative Payment Models in the Quality Payment Program as of November 2019.* Accessed April 21, 2020. https://qpp-cm-dev-content.s3.amazonaws.com/uploads/733/2019%20Comprehensive%20List%20of%20APMs%20Nov%206.pdf.

Coalition to Protect America's Health Care. 2020. "About." Facebook. Accessed April 22. www.facebook.com/protectcare/info.

Collins, P. M., Jr. 2008. *Friends of the Supreme Court: Interest Groups and Judicial Decision Making*. New York: Oxford University Press.

Edwards, G. C., M. P. Wattenberg, and R. L. Lineberry. 2012. *Government in America: People, Politics, and Policy*, 11th ed. New York: Pearson.

Feldstein, P. J. 2019. *The Politics of Health Legislation: An Economic Perspective*, 7th ed. Chicago: Health Administration Press.

Forrest, C. B., D. Martin, E. Holve, and A. Millman. 2008. *Health Services Research Doctoral Core Competencies: Final Report*. Accessed April 22, 2020. http://archive.ahrq.gov/funding/hsrcomp08/hsrcomp08.html.

Girgis, L. 2015. "Is the AMA Really the Voice of Physicians in the US?" *PhysiciansWeekly.com*. Published June 9. www.physiciansweekly.com/is-the-ama-really-the-voice-of-physicians-in-the-us.

Godwin, R. K., S. Ainsworth, and E. Godwin. 2013. *Lobbying and Policymaking: The Public Pursuit of Private Interests*. Washington, DC: CQ Press.

Green, J. 1995. "High-Court Ruling Protects Hospital-Bill Surcharges." *AHA News* 31 (18): 1.

Hacker, J. S. 2010. "The Road to Somewhere: Why Health Reform Happened; or Why Political Scientists Who Write About Public Policy Shouldn't Assume They Know How to Shape It." *Perspectives on Politics* 8 (3): 861–76.

———. 1997. *The Road to Nowhere*. Princeton, NJ: Princeton University Press.

Herrnson, P. S., R. G. Shaiko, and C. Wilcox. 2005. *The Interest Group Connection: Electioneering, Lobbying, and Policymaking in Washington*, 2nd ed. Washington, DC: CQ Press.

Itkowitz, C. 2018. "Senate Easily Passes Sweeping Opioid Legislation, Sending to President Trump." *Washington Post*. Published October 3. www.washingtonpost.com/politics/2018/10/03/senate-is-poised-send-sweeping-opioids-legislation-president-trump.

Johnson, H., and D. S. Broder. 1996. *The System: The American Way of Politics at the Breaking Point*. Boston: Little, Brown.

Kaiser Family Foundation. 2013. "Kaiser Health Tracking Poll: December 2013." Published December 20. www.kff.org/health-reform/poll-finding/kaiser-health-tracking-poll-december-2013.

———. 2009. "Kaiser Health Tracking Poll: July 2009." Published July. www.kff.org/wp-content/uploads/2013/01/7945.pdf.

Kamal, R., D. McDermott, and C. Cox. 2019. "Total Health Expenditures Have Increased Substantially Over the Past Several Decades." Published December 20. www.healthsystemtracker.org/chart-collection/u-s-spending-healthcare-changed-time/#item-nhe-trends_total-national-health-expenditures-us-billions-1970-2018.

Kersh, R. 2014. "Ten Myths About Health Lobbyists." In *Health Politics and Policy*, 5th ed., edited by J. A. Morone and D. Ehlke, 236–53. Stamford, CT: Cengage Learning.

Kingdon, J. W. 2010. *Agendas, Alternatives, and Public Policies*, 2nd ed. Upper Saddle River, NJ: Pearson Education.

McCoy, M. S., M. Carniol, K. Chockley, J. W. Urwin, E. J. Emanuel, and H. Schmidt. 2017. "Conflicts of Interest for Patient Advocacy Organizations." *New England Journal of Medicine* 376: 880–85.

Morone, J. A. 2014. "The Presidency." In *Health Politics and Policy*, 5th ed., edited by J. A. Morone and D. Ehlke, 56–75. Stamford, CT: Cengage Learning.

Ornstein, N. J., and S. Elder. 1978. *Interest Groups, Lobbying and Policymaking*. Washington, DC: Congressional Quarterly Press.

Patient-Centered Outcomes Research Institute (PCORI). 2017. "Our Funding." Updated January. www.pcori.org/about-us/financials-and-reports/our-funding/.

Price, D. 1978. "Policymaking in Congressional Committees: The Impact of 'Environmental' Factors." *American Political Science Review* 72 (2): 548–75.

Redhead, C. S. 2017. "Appropriations and Fund Transfers in the Patient Protection and Affordable Care Act (ACA)." Congressional Research Service. Published February 7. www.fas.org/sgp/crs/misc/R41301.pdf.

Rostron, A. 2018. "The Dickey Amendment on Federal Funding for Gun Research: A Legal Dissection." *American Journal of Public Health*. Published June 6. https://ajph.aphapublications.org/doi/full/10.2105/AJPH.2018.304450.

Schlesinger, M. 2014. "Public Opinion." In *Health Politics and Policy*, 5th ed., edited by J. A. Morone and D. Ehlke, 214–35. Stamford, CT: Cengage Learning.

Shannon. 2009. "DC Mythbusting: 'Lobbyist' Coined at Willard Hotel." We Love DC. Published June 3. www.welovedc.com/2009/06/09/dc-mythbusting-lobbyist-coined-at-willard-hotel.

Skidmore, M. 1970. *Medicare and the American Rhetoric of Reconciliation*. Tuscaloosa, AL: University of Alabama Press.

Steinberg, E. P., and B. R. Luce. 2005. "Evidence Based? Caveat Emptor!" *Health Affairs* 24 (1): 80–92.

Stracqualursi, V. 2019. "Congress Agrees to Millions in Gun Violence Research for the First Time in Decades." CNN. Published December 17. www.cnn.com/2019/12/17/politics/gun-research-congress-spending-bill-cdc-trnd/index.html.

US Congress. 1996. "Omnibus Consolidated Appropriations Act." P.L. 104–208. Washington, DC: GPO.

US Department of State. 2004. *Outline of U.S. Legal System*. Accessed April 22. https://usa.usembassy.de/etexts/gov/outlinelegalsystem.pdf.

Weissert, C. S., and W. G. Weissert. 2019. *Governing Health: The Politics of Health Policy*, 5th ed. Baltimore: Johns Hopkins University Press.

Yankelovich, D., and W. Friedman. 2010. "How Americans Make Up Their Minds: The Dynamics of the Public's Learning Curve and Its Meaning for American Life." In *Toward Wiser Public Judgment*, edited by D. Yankelovich and W. Friedman, 1–8. Nashville, TN: Vanderbilt University Press.

CHAPTER

6

POLICY FORMULATION: DEVELOPMENT OF LEGISLATION

Learning Objectives

After reading this chapter, you should be able to

- describe the policy formulation phase of policymaking;
- list and describe the steps in the choreography of legislation development;
- discuss the drafting of legislative proposals, including the forms they can take;
- discuss the legislative committee and subcommittee structure of Congress;
- identify and describe the roles of the key congressional committees and subcommittees with health policy jurisdiction; and
- describe the federal and state budget legislative development processes.

As we noted in chapters 4 and 5, the formulation phase of health policymaking is made up of two distinct and sequential parts: agenda setting and legislation development. Chapter 5 focused on agenda setting; in this chapter we turn our attention to the development of legislation. Understanding the agenda setting process and the development of legislation is foundational to appreciating the policymaking process fully.

As with the discussion of agenda setting in chapter 5, this discussion of legislation development is confined almost exclusively to its occurrence at the federal level of government. However, state and local governments develop legislation using a similar approach. The problems for which legislation is developed differ at each level, but the general process framework is remarkably similar.

The result of the entire formulation phase of policymaking is public policy in the form of new public laws or amendments to existing laws. New health-related laws or amendments originate from the policy agenda. Recall that the health policy agenda is established through the interactions of a diverse array of problems, possible solutions to those problems, and the dynamic political circumstances that relate to the problems and to their potential solutions. Combinations of problems, potential solutions, and political circumstances that achieve priority on the policy agenda move on to the next component of the policy formulation phase: legislation development (see the darkly shaded portion of exhibit 6.1).

The laws and amendments to existing laws that result from the formulation phase of policymaking are tangible. They can be seen and read in a number of places (see appendix 2.2). The US Constitution prohibits the enactment of laws that are not specifically and directly made known to the people who are to be bound by them. In practice, federal laws are published immediately on enactment. Of course, it is incumbent on people who might be affected by laws to know of them and to be certain that they understand the effects of those laws. Health professionals should devote time and attention to the potential and real impact of relevant laws and amendments and be aware of the continually evolving nature of health policy.

At the federal level, enacted laws are first printed in pamphlet form called *slip law*. Later, laws are published in the *US Statutes at Large* and eventually incorporated into the *US Code*. The *Statutes at Large*, published annually, contains the laws enacted during each session of Congress. In effect, it is a compilation of all laws enacted in a particular year. The *US Code* is a complete compilation of all the nation's laws. A new edition of the code is published every six years, with cumulative supplements published annually. Federal public laws can be found and reviewed at www.congress.gov.

The Choreography of Legislation Development

Development of legislation is the point in policy formulation at which specific legislative proposals, which are characterized in chapter 5 as hypothetical or unproved potential solutions to the problems they are intended to address, advance through a series of steps that can end in new or amended public laws. These steps, not unlike those of a complicated dance, are specified or choreographed. The steps followed at the federal level are shown schematically in exhibit 6.2. A variation of these steps was briefly introduced and described in chapter 3. Only when all of the steps are completed does a new public law or, far more typically, an amendment to a previously enacted law, result. The steps that make up the development of legislation activity provide the framework for most of the discussion in this chapter.

EXHIBIT 6.1

Policymaking Process: Development of Legislation in the Formulation Phase

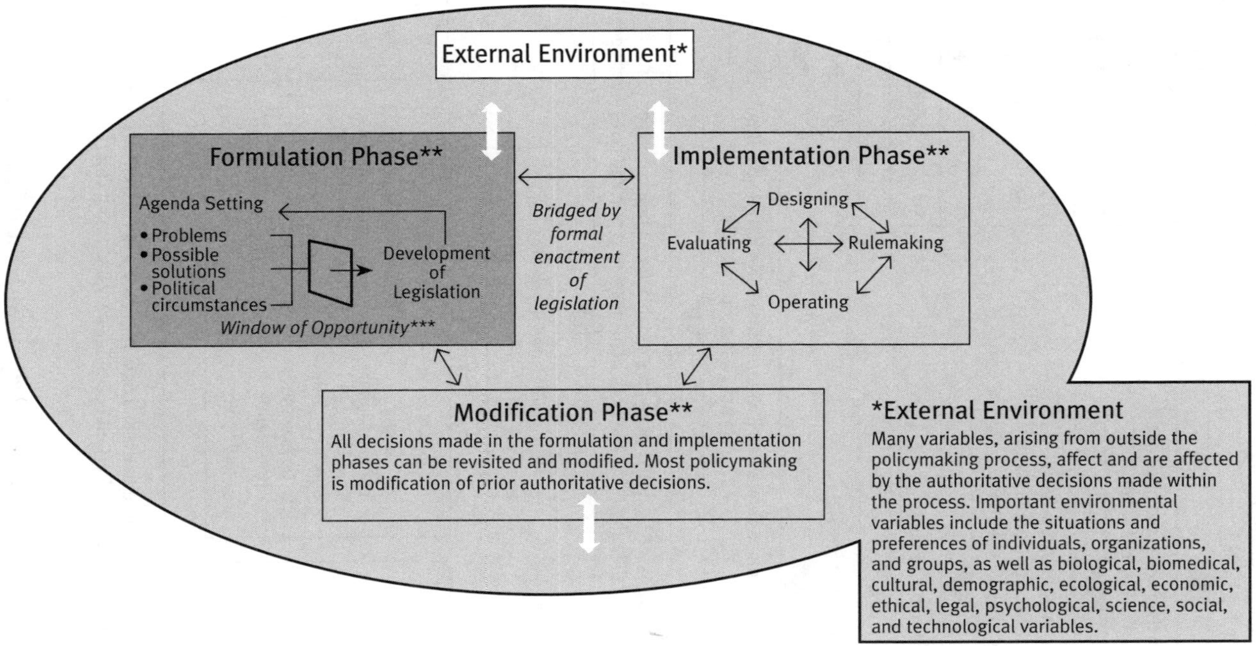
External Environment*
Formulation Phase**
Agenda Setting
• Problems
• Possible solutions
• Political circumstances
Development of Legislation
Window of Opportunity***
Bridged by formal enactment of legislation
Implementation Phase**
Designing
Evaluating
Rulemaking
Operating
Modification Phase**
All decisions made in the formulation and implementation phases can be revisited and modified. Most policymaking is modification of prior authoritative decisions.
*External Environment
Many variables, arising from outside the policymaking process, affect and are affected by the authoritative decisions made within the process. Important environmental variables include the situations and preferences of individuals, organizations, and groups, as well as biological, biomedical, cultural, demographic, ecological, economic, ethical, legal, psychological, science, social, and technological variables.

Policymakers in all three branches of government make policy in the form of position-appropriate, or authoritative, decisions. Their decisions differ in that the **legislative branch is primarily involved in formulation, the **executive branch** is primarily involved in implementation, and both are involved in modification of prior decisions or policies. The **judicial branch** interprets and assesses the legality of decisions made within all three phases of the policymaking process.

***A window of opportunity opens for possible progression of issues through formulation, enactment, implementation, and modification when there is a favorable confluence of problems, possible solutions, and political circumstances.

EXHIBIT 6.2
The Steps in Legislation Development

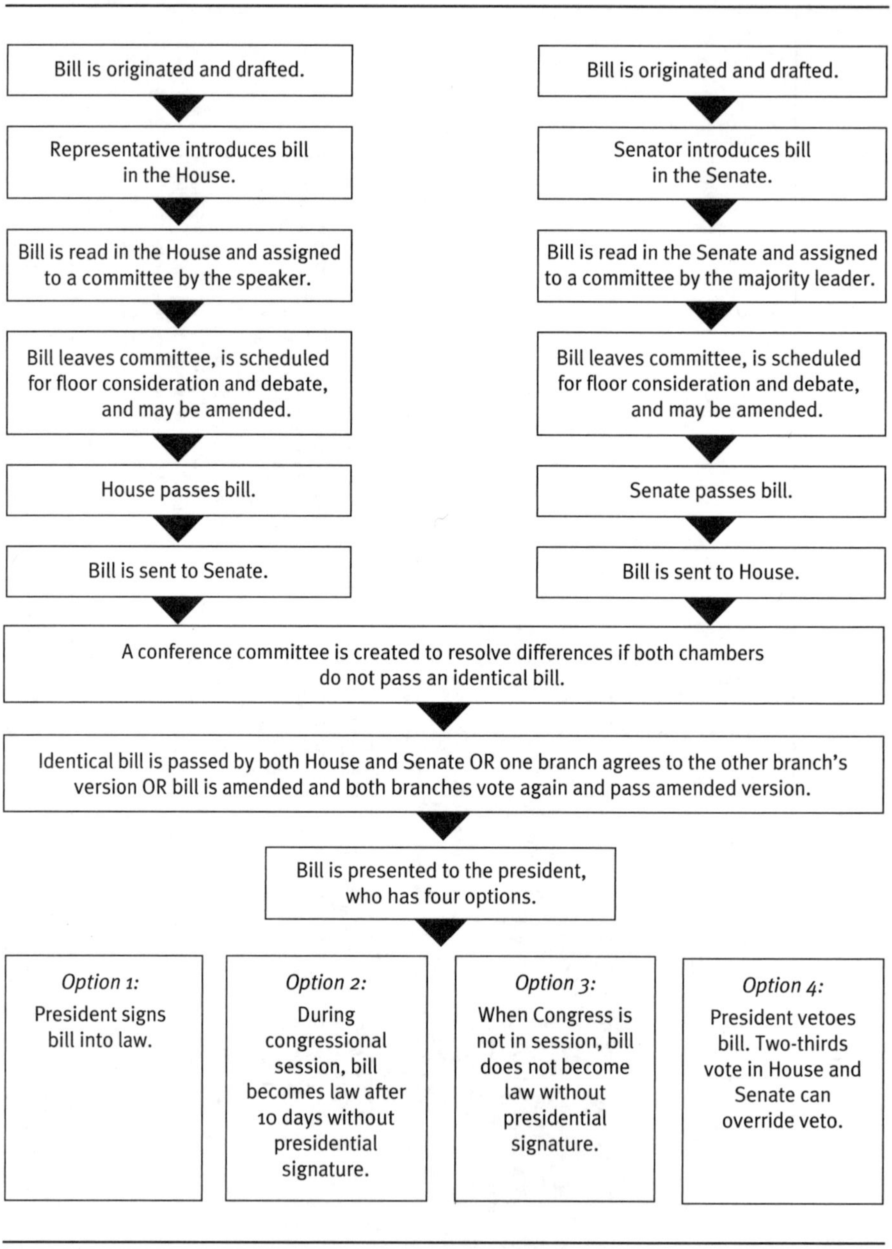
Bill is originated and drafted.
Representative introduces bill in the House.
Bill is read in the House and assigned to a committee by the speaker.
Bill leaves committee, is scheduled for floor consideration and debate, and may be amended.
House passes bill.
Bill is sent to Senate.
Bill is originated and drafted.
Senator introduces bill in the Senate.
Bill is read in the Senate and assigned to a committee by the majority leader.
Bill leaves committee, is scheduled for floor consideration and debate, and may be amended.
Senate passes bill.
Bill is sent to House.
A conference committee is created to resolve differences if both chambers do not pass an identical bill.
Identical bill is passed by both House and Senate OR one branch agrees to the other branch's version OR bill is amended and both branches vote again and pass amended version.
Bill is presented to the president, who has four options.
Option 1: President signs bill into law.
Option 2: During congressional session, bill becomes law after 10 days without presidential signature.
Option 3: When Congress is not in session, bill does not become law without presidential signature.
Option 4: President vetoes bill. Two-thirds vote in House and Senate can override veto.

Source: Adapted from J. B. Teitelbaum and S. E. Wilensky, 2013, *Essentials of Health Policy and Law*, 2nd ed., Burling, MA: Jones and Bartlett Learning. www.jblearning.com. Reprinted with permission.

Legislation development begins with the origination of ideas for legislation and extends through the enactment of some of those ideas into law or the amendment of existing laws. The steps of this process apply equally whether the resulting legislation is a new law or an amendment. Sullivan (2007) provides an extensive description of the steps through which federal legislation is developed. Similarly, most states include descriptions of their legislative processes on their

EXHIBIT 6.3
State Legislative Process

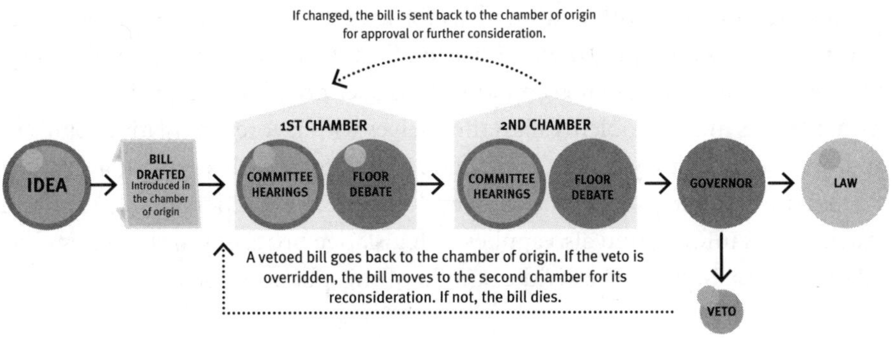

Source: National Conference of State Legislatures (2020).

websites. For example, the Kansas Legislature publishes a PDF highlighting the process (Kansas Legislature 2019). Exhibit 6.3 illustrates the generic steps in the state legislative process.

At the federal level, the path through which legislation is developed begins with ideas for proposed legislation or bills in the agenda-setting stage, extends through formal drafting of legislative proposals and several other steps, and culminates in the enactment of laws derived from some of the proposals. In practice, only a fraction of the legislative proposals that are formally introduced in a Congress—the two annual sessions spanning the terms of office of members of the House of Representatives—are enacted into law. For example, the 116th Congress spanned the period from January 3, 2019, to January 3, 2021. (Refer to exhibit 4.2 for details regarding the number of bills introduced and the percentage that become law.) Proposals that are not enacted by the end of the congressional session in which they were introduced die and must be reintroduced in the next Congress to be considered further.

As the bridge between policy formulation and implementation (shown in exhibit 6.1), formal enactment of proposed legislation into new or amended law represents a significant transition between these two phases of the overall public policymaking process. The focus in this chapter is on ways in which public laws are developed and enacted in the policymaking process; their implementation is discussed in chapter 7.

As we described in chapter 5, individuals, health-related organizations, and the interest groups to which they belong are instrumental in the agenda setting that precedes legislation development. They also actively participate in the development of legislation: Once a health policy problem or issue achieves an actionable place on the policy agenda and moves to the next stage of policy formulation—development of legislation—those with concerns and preferences often continue to seek to exert influence.

Individuals and health-related organizations and interest groups can participate directly in originating ideas for legislation, helping with the actual drafting of legislative proposals, and attending the hearings sponsored by legislative committees. When competing bills seek to address a problem, those with interests in the problems align themselves with favored legislative solutions and oppose those they do not favor. The following sections present a detailed discussion of the steps in legislation development at the federal level, although much of this information also applies to legislative processes in the states. The following box highlights a vivid example of this phenomenon.

The 21st Century Cures Act: A Legislative Grab Bag

In chapter 5, we discussed how the confluence of problems, possible solutions, and political circumstances can combine to create a window of opportunity for legislation to be written and enacted intended to address the problem. Sometimes these events occur when multiple issues are incorporated into a single piece of legislation; this bill may overcome the political controversy associated with the solutions for each individual problem. This technique represents not merely the confluence of problems, political circumstances, and potential solutions for *one* problem, but for *multiple* problems. Put another way, sometimes the whole is greater than the sum of its parts.

The 21st Century Cures Act of 2016 (P.L. 114-255) is an example of this phenomenon, and it is yet another significant (and, at more than 900 pages, massive) piece of healthcare-related legislation. Brief summaries can be found in four of the summaries of federal legislation in appendix 1.3: "Food and Drug Safety," "Behavioral and Developmental Health," "System Infrastructure," and "Access to Care." As you can see, this bill dealt with four discrete topics. Moreover, this legislation enjoyed wide bipartisan support, passing the House 392–26 and the Senate 94–5.

The success of this legislation lies in the fact that it became a legislative grab bag. The final bill included a number of controversial ideas. Indeed, most of its elements, standing alone, would face a more difficult legislative path for either lack of salience or intensity of conflict. By incorporating multiple problems along with multiple solutions, the positive response by some policymakers to their favored issues overcame their negative reaction to one (or more) of the other problems.

As noted in chapter 5, conflictive issues that create intense disagreements among interest groups, or those that pit the interests of groups against the larger public interest, face problematic legislative paths. Legislation with relatively low salience and high conflict is unlikely to be enacted. A brief look at a few of the factors related to certain issues included in the 21st Century Cures Act are shown in exhibit 6.4.

EXHIBIT 6.4
Selected Issues in the 21st Century Cures Act

Issue	Problem Addressed	Legislative Challenge
Accelerated drug approval	Shorten time to get life-saving medicines to market	Relaxing scientific safeguards that ensure safety and efficacy of drugs
Increased awareness of and funding of treatment for mental health and substance abuse disorders	Elevate mental health and substance abuse to a more equal level with medical/surgical issues	These illnesses are stigmatized; lack salience for some policymakers; are difficult to understand
Increased funding for research	Discover new disease treatments	Existing budget deficit and national debt; some legislative ambivalence toward science
Enhanced sharing of electronic health record data	Facilitate care regardless of patient location	Privacy concerns

The initial version of the bill introduced in 2015 dealt only with the accelerated regulatory process for approval of new drugs and medical devices. On its face, this seems a reasonable thing: get efficacious drugs to the market fast so they can help patients who need them.

The flip side of this issue, however, is loosening scientific standards currently necessary for drug approval. In a phrase, this bill would allow the Food and Drug Administration to approve new drugs based on the "real-world evidence" of observation and insurance claims data, eliminating the scientific gold standard for assessing meaningful testing: the double-blind clinical trial. This modification was advocated for by the pharmaceutical industry, often referred to as *big pharma*, which clearly had a profit motive for its member companies as part of its underlying rationale. A substantial number of people—including members of Congress—are suspicious of big Pharma, if not downright hostile, citing ever-increasing drug prices and direct-to-consumer advertising, among other reasons. Approving this new, less rigorous standard for drug approval was and would continue to be highly controversial.

(continued)

Likewise, increasing funding for National Institutes of Health (NIH) research, while not as high profile as pharmaceutical issues, certainly has its supporters among scientists in universities and medical centers. At the same time, however, those interests would be confronted by budget hawks in the legislative process (policymakers who want to hold the line on new spending). Avoiding new spending is generally an easier vote than justifying an increase. Similarly, approving new funding and enhanced organizational stature for mental health and substance abuse disorders may not be particularly controversial, but they lack salience: the issue is complicated to understand; more complicated to explain; and, in general, lacks political appeal.

The transmittal of patient information across multiple platforms may help provide care for patients regardless of location; for many, however, this capacity represents an unacceptable threat to patient privacy. Again, electronic health record portability is a complex issue that defies easy explanation, and politicians would find it politically easier to vote down reform than to explain their reasoning for supporting change.

Each of these issues alone would face a difficult path. This is not to say they could not carry the day, but it is safe to say that some would not and others would face a contentious debate. Each solution attempts to address a legitimate problem; each confronts challenging political circumstances ranging from ambivalence to overt hostility.

In 2016, however, the various advocates for these respective interests began to form alliances. Legislators in favor of a solution to one problem might find sufficient political upside in that issue to overcome their opposition to the solution in another. For example, the members of Congress likely to vote against reducing the standards necessary to win approval for a new drug are, more or less, the same members who favor increasing health-related research capacity. Thus, combining the deregulation issue with more money for the NIH produces a plausible political win for both groups because it is also highly likely that those favoring deregulation are budget hawks and vote against new funding for the NIH.

This is why they say politics makes strange bedfellows. This same concept applies to the other issues in the bill as well. Basically, it became an exercise in trading one set of political interests for another as liberals and conservatives coalesced to produce an overwhelming majority in favor of the *combined* legislation.

However, this legislation is not only a story about political logrolling, where the members of Congress look after each other's pet interests. It is also about interest group behavior. In this case, as this coalition began to assemble, it did so with the help of lobbyists. More than 400 companies and organizations registered to lobby on this bill. A stunning 1,455 individual lobbyists registered on behalf of affected interest groups—nearly three lobbyists for each member of Congress (435 House members and 100 senators).

In the end, whether you see this bill as a victory for the public interest, a victory for special interest groups, or a combination of both is a matter of political perception. Regardless of one's perspective, however, the 21st Century Cures Act is a good example of the power of interest groups to create coalitions that ultimately produce a successful result for their respective interests (Hiltzik 2016; Kaplan 2016; Lupkin 2016; Ornstein 2015).

Originating and Drafting Legislative Proposals

The development of legislation begins with the conversion of ideas, hopes, and hypotheses about how problems might be addressed through changes in policy—ideas that emerge from agenda setting—into concrete legislative proposals or bills (see exhibit 6.2). Proposed legislation can be introduced in one of four forms. Two of the forms, bills and joint resolutions, are used for making laws. The other two forms of proposed legislation, simple resolutions and concurrent resolutions, are used to handle matters of congressional administration or for expressing nonbinding policy views.

Forms of Legislative Proposals

The discussion of originating and drafting legislative proposals presented here focuses on bills because they are the most common way for legislation to emerge. Using conventions developed over time for the subject matter involved, Congress selects between two options for introducing legislative proposals: bills and joint resolutions. Although bills are much more common than joint resolutions, a good example of a routinely used joint resolution is one to continue appropriations beyond the end of a fiscal year (FY), when the regular appropriations bills for the next year have not been completed. This joint resolution is called a *continuing resolution* (CR) (US House of Representatives Office of the Legislative Counsel 2020a).

For a bill or a joint resolution to become law, it must pass both the House of Representatives and the Senate and be signed by the president. Even if a bill or joint resolution is passed and presented to the president, it can be vetoed. Such vetoed legislation can become law if Congress overrides the veto by a two-thirds vote. The legislation can also become law if the president takes no

EXHIBIT 6.5
Comparison of Forms of Legislative Proposals

Forms of Legislative Proposals	Passage Required by . . .	Presented to President?	Result	Example
Bill	Both House of Representatives and Senate	Yes	Law	H.R. 259 (116th Congress) P.L. 116-3
Joint resolution	Both House of Representatives and Senate	Yes	Law	H.J. Res. 31 (116th Congress) P.L. 116-6
Concurrent resolution	Both House of Representatives and Senate	No	Not law (binding only in certain matters of congressional administration)	S. Con. Res. 22 (a concurrent resolution on the climate crisis; 116th Congress)
Simple resolution	Either House of Representatives or Senate	No	Not law (binding only as to certain matters of adminis-tration of the house that passed it)	S. Res. 452 (supporting the goals of World AIDS day; 116th Congress)

Source: Adapted from US House of Representatives Office of the Legislative Counsel (2020a).

action for a period of ten days while Congress is in session. There is no legal difference and little practical difference between a bill and a resolution, and they are not differentiated operationally here.

Simple resolutions (passed in either the House of Representatives or the Senate) and concurrent resolutions (passed in both the House of Representatives and the Senate) are not presented to the president because they do not become law. Exhibit 6.5 summarizes the four forms that legislative proposals can take.

Origins of Ideas for Public Policies

Ideas for public policies originate in many places. One source is members of the House of Representatives and the Senate. In fact, many Congress members are elected, at least in part, on the basis of the legislative ideas they expressed in their campaigns. Promises to introduce certain proposals, made specifically to the constituents whom candidates seek to represent, are core aspects of the American form of government and frequent sources of eventual legislative proposals. Once in office, legislators may become more aware of and knowledgeable about the need to amend or repeal existing laws or enact new laws as their understanding of the problems and potential solutions that face their constituents or the larger society evolves.

But legislators are not the only source of ideas for laws or amendments. Individual citizens, health-related organizations, and interest groups representing many individuals or organizations may petition the government—a right guaranteed by the First Amendment—and propose ideas for the development of policy in the form of laws or amendments. In effect, such petitions result directly from the participation of individuals, organizations, and groups in agenda setting, as described in chapter 5. Much of the nation's policy originates in this way because certain individuals, organizations, and interest groups have considerable knowledge of the problem–potential solution combinations that affect them or their members.

Individuals, organizations, and groups also participate in the development of legislation. Interest groups tend to be especially influential in legislation development, as they are in agenda setting, because of their pooled resources. Well-staffed interest groups, for example, can draw on the services of legislative draftspersons to transform ideas and concepts into suitable legislative language.

An increasingly important source of ideas for legislative proposals is "executive communication" from members of the executive branch to members of the legislative branch. Such communications, which also play a role in agenda setting, usually take the form of a letter from a senior member of the executive branch such as a member of the president's cabinet, the head of an independent agency, or even the president. These communications typically include comprehensive drafts of proposed bills. They are sent simultaneously to the Speaker of the House of Representatives and the president of the Senate, who can insert them into the legislation development procedures at appropriate places.

The executive branch's role as a source of policy ideas is based in the US Constitution. Although the Constitution establishes a government characterized by the separation of powers, Article II, Section 3, imposes an obligation on the president to report to Congress from time to time on the state of the union and to recommend such policies in the form of laws or amendments as the president considers necessary, useful, or expedient. Many of the executive communications to Congress follow up on ideas first aired in annual presidential State of the Union addresses to Congress.

Executive communications that pertain to proposed legislation are referred by the legislative leaders who receive them to the appropriate legislative committee or committees that have jurisdiction in the relevant areas. The chairperson of an affected committee may introduce the bill either in the form in which it was received or with whatever changes the chairperson considers necessary or desirable. Only members of Congress can actually introduce proposed legislation, no matter who originates the idea or drafts the proposal.

As a matter of comity, the congressional committees will introduce legislative requests from the executive branch even when the majority of the House or Senate and the president are not of the same political party, although there is no constitutional or statutory requirement to do so. The committee's jurisdiction is based on the proposal's subject matter. The committee or one of its subcommittees considers the proposed legislation to determine whether the bill should be introduced.

The most important regular executive communication is the proposed federal budget the president transmits annually to Congress (Oleszek 2014). Recently prepared budgets and related supporting documents are available from the Office of Management and Budget (OMB; www.whitehouse.gov/omb/budget). While the budget process will be addressed in more detail later in this chapter, in broad terms, there are 12 subcommittees of the appropriations committees of the House and Senate. Those subcommittees use the president's budget proposal, together with supportive testimony by officials of the various executive branch departments and agencies, individuals, organizations, and interest groups as the basis of the appropriation bills that these subcommittees draft.

Drafting Legislative Proposals

Drafting legislative proposals is an art, one requiring considerable skill, knowledge, and experience. Any member of the Senate or House of Representatives can draft bills, and these legislators' staffs are usually instrumental in the process, often with assistance from the Office of Legislative Counsel of either the House or the Senate (nonpartisan organizations that provide the same services to members of either party, both in their respective bodies).

Office of Legislative Counsel

"The Office of the Legislative Counsel provides legislative drafting services to the committees and Members of the House of Representatives on a non-partisan, impartial, and confidential basis. Our goal is to work with committees and Members to understand their policy preferences in order to implement those preferences through clear, concise, and legally effective legislative language" (US House of Representatives Office of Legislative Counsel 2020b). Information on how the Office of the Legislative Counsel in the House of Representatives supports legislation development is available at https://legcounsel.house.gov. Information on how the Senate's Office of the Legislative Counsel supports legislation development is available at www.senate.gov.

When bills are drafted in the executive branch, trained legislative counsels are typically involved. These counsels work in several executive branch departments, and their work includes drafting bills to be forwarded to Congress. Similarly, proposed legislation that arises in the private sector, typically from interest groups, is drafted by people with expertise in this intricate task.

No matter who drafts legislation, however, only members of Congress can officially sponsor a proposal, and the legislative sponsors are ultimately responsible for the language in their bills. Bills commonly have multiple sponsors and many cosponsors. Once ideas for solving problems through policy are drafted in legislative language, they are ready for the next step: introduction for formal consideration by Congress.

On occasion, legislation drafting is undertaken as a public–private partnership (Hacker 1997, 2010). Such legislation drafting has occurred twice in recent decades in the health policy arena. Although the health security proposal the Clinton administration drafted was formally introduced in Congress, it was not enacted into law. The Affordable Care Act (ACA), on the other hand, was formally introduced and moved through the other steps in legislation development before it was enacted into law.

Health Security Act

In the first example, in late 1993, after many months of feverish drafting by a team including some of the nation's foremost health policy experts, President Bill Clinton presented his proposal for legislation that would fundamentally reform the American healthcare system. The document, 1,431 pages in length, outlined the drafters' vision of the way health services should be provided and financed in the United States. The proposal was in the form of a comprehensive draft of a bill (to be called the Health Security Act) that could potentially be enacted into law.

However, the proposal faced a long and difficult path from legislation development to possible enactment. Hacker and Skocpol (1997, 315–16) noted that "President Clinton sought to enact comprehensive federal rules that would, in theory, simultaneously control medical costs and ensure universal insurance coverage. The bold Health Security initiative was meant to give everyone what they wanted, delicately balancing competing ideas and claimants, deftly maneuvering between major factions in Congress, and helping to revive the political prospects of the Democratic Party in the process."

In the end, the Clinton health reform proposal failed to make it successfully through the remaining steps in legislation development to enactment into law (Johnson and Broder 1996; Skocpol 1996). Peterson (1997, 291) characterized the failure of this proposal as a situation in which "the bold gambit of comprehensive reform had once again succumbed to the power of antagonistic stakeholders, a public paralyzed by the fears of disrupting what it already had, and the challenge of coalition building engendered by the highly decentralized character of American government." The other political flaw in the Clinton proposal was that, while there was stakeholder input, the legislation was drafted under a cloak of secrecy. Congress was presented with the complete plan—a plan that fundamentally reengineered the health services delivery system– that left little room for meaningful congressional input. By not engaging in the usual vetting process with professionals from agencies and members of Congress, the Clinton administration missed the opportunity to build support for the proposal early in the process (Johnson and Broder 1996).

The Affordable Care Act

The second example of developing legislation through a public–private partnership led to a more successful outcome. The ACA was enacted in 2010. (See appendix 1.1, an overview of the ACA.) There have been difficulties in implementing this law and extraordinary attempts have been made to repeal it (Jost 2014), but this legislation was successfully developed into public law, and a complex law at that.

Technically, in March 2010, the 111th Congress enacted the ACA (P.L. 111-148). The law was substantially amended by the health provisions in the Health Care and Education Reconciliation Act of 2010 (P.L. 111-152). Several other laws that were subsequently enacted made more targeted changes to specific ACA provisions. The ACA emerged from bills in the House of Representatives and the Senate. In the Senate, two committees—the Committee on Health, Education, Labor and Pensions (HELP) and the Committee on Finance—participated in the drafting. The law was formed in an amazingly convoluted series of negotiations involving numerous members of Congress working through various committees, the administration, congressional and administration staff, external stakeholders such as the pharmaceutical and insurance industries, and the professionals who wrote the actual language of the law. Cannan (2013) wrote a thorough history of the ACA's dynamic path through the legislation development step.

One political reality of the ACA was that the Obama administration had learned—or in the eyes of some, overlearned—the lessons of Clinton's proposal. The Obama administration plan built on the existing system of private insurance. At the same time, however, the administration presented Congress not with any draft legislation, but with an overarching set of principles crafted through negotiations with stakeholder groups. In essence, the administration asked Congress to draft the legislation from scratch. This strategy contributed to the confusion associated with the legislative process (Altman and Shactman 2011).

The ACA had multiple goals. Among the most important were to increase access to affordable health insurance for the millions of Americans without coverage and make health insurance more affordable for those already covered. While largely relying on the existing system of commercial insurance, the act made numerous changes in the way healthcare is financed, organized, and delivered. Among its many provisions, the ACA restructured the private health insurance market, set minimum standards for health coverage, created a mandate for most US residents to obtain health insurance coverage, and provided for the establishment of state-based insurance exchanges for the purchase of private health insurance. Federal subsidies in the form of tax credits were made available to certain classes of individuals and families to reduce the cost of purchasing coverage through the exchanges. The ACA also expanded eligibility for Medicaid dramatically; amended the Medicare program in ways that were intended to reduce the growth in Medicare spending; imposed an excise tax on insurance plans found to have high premiums; and made numerous other changes to the tax code, Medicare, Medicaid, the Children's Health Insurance Program (CHIP), and many other federal programs. Full implementation of the law involved all the major healthcare stakeholders, including the federal and state governments, as well as employers, insurers, and healthcare providers (Redhead et al. 2012).

Packed into 1,024 pages, the ACA is a product of input from many sources. For example, the individual mandate provision requiring most residents to obtain health insurance, coupled with public subsidies for many, has deep historical roots in previous health reform attempts. The conservative Heritage Foundation proposed an individual mandate as an alternative to single-payer healthcare as far back as 1989 (Avik 2012). In 2006, Massachusetts enacted health reform at the state level that included an individual mandate and an insurance exchange (Wees, Zaslavsky, and Ayanian 2013). The individual mandate, despite its deep historical roots, is also highly controversial (see the policy snapshots for parts 1 and 3).

The ACA was the product of a bitterly partisan struggle. In the wake of that struggle, the ACA has been repeatedly attacked in both legislative and judicial forums, mostly from the political right. In the Democratic presidential primaries of 2020, however, the political left increasingly advocated for "Medicare for all." From a policymaking perspective, the underlying lesson is clear: Policy initiatives that enjoy broad-based, bipartisan support, such as Medicare, Medicaid, and CHIP, are more likely to achieve the desired result and less likely to be subject to attack, either in the legislative or judicial branches, than those enacted on the barest of partisan margins.

Introducing and Referring Proposed Legislation to Committees

Members of the Senate and the House of Representatives who have chosen to sponsor or cosponsor legislation introduce their proposals in the form of bills (see exhibit 6.2). On occasion, identical bills are introduced in the Senate and House for simultaneous consideration. When bills are introduced in either chamber of Congress, they are assigned a sequential number (e.g., H.R. 1, H.R. 2, H.R. 3, etc.; S. 1, S. 2, S. 3, etc.) based on the order of introduction by the presiding officer and are referred to the appropriate standing committee or committees for further study and consideration. Exhibit 6.6 illustrates the path of a bill introduced in the House of Representatives through its enactment into public law.

EXHIBIT 6.6
Path to a Public Law: H.R. 3253—Sustaining Excellence in Medicaid Act of 2019

Date	Chamber	Action
6/13/2019	House	Introduced in the House
6/13/2019	House	Referred to the House Committee on Energy and Commerce
6/18/2019, 2:45 p.m.	House	Mrs. Dingell moved to suspend the rules and pass the bill as amended
6/18/2019, 2:46 p.m.	House	Considered under suspension of the rules
6/18/2019, 2:46 p.m.	House	DEBATE—The House proceeded with 40 minutes of debate
6/18/2019, 3:06 p.m.	House	At the conclusion of debate, the Yeas and Nays were demanded and ordered. Pursuant to the provisions of clause 8, rule XX, the Chair announced that further proceedings on the motion would be postponed.
6/18/2019, 9:18 p.m.	House	Considered as unfinished business
6/18/2019, 9:50 p.m.	House	On motion to Suspend the Rules and pass the bill, as amended, Agreed to by 371–46 (Vol. 165, # 102, page H4706 *Congressional Record*)
6/19/2019	Senate	Received in the Senate; read twice
7/25/2019	Senate	Measure laid before the Senate by unanimous consent
7/25/2019	Senate	S. Amendment (SA 930) proposed by Senator Scott–FL for Senator Blunt–MO in the nature of a substitute
7/25/2019	Senate	S. Amendment (SA 930) agreed to in Senate by Unanimous Consent
7/25/2019	Senate	Passed Senate with amendment by Voice Vote
7/25/2019	Senate	Message on Senate action sent to the House
7/30/2019, 11:34 a.m.	House	Mr. Norton asked unanimous consent to take from the Speaker's Table and agree to the Senate Amendment
7/30/2019, 11:34 a.m.	House	On motion that the House agree to the Senate Amendment Agreed to without objection

(continued)

EXHIBIT 6.6

Path to a Public Law: H.R. 3253—Sustaining Excellence in Medicaid Act of 2019 *(continued)*

Date	Chamber	Action
7/30/2019, 11:34 a.m.	House	Motion to reconsider laid on the table Agreed to without objection
8/1/2019	House	Presented to the President
8/6/2019		Signed by the President
8/6/2019		Became Public Law No. 116-39

Note: The path is not always as straightforward as is portrayed here. In this case, there was little or no controversy, no committee amendments, and only minor amendments in the Senate, to which the House of Representatives agreed without a conference committee. At times a bill in one house may completely replace a bill from the house of origin. For the detailed history that includes all the references to the *Congressional Record* as well as the summary quoted earlier, see Congress.gov (2019a).

Source: Data from Congress.gov (2019a).

The US Congress reports that

> this bill alters several Medicaid programs and funding mechanisms. Specifically, the bill
>
> - makes appropriations through FY 2024 for, and otherwise revises, the Money Follows the Person Rebalancing Demonstration Program;
> - allows state Medicaid fraud control units to review complaints regarding patients who are in noninstitutional or other settings;
> - temporarily extends the applicability of Medicaid eligibility criteria that protect against spousal impoverishment for recipients of home and community-based services;
> - temporarily extends the Medicaid demonstration program for certified community behavioral health clinics;
> - repeals the requirement, under the Medicaid Drug Rebate Program, that drug manufacturers include the prices of certain authorized generic drugs when determining the average manufacturer price (AMP) of brand-name drugs (also known as a "blended AMP"), and excludes manufacturers from the definition of "wholesalers" for purposes of rebate calculations; and
> - increases funding available to the Medicaid Improvement Fund beginning in FY 2021 (Congress.gov 2019a).

Legislative Committees and Subcommittees

The Senate and the House of Representatives are organized into legislative committees and subcommittees. The committee structure of Congress is crucial to the development of legislation. Committee and subcommittee deliberations provide the settings for intensive and thorough consideration of legislative proposals and issues. Exhibit 6.7 shows the current legislative committee structure of the US Congress.

EXHIBIT 6.7
Congressional Committees for the 116th Congress, January 2019–January 2021

House	Senate
Agriculture	Agriculture, Nutrition and Forestry
Appropriations	Appropriations
Armed Services	Armed Services
Budget	Banking, Housing and Urban Affairs
Education and Labor	Budget
Energy and Commerce	Commerce, Science and Transportation
Ethics	Energy and Natural Resources
Financial Services	Environment and Public Works
Foreign Affairs	Finance
Homeland Security	Foreign Relations
House Administration	Health, Education, Labor and Pensions
Judiciary	Homeland Security and Governmental Affairs
Natural Resources	Judiciary
Oversight and Reform	Small Business and Entrepreneurship
Rules	Veterans' Affairs
Science, Space and Technology	
Small Business	
Transportation and Infrastructure	
Veterans' Affairs	
Ways and Means	
Special, Select and Other Committees	
Permanent Select Committee on Intelligence	Aging
Select Committee on the Climate Crisis	Ethics
Select Committee on the Modernization of Congress	Indian Affairs
	Intelligence
	Senate Narcotics Caucus
Joint Committees	
Joint Committee on Printing	
Joint Committee on the Library	
Joint Economic Committee	
Joint Taxation Committee	

Source: Congress.gov (2019b).

Each standing committee has jurisdiction over a certain area of legislation, and all bills that pertain to a particular area are referred to its committee. Information about the committees is available on their websites, which can be accessed through www.congress.gov. Committees are divided into subcommittees to facilitate work. For example, the Ways and Means Committee of the House of Representatives has six subcommittees: Health, Human Resources, Oversight, Select Revenue Measures, Social Security, and Trade.

Sometimes the content of a bill calls for assignment to more than one committee. In this case, the bill is assigned to multiple committees either jointly or, more commonly, sequentially. For example, the Clinton administration's Health Security plan was introduced simultaneously in the House and the Senate as H.R. 3600 and S. 1757. Because of its scope and complexity, the bill was then referred jointly to ten House committees and two Senate committees for consideration and debate.

Membership on the various congressional committees is divided between the two major political parties. The proportion of members from each party is determined by the majority party, using a ratio of majority to minority members. In other words, the more there are of one party in either house, the more members from that party will serve on committees, with concomitantly fewer member of the minority party. Legislators typically seek membership on committees that have jurisdiction in their particular areas of interest and expertise. The interests of their constituencies typically influence the interests of policymakers. For example, members of the House of Representatives from agricultural districts or financial centers often prefer to join committees that deal with these areas. The same is true of senators in terms of whether they hail from primarily rural or highly urbanized states, from the industrialized Northeast, or from the more agrarian West. The seniority of committee members follows the order of their appointment to the committee.

The majority party in each chamber also controls the appointment of committee and subcommittee chairpersons. These chairpersons exert great power in the development of legislation because they determine the order and the pace in which the committees or subcommittees they lead consider legislative proposals.

Each committee has a professional staff to assist with administrative details involved in its consideration of bills. Under certain conditions, a standing committee may also appoint consultants on a temporary or intermittent basis to assist the committee in its work. By virtue of expert knowledge, the professional staff members who serve committees and subcommittees are key participants in legislation development.

Committees with Health Policy Jurisdiction

Although no congressional committee is devoted exclusively to the health policy domain, several committees and subcommittees have jurisdiction in health-related legislation development. In recent decades, health has been an especially important and prevalent domain in the federal and state policy agendas. The committees and subcommittees with jurisdiction for health matters have been busy.

At the federal level, there is some overlap in the jurisdictions of committees with health-related legislative responsibilities. Most general health bills are referred to the House Committee on Energy and Commerce and the Senate HELP Committee. However, any bills involving taxes and revenues must be referred to the House Committee on Ways and Means and the Senate Committee on Finance. These two committees have substantial health policy jurisdiction because so much health policy involves taxes as a source of funding. The main health policy interests of these committees are outlined here.

- *Committee on Finance* (www.finance.senate.gov), *with its Subcommittee on Health Care.* This Senate committee has jurisdiction over health programs under the Social Security Act and health programs financed by a specific tax or trust fund. This role gives the committee jurisdiction over matters related to the ACA, Medicare, and Medicaid.
- *Committee on Health, Education, Labor, and Pensions* (www.help.senate.gov), *with its Subcommittees on Children and Families, Employment and Workplace Safety, and Primary Care and Aging.* This Senate committee's jurisdiction encompasses most of the agencies, institutes, and programs of the Department of Health and Human Services (HHS), including the Food and Drug Administration, the Centers for Disease Control and Prevention, the National Institutes of Health, the Administration on Aging, the Substance Abuse and Mental Health Services Administration, and the Agency for Healthcare Research and Quality. The committee also oversees public health and health insurance policy.
- *Committee on Ways and Means* (http://waysandmeans.house.gov), *with its Subcommittee on Health.* This House committee has jurisdiction over bills and matters that pertain to providing payments from any source for healthcare, health delivery systems, or health research. The jurisdiction of the Subcommittee on Health includes bills and matters related to the healthcare programs of the Social Security Act (including Titles XVIII and XIX, which are the Medicare and Medicaid programs), portions of the ACA, and tax credit and deduction provisions of the Internal Revenue Code dealing with health insurance premiums and healthcare costs.
- *Committee on Energy and Commerce* (http://energycommerce.house.gov) *with its subcommittees, including those on Health and on Environment and the Economy.* This House committee has jurisdiction

over all bills and matters related to public health and quarantine; hospital construction; mental health; biomedical research and development; health information technology, privacy, and cybersecurity; public health insurance (Medicare, Medicaid) and private health insurance; medical malpractice insurance; the regulation of food and drugs; drug abuse; HHS; the Clean Air Act; and environmental protection in general, including the Safe Drinking Water Act.

Legislative Committee and Subcommittee Operations

Depending on whether the chairperson of a committee has assigned a bill to a subcommittee, either the full committee or the subcommittee can, if it chooses, hold hearings on the bill. At these public hearings, members of the executive branch, representatives of health-related organizations and interest groups, and other individuals can present their views and recommendations on the legislation under consideration. For example, from the 116th Congress, no fewer than nine bills pertaining to universal healthcare were introduced. A partial rendition includes HR 1277, the State Public Option Act; HR 1384, the Medicare for All Act; HR 2452, the Medicare for America Act; and HR 584, the Incentivizing Medicaid Expansion Act. (For a complete list see House Committee on Energy and Commerce.)

All of these bills were referred to the House Committee on Energy and Commerce. The health subcommittee conducted a hearing on all of the proposals en masse on December 10, 2019. Appendix 2.3 provides an example of testimony at a hearing related to this issue before the House Subcommittee on Health of the Committee on Energy and Commerce.

Following such hearings, and there may be a number of them for a bill, members of committees or subcommittees mark up the bills they are considering. This term refers to going through the original bill line by line and making changes. Sometimes, when similar bills or bills addressing the same issue have been introduced, they are combined in the markup process. In cases of subcommittee involvement, when the subcommittee has completed its markup and voted to approve the bill, it reports out the bill to the full committee with jurisdiction.

When no subcommittee is involved, or when a full committee has reviewed the work of a subcommittee and voted to approve the bill, the full committee reports out the bill for a vote, this time to the floor of the Senate or House. At this point, the administration can formally weigh in with support for or opposition to a bill. This input is issued through a statement of administration policy, examples of which are available at OMB (2020b).

Administration officials also may be called on to testify to either the committee or subcommittee. If a committee votes to report a bill favorably, a member of the committee staff writes a report in the name of a committee member. This report is an extremely important document. The committee report describes the purposes and scope of the bill and the reasons the committee recommends its approval by the entire Senate or House. As an example, the report for H.R. 1014 can be read at the congressional website (www.congress.gov/bill/110th-congress/house-bill/1014).

Committee reports are useful and informative documents in the legislative history of a public law or amendments to it. These reports are used by courts in considering matters related to particular laws that have been enacted and by executive branch departments and agencies as guidance for implementing enacted laws and amendments. They provide information regarding legislative intent for courts, attorneys, agencies, and others who may be interested in the history, purpose, and meaning of enacted legislation.

Generally, a committee report contains an analysis in which the purpose of each section of a bill is described. All changes or amendments to existing law that the bill would require are indicated in the report, and the text of laws the bill would repeal are set out. The report begins by describing and explaining committee amendments to the bill as it was originally referred to the committee. Executive communications pertaining to the bill are usually quoted in full in the report. Witness testimony is likewise either included directly or included by reference in the report.

From Committee to the President

Following approval of a bill by the full committee with jurisdiction, the bill and its report are discharged from the committee. The House or Senate receives it from the committee and places it on the legislative calendar for floor action (see exhibit 6.2).

Bills can be further amended in debate on the House or Senate floor. However, because great reliance is placed on the committee process in both chambers of Congress, amendments to bills proposed from the floor require considerable support. Indeed, in the House, a bill may not be assigned a rule that permits amendments. In the Senate, in order to avoid a filibuster, sometimes an amendment will need 60 votes to succeed.

Once a bill passes in either the House or the Senate, it is sent to the other chamber. The step of referral to a committee with jurisdiction, and perhaps then to a subcommittee, is repeated, and another round of hearings, markup, and eventual action may or may not take place. If the bill is again reported out of committee, it goes to the involved chamber's floor for a final vote. If it is passed in the second chamber, any differences in the House and Senate versions of a bill must be resolved in conference committee. At that point, both houses must adopt identical versions of the conference committee report before the bill is sent to the White House for action by the president.

Conference Committee Actions on Proposed Legislation

To resolve differences in a bill that both chambers of Congress have passed, a conference committee (see exhibit 6.2) may be established (US Senate 2014). On occasion, the initial house will accede to the amendments from the other chamber, as occurred in our example in exhibit 6.5. Conferees are usually the ranking members of the committees that reported out the bill in each chamber. If they can resolve the differences, a conference report is written and both chambers of Congress vote on it. If the conferees cannot reach agreement, or if either chamber does not accept the report, the bill dies. However, if both chambers accept the conference report, the bill is sent to the president for action. The conference committee process is described more fully in appendix 2.4.

Presidential Action on Proposed Legislation

The president has several options regarding proposed legislation that has been approved by both the House and the Senate (see exhibit 6.2). The president can sign the bill, in which case it immediately becomes law. The president can veto the bill, in which case it must be returned to Congress along with an explanation for the rejection. A two-thirds vote in both chambers of Congress can override a presidential veto. The president's third option is neither to veto the bill nor to sign it. In this case, the bill becomes law in ten days, but the president has made a political statement of disfavor regarding the legislation. A fourth option may apply when the president receives proposed legislation near the close of a congressional session; the bill can be pocket vetoed if the president does nothing about it until the Congress is adjourned. In this case, the bill dies.

Legislation Development for the Federal Budget

Because enactment of legislation related to the federal government's annual budget is so crucial to the government's performance and the well-being of the American people, special procedures have been developed to guide this process. The Congressional Budget and Impoundment Control Act of 1974 and the Balanced Budget and Emergency Deficit Control Act of 1985 and their subsequent amendments provide Congress with the process through which it establishes target levels for revenues, expenditures, and the overall deficit for the coming FY. The budget process is designed to coordinate decisions on sources and levels of federal revenues and on the objectives and levels of federal expenditures. Such decisions affect other policy decisions, including those that pertain to health.

A distinctive feature of legislation development for the budget is the president's role. The president is required to submit a budget request to Congress each year to initiate the process. By doing so, the president establishes the starting point and the framework for the annual process of legislation development for the federal budget. Once the president submits a budget request, the legislative process for federal budget making unfolds in distinct stages. First, Congress drafts and approves a budget resolution that provides the framework for overall federal government taxation and spending for various agencies and programs for the upcoming year. Next, the agencies and programs are authorized by way of establishment, extension, or modification. This authorization must take place before any money can be appropriated for an agency or program, which is the final stage of federal budget making.

The federal budgeting process is enormously complex. It "entails dozens of subprocesses, countless rules and procedures, the efforts of tens of thousands of staff persons in the executive and legislative branches, millions of work hours each year, and the active participation of the president and congressional leaders, as well as other members of Congress and executive officials" (Heniff, Lynch, and Tollestrup 2012, ii). Several federal agencies play especially important research and oversight roles in the budgeting process. These include the OMB, the Government Accountability Office (GAO), and the Congressional Budget Office (CBO).

Exhibit 6.8 shows the actions and timeline through which the annual federal budget is supposed to be developed. As noted earlier, the schedule begins when the president submits a budget request to Congress. Appendix 2.5 describes these steps in greater detail.

EXHIBIT 6.8
Steps in the Federal Budget Process

Action Steps	Timeline
1. President submits budget request to Congress.	First Monday in February
2. House and Senate Budget Committees pass budget resolutions.	April 15
3. House and Senate Appropriations Subcommittees mark up appropriations bills.	June 10
4. House and Senate vote on appropriations bills and reconcile differences.	June 30
5. President signs each appropriations bill and the budget becomes law.	October 1
6. Congress passes continuing resolutions until budget is in place.	As needed
7. Audit and review of expenditures.	Ongoing

Source: Data from Amadeo (2019), USA.gov (2019).

President's Budget Request

The president's budget, officially referred to as the *Budget of the United States Government* (www.whitehouse.gov/omb/budget), is required by law to be submitted to Congress no later than the first Monday in February (see step 1 in exhibit 6.8). The budget request by the president includes estimates of spending, revenues, borrowing, and debt. In addition, it includes policy and legislative recommendations and detailed estimates of the financial operations of federal agencies and programs. The president's budget request plays three important roles. First, the budget request tells Congress what the president recommends for overall federal fiscal policy. Second, it lays out the president's priorities for spending on health, defense, education, and so on. Finally, the budget request signals to Congress the spending and tax policy changes the president prefers (Center on Budget and Policy Priorities 2020).

The president's budget is only a request to Congress, which can do as it pleases. Even so, the formulation and submission of the budget request is an important tool in the president's direction of the executive branch and of national policy. The president's proposals often influence congressional revenue and spending decisions, though the extent of the influence varies from year to year and depends on such variables as political circumstances and the condition of the economy (Heniff, Lynch, and Tollestrup 2012).

Preparation of the president's budget typically begins at least nine months before it is submitted to Congress. Therefore, preparation begins about 17 months before the start of the FY to which a budget pertains. The early stages of budget preparation occur in federal agencies, primarily in the OMB.

Congressional Budget Resolution

On receiving the president's budget request, Congress begins the months-long process of reviewing the request (step 2 in exhibit 6.8). Based on the review process, which may include hearings to question administration officials, the House and Senate Budget Committees draft their budget resolutions. These resolutions go to the House and Senate floors, where they can be amended (by a majority vote). A House–Senate conference then resolves any differences, and a reconciled version is voted on in each chamber.

Because the budget resolution is a "concurrent" congressional resolution, it is not signed by the president and is not a law. The concurrent resolution is the congressional statement of spending priorities—the legislative counterbalance to the executive branch budget. Budget resolutions are supposed to be passed by April 15, but often are not. Resolutions may not be passed because of disagreements about spending levels and priorities. On occasion, no budget resolution is passed, in which case the previous year's resolution remains in effect. Congress has failed to pass a budget resolution by the April 15 deadline on many occasions. When Congress fails to do so, the House can begin to work on most of the appropriations bills without a budget resolution after one month. The Senate can also do so if a majority of senators favors proceeding. In the early part of the twenty-first century, owing to hyperpartisanship, Congress had substantial difficulty establishing a congressional budget and passing the necessary 12 appropriations bills.

Congressional Appropriations Process

Before appropriations can be made to any agency or program, they first must be authorized. Authorization can occur through a law that establishes a program or agency and sets the terms and conditions under which it operates or by a law that specifically authorizes appropriations for that program or agency. Assuming that authorization has occurred, federal spending for agencies and programs occurs in two main forms: mandatory and discretionary. Primarily, mandatory spending, also known as direct spending, is for entitlement programs such as Medicare, Medicaid, and Social Security. The ACA contains some mandatory programs such as the Prevention and Public Health Fund, for example. Mandatory spending is under the jurisdiction of the legislative committees of the House and Senate. The House Ways and Means Committee and the Senate Finance Committee are most responsible for mandatory spending decisions. Discretionary spending decisions occur in the context of annual appropriations acts. All discretionary spending is under the jurisdiction of the appropriations committees in the House and the Senate (Tollestrup 2012).

The appropriations acts passed by Congress provide federal agencies and programs legal authority to incur obligations. These acts also grant the Treasury Department the authority to make payments for designated purposes (Heniff, Lynch, and Tollestrup 2012). Steps 3 and 4 in exhibit 6.8 constitute the federal appropriations process. Based on the guidance provided by the budget resolution, the House and Senate Appropriations Committees allocate spending levels to their 12 subcommittees, which then determine funding levels for the agencies and programs under their jurisdiction. The subcommittees include those for labor, health and human services, education, and related agencies as well as 11 others in each chamber of Congress.

As with delays in Congress failing to pass a budget resolution by the deadline, disagreements over spending levels and priorities also delay the work of the appropriations committees' subcommittees. When some or all of the appropriations subcommittees fail to pass their spending bills, the bills can be grouped into a single appropriations bill, called an omnibus bill, and sent to the floor of the House or Senate for a vote.

President Signs Appropriations Bills

For the federal budget to become law, the president must sign each appropriations bill passed by Congress (step 5 in exhibit 6.8). Only then is the budget process complete for the year. Rarely, however, is this work completed by the September 30 deadline so that the budget can become law on October 1. When appropriations bills are stalled, the Congress must pass a CR to permit government agencies to continue with normal routines as if then-current spending levels were in effect.

At times even this small, incremental step becomes challenging to the point of dysfunction. When that occurs, the government shuts down. At times, this has been only a partial shutdown because some, but not all, of the appropriations bills have passed. Agencies implicated in the bills not passed will shut down; those whose appropriations have been enacted proceed to function under the new funding levels (step 6 in exhibit 6.8). The alternative to a CR is to shut down the nonessential activities of the federal government. Both CRs and shutdowns are problematic for the agencies and programs operating under the federal budget.

Audit and Review of Expenditures

Even when the federal budget for a given FY is completed and operating, however, the budgeting cycle continues. Review and evaluation of expenditures are continual, along with legislative oversight and targeted auditing by the GAO, an independent, nonpartisan agency that works for Congress. Among its duties are "auditing agency operations to determine whether federal funds are being spent efficiently and effectively; investigating allegations of illegal or improper activities; and reporting on how well government programs and policies are meeting their objectives" (GAO 2020). The CBO produces "independent analyses of budgetary and economic issues to support the Congressional Budget process" (CBO 2020). Among its products is a monthly analysis of federal spending and revenue totals for the previous month, current month, and FY to date. The Office of Management and Budget (OMB) works directly for the president and has major responsibility for budget development and execution and oversight of agency and program performance (OMB 2020a).

Legislation Development for State Budgets

The states also develop budget legislation, although the process varies from state to state. In all states, however, the budget is among the most—if not *the* most—important mechanisms for establishing policy priorities. Despite the variability in state processes, some general concepts within a framework may be observed. Note the typical timeframes for different parts of the process in exhibit 6.9.

EXHIBIT 6.9
Steps in the State Budget Process

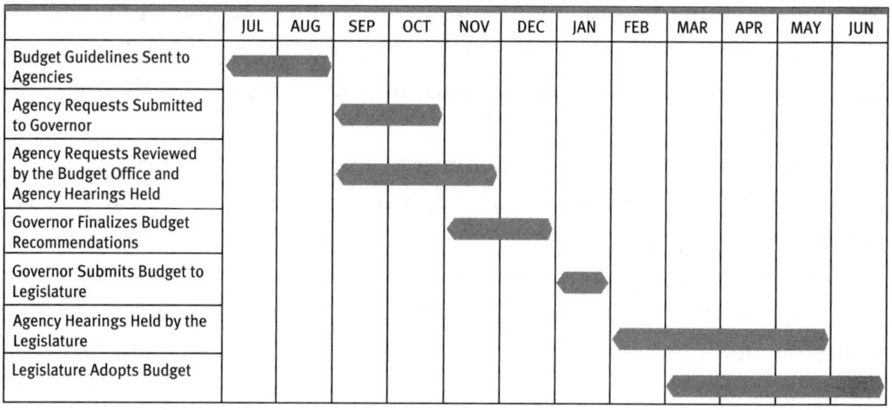

Source: Reprinted from National Association of State Budget Officers (2020).

Stage 1: Budget Preparation

The budget office, in most states housed in the executive branch, sends instructions to agencies outlining format and other parameters with which agencies must comply. Agencies respond with requests. The budget office will then prepare a draft budget based on the governors' priorities. At this juncture, the governor or the budget office may hold hearings or meetings with department heads to permit them an opportunity to appeal for agency priorities.

The governor's budget, the result of the preparation stage, is finalized (usually in January) and submitted to a joint session of the general assembly through the governor's budget address in early February.

Note there is some variation in the calendar, in part because of what date the state has chosen as the beginning of its FY. Forty-six states use a July 1 FY; New York uses April 1; Texas uses September 1; Alabama, Michigan, and the District of Columbia all use October 1, the same date used by the federal government.

The revenue estimating process is also important. Most states have a balanced budget requirement; 39 states cannot carry forward any deficit, which is effectively a balanced budget requirement (White 2017).

Stage 2: Legislative Review and Approval

On receiving the budget, the respective house and senate committees with jurisdiction over the budget hold hearings to review agency requests for funds. Cabinet secretaries and others participate in these hearings, which provide legislators with an opportunity to review the specific programmatic, financial, and policy aspects of each agency's programs and requests. At the same time, legislative staff members analyze the details of the proposals. These review activities provide interest groups with their greatest opportunities to influence the outcome in specific areas by interacting with the legislature. The legislature makes its decisions on the budget in the form of appropriations bills.

Unlike the federal government, the state's chief executive in 44 states has the power of line-item veto, which means the governor can reduce or eliminate, but not increase, specific items in the budget legislation. Line-item veto power allows the governor to insist on certain items in the budget and exert additional influence over the legislative process before the budget legislation reaches the governor's desk.

Stage 3: Budget Execution

The governor's signing appropriations legislation signals the beginning of the execution stage of the budget cycle. Next, the budget office issues detailed spending plans and instructions. The agencies rebudget the funds appropriated in the legislation. The governor assumes responsibility for implementing the budget, although the various state agencies share this responsibility and the state's budget office is highly involved. In 33 states, the governor has the authority to withhold funds from agencies even if the money has been appropriated by the legislature. The predominant reason for this authority and its use is a shortfall of revenue (White 2017).

> For detailed information on state budget processes for all 50 states, see *Budget Processes in the States* at www.nasbo.org/reports-data/budget-processes-in-the-states.

Stage 4: Audit

States monitor and review agency performance and may conduct program audits or evaluations of selected programs. In addition, states have a financial postaudit. Audits may be administrative reviews or more official performance audits with published results available to other government officials and the public. Agency officials or the legislature will act on significant audit findings and recommendations.

From Formulation to Implementation

When a legislature, whether the US Congress or a state legislature, approves proposed legislation, and the chief executive, whether the president or a governor, signs it, the policymaking process crosses an important threshold. The point at which proposed legislation is formally enacted into law is the point of transition from policy formulation to policy implementation. As shown in exhibit 6.1, the formal enactment of legislation bridges the formulation and implementation phases of policymaking and triggers the implementation phase. Policy implementation is considered in the next chapter.

Summary

The policy formulation phase of policymaking involves agenda setting and the development of legislation. Agenda setting, which we discussed in chapter 5, entails the confluence of problems, possible solutions to those problems, and political circumstances that creates a window of opportunity for certain problem–possible solution combinations to progress to the development of legislation.

Legislation development, the other component of policy formulation and the central topic of this chapter, follows carefully choreographed steps that include the drafting and introduction of legislative proposals, their referral to appropriate committees and subcommittees, House and Senate floor action on proposed legislation, conference committee action when necessary, and presidential action on legislation voted on favorably by the legislature. These steps apply whether the legislation is new or, as is often the case, an amendment of prior legislation.

The tangible final products of legislation development are new public laws, amendments to existing ones, or budgets, in the case of legislation development in the budget process. At the federal level, laws are first printed in pamphlet form called *slip law*. Subsequently, laws are published in the *Statutes at Large* and then incorporated into the *US Code*.

Review Questions

1. Discuss the link between agenda setting and the development of legislation.
2. Describe the steps in legislation development.
3. Discuss the various sources of ideas for legislative proposals.
4. What congressional legislative committees are most important to health policy? Briefly describe their roles.
5. Describe the federal budget process. Include the relationship between the federal budget and health policy in your response.

References

Altman, S., and D. Shactman. 2011. *Power, Politics and Universal Health Care.* Amherst, NY: Prometheus Books.

Amadeo, K. 2019. "Federal Budget Process." Published March 13. www.thebalance.com/federal-budget-process-3305781.

Avik, R. 2012. "The Tortuous History of Conservatives and the Individual Mandate." *Forbes.* Published February 7. www.forbes.com/sites/theapothecary/2012/02/07/the-tortuous-conservative-history-of-the-individual-mandate/.

Cannan, J. 2013. "A Legislative History of the Affordable Care Act: How Legislative Procedure Shapes Legislative History." *Law Library Journal* 105 (2): 131–73.

Center on Budget and Policy Priorities. 2020. "Policy Basics: Introduction to the Federal Budget Process." Updated April 2. www.cbpp.org/cms/index.cfm?fa=view &id=155.

Congress.gov. 2019a. "Sustaining Excellence in Medicare Act of 2019." Published August 6. www.congress.gov/bill/116th-congress/house-bill/3253.

———. 2019b. "Committees of the U.S. Congress." Accessed December 31. www.congress.gov/committees.

Congressional Budget Office (CBO). 2020. "Introduction to CBO." Accessed January 15. www.cbo.gov/about/overview.

Government Accountability Office (GAO). 2020. "About GAO." Accessed January 15. www.gao.gov/about/index.html.

Hacker, J. S. 2010. "The Road to Somewhere: Why Health Reform Happened; Or Why Political Scientists Who Write About Public Policy Shouldn't Assume They Know How to Shape It." *Perspectives on Politics* 8 (3): 861–76.

———. 1997. *The Road to Nowhere.* Princeton, NJ: Princeton University Press.

Hacker, J. S., and T. Skocpol. 1997. "The New Politics of U.S. Health Policy." *Journal of Health Politics, Policy and Law* 22 (2): 315–38.

Heniff, B., Jr., M. S. Lynch, and J. Tollestrup. 2012. *Introduction to the Federal Budget Process.* Congressional Research Service. Published December 3. https://fas.org/sgp/crs/misc/98-721.pdf.

Hiltzik, M. 2016. "21st Century Cures Act: A Huge Handout to the Drug Industry Disguised as a Pro-Research Bounty." *Los Angeles Times.* Published December 5. www.latimes.com/business/hiltzik/la-fi-hiltzik-21st-century-20161205-story.html.

Johnson, H., and D. S. Broder. 1996. *The System: The American Way of Politics at the Breaking Point.* New York: Little, Brown.

Jost, T. S. 2014. "Implementing Health Reform: Four Years Later." *Health Affairs* 33 (1): 7–10.

Kansas Legislature. 2019. "How a Bill Becomes Law." Accessed December 31. www.kslegislature.org/li/m/pdf/how_bill_law.pdf.

Kaplan, S. 2016. "Winners and Losers of the 21st Century Cures Act." STAT. Published December 5. www.statnews.com/2016/12/05/21st-century-cures-act-winners-losers.

Lupkin, S. 2016. "Legislation That Would Shape FDA and NIH Triggers Lobbying Frenzy." NPR. Published November 25. www.npr.org/sections/health-shots/2016/11/25/503176370/legislation-that-would-shape-fda-and-nih-triggers-lobbying-frenzy.

National Association of State Budget Officers. 2020. "Budget Processes in the States." Accessed January 6. www.nasbo.org/reports-data/budget-processes-in-the-states.

National Conference of State Legislatures. 2020. "State Legislative Process." Accessed January 15. www.ncsl.org/portals/1/Media/modal_bootstrap.htm.

Office of Management and Budget (OMB). 2020a. "Office of Management and Budget." White House. Accessed January 15. www.whitehouse.gov/omb.

———. 2020b. "Statements of Administration Policy." White House. Published May 14. www.whitehouse.gov/omb/statements-of-administration-policy.

Oleszek, W. J. 2014. *Congressional Procedures and the Policy Process*, 9th ed. Thousand Oaks, CA: CQ Press.

Ornstein, N. 2015. "A Bipartisan Victory for Medical Research in Congress." *Atlantic*. Published July 13. www.theatlantic.com/politics/archive/2015/7/21st-century-cures-act-bipartisan/398369.

Peterson, M. A. 1997. "Introduction: Health Care into the Next Century." *Journal of Health Politics, Policy and Law* 22 (2): 291–313.

Redhead, C. S., H. Chaikind, B. Fernandez, and J. Staman. 2012. "ACA: A Brief Overview of the Law, Implementation, and Legal Challenges." Congressional Research Services. Published July 3. https://fas.org/sgp/crs/misc/R41664.pdf.

Skocpol, T. 1996. *Boomerang: Clinton's Health Security Effort and the Turn Against Government in U.S. Politics.* New York: Norton.

Sullivan, J. V. 2007. *How Our Laws Are Made.* Government Printing Office. Published July 25. www.gpo.gov/fdsys/pkg/CDOC-110hdoc49/pdf/CDOC-110hdoc49.pdf.

Teitelbaum, J. B., and S. E. Wilensky. 2013. *Essentials of Health Policy and Law*, 2nd ed. Burlington, MA: Jones & Bartlett Learning.

Tollestrup, J. 2012. *The Congressional Appropriations Process: An Introduction.* Washington, DC: Congressional Research Service Report R42388. Updated November 30. www.senate.gov/CRSpubs/8013e37d-4a09-46f0-b1e2-c14915d498a6.pdf.

USA.gov. 2019. "Budget of the U.S. Government." Updated October 10. www.usa.gov/budget#item-213709.

US House of Representatives Office of the Legislative Counsel. 2020a. "HOLC Guide to Drafting Legislation." Accessed April 27. https://legcounsel.house.gov/HOLC/Drafting_Legislation/Drafting_Guide.html.

———. 2020b. "Welcome to the Office of Legislative Counsel of the U.S. House of Representatives." Accessed April 26. https://legcounsel.house.gov.

US Senate. 2014. "Senate Glossary." Accessed March 23. www.senate.gov/reference/glossary_term/conference_committee.htm.

Wees, P., A. M. Zaslavsky, and J. Z. Ayanian. 2013. "Improvements in Health Status After Massachusetts Health Care Reform." *Milbank Quarterly* 91 (4): 663–89.

White, K. V. 2017. "State Budget Process: A Comparative Analysis." Council of State Governments. Accessed January 6, 2020. http://knowledgecenter.csg.org/kc/system/files/White2017.pdf.

APPENDIX

2.1

TYPES OF ADVOCACY GROUPS

This list, prepared by the Center for Responsive Politics, describes the various groups allowed to be involved in financing political campaigns.

501(c) Groups

Nonprofit, tax-exempt groups organized under Section 501(c) of the Internal Revenue Code that can engage in varying amounts of political activity, depending on the type of group. For example, 501(c)(3) groups operate for religious, charitable, scientific or educational purposes. These groups are not supposed to engage in any political activities, though some voter registration activities are permitted. 501(c)(4) groups are commonly called "social welfare" organizations that may engage in political activities, as long as these activities do not become their primary purpose. Similar restrictions apply to Section 501(c)(5) labor and agricultural groups, and to Section 501(c)(6) business leagues, chambers of commerce, real estate boards and boards of trade.

527 Group

A tax-exempt group organized under Section 527 of the Internal Revenue Code to raise money for political activities. These groups are typically parties, candidates, committees or associations organized for the purpose of influencing an issue, policy, appointment or election, be it federal, state or local. Such organizations can raise unlimited funds from individuals, corporations or labor unions, but they must register with the IRS [Internal Revenue Service] and disclose their contributions and expenditures.

Hybrid PACs (Carey Committees)

A Carey committee is a hybrid political action committee [PAC] that is not affiliated with a candidate and has the ability to operate both as a traditional PAC, contributing funds to a candidate's committee, and as a super PAC, which makes independent expenditures. To do so, Carey committees must have a separate bank account for each purpose. The committee can collect unlimited contributions from almost any source for its independent expenditure account, but may not use those funds for its traditional PAC contributions.

Political Action Committee (PAC)

A political committee that raises and spends limited "hard" money contributions for the express purpose of electing or defeating candidates. Organizations that raise soft money for issue advocacy may also set up a PAC. Most PACs represent business, such as the Microsoft PAC; labor, such as the Teamsters PAC; or ideological interests, such as the EMILY's List PAC or the National Rifle Association PAC. An organization's PAC will collect money from the group's employees or members and make contributions in the name of the PAC to candidates and political parties. Individuals contributing to a PAC may also contribute directly to candidates and political parties, even those also supported by the PAC. A PAC can give $5,000 to a candidate per election (primary, general or special) and up to $15,000 annually to a national political party. PACs may receive up to $5,000 each from individuals, other PACs and party committees per year. A PAC must register with the Federal Election Commission within 10 days of its formation, providing the name and address of the PAC, its treasurer and any affiliated organizations.

Source: Reprinted with permission from Center for Responsive Politics. 2020. "Types of Advocacy Groups." OpenSecrets.org. Accessed April 29. www.opensecrets.org/527s/types.php.

APPENDIX

2.2

NATIONAL INSTITUTE OF BIOMEDICAL IMAGING AND BIOENGINEERING ESTABLISHMENT ACT

P.L. 106-580
106th Congress

To amend the Public Health Service Act to establish the National Institute of Biomedical Imaging and Bioengineering.

Be it enacted by the Senate and House of Representatives of the United States of America in Congress assembled,

SECTION 1. SHORT TITLE.

This Act may be cited as the "National Institute of Biomedical Imaging and Bioengineering Establishment Act."

SEC. 2. FINDINGS.

The Congress makes the following findings:

(1) Basic research in imaging, bioengineering, computer science, informatics, and related fields is critical to improving health care but is fundamentally different from the research in molecular biology on which the current national research institutes at the National Institutes of Health (NIH; www.nih.gov) are based. To ensure the development of new techniques and technologies for the 21st century, these disciplines therefore require an identity and research home at the NIH that is independent of the existing institute structure.

(2) Advances based on medical research promise new, more effective treatments for a wide variety of diseases, but the development of new, non-invasive imaging techniques for earlier detection and diagnosis of disease is essential to take full advantage of such new treatments and to promote the general improvement of health care.

(3) The development of advanced genetic and molecular imaging techniques is necessary to continue the current rapid pace of discovery in molecular biology.

(4) Advances in telemedicine, and teleradiology in particular, are increasingly important in the delivery of high-quality, reliable medical care to rural citizens and other underserved populations. To fulfill the promise of telemedicine and related technologies fully, a structure is needed at the NIH to support basic research focused on the acquisition, transmission, processing, and optimal display of images.

(5) A number of Federal departments and agencies support imaging and engineering research with potential medical applications, but a central coordinating body, preferably housed at the NIH, is needed to coordinate these disparate efforts and facilitate the transfer of technologies with medical applications.

(6) Several breakthrough imaging technologies, including magnetic resonance imaging (MRI) and computed tomography (CT), have been developed primarily abroad, in large part because of the absence of a home at the NIH for basic research in imaging and related fields. The establishment of a central focus for imaging and bioengineering research at the NIH would promote both scientific advance[s] and United States economic development.

(7) At a time when a consensus exists to add significant resources to the NIH in coming years, it is appropriate to modernize the structure of the NIH to ensure that research dollars are expended more effectively and efficiently and that the fields of medical science that have contributed the most to the detection, diagnosis, and treatment of disease in recent years receive appropriate emphasis.

(8) The establishment of a National Institute of Biomedical Imaging and Bioengineering at the NIH would accelerate the development of new technologies with clinical and research applications, improve coordination and efficiency at the NIH and throughout the Federal Government, reduce duplication and waste, lay the foundation for a new medical information age, promote economic development, and provide a structure to train the young researchers who will make the path-breaking discoveries of the next century.

SEC. 3. ESTABLISHMENT OF NATIONAL INSTITUTE OF BIOMEDICAL IMAGING AND BIOENGINEERING.

(a) In General.—Part C of Title IV of the Public Health Service Act (42 U.S.C. 285 et seq.) is amended by adding at the end the following subpart:

Subpart 18—National Institute of Biomedical Imaging and Bioengineering

PURPOSE OF THE INSTITUTE

Sec. 464z. (a) The general purpose of the National Institute of Biomedical Imaging and Bioengineering (in this section referred to as the "Institute") is the conduct and support of research, training, the dissemination of health information, and other programs with respect to biomedical imaging, biomedical engineering, and associated technologies and modalities with biomedical applications (in this section referred to as "biomedical imaging and bioengineering").

(b)(1) The Director of the Institute, with the advice of the Institute's advisory council, shall establish a National Biomedical Imaging and Bioengineering Program (in this section referred to as the "Program").

(2) Activities under the Program shall include the following with respect to biomedical imaging and bioengineering:

(A) Research into the development of new techniques and devices.

(B) Related research in physics, engineering, mathematics, computer science, and other disciplines.

(C) Technology assessments and outcomes studies to evaluate the effectiveness of biologics, materials, processes, devices, procedures, and informatics.

(D) Research in screening for diseases and disorders.

(E) The advancement of existing imaging and bioengineering modalities, including imaging, biomaterials, and informatics.

(F) The development of target-specific agents to enhance images and to identify and delineate disease.

(G) The development of advanced engineering and imaging technologies and techniques for research from the molecular and genetic to the whole organ and body levels.

(H) The development of new techniques and devices for more effective interventional procedures (such as image-guided interventions).

(3)(A) With respect to the Program, the Director of the Institute shall prepare and transmit to the Secretary and the Director of NIH a plan to initiate, expand, intensify, and coordinate activities of the Institute with respect to biomedical imaging and bioengineering. The plan shall include such comments and recommendations as the Director of the Institute determines appropriate. The Director of the Institute shall periodically review and revise the plan and shall transmit any revisions of the plan to the Secretary and the Director of NIH.

(B) The plan under subparagraph (A) shall include the recommendations of the Director of the Institute with respect to the following:

(i) Where appropriate, the consolidation of programs of the National Institutes of Health for the express purpose of enhancing support of activities regarding basic biomedical imaging and bioengineering research.

(ii) The coordination of the activities of the Institute with related activities of the other agencies of the National Institutes of Health and with related activities of other Federal agencies.

(c) The establishment under section 406 of an advisory council for the Institute is subject to the following:

(1) The number of members appointed by the Secretary shall be 12.

(2) Of such members—

(A) six members shall be scientists, engineers, physicians, and other health professionals who represent disciplines in biomedical imaging and bioengineering and who are not officers or employees of the United States; and

(B) six members shall be scientists, engineers, physicians, and other health professionals who represent other disciplines and are knowledgeable about the applications of biomedical imaging and bioengineering in medicine, and who are not officers or employees of the United States.

(3) In addition to the ex officio members specified in section 406(b)(2), the ex officio members of the advisory council shall include the Director of the Centers for Disease Control and Prevention, the Director of the National Science Foundation, and the Director of the National Institute of Standards and Technology (or the designees of such officers).

(d)(1) Subject to paragraph (2), for the purpose of carrying out this section:

(A) For fiscal year 2001, there is authorized to be appropriated an amount equal to the amount obligated by the National Institutes of Health during fiscal year 2000 for biomedical imaging and bioengineering, except that such amount shall be adjusted to offset any inflation occurring after October 1, 1999.

(B) For each of the fiscal years 2002 and 2003, there is authorized to be appropriated an amount equal to the amount appropriated under subparagraph (A) for fiscal year 2001, except that such amount shall be adjusted for the fiscal year involved to offset any inflation occurring after October 1, 2000.

(2) The authorization of appropriations for a fiscal year under paragraph (1) is hereby reduced by the amount of any appropriation made for such year for the conduct or support by any other national research institute of any program with respect to biomedical imaging and bioengineering.

(b) USE OF EXISTING RESOURCES.—In providing for the establishment of the National Institute of Biomedical Imaging and Bioengineering pursuant to the amendment made by subsection (a), the Director of the National Institutes of Health (referred to in this subsection as "NIH")—

(1) may transfer to the National Institute of Biomedical Imaging and Bioengineering such personnel of NIH as the Director determines to be appropriate;

(2) may, for quarters for such Institute, utilize such facilities of NIH as the Director determines to be appropriate; and

(3) may obtain administrative support for the Institute from the other agencies of NIH, including the other national research institutes.

(c) CONSTRUCTION OF FACILITIES.—None of the provisions of this Act or the amendments made by the Act may be construed as authorizing the construction of facilities, or the acquisition of land, for purposes of the establishment or operation of the National Institute of Biomedical Imaging and Bioengineering.

(d) DATE CERTAIN FOR ESTABLISHMENT OF ADVISORY COUNCIL.—Not later than 90 days after the effective date of this Act under section 4, the Secretary of Health and Human Services shall complete the establishment of an advisory council for the National Institute of Biomedical Imaging and Bioengineering in accordance with section 406 of the Public Health Service Act and in accordance with section 464z of such Act (as added by subsection (a) of this section).

(e) CONFORMING AMENDMENT.—Section 401(b)(1) of the Public Health Service Act (42 U.S.C. 281(b)(1)) is amended by adding at the end the following subparagraph:

(R) The National Institute of Biomedical Imaging and Bioengineering.

SEC. 4. EFFECTIVE DATE.

This Act takes effect October 1, 2000, or upon the date of the enactment of this Act, whichever occurs later.

Approved December 29, 2000.

Source: National Institute of Biomedical Imaging and Bioengineering Establishment Act of 2000, Pub. L. No. 106-580, 114 Stat. 3088 (2000). Accessed January 16, 2014. www.gpo.gov/fdsys/pkg/PLAW-106publ580/pdf/PLAW-106publ580.pdf.

APPENDIX

2.3

STATEMENT OF THE AMERICAN HOSPITAL ASSOCIATION FOR THE COMMITTEE ON ENERGY AND COMMERCE SUBCOMMITTEE ON HEALTH OF THE U.S. HOUSE OF REPRESENTATIVES "PROPOSALS TO ACHIEVE UNIVERSAL HEALTH CARE COVERAGE," DECEMBER 10, 2019

On behalf of our nearly 5,000 member hospitals, health systems and other health care organizations, our clinician partners—including more than 270,000 affiliated physicians, 2 million nurses and other caregivers—and the 43,000 health care leaders who belong to our professional membership groups, the American Hospital Association (AHA) appreciates the opportunity to submit for the record our comments on "Proposals to Achieve Universal Health Care Coverage."

America's hospitals and health systems are committed to the goal of affordable, comprehensive health insurance for every American and believe we should build upon and improve our existing system to increase access to coverage of comprehensive health benefits. However, "Medicare for All" and other public option and buy-in proposals are not the solution.

Our detailed comments follow.

The Importance of Health Coverage

Meaningful health care coverage is critical to living a productive, secure and healthy life. Studies confirm that coverage improves access to care; supports positive health outcomes, including an individual's sense of their own health and wellbeing; incentivizes appropriate use of health care resources; and reduces financial strain on individuals and families. Coverage has broader community benefits as well, from ensuring adequate resources to maintaining critical health care infrastructure to being associated with decreased crime. We, therefore, appreciate Congress' focus on opportunities to close the remaining coverage gaps and achieve comprehensive health coverage for every American.

Despite recent coverage gains, approximately 9% of the U.S. population remains uninsured, a number that has increased over the past two years. The remaining uninsured tend to be young adults, disproportionately Hispanic and workers in lower-income jobs. Many of the uninsured are likely eligible for but not enrolled in subsidized coverage, including through Medicaid, the Health Insurance Marketplaces or their employers. For example, millions of the lowest-income uninsured could be covered if all states expanded Medicaid.

Single-Payer, Public-Option and Buy-in Proposals Are the Wrong Approach

While the AHA shares the objective of achieving health coverage for all Americans, we do not agree that a government-run, single-payer model is right for this country. Such an approach would upend a system that is working for the vast majority of Americans, and throw into chaos one of the largest sectors of the U.S. economy. Moreover, we are concerned that the alternative approaches being considered—mainly those creating opportunities to buy government-run health insurance coverage through one of the existing public programs or a new program—are equally detrimental to the health care system, without achieving the desired coverage results.

Payment under existing public programs, including Medicare and Medicaid, historically reimburse providers at less than the cost of delivering services. For example, Medicare and Medicaid reimbursed only 87 cents for every dollar spent by hospitals caring for these patients in 2017—a shortfall in payments of $53.9 billion for Medicare and $22.9 billion for Medicaid. Chronic underpayment can lead to access issues for seniors as some providers, especially physicians, may limit the number of Medicare patients they take or stop seeing them altogether. Indeed, hospitals and health systems only are able to stay open today to the extent commercial coverage makes up for the losses sustained providing care to beneficiaries of public programs. Congress' own advisory group, the Medicare Payment Advisory Commission (MedPAC), reported in its March 2019 report that hospitals had a negative 9.9% Medicare margin in 2017, on average, and projects that hospital Medicare margins will decline to negative 11% in 2019, the lowest such margin ever recorded.

Results from a recent study give some idea of the financial impact on the health care system of shifting more, or all, Americans into programs based on Medicare rates. The study found that a proposal to create a government-run, Medicare-like health plan on the individual exchange could create the largest ever cut to hospitals—nearly $800 billion—and be disruptive to the employer-sponsored and non-group health insurance markets. At the same time, this proposal would result in only a modest drop in the number of uninsured as compared to the 9 million Americans who would gain insurance by taking advantage of building upon the existing public/private coverage framework.

Even if the legislative proposals being considered today increased hospital reimbursement rates above current Medicare and Medicaid rates, our members' experience suggests that the government does not always act as a reliable business partner. Delays in payment and retroactive changes to reimbursement policies leave providers at risk of inadequate payment. Politicization means that providers cannot always trust that the rules of today will be the rules of tomorrow, which presents a challenging—if not impossible—environment for large, complex organizations. Recent examples of the uncertainty of working with government include the defunding of critical elements of the Health Insurance Marketplaces, including outreach and education, and cuts to the Medicare and Medicaid programs to offset spending on other priorities.

We also are deeply concerned that implementing any of these new proposals would seriously distract from the important delivery system reform work already underway. Hospitals and health systems have invested billions of dollars in technology and delivery system reforms to improve care, enhance quality and reduce costs. These proposals to revamp the system could easily stymie these improvement efforts by, at best, diverting attention and, at worst, being deemed irrelevant if the government can simply ratchet down provider rates to achieve spending objectives.

Finally, creating such fundamental shifts to the health care system would be highly disruptive not only to health coverage, but also to the broader economy. For example, almost half of all Americans, roughly 156 million people, receive coverage through an employer and these enrollees report being satisfied with their current coverage. Not only would a single-payer system move over 240 million people into some new form of coverage, it could radically alter the coverage of the more than 55 million people currently enrolled in the Medicare program, including the tens of millions who have voluntarily opted to enroll in Medicare Advantage.

Ways to Promote Better Care for America

Health coverage is too important to risk the potential disruption these legislative proposals would cause. The better path to achieving comprehensive coverage for all Americans lies in continuing to build on the progress made over the past decade. To advance our objective of covering all Americans, we support:

- Continued efforts to expand Medicaid in non-expansion states, including providing the enhanced federal matching rate to any state, regardless of when it expands. This would give newly expanded states access to three years of 100% federal match, which would then scale down over the next several years to the permanent 90% federal match.

- Providing federal subsidies for more lower- and middle-income individuals and families. Many individuals and families who do not have access to employer-sponsored coverage earn too much to qualify for either Medicaid or marketplace subsidies and, yet, struggle to afford coverage. This is particularly true for lower-income families who would be eligible for marketplace subsidies except for a "glitch" in the law that miscalculates how much families can afford. We support both expanding the eligibility limit for federal marketplace subsidies to middle-income families and fixing the "family glitch" so that more lower-income families can afford to enroll in coverage.
- Strengthening the marketplaces to improve their stability and the affordability of coverage by reinstituting funding for cost-sharing subsidies and reinsurance mechanisms and reversing the expansion of "skinny" plans that siphon off healthier consumers from the marketplaces, driving up the cost of coverage for those who remain.
- Robust enrollment efforts to connect individuals to coverage. The majority of the uninsured are likely eligible for Medicaid, subsidized coverage in the marketplace or coverage through their employer. We need an enrollment strategy that connects them to—and keeps them enrolled in—coverage. This requires adequate funding for advertising and enrollment efforts, as well as navigators to assist consumers in shopping for and selecting a plan.

We also must ensure the long-term sustainability of Medicare, Medicaid and other programs that so many Americans depend upon for coverage.

May 2019 CBO Report

In May, the Congressional Budget Office released a report examining the possible components of a single-payer system and their potential impact on health care. This report makes clear that establishing a single-payer system would be a "major undertaking that would involve substantial changes in the sources and extent of coverage, provider payment rates and financing methods of health care in the United States."

The CBO report details possible implications of paying providers Medicare rates in a single-payer system and states "such a reduction in provider payment rates would probably reduce the amount of care supplied and could also reduce the quality of care." The instability of changes to the health care system with a "Medicare for All" type system could have the unintended impact of jeopardizing access to care for everyone. This report raises serious concerns that we believe Congress should listen to and we would urge caution in moving forward with any system that would decrease availability of care or add to the length of time for availability of service.

Conclusion

The AHA appreciates the Committee holding this hearing and we look forward to working with Congress on this important issue. We believe we should come together and build upon and improve our existing system to increase access to coverage and comprehensive health benefits.

Source: American Hospital Association, 2019, "Statement of the American Hospital Association for the Committee on Energy and Commerce Subcommittee on Health of the U.S. House of Representatives 'Proposals to Achieve Universal Health Care Coverage,'" published December 10, www.aha.org/testimony/2019-12-10-aha-statement-proposals-achieve-universal-health-care-coverage.

APPENDIX

2.4

CONFERENCE COMMITTEES

Legislation can take many twists and turns along the path to enactment into law. It must go through subcommittees and then committees (in the House, each bill must have its own rule governing debate). Next, the leadership will assign a bill to a place on the calendar, and the originating house then considers it on the floor. If the bill passes through all these steps, it undergoes a similar process in the other chamber—subcommittee, committee, calendar assignment, then consideration by the second chamber. If the bill makes it through all this, then it goes to the president for veto or signature.

But what happens if the House and Senate pass different versions of the same bill? Regardless of the significance of the differences, they must be resolved so that both houses approve an identical piece of legislation. What follows is a summary of the conference committee process; the summary was prepared as part of a more extensive report by the Congressional Research Service.

The Constitution requires that the House and Senate approve the same bill or joint resolution in precisely the same form before it is presented to the President for his signature or veto. To this end, both houses must pass the same measure and then attempt to reach agreement about its provisions.

The House and Senate may be able to reach agreement by an exchange of amendments between the houses. Each house has one opportunity to amend the amendments from the other house, so there can be Senate amendments to House amendments to Senate amendments to a House bill. House amendments to Senate bills or amendments are privileged for consideration on the Senate floor; Senate amendments to House bills or amendments generally are not privileged for consideration on the House floor. In practice, the House often disposes of amendments between the houses under the terms of a special rule reported by the Rules Committee. The Senate sometimes disposes of House amendments by unanimous consent, but the procedures associated with the exchange of amendments can become complicated.

Alternatively, the House and Senate can each disagree to the position of the other on a bill and then agree to create a conference committee to propose a package settlement of all their disagreements. Most conferees are drawn from the standing committees that had considered the bill initially. The House or

Senate may vote to instruct its conferees before they are appointed, but such instructions are not binding.

Conferees generally are free to negotiate in whatever ways they choose, but eventually their agreement must be approved by a majority of the House conferees and a majority of the Senate conferees. The conferees are expected to address only the matters on which the House and Senate have disagreed. They also are expected to resolve each disagreement within the scope of the differences between the House and Senate positions. If the conferees cannot reach agreement on an amendment, or if their agreement exceeds their authority, they may report that amendment as an amendment in true or technical disagreement.

On the House and Senate floors, conference reports are privileged and debatable, but they are not amendable. The Senate has a procedure to strike out portions of the conference agreement that are considered, under Senate rules, to be "out of scope material" or "new directed spending provisions." The House also has a special procedure for voting to reject conference report provisions that would not have been germane to the bill in the House. After agreeing to a conference report, the House or Senate can dispose of any remaining amendments in disagreement. Only when the House and Senate have reached agreement on all provisions of the bill can it be enrolled for presentation to the President.

Source: E. Rybicki. 2019. "Summary." In *Resolving Legislative Differences in Congress: Conference Committees and Amendments*, Congressional Research Service, Report 98-696. Updated May. https://fas.org/sgp/crs/misc/98-696.pdf.

APPENDIX

2.5

INTRODUCTION TO THE FEDERAL BUDGET PROCESS

The not-for-profit Center on Budget and Policy Priorities conducts nonpartisan research and analysis on various government policies. The center published the following "backgrounder" explaining how the federal government prepares a budget.

This backgrounder describes the laws and procedures under which Congress decides how much money to spend each year, what to spend it on, and how to raise the money to cover some or all of that spending. The Congressional Budget Act of 1974 lays out a formal framework for developing and enforcing a "budget resolution" to guide the process but in recent years the process has not always worked as envisioned.

In this backgrounder, we address:

- the President's annual budget request, which is supposed to kick off the budget process;
- the congressional budget resolution—how it is developed, what it contains, and what happens if there is no budget resolution;
- how the terms of the budget resolution are enforced in the House and Senate;
- budget "reconciliation," an optional procedure used in some years to facilitate the passage of legislation amending tax or entitlement law; and
- statutory deficit-control measures—spending caps, pay-as-you-go requirements, and sequestration.

Step One: The President's Budget Request

The process starts when the President submits a detailed budget request for the coming fiscal year, which begins on October 1. (The President's request is supposed to come by the first Monday in February, but sometimes the submission is delayed, particularly when a new Administration takes office or congressional action on the prior year's budget has been delayed.) This budget

Spending, Revenues, and the Deficit

In trillions of dollars, fiscal year 2019

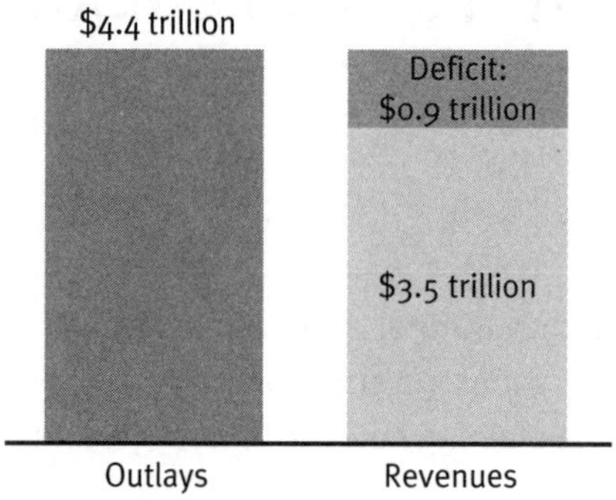

Source: Office of Management and Budget.

request—developed through an interactive process between federal agencies and the President's Office of Management and Budget (OMB) that begins the previous spring (or earlier)—plays three important roles.

First, it tells Congress what the President recommends for overall federal fiscal policy: (a) how much money the federal government should spend on public purposes; (b) how much it should take in as tax revenues; and (c) how much of a deficit (or surplus) the federal government should run, which is simply the difference between (a) and (b). In most years, federal spending exceeds tax revenues and the resulting deficit is financed through borrowing (see chart).

Second, the President's budget lays out his relative priorities for federal programs—how much he believes should be spent on defense, agriculture, education, health, and so on. The President's budget is very specific, recommending funding levels for individual "budget accounts"—federal programs or small groups of programs. The budget typically sketches out fiscal policy and budget priorities not only for the coming year but also for the subsequent nine years. The budget is accompanied by supporting volumes, including historical tables that set out past budget figures.

The third role of the President's budget is signaling to Congress the President's recommendations for spending and tax policy changes. As discussed below, the budget comprises different types of programs, some that require new funding each year to continue and others that do not require annual action by Congress. While the President must recommend funding levels for annually appropriated programs, he need not propose legislative changes for ongoing parts of the budget already funded by prior laws.

- **Annually appropriated programs.** These programs fall under the jurisdiction of the House and Senate Appropriations Committees.

Funding for these programs must be renewed each year to keep government agencies open and the programs in this category operating. These programs are known as "discretionary" because the laws that establish those programs leave Congress with the discretion to set the funding levels each year. That doesn't mean the programs are optional or unimportant, however. For example, almost all defense spending is discretionary, as are the budgets for a broad set of public services, including environmental protection, education, job training, border security, veterans' health care, scientific research, transportation, economic development, some low-income assistance, law enforcement, and international assistance. Altogether, discretionary programs make up about one-third of all federal spending. The President's budget spells out how much funding he recommends for each discretionary program.

- **Taxes, "mandatory" or "entitlement" programs, and interest.** Nearly all of the federal tax code is set in ongoing law that either remains in place until changed or requires renewal only periodically. Similarly, more than one-half of federal spending is also governed by ongoing laws. This category is known as "mandatory" spending. It includes the three largest entitlement programs (Social Security, Medicare, and Medicaid) as well as certain other programs (including SNAP, formerly food stamps; federal civilian and military retirement benefits; veterans' disability benefits; and unemployment insurance) that are not controlled by annual appropriations. Interest on the national debt is also paid automatically, with no need for new legislation. (There is, however, a separate limit on how much the Treasury can borrow. This "debt ceiling" must be raised or suspended through separate legislation when necessary.)

  As noted, the President's budget does not need to include recommendations to ensure the continuation of ongoing mandatory programs and revenues, but it will nonetheless typically include proposals to alter some mandatory programs and some aspects of revenue law.

- **Recommendations for mandatory programs** typically spell out changes to eligibility criteria and levels of individual benefits but do not usually propose binding funding limits. Rather, funding for these programs is effectively determined by the eligibility and benefits rules set in law.
- **Changes to the tax code will increase or decrease taxes.** Such proposals will be reflected as a change in the amount of federal revenue that the President's budget projects will be collected the next year or in future years, relative to what would otherwise be collected.

Components of Federal Spending, Fiscal Year 2019

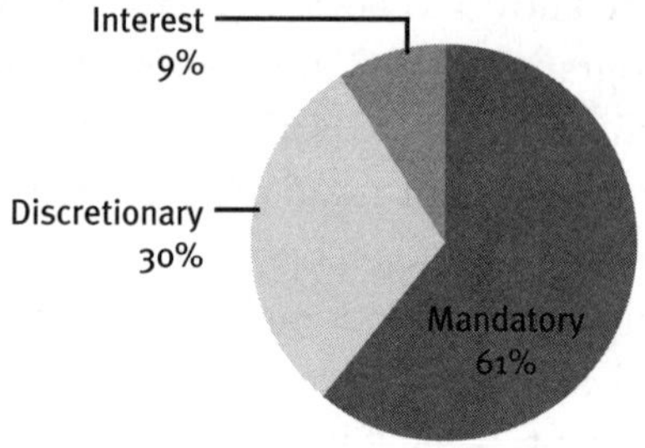

Source: Office of Management and Budget.

Step Two: The Congressional Budget Resolution

Next, Congress generally holds hearings to question Administration officials about their requests and then develops its own budget plan, called a "budget resolution." This work is done by the House and Senate Budget Committees, whose primary function is to draft and enforce the budget resolution. Once the Budget Committees pass their budget resolutions, the resolutions go to the House and Senate floors, where they can be amended (by majority vote). A House–Senate conference then resolves any differences, and the budget resolution for the year is adopted when both houses pass the conference agreement.

The budget resolution is a "concurrent" congressional resolution, not an ordinary bill, and therefore does not go to the President for his signature or veto. It also requires only a majority vote to pass, and its consideration is one of the few actions that cannot be filibustered in the Senate. Because it does not go to the President, a budget resolution cannot enact spending or tax law. Instead, it sets targets for other congressional committees that can propose legislation directly providing or changing spending and taxes.

Congress is supposed to pass the budget resolution by April 15, but it often takes longer. In recent years it has been common for Congress not to pass a budget resolution at all. When that happens, the previous year's resolution, which is a multi-year plan, stays in effect, although the House, the Senate, or both can and typically do adopt special procedures to set different spending levels (see box on page 319: What If There Is No Budget Resolution?).

- **What is in the budget resolution?** Unlike the President's budget, which is very detailed, the congressional budget resolution is a very simple document. It consists of a set of numbers stating how much Congress is supposed to spend in each of 19 broad spending categories (known as budget "functions") and how much total revenue the

Federal Spending, Fiscal Year 2019

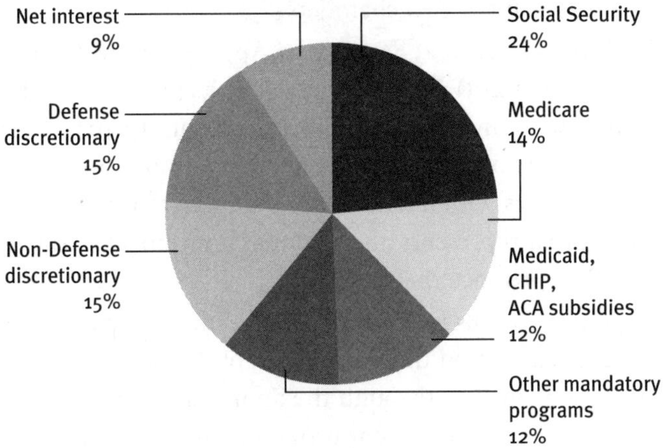

Source: Office of Management and Budget.

government will collect, for each of the next five years or more. (The Congressional Budget Act requires that the resolution cover a minimum of five years, though Congress now generally chooses ten years.) The difference between the two totals—the spending ceiling and the revenue floor—represents the deficit (or surplus) expected for each year.

- **How spending is defined: budget authority versus outlays.** The spending totals in the budget resolution are stated in two different ways: the total amount of "budget authority," and the estimated level of expenditures, or "outlays." Budget authority is how much money Congress allows a federal agency to commit to spend; outlays are how much money actually flows out of the federal Treasury in a given year. For example, a bill that appropriated $50 million for building a bridge would provide $50 million in budget authority for the coming year, but the outlays might not reach $50 million until the following year or even later, when the bridge actually is completed.

  Budget authority and outlays thus serve different purposes. Budget authority represents a limit on the new financial obligations federal agencies may incur (by signing contracts or making grants, for example), and is generally the focus of Congress' budgetary decisions. Outlays, because they represent actual cash flow, help determine the size of the overall deficit or surplus.
- **How committee spending limits get set: 302(a) allocations.** The report that accompanies the budget resolution includes a table called the "302(a) allocation." This table takes the spending totals that are laid out by budget function in the budget resolution and distributes

them by congressional committee instead. The House and Senate tables are different from one another, since committee jurisdictions vary somewhat between the two chambers.

In both the House and Senate, the Appropriations Committee receives a single 302(a) allocation for all of its programs. It then decides on its own how to divide this funding among its 12 subcommittees, creating what are known as 302(b) sub-allocations. Similarly, the various committees with jurisdiction over mandatory programs each get an allocation that represents a total dollar limit on all of the spending legislation they produce that year.

The spending totals in the budget resolution do not apply to "authorizing" legislation that merely establishes or changes rules for federal programs funded through the annual appropriations process. Unless it changes an entitlement program (such as Social Security or Medicare), authorizing legislation does not actually have a budgetary effect. For example, the education committees could produce legislation that authorizes a certain amount to be appropriated on the Title I education program for disadvantaged children. However, none of that money can be spent until the annual Labor-Health and Human Services-Education appropriations bill—which includes education spending—sets the actual dollar level for Title I funding for the year, which is frequently less than the authorized limit.

Often the report accompanying the budget resolution contains language describing the assumptions behind it, including how much it envisions certain programs being cut or increased. These assumptions generally serve only as guidance to the other committees.

The budget resolution can also include temporary or permanent changes to the congressional budget process.

Step Three: Enacting Budget Legislation

Following adoption of the budget resolution, Congress considers the annual appropriations bills, which fund discretionary programs in the coming fiscal year, and considers legislation to enact changes to mandatory spending or revenue levels within the dollar constraints specified in the budget resolution. Mechanisms exist to enforce the terms of the budget resolution during the consideration of such legislation, and a special mechanism known as "reconciliation" exists to expedite the consideration of mandatory spending and tax legislation.

Enforcing the Terms of the Budget Resolution

The main enforcement mechanism that prevents Congress from passing legislation that violates the terms of the budget resolution is the ability of a single member of the House or the Senate to raise a budget "point of order" on the floor to block such legislation. In some recent years, this point of order has not been particularly important in the House because it can be waived there by a simple majority vote on a resolution developed by the leadership-appointed Rules Committee, which sets the conditions under which each bill will be considered on the floor.

However, the budget point of order is important in the Senate, where any legislation that exceeds a committee's spending allocation—or cuts taxes below the level allowed in the budget resolution—is vulnerable to a budget point of order on the floor that requires 60 votes to waive.

What If There Is No Budget Resolution?

Congress has seldom completed action on the budget resolution by the April 15 target date specified in the Budget Act, and it failed to complete action on a resolution for fiscal years 1999, 2003, 2005, 2007, each year from 2011 through 2015, and 2019. In the absence of a budget resolution, the House and Senate typically enact separate budget targets, which they "deem" to be a substitute for the budget resolution. Such deeming resolutions typically provide spending allocations to the Appropriations Committees but may serve a variety of other budgetary purposes. Unless the House or Senate agrees to such a deeming resolution, the multi-year revenue floors and spending allocations for mandatory programs that had been agreed to in the most recent budget resolution remain in effect.

The Bipartisan Budget Act of 2013, described below, took a different tack, establishing a "Congressional Budget" for fiscal years 2014 and 2015 in statute as an alternative to the concurrent budget resolution called for in the Congressional Budget Act, including new appropriations targets for discretionary programs for each of those years. The Bipartisan Budget Act of 2015 did the same for the Senate for fiscal year 2017. And the Bipartisan Budget Act of 2018 did the same for both chambers for fiscal years 2018 and 2019, even though a budget resolution for 2018 had been agreed to by Congress three and a half months earlier.

Appropriations bills (or amendments to them) must fit within the 302(a) allocation given to the Appropriations Committee as well as the committee-determined 302(b) sub-allocations for the coming fiscal year. Entitlement bills (or any amendments offered to them) must not exceed the budget resolution's 302 allocation for the applicable committee and must not cause revenues to fall below the revenue floor, both in the first year and over the total multi-year period covered by the budget resolution. The cost of a tax or entitlement bill is determined (or "scored") by the Budget Committees, nearly always by relying on estimates provided by the nonpartisan Congressional Budget Office (CBO). CBO measures the cost of tax or entitlement legislation against a budgetary "baseline" that projects mandatory spending and tax receipts under current law.

The Budget "Reconciliation" Process

From time to time, Congress makes use of an optional, special procedure outlined in the Congressional Budget Act known as "reconciliation" to expedite the consideration of mandatory spending and tax legislation. This procedure was originally designed as a deficit-reduction tool, to force committees to produce spending cuts or tax increases called for in the budget resolution. However, it was used to enact tax cuts several times during the George W. Bush Administration and again under the Trump Administration in 2017, thereby increasing projected deficits.

- **What is a reconciliation bill?** A reconciliation bill is a single piece of legislation that typically includes multiple provisions (generally developed by several committees), all of which directly affect the federal budget—whether mandatory spending, taxes, or both. A reconciliation bill, like the budget resolution, cannot be filibustered by the Senate, so it only requires a majority vote to pass.
- **How does the reconciliation process work?** If Congress decides to use the reconciliation process, language known as a "reconciliation directive" must be included in the budget resolution. The reconciliation directive instructs committees to produce legislation by a specific date that meets certain spending or tax targets. (If they fail to produce this legislation, the Budget Committee chair generally has the right to offer floor amendments to meet the reconciliation targets for them, a threat which usually produces compliance with the directive.) The Budget Committee then packages all of these bills together into one bill that goes to the floor for an up-or-down vote, with limited opportunity for amendment. After the House and Senate resolve the

differences between their competing bills, a final conference agreement is considered on the floor of each chamber and, if adopted, then goes to the President for his signature or veto.

- **Constraints on reconciliation: the "Byrd rule."** While reconciliation enables Congress to bundle together several different provisions from different committees affecting a broad range of programs, it faces one major constraint: the "Byrd rule," named after the late Senator Robert Byrd of West Virginia. This Senate rule provides a point of order against any provision of (or amendment to) a reconciliation bill that is deemed "extraneous" to the purpose of amending entitlement or tax law. If a point of order is raised under the Byrd rule, the offending provision is automatically stripped from the bill unless at least 60 senators vote to waive the rule. This makes it difficult, for example, to include any policy changes in a reconciliation bill unless they have direct fiscal implications. Under this rule, changes in the authorization of discretionary appropriations are not allowed, nor, for example, are changes to civil rights or employment law or even the budget process. Changes to Social Security also are not permitted under the Byrd rule, even if they are budgetary.

  In addition, the Byrd rule bars any entitlement increases or tax cuts that cost money beyond the five (or more) years covered by the reconciliation directive, unless other provisions in the bill fully offset these "out-year" costs.

What If Appropriations Bills Are Not Passed on Time?

If Congress does not complete action on an appropriations bill before the start of the fiscal year on October 1, it must pass, and the President must sign, a continuing resolution (CR) to provide stopgap funding for affected agencies and discretionary programs. If Congress doesn't pass or the President will not sign a CR because it contains provisions he finds unacceptable, agencies that have not received funding through the ordinary appropriations process must shut down operations.

A dispute between President Trump and Congress over border wall funding led to a 35-day shutdown of federal agencies under nine different departments starting December 22, 2018. A dispute over delay or defunding of health reform legislation between President Obama and congressional Republicans led to a 16- day shutdown of ordinary government operations beginning October 1, 2013. And a dispute between President Clinton and congressional Republicans in the winter of 1995–96 produced a 21-day shutdown of substantial portions of the federal government.

Statutory Deficit-Control Mechanisms

Separately from the limits established in the annual budget process, Congress operates under statutory deficit-control mechanisms that prevent tax and mandatory spending legislation from increasing the deficit and that constrain discretionary spending.

- **PAYGO.** Under the 2010 Statutory Pay-As-You-Go (PAYGO) Act, any legislative changes to taxes or mandatory spending that increase projected multi-year deficits must be "offset" or paid for by other changes to taxes or mandatory spending that reduce deficits by an equivalent amount. Violation of PAYGO triggers across-the-board cuts ("sequestration") in selected mandatory programs to restore the balance between budget costs and savings. (In addition, the House and Senate each enforce the PAYGO principle though similar internal rules, independent of the Congressional Budget Act.)
- **Discretionary funding caps.** The 2011 Budget Control Act (BCA) imposed limits or "caps" on the level of discretionary appropriations for defense and for non-defense programs in each year through 2021. Appropriations in excess of the cap in either category trigger sequestration in that category to reduce funding to the capped level.
- **BCA sequestration.** On top of any sequestration triggered by PAYGO or funding cap violations, the BCA also requires additional sequestration each year through 2021 in discretionary and select mandatory programs, split evenly between defense and non-defense funding. This BCA sequestration was implemented as a result of the failure of a joint select committee that had been created by the BCA to propose a legislative plan in the fall of 2011 that would reduce deficits by $1.2 trillion over ten years. In the case of discretionary programs, for 2014 and after, this special sequestration mechanism operates by reducing the appropriations caps below the level that the BCA originally set.

If budget legislation violates these statutes, the applicable sequestration penalties occur automatically, unless Congress also modifies the requirements. For example, policymakers modified the 2013 BCA sequestration requirement in the American Taxpayer Relief Act of 2012. Similarly, the Bipartisan Budget Act of 2013, worked out by Senate Budget Committee Chair Patty Murray (D-WA) and House Budget Committee Chair Paul Ryan (R-WI), reduced sequestration cuts in 2014 and 2015 while extending BCA sequestration of mandatory programs through 2023. Congress approved two subsequent budget deals in 2015 and 2018 to provide even bigger relief for 2016–2017 and 2018–2019, respectively.

Conclusion

The annual federal budget process begins with a detailed proposal from the President; Congress next develops a blueprint called a budget resolution that sets limits on how much each committee can spend or reduce revenues in bills considered over the course of the year; and the terms of the budget resolution are then enforced against individual appropriations, entitlement bills, and tax bills on the House and Senate floors. In addition, Congress sometimes uses a special procedure called "reconciliation" to facilitate the passage of deficit-reduction legislation or other major entitlement or tax legislation. Moreover, budget legislation is subject to statutory deficit-control requirements. Legislation implementing a budget resolution that violates those requirements could trigger across-the-board budget "sequestration" cuts to offset the violations.

Source: Center on Budget and Policy Priorities. 2019. "Policy Basics: Introduction to the Federal Budget Process." Published July 8. www.cbpp.org/research/policy-basics-introduction-to-the-federal-budget-process.

PART

3

POLICY IMPLEMENTATION AND JUDICIAL REVIEW

Parts 1 and 2 examined health, the context of health policy, and the legislative process in creating health policy. Part 3 carries consideration of the policymaking process to its next steps: implementation and judicial review.

To be clear, not every policy invites judicial review. However, every policy is, to be a policy at all, implemented. Policy implementation is a bit like the old saying: That's where the rubber hits the road. It becomes a real, living *thing* at that point, taking on a life of its own. When that happens, generally, the process moves forward without significant incident. In the case of a controversial policy, however, or in the case of a questionable judgment by the implementing agency, a court will be "invited" to review the law and the facts to determine whether the application of the policy is within the meaning of the law.

Part 3 begins with just such a circumstance. The plaintiffs in the case that serves as the policy snapshot did not think the administrative agency charged with implementation of this particular section of the Affordable Care Act (ACA) correctly interpreted the law; that interpretation then placed them within the ambit of the ACA, which the plaintiffs did not want.

So, we begin with one of the elements of implementation before delving into the detail of implementation and how it is that courts become a part of the policy process.

POLICY SNAPSHOT

CHALLENGING ADMINISTRATIVE REGULATIONS: ANOTHER EXAMPLE OF POLICYMAKING LITIGATION

You may recall the policy snapshot introducing part 1, "The Affordable Care Act: A Cauldron of Controversy," which was a review of *NFIB v. Sebelius.* That case dealt with two of the major initiatives in the Affordable Care Act (ACA) to increase the number of citizens with health insurance: first, by expanding Medicaid; and second, instituting the individual mandate requiring all nonexempt people to acquire health insurance. *NFIB* rendered decisions as to the constitutionality of both measures. The decision to uphold the constitutionality of the individual mandate, albeit on different grounds than those advanced by the government, opened the door to subsequent litigation on the issue pursued by opponents of the ACA.

King v. Burwell (135 S. Ct. 2480), decided in 2015, presents a good opportunity to see how the courts establish health policy while providing the reader an opportunity to review an important question regarding the ACA. The focus here will be on the individual mandate and related issues pertaining to implementation of a legislative requirement by an administrative agency.

The lawsuit was brought by Mr. David King and three other residents of Virginia. The plaintiffs contended that they should be exempted from the individual mandate of the ACA, which requires all individuals to obtain conforming insurance coverage or be subjected to the "Shared Responsibility Payment" authorized by the ACA. (See discussion in *NFIB v. Sebelius*, the policy snapshot in part 1.)

Their legal argument was that without the tax credits and subsidies available through the ACA, the cost of insurance to the plaintiffs would exceed 8 percent of their adjusted gross income, which is one of the exceptions to the individual mandate. The plaintiffs further contended that they were not eligible for the tax credits and subsidies contemplated by the ACA, because the Commonwealth of Virginia had not established a state exchange, as referenced in the statute, but rather had a federal exchange, and that such an exchange did not have the legal authority to grant the ACA's tax credits and subsidies.

The ACA allows each state the opportunity to establish an exchange, but provides that the federal government will establish "such Exchange" if the State does not (42 U. S. C. §§18031, 18041, as cited in *King v. Burwell*, 989, 2015). In implementing the legislation (discussed more generally and in greater detail in chapter 8), the Internal Revenue Service (IRS) promulgated a regulation that interpreted "such Exchange" to include both a "federal exchange" as well as a "state exchange," in effect, concluding that, for the purposes of administration of the ACA and its related tax credits and subsidies, a federal exchange and a state exchange are the same thing. Mr. King and his fellow plaintiffs contend that the IRS incorrectly interpreted this statutory provision—that it lacked the legal authority to conclude a federal exchange was the same as the state exchange. In essence, the plaintiffs are claiming that the IRS was acting legislatively in adopting this regulation. As a consequence, the plaintiffs claimed that the regulation was unlawful and that, therefore, the exchange in Virginia could not legally confer the tax credits and subsidies contemplated in the act because it was not an exchange authorized by the act. Plaintiffs further contended that, in the absence of such tax credits and subsidies, their costs for health insurance would exceed the 8 percent exception threshold; therefore, they further contended that the individual mandate did not apply to them. If the plaintiffs in this case were to be eligible for such tax credits and subsidies, they would be compelled to comply with the individual mandate. Because they objected to the individual mandate, its application to them caused them harm by forcing them to acquire health insurance that complied with the ACA or pay the Shared Responsibility Payment. The application of the individual mandate to them in a scheme that they asserted lacked legal authority was the grievance that gave them standing to bring the case.

The plaintiffs began the case with the filing of a complaint in the federal district court for the Eastern District of Virginia. (The case was filed in February 2014 as *King v. Sebelius*, but the name was changed when Sylvia Burwell replaced Kathleen Sebelius as secretary of the Department of Health and Human Services.) The government then filed an answer. Taken together, the two documents joined the question for the court to consider. The defendant (the US government, through the secretary of Health and Human Services) filed a motion to dismiss. The District Court dismissed the suit, ruling that the IRS regulation was a proper use of its authority.

This was a case of *first impression*, meaning that this is a novel legal question not previously litigated. As a consequence, there was no precedent for the court to rely on in reaching its conclusion. There are, however, rules of construction that provide guidance to a court in how to construe the meaning of a statute, particularly the rule of deference. As we will see shortly, these are also subject to interpretation about which there may be disagreement.

In *King*, we see several roles being played by the court. First, the court is acting as a constitutional referee in determining whether the IRS overstepped its administrative authority by legislating through the adoption of a regulation. Second, the court is acting as a meaning giver by defining the term "such exchange" as referenced in the statute. Finally, the court is acting as a rights protector with regard to the legal obligation of the plaintiff.

As referenced above, the court found that the IRS had *not* exceeded its authority in adopting the regulation; that the regulation applied to a federal exchange; and, therefore, the federal exchange could confer the tax credits and subsidies subject to the terms of the ACA. Accordingly, the plaintiffs would be eligible for the tax credits and subsidies contemplated in the act and, therefore, the plaintiffs' costs would not exceed 8 percent of their adjusted gross income. By that rationale, the individual mandate would apply to them and they would be required to obtain health insurance coverage.

Upon the dismissal, the plaintiffs appealed to the Fourth Circuit Court of Appeals. That court upheld the dismissal, opining that the IRS had the legal authority to interpret the language in the statute the way it did. With that in mind, the Fourth Circuit said the IRS had correctly interpreted the statute and that, therefore, the subsidies were legally available in both state and federal exchanges. With that finding, the plaintiffs were eligible for the applicable tax credits and subsides, so therefore, the plaintiffs would be required to comply with the individual mandate. King and his fellow plaintiffs then appealed to the Supreme Court.

In another case, however, decided by the District of Columbia (DC) Circuit Court of Appeals at approximately the same time, the court reached the opposite conclusion. In 2014, in *Halbig v. Burwell*, the DC Circuit found that the IRS interpretation of the statute and subsequent regulation went beyond congressional intent; that the regulation lacked legal authority; and that, therefore, subsidies flowing from a federal exchange were illegal. This finding presented a conflict among the circuits of the US Courts of Appeal, with the ruling in one circuit directly contradicting the ruling in another. This difference of opinion between the courts made the question ripe for consideration by the Supreme Court; on appeal, the US Supreme Court would grant a writ of certiorari to hear the case.

Ultimately, in *King v. Burwell*, the Supreme Court upheld the Fourth Circuit decision and found that the IRS did not exceed its authority and that the regulation appropriately interpreted the statute. This result meant that residents in states with a federal exchange were eligible for tax credits and subsidies incorporated in the ACA and that, therefore, the individual mandate applied in those states just as it would in states with a state exchange. Thus, the court was both a meaning giver regarding the conformity of the regulation to the statute and a rights protector (in this case, however, placing limitations of the individual rights) with regard to the plaintiffs' legal obligations.

By upholding the IRS interpretation of the portion of the ACA that dealt with federal and state exchanges, the court upheld the legality of the individual mandate. This policy outcome is important because under the terms of the ACA, the individual mandate is responsible for approximately 8 million people having insurance who might not otherwise obtain coverage (Antos and Capretta 2018).

Reference

Antos, J. R., and J. C. Capretta. 2018. "CBO's Revised View of Individual Mandate Reflected in Latest Forecast." *Health Affairs.* Published June 7. www.healthaffairs.org/do/10.1377/hblog20180605.966625/full.

CHAPTER

7

POLICY IMPLEMENTATION

Learning Objectives

After reading this chapter, you should be able to

- describe the responsibilities of the executive, legislative, and judicial branches of government in policy implementation;
- explain why the Centers for Medicare & Medicaid Services (CMS) is an important policy-implementing organization;
- discuss the management challenges CMS faces in carrying out its policy implementation responsibilities;
- describe the four key activities of policy implementation;
- outline the federal rulemaking process;
- discuss the role of interest groups in rulemaking; and
- list and discuss three key variables in policy operation.

In this chapter, we shift our focus from policy formulation to policy implementation, with particular emphasis on the Centers for Medicare and Medicaid Services (CMS). As outlined in chapter 4 and described in more detail in chapters 5 and 6, policy formulation consists of two interrelated activities—agenda setting and legislation development. Sometimes these activities lead to policies in the form of new or amended public laws. The enactment of laws and amendments marks the transition from the formulation phase to the implementation phase of policymaking, although the boundary between the two phases is porous and two-way, as shown in exhibit 7.1.

As noted earlier, without implementation, policies are only paper and rhetoric. Organizations charged with implementing policies, primarily the departments and agencies in the executive branches of governments, are established and maintained to carry out the intent of public laws as enacted by the legislative branch. An implemented law or amendment can affect one or more determinants of health by changing the physical or social environment in which people live and work, by affecting their behavior and even their biology, and by influencing the availability and accessibility of health services. Departments and agencies charged with implementation conduct various activities to execute the policies. These activities and their interrelationships are shown in the darkly shaded portion of exhibit 7.1.

The implementation phase of public policymaking involves managing human, financial, and other resources to achieve the objectives embodied in the enacted legislation. These activities—designing, rulemaking, operating, and evaluating—are the essence of what organizations do to implement public policies. This chapter will examine these activities, with a focus on CMS. As administrative agencies go about implementing the policies formulated in the legislative phase, agency staff must make additional decisions, which may also be considered policy, as they are authoritative decisions made by agencies empowered to do so. As a result, people in these organizations both implement policies and make other, related policies.

Depending on the scope of the policies being implemented, the managerial tasks involved can be simple and straightforward, or they can require massive effort. The implementation of the Affordable Care Act (ACA), for example, was a monumental and challenging management undertaking. It involved changing how insurance companies did underwriting and required many small employers to add coverage and large employers to expand benefits. Moreover, the ACA called for the expansion of Medicaid (rendered optional, but nonetheless creating a management challenge); established federal (or state) health insurance exchanges; and engaged three federal agencies (Health and Human Services, Labor, and Treasury) in regulatory detail (Jost 2014).

In this chapter, we focus on the CMS (www.cms.gov) as an exemplar of an implementing agency or organization emphasizing the essential activities of implementation: designing, rulemaking, operating, and evaluating. Each of these core activities is discussed in the following sections.

First, however, we discuss an important feature of public policymaking in the United States: how the three branches of government share responsibility for policy implementation. As noted earlier, during implementation, more responsibility for policymaking shifts from the legislative branch to the executive branch, although implementation is a shared responsibility among the branches of government. While the executive branch role is central to the act of implementing policy, the legislative branch oversees implementation and appropriates funding for it. The judicial branch also plays a role, when there is an appropriate case or controversy, as described in detail in chapter 8. Each branch's implementation responsibility is described in the following sections, beginning with the executive branch agencies.

EXHIBIT 7.1

Policymaking Process: Implementation Phase and Activities

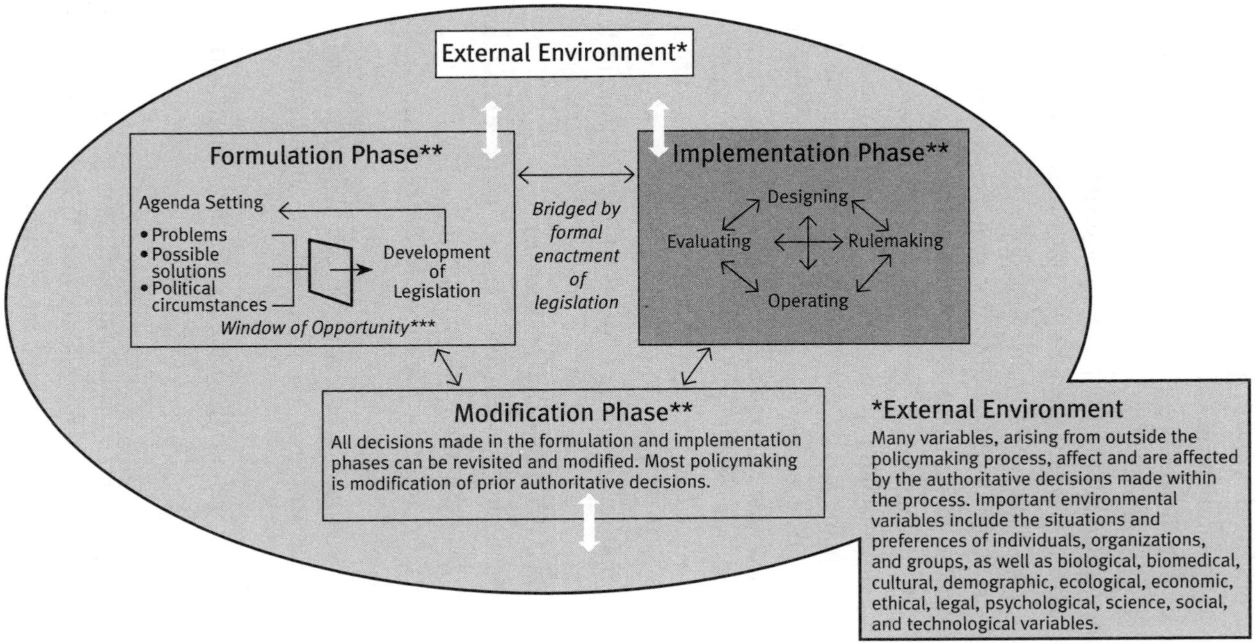
External Environment*
Formulation Phase**
Agenda Setting
• Problems
• Possible solutions
• Political circumstances
Development of Legislation
Window of Opportunity***
Bridged by formal enactment of legislation
Implementation Phase**
Designing
Evaluating
Rulemaking
Operating
Modification Phase**
All decisions made in the formulation and implementation phases can be revisited and modified. Most policymaking is modification of prior authoritative decisions.
*External Environment
Many variables, arising from outside the policymaking process, affect and are affected by the authoritative decisions made within the process. Important environmental variables include the situations and preferences of individuals, organizations, and groups, as well as biological, biomedical, cultural, demographic, ecological, economic, ethical, legal, psychological, science, social, and technological variables.

Policymakers in all three branches of government make policy in the form of position-appropriate, or authoritative, decisions. Their decisions differ in that the **legislative branch is primarily involved in formulation, the **executive branch** is primarily involved in implementation, and both are involved in modification of prior decisions or policies. The **judicial branch** interprets and assesses the legality of decisions made within all three phases of the policymaking process.

***A window of opportunity opens for possible progression of issues through formulation, enactment, implementation, and modification when there is a favorable confluence of problems, possible solutions, and political circumstances.

Policy Implementation: Roles of Each Branch

Although the implementation of policies is different from their formulation by legislative bodies of governments, authoritative decisions are also made during implementation. In other words, policy is being made in both the formulation and the implementation phases of the process shown in exhibit 7.1. As we will see in chapter 9, policymaking (or authoritative decision-making) continues in the modification phase.

In the implementation phase of policymaking, in addition to the fact that policy is being made as authoritative decisions, two important management aspects must come into play simultaneously. First, the organizations must, by definition, manage the implementation of policy. Second, the managers of these organizations must also oversee their own organizations.

Effective management of entities such as CMS or any of many other implementing organizations in the executive branch requires managers to do essentially what managers of all kinds of organizations do. Organizational management can be defined generically as a "process, composed of interrelated social and technical functions and activities, occurring in a formal organizational setting for the purpose of helping establish objectives and accomplishing the predetermined objectives through the use of human and other resources" (Longest and Darr 2014, 255). This definition explains what effective managers do. For example, in managing CMS as an organization, its leaders must:

- understand CMS's mission and objectives;
- analyze variables in CMS's external environment, assess their importance, and respond to them appropriately;
- assemble and organize the resources necessary to achieve the mission and objectives;
- determine the processes necessary to accomplish the mission and objectives and ensure that the processes are carried out effectively and efficiently; and
- lead others in contributing to the accomplishment of CMS's mission and objectives.

However, beyond the traditional management responsibilities involved in running a large and complex organization, CMS's leaders must also lead and manage the implementation of appropriately formulated policies for which CMS bears implementation responsibility. We consider this latter form of management here. Information on the more traditional form of managing in formal organizational settings can be found in the general management literature, which is abundant. See, for example, Daft (2018).

The Role of the Executive Branch

Virtually all executive branch organizations exist primarily to implement the laws enacted by the legislative branch. These organizations and agencies include the Department of Health and Human Services (HHS), the Department of Justice (DOJ), and subdivisions of those departments. Other of these executive organizations include independent federal agencies such as the Environmental Protection Agency (EPA), the Consumer Product Safety Commission, and the Food and Drug Administration (FDA).

CMS is one example of an implementing organization. This federal agency is located organizationally within HHS (exhibit 7.2). The agency was established specifically to implement the Medicare and Medicaid programs. In addition, CMS now has major responsibilities for implementing the ACA, which requires that it coordinate with states to establish health insurance marketplaces, expand Medicaid, and regulate private health insurance plans, among other things. We use CMS as an exemplar because it is so heavily involved in implementing important health policies such as Medicare, Medicaid, and the ACA. First, however, we consider the roles of the legislative branch and the judicial function in policy implementation.

Legislative Oversight of the Executive Branch

The legislative branch maintains oversight responsibility of the implementation phase. The Congressional Research Service defines *oversight* as "reviewing, monitoring and supervising the implementation of public policy by the executive branch" (Davis et al. 2020, 1). Legislative branch oversight has a long history, having been mandated by the Legislative Reorganization Act of 1946. Generally, legislative oversight is intended to accomplish the following (Garvey and Oleszek 2004):

- Ensure that the implementing organizations adhere to congressional intent
- Improve the efficiency, effectiveness, and economy of the government's operations
- Assess the ability of the implementing organizations and individuals to manage and accomplish implementation, including investigation of alleged instances of inadequate management, waste, fraud, dishonesty, or arbitrary and capricious action
- Ensure that implementation of policies reflects the public interest

Effective legislative oversight is accomplished through several means. One powerful technique involves the funding appropriations to continue the implementation of many congressionally enacted policies. Although some health

EXHIBIT 7.2
Organization Chart of the Department of Health and Human Services (HHS)

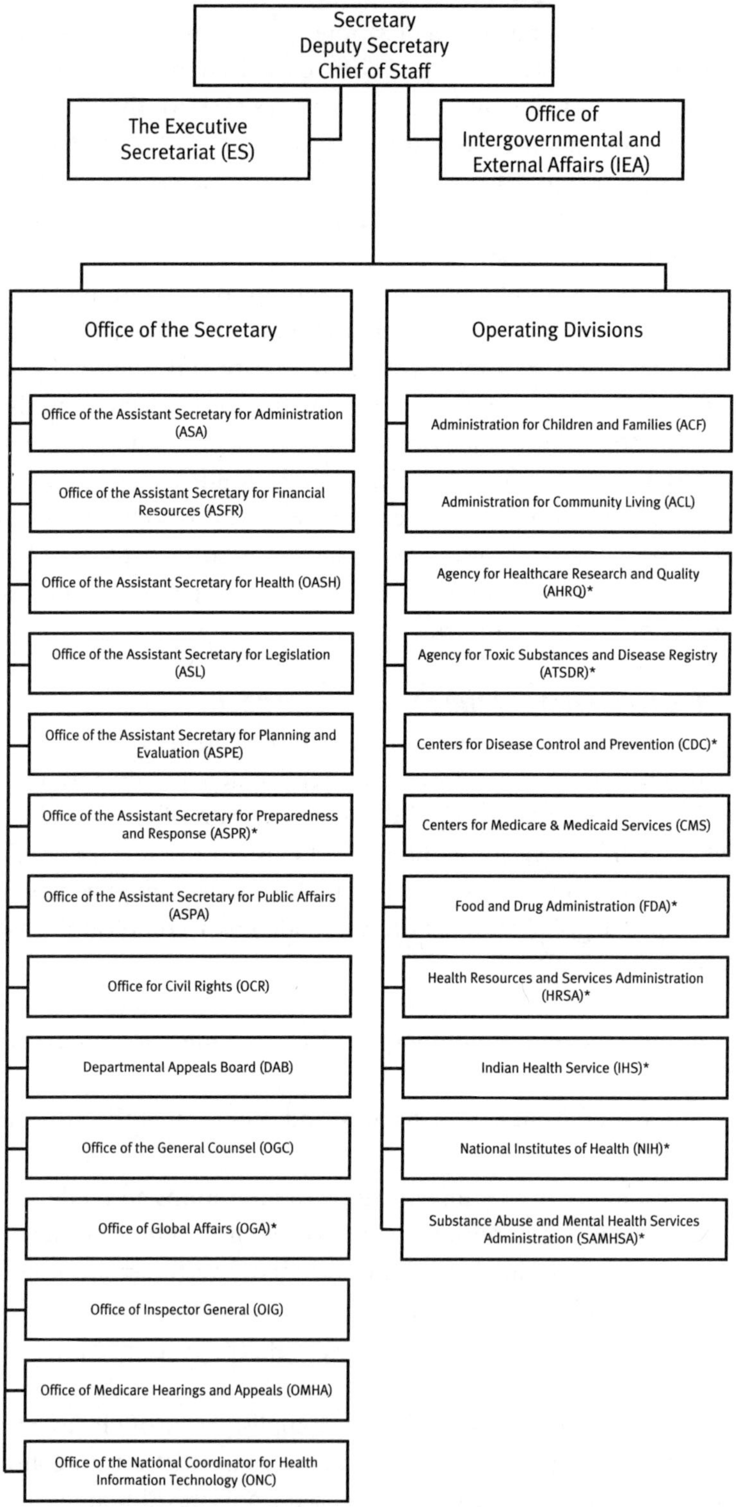

*Component of the Public Health Service.

Source: HHS (2020b).

policies, such as the Medicare program, are entitlements, others require annual funding through appropriations acts. Examples include the research programs of the National Institutes of Health; the health activities of the Department of Veterans Affairs; and the activities of the US Public Health Service, the Centers for Disease Control and Prevention (CDC), and the FDA. The House and Senate appropriations committees review the performance of these and similar organizations in carrying out their implementation responsibilities. Implementation inadequacies—real or perceived—may be reflected in the budgets that Congress appropriates for the implementing organizations.

Other means of oversight include direct contact between members of Congress and their staffs and the executive branch personnel who are involved in implementing policies as well as the use of implementation oversight agencies, including the Congressional Budget Office and the Government Accountability Office (Davis et al. 2020; Nadel 1995; Oleszek et al. 2020).

Legislative oversight extends beyond appropriations. Each standing committee of the House and Senate has certain oversight responsibilities. Those for the House standing committees, for example, are spelled out in Clause 2 of Rule X of the Rules of the House of Representatives for the 116th Congress (US House of Representatives 2019). Rule X requires that early in the first session of a Congress, each standing committee shall, in a meeting that is open to the public and with a quorum present, adopt its oversight plan for that Congress. Clause 2(b)(1) of Rule X states the following:

> In order to determine whether laws and programs addressing subjects within the jurisdiction of a committee are being implemented and carried out in accordance with the intent of Congress and whether they should be continued, curtailed, or eliminated, each standing committee (other than the Committee on Appropriations) shall review and study on a continuing basis:
>
> - the application, administration, execution, and effectiveness of laws and programs addressing subjects within its jurisdiction;
> - the organization and operation of Federal agencies and entities having responsibilities for the administration and execution of laws and programs addressing subjects within its jurisdiction;
> - any conditions or circumstances that may indicate the necessity or desirability of enacting new or additional legislation addressing subjects within its jurisdiction (whether or not a bill or resolution has been introduced with respect thereto); and
> - future research and forecasting on subjects within its jurisdiction.

Appendix 3.1 shows a typical oversight plan from the House Committee on Energy and Commerce, a committee with important oversight responsibilities for health policy.

Judicial Review

Enacted legislation and the rules made to guide its implementation can be challenged in the courts (see chapter 8). Two notable examples were presented as "policy snapshots" at the beginnings of parts 1 and 3. Those examples represent appeals of either legislative activity (*National Federation of Independent Business (NFIB) v. Sebelius*; part 1) or administrative activity (*King v. Burwell*; part 3). The judicial branch of the government litigated questions of the constitutionality of those respective actions. More commonly, appeals of specific agency decisions are appeals to administrative law judges. These judges are *not* part of the judicial branch as it was created in Article III of the Constitution, but they serve an important judicial function.

Administrative law judges in the implementing agencies hear the appeals of people or organizations that are dissatisfied with how the implementation of a policy affects them. For example, the Office of Administrative Law Judges (www.epa.gov/oalj) is an independent office in the Office of the Administrator of EPA. In other words, these administrative law judges are part of the executive branch but are insulated by law within the agency of which they are a part. These judges conduct hearings and render decisions in proceedings between the EPA and people, businesses, government entities, and other organizations that are regulated under environmental laws. They also preside over enforcement and permit proceedings under the Administrative Procedure Act, and they conduct other proceedings involving alleged violations of environmental laws, including the following:

- Clean Air Act
- Clean Water Act
- Comprehensive Environmental Response, Compensation, and Liability Act
- Emergency Planning and Community Right-to-Know Act
- Federal Insecticide, Fungicide, and Rodenticide Act
- Marine Protection, Research, and Sanctuaries Act
- Safe Drinking Water Act
- Solid Waste Disposal Act, as amended by the Resource Conservation and Recovery Act
- Toxic Substances Control Act
- Subchapter II of the Toxic Substances Control Act, known as the Asbestos Hazard Emergency Response Act

Federal administrative law judges are certified by the Office of Personnel Management and are ensured decisional independence. Decisions issued by these judges at the EPA are subject to review by the Environmental Appeals Board. The initial decision of these judges—unless a party appeals to the board, or if the board itself elects to review the initial decision—becomes the EPA's final order. Such an order may still be appealed to the federal district court in an appropriate circumstance.

To be clear, however, these administrative law judges are not federal judges created under the auspices of Article III of the Constitution. These are judges housed in the executive branch—*Article II judges*—who have only limited authority and jurisdiction related to the agency to which they are connected.

The legislative branch oversees implementation and the judicial function, whether in the executive branch or in the judicial branch, and interprets and referees questions of implementation in appropriate cases. The following box presents CMS as an example of a federal implementing organization. This example highlights important aspects of policy implementation described in this chapter.

CMS: Exemplar Implementing Agency

As shown in exhibit 7.2, CMS is an operating division within HHS. CMS is the largest purchaser of healthcare in the United States, currently paying for almost one-third of the nation's health expenditures. In fiscal year (FY) 2020, CMS's budget for benefit outlays and operations was about $1.16 trillion (CMS 2019). The organization provides health benefits to approximately 145 million Medicare, Medicaid, and Children's Health Insurance Program (CHIP) beneficiaries, or approximately 44 percent of Americans. With implementation of the ACA, CMS provides benefits to millions of additional people (HHS 2020a). CMS is indeed a large and especially important health policy implementing organization.

Legislative History

Created in 1977 as the Health Care Financing Administration, the agency brought together, under unified leadership, implementation responsibility and authority for the two largest federal healthcare programs—Medicare and Medicaid. The agency has evolved over time, for example, changing its name to CMS in 2001. The brief history described here is drawn from the agency's budget justification document for FY 2015, especially the executive summary (HHS 2017).

Throughout CMS's evolution, new legislation keeps significantly expanding the organization's implementation responsibilities. CHIP was added to its responsibilities in 1997. In 2003, the Medicare Prescription Drug, Improvement, and Modernization Act added a prescription drug benefit, creating substantial new implementation responsibilities. In 2005, the Deficit Reduction Act created a Medicaid Integrity Program to address

(continued)

fraud and abuse in the Medicaid program. The Tax Relief and Health Care Act of 2006 established a physician quality reporting program and quality improvement initiatives and increased CMS's program integrity efforts. The Medicare Improvements for Patients and Providers Act of 2008 extended and expanded the physician quality reporting program and established an electronic prescribing incentive program. It also established value-based purchasing for end-stage renal disease services. The Children's Health Insurance Program Reauthorization Act of 2009 improved outreach, enrollment, and access to benefits in the Medicaid and CHIP programs and mandated development of child health quality measures and reporting for children enrolled in these programs. The American Recovery and Reinvestment Act of 2009 provided investments for technological advances, including health information technology and the use of electronic health records, along with prevention and wellness activities.

The 2010 ACA contained numerous provisions affecting CMS's traditional role in Medicare, Medicaid, and CHIP. For example, there was a major expansion of the Medicaid program and a two-year extension of CHIP. Other provisions included the establishment of a new Federal Coordinated Health Care Office in CMS to improve care for beneficiaries who are eligible for both Medicare and Medicaid and the gradual elimination of the Medicare prescription drug coverage gap. The ACA also provided for such payment reform as bundled payments (a single global payment for all providers in an episode of care), quality improvement incentives, and the creation of a CMS Innovation Center to explore different care delivery and payment models in Medicare, Medicaid, and CHIP.

In 2011, CMS became responsible for the implementation of the ACA's consumer protections and private health insurance provisions. Among these provisions were new coverage options for previously uninsured Americans with preexisting conditions and reimbursement for employers to help defray the cost of providing health benefits for early retirees, their spouses, and their dependents. Other provisions included new requirements for the market conduct of private healthcare insurers and new consumer outreach and education efforts to help consumers assess their options and determine their eligibility for public health programs. In 2014, CMS worked with states to create new health insurance marketplaces. Exhibit 7.3 presents the organizational structure of CMS at that time. In 2015, CMS became responsible for implementing a new merit-based incentive payment system for providers as part of the Medicare Access and CHIP Reauthorization Act (MACRA), P.L. 114-10. In addition, MACRA established processes for developing, evaluating, and adopting alternative payment mechanisms. As the title of the legislation suggests, MACRA also reauthorized and funded CHIP for an additional two years (Hahn and Blom 2015).

EXHIBIT 7.3
Organization Chart of the Centers for Medicare & Medicaid Services, 2014

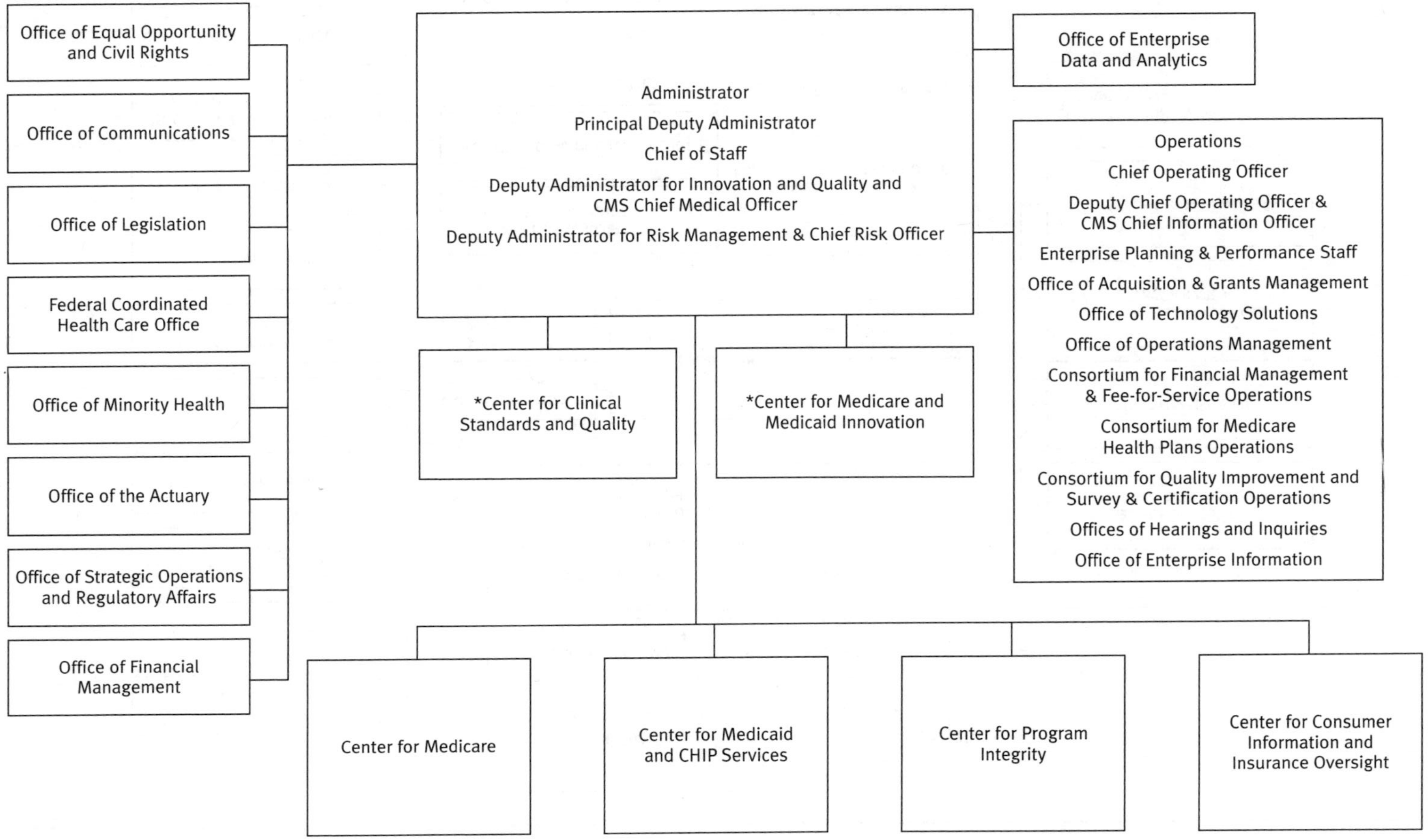

*Reports to Deputy Administrator for Innovation and Quality.

Source: HHS (2014).

EXHIBIT 7.4
Organization Chart of the Centers for Medicare & Medicaid Services, 2020

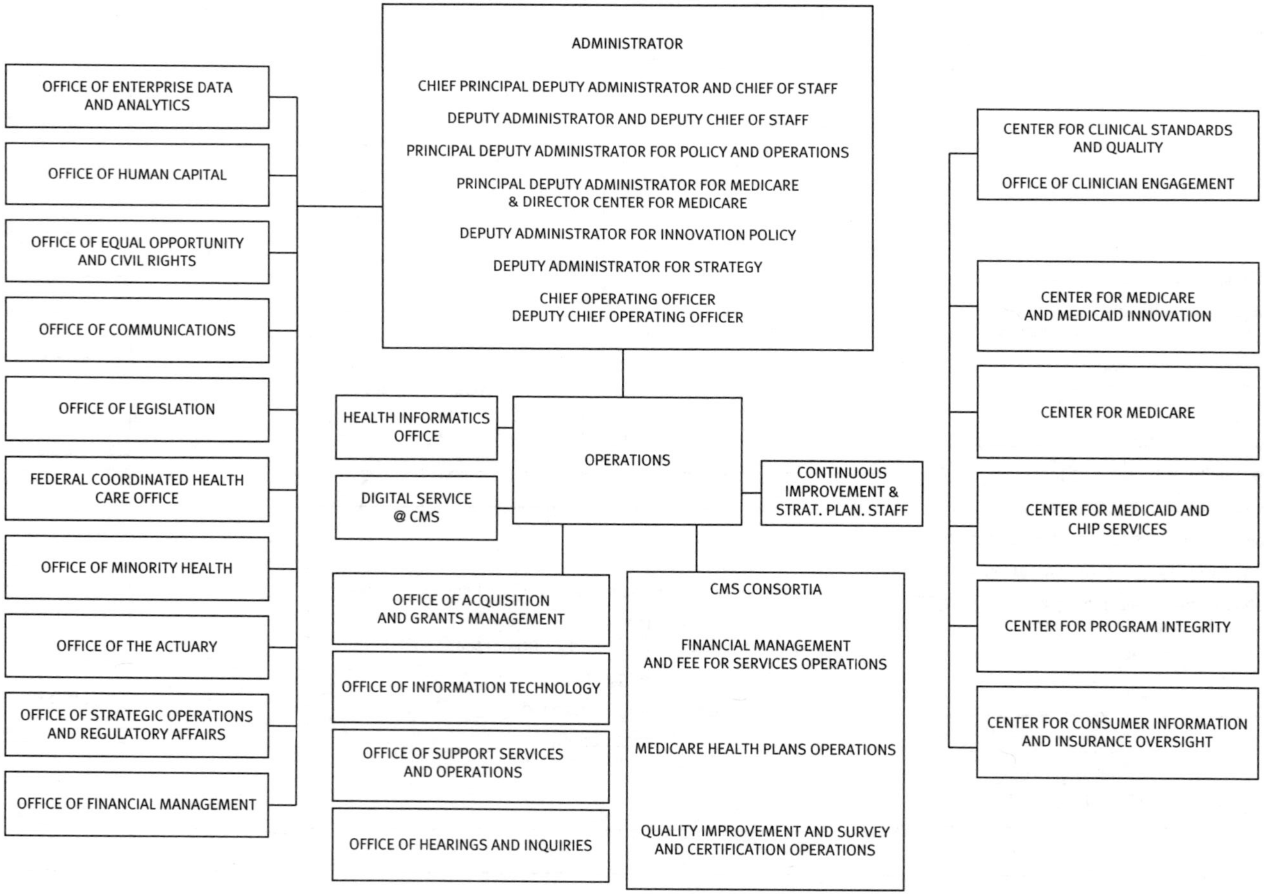

Source: HHS (2020b).

CMS was redesigned in the intervening years between 2014 and 2019 (see exhibit 7.4, which was taken from a CMS budget request for FY 2020). The Office of Human Capital was added, and the changing technology around digital information precipitated the creation of the Health Informatics Office. The Enterprise Performance and Planning staff has changed its focus and is relabeled Continuous Improvement and Strategy Planning. In addition, both the Financial Management group and the Grants Management group provide greater emphasis on fiscal integrity in the agency. As the "Evaluating" section will discuss, some of these changes are in response to findings from the Office of the Inspector General, whose function includes the evaluation of agency performance.

Critical Components of CMS

While a number of components in CMS have been recast or changed, several centers continue to constitute critical elements, contributing to the agency's core mission:

- Center for Medicare
- Center for Medicaid and CHIP Services
- Center for Consumer Information and Insurance Oversight
- CMS Innovation Center
- Center for Clinical Standards and Quality
- Center for Program Integrity

Detailed descriptions of these mission-critical centers are included in appendix 3.2.

CMS's large, complex structure helps it manage a wide variety of issues connected to its main mission, which is to serve Medicare and Medicaid beneficiaries by effectively managing those programs. Organizational design is only a starting point. In implementing policy, an agency needs to set forth rules and regulations that provide the details not included in the broad contours of legislation.

Designing Policy Implementation

Continuing with CMS as an example of an implementing organization, we turn to the first of four implementation activities: designing. This activity involves efforts to establish the agenda of an implementing organization, to plan how to address the agenda, and to carry out the plans. Sometimes, designing is straightforward and largely determined by which continuing, new, or revised policies an organization must implement.

Normally, an implementing organization's work agenda might remain stable from year to year, with some routine changes occurring. But policy shifts may sometimes be significant enough to require the redesign of part of an agency. The additional implementing responsibilities given to CMS by the ACA are a good example of this phenomenon. In effect, the ACA created major additions to CMS's implementation responsibilities, including the expansion of Medicaid, the coordination with states to establish health insurance marketplaces, and care innovation.

Faced with these added implementation responsibilities, CMS had to plan how it would carry them out and organize itself to meet the responsibilities. For policy-implementing organizations, design is an ongoing process. Regardless of its pace, change is a constant. Even routine minor shifts in policy might require a revision in the organizational structure. Managers cannot simply design the organization once and then turn their attention elsewhere. Instead, this task involves continuous redesign. Some of the circumstances under which managers of implementing organizations must redesign include the following:

- *Significant change in an implementing organization's external environment:* This change could be a new or an amended public law for the organization to implement or a change in the rules that affect the operationalization of public laws. Environmental changes might also include a major reduction in the organization's budget or a reorganization initiative undertaken in the executive branch.
- *New technologies or new implementation responsibilities:* A redesign may be required to channel necessary resources into the new activities. Conversely, when old technologies are abandoned or when previous responsibilities are shifted elsewhere, new structural arrangements may be necessary.
- *Change in management personnel:* Leadership changes are routine in the executive branch organizations that implement policy. People move into and out of public service. Administrations change. Changes at or near the top level of organizations often stimulate redesign. New leadership provides an opportunity to rethink the way the organization is designed and how it conducts its work. New managers typically view their organization's design from a fresh perspective and may want to have its design reflect their own ideas and preferences.
- *Large-scale design changes involving substantial reorganization in the context of larger change programs:* For example, the creation of the Health Informatics Office and the Digital Services Office within CMS significantly changed the organizational chart of CMS (see exhibits 7.3 and 7.4).
- *Significant changes in implementation responsibilities:* A shift in responsibilities can also trigger changes in an agency's organizational structure. For example, the new responsibilities given to CMS under

the ACA for market reforms and consumer protections in the private health insurance market caused CMS to establish the Center for Consumer Information and Insurance Oversight (exhibit 7.3). The ACA also specified that CMS would house the CMS Innovation Center and would help coordinate agencywide efforts to promote experimentation and innovation in payment and delivery models, reduce disparities in healthcare outcomes, promote primary care, and improve patient protections.

CMS's organizational responses to the ACA and subsequent legislative enactments provide a useful example of the importance of design in implementing policy. Designing—involving establishment of the working agenda and developing plans for how the work will be accomplished, organizing the agency to perform the work, directing the staff, and controlling results—is the essence of management.

Another example of organizational redesign, but at the hands of Congress, is the Helping Families in Mental Health Crisis Act (passed as part of the 21st Century Cures Act). In an effort to improve the visibility of mental health and substance use disorders as a health issue, Congress changed the title Administrator of Substance Abuse and Mental Health Services Administration to Assistant Secretary for Mental Health and Substance Abuse and increased the responsibilities of the office.

Rulemaking

Rules and rulemaking are important aspects of policy implementation. Rulemaking has a long history. The Administrative Procedure Act of 1946 defines a *rule* as "the whole or part of an agency statement of general or particular applicability and future effect designed to implement, interpret, or prescribe law or policy" (*US Code* 1946). Enacted laws are seldom explicit enough to guide their own implementation completely. Rather, they tend to be relatively vague, leaving it to the implementing organizations to specify, publish, and circulate the rules or regulations (remember, *rules* and *regulations* have the same meaning in the policy context and will be used interchangeably here) that will guide the law's actual operation. For this reason, *rulemaking*, the process through which federal agencies develop, amend, or repeal rules, is an early and vital step in public policy implementation in the United States (Kerwin and Furlong 2018).

Exhibit 7.5 outlines the process most federal agencies are required to follow in writing or revising a rule. Federal agencies issue approximately three thousand final rules (or sets of rules) annually on a great range of topics, such as the timing of bridge openings on some of the nation's rivers and the permissible levels of arsenic and other contaminants in drinking water.

EXHIBIT 7.5
The Federal Rulemaking Process

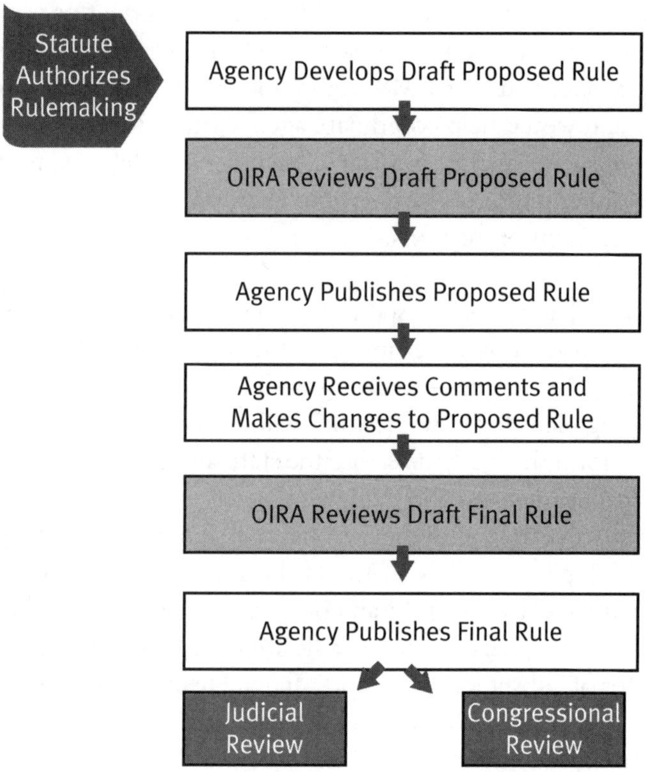

Note: OIRA, Office of Information and Regulatory Affairs (part of the Office of Management and Budget).
Source: Adapted from Carey (2019).

As shown at the top of exhibit 7.5, the federal rulemaking process begins when Congress takes an action (usually the enactment of a new law or an amended one) that either requires or authorizes an implementing organization in the executive branch to write and issue rules. Much rulemaking is driven by the formulation phase, where new laws or amendments to existing ones typically require rules to guide implementation. However, the process is not exclusively determined by legislative action. An implementing agency can decide to undertake rulemaking for several other reasons, including these, as described by the Office of the Federal Register (2020).

- New technologies or new data on existing issues;
- Concerns arising from accidents or various problems affecting society;
- Recommendations from Congressional committees or federal advisory committees;

- Petitions from interest groups, corporations, and members of the public;
- Lawsuits filed by interest groups, corporations, States, and members of the public;
- Presidential directives;
- "Prompt letters" from the Office of Management and Budget (OMB);
- Requests from other agencies;
- Studies and recommendations of agency staff.

No matter what triggers the rulemaking, any rules formally established by executive departments and agencies have legal effect. Because rules or regulations are authoritative decisions made in government to guide the decisions, actions, and behavior of others, the rules are, by definition, policies. These policies are codified in the *Code of Federal Regulations* (CFR 2020).

The delegation of rulemaking authority to implementing agencies is an essential feature of rulemaking, although Congress does not relinquish involvement in the process. As shown at the bottom of exhibit 7.5, Congress and the courts can determine that a rule must be returned to an earlier point in the process for further action or even that a rule be vacated.

Rules of Rulemaking

The promulgation of rules is itself guided by certain rules and protocols, primarily set forth in the Federal Register Act of 1935 and the Administrative Procedure Act of 1946. Key among these protocols is the requirement that implementing agencies publish *proposed* rules (the third step in exhibit 7.5).

Publishing a proposed rule enables those who would be affected by it to participate in the rulemaking before its adoption as a final rule. Proposed and final rules are published in the *Federal Register*, a daily publication that provides a uniform system for publishing presidential and federal agency documents. It includes the following major sections: Presidential Documents, Rules and Regulations, Proposed Rules, and Notices. The *Federal Register*, along with many other federal documents, can be read at a website maintained by the Government Printing Office (www.gpo.gov/fdsys).

A proposed rule is effectively a *draft* of a rule or set of rules that will guide the implementation of a law while the final rules are under development. Rules can be added, deleted, or modified; thus, rulemaking is an ongoing component in the life of any public law. The publication of a proposed rule is an open invitation for all parties with an interest in the rule to react before it becomes final.

A Rulemaking Example

One example of a controversy in Medicare (and healthcare in general) is the issue of cost to the consumer. Specifically, patients frequently lack sufficient—if any—information on the cost of a treatment or procedure until after the fact. Many times, the provider's bill is large and comes as a complete surprise to the patient and the family. CMS has proposed a rule to force healthcare providers to be transparent about pricing. Part of the notice of the proposed rule can be found in appendix 3.3.

This issue of cost transparency—or lack thereof—provides an example of administrative policymaking from the initiation of a proposed regulation, to the notice of the proposed rule, to a period of public comment. In this example, President Donald Trump issued an executive order directing elements of his administration to take action on price transparency (see appendix 3.4 for full text of the order). In his executive order, issued June 24, 2019, the president directed the secretary of Health and Human Services to promulgate, within 60 days, regulations within the parameters of existing law to promote price transparency.

Readers might notice that the date of the proposed rule did not quite meet the 60-day deadline imposed in the executive order. The slight delay is not critical; the rule is consistent with what the president intended to accomplish.

Finally, appendix 3.5 presents an example of a comment from the public received in response to the notice of the proposed rule. This comment was chosen from more than two thousand received. All the comments may be seen at Regulations.gov (2020). For complete information on the regulation related to transparency in pricing, see *Federal Register* (2019).

The Role of Interest Groups

Every policy affects one or more interest groups. Because rules established to implement health-related public laws often target members of interest groups, these groups routinely seek to influence rulemaking. Regulatory policies are implemented to prescribe and control the actions, behaviors, and decisions of certain individuals or organizations. Allocative policies provide income, services, or other benefits to some individuals or organizations at the expense of others. Interest groups that represent the individuals and organizations directly affected by such policies are actively interested in all aspects of policymaking, including rulemaking. As chapter 2 discussed, interest groups in health policy markets tend to be well organized and aggressive in pursuing their preferences, seeking to influence the formulation and implementation of policies that affect them (see the following box).

An Example of Interest Group Engagement: Patient Data

The implementation of any complex health-related law involves interaction between implementing organizations and the affected interest groups (Doonan 2013). Health policy is replete with examples of interest groups that influence, or attempt to influence, the rulemaking process. Part of the 21st Century Cures Act has a substantial discussion on rulemaking (see chapter 6). The newest battleground among various players in the healthcare sector is taking place over the availability of patient data and its uses. The sector grapples with the conflict between privacy and the interoperability of healthcare data systems. Concordantly, there are also economic interests at stake. Some organizations have already become significant purveyors of data management systems to healthcare organizations. Other entities, seeking to be disruptors in the healthcare market, are attempting to broaden access to patient data so they can enter this important and lucrative arena.

That availability and use of patient data relates to regulations arising from the Health Insurance Portability and Accountability Act (HIPAA), to be adopted as a result of a mandate in the 21st Century Cures Act to accelerate the interoperability of electronic health records nationwide (Sarata 2016). Specifically, the Office of National Coordinator for Health Information Technology is directed to develop a uniform standard for data sharing. (This office is a function within the Office of the Secretary of HHS.) This standard would facilitate the seamless exchange of information, irrespective of device. One observer compared this uniform standard to Bluetooth technology (Rae-Dupree 2020).

As healthcare continues to evolve, increasingly more companies that do not fit the traditional mold of hospitals, ambulatory surgical centers, or physician offices are entering the healthcare marketplace. These organizations need to consider the requirements of health services delivery as they come to this new market. Such companies as Amazon, Apple, Google, and Microsoft are promoting greater accessibility to individual patient data through application programming interfaces (APIs). These APIs would give a patient and various healthcare providers access to the individual patient's data. With this arrangement, or "back-door" access to existing electronic health records, a provider—or the patient—could use virtually any device to obtain health information such as diagnoses and procedures without the need for complete documents.

(continued)

A unique identifier is assigned to each discrete segment of information, enabling nearly universal access regardless of the location of the data.

The CARIN Alliance promotes advancing the broader use of data. The alliance is "led by distinguished risk-bearing providers, payers, consumers, pharmaceutical companies, consumer platform companies, health IT companies, and consumer-advocates who are working collaboratively with other stakeholders in government to overcome barriers in advancing consumer-directed exchange across the U.S." (CARIN Alliance 2020).

Conversely, groups with a large market share of health records and data question the wisdom of enhancing access to data for fear that individual privacy rights may be violated.

Not only are individual privacy issues at stake, but the economics underlying the issue are substantial. One analysis indicated the electronic health record market could grow to $35 billion by 2025 (Rae-Dupree 2020). So, too, is the way care is delivered and received. By early 2020, this issue of enhanced availability of patient data remained unresolved, though it would seem that the continuing evolution of healthcare will require continued change in how healthcare providers use and distribute patient data. For representative positions on this issue, see appendixes 3.6 and 3.7.

Lobbying and other forms of influence become especially intense when some interest groups strongly support the formulation of a particular law or the manner in which it is to be implemented, and other groups oppose it. Policymakers almost always face this dilemma in the formulation and implementation of policies. As we noted in chapter 2, legislators in such situations will seek to maximize their net political support through their decisions and actions (see the accompanying box on lobbying). Those responsible for the management of

A Cautionary Word About Lobbying

Most health administration professionals will never need to be concerned about lobbying. Hopefully, as engaged citizens you may call or write an elected representative or an appointed official. If, however, you find yourself becoming more deeply engaged on behalf of your organization or interest group, be aware that you are subject to certain ethical considerations and legal obligations. Chapter 10 discusses these issues.

EXHIBIT 7.6
Typical Policy Preferences of Selected Health-Related Individuals and Organizations

Federal Government
- Deficit reduction/increased surpluses
- Control over growth of Medicare and Medicaid expenditures
- Fewer uninsured citizens
- Slower growth in healthcare costs

Employers
- Simplified benefit administration
- Elimination of cost shifting
- No mandates

Insurers
- Administrative simplification
- Elimination of cost shifting
- Slower growth in healthcare costs
- No mandates

Individual Practitioners
- Income maintenance/growth
- Professional autonomy
- Malpractice reform

Suppliers
- Continued demand
- Sustained profitability
- Favorable tax treatment

State Government
- Medicaid funding relief
- More Medicaid flexibility
- Fewer uninsured citizens
- More federal funds and slower growth in healthcare costs

Consumers
- Insurance availability
- Access to care (with choices)
- Lower deductibles and copayments
- Lower premiums

Technology Producers
- Continued demand
- Sustained research funding
- Favorable tax treatment

Provider Organizations
- Improved financial condition
- Administrative simplification
- Less uncompensated care
- Better reimbursement rates

Professional Schools
- Continued demand
- Student subsidies

implementing agencies and organizations are likely to do the same. The result is that rulemaking is often influenced by interest group preferences, with the more politically powerful groups exerting the greatest influence.

The potential for conflicting interests among groups concerned with health policy can be seen in exhibit 7.6. Although some similarities exist among the preferences of the various categories, there are also important differences. Policymakers can anticipate that these individuals and organizations, largely working through interest groups, will seek to ensure that any enacted policies reflect the interest groups' preferences and that these preferences influence the subsequent implementation of such policies.

Other Interactions Between Rulemakers and Those Affected by the Rules

In certain instances, especially when rule development seems likely to be unusually difficult or to attract severe disagreement, or when continual revision is expected, the implementing organization may make special provisions.

For example, after passage of the Health Maintenance Organization Act (P.L. 93-222) in 1973, HHS organized a series of task forces, some of whose members came from outside the organization, to help develop the proposed rules for implementing the law. This strategy produced rules that were more acceptable to those who would be affected by them.

Another strategy used to support rulemaking is the creation of advisory commissions that can provide informed expertise from multiple perspectives. In addition, after enactment of the 1983 Amendments to the Social Security Act (P.L. 98-21), which established the prospective payment system for Medicare reimbursement, Congress established the Prospective Payment Assessment Commission (ProPAC) to provide nonbinding advice to the Health Care Financing Administration (now CMS) in implementing the reimbursement system. A second commission, the Physician Payment Review Commission (PPRC), was established later to advise Congress and CMS regarding payment for physicians' services under the Medicare program. The Balanced Budget Act of 1997 (P.L. 105-33) replaced both commissions with a new commission—the Medicare Payment Advisory Commission (MedPAC; www.medpac.gov)—which incorporates and expands the roles of ProPAC and PPRC. Appendix 3.8 briefly describes MedPAC's role.

After laws have been enacted by legislatures, after the implementing agencies have designed plans and structures to implement the laws, and after the initial rules necessary for implementing the legislation have been promulgated, policy implementation enters an operational phase (see exhibit 7.1).

Operating

As policies become operational, those who implement them are required to follow the rules developed to guide that implementation according to the legislative mandate. Ideally, a smooth transition from legislation to the actual operation of the policy is exactly what happens. However, implementation does not always go smoothly. Some individuals with implementing responsibilities may disagree with the purposes of the enacted laws and may seek to stall, alter, or even subvert the laws in their implementation phases. These individuals' power to affect the final outcomes and consequences of policies should not be underestimated. They hold an authority equivalent to that of executives in private-sector organizations with operational responsibilities for organizational missions and objectives.

If a policy in the form of a public law is intended to protect people from exposure to toxic substances in their environments, for example, its operation entails the activities involved in actually providing such protection. Operational activities in this situation might include measuring and assessing dangers from substances in the environment or imposing fines as a means to prevent or restrict environmental pollution.

CMS's FY 2014 budget request sought the funding needed to administer CMS's traditional programs—including Medicare, Medicaid, and CHIP—as well as the health insurance marketplaces, new private health insurance provisions, and consumer protections enacted by the ACA (CMS 2013). In essence, this list represents the main operating activities of CMS.

The description of the operation of Medicare Parts A and B provided in appendix 3.9 is abstracted from CMS's FY 2014 Justification of Estimates for Appropriations Committees. Medicare has four parts: Part A is hospital insurance, and Part B is supplemental medical insurance. Part C, also known as Medicare Advantage, offers comprehensive Parts A and B benefits in a managed care setting through private healthcare companies. Medicare Part D provides voluntary prescription drug coverage. This description of policy operation in appendix 3.9 is limited to Parts A and B.

Key Variables in Operating Policies

The success of any policy's operation depends on many variables, including how the policy is designed or constructed, the characteristics of the organizations charged with implementation, and the capabilities of the implementing organizations' managers. Each of these variables is examined in the sections that follow.

The Effect of a Policy's Design on Operation

As with any writing intended to influence the actions, behaviors, or decisions of others, the way laws are written affects how they are subsequently implemented. The effect can be seen throughout implementation. For example, the ACA assigned new responsibilities to CMS and explicitly directed the agency to engage in certain implementation activities. The design or construction of a policy includes its objectives, the hypotheses or causal relationships embedded in it, and the degree of flexibility allowed those responsible for implementation. As with laws, the design of other forms of policies heavily influences their implementation. For example, the presidential executive order in appendix 3.4 gives specific guidance as to who is authorized to do what in implementing the order.

Objectives of the Policy

Well-written laws always include clearly articulated objectives aligned with one another, although these are only one element of a good policy. When those who are responsible for implementation know what a law is intended to accomplish—what its objectives are—they can more easily operate the programs and procedures embedded in it.

If a single policy contains multiple conflicting objectives, implementation can be extremely difficult. In one study, managers with implementation responsibility for Medicare reported that they were often torn by the competing demands imposed by the multiple objectives established for the program

(Gluck and Sorian 2004). This study notes that these managers were simultaneously required under Medicare to

- serve Medicare beneficiaries' healthcare needs;
- protect the financial integrity of the program and preserve the solvency of the Medicare trust funds;
- make sure payments to providers were adequate to ensure their participation in the program;
- ensure the quality of services provided to program beneficiaries;
- guard against fraud and abuse in the program's operation;
- work with numerous private contractors, ensuring their quality and keeping them satisfied with the relationship; and
- work with states, respond to congressional oversight, and serve the political and policy priorities of the executive branch.

For example, one challenging directive of the program read as follows: "Medicare managers must ensure adequate participation in Medicare by healthcare providers, but also see to it that providers meet performance and quality standards" (Gluck and Sorian 2004, 65).

Hypothesis of the Policy

Vague or conflicting objectives are not the only problems that can hinder a policy's operation. The procedural paradigm set forth in a public law can also be flawed. Embedded in every policy, even if only implicitly, is a theory, or hypothesis, about the effect of operating the policy: If someone does *a*, then *b* will result. Only in a perfect world, of course, would a hypothesis be entirely plausible. Plausible or not, however, a policy's underlying hypothesis will affect its implementation.

For example, when the Older Americans Act (OAA) was introduced in 1965, it had a clear underlying hypothesis. The act aimed to provide resources necessary for public and private social service providers to meet the social service needs of the nation's older adult population. The original act received wide bipartisan support and has endured, with amendments, to the present day. The hypothesis of OAA was simple and correct: Establish mechanisms to provide needed services to older individuals, and the services will be provided and consumed.

Degree of Flexibility (or Vagueness) in the Policy

Another aspect of policy construction that can significantly affect implementation is the nature and extent of any decisions left to the implementing organizations. These decisions may be necessitated by directive language in a law, by what a law does not say, or by confusing or vague language in a law. Although some flexibility in developing policy implementation rules can be advantageous, vague directives can create problems for those with implementation responsibilities.

The Occupational Safety and Health Act of 1970 (P.L. 91-596), for example, contained vague directives and phrases that created significant problems for its implementers. Section 2 of the law stressed the importance of fostering healthful working conditions "insofar as possible" rather than specifying objectives or targets for achieving reductions in occupational injuries or diseases. In Section 6, the statute authorized the secretary of labor, in implementing the law, to issue standards dealing with toxic substances in the workplace "to the extent feasible." These kinds of phrases facilitate agreement among legislators precisely because they are vague and the exact definition can be in the eyes of the beholder. Conversely, from a regulatory standpoint, such vagueness can be vexatious. Implementers spent considerable time and energy deciding if "to the extent feasible" meant that they could take into account their actions' economic costs to employers in establishing standards for workplace toxic substances. In these instances, effective implementation was impeded by the policy's imprecise language.

Language that is too restrictive can also impede the implementation of a policy. In contrast with the imprecise language in the Occupational Safety and Health Act, Congress wrote into the law a precise and extremely restrictive range of fines that could be assessed against firms that violated standards. For less serious violations, the fine would be $1,000. For serious, willful violations, the fine could be up to $10,000. This precise, set range brings up the question of whether the limits on these fines are too low to be effective deterrents, especially for large, profitable enterprises. In this way, the effective operation of the law may be impeded by such specific language.

The Older Americans Act Amendments of 2006 (P.L. 109-365), which reauthorized OAA, provided extensive implementation guidance. However, considerable flexibility was left to the implementing organization, the Administration on Aging. Much of the language in the law, while providing detailed information about what was to be accomplished in implementation, left to the administration's managers a great deal of flexibility on how to accomplish these responsibilities. For example, the 2006 policy added provisions on elder justice, which was defined in the law as the "effort to prevent, detect, treat, intervene in, and respond to elder abuse, neglect, and exploitation and to protect elders with diminished capacity while maximizing their autonomy." The law provided guidance for addressing elder justice in Section 201:

> [The law] authorizes the Assistant Secretary for Aging to designate within the Administration on Aging responsibility for elder abuse prevention and services. Assigns to the Assistant Secretary the duty of developing objectives, priorities, policy, and a plan for: (1) facilitating the implementation of an elder justice system in the U.S.; (2) supporting states' efforts in carrying out elder justice programs; (3) establishing

> federal guidelines and disseminating best practices for uniform data collection and reporting by states; (4) collecting and disseminating data relating to the abuse, neglect, and exploitation of older individuals (abuse); (5) establishing an information clearinghouse; (6) researching such abuse; (7) providing technical assistance to states and other entities; (8) conducting a study concerning the degree of abuse; and (9) promoting collaborative efforts and diminishing duplicative efforts in elder justice programs in all levels of government.

This wording gave the Administration on Aging explicit direction for what was to be done, leaving the organization's managers to decide how it was to be done, for the most part. This flexibility facilitated the operation of these provisions.

In recent decades, Congress has tended to enact longer and more detailed laws to enhance their implementation. The pages of rules and other guidance to help shape implementation add up quickly. For example, the Medicare Prescription Drug Improvement and Modernization Act of 2003 is 416 pages long, and the PDF version of the ACA is 974 pages long (Office of the Legislative Counsel 2010).

Characteristics of Implementing Organizations

A policy is effectively implemented when one or more organizations operate the enacted legislation, ideally in a manner that realizes the intent behind the legislation. As we noted earlier, the bulk of implementation responsibilities rests with executive branch organizations. For example, CMS is primarily responsible for implementing Medicare, the FDA primarily implements many of the nation's food and drug policies, and state insurance departments are responsible for implementing the states' policies on health insurance.

Operational success requires a good fit between an implementing organization and the objectives of the policies it implements. Fit is determined by whether (1) the organization is sympathetic to a policy's objectives and (2) the organization has the necessary resources—authority, money, personnel, status or prestige, information and expertise, technology, and physical facilities and equipment—to implement a policy effectively.

An implementing organization's agreement with the objectives of a policy depends on the attitudes and perspectives of its senior leaders and managers. These people ensure that the necessary support for implementation is garnered. At CMS, for example, these people include the administrator, the principal deputy administrator, the chief operating officer of the agency, and the managers of CMS's centers (you may wish to review exhibit 7.4).

If an implementing organization's leaders are not sympathetic to the policies they are responsible for implementing, the leaders are unlikely to protect those policies from unwarranted amendments or intrusions by nonsupporters. Legislators who are hostile to a policy and those who seek to influence those legislators pose a particular threat. Strong allies in the legislative branch and among interest groups can assist with this protective task, but much of the responsibility rests with the leaders of the implementing organization.

The connection between any organization's resources and its capacity to fulfill its purposes is straightforward. CMS's budget and staff must be adequate matches for the implementation challenges facing the organization.

Another factor in the fit between an implementing organization and the policies it is supposed to implement is technology. Organizations rely on a variety of methods and technologies to implement policies. Just as policies differ substantially (e.g., the distinction between allocative and regulatory policies, as described in chapter 1), the technologies needed to implement them also differ (Dye 2012).

Regulatory policies require implementation technologies that prescribe and control the behaviors of whoever is being regulated. Such technologies include capacity for rule promulgation, investigatory capacity, and ability to impose sanctions. Allocative policies, on the other hand, require technologies through which implementing organizations deliver income, goods, or services. Such technologies include tools that target recipients or beneficiaries, determine eligibility for benefits, and manage the supply and quality of goods or services provided through the policy. For instance, the Occupational Safety and Health Administration relies heavily on regulatory technologies as it seeks to protect workers from hazards in the workplace. In contrast, CMS relies heavily, although not exclusively, on allocative technologies in the operation of Medicare, Medicaid (including the ACA-based Medicaid expansion), and CHIP. In fulfilling some of its implementation responsibilities under the ACA, CMS relies increasingly on regulatory technologies.

Only when the leaders of an implementing organization are fully sympathetic to a policy's objectives and have adequate operational resources, including the appropriate technologies to get the job done, can they effectively carry out their implementation duties. Even then, however, other factors, including the contributions of the organization's managers, affect the degree of success achieved.

The Capabilities of Managers

Managers make a difference in implementation (Trattner and McGinnis 2004). Management is essential in any purposeful organization. Someone must determine, initiate, integrate, and oversee the work of others. Senior-level managers in implementing organizations have a variety of responsibilities:

- Building support for the organization's purposes and priorities among internal and external stakeholders, especially among administrative branch superiors, legislators with oversight responsibility for the organization, and relevant interest groups

- Striking a workable balance between the economic and professional interests of the organization's members, the demands and preferences of its external stakeholders, and the public interest the organization is required to serve
- Negotiating and maintaining effective relationships with people and organizations that, regulated by or otherwise affected by the implementing organization, supply resources to the implementing organization or with which the implementing organization must work closely in implementing the policy

Effective implementing organizations need leaders and managers who can develop and instill a common vision of what the organization is to accomplish and how it is to be accomplished and who can stimulate determined and widespread adherence to that vision. They must focus on decisions and activities that affect the entire organization, including those intended to ensure its survival and overall well-being. They must establish missions and objectives; inculcate appropriate values in the individuals who make up the organization; manage the organizational culture; build intraorganizational and interorganizational coalitions; and interpret and respond to challenges and opportunities presented by the external environment (Longest and Darr 2014).

As in any organization, the managers of implementing agencies can benefit from knowing the histories and experiences of their organization. Managerial performance can benefit from a number of attributes:

- Long-standing shared values and commonly accepted norms help shape the organization's mission and operating practices and resolve conflicts among competing views.
- A history of success in implementing policies helps legitimize the organization's claims for support from internal and external stakeholders.
- A history of effective relationships with oversight actors and relevant interest groups and the availability of adequate financial resources provide a sense of organizational pride, stability, self-determination, and autonomy.

Basic management skills—especially in communication, conflict resolution, and motivation—also facilitate management effectiveness. Managers who can effectively communicate their views and preferences have a distinct advantage in guiding the behaviors of their followers. Similarly, successful managers can minimize conflict, mobilize widespread commitment to their preferences for the organization, and motivate stakeholders to help realize these preferences.

The ACA in particular underscores the need for managers to engage with other entities and stakeholders outside CMS. States that established health insurance exchanges, as well as parts of the Department of Justice and the Department of Treasury, all became "partners" with CMS in the implementation of the ACA.

The ability of managers of implementing organizations to collaborate with other entities is increasingly important to successful implementation. This capability includes the skills to create and maintain multiparty organizational arrangements; to negotiate complex agreements, perhaps even contracts, that sustain these arrangements; and to produce mutually beneficial outcomes through such arrangements.

The ability to develop shared cultures, or at least to minimize the differences that exist in the cultures of collaborating entities, is crucial to establishing and maintaining effective intergovernmental, interorganizational, or interagency collaborations. In this context, culture is the pattern of shared values and beliefs ingrained in an organization or agency over time that influences the behaviors and decisions of the people in it. Because collaborating organizations frequently have different cultures, the relationships between them can be complicated.

When more than one level of government, organization, or agency is involved in the implementation of a policy, as is frequently the case, the capability of the implementing organizations to collaborate in a coordinated manner is important to success. As was described earlier for the ACA, laws often require an implementing agency to coordinate or collaborate with other agencies.

Rarely does a single organization implement a health policy, and never does it do so when the scope of the policy is large. The responsibility for implementing the Medicaid program, for example, does not rest entirely with a single organization. CMS must work with the Medicaid agencies in each state and with such private-sector organizations as hospitals, nursing homes, and health plans. Successful implementation of the Medicaid program depends heavily on interactions among these and other organizations.

Collaborative capabilities are even more important when several implementing organizations must coordinate their responsibilities for a variety of policies intended to address a particular problem. A chief executive (president or governor) often issues an executive order directing two or more agencies to collaborate or to establish a mechanism to facilitate collaboration. For example, President Barack Obama issued Executive Order 13544 to establish the National Prevention, Health Promotion, and Public Health Council in 2010 (White House of President Barack Obama 2010). The ACA called for the establishment of this council, one of whose purposes stated in the executive order is to "provide coordination and leadership at the Federal level, and among all executive departments and agencies, with respect to prevention, wellness, and health promotion practices, the public health system, and integrative health care in the United States." This council was abolished by the Trump administration.

A Caveat to Organizational Culture and Management Capability

For effective implementation, a policy should be assigned to an agency with a culture supportive of that policy. Agency managers must also foster support for the policy. But in a governmental context, leaders and agency culture may be subject to the political winds of the moment. For this reason, such support may be more than ephemeral. In other words, if an administration comes to power and has a different worldview about how to approach the health policy challenges, administration staff may appoint leaders who are not interested in advancing the agency's existing mission or agenda. Simply put, if the new leaders are unconcerned about the mission, they may create a culture hostile to initiatives traditionally assigned to an agency.

Evaluating

The last core activity in implementing policy, critical to the ongoing success of the implementing organization, is evaluating it (see exhibit 7.1). This activity brings the other elements of implementation full circle and can lead to new rounds of designing, rulemaking, and operating.

At its most basic level, *evaluating* something means determining "its merit, worth, value, or significance" (Patton 2012, 2). When managers of implementing organizations evaluate a policy or some component part of it, they are interested in determining its value among other things. However, these determinations are made by seeking answers to more practical questions. Examples of these questions include the following: Is the policy being effectively implemented? How effective is the policy or some component of it? Were the policy's objectives or part of them achieved? What are the strengths and weaknesses of the policy or some part of it? To what extent do the benefits of the policy or part of it justify the costs? Does the policy or a component of it deserve continued funding? Increased funding? There are many ways that these and other, similar questions can be answered.

Policy evaluation can be defined as systematically collecting, analyzing, and using information to answer basic questions about a policy and ensuring that those answers are supported by evidence. As discussed earlier, a policy typically has a plausible model of how it should work: a hypothesis, or a theory, embedded in it. Of course, some policies have no explicitly articulated theory as their basis. Also, as discussed earlier, when a policy hypothesis is present, even if only implicitly, the underlying theory can be expressed as follows: If inputs or resources *a*, *b*, and *c* are assembled and processed by doing *m*, *n*, and *o* with them, then the results will be *x*, *y*, and *z*. The important point here is that using their underlying hypotheses as guidelines, policies can be described in terms of the interrelationships between the inputs and resources available for them, what is done with the resources, and the results achieved.

Evaluation Identifies Challenges

Evaluations can take several forms. Among the most widely used types are process and outcome evaluations, formative and summative evaluations, and cost–benefit and cost-effectiveness evaluations. Each of these types of evaluations has specific characteristics, as follows (Office of Planning, Research and Evaluation 2010):

- *Process evaluation* examines the extent to which a policy or a component of it is operating as intended by assessing ongoing operations. A process evaluation involves collecting data that describes operations in detail. Data can include such variables as the types and levels of services being provided, the location of service delivery, sociodemographic characteristics of those being served, and the linkages with collaborating agencies.
- *Outcome evaluation* assesses the extent to which a policy or a component of it produces outcomes as measured in terms of specific variables or data elements. The actual results are compared with the expected results from the policy. This type of evaluation is also known as impact evaluation and is sometimes also referred to as a *summative evaluation*.
- *Formative evaluation* is a type of process evaluation of a new or amended policy or a component of it. This evaluation collects data on operations so that any needed modifications can be made in the early stages of policy implementation. Formative evaluations provide managers with feedback on what aspects of a policy are working and those that need to be changed.
- *Cost–benefit evaluation* compares the relative costs of operating a policy or component (expenses, staff salaries, etc.) with the benefits (gains to individuals or society) the policy generates. For example, a policy guiding an intervention to reduce cigarette smoking would focus on the difference between the dollars expended for converting smokers into nonsmokers with the dollar savings from reduced medical care for smoking-related disease, days lost from work, and the like.
- *Cost-effectiveness evaluation* compares the relative costs of operating a policy or component with the extent to which the policy or component met its objectives. For example, evaluating a policy to guide an intervention to reduce cigarette smoking on a cost-effectiveness basis would estimate the dollars that had to be expended to convert each smoker into a nonsmoker.

The following box provides an example of how the Office of the Inspector General (OIG) for HHS can identify opportunities for improvement in how CMS performs its functions.

The OIG and Evaluation

Information about the nature and extent of the challenges CMS faces in managing implementation can be found in an annual summary of the top management challenges facing HHS, prepared by the OIG (2019). Although the summary pertains to all of HHS, CMS faces all the significant challenges currently included on the OIG list in its implementing activities. The OIG's list of challenges for HHS in 2019 was as follows (OIG 2019):

- Ensuring the financial integrity of HHS programs
- Delivering value, quality, and improved outcomes in Medicare and Medicaid
- Protecting the health and safety of HHS beneficiaries
- Safeguarding public health
- Harnessing data to improve the health and well-being of individuals
- Working across the government to provide better service to HHS beneficiaries

While the top challenges for any given year are important, the longer-term trends that the OIG identified as challenges to the agency may be of more interest. In this respect, from 2015 through 2019, three categories emerge: (1) program and financial integrity for Medicare and Medicaid, (2) the quality and value of care, and (3) the use of data and its security.

Medicare and the federal portion of Medicaid spending totals more than $1 billion. For some people, regrettably, this enormous expenditure looks like a prime opportunity to defraud the government. Preventing waste, fraud, and abuse—issues associated with financial and program integrity—are central to the OIG's efforts. Perhaps the cruelest example of this perfidy comes from the operator of a chain of hospice facilities and a physician who were convicted of defrauding the government of approximately $154 million. They enrolled patients with long-term incurable diseases, falsely telling them that they had less than six months to live and even sending chaplains to lie to the patients. In fact, the patients were not expected to die within six months, as is required to qualify for hospice services. However, the defendants kept the patients on services for multiple years to increase revenue. Clearly, reining in those who willfully steal from the system is an ongoing concern. Consider some other examples of challenges that the OIG faced in 2019 and 2020 (HHS 2019):

1. In several unrelated cases, physicians in Philadelphia, Detroit, Los Angeles, and New Jersey were convicted for unlawful distribution of a variety of opioids.
2. In a New York–based money-laundering and kickback scheme, the convicted individual referred Medicare and Medicaid patients to a clinic in exchange for kickbacks; the clinic fraudulently billed Medicare and Medicaid for nearly $100 million.
3. A home health care provider in Detroit was convicted of a $1.5 million kickback scheme.
4. An assisted-living and nursing-home operator in Florida was convicted in a years' long $37 million scheme in which he bribed physicians to admit patients to his facilities where he provided substandard care.

Sadly, many providers and other individuals are willing to cheat to gain more money from these programs. It is no surprise, therefore, that program and financial integrity (or related issues such as financial management) are listed regularly as a challenge for HHS.

Another key, regularly recurring issue for HHS is quality and value of care. Value is, of course, at least partly related to efficiency or the absence of waste, as in "waste, fraud, and abuse" as defined in the 2017 False Claims Act (31 US Code Sections 3729–3733). At least part of quality and value of care is tied to what may more broadly be termed *program and financial integrity*. Aside from that bit of overlap in program and financial integrity, however, the function of the OIG is to uncover shortcomings in services purchased by CMS and to provide recommendations about those lapses. Thus, a review of several years of the top management challenges reveals several examples of activity in the area of waste, fraud, and abuse. The OIG recommended the development of meaningful measures of quality and outcomes of services provided through the auspices of Medicare and Medicaid.

Compliance with regulations is another fertile area. The OIG found, for example, that some nursing home providers were not rendering services consistent with their healthcare plans. When the patients developed a urinary tract infection (a common development in that environment) and were not treated appropriately, the patients often had to be hospitalized. Hospitalization is a costly, and an entirely avoidable, development. The OIG likewise has uncovered that many children eligible for Medicaid were not receiving dental care services. And for home- and community-based services and personal care services, the OIG recommended a Five Star program to recognize the providers that meet service standards, thus motivating members of the industry to improve their care (HHS 2020c).

The use of data and its security have been a source of interest for several years as a management or performance challenge. HHS spends more than $5 billion on information technology, using and providing data across hundreds of thousands of platforms. The OIG report from 2018 perhaps captures this issue most effectively (HHS 2018):

> The environment in which HHS must protect its systems is complex, with ever-increasing volumes of data residing in many places and with many entities and individuals, and with continued expansion of the Internet of Things, including networked medical devices. Those possessing health and human services data—including public stakeholders—have cybersecurity responsibilities, which include ensuring effective people, processes, and technologies are in place to protect HHS data. The Department's challenges are, thus, multifaceted and include protecting data on internal systems, overseeing the cybersecurity of data in cloud environments, and ensuring that providers, grantees, and contractors are adhering to sound cybersecurity principles.

These are but a few examples of the evaluation mechanisms that take place in the implementation of policy. They are pertinent here to show the breadth of issues confronting the agency that manages the Medicare and Medicaid programs incident to implementing congressional mandates.

The range of issues is much broader than portrayed in these examples. The implementation and management of health insurance exchanges, the health and safety of program beneficiaries, food and drug safety, the protection of the public health—and more—are all areas in the HHS portfolio and present perennial management and performance challenges. And as one might expect, the number of challenges and their subject matter change from year to year. The three discussed above are present in one form or another over multiple years. For an example of the reporting of these challenges, see the partial 2019 OIG report about program and financial integrity in appendix 3.10.

Timing of Evaluations

Another consideration for policy evaluation is when in the life of a policy the evaluation occurs. This continuum can be organized as ex ante policy evaluation, policy maintenance, policy monitoring, and ex post policy evaluation (Patton, Sawicki, and Clark 2012):

- *Ex ante policy evaluation*, also called *anticipatory* or *prospective evaluation*, mainly influences agenda setting, whether it occurs in the original formulation of a policy or in its subsequent modification.

- *Policy monitoring* is typically undertaken to help ensure that policies are implemented as their formulators designed them to be implemented. It is relatively straightforward and constitutes part of legislative oversight and managerial control in implementation. Consequently, monitoring can play a powerful role in identifying when and how to change a policy, either by reformulating it or by making changes in its implementation, both in rules and in operations. Such monitoring frequently provides valuable information for subsequent ex post analysis.
- *Ex post policy evaluation*, also called *retrospective evaluation,* is a way to determine the real value of a policy. This determination depends on an assessment of the degree to which a policy's objectives are achieved through its implementation.

Support for Policy Evaluation and Policy Analysis

The legislative and executive branches of the federal government are involved in policy evaluation and other forms of analysis because they are interested in the performance of the policies they enact and implement. Key federal policy analytical organizations are briefly described in the following sections. The first two agencies are executive branch organizations, and the next three are part of the legislative branch. The analytical work done by all five agencies supports policy formulation and implementation.

Agency for Healthcare Research and Quality

The Agency for Healthcare Research and Quality (AHRQ; www.ahrq.gov) was originally established in 1989 as the Agency for Health Care Policy and Research. It was reauthorized with a name change to AHRQ in 1999. The agency's mission is to "produce evidence to make health care safer, higher quality, more accessible, equitable, and affordable, and to work with HHS and other partners to make sure that the evidence is understood and used" (AHRQ 2014).

AHRQ has a staff of about 300 people, with an annual budget exceeding $400 million. Approximately 80 percent of the agency's budget is used to support grants and contracts intended to improve healthcare. AHRQ currently has several priority areas of focus:

- Improve healthcare quality by accelerating the implementation of patient-centered outcomes research.
- Make healthcare safer.
- Increase accessibility by evaluating ACA coverage expansions.
- Improve healthcare affordability, efficiency, and cost transparency.

The agency's duties to evaluate ACA coverage expansions provide a good example of the role of evaluation in policy implementation. AHRQ, in collaboration with the Office of the Assistant Secretary for Planning and Evaluation and CMS, will evaluate the effects of the Medicaid and Marketplace coverage expansions under provisions in the ACA. In conducting the evaluations, AHRQ will focus on gathering evidence that will help the secretary of HHS and Congress make better-informed decisions about the implementation of the ACA. The evaluations will be designed to determine the effects of the coverage expansions on access, the reduction of disparities, outcomes, financial security, and employer offers and coverage take-up.

CMS Innovation Center

The CMS Innovation Center (www.innovation.cms.gov) was established by the ACA as part of CMS to test "innovative payment and service delivery models to reduce program expenditures . . . while preserving or enhancing the quality of care" for individuals who receive Medicare, Medicaid, or CHIP benefits. In establishing the center, Congress provided the secretary of HHS with the authority to expand the scope and duration of a model being tested through rulemaking, including the option of testing on a nationwide basis. For the secretary to exercise this authority, a model must either reduce spending without reducing the quality of care or improve the quality of care without increasing spending, and the model must not deny or limit the coverage or provision of any benefits. These determinations are based on evaluations performed by CMS and certified by CMS's chief actuary.

The CMS Innovation Center is working on several overarching priorities. It is testing new payment and service delivery models, evaluating the results, and advancing best practices. The center is also engaging a broad range of stakeholders to develop additional models for testing; it has divided its models into seven categories, as follows (CMS 2014):

Accountable Care

Accountable Care Organizations and similar care models are designed to incentivize health care providers to become accountable for a patient population and to invest in infrastructure and redesigned care processes that provide for coordinated care, high quality and efficient service delivery.

Bundled Payments for Care Improvement

Medicare currently makes separate payments to various providers for the services they furnish to the same beneficiary for a single illness or course of treatment (an episode of care). Offering these providers a single, bundled payment for an episode of care makes them jointly accountable for the patient's care. It also allows providers to achieve savings based on effectively managing resources as they provide treatment to the beneficiary throughout the episode.

Primary Care Transformation

Primary care providers are a key point of contact for patients' health care needs. Strengthening and increasing access to primary care is critical to promoting health and reducing overall health care costs. Advanced primary care practices—also called "medical homes"—utilize a team-based approach, while emphasizing prevention, health information technology, care coordination, and shared decision making among patients and their providers.

Initiatives Focused on the Medicaid and CHIP Population

Medicaid and the Children's Health Insurance Program (CHIP) are administered by the states but are jointly funded by the federal government and states. Initiatives in this category are administered by the participating states.

Initiatives Focused on the Medicare–Medicaid Enrollees

The Medicare and Medicaid programs were designed with distinct purposes. Individuals enrolled in both Medicare and Medicaid (the "dual eligibles") account for a disproportionate share of the programs' expenditures. A fully integrated, person-centered system of care that ensures that all their needs are met could better serve this population in a high quality, cost effective manner.

Initiatives to Speed the Adoption of Best Practices

Recent studies indicate that it takes nearly 17 years on average before best practices—backed by research—are incorporated into widespread clinical practice—and even then the application of the knowledge is very uneven. The Innovation Center is partnering with a broad range of health care providers, federal agencies, professional societies and other experts and stakeholders to test new models for disseminating evidence-based best practices and significantly increasing the speed of adoption.

Initiatives to Accelerate the Development and Testing of New Payment and Service Delivery Models

Many innovations necessary to improve the health care system will come from local communities and health care leaders from across the entire country. By partnering with these local and regional stakeholders, CMS can help accelerate the testing of models today that may be the next breakthrough tomorrow.

Government Accountability Office

The Government Accountability Office (GAO; www.gao.gov) is the investigative arm of Congress. It is often called the "congressional watchdog" because it investigates how the federal government spends taxpayer dollars. The agency advises Congress and the heads of executive branch agencies on making government more efficient, effective, ethical, equitable, and responsive. The stated mission of GAO is to "support the Congress in meeting its constitutional responsibilities and to help improve the performance and ensure the accountability of the federal government for the benefit of the American people" (GAO 2014). The agency seeks to provide Congress with timely information that is objective, nonpartisan, and fair.

In carrying out its mission, GAO audits and analyzes a host of programs and activities that arise from the implementation of federal policies. Organizationally, the office is under the direction of the comptroller general of the United States, who is appointed by the president, with the advice and consent of the Senate, to a 15-year term. This organizational structure gives GAO a level of independence and continuity of leadership—a level that is rare in government. The Budget and Accounting Act of 1921 established the organization for the limited purpose of independently auditing federal agencies. Over the years, however, Congress has expanded GAO's audit authority, added extensive new responsibilities, and strengthened the organization's ability to perform its work independently.

GAO does its work largely at the request of congressional committees or subcommittees or by mandate of public laws or committee reports. In fact, the office is required to perform work requested by committee chairpersons and assigns equal status to requests from ranking minority members of congressional committees. When possible, GAO also responds to requests for analyses and audits from individual members of Congress. The agency supports congressional oversight in several ways (GAO 2014):

- Auditing agency operations to determine whether federal funds are being spent efficiently and effectively
- Investigating allegations of illegal and improper activities
- Reporting on how well government programs and policies are meeting their objectives
- Performing policy analyses and outlining options for congressional consideration

Because GAO conducts a wide range of analyses, its staff is drawn from various disciplines, including accounting, law, public and business administration, economics, and the social and physical sciences. The work is organized so that each staff member concentrates on a specific subject area, facilitating the development of expertise in that area. When an analytical assignment requires specialized experience not available inside GAO, outside experts assist the permanent staff.

Congressional Budget Office

The Congressional Budget Office (CBO; www.cbo.gov) was created by the Congressional Budget and Impoundment Control Act of 1974. The agency's mission is to provide Congress with the objective, timely, and nonpartisan information analyses and estimates required for the congressional budget process. Compared with the missions of Congress's other support agencies—the Congressional Research Service (CRS) and the GAO—CBO's mission is narrow and focused. Even so, because the federal budget covers a broad array of activities, the agency is involved in wide-ranging health policy issues.

The Congressional Budget and Impoundment Control Act of 1974 requires CBO to produce a cost estimate for every bill "reported out" (approved) by a congressional committee. CBO's cost estimates show how the legislation would affect spending or revenues over the subsequent five years or more. They also provide information about the proposal and explain how CBO prepared the estimate.

CBO's primary responsibility is to assist the congressional budget committees with the matters under their jurisdiction—principally the congressional budget resolution and its enforcement. To help the budget committees enforce the resolution, CBO provides estimates of the budgetary costs of legislation approved by the various congressional committees and tracks the progress of spending and revenue legislation.

Overall, CBO's services can be grouped into four categories: helping Congress formulate budget plans, helping it stay within the scope of these plans, helping it assess the impact of federal mandates, and helping it consider the impact of policies on the federal budget. In the last role, for example, CBO analysts examine current and proposed policies, sometimes suggesting alternative approaches and projecting how the alternatives would affect current programs, the federal budget, and the economy. In line with its nonpartisan mandate, CBO does not offer specific policy recommendations.

Congressional Research Service

CRS (www.loc.gov/crsinfo/about) is another analytical resource available to members of Congress. Established in 1914 through legislation creating a separate department in the Library of Congress, the Legislative Reference Service was to provide Congress with information and analysis that would allow the legislature to make more informed decisions. The Legislative Reorganization Act of 1970 renamed the agency and significantly expanded its responsibilities. Today, the CRS's mission is to serve "the Congress throughout the legislative process by providing comprehensive and reliable legislative research and analysis that are timely, objective, authoritative, and confidential, thereby contributing to an informed national legislature" (CRS 2012).

As a legislative branch organization, CRS serves as a shared staff to congressional committees and members, assisting at every stage of the legislative process—from the early considerations in agenda setting that precede bill drafting, through committee hearings and floor debate, to the oversight and modification of enacted laws and various agency activities. CRS operates in many ways as an extension of, or supplement to, the members' own office staff. The agency's staff includes more than 400 policy analysts, attorneys, information professionals, and experts in a variety of disciplines: law, economics, foreign affairs, defense and homeland security, public administration, education, healthcare, immigration, energy, environmental protection, science, and technology.

CRS is organized into five interdisciplinary research divisions, which are clustered around American law; domestic social policy; foreign affairs, defense, and trade; government and finance; and resources, science, and industry. A knowledge services group serves the five divisions. In each division, CRS analysts and specialists are organized into smaller sections that focus on specific areas of public policy such as education, labor, taxes, and health.

CRS provides its services in many forms, including the following (CRS 2013):

- Reports on major policy issues
- Tailored confidential memoranda, briefings, and consultations
- Seminars, workshops, and expert congressional testimony
- Responses to individual inquiries

With an understanding of the implementation phase of policymaking, we now move on to chapter 8, which looks at judicial review in policymaking. Then, in part 4, we will examine the modification phase of policymaking and how healthcare professionals can build policy competence.

Summary

The implementation phase of public policymaking involves managing human, financial, and other resources in ways that facilitate achievement of the objectives embodied in enacted legislation. The implementing organizations, primarily the departments and agencies in the executive branches of governments, are established and maintained and the people in these organizations are employed to carry out the intent of public laws and amendments to them as enacted by the legislative branch.

Implementation is carried out through the interrelated set of activities shown in the implementation phase in exhibit 7.1: designing, rulemaking, operating, and evaluating. As the bidirectional arrows in the exhibit suggest, implementation may involve repeated rounds of these activities.

Designing involves establishing the agenda of an implementing organization, planning how to address the agenda, and organizing to carry out the plans. Sometimes this process is straightforward, but at other times it can be difficult. Designing the implementation of the ACA, for example, remains a challenge for CMS.

Rulemaking is an especially important and necessary part of policymaking because enacted laws are seldom explicit enough concerning the steps required to guide their full implementation. Implementing organizations routinely promulgate rules to guide the operation of enacted laws. The drafting and issuing of rules are themselves guided by certain rules and established procedures that ensure that those affected by a policy will have ample opportunity to participate in the rulemaking associated with its implementation. Interest groups may be heavily involved in rulemaking because they frequently express their preferences about rules.

Operating policies put the rules (and thus the law) into effect. If the objective of a policy is to expand Medicaid enrollment, for example, its operation means adding new enrollees. Operation requires that those who implement policies follow the rules promulgated to guide that implementation according to the mandates inherent in the laws.

Evaluating the implemented policy brings the other elements of designing, rulemaking, and operating full circle. Policy evaluation is defined as systematically collecting, analyzing, and using information to answer basic questions about a policy. When managers of implementing organizations evaluate a policy, or some part of it, they are interested in determining answers to such questions as these: Was the policy effectively implemented? How effective is the policy or component? Were the policy's or component's objectives achieved? What are the strengths and weaknesses of the policy or component? To what extent do the benefits of the policy or part of it justify its costs? Does the policy or component deserve continued funding? Increased funding? There are many ways that these and other, similar questions can be answered because there are several types of evaluations. In addition, implementing organizations can turn to several organizations, including AHRQ, CMS Innovation Center, GAO, CBO, and CRS, for help with evaluations.

Review Questions

1. Describe in general terms the implementation phase of public policymaking, including the responsibility of each branch of government.
2. Describe the designing activity in policy implementation.
3. Discuss the federal rulemaking process, including the role of interest groups.
4. Describe the operating activity in policy implementation.
5. Describe the evaluating activity in policy implementation.
6. List and briefly describe five organizations that support policy evaluation.

7. Discuss legislative oversight of policy implementation.
8. What are some of the important activities in CMS?
9. Describe CMS's key functions with regard to Medicare and Medicaid.
10. Discuss the challenges CMS faces in managing the health insurance marketplaces.

References

Agency for Healthcare Research and Quality (AHRQ). 2014. "About Us." Accessed February 13, 2020. www.ahrq.gov/about/index.html.

Carey, M. P. 2019. *An Overview of Federal Regulations and the Rulemaking Process.* Congressional Research Service Report IF 10003. Published January 7. https://crsreports.congress.gov/product/pdf/IF/IF10003.

CARIN Alliance. 2020. "The CARIN Alliance." Accessed January 24. www.carinalliance.com.

Centers for Medicare & Medicaid Services (CMS). 2019. *National Health Expenditures.* December 17. Accessed January 15, 2020. www.cms.gov/Research-Statistics-Data-and-Systems/Statistics-Trends-and-Reports/NationalHealthExpendData.

———. 2014. "Innovation Models." Accessed February 13. https://innovation.cms.gov/innovation-models#views=models.

———. 2013. "Justification of Estimates for Appropriations Committees, FY 2014." Accessed February 11, 2014. www.cms.gov/About-CMS/Agency-Information/PerformanceBudget/Downloads/FY2014-CJ-Final.pdf.

Code of Federal Regulations (CFR). 2020. Washington, DC: Government Printing Office. Accessed June 1. www.gpo.gov/fdsys/browse/collectionCfr.action?collectionCode=CFR.

Congressional Research Service (CRS). 2013. "About CRS." Library of Congress. Updated May 1. www.loc.gov/crsinfo/about.

———. 2012. "History and Mission." Library of Congress. Updated November 15. www.loc.gov/crsinfo/about/history.html.

Daft, R. L. 2018. *Management*, 13th ed. Boston: Cengage Learning.

Davis, C., W. J. Oleszek, B. Wilhelm, C. T. Brass, I. A. Brudnick, M. P. Carey, S. J. Eckman, W. T. Egar, K. A. Francis, M. J. Oleszek, R. E. Petersen, J. R. Straus, and M. M. Stuessy. 2020. *Congressional Oversight Manual.* RL 30240, Washington, DC: Congressional Research Service.

Doonan, M. T. 2013. *American Federalism in Practice: The Formulation and Implementation of Contemporary Health Policy.* Washington, DC: Brookings Institution Press.

Dye, T. R. 2012. *Understanding Public Policy*, 14th ed. Upper Saddle River, NJ: Pearson Education.

Federal Register. 2019. "Transparency in Coverage." Published November 27. www.federalregister.gov/documents/2019/11/27/2019-25011/transparency-in-coverage.

Garvey, T., and W. J. Oleszek. 2004. *Congressional Oversight and Investigations.* Focus IF 10015. Washington, DC: Congressional Research Service.

Gluck, M. E., and R. Sorian. 2004. *Administrative Challenges in Managing the Medicare Program.* American Association of Retired Persons Report #2004-15. Washington, DC: American Association of Retired Persons.

Government Accountability Office (GAO). 2014. "About GAO." Accessed February 21. http://gao.gov/about/index.html.

Hahn, J., and K. B. Blom. 2015. *The Medicare Access and CHIP Reauthorization Act.* R 43962. Washington, DC: Congressional Research Service.

Jost, T. S. 2014. "Implementing Health Reform: Four Years Later." *Health Affairs* 33 (1): 7–10.

Kerwin, C. M., and S. R. Furlong. 2018. *Rulemaking: How Government Agencies Write Law and Make Policy*, 5th ed. Washington, DC: CQ Press.

Longest, B. B., Jr., and K. Darr. 2014. *Managing Health Services Organizations and Systems*, 6th ed. Baltimore, MD: Health Professions Press.

Nadel, M. 1995. "Congressional Oversight of Health Policy." In *Intensive Care: How Congress Shapes Health Policy*, edited by T. E. Mann and N. J. Ornstein, 127–42. Washington, DC: American Enterprise Institute and the Brookings Institution.

Office of Inspector General (OIG). 2019. *2019 Top Management and Performance Challenges Facing HHS.* Accessed January 12, 2020. http://oig.hhs.gov/reports-and-publications/top-challenges/2019.

Office of Planning, Research and Evaluation. 2010. *The Program Manager's Guide to Evaluation*, 2nd ed. Washington, DC: US Department of Health and Human Services (HHS), Administration for Children and Families, Office of Planning, Research and Evaluation.

Office of the Federal Register. 2020. "A Guide to the Rulemaking Process." Accessed February 9. www.federalregister.gov/uploads/2011/01/the_rulemaking_process.pdf.

Office of the Legislative Counsel. 2010. "Compilation of Patient Protection and Affordable Care Act." 111th Congress, 2nd session. May 1. https://housedocs.house.gov/energycommerce/ppacacon.pdf.

Oleszek, W. J., M. J. Oleszek, E. Rybicki, and B. Heniff. 2020. *Congressional Procedures and the Policy Process*, 11th ed. Thousand Oaks, CA: CQ Press.

Patton, C. V., D. S. Sawicki, and J. J. Clark. 2012. *Basic Methods of Policy Analysis and Planning*, 3rd ed. Upper Saddle River, NJ: Pearson Education.

Patton, M. Q. 2012. *Essentials of Utilization-Focused Evaluation.* Thousand Oaks, CA: Sage.

Rae-Dupree, J. 2020. *How Fast Can a New Internet Standard for Sharing Patient Data Catch Fire?* January 22. Published January 22. https://khn.org/news/how-fast-can-a-new-internet-standard-for-sharing-patient-data-catch-fire/.

Regulations.gov. 2020. "Transparency in Coverage CMS-9915-P." Public comments. Accessed June 1. www.regulations.gov/docketBrowser?rpp=25&so=DESC&sb=commentDueDate&po=25&dct=PS&D=CMS-2019-0163.

Sarata, A. K. 2016. *The 21st Century Cures Act (Division A of PL 114-255)*. CRS Report R44720. Washington, DC: Congressional Research Service.

Trattner, J. H., and P. McGinnis. 2004. *The 2004 Prune Book: Top Management Challenges for Presidential Appointees*. Washington, DC: Brookings Institution Press and the Council for Excellence in Government.

US Department of Health and Human Services (HHS). 2020a. "Centers for Medicare and Medicaid Services, Justification of Estimates for Appropriations Committees, FY 2020." Accessed January 11. www.cms.gov/About-CMS/Agency-Information/PerformanceBudget/FY2020-CJ-Final.pdf.

———. 2020b. "HHS Organizational Chart." Accessed January 11. www.hhs.gov/about/agencies/orgchart/index.html.

———. 2020c. *Office of the Inspector General: Archives Top Management & Performance Challenges*. Accessed January 12. www.oig.hhs.gov/reports-and-publications/archives/top-challenges.

———. 2019. "Medicare Fraud Strike Force." HHS Office of the Inspector General. May 31. Accessed January 12, 2020. https://oig.hhs.gov/fraud/strike-force.

———. 2018. "2018 Top Management and Performance Challenges." Office of the Inspector General. Accessed January 12, 2020. www.oig.hhs.gov/reports-and-publications/archives/top-challenges.

———. 2017. "Centers for Medicare and Medicaid Services, Justification of Estimates for Appropriations Committee, FY 2017." Accessed June 7. www.cms.gov/About-CMS/Agency-Information/PerformanceBudget/Downloads/FY2017-CJ-Final.pdf.

———. 2014. "CMS Organizational Chart." Accessed January 7, 2015. www.cms.gov/About-CMS/Agency-Information/CMSLeadership/Downloads/CMS_Organizational_Chart.pdf.

US House of Representatives. 2019. "Rules of the US House of Representatives." Published January 11. https://rules.house.gov/sites/democrats.rules.house.gov/files/documents/116-House-Rules-Clerk.pdf.

White House of President Barack Obama. 2010. "Executive Order 13544: Establishing the National Prevention, Health Promotion, and Public Health Council." Published June 10. https://obamawhitehouse.archives.gov/the-press-office/executive-order-establishing-national-prevention-health-promotion-and-public-health.

CHAPTER

8

ROLE OF THE JUDICIAL BRANCH IN HEALTH POLICY AND POLICYMAKING

Learning Objectives

After reading this chapter, you should be able to

- understand how the role of the judicial branch in policymaking differs from the roles of the legislative and executive branches;
- understand the three core roles played by courts in policymaking: constitutional referee, interpreter, and rights protector;
- understand critical structural features of the judicial branch;
- understand the concepts of separation of powers, judicial review, and institutional competence;
- appreciate the importance of the states' police power in health policymaking;
- define the Constitution's supremacy clause;
- identify the three most common areas of disputes requiring courts to act as referees; and
- appreciate the importance of *National Federation of Independent Business (NFIB) v. Sebelius.*

As noted in chapter 1, health policies established in the public sector take the form of laws, rules or regulations, other implementation decisions, and judicial decisions.* All these forms are authoritative decisions and, thus, policies. The nation's constitutionally determined structure (see exhibit 2.1 for the resulting organization chart of the federal government) requires that the legislative branch enact laws, that the executive branch make additional policy to implement the laws, and that the judicial branch, especially through the courts, play a different and less direct part in policymaking (Anderson 1992; Teitelbaum and Wilensky 2013). This chapter explores the vital part the courts play in health policymaking.

* The author thanks Mary Crossley, professor of law, University of Pittsburgh School of Law, for her contribution to this chapter.

Like the rest of this book, this chapter on judicial issues will focus on federal courts. This is not to discount the importance of state courts, but because the major cases related to health policy most frequently come through the federal system, that is a more appropriate focus for this chapter.

Most states' court structures mirror the federal system: There is a trial-level court, an appellate court, and a court of final determination, generally a state supreme court. The variety of courts at the state and local level of special jurisdiction are generally not engaged in decisions related to health policy.

This chapter will explain the structure, role, and function of courts and how these matters relate to health policymaking. Specific cases will serve as examples. The scope of health-related issues arising in the federal court system is vast. Overall, our focus will be, as it has been in other chapters, on policymaking related to health services delivery. That said, however, we should also consider the courts' interaction with policy on social issues that bear directly on health-related questions. This chapter will address those matters in a more condensed form. They are important, to be sure. The primary focus here, however, will be on matters related to management and leadership in health services organizations.

Structure of the Judicial Branch

Two structural features of the judiciary are critical to appreciating how court decisions can affect health policy. First, the judiciary is part of a tripartite system of government, where power is shared among the three branches of the federal government: executive, legislative, and judicial. Second, the judiciary exists in a federalist system of government, where the authority to make policy is shared between the federal and state governments.

The extensive sharing of power in government, across branches and between levels, gives rise to disputes about whether a particular exercise of power is legitimate or overreaching or is correctly exercised at the federal or state level. Deciding those disputes is the essence of the core *refereeing* role of the courts. For example, in this chapter, we will discuss court cases that decided whether regulations promulgated by an implementing organization in the executive branch (referred to in this chapter simply as *administrative agencies*) improperly usurped the legislative authority to make laws. We will also examine cases that considered whether state legislative attempts to enact health reform were invalid because an act of Congress had "preempted" state authority in a particular area. (Refer to chapter 2 for full discussion on the three branches of government and the separation of powers.)

Courts in a Tripartite System of Government

As noted previously, under the US Constitution the judiciary is one of three coequal branches of government, each with its own responsibilities and authority. Article III of the US Constitution vests judicial power in the US Supreme Court and grants Congress the right to establish such inferior courts as it "may from time to time ordain and establish" (Constitutional Convention 1789). In an effort to protect judges from the pernicious predilections of politics, Article III also provides for lifetime appointments for judges.

Congress has acted to create other courts, creating a trial-level court (the US District Court) and an appellate-level court (the US Court of Appeals). The federal district courts are sometimes coterminous with state boundaries, although states with large populations have multiple federal district courts. The US Court of Appeals is divided into 13 *circuits*, one for the District of Columbia and the rest composed of multiple states. (Because the District of Columbia is home of the federal government, many—but by no means all—cases against the federal government arise there, generating sufficient volume to justify a circuit unto itself.)

In the federal judicial system, most cases begin at the trial level—the district court. Should a party be dissatisfied with the outcome, they are entitled as a matter of right to appeal to the appropriate circuit court of appeal. Once that court has made a determination, the matter is most likely over. A party may file a writ of certiorari to the US Supreme Court, but there is no guarantee the case will be accepted. Indeed, of the more than 7,000 requests filed annually, the Supreme Court generally agrees to hear only 100 to 150 cases (US Courts 2019).

Taken together, these courts all represent the judicial branch of the federal government. Just as congressional action is limited to certain enumerated matters defined in Article II of the Constitution, courts created under Article III, the federal courts, have jurisdiction (the legal authority to make decisions or, technically, to enter judgments) only over certain types of cases and controversies.

The US District Court is considered a court of *limited jurisdiction*. It can only hear and decide a *case or controversy* if there is a question of federal law or the Constitution, in other words, a legal question emanating from federal law. This court may also hear and decide cases if the parties to the lawsuit live or are incorporated in different states—a situation referred to as *diversity jurisdiction*. For example, if a person from Kansas should fall ill while visiting California and subsequently be the victim of medical malpractice, the individual might well bring the lawsuit against the healthcare provider either in a California state court or in a federal district court in California. The individual could not sue in Kansas, because the Kansas state courts and the federal district court in Kansas have no *personal* jurisdiction over a provider in California. In other words, there would be no way to enforce a judgment the plaintiff may receive. The decision of whether to sue in the local state court or in federal court is a matter of legal strategy that lies outside the scope of this book.

Each state also has its own system of courts to adjudicate legal disputes. Each of these systems is established by its state constitution, and like the federal courts, the state courts operate within a tripartite system of state government. Unlike federal courts, however, state court systems have general jurisdiction over a wide range of cases—basically all cases except a narrow range that can be brought only in federal court (e.g., cases against the United States or cases brought under certain federal laws or statutes). As a result, the large majority of lawsuits are filed in state courts.

Within the framework of a *tripartite government*, there are three concepts vital to understanding the judicial branch's scope of power: separation of powers, judicial review, and institutional competence.

Separation of Powers

As noted earlier, at both the federal and the state levels, the court system shares governmental authority with the legislative and executive branches of government. Under the Constitution's framework, these branches are separate from one another and equally powerful in different ways. Through this *separation of powers*, each branch exercises distinctive but limited powers, a feature the framers of the Constitution shaped to prevent the tyranny that can flow from the concentration of power.

No branch is truly independent of the others, however, because each one's power is limited or checked by powers that the Constitution assigns to the other branches. For example, the Constitution gives the legislative branch the power to enact laws, but the president can veto a law that Congress passes and the judicial branch can determine that an act of Congress violates the Constitution. Similarly, while the president has the authority to appoint federal judges, the nominees must be confirmed by the Senate. Further, federal courts can judicially review the constitutionality of executive branch and legislative branch actions. These are only examples of a broader set of constitutional checks that seek to strike a balance of governmental power among the three branches. The branches are separate but interrelated, as conceptualized in exhibit 8.1.

Judicial Review

The judicial branch has the exclusive power of *judicial review*—the power to interpret the Constitution to determine whether an act by a legislative body or an executive official exceeds constitutional limits. This power of judicial review is not expressly granted in the Constitution's text; instead, it is itself the

EXHIBIT 8.1
Relationship of the Branches of the US Government

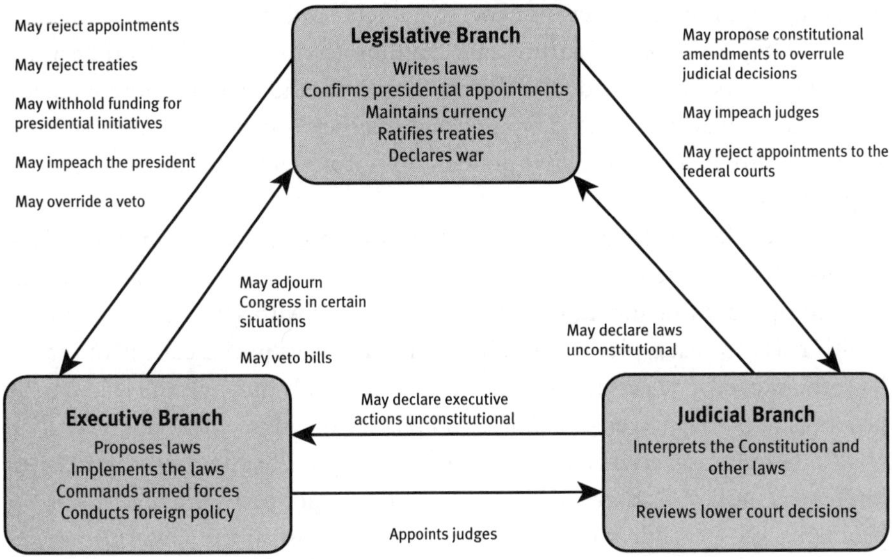

product of judicial decision-making in a landmark case (*Marbury v. Madison*) decided in 1803. While lower federal courts interpret the Constitution to assess a law's constitutionality, decisions invalidating laws are, as a practical matter, typically appealed to the Supreme Court, which thus becomes the final arbiter of constitutional questions.

A court's power to interpret the Constitution to strike down laws enacted by Congress or an executive branch action is potentially enormous. Over the decades, however, the Supreme Court has prudently fashioned limits on when it will engage in judicial review, and the other branches have yielded to the Court in its exercise of this power. Nonetheless, Supreme Court decisions holding a law unconstitutional are often cited in the political realm as prime examples of judicial activism (or policymaking by the courts). Judicial review is the power courts use to shape or constrain health policy by limiting (or validating) another branch's formulation or implementation of this policy.

Institutional Competence

Although the division of authority was constitutionally established as a means of protecting against a concentration of governmental power, the division is also in accord with the concept that each branch of government has its own particular *institutional competence*. As Gostin (1995) suggests, each branch of government possesses specific strengths and weaknesses relevant to policymaking in general and to health policymaking in particular. For example, the legislative branch, through agenda setting and legislation development, can investigate broadly the real-world conditions that require a policy response, including tapping into relevant expertise when needed.

In theory, the legislature can examine the big picture to determine whether new policy is needed and what form it should take. Because its members must regularly be elected or reelected, they are publicly accountable; their accountability helps ensure that policies do not deviate substantially from the popular will.

Once the legislature has formulated a new policy, the executive branch is responsible for implementing and enforcing it. For many health policies dealing with complicated financing or delivery systems or with scientifically complex health risks, for example, the administrative agencies in the executive branch have the expertise necessary to flesh out policy details through the rulemaking process and perhaps to ensure policy compliance through enforcement actions.

By contrast, courts are not institutionally well suited to formulate or implement policy. Rather than looking at the larger picture of health policy problems and possible solutions, courts must focus on the lawsuit immediately in front of them. A judge's or jury's understanding of the facts is shaped by the parties' presenting evidence in an adversarial process—facts that may be highly germane to the parties' dispute but that may not shed light on social, economic, or health conditions more broadly. Moreover, while judges hearing cases have considerable expertise in interpreting and applying the law, they typically lack the requisite education that would enable them to undertake a sophisticated evaluation of the scientific, economic, or ethical questions inherent in policymaking in general.

Thus, the division of labor among the three branches of government, each with particular competence, is not only constitutionally mandated but also arguably effective in allocating to each branch the policy-related tasks for which it is best equipped. Of course, these theories about how things should work don't always play out in the messy arena of real-life governing. The judgment of legislators, which in theory should be focused on the public interest, may be compromised by ideological commitments or by the influence of politically powerful interest groups. Administrative agencies similarly may be subject to powerful interest group pressure or ideological direction. Even the courts themselves are not immune from political pressures. Although no system of government is perfect or always lives up to ideal standards, the US system of government, featuring its checks and balances, has stood the test of time for nearly 250 years.

Courts in a Federal System of Government

Because governmental power in the United States is shared between the national and state governments, the power-sharing relationships in the different levels of government shape many aspects of government. These relationships affect

EXHIBIT 8.2
Federal and State Relationships

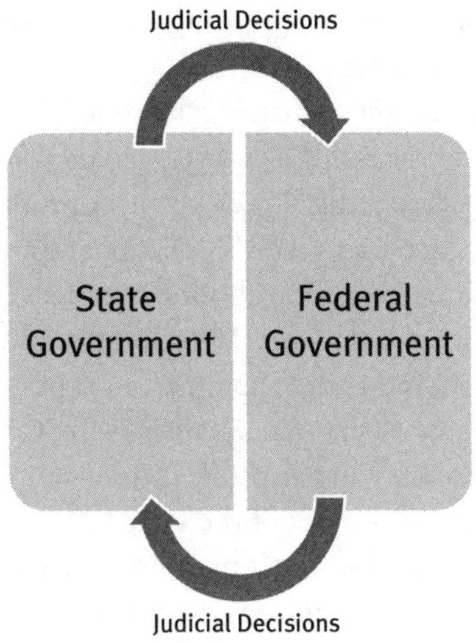

the functioning of courts, and judicial decisions affect the boundaries of these relationships. As detailed in chapter 3, the distribution of power—meaning the authority to govern, including formulating and implementing policy—is often distributed between the federal government and the states (exhibit 8.2).

The Constitution lists a number of powers that the federal government can exercise (e.g., the powers to tax and spend funds to provide for the nation's defense and general welfare, to regulate interstate and foreign commerce, and to regulate immigration), and that list establishes the boundaries of federal authority. In short, the federal government is often said to be a government of limited powers.

In contrast, the Tenth Amendment of the Constitution makes clear that all governmental powers not accorded to the federal government are "reserved to the States." This broad scope of governmental power includes the states' "police power," which is their ability to regulate a wide range of areas to protect the health and safety, property rights, and much of what is related to the day-to-day life of their citizens.

As discussed earlier, this division of governmental authority is evident in health policy. For example, many state-enacted public health measures, such as laws requiring vaccination or newborn screening, represent exercises of the police power. The states also retain the power to regulate the practice of medicine, the provision of healthcare services, and insurance, including health insurance. The federal government, by contrast, has used its spending authority to establish federal health insurance programs such as Medicaid and Medicare, its taxing power to fund those programs, and its power to regulate interstate commerce to control the marketing of tobacco and prescription drugs. Moreover, the federal government has used its taxing and spending power to shape national policy by engaging the states through a combination of grants-in-aid and restrictions.

Questions about whether a matter can properly be addressed by Congress or is properly reserved to the states, however, can be contentious politically and legally and typically require judicial resolution. A prominent example is *King v. Burwell*, discussed in detail in part 3's policy snapshot (page 327). This case asked the politically charged question about Congress's constitutional authority to require individuals to purchase health insurance as part of the Affordable Care Act (ACA), a question that the Supreme Court ultimately decided in 2015.

Another important aspect of federalism is the Constitution's *supremacy clause*, which states that the Constitution and federal laws authorized by the Constitution are the "supreme law of the land." As a result of the supremacy clause, federal laws may be found to preempt any state laws regulating the same subject. As we will see, when some states sought to enact health reform measures in the 1990s and 2000s, they were constrained by judicial applications of federal preemption under the supremacy clause. Federal preemption has also limited state courts' ability to apply state tort law to compensate consumers harmed by unsafe products, such as pharmaceuticals, regulated by federal law.

In summary, the Constitution creates a system in which the power to govern is shared—shared between the legislative, executive, and judicial branches of government and between the federal and state governments. But in any system premised on sharing, situations arise when one participant claims that another is taking more than its allotted portion. When these questions arise in our constitutional democracy (e.g., when a state asserts that the federal government is encroaching on rights reserved to the states, as we saw in *NFIB v. Sebelius*, or when, as we saw in *King v. Burwell*, individuals assert that the government is overreaching its authority), the courts are responsible for settling these questions. Having put the courts—the judicial branch—in context within the three branches of government and in the federalist system, we turn to the core roles courts play in those frameworks.

Three Core Roles of the Courts

Courts are uniquely situated to perform three core roles, described below, because of their constitutional standing as separate from the other branches of government. Courts are an *independent* judiciary. How courts make health policy decisions and how their decisions in turn may affect other health policies and policymaking goes hand in glove with their role in US society. In effect, we want to consider what courts actually do and how they do it to appreciate more fully how judicial decisions affect health policy.

The judicial branch of government, through the courts, plays a significant part in policymaking by serving three roles, *referee*, *interpreter*, and *rights protector*:

- *Constitutional referee:* deciding disputes about the extent of the checks and balances enjoyed by each of the three branches. In performing this role, courts define the scope of constitutional authority of the legislative and executive branches.
- *Interpreters:* analyzing laws with unclear language and applying them to a particular dispute. In performing this role, courts clarify the meaning of a law.
- *Rights protectors:* vindicating (or rejecting) the legal or constitutional rights of parties who come to court alleging a violation of their rights. In performing this role, courts act as *rights protectors* (or rights limiters).

Considering that courts have no formal institutional role in either formulating policy (as the legislative branch does) or in implementing policy (as the executive branch does), we ask the central question in this chapter: How do courts—acting as constitutional referees, interpreters, and rights protectors—affect health policy and policymaking?

Before examining these core roles more closely, we need to make two general points. First, the three roles of courts are not mutually exclusive. A single lawsuit may call on a court to play more than one role simultaneously. For example, if an individual claims that a government action violates the person's constitutional rights, the court hearing the case may need to decide on the existence and scope of the asserted constitutional right (its interpreter role) and then determine whether the government's action impermissibly infringes on that right (its rights-protector role).

Second, judicial decisions affect both the public and the private sectors. As discussed in chapter 1, policy is made in each of these sectors. Consequently, the judicial decisions made by courts affect decisions made by actors in both sectors. This point is important because of the heavy US reliance on the private sector for healthcare financing and delivery.

The three core roles that courts play in policymaking may be visualized in a simple Venn diagram consisting of three overlapping circles, one for each of the judicial roles outlined previously (exhibit 8.3). The diagram reflects that some cases potentially represent a point where the court must play two of its core roles to resolve the parties' dispute; some cases (those represented by the space where all three circles intersect) would require a court to perform all three roles simultaneously. (The diagram is conceptual, not proportional.)

Many decisions that affect cost and quality of healthcare, and access to it, are decentralized and privatized. For example, until the enactment of the

EXHIBIT 8.3
The Roles of Courts in Policymaking

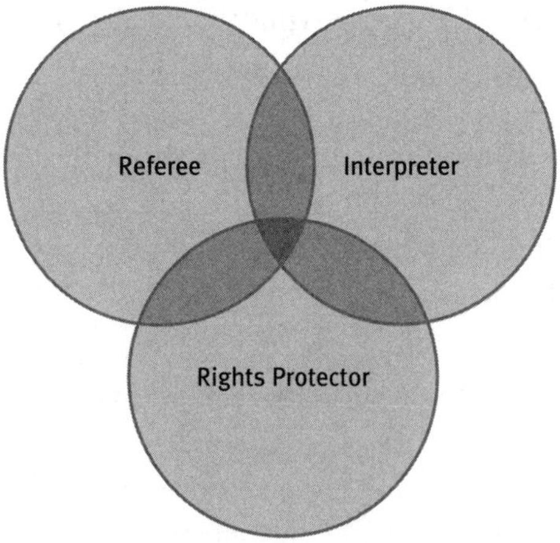

ACA, employers had complete discretion to decide whether to provide insurance coverage for their employees, and insurers (whether traditional insurance companies or managed care plans) had great latitude in deciding what benefits to provide as part of their plans. Likewise, before passage of the ACA, individuals were free to choose not to have health insurance. In effect, the aggregated decisions by private-sector actors provided the answers to many questions that might have been addressed through public policy, but were not. The ACA helped answer some of these questions, but those legislative constructs have been the subject of considerable litigation where the courts have had to assume one or more of the three core roles.

As we examine the three core roles of the courts, we also need to understand how they can perform those roles. A court is limited to *cases and controversies* that come before it. In these cases, it must *interpret the law* and apply it to the facts of the case while *following precedent* of higher court decisions.

Resolving Cases and Controversies

Courts function in a reactive mode. They act only in response to lawsuits properly filed and subject to the courts' jurisdiction. Except in the rare situations when a court is authorized to declare its opinion on a legal question in the absence of a live controversy (by issuing a *declaratory judgment* or an *advisory opinion*), courts address legal questions in concrete disputes, not in the abstract or in anticipation of possible future disputes.

Courts resolve those legal questions in an adversarial system in which attorneys advocate for their parties' positions, arguing legal authority and factual evidence particular to the case. The trial court (which sometimes relies on a jury to determine what version of disputed facts is true) renders a decision resolving the dispute between the parties. If one or both parties disagree with the trial court's resolution and can point to an error in how the court reached that resolution, they may choose to appeal the decision to an appellate court. In a case or controversy, a court can act as referee, interpreter, or rights enforcer.

As noted earlier, an appeal to the Supreme Court has a small chance of actually being heard and decided.

Identifying, Interpreting, and Applying the Law

The central function of the judicial system at the trial level in the United States is to apply the law to the facts of a particular case to resolve a dispute between the parties involved. The dispute may be as mundane as whether a prescription was filled properly by the pharmacy, or it may be as momentous as whether an act of Congress violated an individual's constitutional rights. In any case, the court must identify which law applies, what that law means, and how it applies to facts of the case before it.

The law to which the courts look in deciding a dispute derives from multiple sources of potentially binding legal authority. These sources of law include constitutions (federal and state), laws or statutes passed by legislative bodies, rules and regulations issued by implementing organizations and agencies, and the common law (a term referring to the body of judge-made law). In addition, in contract disputes between private litigants, a court is called on to enforce terms that the parties have themselves agreed to; in these cases, the court is effectively applying the parties' *private law*.

When the language of the law—in whatever form—is clear, the matter is generally settled out of court. Consequently, many of the cases that courts are called on to decide raise legal questions for which the law's answer is uncertain. In these situations, the courts must give meaning to the written word.

This uncertainty often centers on determining what the general language used in a constitution or statute (or another source of law) means when applied to a specific case. As described in chapter 3, the distinction between the role of the states and the federal government is open to interpretation because the US Constitution is itself fairly short and written mostly in general terms. The brief and general nature of the document has produced endless controversy about the interpretation of its terms. In this vein, the court is not only giving meaning to, or interpreting, the language of the applicable clause but also acting as referee regarding constitutional boundaries. When individuals claim that their constitutional rights are violated, then the court becomes a rights enforcer while interpreting the relevant language.

While statutes are longer and more definitive, and administrative regulations even more so, it is beyond the ability of any policymaker to anticipate and provide for every situation that may arise. As a result, courts regularly must give meaning to a source of law that is ambiguous or vague, so that it can then apply the law to resolve the dispute at hand. In the later discussion on courts as interpreters, we will explore several examples of how courts' interpretations of the law have shaped health policy.

The Conservative Influence of Precedent

In interpreting the law, courts exercise significant power. That power, however, is subject to a restraint found in judicial adherence to the principle of stare decisis (meaning "to stand by a decision"). This principle dictates that a court should decide legal questions (like a law's meaning) consistently with how the question has been decided previously by the same court or any court superior to it in the judicial hierarchy. For example, a federal district court follows the precedent of its own prior decisions, decisions of the circuit court of appeals for its federal judicial circuit, and decisions of the US Supreme Court. Reliance on precedent means that a court deciding a new case will be guided by how courts have decided previous, similar cases, thus ensuring some level of stability, predictability, and consistency in the law and satisfying the basic precept of justice that "like cases should be treated alike."

The power of precedent is not absolute, however, and the Supreme Court may overrule a prior decision if a majority of the Court becomes convinced that the prior case was wrongly decided and has produced a rule that is unworkable, particularly in light of changes in society. Perhaps the most notable instance of this principle is in the Court's 1954 decision of *Brown v. Board of Education*. *Brown* directly and succinctly overturned the Court's 1896 decision of *Plessy v. Ferguson*, which held that public facilities could be segregated as long as they were "separate but equal." In reaching its conclusion that *Plessy* was simply wrong, the *Brown* court said, "Separate educational facilities are inherently unequal."

Understanding basic concepts of how a court provides rationale for its decisions, we turn now to its three core roles and some specific examples.

Courts Acting as Referees

When the complexity of the policymaking process depicted in exhibit 4.1 is considered, the frequent need for refereeing disputes between various parties is apparent. These disputes arise primarily in three areas: (1) questions of the extent of congressional authority, (2) questions of the power of implementing agencies, and (3) questions of federalism pertaining to federal and state levels of government. Each of these areas is considered in the following sections, with actual case examples.

Refereeing Questions of Congressional Authority

Our discussion of how courts act as constitutional referees to affect health policy begins with one of the most celebrated or reviled, depending on one's opinion about the ACA, Supreme Court decisions in recent times. For this discussion, we return to *NFIB v. Sebelius*, discussed in the policy snapshot "The Affordable Care Act: A Cauldron of Controversy" at the beginning of part 1. This lawsuit challenged the constitutional authority of Congress to enact, as part of the ACA, a requirement that individuals have health insurance or pay a fine to the federal government. This so-called individual mandate is a crucial piece in the ACA's attempt to ensure near-universal health coverage for Americans.

To recap briefly the discussion in the snapshot, the ACA builds on the nation's existing structure of private health insurance but restricts insurers' ability to limit or deny coverage or charge higher premiums for persons with preexisting health conditions. With those changes, the cost of health insurance could be expected to rise sharply unless people who are relatively healthy and young also enroll in health plans. The individual mandate, coupled with tax subsidies for low-income individuals, supplied the mechanism to get those young and healthy "good risks" to purchase health insurance. Conceptually, this mechanism would satisfy the concerns of health insurance companies to create larger risk pools and increase access to care for millions of formerly uninsured Americans.

The law's opponents, however, objected that Congress did not have the constitutional authority to enact the individual mandate as part of the ACA. As discussed, the Constitution limits Congress's powers to legislate, and in *NFIB v. Sebelius*, the Supreme Court considered the constitutionality of the individual mandate. Proponents of the ACA argued that the power to regulate interstate commerce (articulated in the commerce clause of the Constitution) extended to Congress's ability to mandate the purchase of health insurance as part of a comprehensive regulatory scheme affecting the financing and delivery of healthcare.

The Supreme Court historically has interpreted the commerce clause expansively, permitting Congress to regulate any economic activity that substantially affects interstate commerce. Because of the scope and economic importance of the healthcare and health insurance industries, this expansive reading of the commerce clause has supported a broad exercise of congressional power in health-related fields.

As for the individual mandate, proponents asserted that the failure of millions of Americans to have health insurance undoubtedly affected interstate commerce. The Supreme Court, however, disagreed and held that the individual mandate did not regulate existing commercial activity; instead, the mandate compelled individuals to engage in the activity of purchasing insurance. The Court was unwilling to extend Congress's commerce clause authority to permit regulation of individuals not already acting in the market, fearing that to do so, in the Court's words, "would open a new and potentially vast domain to congressional authority."

Many court watchers had assumed that if the Supreme Court held that the individual mandate was not authorized under the commerce clause, the justices would then strike down this linchpin of the ACA, thus crippling the health reform law. To their surprise, the Court proceeded to consider other sources of constitutional authority for the individual mandate and ultimately upheld it as an exercise of Congress's constitutionally based taxing power. Although the law itself refers to the payment that persons who do not have health insurance must make to the government as a "penalty," the Court reasoned that Congress did not mean for the payment to punish persons for failing to purchase insurance. Instead the Court viewed the payment as a way to induce people to purchase coverage and to raise revenue—both of which are characteristic of taxes. Because the Court framed the individual mandate as a tax on persons who do not purchase health insurance, the mandate was determined to be within the scope of Congress's taxing powers and, hence, constitutional.

NFIB v. Sebelius vividly illustrates how courts can affect health policy through their refereeing role and their interpreter role. Although the Supreme Court's decision neither formulated nor implemented policy, the Court, through judicial review, validated a crucial piece of the most sweeping health reform legislation in a generation. A Court decision striking down the individual mandate as beyond Congress's constitutional authority would have severely weakened the ACA.

As referees, courts have the power to rein in legislative policymaking by deciding that a policy exceeds constitutional bounds. And although the Supreme Court upheld the individual mandate under the taxing power, many commentators suggest that its commerce clause holding portends future limitations on congressional power. Finally, as we'll discuss later, judicial decisions on the scope of congressional authority also may have implications for the federal government and states' sharing of power to make health policy.

Refereeing the Power of Administrative Agencies

As we saw in chapter 7, when Congress (or a state legislature) enacts a policy, it expects certain agencies in the executive branch to implement them. In formal terms, Congress delegates implementation authority to administrative agencies in the executive branch. This authority includes the ability, indeed the responsibility, to write and issue rules and regulations that flesh out the details of a legislatively enacted policy and establish specific standards for regulated parties' compliance with the legislation.

Agencies also enforce those standards, and when a dispute arises about an agency's implementation and enforcement activities (e.g., when an individual disputes the Social Security Administration's determination that the person is not disabled enough to receive Social Security disability benefits), the agency may adjudicate those disputes. However, when a dispute arises about an agency's authority to act in a particular way, the courts are called on to resolve those disputes.

Judicial decisions concerning the validity of an agency's exercise of authority can have an significant impact on health policy. For example, the *King v. Burwell* decision affected the viability of the individual mandate as a tool to broaden the insurance pool and consequently to restrain increases in premiums.

Although all challenges to agency action address whether an agency has somehow exceeded its proper authority, three types of challenges can arise. First, a party may challenge an agency's rule or regulation as an unreasonable interpretation of what Congress charged it to do. A second type of challenge is similar, but goes further in asserting that the agency's promulgation of rules and regulations exceeds the scope of the authority Congress delegated to it. Third, a rule or regulation may be challenged as essentially legislative, not administrative, and thereby as encroaching on legislative branch functions. In these situations, the claim is that the agency has usurped the legislative role by going beyond its role in implementing or enforcing the legislature's policy. Some cases will illustrate each type of challenge.

Unreasonable Interpretation of Authority

Even when Congress clearly delegates to an agency the responsibility for issuing rules or regulations on a particular matter, questions may arise about whether the resulting rules or regulations legitimately interpret the authorizing statute. A core precept of administrative law, established by the Supreme Court, is that courts ordinarily should uphold an agency's reading of a law it is responsible for implementing, as long as that reading is permissible (Jost 2004; Richards 2007). This *rule of deference* to agency judgment applies when a law being implemented is silent or ambiguous on some implementation issue. If the law speaks specifically to the issue, the rule does not apply. The rule of deference gives agencies a good deal of leeway in interpreting ambiguous language and filling gaps in laws and prevents courts from simply substituting their own judgment about how best to fulfill the legislature's policy objectives for the agency's judgment.

A contemporary example of this type of dispute can be found in *King v. Burwell*. The Court accorded deference to the Internal Revenue Service in interpreting the meaning of "such exchange," as used in the statute.

Agency Exceeding the Scope of Delegated Authority

Sometimes, the judicial challenge to an agency's implementation of a health policy considers whether the agency has overstepped its delegated authority. In the 1938 Food, Drug, and Cosmetic Act (FDCA), Congress delegated to the US Food and Drug Administration (FDA) the authority to regulate drugs and medical devices to make sure they are "safe and effective."

In 1996, after decades of mounting evidence about the health risks of tobacco and new revelations of tobacco industry deception and efforts to manipulate cigarettes' nicotine levels to enhance addictiveness, the FDA issued regulations designed to restrict the marketing and accessibility of tobacco products to children and adolescents (Gostin 2009). The FDA's rationale was that new evidence confirmed that nicotine was a "drug" and that cigarettes and other tobacco products were "devices" delivering it to users. Thus, the FDA viewed the development and issuance of these rules and regulations as properly within the scope of its authority as granted by the FDCA.

Tobacco companies challenged the rules in court, arguing that the rules exceeded the FDA's delegated authority under the FDCA. The case ultimately reached the Supreme Court, which in 2000, in *FDA v. Brown & Williamson Tobacco Corp.*, held that the FDA lacked any authority to regulate tobacco products.

To reach this conclusion, the Court relied on the interplay of the FDCA's regulatory goal of ensuring that marketed drugs and devices are safe and Congress's passage of other laws specifically regulating tobacco. In short, the Court reasoned that Congress had made clear in other legislation that tobacco products could continue to be sold in the United States, but that regulating tobacco to ensure safety would actually require its removal from the market. In light of this reasoning, the Court found that Congress, in enacting the FDCA, did not intend to give the FDA the authority to regulate tobacco. In this case, the conclusion was not simply that *how* the FDA had regulated tobacco was inconsistent with Congress's policy directives; instead, the Court concluded that any FDA regulation of tobacco was undertaken in the absence of congressionally delegated authority and, thus, was unlawful.

Agency Exercise of Legislative Prerogative

A third type of challenge to administrative agency authority arises from questions about whether an agency has gone beyond developing and issuing rules and regulations intended to implement the legislature's policy and is, instead, exercising legislative authority. Challenges asserting this type of misuse of authority more often arise at the state level. Although the legislative branch at either level of government can delegate to an executive branch agency the authority to interpret and implement a health policy enacted by the legislature, it cannot constitutionally delegate responsibility for making the broad policy judgments inherent in legislating. Any attempt by an agency to make policy judgments found by a court to be legislative in nature will be invalid.

In *New York Statewide Coalition of Hispanic Chambers of Commerce v. New York City Department of Health and Mental Hygiene*, a judicial determination struck down the New York City Board of Health's partial ban on the sale of sugary drinks larger than 16 ounces. The rationale for the decision was that the board had made a policy decision reserved for the legislative branch (Mariner and Annas 2013). The Board of Health, which is part of the city's Department of Health and Mental Hygiene, adopted the rule—popularly referred to as the "Big Gulp Ban"—as part of a broad effort to combat obesity. But the court decided that the city charter's grant of authority to the Board of Health did not permit the board to ban the sale of a legal item even if it was a means of combating a chronic disease.

According to the court, any decision to take such a step (and to create a complex set of exceptions to the rule, as the board had done) belongs properly to the legislature, in this case, the New York City Council. By this reasoning, when the board adopted the rule, it overreached and acted like a legislature, violating the constitutional separation of powers. According to the judge, such a ban could be made only by an elected city council, not by a board appointed by the mayor. In June 2014, the highest court in New York State affirmed that decision, in *New York Statewide Coalition of Hispanic Chambers of Commerce v. New York City Department of Health and Mental Hygiene.*

Refereeing Federalism Questions

As noted earlier and discussed extensively in chapter 3, both the federal and the state governments have constitutional authority to make health policy, although the scope of their authority differs. Congress's authority is limited to the exercise of its enumerated constitutional powers, while all other powers are reserved to the states. This section explores how court decisions settling conflicts between federal and state authority can affect health policy. As we will see, the existence and exercise of federal power sometimes limits states' ability to make health policy relating to a particular concern, but in other instances, state interests may constrain the exercise of federal power. In yet other situations, both the federal and the state governments can make policy in a certain area as long as their policies (often in the form of rules or regulations) do not conflict.

Cooperative Federalism Versus Federal Coercion: *NFIB* Revisited

As we saw in chapter 3, and as further demonstrated in *NFIB v. Sebelius*, the federal government cannot constitutionally compel a state to enact a particular policy. Nor can the federal government "commandeer" state employees to implement policies adopted by Congress. Pursuant to its constitutional spending power, however, Congress can provide the states with financial incentives to pursue certain policy objectives. As described earlier, this movement toward cooperative federalism first occurred in the healthcare domain with the Sheppard-Towner legislation of 1921. A more current example of the use of this motivational power was the creation of the Medicaid program in 1965. The program was voluntary for the states, the federal government having guaranteed to provide partial funding for the states according to a wealth-related formula. (Arizona, for example, did not adopt Medicaid until 1982, even though the program had been created 17 years earlier.)

Within the concept of cooperative federalism, the federal and state governments act autonomously, but their policy interventions are cooperative. While largely positive, cooperative federalism does raise the possibility that the federal government's financial inducement to a state—if extremely strong—could effectively override the state's autonomy in formulating policy.

Implementation of the ACA, for example, relies heavily on cooperative federalism, but one aspect of the law was judged to violate federalism principles. The Supreme Court did not like the gun-to-the-head approach taken in the ACA to "encourage" states to expand their Medicaid programs (Kaiser Family Foundation 2012).

The ACA originally conditioned continued federal Medicaid matching funds on each state's expanding its Medicaid eligibility criteria from coverage primarily for specific categories of poor people to a program covering everyone with income below a certain threshold. Under the terms of the ACA, a state that chose not to expand coverage would lose *all* federal matching funds for its Medicaid program.

Opponents argued that when Congress threatened the loss of all federal Medicaid funding if a state did not expand its Medicaid program, the legislature had acted coercively and thus exceeded its spending power authority. A majority of the Supreme Court in *NFIB v. Sebelius* agreed. According to Chief Justice John Roberts, the amount of federal funding that states stood to lose if they did not expand their Medicaid eligibility criteria was so large that the law left states with no real choice. Instead, the threatened loss of funding was, in Chief Justice Roberts's words, like a "gun to the head" of the states. From this perspective, Congress was unconstitutionally compelling states to expand Medicaid under the guise of making a constitutionally valid conditional grant of federal funds.

Once the Court found this essentially mandatory Medicaid expansion unconstitutional, the question became what effect that finding would have on the health reform law. One possibility (which four dissenting justices endorsed) was that the unconstitutionality justified striking down the entire law. Another, less drastic result could have been to sever the Medicaid expansion from the rest of the ACA and to strike down only the expansion provisions as unconstitutional. That result would have left in force the health insurance market reforms, the individual mandate, and numerous other provisions of the ACA. But the failure to expand Medicaid would mean that the approximately 17 million uninsured, low-income people expected to benefit would not receive coverage.

Instead, a majority of the Court concluded that it could remedy the unconstitutionally coercive nature of the Medicaid expansion simply by removing the coercion; the remedy was to deny the federal government's ability to withhold *all* Medicaid matching funds from states choosing not to expand. This remedy left states the option: choose either to expand their Medicaid population and receive federal funding for the expanded population or to maintain their Medicaid program at pre-ACA coverage levels, without losing their existing funding.

The Medicaid-expansion part of the *NFIB v. Sebelius* decision dramatically demonstrates the Court's power to affect health policy, particularly as the policy relates to the balance of power in a federalist system of government. It was within the scope of the Court's judicial review powers to strike down the health reform law entirely as unconstitutional. Doing so would have rendered moot all the legislative and executive branch efforts to enact and implement the law. But even though the Supreme Court found that Congress exceeded its constitutional authority by attempting to coerce states to expand their Medicaid programs, the Court adopted its more modest remedy so that it could avoid unnecessary judicial intrusion on the legislative authority to formulate policy. In effect, the Court's decision permitted Congress to adopt the Medicaid expansion as a way to increase insurance coverage in states that cooperated, but denied its ability to compel states to go along with that policy.

We examined the development of national federalism in chapter 4, noting that the contemporary model of federalism emanates from the federal government to the states in the form of statutes, regulations, and waivers. Medicaid expansion is a good example. The Trump administration, however, used the federalism philosophy in a different way. By 2018 and 2019, federal waivers had been approved for states to reduce their Medicaid costs by effectively limiting enrollment through the imposition of work or community service requirements. Some groups objected to this new model. Multiple suits were filed against the federal government over the issue of work requirements for Medicaid beneficiaries, with advocacy groups starting litigation in Arkansas, Indiana, Kentucky, Michigan, and New Hampshire. The groups claimed that the requirements defeated the objective of expanding insurance coverage for those who cannot afford it. The implicit message in referencing those measures and resulting lawsuits here is to underscore the court system's inherent availability to advocates of all sides of an issue. In *King* and *NFIB*, litigation was brought by those who wanted to repeal, strike down, or diminish the impact of the ACA. The lawsuits discussed here, however, were instigated by those who wanted to defend the ACA or strengthen its effect against what they saw as administrative efforts to attenuate its scope.

The Supremacy Clause and Federal Preemption

The Supreme Court's decision in *NFIB v. Sebelius* regarding the Medicaid expansion used the spending clause of the Constitution to constrain Congress's ability to induce states' compliance with federal health policy objectives. The more typical power-sharing disputes between the federal government and states, however, involve the supremacy clause of the Constitution.

As noted earlier, the supremacy clause declares the Constitution and federal laws authorized by the Constitution the "supreme law of the land." Its effect is to permit Congress, by enacting a law on a particular topic, to preempt state laws in that area, that is, to prevent states from acting in that area of the law addressed by congressional action. The preemption may extend to state common-law actions (e.g., negligence or product liability lawsuits) and to statutory law. As a result, questions have arisen about the validity of state health policy initiatives in diverse areas. For example, concerning a state-mandated hospital budget review for cost-containment purposes and a state law prohibiting a form of hazardous waste disposal, the state was not preempted. On the other hand, the state was preempted for a state law imposing burdensome requirements on "navigators" charged by the ACA to help consumers use insurance exchanges to enroll in health plans.

As these examples suggest, federal laws do not always preempt state laws or regulations, and part of the courts' role as constitutional referees is to determine when the supremacy clause and federal preemption apply. The central issue in determining preemption is whether the federal policymakers intended the federal law to displace state laws on the same subject. If a federal law explicitly includes a stated purpose of preempting state laws on the same subject, then a court simply interprets the statute's preemption language to determine whether the state law being challenged falls within the scope of preemption. The courts had to make such a decision, for example, when the Massachusetts attorney general issued regulations that prohibited retailers from using self-service displays of cigarettes and that banned outdoor advertising of cigarettes in any location within a thousand feet of a school. Cigarette manufacturers and retailers challenged the regulations as preempted by the Federal Cigarette Labeling and Advertising Act (FCLAA).

The FCLAA prescribes mandatory health warnings for cigarette packaging and advertising and contains an express preemption of state prohibitions "based on smoking and health" relating to cigarette advertising. Massachusetts argued that this preemption did not extend to state regulation of the location of cigarette advertising, as opposed to the content of cigarette advertising, an argument that some lower federal courts accepted. In 2001, however, the Supreme Court held in *Lorillard Tobacco Co. v. Reilly* that Congress intended to preempt all health-motivated state regulation targeting cigarette advertising, including location restrictions. According to the Court, Congress's decision in the FCLAA to require health warnings on cigarette packaging and advertising and to include a broad preemption clause meant that Massachusetts could not implement its own policy to decrease youth exposure to cigarette advertising by regulating its location.

Even when Congress does not expressly state its intent to preempt state law, a court may find that preemptive intent is implicit in a federal policy. Perhaps the easiest case for finding preemption is when a state law directly conflicts with a federal law. If it would be physically impossible to comply with both the federal and the state requirements, a court will invoke the supremacy clause to invalidate the state law. In sum, judicial decisions determining the existence and scope of federal preemption of state law in health-related areas establish a balance of authority between the states and the federal government.

Courts Acting as Interpreters

As noted earlier, a second core role for courts is interpreting laws whose meaning or application to a particular dispute is somehow unclear. In this role, courts function as *interpreters* by clarifying the sense of laws. How courts perform their role as interpreters of the law can shape the direction or evolution of health policies. In some situations, of course, the law is entirely clear and needs no interpretation, but the facts are in dispute. For example, in a personal injury lawsuit, it may be perfectly clear that the defendant will be liable to the plaintiff for injuries sustained in a car accident if the driver ran a red light before hitting the other car. But a factual dispute may exist about whether the light was red when the defendant went through the intersection. In that case, the court's primary role is that of fact-finder. Often, however, courts need to act as interpreters.

Courts play the interpreter role in most lawsuits. In each of the cases discussed in the previous section, for example, a court had to interpret the Constitution or a law to decide whether a branch of government had acted within the bounds of its constitutional authority or how power should be shared between the federal and state governments.

The cases examined in this section, however, highlight how courts' interpretation of the language of laws can determine the law's impact on health policy. We will see that court decisions sometimes play an important role in establishing the effects of legislative action. The cases in this section will also preview the final section's discussion of cases in which the courts' predominant role is to enforce rights claimed pursuant to contracts, statutes, or the Constitution. In those cases, courts may first have to interpret the relevant source of law to determine the existence and scope of the right claimed.

In many situations, the courts' interpretation of laws effectively delineates the policy implications of Congress's handiwork. In looking again at how broadly to interpret preemptive language in a federal law, we will see how courts' parsing of the preemption clause in a law having little to do with health has substantially affected states' ability to pursue state-level healthcare reforms. The discussion will then turn to judicial interpretations of statutes that regulate the conduct of actors in the healthcare marketplace and create rights on the part of healthcare consumers.

Employee Retirement Income Security Act Preemption and State Health Reform

When Congress enacted the Employee Retirement Income Security Act (ERISA) in 1974, its main goal was to create a federal regulatory scheme for employer-sponsored pension plans to make sure they met certain standards for protecting employees. Congress, however, drafted the law to apply to employee benefit plans more broadly, including healthcare benefit plans. The law does not require employers to offer any particular benefit but instead sets up uniform standards for administering whatever benefits are offered. By displacing all state regulation of employee benefit plans, Congress wanted to encourage employers to establish plans. This preemption of state law would permit large multistate employers to avoid having to comply with varying and potentially conflicting plan regulations in different states.

To that end, ERISA includes a broadly worded preemption clause stating that it preempts all state laws that "relate to" employee benefit plans covered by ERISA. Although Congress wanted to establish the regulation of employee benefit plans—and particularly pensions—as an area of exclusive federal concern, many members were concerned about unduly intruding on areas of traditional state regulation. Therefore, Congress qualified ERISA's preemption clause with a "savings" clause, which effectively saves from preemption any state law that "regulates insurance." Thus, in essence, state laws that relate to employment benefit plans are preempted, but a state can regulate insurance companies. Such regulatory power has been within the ambit of state regulation since the founding days of the republic.

The situation gets even more complicated when an employer provides health coverage for its employees by self-insuring (i.e., by acting as the insurer itself) rather than by purchasing contracts of insurance from an insurance company. ERISA anticipated this possibility. The statute includes in the savings clause an exception stating that an employee benefit plan should not be deemed to be in the business of insurance for purposes of applying the savings clause. The simple effect of this "deemer clause" is to modify the description provided earlier: State laws that relate to employment benefit plans are preempted, *but* a state can regulate insurance companies, *except for* an employee benefit plan that self-insures to provide health benefits, according to a 2003 Supreme Court ruling in *Kentucky Assn. of Health Plans, Inc. v. Miller*. Language like this and complex legal provisions including exceptions to exceptions ensure a continuing vital role as interpreters for the courts.

For several decades after ERISA's enactment, the combination of the law's preemption clause, its savings clause, and its deemer clause produced a steady stream of lawsuits probing the precise scope of ERISA's preemption of state health policies. Typically, employers or insurance companies filed these lawsuits to argue that a state law could not be enforced against them, because the law was preempted by ERISA. The lawsuits required courts to interpret ERISA's statutory language to make decisions with important implications for states' ability to enforce their health policies.

Further complicating matters, some of the language in this law that courts were interpreting is vague. (What does it mean for a state law to "relate to" an employee benefit plan? What kinds of state laws "regulate insurance"?) This vagueness left courts with a good deal of interpretive latitude. Indeed, numerous decisions by courts, including the Supreme Court, about how to interpret ERISA's preemption provisions over time have swung from an expansive understanding of the law's preemptive effect to a more limited one. According to Furrow and colleagues (2013, 370), ERISA preemption lawsuits have included "over twenty Supreme Court decisions and hundreds of state and federal lower court decisions." As a result, states' ability to pursue health policies having any connection to employer-provided health insurance over time has waned and, more recently, waxed.

A few examples help illustrate the role courts have played in disabling or enabling state health policies arguably related to ERISA. For several decades, many state legislatures passed laws requiring health insurers to include in their policies certain types of coverage (e.g., mental health coverage, maternity coverage). Because these mandated-benefit laws applied to policies purchased as part of an employee benefit plan, insurers argued that the laws were preempted by ERISA. By interpreting the interaction of the preemption clause and the savings clause in *Metropolitan Life Insurance Co. v. Massachusetts*, the Supreme Court held that a state law mandating coverage of certain mental health benefits did "relate to" employee benefit plans but was saved from preemption as a law that "regulates insurance." In that 1985 case, the Court went on to apply the deemer clause, concluding that the mandated-benefit law could not be enforced against a self-insured plan providing health coverage to employees. As a result, workers whose employers bought group coverage from an insurance company would receive the benefit, but employees of self-insured employers might not. This outcome both frustrated the state's policy goal of ensuring coverage of the mental health services and provided additional incentive for employers to self-insure to avoid mandated benefits and other state regulation.

As Jacobson (2009, 88) describes, expansive judicial interpretations of ERISA's preemption provisions at least through the mid-1990s meant that, even as federal policymakers unable to enact comprehensive national health reform encouraged states to pursue their own reforms, a federal law "imperil[ed] aggressive state health coverage experiments." Since the mid-1990s, several Supreme Court decisions have suggested that lower courts should interpret ERISA's "relate to" language in the preemption clause more narrowly (which would shrink the law's preemptive scope) and should interpret the "regulates insurance" language in the savings clause more broadly (which would enlarge states' ability to adopt policies implicating health coverage). For example, in *New York State Conference of Blue Cross & Blue Shield Plans v. Travelers Insurance Company* in 1995, the Supreme Court found that a New York law imposing hospital bill surcharges on most commercial insurers survived preemption. Although the surcharge law had some economic effect on employee benefit plans, the Court read ERISA's "relates to" language as not extending to such an indirect effect.

In 2003, in *Kentucky Assn. of Health Plans, Inc. v. Miller*, the Supreme Court interpreted the savings clause to uphold a Kentucky "any willing provider" law (requiring health plans to permit any willing provider to join their networks) as a law that "regulates insurance." In that case, the Court adopted a new approach, more permissive of state regulation, for determining whether a state law "regulates insurance" for purposes of ERISA's savings clause. Thus, evolving judicial interpretations of ERISA's preemption provisions have alternately constrained and permitted many state health policies.

Laws Regulating Health Markets and Clarifying Consumer Rights

Besides determining the breadth of federal preemption in the health policy domain, judicial interpretations of the substantive provisions of laws affect health policy and policymaking in other ways. Almost any law can require some judicial explication to clarify its meaning in a particular circumstance. Courts, however, are most likely to be called on to interpret when (1) legislative language is vague, with multiple plausible meanings, and (2) a party trying to claim a right or avoid regulation under the statute has enough at stake to litigate its meaning.

Regulating Health Markets

When a public entity (e.g., an administrative agency with enforcement authority, such as the Centers for Medicare & Medicaid Services or a state attorney general) brings a lawsuit to enforce a law's regulatory provisions, the court's interpretive judgment most obviously determines whether enforcement will succeed in the case. The court may also signal to the enforcer and other regulated parties the types of conduct that might (or might not) trigger enforcement actions in the future. For example, in a 1982 case, *Arizona v. Maricopa County Medical Society*, the Supreme Court interpreted federal antitrust law (specifically, the Sherman Act's rule against price-fixing) to find that the agreements among physicians setting the maximum fees to be charged to policyholders were illegal per se. This decision signaled to doctors and other actors in health markets that neither physicians' status as professionals nor the judiciary's relative inexperience with applying antitrust law to the healthcare industry would immunize them from antitrust liability (Hammer and Sage 2002). From a policy perspective, the court decision also gave a green light to regulators to proceed with enforcement actions in the health field in an effort to spur competition, efficiency, and cost savings.

Many laws create rights on the part of individuals to enforce the law through private lawsuits (or administrative adjudications). In cases involving such laws, such as the Emergency Medical Treatment and Active Labor Act (EMTALA), discussed later, a court decision interpreting unclear statutory language determines the current plaintiff's ability to prevail and the exposure of regulated parties to future similar suits.

Clarifying Consumer Rights

Congress enacted EMTALA in 1986 to address the problem of emergency rooms' "dumping" patients (refusing to see them or sending them immediately to a public hospital) because the patient was uninsured and unable to pay potentially large hospital bills (Perez 2007). In formulating EMTALA as a response to this problem, Congress knew precisely what problem it wanted to address. The language it used in the law, however, failed in several respects to make clear exactly what the law obligated hospitals to do and, by extension, which damages patients harmed by violations had a right to recover and when patients could pursue those rights. The most glaring of the law's ambiguities is the requirement that a hospital covered by EMTALA provide an "appropriate medical screening examination" to any person who comes to an emergency room seeking treatment.

EMTALA does not define the phrase "appropriate medical screening examination," and the text of the law provides only a few clues as to what Congress meant. The law provides only that the screening examination is to be "within the capability of the hospital's emergency department" and that its purpose is "to determine whether or not an emergency medical condition . . . exists." As a result, when patients who suffered some kind of harm after visiting a hospital emergency room sued the hospital for violating EMTALA, it was left to the courts to distinguish an "appropriate medical screening examination" from one that somehow fell short of EMTALA's requirements.

As the court put it in a 1990 case, *Cleland v. Bronson Health Care Group, Inc.*, the word *appropriate* is "one of the most wonderful weasel words in the dictionary, and a great aid to the resolution of disputed issues in the drafting of legislation." In other words, *appropriate* is a handy term for promoting agreement among legislators, precisely because it sounds good while having no specific meaning.

As plaintiffs filed lawsuits alleging violations of EMTALA, the courts had to give some meaning to "appropriate medical screening examination." In doing so, they relied on the clues in the rest of the law and evidence of Congress's intent in enacting the law. It was clear that Congress did not intend to create a new federal cause of action for medical malpractice or negligent medical care, and accordingly, the courts consistently have rejected any argument that an "appropriate" screening requires compliance with particular medical standards.

The courts have been less consistent in developing tests for what makes a screening inappropriate. Most of the federal circuit courts of appeals have adopted one standard: A hospital's screening of a patient should be considered appropriate if it is similar to the screening the hospital typically gives patients with similar symptoms. But some of these courts have used a slightly different approach. Because the Supreme Court has not addressed this question, no definitive answer exists. With Congress's use of vague language in EMTALA, therefore, the standard a hospital is held to in screening an emergency room patient may depend on which federal circuit the hospital is located in. Thus, one downside of relying on courts to give meaning to a policy is that—unless the Supreme Court provides a definitive interpretation—judicial interpretations of the legislature's policy objectives may be inconsistent.

Courts Acting as Rights Enforcers

As the discussion of the courts' EMTALA interpretations show, courts can play multiple roles in a single lawsuit. For example, in a patient's lawsuit alleging that a hospital failed to provide an "appropriate medical screening examination," the court must first give meaning to the statutory requirement; then it applies that requirement to the plaintiff's factual scenario. In doing the latter, the court decides whether the hospital violated the plaintiff's statutory right to the required screening and consequently owes the plaintiff a monetary judgment. In these cases, the court acts as both interpreter and rights enforcer. Other laws on both the federal and the state levels also create health-related rights for patients and providers, and individuals who believe that their rights have been violated may seek remedies through the courts.

This section, however, will focus primarily on how the courts' enforcement of (or limitation or denial of) common-law rights and constitutional rights can affect health policy. We will first consider how judicial resolution of claims brought by health plan subscribers against the entities managing their plans can affect health policy. We revisit the subject of ERISA preemption, which has severely limited plan members' ability to sue for a denial of benefits. This section and the rest of the chapter then consider how court decisions involving constitutional rights of both individuals and corporations have significantly shaped health policy.

Enforcement of Contract and Tort Rights: ERISA Preemption Revisited

Traditionally, a subscriber to a health insurance plan who believed that the plan manager had improperly refused to pay for covered benefits could sue the plan manager in state court for breach of contract. The lawsuit would require the court to interpret and apply language in the health insurance policy (e.g., whether a particular treatment prescribed for the subscriber fell under the policy's exclusion of "experimental" treatments). And in a managed care setting, if a health plan also employed physicians and other providers, subscribers might file a tort action against the plan if they believed they had suffered injury because the doctor had skimped on their care to save the plan money. That tort action would require the court to decide whether the doctor had acted negligently in making medical decisions or treating the plaintiffs.

Over the past several decades, however, courts have regularly found that ERISA preempts contract and tort lawsuits brought by plaintiffs who receive their health coverage through employer-sponsored health plans. As discussed, ERISA preempts state laws—including common-law contract and tort claims—that "relate to" employee benefit plans. Courts have interpreted ERISA's "relate to" preemption language broadly and have also invoked another ERISA provision that limits remedies for the denial of benefits to a remedy provided by ERISA itself. As a result, courts have kept dissatisfied subscribers from pursuing state law claims, leaving them only the option of going after the remedy provided for in the law itself. The remedy provided by ERISA, however, is limited, permitting a plan member to recover only the value of the benefit that was improperly denied. In contrast, a broader range of remedies (and more generous damages awards) is available to a subscriber who prevails in a contract or tort action. Thus, the preemption of state law claims has disadvantaged health plan subscribers who have claimed they had been harmed by health plan decisions to limit their care.

Moreover, as Jacobson (2009) points out, these judicial decisions also have had important policy implications. Because the preemption decisions limited the remedies available to plan members, they also limited the liability exposure of managed care plans. If the plan was sued and it lost, it would have to pay the injured subscriber only the value of the benefit it should have provided at the outset. This judicial application of ERISA to provide plans protection from potential liability for a full range of economic, pain and suffering, and punitive damages effectively gave managed care organizations the go-ahead to employ a variety of techniques to control costs aggressively.

At the same time, however, as news media began covering the plight of injured plan beneficiaries who were left without a meaningful remedy, the court decisions also prompted state legislatures and Congress to consider possible legislative fixes in the form of a patients' bill of rights that would provide some kind of protections to health plan enrollees. Although congressional efforts in the 1990s and early 2000s to enact a federal patients' bill of rights ultimately failed, several states enacted such reforms (Law 2002). Thus, the story of ERISA's preemption of health plan subscriber claims illustrates how courts' denial of subscribers' common-law rights catalyzed efforts to enact statutory protections.

Enforcement of Constitutional Rights

In contrast to the common law, which typically creates rights between private parties, the Constitution creates private rights against the exercise of governmental authority. Although state constitutions are also sources of important individual rights, this discussion focuses on the US Constitution. While both the constitutional separation of powers and the federalism provisions prevent the concentration of power in any one branch of government and limit the government's authority to act in the first instance, the Bill of Rights and the Fourteenth Amendment guard certain rights of individuals (and, sometimes, corporations) against governmental intrusion. For health policy purposes, the most important of these constitutional rights are found in the First Amendment (with its protection of free speech and religious freedom) and the Fourteenth Amendment (with its guarantees of equal protection and due process). Persons seeking the vindication of their constitutional rights call on the courts to claim those rights.

As Gostin (1995) points out, the courts have played their most robust—and most controversial—role in making policy decisions with respect to constitutional rights in health-related matters. By recognizing constitutional protections of individual rights relating to reproduction (both contraception and abortion rights) and end-of-life decision-making, the Supreme Court has addressed issues that are socially divisive and that legislatures had often failed to address. As a result, the "judiciary . . . has sometimes acted as a pathfinder when there was a paucity of established policy" (Gostin 1995, 345).

The effect of the Supreme Court's decisions on legislatures' ability to formulate policies on reproductive and end-of-life rights varies, though. The Court's decisions in the 1960s and 1970s establishing individual rights relating to contraception and abortion limited states' ability to enact policies regulating these areas. But subsequent Court decisions have eroded those limitations, emboldening state legislatures in recent years to enact a plethora of laws regulating abortion. By contrast, while assuming the Constitution provides some protection to individual autonomy in end-of-life decisions, as it did in the 1990 *Cruzan v. Director, Missouri Department of Health* case, the Court has been unwilling to declare that individuals have an absolute right either to terminate medical treatment or to receive physician assistance in dying. This reluctance largely leaves policy decisions about end-of-life care to state legislatures, many of which have enacted laws in this legal domain.

The ability to assert constitutional rights is not limited to individuals; the Supreme Court has recognized that corporations may also claim some constitutional protections. Corporations' success in convincing courts to recognize their First Amendment rights to free speech vividly illustrates how court decisions can affect health policy and, in particular, the government's ability to protect public health through its tobacco policy.

In 2009 (nine years after the Supreme Court held that the FDA did not have the delegated authority under the FDCA to regulate tobacco), Congress passed the Family Smoking Prevention and Tobacco Control Act (P.L. 111-31), granting the FDA that authority. One provision of that act mandates that the FDA develop new written health warnings to go on cigarette packages and select images to accompany those textual warnings (Orentlicher 2013).

In 2011, the FDA made public the nine images it proposed to place on cigarette packages; some of the images were quite disturbing. Tobacco companies filed First Amendment challenges to the statutory mandate that the FDA develop graphic warnings for cigarette packages and the actual images the FDA selected. The challenges essentially asserted a violation of the companies' First Amendment right to free speech, arguing that the government did not have a strong enough interest in promulgating the graphic warnings to be able to compel the companies to "speak" against their own interest by including the warnings on their product (Berman 2009; Cortez 2013). In 2012, in *Discount Tobacco City & Lottery, Inc. v. United States*, a federal circuit court of appeals upheld Congress's authority to require graphic warnings. But that same year, in *R.J. Reynolds Tobacco Co. v. FDA*, another circuit court of appeals found that compelling tobacco companies to include the images chosen by the FDA on their cigarette packages would violate the companies' First Amendment rights.

What happened next is telling. Normally, when federal courts of appeals from different circuits disagree on the constitutionality of a federal law, the issue is ripe for Supreme Court review. But rather than risk a Supreme Court decision that might establish new precedent broadly limiting the government's ability to protect the public's health by requiring warnings on dangerous products, the FDA chose to withdraw its proposed graphic warnings and announced that it would work on developing new images. That was in 2012. The issue languished for seven years. In late 2019, the FDA reworked the images and drafted a new rule, including new graphic images the agency hoped would be more certain to withstand constitutional scrutiny. The proposed new rule with the new images was posted on August 16, 2019. The initial comment period on the new rule was closed, then reopened and concluded October 15, 2019 (FDA 2019). The final rule was expected in March 2020 (Yorgancioglu 2019) but was postponed because of the COVID-19 pandemic (FDA 2020). From there will come either new images on cigarette packages or another challenge in court from the tobacco trade association and others. The tobacco companies' ability to resort to the courts to block the FDA's proposed graphic warnings demonstrates how an expansive judicial understanding of corporate First Amendment rights can constrain the government's pursuit of health policy

Courts often become arenas in which disputes over all manner of society's conflicts are resolved. These questions arise in health policy, discrimination based on race, and a host of social questions, several of which are highlighted in the following box.

The Courts as Agents of Social Change

The focus of this chapter has been on activities of the courts in the general topic of health services or health services delivery and access. The courts have made rulings that have particular application in health services delivery or availability of insurance coverage. Those issues, along with gender- and race-based discrimination, have received special consideration in our society.

Roe v. Wade, for example, decided in 1973, struck down a Texas statute banning abortion. The Supreme Court said that a woman was guaranteed the liberty of terminating a pregnancy as a right to privacy under the Fourteenth Amendment of the Constitution. The Court further opined that the government did have an interest in regulating abortion to protect the health of women and children. Thus, the Court reasoned that a woman's right to terminate a pregnancy in the first trimester should be unfettered—that it is an absolute right; that, in the second semester, the government could impose "reasonable" regulation; and that, in the third trimester, abortion should not be permitted. This decision touched off a national debate that continues today. Subsequently, in *Planned Parenthood of Southeastern Pennsylvania v. Casey* in 1992, the Supreme Court abandoned its trimester framework and adopted a "fetal viability" test. Without belaboring the point, several court decisions since 1973 and many states over the past several decades have adopted—sometimes successfully, sometimes not—a variety of restrictions on a woman's right to an abortion. Both *Roe v. Wade* and *Planned Parenthood of*

Southeastern Pennsylvania v. Casey fall in the constitutional-referee role and the rights-protector role played by the courts.

Irrespective of one's beliefs regarding this important healthcare issue, an interesting policy-related aspect is how the issue represents the never-ending policy loop. Further, the Court decisions represent the ongoing tension in the federalism context as some states adopt legislation that stretches the court's restrictions as far as they can. *Casey* was an example of that reach, as the Pennsylvania statute in that court case included a requirement that the husband be notified prior to the pregnancy termination. Parental consent has been another area of contention in the abortion issue as it relates to minors. The only real conclusion one can reach about this issue is that it will continue to be debated in one fashion or another. And it further demonstrates the accessibility of the courts to all sides of the debate.

A corollary case arose from the ACA. Regulations adopted by the Department of Health and Human Services (HHS) pursuant to the ACA required health insurance to include coverage for contraception. While not-for-profit organizations associated with a faith that objects to birth control were exempted, for-profit organizations were not. In *Burwell v. Hobby Lobby Stores, Inc.* in 2014, three closely held for-profit corporations filed suit to enjoin enforcement of the regulation as it applied to them. They cited the Religious Freedom Restoration Act of 1993 as justification for their position. In a five-to-four decision, the Supreme Court held that since the applicable HHS regulations would require the corporations to engage in conduct contrary to their sincere religious beliefs (these "closely held" corporations are essentially family-owned), the companies should therefore be exempted from the ambit of those regulations.

The Supreme Court has acted in other ways that have a broad impact on our society as well. In *Loving v. Virginia* in 1967, the Court ruled that statutes banning interracial marriage were unconstitutional. Further, in *Obergefell v. Hodges* in 2015, the Court ruled that the due process clause and the Fourteenth Amendment equal protection clause guaranteed same-sex marriage as a fundamental right. In each of these cases, the Court declared state statutes unconstitutional, overturning lower court rulings upholding the same.

The Supreme Court's impact on health policy is as vast as state and federal decisions combined. Given the proper circumstances, either state or federal decisions can reach the Supreme Court. The health policy issues that fall under the penumbra of court jurisdictional influence are limitless, ranging from seat belt and helmet laws to gun safety, tobacco use, drug use, and more. The aforementioned decisions—whether one agrees or disagrees with them—have implications for healthcare and health policy. Likewise, court decisions about pollution, immigration, insurance coverage, and other concerns will all affect the delivery of health services. As we have seen, the courts and the legislative and executive branches of government at both the federal and the state levels influence important social issues that affect health. These social issues will be addressed in more detail in chapter 10.

Summary

In the drama of policymaking, courts do not typically play the leading role. The cases discussed in this chapter, however, demonstrate that the courts frequently do play an important supporting role that may shape or constrain policy formulation and implementation. The courts' traditional roles include performing judicial review of government action, interpreting the law, and applying the law to settle disputes between litigating parties. By acting as constitutional referees, interpreters, and rights enforcers, courts have affected the development of numerous health policies in various areas, including national health reform, tobacco policy, and the regulation of employer-provided health insurance.

Review Questions

1. Discuss the three traditional core roles of courts in the US constitutional scheme of government.
2. Explain how courts affect health policymaking by acting as constitutional referees.
3. Explain how courts affect health policymaking by acting as interpreters.
4. Explain how courts affect health policymaking by acting as rights protectors.
5. Explain how a court is only allowed to consider a "case or controversy."
6. What does it mean for a court to be an interpreter?
7. What is the impact of stare decisis?
8. What is the supremacy clause of the US Constitution?
9. What implications does a tripartite system of government have for the courts?

10. What implications does a federal system of government have for the courts?
11. Discuss the concepts of separation of powers, judicial review, and institutional competence.

References

Anderson, G. F. 1992. "The Courts and Health Policy: Strengths and Limitations." *Health Affairs* 11 (4): 95–110.

Berman, M. L. 2009. "Smoking Out the Impact of Tobacco-Related Decisions on Public Health Law." *Brooklyn Law Review* 75 (1): 1–61.

Constitutional Convention. 1789. "America's Founding Documents." *National Archives.* Accessed December 1, 2019. www.archives.gov/founding-docs/constitution-transcript#toc-article-iii-.

Cortez, N. 2013. "Do Graphic Tobacco Warnings Violate the First Amendment?" *Hastings Law Journal* 64 (5): 1467–1500.

Furrow, B. R., T. L. Greaney, S. H. Johnson, T. S. Jost, and R. L. Schwartz. 2013. *Health Law: Cases, Materials, and Problems*, abridged 7th ed. St. Paul, MN: West Academic.

Gostin, L. O. 2009. "FDA Regulation of Tobacco: Politics, Law, and the Public's Health." *Journal of the American Medical Association* 302 (13): 1459–60.

———. 1995. "The Formulation of Health Policy by the Three Branches of Government." In *Society's Choices: Social and Ethical Decision Making in Biomedicine*, edited by F. E. Bulger, E. M. Bobby, and H. V. Fineberg, 335–57. Washington, DC: National Academy Press.

Hammer, P. J., and W. M. Sage. 2002. "Antitrust, Health Care Quality, and the Courts." *Columbia Law Review* 102 (3): 545–649.

Jacobson, P. D. 2009. "The Role of ERISA Preemption in Health Reform: Opportunities and Limits." *Journal of Law, Medicine & Ethics* 37 (suppl. 2): 86–100.

Jost, T. S. 2004. "Health Law and Administrative Law: A Marriage Most Convenient." *St. Louis University Law Journal* 49: 1–34.

Kaiser Family Foundation. 2012. *A Guide to the Supreme Court's Decision on the ACA's Medicaid Expansion.* Published August 1. http://kff.org/health-reform/issue-brief/a-guide-to-the-supreme-courts-decision.

Law, S. A. 2002. "Do We Still Need a Federal Patients' Bill of Rights?" *Yale Journal of Health Policy, Law & Ethics* 3 (1): 1–34.

Mariner, W. K., and G. J. Annas. 2013. "Limiting 'Sugary Drinks' to Reduce Obesity—Who Decides?" *New England Journal of Medicine* 368 (19): 1763–65.

Orentlicher, D. 2013. "The FDA's Graphic Tobacco Warnings and the First Amendment." *New England Journal of Medicine* 369 (3): 204–6.

Perez, V. K. 2007. "EMTALA: Protecting Patients First by Not Deferring to the Final Regulations." *Seton Hall Circuit Review* 4 (1): 149–85.

Richards, E. P. 2007. "Public Health Law as Administrative Law: Example Lessons." *Journal of Health Care Law and Policy* 10 (1): 61–88.

Teitelbaum, J. B., and S. E. Wilensky. 2013. "Law and the Legal System." In *Essentials of Health Law and Policy*, 2nd ed., 31–44. Burlington, MA: Jones & Bartlett Learning.

US Courts. 2019. *The Supreme Court.* Accessed December 1. www.uscourts.gov/about-federal-courts/educational-resources/about-educational-outreach/activity-resources/about.

US Food and Drug Administration (FDA). 2020. "Cigarette Labeling and Health Warning Requirements." Updated June 17. www.fda.gov/tobacco-products/labeling-and-warning-statements-tobacco-products/cigarette-labeling-and-health-warning-requirements.

———. 2019. "FDA Proposes New Health Warnings for Cigarette Packs and Ads." Published November 8. www.fda.gov/tobacco-products/labeling-and-warning-statements-tobacco-products/fda-proposes-new-health-warnings-cigarette-packs-and-ads.

Yorgancioglu, D. Z. 2019. "Updating Required Warnings for Cigarette Packages and Advertisements (Proposed Rule, 84 FR 42754)." SciPol. Published November 15. https://scipol.duke.edu/track/84-fr-42754-tobacco-products-required-warnings-cigarette-packages-and-advertisements.

Cases Cited

Arizona v. Maricopa County Medical Society. 457 US 332 (US Supreme Court, June 18, 1982).

Brown v. Board of Education. 347 US 483 (US Supreme Court, 1954).

Burwell v. Hobby Lobby Stores, Inc. 134 S. Ct. 2751 (US Supreme Court, June 30, 2014).

Cleland v. Bronson Health Care Group, Inc. 917 F.2d 266 (6th Circuit US Court of Appeals, October 24, 1990).

Cruzan v. Director, Missouri Department of Health. 497 US 261 (US Supreme Court, June 25, 1990).

Discount Tobacco City & Lottery, Inc. v. United Sates. 674 3d 509 (6th Circuit US Court of Appeals, March 19, 2012).

FDA v. Brown & Williamson. 529 U.S. 120 (US Supreme Court, March 21, 2000).

Kentucky Assn. of Health Plans, Inc. v. Miller. 538 U.S. 329 (US Supreme Court, April 2, 2003).

King v. Burwell. 135 S. Ct. 2480 (US Supreme Court, June 25, 2015).

Lorillard Tobacco Co. v. Reilly. 533 US 525 (US Supreme Court, June 28, 2001).

Loving v. Virginia. 388 US 1 (US Supreme Court, June 12, 1967).

Marbury v. Madison. 5 US 137 (US Supreme Court, February 24, 1803).
Metropolitan Life Insurance Co. v. Massachusetts. 471 US 724 (US Supreme Court, June 3, 1985).
New York State Conference of Blue Cross & Blue Shield Plans v. Travelers Insurance Company. 541 US 645 (US Supreme Court, April 26, 1995).
New York Statewide Coalition of Hispanic Chambers of Commerce v. New York City Department of Health and Mental Hygiene. 16 N.E.3d 538 (New York Court of Appeals, June 26, 2014).
NFIB v. Sebelius. 567 US 519 (US Supreme Court, June 28, 2012).
Obergefell v. Hodges. 576 US 644 (US Supreme Court, June 26, 2015).
Planned Parenthood of Southeastern Pennsylvania v. Casey. 505 US 833 (US Supreme Court, June 29, 1992).
Plessy v. Ferguson. 167 US 537 (US Supreme Court, 1896).
R.J. Reynolds Tobacco Co. v. FDA. 696 F 3d 1205 (DC Circuit, US Court of Appeals, August 24, 2012).
Roe v. Wade. 1973. 410 U.S. 113 (US Supreme Court, January 22).

APPENDIX

3.1

TYPICAL PLAN FOR LEGISLATIVE OVERSIGHT

The following oversight plan, reprinted here in its entirety, was set forth by members of the House Committee on Energy and Commerce.

Authorization and Oversight Plan of the Committee on Energy and Commerce U.S. House of Representatives, 115th Congress

During the 115th Congress, the Committee on Energy and Commerce will hold hearings and conduct rigorous oversight over matters within its jurisdiction. The Committee will conduct thorough oversight, reach conclusions based on an objective review of the facts, and treat witnesses fairly. The Committee will request information in a responsible manner that is calculated to be helpful to the Committee in its oversight responsibilities. The Committee's oversight functions will focus on: 1) cutting government spending through the elimination of waste, fraud, and abuse and 2) ensuring laws are adequate to protect the public interest or are being implemented in a manner that protects the public interest, without stifling economic growth. The Committee will use the information it collects through its oversight to inform the reauthorization of certain lapsed programs within its jurisdiction.

Health and Healthcare Issues

Patient Protection and Affordable Care Act

To aid in legislative efforts to replace the Patient Protection and Affordable Care Act (PPACA), the Committee will continue to examine issues related to the Department of Health and Human Services (HHS) implementation of PPACA, Public Law 111-148, and the related Health Care and Education Reconciliation Act of 2010, Public Law 111-152. It is critical that the Committee understand decisions made in drafting and implementing PPACA so that it can replace PPACA with better solutions focused on helping consumers. The Committee will examine the continuing impact of PPACA and its implementing regulations on the economy, consumers, and the health care industry. The Committee will also examine the status and future of employer-sponsored health care plans as well as the effects of PPACA's enactment on the States. The Committee will continue to monitor the law's effects on individuals as well as the regulations and requirements imposed on small and large businesses.

Centers for Medicare and Medicaid Services

The Committee will review the management, operations, and activity of the Centers for Medicare and Medicaid Services (CMS) and the programs it administers. The Committee will examine and review Medicare and Medicaid management and activity as it relates to ongoing Committee efforts to prevent bias, waste, fraud, and abuse in Federal health care programs. The Committee will investigate the process by which CMS implements statutory formulas to set prices for Medicare payment, as well as the effectiveness of those formulas. The Committee will investigate the processes by which CMS prevents bias, waste, fraud, and abuse in the award of government contracts.

Food and Drug Administration and Drug Safety

The Committee will review whether the Food and Drug Administration (FDA) is ensuring that regulated drugs are safe, effective, and available to American patients in an expeditious fashion. The Committee will also explore the interplay between these policies and drug innovation, both in the United States and abroad. Further, the Committee will examine FDA's enforcement of current drug safety laws and the issues involved in protecting the nation's supply chains against economically motivated and other forms of adulteration, including those posed by illegal drug supply chains and economically-motivated adulteration. The Committee will examine whether FDA's reorganization efforts are improving the effectiveness of product reviews, or worsening delays and inefficiency in decision-making. The Committee will review FDA's efforts to improve and modernize import-safety screening, and the management of its foreign inspection program.

Public Health and Pandemic Preparedness

The Committee will examine the roles of various Federal agencies involved in insuring and protecting the public health, including the implementation and management of these programs. In particular, the Committee will review Federal efforts on the opioid epidemic, pandemic preparedness, including influenza preparedness, the United States' response to the spread of the Zika virus, and other emerging infectious disease threats from abroad. The Committee will continue to evaluate the Federal response to the opioid epidemic, the Zika virus, and other public health emergencies to better understand the operation and efficacy of key public health programs and to address broader concerns about national all-hazards preparedness and response capacity. Further, the Committee will monitor related spending to ensure the appropriate and efficient use of Federal tax dollars.

21st Century Cures and Mental Health Reforms

In the 115th Congress, the Committee will examine implementation of the 21st Century Cures Act, landmark legislation that will expedite the discovery, development, and delivery of new treatments and cures. The legislation also included meaningful mental health reforms. The Committee will ensure that HHS and its component agencies, including FDA and the National Institutes of Health, and other relevant agencies implement the legislation in a manner that will quickly deliver the benefits provided by the law. The Committee will conduct oversight of the implementation of and work done by the newly-created Assistant Secretary for Mental Health, an office which will be responsible for HHS mental health programs and policies. The Committee will also examine regulations drafted to implement the 21st Century Cures Act to ensure they comport with the intent of Congress, and will monitor funding provided by the legislation to ensure that it is appropriately spent.

Energy and Environment Issues

National Energy Policy

During the 115th Congress, the Committee will examine issues relating to national energy policy, including U.S. policies that relate to the exploration, production, distribution, and consumption of electricity, oil and natural gas, coal, hydroelectric power, nuclear power, and renewable energy. The Committee will examine the impact of government policies and programs on the efficient exploration, production, storage, supply, marketing, pricing, and regulation of domestic energy resources, including issues relating to the nation's energy infrastructure. The Committee will continue to examine safety and security issues relating to energy exploration, production, and distribution.

Electricity System and Electric Utility Markets

During the 115th Congress, the Committee will undertake a comprehensive review of the nation's electricity system. This effort will include a review of the federal electricity policies of the Department of Energy (DOE) and the Federal Energy Regulatory Commission (FERC) to ensure that those policies promote competitive wholesale power markets, transmission, generation infrastructure upgrades, and compliance with relevant statutes. It will also examine the activities of the DOE and FERC relating to electric industry restructuring, protection of consumers, and the development of efficient and vigorous wholesale markets for electricity. It will also continue to examine the activities of the DOE and FERC with respect to Environmental Protection Agency (EPA) regulations affecting the electricity sector, including regulatory requirements that may impact consumer prices and reliability of the electricity grid.

Energy Efficiency Mandates

The Committee will continue to assess federal programs setting energy efficiency standards for motor vehicles, crafted by EPA and the National Highway Traffic Safety Administration (NHTSA), and home appliances, crafted by DOE, to ensure that the programs are implemented in a manner that maximizes the benefit to consumers. In the case of motor vehicle standards, the Committee will also assess the merit of having two federal agencies operating parallel efficiency programs.

Management of the Department of Energy and Its National Laboratories

The Committee will continue to oversee the governance, management, and operations issues at DOE, including oversight, management, and operations of the National Nuclear Security Administration (NNSA) and the national laboratories.

The Committee's oversight work will include review of the implementation of security and safety reforms at NNSA and DOE facilities, ongoing safety and security matters, and the Office of Environmental Management's cleanup program. This work will also include the Committee's special oversight functions over programs and activities relating to nonmilitary energy research and development.

Yucca Mountain

The Committee will continue to examine the actions of DOE and the NRC in connection with obligations of these agencies under the Nuclear Waste Policy Act, including licensing activities for the Yucca Mountain repository.

DOE Energy Grant and Loan Programs

The Committee will continue to review management and implementation of clean energy and advanced technology grant and loan programs authorized under the Energy Policy Act of 2005 and other statutes; the development of new technologies, products, and businesses including clean energy, advanced coal, nuclear, and other technologies; and the impact of DOE grant, cost-sharing, and loan spending on the domestic supply, manufacture and commercial deploymentof clean and advanced energy products and other technologies.

The Nuclear Regulatory Commission

The Committee will continue to review the activities of the Nuclear Regulatory Commission (NRC). The Committee will examine NRC's budget requests and conduct oversight of the manner in which the Commission discharges its various responsibilities, including licensing activity, the safety and security of nuclear power facilities and nuclear materials licensees, and the Commission's regulatory actions.

Clean Air Act

The Committee will continue to review significant rulemakings under the Clean Air Act and the potential economic and job impacts of those rulemakings on the energy, manufacturing, industrial, and construction industries, and other critical sectors of the U.S. economy, as well as any public health and environmental benefits of the regulations. The Committee's review will include oversight of the EPA's decisions, strategies, and actions to meet Clean Air Act standards, and the current role of cost, employment and feasibility considerations in Clean Air Act rulemakings. The Committee will also continue to review EPA's implementation of the Renewable Fuel Standard.

Climate Change

The Committee will continue to monitor international negotiations on efforts to control greenhouse gas emissions in connection with concerns about global climate change. In addition, the Committee will examine the EPA's efforts to regulate domestic greenhouse gas emissions under the Clean Air Act based on its endangerment findings. The Committee will consider whether such agreements and regulatory efforts are scientifically well grounded. The Committee will also review the activities undertaken in this area by DOE, HHS, and other agencies within the Committee's jurisdiction, including efforts to prepare for and respond to weather events and natural disasters in the future.

EPA Management and Operations

The Committee will conduct general oversight of the EPA, including review of the agency's funding decisions, resource allocation, grants, research activities, enforcement actions, relations with State and local governments, public transparency, and respect for economic, procedural, public health, and environmental standards in regulatory actions. In addition, the Committee will review the government's activities in hydraulic fracturing research and regulation.

Assessment and Management of Chemical Substances

The Committee will monitor EPA implementation of reforms made to title I of the Toxic Substances Control Act. These efforts will include program management and the use of chemical risk analysis in environmental assessment programs. The Committee will also review deadline management and consistency of implementation, ensure that confidential business information is protected from unwarranted disclosure, and make certain that EPA provides the appropriate consideration of risks and their trade-offs during the evaluation and regulatory process.

Drinking Water Infrastructure and Regulation

The Committee will conduct oversight of the operation of the Drinking Water State Revolving Loan Fund program authorized under Section 1452 of the Safe Drinking Water Act. Included will be an examination of State funding uses, efficiencies that could be realized in managing this funding that maximize its effectiveness, and the use of this funding for leveraging other investments. In addition, the Committee will conduct oversight of EPA regulatory actions under Section 1412 of the Safe Drinking Water Act and the protocol it uses to issue health advisories under the same section of law.

Solid and Hazardous Waste Management

The Committee will review EPA implementation of various regulatory programs established under the most recent administration, including regulations regarding the definition of solid waste and coal ash.

CERCLA (Superfund) and Brownfields

The Committee will monitor EPA implementation of the Comprehensive Environmental Response Compensation & Liability Act (CERCLA). These efforts will include an examination of State cleanup programs and a comprehensive analysis regarding whether cleanup under State programs would result in greater efficiency in the process. The Committee will also conduct oversight of EPA regulatory actions under CERCLA, in particular the current rule making for financial assurance under CERCLA Section 108(b). The Committee will also examine the EPA brownfields program, including statutory implementation, the challenges of program operation, and whether changes to the program would result in more effective and efficient cleanup and redevelopment of abandoned and blighted properties.

Communications and Technology Issues

A Modern Communications Framework for the Innovation Age

The Committee will continue to exercise its jurisdiction over wired and wireless communications to ensure our nation's policies governing voice, video, audio, and data services are promoting investment, innovation, and job creation. The country's current regulatory regime takes a siloed approach in which different technological platforms—such as wireline, wireless, broadcast, cable, and satellite—are regulated differently based on regulations that may be decades old. As we move deeper into the Internet era, however, providers are increasingly using these platforms to offer the same or similar services. The Committee will examine whether these regulations should be updated to better meet the communications needs of the country and to ensure its citizens enjoy cutting edge services and the economic benefits they bring.

Federal Communications Commission

During the 115th Congress, the Committee will conduct oversight of the Federal Communications Commission (FCC), including the efforts to reverse the reclassification of Broadband Internet Access Service as a telecommunications service subject to Title II of the Communications Act of 1934 and efforts to bring transparency and accountability to the Commission's processes. The Committee will also continue to conduct oversight of the FCC's decisions and their impact on innovation and the U.S. economy. Among other things, the Committee will evaluate the impact generally of FCC actions on voice, video, audio, and data services, and on public safety. The Committee will pay particular attention to whether the FCC conducts cost-benefit and market analyses before imposing regulations.

Spectrum Management

The Committee will conduct oversight of the Federal Communications Commission's and the National Telecommunications and Information Administration's (NTIA) management and allocation of the nation's spectrum for commercial and government use. Spectrum is increasingly being used to provide voice, video, audio, and data services to consumers and to serve the needs of our nation's government agencies. The Committee will evaluate spectrum-management policies to ensure efficient use of the public airwaves for innovative communications services. The Committee will also examine whether plans for allocating spectrum maximize broadband deployment and encourage investment. The Committee will pay particular attention to FCC and NTIA implementation of the Middle Class Tax Relief and Job Creation Act of 2012 and the Bipartisan Budget Act of 2015, which included provisions intended to make more spectrum available for mobile broadband services, as well as raise billions in spectrum auction proceeds.

Availability of Broadband

The Committee will investigate whether regulatory policies are helping or hindering broadband deployment. In particular, the Committee will examine the need for reforms to State and Federal permitting processes to speed the deployment of fiber optic systems and 5G wireless services. Additionally, the

Committee will conduct oversight of funding mechanisms for broadband deployment and adoption, including the $9 billion per year Universal Service Fund. Specifically, the Committee will examine what procedures are in place to control waste, fraud, and abuse, whether the funds are appropriately targeted, and the impact of the funding on jobs and the economy.

Internet

The Committee will exercise its jurisdiction over wired and wireless communications to ensure continued growth and investment in the Internet. In particular, the Committee will monitor efforts to employ the multi-stakeholder model of Internet governance—in which governmental and non-governmental entities develop best practices for the management of Internet networks and content. The Committee will also monitor international efforts to replace multistakeholder governance with domestic regulation and international multilateral institutions.

Public Safety Communications

The Committee will examine whether the communications needs of first responders are being met. The Committee will examine the progress being made to ensure that first responders have interoperable communications capabilities with local, State, and Federal public safety officials. The Committee will also examine the progress being made by the First Responder Network Authority (FirstNet) in carrying out the mandates of the Middle Class Tax Relief and Job Creation Act of 2012. Specifically, the progress made in finding private sector partners to develop an interoperable public safety broadband network and implementation of the network. In addition, the Committee will conduct oversight regarding the implementation of legacy 911 and Next Generation 911 (NG911) services. The Committee will review efforts to promote deployment of these advanced systems and challenges to realizing ubiquitous NG911.

Digital Commerce and Consumer Protection

Privacy and Security

In the 115th Congress, the Committee will examine issues relating to the privacy and security of methods, information and data collected by businesses about consumers and the potential for improving protection without undercutting innovative uses that benefit consumers and the economy. Further, the Committee will continue to review the manner in which fraud and other criminal activities affect e-commerce. The Committee will also explore how privacy and cybersecurity policies should treat the burgeoning Internet of Things.

Self-Driving Vehicles

The Committee will examine the policy framework being put into place for self-driving vehicles. Self-driving vehicles hold the promise to greatly reduce traffic fatalities, while at the same time expanding mobility to additional subsets of Americans and doing so with less impact on the environment. It is critical that this technology is encouraged through smart approaches and to ensure that the potential of revolutionary change to the industry is not curtailed by unnecessary regulation.

Manufacturing

The Committee will explore the state of manufacturing in the United States to identify factors that are hampering or furthering U.S. competitiveness. The Committee will review the issues presented by the globalization of production and manufacturing networks, including the integrity of products and components assembled overseas and the impact on national security.

Trade

The Committee will examine trade negotiations to ensure that foreign governments are not imposing non-tariff trade barriers, such as regulations or requirements, that harm U.S. businesses, their competitiveness and their ability to support jobs in the United States, especially as it relates to the flow of data across borders.

Department of Commerce Management and Operations

The Committee will conduct oversight of the Commerce Department and complementary or conflicting Federal efforts to promote U.S. manufacturing, exports, and trade, including efforts to lower or eliminate non-tariff barriers and harmonize regulation of products sold internationally where other countries share our health, safety, and consumer protection goals.

Consumer Product Safety Commission Management and Operations

The Committee will continue oversight of the Consumer Product Safety Commission and its implementation and enforcement of laws and regulations relating to the safety of consumer products, including the agency's implementation of Public Law 112-28 and determination of priorities to ensure that it is efficiently and effectively protecting consumers.

NHTSA Management and Operations

The Committee intends to continue oversight of the National Highway Traffic Safety Administration (NHTSA), including the effectiveness of the agency's structure, regulations, research activities, investigations, and enforcement actions pertaining to motor vehicle safety. The committee will be particularly concerned with the way the Administration processes information and its ability to effectively oversee ever advancing safety technologies.

Federal Trade Commission Management and Operations

The Committee will conduct oversight of the Federal Trade Commission's management and operations, including the impact of its decisions and actions on the general public and the business community, its determination of priorities and the need, if any, for refinement of its authorities. In particular, the Committee will explore the FTC's role relative to emerging sectors of the economy and its jurisdiction relative to new technologies.

Miscellaneous

Cybersecurity

The Committee will exercise its jurisdiction over cybersecurity to ensure the country is well protected while at the same time avoiding one-size-fits all approaches that hinder the flexibility of commercial and governmental actors to combat the rapidly evolving threats. The Committee will also review the efforts of agencies within its jurisdiction to secure their networks consistent with the Homeland Security Act of 2002. In doing so, the Committee will explore current cybersecurity threats and strategies to address those threats. The Committee will also examine government initiatives to improve cybersecurity both in the public and private sectors, and review efforts at agencies within the Committee's jurisdiction to regulate cybersecurity. The Committee will also examine the security of the Internet of Things, discovery and disclosure of cybersecurity vulnerabilities, the National Institute of Standards and Technology (NIST) Cybersecurity Framework, and the recently released report from the Presidential Commission on Enhancing Cybersecurity.

Bioterrorism Preparedness and Response

The Committee will continue its examination of the roles of HHS agencies in assisting the nation's detection, warning capability, and response to potential biological attacks. In addition, the Committee will evaluate the potential impact and preparedness of the nation's public health system. The Committee will continue to review the implementation of the Public Health Security and Bioterrorism Preparedness and Response Act of 2002 by HHS, and the extent of the coordination between HHS and the Department of Homeland Security (DHS), especially as it relates to Project Bioshield.

Federal Oversight of High-Containment Bio Laboratories

The Committee will examine issues related to high-containment bio laboratories, which handle some of the world's most exotic and dangerous diseases, including anthrax, smallpox, foot and mouth disease, and Ebola virus. Among the issues under review are the adequacy of the security and practices of high-containment bio laboratories, Federal efforts to oversee the laboratories, and whether some of these efforts are duplicative and overlapping. The Committee will continue its oversight into issues raised by the improper storage and handling of Federal select agents at CDC, NIH, and FDA labs.

Anti-Terrorism Security for Chemical Facilities

The Committee will continue its oversight of DHS's implementation of the Chemical Facilities Anti-Terrorism Program, originally authorized in Section 550 of Public Law 109-295, the Homeland Security Appropriations Act of 2007. The Committee will continue to examine whether taxpayer funds are spent prudently and the extent to which DHS is advancing the purpose of securing chemical facilities against terrorist threats.

Government Scientific and Risk Assessment Programs

During the 115th Congress, the Committee will examine issues relating to the numerous Federal science programs assessing public health risks, including the Integrated Risk Information System at the EPA, the Report on Carcinogens produced by the National Toxicology Program at HHS, and assessments proposed or ongoing in other Federal departments and agencies. The Committee will review programs to assess the objectives, transparency, and integrity of scientific assessments that inform regulatory and public health policies.

Controlling Spending

The Committee will examine Departments and agencies under its jurisdiction to assure adequate and prompt implementation of recommendations from the Administration, the Offices of Inspectors General, the Government Accountability Office, and other sources to achieve cost savings or eliminate wasteful spending.

Critical Infrastructure

In June 2006, the Bush Administration issued a National Infrastructure Protection Plan. This plan created a process by which DHS is to identify critical assets and assess their vulnerabilities and risks due to loss or natural disaster.

During the 115th Congress, the Committee will review the Department's activities with respect to identifying high-priority assets and implementing plans to protect these assets in areas within the Committee's jurisdiction. The Committee will also examine the activities of DOE, FERC, and other Federal agencies related to the physical and cybersecurity of the nation's energy infrastructure. Further, the Committee will examine the roles and responsibilities of the private sector, which owns and operates the bulk of the nation's critical infrastructure assets.

Nuclear Smuggling

The Committee will continue to monitor Federal government and private sector efforts at border crossings, seaports, and mail facilities. The Committee's review will analyze and assess U.S. Customs and Border Protection and the Department of Energy's efforts, including international efforts, aimed at detecting and preventing the smuggling of dangerous commerce, particularly nuclear and radiological weapons of mass destruction.

Authorization of Programs Within the Jurisdiction of the Committee on Energy and Commerce

During the 115th Congress, as part of both its oversight and legislative agenda, the Committee on Energy and Commerce will review the authorizations of agencies and programs within its jurisdiction and, specifically with regard to lapsed authorizations, determine whether the program should be reauthorized or terminated. Each subcommittee will conduct oversight of these programs and offices, including hearings, outreach to the Executive Branch, and requests for information in order to gather the necessary information to support these determinations.

The Committee plans to dedicate considerable time in the 115th Congress to examining the policies of the Patient Protection and Affordable Care Act (PPACA) and then developing legislation to improve health care delivery and treatment and lower costs for families. When the PPACA was enacted in 2010, it authorized dozens of individual programs. Some of these programs received indefinite, or "such sums" authorizations, and others were authorized at a specific level. Since 2010, the authorizations for most of these programs have expired; some have continued to receive appropriations while others have not. The Committee expects to consider the now-lapsed programs that the law authorized and determine which ones should be reauthorized. The Committee's oversight of the PPACA, as described previously in this document, will necessarily inform how the Committee will advance alternative solutions to the PPACA and either reauthorize or terminate the programs first authorized by that law. The Committee plans to work closely with the Department of Health and Human Services and the Executive Branch when making decisions about individual programs.

In addition to examining the lapsed authorizations contained within the ACA, the Committee in the first session of the 115th Congress will work on the reauthorization of two key programs before they expire: the State Children's Health Insurance Program (SCHIP), last authorized in the Medicare Access and CHIP Reauthorization Act of 2015 and expiring in 2017, and the Food and Drug Administration (FDA) User Fees, including the Prescription Drug User Fee Act (PDUFA) and Generic Drug User Fee Amendments (GDUFA). The reauthorization of both programs will require multiple hearings and may involve extensive negotiations.

With regard to the Committee's jurisdiction over energy and the environment, a number of the energy and environment programs within the Committee's jurisdiction have lapsed but continue to receive appropriations. The bulk of the lapsed programs are within the Committee's energy jurisdiction, including the Energy Policy Act of 2005 (P.L. 109-58) and the Energy Independence and Security Act of 2007 (P.L. 110-140). In addition, there are various lapsed programs within the Clean Air Act; the Safe Drinking Water Act; the Toxic Substances Control Act; the Nuclear Waste Policy Act; the Solid Waste Disposal Act, also referred to as the Resource Conservation and Recovery Act (RCRA); the Comprehensive Environmental Response, Compensation, and Liability Act of 1980; the Superfund Amendments and Reauthorization Act of 1986; the Energy Act of 2000; the Small Business Liability Relief and Brownfields Revitalization Act; the Pollution Prevention Act; the Department of Energy Organization Act; and the Energy Policy and Conservation Act of 1975.

As many of the programs related to energy and environmental matters have lapsed for more than a decade, and as part of the Committee's ongoing work to modernize energy policy, it is an appropriate time to consider whether these programs should continue, be updated, or be terminated. The Committee plans to collect information as appropriate and to evaluate the relevant programs within the Department of Energy, the Environmental Protection Agency, the Nuclear Regulatory Commission, the Energy Information Administration, the Federal Energy Regulatory Commission, the Department of Homeland Security, and other relevant agencies. Such reauthorization activity will include consideration of programs in relation to current and projected U.S. economic, energy, and environmental conditions.

In addition to the reauthorization work described previously in the health, environment, and energy jurisdictions of the Committee, and as explained in the oversight plan, the Committee plans to lay the groundwork for other reauthorizations in this Congress. Within the jurisdiction of the Subcommittee on Communications and Technology, the oversight of the Federal Communications Commission (FCC) and the NTIA that the Committee pursued in the 114th Congress will continue in the 115th Congress, including the examination of the Federal Communications Commission Authorization Act of 1990 and the

NTIA Organization Act. Finally, within the jurisdiction of the Subcommittee on Digital Commerce and Consumer Protection, the Federal Trade Commission was last reauthorized in 1996, with the authorization expiring at the end of Fiscal Year 1998. The Subcommittee on Digital Commerce and Consumer Protection plans to conduct continued oversight of how the FTC carries out its authorities relating to unfair or deceptive acts or practices, specifically the agency's actions with respect to disruptive and technology-driven markets, innovative products, and services that benefit consumers. The purpose of this oversight work is to clarify the FTC's consumer protection authority in areas where observed harms have plagued consumers and better understand the legal and economic basis for the agency's enforcement actions.

The reauthorization work will require extensive Committee resources and member participation, particularly of the members of the Subcommittee on Health and Subcommittee on Energy. While the Committee expects that the repeal and replacement of the PPACA will be accomplished by the end of the 115th Congress, it is possible that the Committee's work to reauthorize the energy and environment-related programs and agencies will continue into the next Congress.

Source: Reprinted from US House of Representatives. 2018. "Authorization and Oversight Plan of the Committee on Energy and Commerce U.S. House of Representatives, 115th Congress." Accessed June 13, 2020. https://energycommerce.house.gov/sites/democrats.energycommerce.house.gov/files/documents/FC-Org-Mtg-115-Oversight-Plan-20170124.pdf.

APPENDIX

3.2

SOME MISSION-CRITICAL CENTERS OF THE CENTERS FOR MEDICARE & MEDICAID SERVICES

The descriptions provided for the CMS centers included here are adapted and abstracted from CMS's website (CMS 2020).

Center for Medicare

The Center for Medicare serves the following functions:

- Acts as CMS's focal point for the formulation, coordination, integration, implementation, and evaluation of national Medicare program policies and operations.
- Identifies and proposes modifications to Medicare programs and policies to reflect changes or trends in the healthcare industry, program objectives, and the needs of Medicare beneficiaries.
- Coordinates with the Office of Legislation on the development and advancement of new legislative initiatives and improvements.
- Acts as CMS's lead for management, oversight, budget, and performance issues relating to Medicare Advantage, Medicare's prescription drug plans, and Medicare fee-for-service providers and contractors.
- Oversees all CMS collaboration with key stakeholders and other interactions relating to Medicare (i.e., plans, providers, other government entities, advocacy groups, consortia); oversees all communication and dissemination of policies, guidance, and materials to these same stakeholders to understand their perspectives and to drive best practices in the healthcare industry.
- Develops and implements a comprehensive strategic plan, objectives, and measures to carry out CMS's Medicare program mission and goals and to position the organization to meet future challenges with the Medicare program and its beneficiaries.

- Coordinates with the Center for Program Integrity to identify program vulnerabilities and to implement strategies to eliminate fraud, waste, and abuse.

Center for Medicaid and CHIP Services

The Center for Medicaid and CHIP Services serves the following functions:

- Acts as CMS's focal point for the formulation, coordination, integration, implementation, and evaluation of all national program policies and operations relating to Medicaid, the Children's Health Insurance Program (CHIP), and the Basic Health Program (BHP).
- In partnership with states, assists state agencies in successfully carrying out their responsibilities for effective program administration and beneficiary protection and, as necessary, supports states in correcting problems and improving the quality of their operations.
- Identifies and proposes modifications to Medicaid and CHIP program measures, regulations, laws, and policies to reflect changes or trends in the healthcare industry, program objectives, and the needs of Medicaid, CHIP, and BHP beneficiaries.
- Collaborates with the Office of Legislation on the development and advancement of new legislative initiatives and improvements.
- Acts as CMS's lead for management, oversight, budget, and performance issues relating to Medicaid, CHIP, BHP, and the related interactions with the states and stakeholder community.
- Coordinates with the Center for Program Integrity on the identification of program vulnerabilities and implementation of strategies to eliminate fraud, waste, and abuse. Leads and supports all CMS interactions and collaborations relating to Medicaid, CHIP, and BHP with states and local governments, territories, Indian tribes, and tribal healthcare providers, key stakeholders (e.g., consumer and policy organizations and the healthcare provider community) and other federal government entities. Facilitates communication and disseminates policy and operational guidance and materials to all stakeholders. Works to understand stakeholders and consider their perspectives, support their efforts, and develop best practices for beneficiaries across the country and throughout the healthcare system.
- Develops and implements a comprehensive strategic plan, objectives, and measures to carry out CMS's Medicaid, CHIP, and BHP mission and goals and to position the organization to meet future challenges with Medicaid, CHIP, and BHP.

Center for Consumer Information and Insurance Oversight

The Center for Consumer Information and Insurance Oversight serves the following functions:

- Provides national leadership in setting and enforcing health-insurance standards that promote fair and reasonable practices to ensure that affordable, quality healthcare coverage is available to all Americans.
- Provides consumers with comprehensive information on insurance coverage options currently available so they may make informed choices on the best health insurance for themselves and their families; issues consumer assistance grants to states.
- Implements, monitors compliance with, and enforces the new rules governing the insurance market such as the prohibition on rescissions and on preexisting condition exclusions for children. Conducts external appeals for states that do not have that authority.
- Implements, monitors compliance with, and enforces the new rules on medical loss ratio standards and insurance premium rate reviews, and issues premium rate review grants to states.
- Administers the Pre-Existing Condition Insurance Plan and associated grant funding to states, the Early Retiree Reinsurance Program, and the Consumer Operated and Oriented Plan Program.
- Collects, compiles, and maintains comparative pricing data for an internet portal providing information on insurance options, and provides assistance to enable consumers to obtain maximum benefit from the new health insurance system.
- Collects, compiles, and maintains comparative pricing data for the department's website, provides assistance to enable consumers to understand the new health insurance laws and regulations, and establishes and issues consumer assistance grants to states.
- Develops and implements policies and rules governing state-based exchanges, establishes and issues exchange planning and establishment to states, oversees the operations of state-based exchanges, and administers exchanges in states that elect not to establish their own.
- Oversees and directs the development and operations of the back-end and systems functions for healthcare.gov in support of the federally facilitated marketplace, distributed hub services, and multidimensional insurance data analytics systems.

CMS Innovation Center

The CMS Innovation Center serves the following functions:

- Identifies, validates, and disseminates information about new care models and payment approaches to serve Medicare and Medicaid beneficiaries seeking to enhance the quality of health and healthcare and reducing cost through improvements.
- Consults with representatives of relevant federal agencies and clinical and analytical professionals with expertise in medicine and healthcare management (e.g., management of providers, payers, states, businesses, and community agencies) to develop new and effective models of care.
- Creates and tests new models in clinical care, integrated care, and community health, and disseminates information on these models through CMS, Health and Human Services (HHS), states, local organizations, and industry channels.
- Performs rapid cycle evaluation of innovation and demonstration activities to determine effectiveness and feasibility for broader dissemination, scale, and sustainability.
- Works closely with other CMS components and regional offices to study healthcare industry trends and data to design, implement, and evaluate innovative payment and service delivery models and to disseminate information about effective models.
- Builds collaborative learning networks to facilitate collection and analysis of relevant data. Develops the necessary technology to support this activity.
- Develops professionals with expertise in innovation, demonstration, and diffusion to help introduce effective practices across the nation.
- Carries out core business functions (e.g., budget, facilities, HR, communications).

Center for Clinical Standards and Quality

The Center for Clinical Standards and Quality serves the following functions:

- Acts as the focal point for all quality, clinical, and medical science issues; the survey and certification of health facilities; and policies for CMS's programs.
- Provides leadership and coordination for the development and implementation of a cohesive, CMS-wide approach to measuring and promoting quality, and leads CMS's priority-setting process for clinical quality improvement.

- Coordinates quality-related activities with outside organizations; monitors quality of Medicare, Medicaid, and the Clinical Laboratory Improvement Amendments (CLIA).
- Identifies and develops best practices and techniques in quality improvement. The implementation of these techniques will be overseen by appropriate components of CMS.
- Develops and collaborates on demonstration projects to test and promote quality measurement and improvement.
- Develops, tests, evaluates, adopts, and supports performance measurement systems (i.e., quality measures) to evaluate care provided to CMS beneficiaries except for demonstration projects in other components.
- Ensures that CMS's quality-related activities (the survey and certification of facilities), technical assistance, beneficiary information, payment policies, and provider/plan incentives) are fully integrated.
- Carries out the Health Care Quality Improvement Program for the Medicare, Medicaid, and CLIA programs.
- Oversees the planning, policy, coordination, and implementation of the survey, certification, and enforcement programs for all Medicare and Medicaid providers and suppliers and for laboratories under the auspices of CLIA.
- Acts as CMS's lead for management, oversight, budget, and performance issues relating to the survey and certification program and the related interactions with the states.
- Leads in the specification and operational refinement of an integrated CMS quality information system, which includes tools for measuring the coordination of care between healthcare settings. Analyzes data supplied by that system to identify ways to improve care and assess the success of improvement interventions.
- Develops the requirements of participation for providers and plans in the Medicare, Medicaid, and CLIA programs; bases these requirements on statutory change and input from other components.
- Operates the Quality Improvement Organization Program and the End-Stage Renal Disease Network Program in conjunction with regional offices, providing policies and procedures, contract design, program coordination, and leadership in selected projects.
- Identifies, prioritizes, and develops content for clinical and health-related aspects of CMS's consumer information strategy; collaborates with other components to develop comparative provider and plan performance information for consumer choices.
- Prepares the scientific, clinical, and procedural basis for coverage of new and established technologies and services, and provides coverage recommendations to the CMS administrator. Coordinates activities of

CMS's Technology Advisory Committee, and maintains liaison with other departmental components regarding the safety and effectiveness of technologies and services. Prepares the scientific and clinical basis for, and recommends approaches to, quality-related medical review activities of carriers and payment policies.
- Identifies new and innovative approaches, and tests for improving quality programs and lowering costs.

Center for Program Integrity

The Center for Program Integrity serves the following functions:

- Acts as CMS's focal point for all national and statewide Medicare and Medicaid programs and CHIP integrity fraud and abuse issues.
- Promotes the integrity of the Medicare and Medicaid programs and CHIP through provider/contractor audits and policy reviews, the identification and monitoring of program vulnerabilities, and the provision of support to states.
- Recommends modifications to programs and operations as necessary, and works with CMS centers, offices, and the chief operating officer (COO) to effect changes as appropriate.
- Collaborates with the Office of Legislation on the development and advancement of new legislative initiatives and improvements to deter, reduce, and eliminate fraud, waste, and abuse.
- Oversees all CMS collaborations and other interactions with key stakeholders relating to program integrity (e.g., the Department of Justice, the HHS Office of Inspector General, state law enforcement agencies, other federal entities, CMS components) to detect, deter, monitor, and combat fraud and abuse and to take action against those who commit or participate in fraudulent or other unlawful activities.
- In collaboration with other CMS centers, offices, and the COO, develops and implements a comprehensive strategic plan, objectives, and measures to carry out CMS's Medicare, Medicaid, and CHIP program integrity mission and goals and to ensure that program vulnerabilities are identified and resolved.

Reference

Centers for Medicare & Medicaid Services (CMS). 2020. "About CMS." Accessed June 13. www.cms.gov/About-CMS/About-CMS.

APPENDIX

3.3

TRANSPARENCY IN COVERAGE: A PROPOSED RULE

Agency:

Internal Revenue Service, Department of the Treasury; Employee Benefits Security Administration, Department of Labor; Centers for Medicare & Medicaid Services, Department of Health and Human Services.

Action:

Proposed rule.

Summary:

These proposed rules set forth proposed requirements for group health plans and health insurance issuers in the individual and group markets to disclose cost-sharing information upon request, to a participant, beneficiary, or enrollee (or his or her authorized representative), including an estimate of such individual's cost-sharing liability for covered items or services furnished by a particular provider. Under these proposed rules, plans and issuers would be required to make such information available on an internet website and, if requested, through non-internet means, thereby allowing a participant, beneficiary, or enrollee (or his or her authorized representative) to obtain an estimate and understanding of the individual's out-of-pocket expenses and effectively shop for items and services. These proposed rules also include proposals to require plans and issuers to disclose in-network provider negotiated rates, and historical out-of-network allowed amounts through two machine-readable files posted on an internet website, thereby allowing the public to have access to health insurance coverage information that can be used to understand health care pricing and potentially dampen the rise in health care spending. The Department of Health and Human Services (HHS) also proposes amendments to its medical loss ratio program rules to allow issuers offering group or individual health insurance coverage to receive credit in their medical loss ratio calculations for savings they share with enrollees that result from the enrollee's shopping for, and receiving care from, lower-cost, higher-value providers.

Dates:

To be assured consideration, comments must be received at one of the addresses provided below, no later than 5 p.m. on January 14, 2020.

Addresses:

Written comments may be submitted to the addresses specified below. Any comment that is submitted will be shared with the Department of the Treasury (Treasury Department), Internal Revenue Service (IRS) and the Department of Labor (DOL). Please do not submit duplicates.

All comments will be made available to the public. Warning: Do not include any personally identifiable information (such as name, address, or other contact information) or confidential business information that you do not want publicly disclosed. All comments are posted on the internet exactly as received, and can be retrieved by most internet search engines. No deletions, modifications, or redactions will be made to the comments received, as they are public records. Comments may be submitted anonymously.

In commenting, please refer to file code CMS-9915-P. Because of staff and resource limitations, the Departments of Labor, HHS, and the Treasury (the Departments) cannot accept comments by facsimile (FAX) transmission.

Comments must be submitted in one of the following three ways (please choose only one of the ways listed):

1. *Electronically.* You may submit electronic comments on this regulation to www.regulations.gov. Follow the "Submit a comment" instructions.
2. *By regular mail.* You may mail written comments to the following address ONLY: Centers for Medicare & Medicaid Services, Department of Health and Human Services, Attention: CMS-9915-P, P.O. Box 8010, Baltimore, MD 21244-8010.

   Please allow sufficient time for mailed comments to be received before the close of the comment period.
3. *By express or overnight mail.* You may send written comments to the following address ONLY: Centers for Medicare & Medicaid Services, Department of Health and Human Services, Attention: CMS-9915-P,

Mail Stop C4-26-05, 7500 Security Boulevard, Baltimore, MD 21244-1850.

Inspection of Public Comments: All comments received before the close of the comment period are available for viewing by the public, including any personally identifiable or confidential business information that is included in a comment. The comments are posted on the following website as soon as possible after they have been received: www.regulations.gov. Follow the search instructions on that website to view public comments.

For Further Information Contact:

Deborah Bryant, Centers for Medicare and Medicaid Services, (301) 492-4293.

Christopher Dellana, Internal Revenue Service, (202) 317-5500.

Matthew Litton or David Sydlik, Employee Benefits Security Administration, (202) 693-8335.

Customer Service Information: Individuals interested in obtaining information from the DOL concerning employment-based health coverage laws may call the Employee Benefits Security Administration (EBSA) Toll-Free Hotline at 1-866-444-EBSA (3272) or visit DOL's website (www.dol.gov/ebsa). In addition, information from HHS on private health insurance for consumers can be found on the Centers for Medicare & Medicaid Services (CMS) website (www.cms.gov/cciio) and information on health reform can be found at www.healthcare.gov.

Source: Reprinted from Internal Revenue Service, Employee Benefits Security Administration, and Health and Human Services Department. 2019. "Transparency in Coverage." *Federal Register*. Published November 27. www.federalregister.gov/documents/2019/11/27/2019-25011/transparency-in-coverage.

APPENDIX

3.4

EXECUTIVE ORDER ON IMPROVING PRICE AND QUALITY TRANSPARENCY IN AMERICAN HEALTHCARE TO PUT PATIENTS FIRST

By the authority vested in me as President by the Constitution and the laws of the United States of America, it is hereby ordered as follows:

Section 1. *Purpose.* My Administration seeks to enhance the ability of patients to choose the healthcare that is best for them. To make fully informed decisions about their healthcare, patients must know the price and quality of a good or service in advance. With the predominant role that third-party payers and Government programs play in the American healthcare system, however, patients often lack both access to useful price and quality information and the incentives to find low-cost, high-quality care. Opaque pricing structures may benefit powerful special interest groups, such as large hospital systems and insurance companies, but they generally leave patients and taxpayers worse off than would a more transparent system.

Pursuant to Executive Order 13813 of October 12, 2017 (Promoting Healthcare Choice and Competition Across the United States), my Administration issued a report entitled "Reforming America's Healthcare System Through Choice and Competition." The report recommends developing price and quality transparency initiatives to ensure that healthcare patients can make well-informed decisions about their care. In particular, the report describes the characteristics of the most effective price transparency efforts: they distinguish between the charges that providers bill and the rates negotiated between payers and providers; they give patients proper incentives to seek information about the price of healthcare services; and they provide useful price comparisons for "shoppable" services (common services offered by multiple providers through the market, which patients can research and compare before making informed choices based on price and quality).

Shoppable services make up a significant share of the healthcare market, which means that increasing transparency among these services will have a broad effect on increasing competition in the healthcare system as a whole. One study, cited by the Council of Economic Advisers in its 2019 Annual Report, examined a sample of the highest-spending categories of medical cases requiring inpatient and outpatient care. Of the categories of medical cases requiring inpatient care, 73 percent of the 100 highest-spending categories were shoppable. Among the categories of medical cases requiring outpatient care, 90 percent of the 300 highest-spending categories were shoppable. Another study demonstrated that the ability of patients to price-shop imaging services, a particularly fungible and shoppable set of healthcare services, was associated with a per-service savings of up to approximately 19 percent.

Improving transparency in healthcare will also further protect patients from harmful practices such as surprise billing, which occurs when patients receive unexpected bills at highly inflated prices from out-of-network providers they had no opportunity to select in advance. On May 9, 2019, I announced principles to guide efforts to address surprise billing. The principles outline how patients scheduling appointments to receive facility-based care should have access to pricing information related to the providers and services they may need, and the out-of-pocket costs they may incur. Having access to this type of information in advance of care can help patients avoid excessive charges.

Making meaningful price and quality information more broadly available to more Americans will protect patients and increase competition, innovation, and value in the healthcare system.

Sec. 2. *Policy.* It is the policy of the Federal Government to ensure that patients are engaged with their healthcare decisions and have the information requisite for choosing the healthcare they want and need. The Federal Government aims to eliminate unnecessary barriers to price and quality transparency; to increase the availability of meaningful price and quality information for patients; to enhance patients' control over their own healthcare resources, including through tax-preferred medical accounts; and to protect patients from surprise medical bills.

Sec. 3. *Informing Patients About Actual Prices.* (a) Within 60 days of the date of this order, the Secretary of Health and Human Services shall propose a regulation, consistent with applicable law, to require hospitals to publicly post standard charge information, including charges and information based on negotiated rates and for common or shoppable items and services, in an easy-to-understand, consumer-friendly, and machine-readable format using consensus-based data standards that will meaningfully inform patients' decision making and allow patients to compare prices across hospitals. The regulation should require the posting of standard charge information for services, supplies, or fees billed by the hospital or provided by employees of the hospital. The regulation should also require hospitals to regularly update the posted information and establish a monitoring mechanism for the Secretary to ensure compliance with the posting requirement, as needed.

(b) Within 90 days of the date of this order, the Secretaries of Health and Human Services, the Treasury, and Labor shall issue an advance notice of proposed rulemaking, consistent with applicable law, soliciting comment on a proposal to require healthcare providers, health insurance issuers, and self-insured group health plans to provide or facilitate access to information about expected out-of-pocket costs for items or services to patients before they receive care.

(c) Within 180 days of the date of this order, the Secretary of Health and Human Services, in consultation with the Attorney General and the Federal Trade Commission, shall issue a report describing the manners in which the Federal Government or the private sector are impeding healthcare price and quality transparency for patients, and providing recommendations for eliminating these impediments in a way that promotes competition. The report should describe why, under current conditions, lower-cost providers generally avoid healthcare advertising.

Sec. 4. *Establishing a Health Quality Roadmap.* Within 180 days of the date of this order, the Secretaries of Health and Human Services, Defense, and Veterans Affairs shall develop a Health Quality Roadmap (Roadmap) that aims to align and improve reporting on data and quality measures across Medicare, Medicaid, the Children's Health Insurance Program, the Health Insurance Marketplace, the Military Health System, and the Veterans Affairs Health System. The Roadmap shall include a strategy for establishing, adopting, and publishing common quality measurements; aligning inpatient and outpatient measures; and eliminating low-value or counterproductive measures.

Sec. 5. *Increasing Access to Data to Make Healthcare Information More Transparent and Useful to Patients.* Within 180 days of the date of this order, the Secretary of Health and Human Services, in consultation with the Secretaries of the Treasury, Defense, Labor, and Veterans Affairs, and the Director of the Office of Personnel Management, shall increase access to de-identified claims data from taxpayer-funded healthcare programs and group health plans for researchers, innovators, providers, and entrepreneurs, in a manner that is consistent with applicable law and that ensures patient privacy and security. Providing access to this data will facilitate the development of tools that empower patients to be better informed as they make decisions related to healthcare goods and services. Access to this data will also enable researchers and entrepreneurs to locate inefficiencies and opportunities for improvement, such as patterns of performance of medical procedures that are outside the recommended standards of care. Such data may be derived from the Transformed Medicaid Statistical Information System (T-MSIS) and other sources. As part of this process, the Secretary of Health and Human Services shall make a list of priority datasets that, if de-identified, could advance the policies set forth by this order, and shall report to the President on proposed plans for future release of these priority datasets and on any barriers to their release.

Sec. 6. *Empowering Patients by Enhancing Control Over Their Healthcare Resources.* (a) Within 120 days of the date of this order, the Secretary of the Treasury, to the extent consistent with law, shall issue guidance to expand the ability of patients to select high-deductible health plans that can be used alongside a health savings account, and that cover low-cost preventive care, before the deductible, for medical care that helps maintain health status for individuals with chronic conditions.

(b) Within 180 days of the date of this order, the Secretary of the Treasury, to the extent consistent with law, shall propose regulations to treat expenses related to certain types of arrangements, potentially including direct primary care arrangements and healthcare sharing ministries, as eligible medical expenses under Section 213(d) of Title 26, United States Code.

(c) Within 180 days of the date of this order, the Secretary of the Treasury, to the extent consistent with law, shall issue guidance to increase the amount of funds that can carry over without penalty at the end of the year for flexible spending arrangements.

Sec. 7. *Addressing Surprise Medical Billing.* Within 180 days of the date of this order, the Secretary of Health and Human Services shall submit a report to the President on additional steps my Administration may take to implement the principles on surprise medical billing announced on May 9, 2019.

Sec. 8. *General Provisions.* (a) Nothing in this order shall be construed to impair or otherwise affect:

(i) the authority granted by law to an executive department or agency, or the head thereof; or

(ii) the functions of the Director of the Office of Management and Budget relating to budgetary, administrative, or legislative proposals.

(b) This order shall be implemented consistent with applicable law and subject to the availability of appropriations.

(c) This order is not intended to, and does not, create any right or benefit, substantive or procedural, enforceable at law or in equity by any party against the United States, its departments, agencies, or entities, its officers, employees, or agents, or any other person.

DONALD J. TRUMP

THE WHITE HOUSE,

June 24, 2019

Source: Reprinted from Executive Office of the President. 2019. "Improving Price and Quality Transparency in American Healthcare to Put Patients First." Executive order 12877. *Federal Register*. Published June 27. www.federalregister.gov/documents/2019/06/27/2019-13945/improving-price-and-quality-transparency-in-american-healthcare-to-put-patients-first.

APPENDIX

3.5

EXAMPLE OF PUBLIC RESPONSE TO NOTICE OF A FEDERAL PROPOSED RULE

The following letter is one of more than two thousand public comments submitted about a June 2019 presidential executive order proposing rules to promote price transparency in healthcare. Every comment is publicly available at Regulations.gov.

Secretary Azar and Administrator Verma,

Thank you for acknowledging the need for the American public to see the price of their care prior to receiving care.

Price transparency is critical to our citizens, employers, and government to reverse the trend of ever-increasing healthcare costs. Can you imagine going to a grocery store and not knowing the price of an apple until you get the bill, weeks or months after you've eaten it? We as patients deserve to know the REAL price—not an estimate or average—prior to care. We should be able to easily search for it online across providers, insurers, and even cash prices. This rule should apply to all providers, labs, devices, drugs, etc.—not just hospitals. I also urge you to enact a strict penalty for non-compliance. $300/day is nothing to a hospital who can pay its executives' salaries in the millions!

Additionally, I urge you to make both price AND clinical information available to patients in real-time via open, standard APIs. I should be able to export my complete electronic record whenever I want, and the EHI export should not be limited to only certain sections of my record.

I manage the care for myself, my two children, my husband, my aging parents, and a couple friends. In every other facet of our lives, it is easy to access our data, including prices, and share them with whomever we please. Thank you for acknowledging that the system is broken. Transparency is the answer, and through finalizing these rules requiring real price transparency enforced by strict penalties, you can fix the broken system.

Thank you,

Linda

Source: Linda. 2019. Public comment regarding "Centers for Medicare Medicaid Services (CMS) Proposed Rule: Transparency in Coverage CMS-9915-P OFR Display." Regulations.gov. Published December 9. www.regulations.gov/document?D=CMS-2019-0163-0009.

APPENDIX

3.6

POSITION STATEMENT PROMOTING INTEROPERABILITY OF PATIENT DATA

The following letter to the director of the Office of Civil Rights at the US Department of Health and Human Services presents one organization's opinion on proposed modifications to certain Health Insurance Portability and Accountability Act (HIPAA) regulations. Ed Cantwell, the president and CEO of the Center for Medical Interoperability (CMI), a not-for-profit organization whose mission is to "accelerate the seamless exchange of information to improve healthcare for all," argues why interoperability should be promoted.

February 12, 2019

Mr. Roger Severino

Office for Civil Rights

Department of Health and Human Services

200 Independence Avenue SW

Room 509F, HHH Building

Washington, DC 20201

RE: Request for Information on Modifying HIPAA Rules to Improve Coordinated Care, HHS-OCR-0945-AA00, RIN 0945-AA00

Dear Mr. Severino:

Thank you for the opportunity to comment on how Health Insurance Portability and Accountability Act (HIPAA) regulations should be modified to promote care coordination and the transformation to value-based care while preserving the privacy and security of protected health information (PHI). We applaud the Office for Civil Rights (OCR) and the Department of Health and Human Services (HHS) for recognizing the need to improve existing regulations to keep up with the evolving technological ecosystem and to support the ultimate aims of a truly person-centric health care delivery system.

The Center for Medical Interoperability (CMI) is a non-profit organization led by health systems with a mission to *accelerate the seamless exchange of information to improve healthcare for all.* Modeled after centralized labs from other industries, CMI serves as a cooperative research and development lab as well as a test and certification resource to address technical challenges related to comprehensive interoperability, data liquidity, and trust. CMI's CEO-level board of directors identify healthcare industry technology problems that, when solved, will benefit the public good and the healthcare industry. CMI membership is limited to health systems, individuals, and self-insured corporations, but we work with a variety of stakeholders, including medical device manufacturers, electronic health record (EHR) vendors, standards development organizations, and others, to design and engineer the technical infrastructure that will enable comprehensive interoperability, data liquidity, and the trust needed to deliver person-centered medical care.

A sound, long-term strategy for governing the use of digital health information and PHI is necessary to achieve the goal of improved care at lower costs while protecting individual privacy and security. In order for these transformative changes to proceed in alignment with the goals of patients, data stewardship, ownership, permission, and control must be considered and incorporated into current and future privacy and security regulations. The HIPAA Privacy Rule and other regulations should be modified to address challenges and facilitate opportunities in an evolving digital ecosystem. The modification of these regulations should proceed in a way that protects and prioritizes the interests of individuals—and the health systems and clinicians who care for them—while allowing the marketplace to innovate and interact with individuals and their PHI in a responsible and controlled way.

While CMI supports modifying HIPAA to promote effective care coordination and reduce administrative burden, we encourage OCR and HHS to think beyond initiatives that produce incremental improvement in favor of supporting the creation of an expanded national trust and security platform that addresses not only privacy and security but also important topics such as patient identity and interoperability—a current focus for the Centers for Medicare and Medicaid Services (CMS) and the Office of the National Coordinator for Health Information Technology (ONC).

Trust is not only key to achieving the aims of HIPAA, it is critical to the success of all healthcare interoperability and security related regulations and initiatives, like Promoting Interoperability, the proposed rules for information blocking and interoperability and patient access, the Trusted Exchange Framework and Common Agreement, and others. Without trust, a national patient matching and identification initiative will fail. Without trust, provider organizations and patients will not feel safe or comfortable with the external marketplace consuming PHI into applications through an open application programming interface (API). Without trust, healthcare provider organizations will be forced to rely upon only their own internally-curated data instead of working in concert with others. Without trust, medical errors persist and costs rise.

To provide trust, investment in and industry adoption of a trust platform technology architecture, supported by an appropriate governance model, is necessary. This platform will enable secure, comprehensive interoperability and data liquidity throughout the healthcare experience for individuals at the point of care, between care settings, and with the external marketplace. The CMI trust platform approach is based on a distributed, encrypted, ledger-based technology architecture with strong identity and security controls for data access, privacy, integrity, and provenance. This type of solution can connect any number of data sources, including medical devices, EHRs, organizations large and small, and most importantly people in an efficient and secure way allowing for the trusted exchange of information. This approach has many advantages over legacy and point solutions. In addition to being low maintenance and cost-effective, a distributed, encrypted, and ledger-based design is reliable, secure, private, and scalable. We can learn from examples where similar trust platforms have been deployed at scale with remarkable results. Estonia has used distributed, encrypted, and ledger-based technology on a national scale to allow individuals dynamic access to their own digital health data. The Estonia digital citizen approach is the global standard. In practice, these concepts create an environment where all Americans will have a digital longitudinal record of their health and wellness. Because trust is built into the platform through the technology architecture and the associated governance model, the patient becomes a known entity with truly portable PHI recognizable by health systems without concerns for patient matching and identification. A distributed, encrypted trust platform like this is flexible enough to scale across large systems and networks as well as down to the level of the patient within a specific episode of care, enabling an interoperable environment of devices and other modalities not yet seen in healthcare.

This level of trust, security, and connectivity among technologies would improve patient safety and reduce caregiver burden. As a person moves in and out of healthcare settings, his or her data would be omnipresent but secure. The burgeoning marketplace of health applications will continue to flourish as long as it has open access to PHI, but the patient will lose unless all data users have met rigorous standards of trust.

We appreciate the opportunity to provide input during this critical step and urge OCR and HHS to incorporate the principles and recommendations discussed below when considering the future path of HIPAA and related regulations.

Responses to Selected Questions

Questions 1–4

Individuals should be able to access all of their PHI at all times. Access to PHI should be controlled and governed by the individual through use of a trusted and secure platform of electronic exchange. Understanding the limitations of the current system of records and release of information processes, OCR should strike a balance between the patient's right of access to their own PHI and the burdens on health systems to produce such information under any proposed timeline. However, CMI strongly encourages OCR to consider the potential for a trust platform to bring about comprehensive interoperability and data liquidity so that patient requests and their processing are immediate and automated. Now is the time to build upon the investment in EHRs and allow health systems, citizens, and the marketplace to add a trusted personal longitudinal health record.

Question 5

An individual should be able to access his or her PHI from any entity with the information through secure exchange over a trusted platform. However, protections against the unauthorized disclosure of PHI should follow any expansion of the ability to disclose such information.

Congress has clearly stated its intention to allow patients to access their information from businesses willing to provide it to them. Section 4006(b) of the 21st Century Cures Act clarified that "if the individual makes a request to a business associate for access to, or a copy of, protected health information about the individual, or if an individual makes a request to a business associate to grant such access to, or transmit such copy directly to, a person or entity designated by the individual, a business associate may provide the individual with such access or copy, which may be in an electronic form, or grant or transmit such access or copy to such person or entity designated by the individual."[1] Given the current inability of patients to track their health history to build their longitudinal health record, claims information presents a unique opportunity for patients to map their entire health history. CMI believes that unlocking data from more sources will allow patients to better access and use their health information to make more informed decisions and receive better care, but CMI cautions OCR that increasing disclosures without a trust platform could undermine patient privacy and the security of PHI.

Questions 6–12

Given the current structure of health information exchange, health care providers face delays and barriers when attempting to obtain PHI from other covered entities. The adoption and use of a trust platform can transform the mechanics of health information exchange and decrease these delays and barriers. HIPAA does not currently require covered entities to disclose PHI to other covered entities or non-covered entities, and the nature of the fee-for-service payment system disincentivizes these disclosures.

As OCR considers requiring covered entities to disclose PHI when requested by other covered entities for treatment purposes, the treatment and care needs of the individual should be considered above all other concerns. OCR should, however, balance the potential burdens, including costs, placed upon providers to share information with other providers given the current lack of a trust platform.

Given that Congress discouraged information blocking in the 21st Century Cures Act, CMI believes that any changes to requirements for the disclosure of PHI should conform with the regulations related to information blocking.

Questions 13–15

Individuals should have visibility and control over the transmission of their own health information through a trust platform of distributed and encrypted information. Adoption of such a platform could provide the ability for individuals to be much more precise with the permissions and sharing of their health information. The trust platform model allows individuals to securely share only the PHI pertinent to a given interaction. As OCR considers allowing individuals to selectively segment their own health information for disclosure, it should weigh the needs and benefits of sharing complete and accurate information to provide the best possible care to patients and prevent misdiagnosis and death, including death from overdoses. A trust platform will be able to accommodate both the very limited sharing of information as well as the comprehensive sharing of information to conform to whatever the law, regulations, and preferences of the patients and care teams dictate. Any proposed changes to the segmentation of health information should comply with all other health privacy laws and regulations.

Question 16

OCR should ensure that any changes to HIPAA are consistent with rulemaking regarding interoperability and information blocking.

Question 17

The use of a trust platform that allows for patient-mediated exchange of distributed and encrypted health information will allow for more complete and timely disclosure of such data to improve treatment and care coordination.

CMI believes that true person-centric data liquidity will enable a more efficient health system and result in better care for patients while also rendering the minimum necessary standard moot.

Questions 18–20

In a technical sense, one participating organization in a trust platform is no different from any other. A social services agency could be the recipient of data about a person in the exact same way as a healthcare provider organization. Consumer-mediated exchange of health information through a trust platform will establish direct sharing of information with these social services programs, community-based support programs, and other patient supports. CMI believes that cooperation and information sharing among various care providers results in the best patient outcomes. As OCR considers expanding HIPAA disclosures to other aspects of available health and social services, CMI urges the adoption of a trust platform to allow for seamless exchange of PHI through patient control.

Questions 27–42

The current structure of health exchange and antiquated information systems makes accounting for disclosures difficult and expensive. The use of a distributed, encrypted, ledger-based trust platform would simplify accounting for disclosures and allow patient access without burden or cost on the health system. In fact, the responsibility currently held by covered entities would be greatly alleviated. Individuals should have full visibility into their own data usage audit trail, including usage by covered entities, business associates, or any other entity that may be using their PHI. Also, the individual should have full visibility into the reason for the disclosure to covered entities, business associates, and other third parties.

As the volume of available digital health data and the potential applications for that data expand, so does the rapid growth of a new economy and marketplace of entities that have previously been outside of healthcare. While it may be tempting to allow access to PHI for any entity that claims to operate under the banner of "promoting care coordination," *OCR should take note of the broader current consumer privacy debate*. In this new health data ecosystem, the rules and processes that govern and protect PHI must be sensitive to the reality that not all covered entities, business associates, and third parties are created equal. It is important to vet not only the entity that will be using the PHI but also the end to which the PHI will be used. For instance, if a company is requesting PHI to fulfill a treatment purpose but is simultaneously mining, aggregating, and monetizing that data in another business line or product offering, this should be made known to the patient. The consent or authorization to use or disclose PHI should rest solely with the individual and be carefully regulated to avoid violations of personal privacy and security.

Conclusion

The pace of technological change, agile market forces, and increasing use of data in healthcare necessitates a modern approach to the governance of health information. CMI realizes the need for modifications to HIPAA and its Privacy Rule. However, incremental changes that do not envision comprehensive interoperability, data liquidity and trust will not be sufficient to support a value-based and patient-centric health care delivery and payment system.

The current system for accessing and exchanging PHI in America is not capable of addressing the challenges and opportunities related to its protection and use. Without an emphasis on ubiquitous trust in healthcare, exploitation and misconduct are inevitable. Trust is the prerequisite for all digital health initiatives.

CMI proposes a coordinated effort to establish a pervasive trust platform that facilitates the secure transmission and use of PHI among not only covered entities and business associates but the entire marketplace. The CMI trust platform approach is agile enough to ensure robust, person-centered data privacy and security controls while allowing flexibility for long-term growth and innovation in the industry. CMI has begun this work in collaboration with its member organizations, which represent the largest healthcare systems in America, but it cannot succeed on its own. Meaningful progress will require bold and intentional action from government and healthcare leaders.

OCR, CMS, ONC, and other agencies at HHS have the ability to become change agents in this journey. The government is uniquely positioned to create and incent a technological trust platform that will help create a truly learning health system where patients, clinicians, and caregivers win. OCR and HHS should explore and embrace the CMI trust platform approach, and it should use its available levers to compel change and encourage rapid innovation across the industry and marketplace.

It is time to devote the nation's resources and attention to solving the issue that will make it possible to create the patient-centric health care system that we envision. The Center for Medical Interoperability urges OCR, CMS, ONC, and all of HHS to consider our recommendations. We stand ready to assist with HHS's initiatives.

Thank you for your consideration. We welcome the opportunity to work with you and other stakeholders.

Sincerely,

Center for Medical Interoperability

Ed Cantwell, President and CEO

8 City Blvd., Ste. 203

Nashville, TN 37209

Note

1. 42 U.S.C 17935(e)(2) (2016).

Source: Reprinted from E. Cantwell. 2019. Letter to R. Severino, Office for Civil Rights, Department of Health and Human Services, February 12. Center for Medical Interoperability. https://medicalinteroperability.org/publiccomments/CMI_HIPAA_RFI_Response_02_12_2019.pdf.

APPENDIX

3.7

POSITION STATEMENT ON INTEROPERABILITY OF PATIENT DATA: CONCERNS

The following letter by the executive director of the Association of American Physicians and Surgeons presents an excellent counterpoint to comments that promote the interoperability of patient data. The letter argues that interoperability presents risks to patient privacy.

Comments on Docket No. HHS-OCR-0945-AAOO Modifying HIPAA Rules to Improve Coordinated Care

February 11, 2019

Thank you for the opportunity to provide comments on the "Request for Information on Modifying HIPAA Rules to Improve Coordinated Care" Docket No. HHS-OCR-0945-AAOO.

The Association of American Physicians & Surgeons ("AAPS") is a nonprofit membership organization of physicians and surgeons who are mostly in small, independent practices. Founded in 1943 (and celebrating our 75th year), AAPS defends and promotes the practice of private, ethical medicine. AAPS has members in virtually every specialty and State.

We speak out frequently about issues concerning patients and medical practice and have been a longstanding critic of the HIPAA Privacy and Security rules. In 2001 AAPS sued HHS over the agency's implementation of these rules and our suit helped solidify protections for "non-covered entities," and their patients, from harmful aspects of the regulations.

HIPAA Privacy and Security Rules have imposed costly bureaucracy on the practice of medicine that detracts from patient-centered care, without meaningfully protecting patient privacy.

In fact, these rules overall have been destructive of patient control over their personal medical history and records.

Unfortunately, the policies HHS-OCR indicates it is considering in the RFI, rather than moving in a more patient and physician friendly direction, would do further harm.

HHS-OCR states its interest in facilitating "the transformation to value-based health care" and "coordinated care." In practice such objectives are often being implemented in ways contrary to the best interests of patients.

"Value-based" frequently means saving resources for the system, and isn't measured in terms of value to patients. Affordable Care Act penalties tied to hospital readmission are just one recent example. The policy reduced readmission rates but resulted in more patient deaths. "Coordinated Care" often brings in third parties to the physician–patient relationship who have no business interfering in medical care decisions.

Accordingly, from a high-level perspective, we object to the stated goal of the RFI because it conflicts with our mission of putting patients first.

More specifically, AAPS comments on the following items raised in the RFI:

Section a. "Promoting Information Sharing":

1) HHS-OCR asks if HIPAA rules should be modified to further "incentivize, encourage, or require," disclosure of Personal Health Information (PHI) to essentially any entity involved in "care coordination" or "health care operations" without express patient consent. "Care coordination" and "health care operations" are broadly defined meaning that such changes would further improperly exacerbate harm to patient privacy and we would object to any such expansion of non-consented disclosure. (Preamble to section a)
2) HHS-OCR asks if HIPAA rules should be modified to "*require* covered entities to disclose Personal Health Information (PHI) to other covered entities" without express consent of the patient. Currently, the only required disclosures are to the individual patient or to HHS itself. PHI should only be disclosable with the patients' consent except in very limited circumstances. We object to the current HIPAA policy requiring disclosure to HHS-OCR without patient consent. Further we object to any new requirements mandating that patient data be handed over without consent of the patient. (Question 7)
3) HHS-OCR asks whether the ability to disclosure PHI without express patient consent to "multiagency teams" or "social service agencies" should be expanded. No, the patient should need to consent to such disclosures. (Question 19)
4) HHS-OCR raises the possibility of imposing paperwork requirements on physicians who are currently non-covered entities. It also asks

whether "the risks associated with disclosing PHI, to health care providers not subject to HIPAA … outweigh the benefit of sharing PHI." Here, HHS has it upside down. Since HIPAA widely permits the disclosure of PHI without patient consent, it is riskier, from a medical privacy perspective, to have the data in the hands of a HIPAA-covered entity than one that is not covered by HIPAA. In the same light, it would not be productive to impose additional requirements on non-covered entities that serve no protective purpose and that would facilitate data sharing without patient consent. Patient data should not be shared without the patient's consent whether the physician is covered by HIPAA or not. However, data should be released, with patient consent, to persons or entities approved by the patient. (Questions 9 and 10)

5) The RFI also asks whether "population-based case management," "review of service for appropriateness," "utilization review" activities, or "formulary development" should be exempt from the limited protections on patient privacy that do exist in HIPAA. It would be improper to give a virtual army of administrators even more access to patient information than they already have. (Question 17)
6) HHS-OCR asks if patients should have the ability to "opt-out" of certain disclosures. An opt-out provision would be better than no control, but ideally patient data should not be disclosed without consent, i.e. an "opt in" would be required to share patient data. (Question 15)

Section b. "Promoting Parental and Caregiver Involvement":

7) While HIPAA grants unconsented access to PHI, access is simultaneously improperly blocked in circumstances where it should be allowed. HHS-OCR gives a nod to this problem by asking, "Are there circumstances in which parents have been unable to gain access to their minor child's health information . . . because of HIPAA?" Parents should not be blocked from knowing about care provided to their minor children. (Question 24)

Section c. "Accounting of Disclosures":

8) HHS-OCR discusses moving forward with delayed implementation of a HITECH provision requiring that patients have the ability to request a report listing to whom disclosures of PHI from EHRs for "treatment, payment, or healthcare operations (TPO) were made." It would be far more meaningful for patients to be able to restrict disclosure

than to see a list of who their data was disclosed to after the fact. This HITECH measure has something in common with many other HIPAA requirements: they add bureaucratic burdens without actually protecting patient privacy. (Question 42)

Section d. Notices of Privacy Practices:

9) In fact, Section d. raises another example of a regulation that increases costs but does little for patients: the requirement that practices "make a good faith effort" to obtain a patient's signature on a Notice of Privacy Practices (NPP). HHS-OCR asks about the implications of removing this requirement. To the extent that eliminating this mandate would cut red tape, we favor it, especially since the NPP is not generally protective of patient privacy. In fact, patients are reportedly often asked to sign it on a digital signature pad where the text is not readily visible. In addition, staff at medical facilities sometimes incorrectly conclude that a signature on the NPP is a condition of treatment and refuse treatment without a signed form. Given the overall confusion and lack of protection offered by the NPP, we agree it is time for related requirements to end. (Question 45 and 47)

Section e. Additional Ways to Remove Regulatory Obstacles:

10) In Section e. HHS asks for other suggestions "to remove regulatory obstacles . . . while preserving the privacy and security of PHI."

One suggestion is to expand the HITECH provision allowing patients to request restrictions when paying out of pocket for care. In previous rulemaking HHS stated that Medicare patients are able to make use of this provision notwithstanding other regulations that impede their ability to pay for care outside of Medicare. HHS should also grant this same flexibility to Medicaid patients and enrollees in other health plans that may limit their ability to self-pay. Patients should have a clear right to privacy for care they are paying for.

Another suggestion we would ask HHS-OCR to consider is increasing the ability of physicians and other medical professionals to become HIPAA non-covered entities. As we previously stated, HIPAA non-covered entities and their patients have a greater ability to protect patient data than HIPAA covered entities. Unfortunately, physicians claiming non-covered status are increasingly under the impression that they become trapped in HIPAA covered entity status simply because they are helping their patient file prior authorization requests or by receiving payment electronically from an insurer. We would particularly welcome the opportunity to discuss with HHS-OCR bureaucratic burdens non-covered entities encounter and cooperate on solutions. (Question 54)

Thank you for this opportunity to comment. In conclusion, HIPAA regulations are inherently at odds with the principles of patient-centered medicine and patient privacy. We are concerned the RFI signals that further harm to medical privacy rights is forthcoming and ask HHS-OCR to not proceed in a manner that moves in the wrong direction. It is time to re-empower patients with policies that protect them and not empower third parties at their expense.

Sincerely,

Jane M. Orient, M.D.

Executive Director

Association of American Physicians and Surgeons, Inc.

1601 N. Tucson Blvd. Suite 9

Tucson, AZ 85716-3450

Source: J. M. Orient. 2019. "Comments on RFI: 'Modifying HIPAA Rules.'" Association of American Physicians and Surgeons. Published February 11. https://aapsonline.org/comments-on-rfi-modifying-hipaa-rules-to-improve-coordinated-care-.

APPENDIX

3.8

THE ROLE OF THE MEDICARE PAYMENT ADVISORY COMMISSION

The Medicare Payment Advisory Commission (MedPAC), created to ensure that a wide range of expertise would be available to provide input to the US Congress on policymaking issues, describes its role in the following paragraphs.

About MedPAC

The Medicare Payment Advisory Commission (MedPAC) is an independent congressional agency established by the Balanced Budget Act of 1997 (P.L. 10-533) to advise the U.S. Congress on issues affecting the Medicare program. The Commission's statutory mandate is quite broad: In addition to advising the Congress on payments to private health plans participating in Medicare and providers in Medicare's traditional fee-for-service program, MedPAC is also tasked with analyzing access to care, quality of care, and other issues affecting Medicare.

The Commission's 17 members bring diverse expertise in the financing and delivery of health care services. Commissioners are appointed to three-year terms (subject to renewal) by the Comptroller General and serve part time. Appointments are staggered; the terms of five or six Commissioners expire each year. The Commission is supported by an executive director and a staff of analysts, who typically have backgrounds in economics, health policy, public health, or medicine.

MedPAC meets publicly to discuss policy issues and formulate its recommendations to the Congress. In the course of these meetings, Commissioners consider the results of staff research, presentations by policy experts, and comments from interested parties. (Meeting transcripts are available at www.medpac.gov/-public-meetings-). Commission members and staff also seek input on Medicare issues through frequent meetings with individuals interested in the program, including staff from congressional committees and the Centers for Medicare & Medicaid Services (CMS), healthcare researchers, healthcare providers, and beneficiary advocates.

Two reports—issued in March and June each year—are the primary outlet for Commission recommendations. In addition to these reports and others on subjects requested by the Congress, MedPAC advises the Congress through other avenues, including comments on reports and proposed regulations issued by the Secretary of the Department of Health and Human Services, testimony, and briefings for congressional staff.

Source: Reprinted from Medicare Payment Advisory Commission (MedPAC). 2014. "About MedPAC." Accessed April 1. www.medpac.gov/-about-medpac-.

APPENDIX

3.9

OPERATION OF MEDICARE PARTS A AND B

Working with its Medicare contractors, the operation of Medicare Parts A and B by the Centers for Medicare & Medicaid Services (CMS) includes processing claims, enrolling providers in the Medicare program, handling provider reimbursement services, processing appeals, responding to provider inquiries, educating providers about the program, and administering the participating physician/supplier program (PARDOC). These operating activities are described in more detail in the following CMS explanation, which has been adapted for brevity and updated.

Bills/Claims Payments

The Medicare contractors are responsible for processing and paying Part A bills and Part B claims correctly and in a timely manner. By 2014, most providers were submitting their claims in electronic format—99.8 percent for Part A and more than 97.5 percent for Part B.

Provider Enrollment

CMS and its Medicare contractors are responsible for both enrolling providers and suppliers into the Medicare program and ensuring that they continue to meet the requirements for their provider or supplier type. Enrollment includes several verification processes to ensure that Medicare is only paying qualified providers and suppliers. In addition, the Medicare program requires that all new enrollees or those changing their enrollment obtain Medicare payments by electronic funds transfer.

Provider Reimbursement Services

Medicare Part A providers are required to file an annual cost report. In addition to determining the amount paid for overhead items, the cost report is used to finalize prospective add-ons to the payment system and includes such items as payments for graduate medical education, indirect medical education, disproportionate share hospitals (those serving a significantly disproportionate number of low-income patients), and bad debt payments. The contractors' provider reimbursement area performs several activities, most requiring substantial manual effort, including these:

- Reviewing rates to establish and adjust interim reimbursement rates for add-on payments
- Performing quarterly reviews when the provider has elected to be paid on a biweekly basis, in lieu of actual claims payments
- Reviewing payments to all hospice providers to determine if the hospice exceeded the aggregate or inpatient cap
- Maintaining files of provider-specific data (such as the disproportionate share hospital adjustment) to calculate the provider's claims payment
- Maintaining systems such as the provider statistical and reimbursement system, which contains all the claims information needed to settle cost reports, and the system for tracking audit and reimbursement, which tracks the cost report through final settlement
- Determining a hospital's provider-based status, which affects the amount of reimbursement the hospital is entitled to receive
- Reporting and collecting provider overpayments
- Identifying delinquent debt and referring debts to the Treasury Department for collection

Medicare Appeals

The statutorily mandated Medicare appeals process enables beneficiaries, providers, and suppliers to dispute an unfavorable contractor determination, including coverage and payment decisions. There are five levels in the Medicare Parts A and B appeals process. The steps start with the Medicare administrative contractor (MAC) and end with judicial review in federal district court. In FY 2014, for example, CMS had anticipated that the MACs would process 3.8 million redeterminations.

Provider Inquiries

CMS coordinates communication between Medicare contractors and providers to ensure consistent responses. To accomplish this, CMS requires the Medicare contractors to maintain a provider contact center (PCC) that can respond to telephone and written (letters, e-mail, fax) inquiries. The primary goal of the PCC is to deliver timely, accurate, accessible, and consistent information to providers in a courteous and professional manner. These practices are designed to help providers understand the Medicare program and, ultimately, bill for their services correctly.

CMS had estimated that it would receive 34.2 million telephone inquiries in FY 2014. CMS has made a number of efforts that contributed to decreased volume in fee-for-service (FFS) provider calls to MACs' toll-free lines. These efforts have included the following:

- Major improvements in education, including major new lines of educational products associated with FFS Medicare
- Improved CMS and MAC websites that host Medicare information
- Improved outreach to FFS providers through national and local provider association partners, expanded MAC provider electronic mailing lists, and expanded CMS provider electronic e-mail lists
- Increased number of MAC provider internet portals for claims-related transaction information
- Improved training of MAC call center customer service representatives

Participating Physician/Supplier Program (PARDOC)

PARDOC helps reduce the impact of rising healthcare costs on beneficiaries by increasing the number of enrolled physicians and suppliers who participate in Medicare. Participating providers agree to accept Medicare-allowed payments as payment in full for their services. The MACs conduct an annual enrollment process and monitor limiting-charge compliance to ensure that beneficiaries are not being charged more than Medicare allows. Every year, the MACs are instructed to furnish participation enrollment materials to providers. The open enrollment period runs from November 15 through December 31 of each year. CMS has more information about physicians participating in Medicare at www.medicare.gov. The National Participating Physician Directory includes the providers' medical school and year of graduation, any board certification in a specialty, gender, hospitals at which they have admitting privileges, and any foreign language capabilities.

Provider Outreach and Education

The goal of provider outreach and education is to reduce errors by helping providers manage Medicare-related matters on a daily basis and properly bill the Medicare program. The Medicare contractors are required to educate providers and their staff about the fundamentals of the program, policies and procedures, new initiatives, and significant changes, including any of the more than 500 change requests that CMS issues each year. They also identify potential issues by analyzing provider inquiries, claim submission errors, medical review data, comprehensive error rate testing data, and the Recovery Audit Program data.

CMS encourages its contractors to be innovative in their outreach approach and to use a variety of strategies and methods for disseminating information. Techniques include the use of print media, digital resources, telephone calls, educational messages on the general-inquiries phone line, face-to-face instruction, and presentations in classrooms and other settings.

Enterprise Data Centers

The enterprise data centers (EDCs) are the foundation of all CMS production data center operations. Traditionally, the Medicare contractors either operated their own data centers or contracted out these services. As part of its contracting reform initiative, CMS reduced the number of data centers from more than one dozen separate small centers to three large EDCs. CMS manages these contracts and has achieved administrative efficiencies from this consolidation, which also delivers greater performance, security, reliability, and operational control. In addition, the new EDC infrastructure gives CMS flexibility in meeting current and future data-processing challenges. This flexibility is critical as the workloads for FFS claims continue to grow and Medicare claims-processing applications require a more stable environment.

Source: Condensed and adapted from Centers for Medicare & Medicaid Services (CMS). 2014. *Justification of Estimates for Appropriations Committees*, 31–34. Accessed June 13, 2020. www.cms.gov/About-CMS/Agency-Information/PerformanceBudget/Downloads/FY2014-CJ-Final.pdf.

APPENDIX

3.10

EXAMPLE OF CHALLENGES FACED BY THE OFFICE OF INSPECTOR GENERAL AT HEALTH AND HUMAN SERVICES

The following excerpt from the Office of Inspector General 2019 report on challenges the Department of Health and Human Services (HHS) must address shows the extent of the issues HHS must consider for its goal of financial integrity.

Ensuring the Financial Integrity of HHS Programs

The Department of Health and Human Services (HHS or the Department) is the largest civilian agency in the Federal Government, with a $1.2 trillion budget in fiscal year (FY) 2019, representing more than one-third of the total Federal budget. HHS's Medicare program is the Nation's largest health insurer, handling more than 1 billion claims per year. Medicare and Medicaid, the Department's largest programs, comprise 49 percent of the U.S. health care insurance economy. More than 136 million beneficiaries, or more than 40 percent of Americans, rely on these programs for their health insurance, including senior citizens, individuals with disabilities, low-income families and individuals, and patients with end-stage renal disease.

CMS bears the responsibility at HHS for administering these programs. Federal Medicare expenditures totaled $644.8 billion in FY 2019; Federal Medicaid spending totaled $418.7 billion in FY 2019 (with an additional $18.6 billion for the Children's Health Insurance Program (CHIP)).

HHS is also the largest grant-making and fourth-largest contracting agency in the Federal Government. In FY 2018, HHS awarded $109 billion in grants (excluding CMS) and $25 billion in contracts. Responsible stewardship that ensures the transparency and accountability of HHS funds is paramount to making sure that HHS beneficiaries and the American public get the true benefit of this substantial financial investment.

The Department must protect the fiscal integrity of HHS funds and ensure that beneficiaries have access to the services they need, especially in light of looming financial shortfalls in the Medicare program, the expansion of Medicaid services to a larger population, and the increased use of grants as funding tools to achieve program results. HHS should take steps to control costs by ensuring proper pricing for goods and services; reducing improper payments; and preventing, detecting, and prosecuting fraud in HHS programs. The Department must not only manage both the efficient and effective use of funds internally but also oversee the thousands of external funding recipients' use of Federal funds to fulfill HHS's mission.

Controlling Costs by Ensuring Proper Payment for Goods and Services

Whether HHS is paying for medical services, prescription drugs, or complex information technology (IT) solutions, managing what the Department pays and recognizing and remedying payment policies that inadvertently incentivize improper billing or inflate prices are critical to controlling costs.

Medicare

Medicare should act as a prudent payer on behalf of taxpayers and beneficiaries, including instituting payment policies delivering greater value. (See TMC 2 for more information on value-based payment models.) In certain contexts, Medicare payment policies, which are generally set by statute, result in Medicare and beneficiaries paying more for care provided in certain settings than for the same care provided in other settings. For example, Medicare could have potentially saved $4.1 billion over a 6-year period if swing-bed services at critical access hospitals had been paid for at the same rates as at skilled nursing facilities (SNFs). Likewise, Medicare pays hospitals different amounts for the same care depending on whether the hospital admits beneficiaries as inpatients or treats them as outpatients. Some payment policies create financial inequities that actually may drive up Medicare costs without improving care for beneficiaries. For example, the OIG found that Medicare payments to SNFs for therapy greatly exceeded SNFs' costs for that therapy, creating an environment that provides incentives to bill for unnecessary therapy.

Prescription Drug Programs

Vulnerabilities exist in HHS's payment strategies for prescription drugs and biologicals. HHS programs accounted for 40 percent ($136 billion) of the total U.S. prescription drug expenditures in 2017. Increases in prescription drug prices have contributed to the growth in total prescription drug spending. Increases in drug prices may limit patients' access to needed prescription drugs if the out-of-pocket costs become unaffordable. The way that Medicare and Medicaid pay for drugs, in addition to fundamental differences in how the Medicare Part B and Part D programs are structured, can result in additional costs for programs and their beneficiaries. In the Part D program, for example,

OIG found that although there was a 17-percent decrease in Medicare Part D prescriptions for brand-name drugs from 2011 to 2015, there was a 77-percent increase in total reimbursement for these drugs, leading to greater overall Part D spending and higher beneficiary out-of-pocket costs. In the Part B program, OIG found that Medicare would have saved millions of dollars if dispensing fees for several drugs had been aligned with the rates that Part D and State Medicaid programs paid. In addition, CMS includes prices for higher-cost versions of drugs that are not covered under Medicare Part B when setting Part B payment amounts. OIG found that, because CMS included noncovered versions when setting payment for two Part B drugs, Medicare and beneficiaries paid an extra $366 million from 2014 through 2016. HHS must endeavor to limit the impact of high prices on programs and beneficiaries while protecting access to medically necessary drugs. Additionally, the Department should be prepared to address coverage and reimbursement challenges of emerging technologies, such as biosimilars and gene therapies like chimeric antigen receptor T-cell therapy.

Contracts

Better controls in HHS's contracting process could strengthen competition and pricing for HHS-purchased goods and services. OIG has identified vulnerabilities in acquisition planning and monitoring of procurement and contracts. For instance, key HHS contracts may not always undergo Contract Review Board oversight before being awarded, and when awarding contracts, CMS has not always performed thorough reviews of contractors' past performance. Similarly, in the past, CMS and other OpDivs have frequently chosen contract types that place the risk of cost increases solely on the Government.

Reducing Improper Payments

Due to their size, HHS programs account for some of the largest estimated improper payments in the Federal Government. Medicare, Medicaid, and CHIP accounted for $86.1 billion, or 99.6 percent, of the $86.4 billion in improper payments that HHS reported in its FY 2018 Agency Financial Report. Furthermore, insufficient HHS oversight of grant programs and contracts poses risks of significant improper payments and payments for unallowable costs.

Medicare

Traditional Medicare fee-for-service (FFS) accounted for $31.6 billion, or about 37 percent, of the improper payments that HHS reported. Notably, this improper payment rate decreased from 9.5 percent, or $36.2 billion, in FY 2017 to 8.1 percent in FY 2018. This represents positive momentum upon which the Department and CMS can build. However, some types of providers and suppliers pose heightened risk to the financial security of Medicare. For instance, OIG and CMS have identified especially high rates of improper payments for home health, hospice, and SNF care, durable medical equipment (DME), chiropractic services, and certain hospital services. HHS and CMS have taken corrective actions for the Medicare FFS program focusing on specific service areas with high improper payment rates. Although this year's reduction in the improper payment rate was driven by a reduction in improper payments for home health and SNF claims, CMS should take further action to reduce improper payments among certain provider and supplier types and in geographic locations that present a high risk to the financial security of Medicare. Further, CMS should ensure that it is prepared to detect and prevent improper payments in burgeoning areas, such as telemedicine and genetic testing.

Medicaid

Medicaid is a Federal–State financing partnership with the 50 States, 5 territories, and the District of Columbia, each offering its own program variations reflecting State and local needs and preferences. CMS's Payment Error Rate Measurement (PERM) program measures improper payments in Medicaid and CHIP in all 50 States and the District of Columbia using a 17-State 3-year rotation. In FY 2018, the improper payment rate for the Medicaid program was 9.8 percent. OIG audits have identified substantial improper payments to providers across a variety of Medicaid services, including school-based, nonemergency medical transportation, targeted case management, and personal care services. CMS has engaged with State Medicaid agencies to develop corrective action plans that address State-specific reasons for improper payments identified through the PERM program. OIG work has also identified that States are not always correctly determining eligibility of individuals to receive Medicaid benefits, resulting in potential improper payments. Given that CMS will resume the Medicaid eligibility component measurement and report updated national eligibility estimates for FY 2019, the improper payment rate may significantly increase for this fiscal year.

Grants and Contracts

Administering grant programs and contracts requires HHS to implement internal controls to ensure program goals are met and funds are used appropriately. For grant programs, this includes oversight and guidance to award recipients. HHS is responsible for providing up-to-date policies to grant recipients and helping States and other grantees address their own financial management and internal control issues. Without proper internal controls, funds may be misspent, duplication of services may occur, and sub-recipients may not be adequately monitored. OIG has identified grantee-level concerns in several HHS programs, including some Office of Refugee Resettlement (ORR) Unaccompanied Alien Children (UAC) Program grantees reporting unallowable costs and lacking effective systems for administering program funds; and States not sufficiently overseeing their Child Care and Development Fund (CCDF) program payments.

As a critical element of ensuring that grant funds are used appropriately, HHS must track and report improper payment rates for its risk-susceptible grant programs, in keeping with the *Improper Payments Information Act of 2002*. However, since the inception of these reporting requirements, HHS has not reported an improper payment estimate for the Temporary Assistance for Needy Families (TANF) program. States receive block grants ($16.5 billion annually) to design and operate TANF programs. HHS has stated that it does not believe it has the statutory authority to collect from States the data necessary for calculating an improper payment rate for the TANF program. The Office of Management and Budget (OMB) has identified TANF as a risk-susceptible program that must report estimated rates and amounts of improper payments. HHS must continue to pursue needed legislative remedies to develop an appropriate methodology for measuring TANF payment accuracy and report an improper payment estimate for TANF.

In terms of the Department's oversight of contracts, HHS has taken steps to enhance its acquisition systems and better monitor contract closeouts and contract payments. Moreover, CMS has increased its efforts in examining workload statistics for benefit integrity contractors and improving performance outcomes. However, OIG has identified problems with the Department's processes for contract closeouts. CMS relies extensively on contractors to carry out its mission and spends billions of dollars each year in contracts. Because improper payments may be identified and recovered during the closeout process, it is imperative that contracts are closed in accordance with Federal Acquisition Regulation (FAR) requirements. The closeout process, generally, is the last chance for improper contract payments to be detected and recovered, and delayed closeout poses a financial risk to agency funds. OIG found that a large backlog of unfinalized indirect cost rates may have contributed to the untimely closeout of CMS contracts totaling $25 billion. Although CMS has taken steps to improve its closeout and contract management processes, the Department needs to take additional actions to ensure that it is meeting FAR requirements.

Combating Fraud, Waste, and Abuse in HHS Programs

Fraud, waste, and abuse divert needed program resources to inappropriate, unauthorized, or illegal purposes. Effectively fighting fraud, waste, and abuse requires vigilance and sustained focus on preventing problems from occurring in the first place, detecting problems promptly when they occur, and rapidly remediating detected problems through investigations, enforcement, and corrective actions. To accomplish this, HHS must have controls to ensure the proper use of resources and to detect and prevent fraud. The Department should also apply a robust program integrity strategy to protect current and future HHS programs.

Program Integrity Strategies

HHS programs must be designed with program integrity in mind. These strategies must take into account the various methods that HHS uses to implement its programs, including how public and private partners can help in meeting the Department's mission. Additionally, these strategies must include systems and processes to detect and prevent fraud, as well as plans for addressing fraud when it occurs.

Systems and Processes for Detecting and Preventing Fraud

With respect to detecting and preventing fraud and improper payments, CMS's Fraud Prevention System (FPS) serves as an important tool that should be improved to increase its effectiveness. Since 2011, the FPS has continuously run predictive algorithms and other sophisticated analytics nationwide against Medicare FFS claims prior to payment to identify, prevent, and stop fraudulent claims. However, OIG found that the FPS is not as effective in preventing fraud, waste, and abuse in Medicare as it could be and recommended that CMS should make better use of the performance results within its FPS to refine and enhance its predictive analytic models.

In the Medicare and Medicaid programs, States must keep bad actors intent on committing fraud from participating in the programs. With respect to Medicaid in particular, significant problems remain for ensuring all high-risk Medicaid providers undergo criminal background checks. Further, States are not sharing provider enrollment data with Federal and State partners to streamline the Medicaid enrollment process. Sharing these data would reduce the chance for error within any one of the State and Federal databases and help in identifying fraud schemes and other vulnerabilities that cross State lines. CMS should continue to work directly with States to implement tools such as fingerprint-based criminal background checks for high-risk providers. Further, CMS should develop a central repository or "one-stop shop" with provider information that all States and Medicare can use.

Medicare and Medicaid

Schemes to steal money from Medicare and Medicaid take many forms and vary depending on setting and services provided. These fraud schemes can be as simple as billing for services not provided and identity theft or as complex as kickbacks, improper prescribing, deceptive marketing, and money laundering. The perpetrators of fraud schemes range from highly respected physicians to individuals with no prior experience in the health care industry to organized criminal enterprises.

Managed care continues to play an increasingly important role in Medicare and Medicaid. Unlike in FFS, where CMS (Medicare) or the State (Medicaid) pays providers directly for each covered service received by a beneficiary, under managed care, CMS or the State pays a population-based fee to a managed care plan for each person enrolled in the plan. In turn, the plan pays providers for services a beneficiary may require that are included in the plan's contract with CMS or the State. Managed care is the primary delivery system for Medicaid, covering at least some services for more than 80 percent of all enrollees. In Medicare, one-third of beneficiaries are enrolled in Medicare Advantage organizations (MAOs). HHS faces a significant challenge in protecting managed care programs and other non-traditional models against fraud, waste, and abuse.

OIG has found weaknesses in MAOs' and Medicaid managed care organizations' (MCOs) efforts to identify and address fraud and abuse by their providers. CMS requires MAOs and Medicaid MCOs to implement compliance plans that include measures to prevent, detect, and correct instances of fraud, waste, and abuse and non-compliance with CMS's program requirements. However, these plans vary widely among the MAOs, as does the detection of suspected fraud. In Medicaid managed care, program integrity responsibilities are even more dispersed, as they are shared among CMS, States, and MCOs. This makes effective oversight by CMS more complex and challenging.

CMS is working to validate the completeness and accuracy of MAO and Medicaid MCO encounter data and recently has released best practices guidance for MAOs to improve encounter data submission. CMS is also working with States to provide technical assistance and education to identify and share best practices for improving Medicaid MCO identification and referral of cases of suspected fraud or abuse.

CMS should take further actions to ensure the completeness, validity, and timeliness of Medicaid encounter data. Further, CMS should work with its contractors and with States to make improvements in efforts to identify and address fraud and abuse. Additionally, CMS should work to ensure that appropriate information and referrals are sent to law enforcement.

Grants and Contracts

Without adequate oversight and internal controls, grants and contracts are vulnerable to fraud schemes, including embezzlement. HHS has worked to strengthen some of its program integrity efforts focused on grant programs. For instance, it issued guidance to HHS awarding OpDivs about facilitating a review of prospective grantees prior to awarding grants. This information enhances awarding OpDivs' assessment of prospective grant recipients' integrity and potential performance.

Fraud Involving Prescription Opioids

Opioid-related fraud encompasses a broad range of criminal activity, from prescription drug diversion to addiction treatment schemes. OIG investigations show that opioid drug diversion (the redirection of legitimate drugs for illegitimate purposes) is on the rise. Diverted opioid drugs are at high risk to be used inappropriately and create significant harm, including increased risk of overdose. Also at high risk for diversion are potentiator drugs (drugs that exaggerate euphoria and escalate the potential for misuse when combined with opioids) and drugs indicated to treat opioid use disorders (OUDs) (particularly buprenorphine).

OpDivs should improve efforts to identify and investigate potential fraud and abuse in prescription drug programs. For instance, CMS should collect comprehensive data from Medicare Part D plan sponsors. CMS should ensure that national Medicaid data are adequate to detect suspected fraud or abuse. The lack of reliable national Medicaid data hampers enforcement efforts. (See TMC 5.) CMS and States should follow up on prescribers with questionable prescribing patterns to ensure that Medicare Part D and Medicaid are not paying for unnecessary drugs that are being diverted for resale or recreational use. OIG has also recommended that the Indian Health Service (IHS) improve its internal controls against opioid-related fraud, including controls at entry points to sensitive areas of its hospitals to protect its pharmacy inventory from unauthorized access. In addition, the Department must guard against fraud in OUD treatment programs, including, for example, the submission of fraudulent insurance claims for purported OUD treatment and testing services.

Monitoring and Reporting on the Integrity of HHS Programs

HHS must ensure the completeness, accuracy, and timeliness of financial and program information provided to other entities, both internal and external to the Federal Government. Responsible stewardship of HHS programs is vital to operating a financial management and administrative infrastructure that employs appropriate safeguards to minimize risk and provide oversight for the protection of resources. Although HHS continues to maintain a clean opinion on their basic financial statements that culminate the results of their programs, addressing weaknesses in financial management systems and meeting the requirements of the *Digital Accountability and Transparency Act (DATA Act) of 2014* remain challenges for HHS.

Addressing Weaknesses in Financial Management Systems

Financial management systems help OpDivs ensure operational effectiveness and efficiency, financial reporting reliability, and compliance with applicable laws and regulations. OIG continues to find significant deficiencies in internal controls over segregation of duties, configuration management for approved changes to

HHS financial systems, and access to HHS financial systems. HHS must take additional actions to address and resolve these issues, including continuing to work to control user access, ensuring proper approval of and documentation supporting system changes, and ensuring appropriate segregation of duties so that no one employee can both enter and approve information entered into HHS financial management systems.

Meeting the Requirements of the DATA Act of 2014

The DATA Act required agencies to use Government-wide data standards to report financial and award information into USAspending.gov. For FYs 2017, 2019, and 2021, the DATA Act also requires the Inspector General of each agency to determine the accuracy, completeness, timeliness, and quality of these data. In FY 2018, OIG performed an additional audit to follow-up on prior issues and monitor and provide feedback on the progress made by the Department. For FY 2018, OIG's audit of compliance with the DATA Act found that HHS complied with data standards but continued to rely on a manual, labor-intensive process. HHS needs to continue to automate the standardization and transmission of data to the Department of Treasury.

Source: Office of Inspector General (OIG). 2019. "1: Ensuring the Financial Integrity of HHS Programs." In *2019 Top Management and Performance Challenges Facing HHS*, 5–11. Accessed January 12, 2020. http://oig.hhs.gov/reports-and-publications/top-challenges/2019.

PART

4

CHARTING THE FUTURE

In the first three parts of this book, we examined what constitutes health and in what contexts health policy is made. We toured a brief history of federalism in the United States and examined legislative policy. We noted that the identification of a problem, the existence of one or more plausible solutions, and favorable political circumstances comprise the window of opportunity for change. The opening of that metaphorical window leads to agenda setting and development of legislation. Understanding that a policy—or a law—is meaningless unless brought to life through implementation, we examined implementation and the concept of judicial review. In part 4, we now turn to the future. As management scholar Peter Drucker said, "You cannot predict the future, but you can create it" (Cohen 2009, 4). To that end, part 4 is titled "Charting the Future," and it addresses two concepts. Chapter 9 examines policy modification—how to create the future by building on the past. Then, in chapter 10, we discuss the concept of health policy competencies. What does it mean for a health services administrator to be competent with regard to health policy? Chapter 10 will attempt to answer that question in several ways, both in describing what a health service professional can do to gain competency and in suggesting issues and opportunities to apply the competencies they should consider, depending on where, how, and with whom they serve. Taken together, the two chapters invite you to create the future.

Reference

Cohen, W. 2009. *Drucker on Leadership: New Lessons from the Father of Modern Management*. San Francisco: Jossey-Bass.

ENGAGING THE FUTURE

This policy snapshot is unlike the others in parts 1, 2, and 3. Those snapshots related a story about some aspect of policy and the policymaking process. This snapshot invites you to create your own story by engaging the future—to set the path from what is to what will be.

Policy, as we have seen, is continually changing. It usually moves in small increments; once in a generation, a sea change occurs: Social Security in 1935, Medicare and Medicaid in 1965, and the Affordable Care Act in 2010. To be sure, other pieces of major legislation have been enacted between those major events. Examples include the initiation of Part D for Medicare and the 21st Century Cures Act, but none of these initiatives move the policy needle to the same degree that the three major policy transformations mentioned here. Likewise, policy ebbs and flows. For example, during one era, the arc of history is characterized by major policy initiatives in the direction of protecting individuals from the cost of care and shifting the cost to the public sector, despite increasing public expenses. At other times, policymaking will flow in the other direction, seizing on the opportunity to reduce public sector costs and shifting the burden back to the individual, despite the ensuing barrier to care for many.

The root of this confusion is uniquely American among developed countries. As a nation and as a society, we have failed to answer one basic question clearly: Is healthcare an *unconditional right* of every American? Or is it a *commodity* available only to the extent that one can afford it? The correct answer to this question is, in the best of American traditions, up to each individual. Thus, at times the policymaking process responds to societal needs by providing greater public support for access to care. And at other times, policymaking responds to that moment's prevailing public voices and slows public support for access to healthcare. As demonstrated in the policy model used throughout this book, the fluctuation merely represents the changing tide of political, economic, social, and other factors.

Healthcare professionals, however, have chosen to dedicate their time and talents to ensuring high-quality care to as many people as they can. Indeed, as discussed below, they have an ethical obligation to extend this level of care.

With that in mind, how do we propose to answer this root question: Is healthcare a commodity or a basic human right? What is your view, and why? Think about that as you read this snapshot.

As you consider that foundational question, let's review a few facts about the US healthcare system. Chapter 1 explained that estimated healthcare expenditures for the United States in 2018 were $3.647 billion. This amounts to $11,121 per capita and represents 17.8 percent of the US gross domestic product (GDP) (CMS 2019). The average for all Organisation for Economic Co-operation and Development (OECD) countries is $3,992 per capita and 8.8 percent of GDP (Tikkanen 2020).

One measure of effectiveness—or ineffectiveness—of the US healthcare system is maternal mortality. For every 100,000 births in the United States, 17.4 women die. By comparison, that same statistic for Italy is 2 (Zephryn and Declercq 2020). Of additional critical importance, this tragedy is visited disproportionately on women of color: In the United States, African American women are 22 percent more likely to die from breast cancer than white women are and 71 percent more likely to die from cervical cancer. And a stunning 243 percent are more likely to die because of pregnancy and delivery than white women are (Hostetter and Klein 2018).

Exhibits A, B, and C present a more complete picture. The exhibits rank the United States and other selected OECD countries on several measures organized by category for presentation here. In each exhibit, the *lower* the value assigned, the *better* the performance for that indicator.

Exhibit A compares the nations on various spending and utilization indicators. Note that the United States ranks last in the number of doctors per thousand people and last in both spending categories. In short, the United States spends more than does any other OECD country listed, but certainly not because it has too many physicians! Indeed, the United States has, in relative terms, the fewest. Nor can the high spending be attributed to hospital utilization: The country ranks in the middle for hospital utilization, as represented by average length of stay (ALOS).

For the public health indicators shown in exhibit B, it is shocking to note that the United States ranks last in life expectancy and in rates of obesity, multiple chronic conditions, and suicides but second in breast cancer screenings and flu vaccinations (for those over 65). Populations in other countries are, for whatever reason, less obese and less likely to have multiple chronic conditions (many of which are linked to obesity). Conversely, the US ranks worse relative to other OECD countries.

Finally, exhibit C ranks countries on certain indicators of healthcare efficacy. The US top ranking in breast cancer survival suggests that early screening is an effective tool. But unfortunately, the vast disparity in survival rates for African American women, as described earlier, shows that US efficacy for this

EXHIBIT A
Rankings by Country for Healthcare Spending, Infrastructure, and Utilization Indicators

	Country Rank for Each Parameter			
Country	**Spending as % of GDP**	**Per Capita Spending**	**Physicians per 1,000**	**ALOS***
United States	11	11	11	6
Switzerland	10	10	2	5
Germany	9	8	3	11
France	8	4	8	7
Sweden	7	7	4	4
Canada	6	5	10	10
Norway	5	9	1	9
Netherlands	4	6	6	3
United Kingdom	3	2	9	8
Australia	1	3	5	1
New Zealand	1	1	7	2

Source: Adapted from Tikkanen (2020).

*ALOS, average length of stay.

indicator is not distributed equitably. Furthermore, the hypertension discharge statistic is plausibly related to obesity, demonstrating again the importance of nonmedical determinants of health. The data in exhibit C are, again, rankings of the OCED countries represented. And again, the United States is the last in mortality amenable to healthcare and next to last in patients discharged from the hospital with hypertension.

In general, the data represented in these exhibits suggest that the United States spends more than any other country by any measure and achieves poor to middling outcomes with only occasional blips of excellence. For example, exhibit A shows that the United States spends more per capita than does any other OECD nation in the study and that New Zealand spends the least per capita. This is not to say least is best, or that most is bad, per se. The results need to be commensurate with the spending. Spending must be measured against the effectiveness of the healthcare system.

In light of where the United States stands in relation to other OECD countries, consider this question: What kind of future do you want to create for yourself and your fellow inhabitants of the planet earth? Both sides of the right-versus-commodity question have ideas about how to address the issues represented by data in these exhibits.

EXHIBIT B Rankings by Country for Selected Public Health Indicators

	Country Rank for Each Parameter					
Country	**Life Expectancy at Birth**	**% Obese**	**% with Multiple Chronic Conditions**	**Suicides per 100,000**	**Breast Cancer Screen***	**Flu Vaccination†**
United States	11	11	11	11	2	2
Switzerland	1	1	4	4	11	No data
Germany	10	6	7	2	9	8
France	3	5	8	10	10	6
Sweden	5	3	9	3	1	7
Canada	6	7	10	8	8	5
Norway	2	2	5	7	4	9
Netherlands	8	4	1	6	3	4
United Kingdom	9	8	2	1	5	1
Australia	4	9	3	9	7	No data
New Zealand	7	10	6	5	6	3

Source: Adapted from Tikkanen (2020).

*Percentage of women aged 50 to 69 screened.

†Percentage of people older than 65 vaccinated.

Your evaluation of the questions that follow should not be merely a reactive or an instinctive personal opinion. You are invited to present your perspective as an ethical, professional healthcare administrator. Your professional opinion should be informed not only by your expertise but also through the lens of the ethical obligations of a professional healthcare administrator.

To place the right-versus-commodity question in an ethical framework, we may find it useful to center the question on the evolving roles of these five domains:

1. Ethics and the common good
2. Social insurance (Medicare)
3. State governments, Medicaid, and the Affordable Care Act (ACA)
4. Public health
5. Technology

EXHIBIT C
Ranking by Country of Selected Health System Performance Indicators

	Country Rank for Each Parameter			
Country	**Mortality Amenable to Healthcare***	**Hypertension Discharges†**	**5-Year Breast Cancer Survival**	**5-Year Cervical Cancer Survival**
United States	11	10	1	11
Switzerland	1	3	9	2
Germany	10	11	10	8
France	2	9	7	9
Sweden	5	5	3	3
Canada	7	7	4	6
Norway	3	4	5	1
Netherlands	6	1	8	4
United Kingdom	9	2	11	10
Australia	4	8	2	7
New Zealand	8	6	6	5

Source: Adapted from Tikkanen (2020).

* Deaths per 100,000.

† Number of discharges with hypertension per 100,000.

The Evolving Role of Ethics and the Common Good

Everyone in healthcare is a caregiver of some kind. Even in management, the obligation is to the patient and the community at large, not merely other stakeholders and other managers. In the following box is an excerpt from the American College of Healthcare Executives (ACHE) Code of Ethics.

ACHE Code of Ethics
V: The Healthcare Executive's Responsibility to Community and Society

The healthcare executive shall:

A. Work to identify and meet the healthcare needs of the community;
B. Work to identify and seek opportunities to foster health promotion in the community;

(continued)

C. Work to support access to healthcare services for all people;
D. Encourage and participate in public dialogue on healthcare policy issues, and advocate solutions that will improve health status and promote quality healthcare;
E. Apply short- and long-term assessments to management decisions affecting both community and society; and
F. Provide prospective patients and others with adequate and accurate information, enabling them to make enlightened decisions regarding services.

Source: ACHE (2017).

Compared with its peers around the world, the US healthcare system clearly has something amiss. Despite having the world's most expensive healthcare system, our country has poor to middling outcomes (and the occasional exceptional outlier, such as breast cancer survival or flu vaccination). But even in the areas where the United States performs well overall, the system remains stained with disparities affecting people of color. Ethically, the question is what duty or obligation does each of us have with regard to working toward a healthier population and a more efficient and more equitable healthcare services delivery system?

As you review the excerpt in the box, note the following references: "meet . . . healthcare needs of the community," "seek . . . to foster health promotion in the community," and "access to healthcare services for all people." What do those phrases mean to you? They suggest an ethical imperative for the administrative healthcare professional to continually consider the common good as a function of their daily professional lives. In fact, it should be the prism through which you view all the following questions raised in this policy snapshot.

The Evolving Role of Social Insurance

Social insurance is a system in which everyone pays into a pool of money to provide services for a defined group of people. These people are referred to as *beneficiaries* and are, by operation of law and the social insurance concept, entitled to the benefits available from the pool of funds. In the United States, this social insurance system is Medicare Part A, as all employers and employees pay a Medicare tax that is tied to payroll for the benefit of everyone 65 and older and people in a few other specific categories. The future of Medicare Part A, however, is in jeopardy. First, at both current and anticipated levels of spending, which exceed revenue and projected revenue, the Medicare Trust Fund will be out of money by 2026. In 2020, Medicare provided coverage for some 60 million Americans; at $731 billion in 2018, Medicare's cost represented 15 percent of the federal budget. Second, costs are expected to continue to increase because of the aging of the population, longer life expectancy, the increased utilization of services, the intensity of the services required by patients, and general escalating costs in healthcare.[1] The picture is not pretty: more people to serve and more services to provide (especially for chronic conditions), stacked against a finite set of resources (Cubanski, Neuman, and Freed 2019).

Several policy options could address the Medicare funding problem. First, the government could raise taxes incrementally to mitigate the continuing shortfall in the difference between Medicare tax revenue and its trust fund expenditures. Second, the Medicare program could impose a means test to limit the number of people covered—requiring that those in higher income brackets pay an additional sum for coverage. Third, the system could limit the scope of services. Fourth, Congress could impose greater limits on the amounts paid to providers. Fifth, Medicare could be used as leverage to bring more uninsured people into coverage through any of a variety of expansions. For example, some segments of the population could be permitted to buy coverage from Medicare, or the government could implement a single-payer system extending Medicare-like coverage to every American. These ideas reflect some of the proposals from several presidential candidates in the 2020 presidential campaign (Blumeberg et al. 2019). Perhaps the nation could try several of the proposed alternatives simultaneously.

Each of these ideas has salient good and bad points, and whether you consider an idea good or bad depends on your perspective. Limiting payments to providers has a good ring to it to those who see providers as profiteers. Providers, of course, would see it differently. And it may not be sanguine to anyone if providers start dropping out of the program for lack of appropriate reimbursement. Policy options need to be crafted carefully to create equity among the stakeholders—that is, to minimize disparities and cost while maximizing quality of care and access to it.

In the future you wish to create, what option or set of options would you choose? How would you apply the lessons in the ensuing chapters to pursue your objective? What observations would influence your answer? How many issues reflected in the preceding exhibits would be affected by your choices on Medicare? How would you use Medicare to address some of the shortcomings reflected in the exhibits?

The Evolving Role of State Governments: Medicaid, the Affordable Care Act, and Beyond

As described in chapter 3, individual states are playing an increasingly important role in health policy. The ACA delegated an enormous responsibility to state governments in the form of Medicaid expansion and the operation of health insurance exchanges. These policy decisions and the waivers associated with each decision enhanced the states' role in health policy significantly. Likewise, litigation filed by, and on behalf of, state governments by attorneys general and governors may further push this boundary.

Medicaid

In its 2020 configuration, Medicaid covers approximately 20 percent of the population. The federal government is delegating more flexibility to the states with regard to Medicaid. In 2018, the Centers for Medicare & Medicaid Services (CMS) announced new *policy guidance*.[2] It invited states to especially experiment with the work requirements in Section 1115 waivers (discussed in chapter 3) to address the "expansion" population in Medicaid created by the ACA (CMS 2018). In response, in early 2020, seven states had been approved for a waiver to impose work requirements, and ten had pending applications (Kaiser Family Foundation 2020). In an effort to provide still more flexibility to the states, in January 2020, CMS issued additional policy guidance inviting states to submit 1115 waiver applications to convert their Medicaid programs into a block grant (Lynch 2020).

This invitation represents a significant shift in policy that was not authorized by any explicit legislation. The promulgation of this policy guidance is solely an *implementation* decision. Medicaid has historically been an open-ended entitlement that funds the cost of care for defined eligible beneficiaries, regardless of cost. The block-grant proposal gives the states more flexibility, to be sure, but in exchange, the nature of the funding would change from open-ended to a finite sum of money. Furthermore, should the state (under the terms of the policy guidance) save money by operating the program with less funding than was made available in the block grant, the state would share in the savings with the federal government (Kaiser Family Foundation 2020). Consumer groups and advocates for people with low incomes are leery. A legal challenge almost certainly awaits this initiative.

Will the states reduce access to care when costs exceed levels supported by block grants? Would this reduction be consistent with the underlying policy of Medicaid's purpose? Should the federal government undertake other efforts to encourage states to expand Medicaid within the existing framework of the ACA? What role does social justice or addressing healthcare disparities occupy in your thinking? How could states ameliorate some of the US shortcomings reflected in the exhibits?

The Affordable Care Act

States also have substantial responsibility in managing health insurance exchanges and defining some of the benefits available through them. Along with Medicaid, these exchanges could have a dramatic impact on disparities in access to care. Likewise, through the waivers discussed earlier and in chapter 3, health insurance exchanges can meet a variety of goals related to state government costs and social programs.

Partly outside the realm of the federal government, some states have enacted a public-option insurance plan that permits people to buy health insurance coverage directly from the states. New York, Minnesota, and Washington have all enacted some form of public-option health insurance for individuals. Washington's program, effective in 2021, allows individuals to buy into the state's Medicaid program (Commonwealth Fund 2020). Considering these efforts, how might a public-option insurance plan improve the healthcare system?

Legal Challenges

In addition to managing Medicaid and operating health insurance exchanges under the ACA, the states' roles will take on other, unknown dimensions as well. State attorneys general of both parties are showing an increasing appetite for challenging federal initiatives, particularly those emerging from the White House (Rayasam 2020). By mid-2020, Democratic attorneys general had filed 91 lawsuits against the Trump administration. Republican attorneys general filed 52 lawsuits against the Obama administration (Rayasam 2020). Note that at least two of those cases were ACA related: *National Federation of Independent Business (NFIB) v. Sebelius*, in which the lead plaintiff was initially the state of Florida, and *Texas v. United States*. Both these cases challenged the constitutionality of the ACA.

What role should the states play in reforming healthcare services delivery? Should they expand Medicaid? Offer a public option for individuals to purchase? Impose work requirements on Medicaid recipients? Operate a health insurance exchange, or leave it to the federal government? Could any of these policy options affect the indicators in exhibits C-2 or C-3? If states like Colorado or Nevada, or others, undertake a public option and other initiatives to improve health services delivery, is it fair to Americans in other states?

The Evolving Role of Public Health

The penumbra of public health can be incredibly broad. As described earlier in the book, its fundamental activities are assurance, assessment, and policy development. These activities can be applied to restaurant inspection, basic health screenings, and, of course, the spread of infectious disease—the last issue being something that should especially concern all of us. The fundamental activities can be applied to health disparities, to ensure that all who need healthcare do, in fact, receive it. And they can be applied even more broadly to climate change.

As hospitals and health systems move toward population-based health services, they become increasingly closer to the realm of public health. Healthcare organizations engaged in expanding the housing supply or increasing access to healthy food is an emerging concept. Should these ideas continue? Should we have clinical organizations addressing social services related to public health? As a professional healthcare administrator, how much should you do to apply the principles of public health to the healthcare system in addressing broader issues such as disparities in care or climate change? What impact, particularly on the indicators in exhibit B, would such initiatives have?

What would it take to improve life expectancy? What health determinants would affect that measure? It is no secret that obesity, suicides, and chronic conditions are related to this issue. What others? The crisis with substance use disorder? Gun violence? How could the overall health system be changed to improve these indicators?

The Evolving Role of Technology

Technology means many things. One may instantly conjure up images of computers, handheld devices, and servers, for example. Other people may picture MRIs or ultrasound devices. Certainly, these impressions are correct. The management and dispersal of health-related data is an enormous public policy issue, as discussed in chapter 7. The widespread access of individual health information facilitates clinical integration and improved delivery of care for an increasingly mobile society. The converse side of the issue, protecting patient privacy, is equally important, however.

Telehealth is another emerging technology that affects the delivery of care. Telehealth includes such practices as monitoring patients' data remotely while they are at home and specialty consults for patients by phone or video. Further, this technology has been used in intensive care units (ICUs). Telemetry transmits the data, which are accompanied by a real-time video, so that the specialists can remotely monitor the ICU patients. The staff in the ICU can then respond to the patients' needs according to the recommendations or instructions of the specialists using the monitors.

But technology means more than the hardware and software associated with data management and diagnostic and therapeutic devices. It also extends to pharmaceutical applications and human genetics research and treatment.

Gene therapy is emerging as a form of treatment for many human diseases and conditions. Bioengineered blood vessels are a reality; can other body parts be far behind? Pharmaceutical manufacturers have created a new form of drug called biologics, medical products derived or partly derived from biological sources. How will these advances be applied? Can programs such as Medicaid and Medicare work to extend these forms of technology to all who need them? How can these developments be used to improve the nation's rankings in either exhibit B or exhibit C?

The transmission of data is critical to a health system's ability to integrate care for its patients. What ramifications does the electronic sharing of data from system to system across the nation have? How does the transmission of personal health information or keeping it in a data warehouse affect the indicators in any of the exhibits presented here? What advances are most likely to have a salubrious impact on those indicators? Can modern therapies be available to patients through Medicare and Medicaid?

Conclusion

Healthcare managers have both an ethical obligation to improve the lives of individuals involved in their organization and a larger ethical obligation to the community and society. The ACHE Code of Ethics, part of which was presented in a sidebar in this snapshot, exemplifies the standards to which all healthcare leaders should aspire.

Policy modification and health professionals' competencies to bring about change are the topics of part 4. Now that you see the condensed data on the equity and efficacy of the healthcare system, what will you do to address the profession's ethical obligations? The overriding question is, How will you use the tools of modifying policy (chapter 9) and policy competence (chapter 10) to create the future?

The comparisons made at the beginning of this policy snapshot rely on national data that few of us will ever be able to influence directly as policymakers. The sources of those indicators remain beyond the reach of all but a handful of elites (see chapter 2) in the policymaking system. Healthcare has been something of a local endeavor historically. Note how often the term *community* arises in the ACHE ethics excerpt and in a wide variety of other healthcare-related settings and conversations. The ubiquity of this term suggests that each of us can have an impact at the local and, perhaps, state level. In that spirit, look at the health indicators and outcomes for your state and county (County Health Rankings 2020). As you read part 4, ask yourself where you can find your opportunity to make changes using the tools and competencies discussed there.

Notes

1. Life expectancy in the United States had continually increased until 2014, when it plateaued and then declined in 2017 because of "deaths of despair," deaths from drug (opioid) overdose, alcohol abuse, and suicide (Woolf and Shoomaker 2019).
2. Policy guidance, unlike rulemaking, offers no public comment period when it is issued. There are, however, 30-day comment periods at both the federal and the state levels for any 1115 waiver application (CHLPI 2020).

References

American College of Healthcare Executives (ACHE). 2017. "Code of Ethics." Amended November 13. www.ache.org/-/media/ache/ethics/code_of_ethics_web.pdf.

Blumeberg, L. J., J. Holahan, M. Beuttigens, A. Gangopadhyaya, B. Garrett, A. Shartzer, M. Simpson, R. Wang, M. M. Farveault, and D. Arnos. 2019. "Comparing Health Insurance Reform Options: From Building on the ACA to Single Payer." Commonwealth Fund. Published October 16. https://doi.org/10.26099/b4g6-9c54.

Center for Health Law and Policy Innovation (CHLPI). 2020. "Health Care in Motion: Administration Releases a 'Block'-Headed Invitation to Dismantle Medicaid." Published January 31. www.chlpi.org/wp-content/uploads/2013/12/HCIM_1_31_20.pdf.

Centers for Medicare & Medicaid Services (CMS). 2019. "National Health Expenditure Data: Projected." Accessed February 5, 2020. www.cms.gov/Research-Statistics-Data-and-Systems/Statistics-Trends-and-Reports/NationaHealthExpendData/NationalHealthAccountsProjected.html.

———. 2018. "CMS Announces New Policy Guidance for States to Test Community Engagement for Able-Bodied Adults." Published January 11. www.cms.gov/newsroom/press-releases/cms-announces-new-policy-guidance-states-test-community-engagement-able-bodied-adults.

Commonwealth Fund. 2020. "States with Public Coverage Options for Individual Market Consumers." Published January 15. www.commonwealthfund.org/chart/2020/states-public-coverage-options-individual-market-consumers.

County Health Rankings. 2020. "State Reports." University of Wisconsin Population Health Institute, School of Medicine and Public Health. Accessed June 8. www.countyhealthrankings.org.

Cubanski, J., T. Neuman, and M. Freed. 2019. "The Facts on Medicare Spending and Financing." Kaiser Family Foundation. Published August 2. www.kff.org/medicare/issue-brief/the-facts-on-medicare-spending-and-financing.

Hostetter, M., and S. Klein. 2018. "Reducing Racial Disparities in Health Care by Confronting Racism." Commonwealth Fund. Published September 27. www.commonwealthfund.org/publications/newsletter-article/2018/sep/focus-reducing-racial-disparities-health-care-confronting.

Kaiser Family Foundation. 2020. "Medicaid Waiver Tracker: Approved and Pending Section 1115 Waivers by State." Published May 29. www.kff.org/medicaid/issue-brief/medicaid-waiver-tracker-approved-and-pending-section-1115-waivers-by-state.

Lynch, C. 2020. "Letter to State Medicaid Director." Centers for Medicare & Medicaid Services, Center for Medicaid & CHIP Services. Published January 30. www.medicaid.gov/sites/default/files/Federal-Policy-Guidance/Downloads/smd20001.pdf.

Rayasam, R. 2020. "Five AGs Who May Drown a Democratic White House." *Politico*. Published January 25. www.politico.com/news/2020/01/25/5-republican-attorneys-general-who-may-drown-a-democratic-white-house-099374.

Tikkanen, R. 2020. "Multinational Comparisons of Health Systems Data, 2019." Commonwealth Fund. Published January 30. www.commonwealthfund.org/publications/other-publication/2020/jan/multinational-comparisons-health-systems-data-2019.

Woolf, S., and H. Schoomaker. 2019. "Life Expectancy and Mortality Rates in the United States, 1959–2017." *Journal of the American Medical Association* 322 (20): 1996–2016.

Zephryn, L., and E. Declercq. 2020. "To the Point: Measuring Maternal Mortality." Commonwealth Fund. Published February 6. www.commonwealthfund.org/blog/2020/measuring-maternal-mortality.

CHAPTER

9

POLICY MODIFICATION

Learning Objectives

After reading this chapter, you should be able to

- discuss how policy modification brings the policymaking process full circle;
- distinguish between policy modification and policy initiation;
- define *incrementalism* and explain the preference for it in policymaking;
- describe the role each branch of government plays in policy modification;
- explain how modification occurs in policy formulation, particularly in agenda setting and legislation development; and
- explain how policies are modified in the designing, rulemaking, operating, and evaluating activities of policy implementation.

Policymaking is not a perfect process. At times, those involved in a policy's formulation and implementation make mistakes. Similarly, a policy that may seem appropriate at one time may be rendered inappropriate in the future, perhaps as quickly as the next election cycle. The policymaking model used throughout this book is brought full circle by the third phase of the process, ***modification***. Including this phase as part of the policymaking framework is necessary because perfection frequently eludes policymakers in the formulation and implementation phases. Even policy decisions that seem to fit the circumstances when they are made must adjust to accommodate changing circumstances.

If modification were eliminated from the framework, policies would be formulated in their original version and then implemented, and that would be the end of the process—except, of course, for the policies' consequences. In practice, however, policymaking does not work this way. The consequences of policies—including the effects of policies on formulators, implementers, and individuals, organizations, and interest groups outside the process—cause people to seek modification. And because circumstances change throughout the life of the policy, people continuously want to modify it.

At a minimum, individuals, organizations, or interest groups that benefit from a policy may seek modifications that increase or maintain these benefits over time. Similarly, those who are negatively affected by a policy will try to modify it to minimize the disadvantages, or repeal it entirely. In addition, when the policymakers who formulate and implement a public policy observe it in operation, they will evaluate it against their objectives for that policy. When preferences and reality conflict, efforts to modify the policy typically ensue. Some policymakers do not have to see any evidence of performance to want to modify a policy. Opposed to the policy from the outset, they pursue modification if the policy is enacted.

The clearest example of such opposition and pursuit of modification in health policy in recent decades is the continuing battle over the Affordable Care Act (ACA). Beginning with the law's enactment, its repeal or modification has been high on the Republican agenda. Between 2011 and early 2015, there were 56 attempts to repeal or modify the ACA in the Republican-controlled House of Representatives (Pear 2015). These efforts were aimed at complete repeal, with or without replacement, or at many specific provisions of the ACA, including health insurance marketplaces, the individual mandate, and taxes on medical device companies.

Almost every policy has a history. In the case of public laws, an initial version is formulated and then evolves as it is implemented, either through amendments to the original legislation or through new or revised rules and changes in operation. Some policies eventually die—they are repealed by the legislative branch—but most have long and dynamic lives during which they are continually modified in various ways. This chapter addresses the policy modification phase of public policymaking.

The modification of a policy, as shown in the darkly shaded portion of exhibit 9.1, is fundamental to policymaking, which is as a continual cycle of interrelated activities. External changes such as economic swings, demographic shifts, or scientific or technological advances can stimulate modifications in policy. Typically, stakeholders prefer incremental policy changes, which we discuss later in this chapter. Regardless, whether the incentive comes from the supporters or the opponents of any given policy, the pressure for policy modification is relentless.

As this chapter describes, the pressure to modify a policy is exerted at many points in the policymaking process. Authoritative decisions made anywhere in the process are always subject to review and revision. Policy modifications—large and small—emphasize that the separate activities in policymaking are, in reality, highly interactive and interdependent. The next section examines the distinction between policy initiation and policy modification.

EXHIBIT 9.1
Policymaking Process: Modification Phase

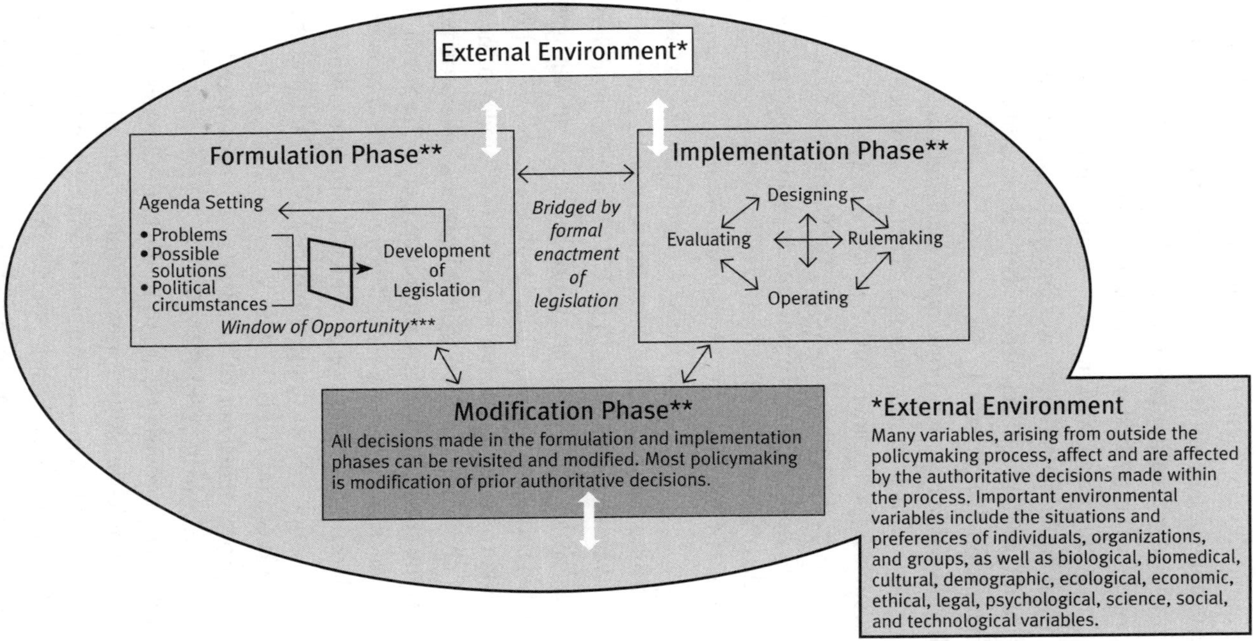
External Environment*
Formulation Phase**
Agenda Setting
• Problems
• Possible solutions
• Political circumstances
Development of Legislation
Window of Opportunity***
Bridged by formal enactment of legislation
Implementation Phase**
Designing
Evaluating
Rulemaking
Operating
Modification Phase**
All decisions made in the formulation and implementation phases can be revisited and modified. Most policymaking is modification of prior authoritative decisions.
*External Environment
Many variables, arising from outside the policymaking process, affect and are affected by the authoritative decisions made within the process. Important environmental variables include the situations and preferences of individuals, organizations, and groups, as well as biological, biomedical, cultural, demographic, ecological, economic, ethical, legal, psychological, science, social, and technological variables.

Policymakers in all three branches of government make policy in the form of position-appropriate, or authoritative, decisions. Their decisions differ in that the **legislative branch is primarily involved in formulation, the **executive branch** is primarily involved in implementation, and both are involved in modification of prior decisions or policies. The **judicial branch** interprets and assesses the legality of decisions made within all three phases of the policymaking process.

***A window of opportunity opens for possible progression of issues through formulation, enactment, implementation, and modification when there is a favorable confluence of problems, possible solutions, and political circumstances.

Policy Modification Versus Policy Initiation

A *new* policy—the establishment of an original public law—is initiated when the confluence of problems, possible solutions, and political circumstances lead to the initial development of legislation in the formulation phase, then its enactment, and then to implementation, including the designing, rulemaking, operating, and evaluating activities needed to put the law into effect. In contrast, the policy is modified when its performance and impact—or perceptions about its performance and impact—require policymakers to revisit the formulation and implementation phases and make changes in legislation or its implementation (see the feedback arrows between modification, formulation, and implementation in exhibit 9.1).

In the United States, new policies are rarely initiated. The modification of existing policy is much more common. The ACA, which amended several existing laws, such as the Public Health Services Act, the Employee Retirement Income Security Act, the Internal Revenue Code, the Social Security Act, and the Medicare Prescription Drug, Improvement, and Modernization Act, is an excellent example of policy modification.

The history of American health policy demonstrates that policymakers can, and on occasion do, initiate entirely new policies. For example, in 1798, Congress established the US Marine Hospital Service to provide medical care for seamen who were sick or disabled. The US Marine Hospital Service was the initial policy from which the US Public Health Service eventually grew. In 1921, Congress enacted the Maternity and Infancy Act (P.L. 67-97), through which grants were made to states to encourage the development of health services for mothers and children. This new policy became the prototype for federal grants in aid to the states. In 1935, Congress enacted the Social Security Act (P.L. 74-271), which initiated the federal government's major entrance into the area of social insurance. This policy, which has been modified many times, now encompasses, among other things, Medicare, Medicaid, and the Children's Health Insurance Program (CHIP). The Veterans' Mental Health and Other Health Care Improvements Act of 2008 (P.L. 110-387) and the American Recovery and Reinvestment Act of 2009 (P.L. 111-5), which also contains extensive health policy provisions, are more recent examples of new policies.

As these examples illustrate, some health or health-related policies are indeed formulated and implemented without being related to prior policies. The vast majority of contemporary health policies, however, spring from existing policies. Because most health policies are derived from revised prior policies, the modification phase is clearly important.

A review of health policies, such as those presented in chapter 3, readily illustrates just how many contemporary health policies are amendments to previously enacted public laws or are otherwise the result of changes—often, a string of changes—in the rules and practices that determine how laws are implemented. In fact, no policy is permanent. Modification of prior policies—whether in the form of decisions representing public laws, implementation rules or regulations, rulings of a court, or operational practices—pervades the entire policymaking process. Perhaps the clearest possible examples of policy modification in practice can be found in the history of Medicare policy, a pattern described in the next section.

Medicare: The Beginning

Medicare's history predates its actual starting point in 1965 and begins with the enactment of the Social Security Act in 1935. From that point forward, however, the establishment and continuation of the Medicare program is largely a matter of modifying previous policies.

The program emerged on the nation's policy agenda largely through the operation of the Social Security program over a span of three decades, from the mid-1930s to the mid-1960s. President Franklin D. Roosevelt formed the Committee on Economic Security in 1934 and charged its members to develop a program that could ensure the "economic security" of the nation's citizens. The committee considered the inclusion of health insurance in the Social Security program from the outset. In fact, sentiment for its inclusion was strong among members of the committee (Oberlander 2003; Starr 2013). But in the end, they decided against recommending the inclusion of health insurance because of the tremendous political burdens associated with such a proposal. The American Medical Association (AMA) in particular strongly opposed the concept.

As stated in the original legislation, the objective of the Social Security Act was "to provide for the general welfare by establishing a system of federal old age benefits, and by enabling the several States to make more adequate provision for aged persons, blind persons, dependent and crippled children, maternal and child welfare, public health, and the administration of their unemployment compensation laws."

Although health insurance was not included among the program's original provisions, its addition was considered from time to time in the ensuing years. President Harry S. Truman considered national health insurance a key part of his legislative agenda. But AMA's continued powerful opposition and the Truman administration's need to divert its attention to Korea in 1950 meant that the president was unable to stimulate the development and enactment of any sort of universal health insurance policy. Faced with dim political prospects for universal health insurance, proponents turned to a much more limited idea—hospital insurance for the aged.

After a number of modest proposals for such insurance, none of which could muster the necessary political support for enactment, two powerful members of Congress, Senator Robert Kerr and Representative Wilbur Mills, passed a bill that provided federal support for state programs that provided health benefits to the aged poor. As discussed in the policy snapshot in part 2, the amendments to the Social Security Act of 1960 (P.L. 86-778) were popularly known as Kerr-Mills. Not until the Democratic margin in Congress was significantly increased in President Lyndon B. Johnson's landslide election in 1964 did a more expansive initiative have much chance of passage.

With Medicare's prospects significantly improved by the 1964 election, Medicare became a high priority among President Johnson's Great Society programs and was enacted as part of the Social Security Amendments of 1965 (P.L. 89-97). Medicare emerged on the nation's policy agenda through a series of attempts to modify the original Social Security Act by expanding the benefits provided to include health insurance. Although these attempts at modifying the original act failed more often than not, they set the stage for the eventual modification that produced the Medicare program.

After the enactment of the 1965 legislation that established the Medicare program, the chronology of related legislation shows a remarkable pattern of evolutionary, incremental modification of a single but massive public policy. The progression of modifications to Medicare continues today, including the addition or removal of benefits, adjustments to eligibility, and different premiums and copayment provisions. Reimbursement rates and payment mechanisms for service providers have also shifted, as have features to ensure the quality and the medical necessity of services (Davis et al. 2019). A brief sample of this history, provided in the box below, illustrates how dynamic the modification of Medicare policy has been. The examples also show the critical role that modification plays in the overall policymaking process. This chronology reflects significant legislative change over time, a pattern likely to continue as long as this complex and expensive program exists. Indeed, considering its current financial challenges, Medicare faces one of the most volatile periods in its history, and many more modifications are likely in the coming years. As described earlier in the book, Medicare pays providers under provisions of Part A (inpatient hospital, home health, skilled nursing facility, and hospice), Part B (physician, outpatient hospital, and other services), Part C (the Medicare Advantage program), and Part D (prescription drugs).

Medicare: A History of Policy Modification

Medicare was enacted in 1965 (P.L. 89-97) in response to the concern that only about half of the nation's adults 65 and older had health insurance and that most of this group had coverage only for inpatient hospital costs. The new program, which became effective July 1, 1966, included Part A coverage for hospital and post-hospital services and Part B coverage for doctors and other medical services. As is the case for the Social Security program, Part A is financed by payroll taxes levied on current workers and their employers; persons must pay into the system for 40 quarters to become entitled to premium-free benefits (self-employed individuals pay both the employer and the employee share of the Medicare tax). Medicare Part B is voluntary, with a monthly premium required of beneficiaries who choose to enroll. Payments to healthcare providers under both Part A and Part B were originally based on the most common form of payment at the time, namely, "reasonable costs" for hospital and other institutional services or "usual, customary and reasonable charges" for physicians and other medical services.

Medicare is considered a social insurance program and is the second-largest such federal program, after Social Security. The 1965 law also established Medicaid, the federal and state health insurance program for poor people; the program was an expansion of previous welfare-based assistance efforts. Some low-income individuals qualify for both Medicare and Medicaid.

In the ensuing years, Medicare has undergone considerable change. P.L. 92-603, enacted in 1972, expanded program coverage to certain individuals younger than 65 (people with disabilities and people with end-stage renal disease) and introduced managed care into Medicare by allowing private insurance entities to provide Medicare benefits in exchange for a monthly capitated payment. This law also began to place limitations on the definitions of reasonable costs and charges to gain some control over program spending, which, even initially, exceeded original projections.

A number of laws enacted in the 1980s and 1990s included provisions designed to further stem the rapid increase in program spending. The laws included modifications to the way payments to providers were determined and efforts to postpone the insolvency of the Medicare Part A trust fund. For example, the legislation tightened the rules governing payments to service providers and limited the annual increases in such payments. The program moved from payments based on reasonable costs and reasonable charges to payment systems under which a predetermined payment amount was established for a specified unit of service. At the same time, beneficiaries received expanded options to obtain covered services through private managed-care arrangements, typically health maintenance organizations. Most Medicare payment provisions were incorporated into larger budget reconciliation bills designed to control overall federal spending.

(continued)

This budget-tightening effort culminated in the enactment of the Balanced Budget Act of 1997 (BBA 97; P.L. 105-33). The law slowed the rate of growth in payments to providers and established new payment systems for certain categories of providers; included in the law was the establishment of sustainable growth rate methodology for determining the annual update to Medicare physician payments. BBA 97 also established the Medicare+Choice program (also referred to as Medicare Part C), which expanded private plan options for beneficiaries and changed the way most of these plans were paid. BBA 97 further expanded preventive services covered by the program.

With the passage of BBA 97, Congress became concerned that the cuts in payments to providers were somewhat larger than originally anticipated. Therefore, it passed legislation in 1999 (the Balanced Budget Refinement Act of 1999, or BBRA; P.L. 106-113) and 2000 (Medicare, Medicaid, and SCHIP [State Children's Health Insurance Program] Benefits Improvement and Protection Act of 2000, or BIPA; P.L. 106-554) to mitigate the impact of BBA 97 on providers.

In 2003, Congress enacted the Medicare Prescription Drug, Improvement, and Modernization Act of 2003 (also called the Medicare Modernization Act, or MMA; P.L. 108-173), which included a major benefit expansion (prescription drugs—Part D) and placed increasing emphasis on the private sector to deliver and manage benefits. The MMA included several provisions:

1. It created a new voluntary outpatient prescription drug benefit to be administered by private entities.
2. It replaced the Medicare+Choice program with the Medicare Advantage (MA) program and raised government payments to MA plans to increase availability for beneficiaries.
3. The act introduced the concept of income testing into Medicare, with higher-income persons paying larger Part B premiums, beginning in 2007.
4. The MMA modified some provider payment rules.
5. It expanded covered preventive services.
6. Finally, the act created a process for overall program review if general revenue spending exceeded a specified threshold.

During the 109th Congress, two laws were enacted that incorporated minor modifications to Medicare's payment rules: the Deficit Reduction Act of 2005 (DRA; P.L. 109-171) and the Tax Relief and Health Care Act of

2006 (TRHCA: P.L. 109-432). In the 110th Congress, additional changes were incorporated in the Medicare, Medicaid, and SCHIP Extension Act of 2007 (MMSEA; P.L. 110-173) and the Medicare Improvements for Patients and Providers Act of 2008 (MIPPA; P.L. 110-275).

The 111th Congress enacted comprehensive health reform legislation that, among other things, made statutory changes to the Medicare program. The Patient Protection and Affordable Care Act (ACA; P.L. 111-148), enacted on March 23, 2010, included numerous provisions affecting Medicare payments, payment rules, covered benefits, and the delivery of care. The Health Care and Education Affordability Reconciliation Act of 2010 (the Reconciliation Act, or HCERA; P.L. 111-152), enacted on March 30, 2010, made changes to a number of Medicare-related provisions in the ACA and added several new provisions. Included in the ACA, as amended, are seven provisions:

1. Constrain Medicare's annual payment increases for certain providers
2. Change payment rates in the MA program so that they more closely resemble those in fee-for-service (FFS) plans
3. Reduce payments to hospitals that serve a large number of low-income patients
4. Create an Independent Payment Advisory Board to make recommendations to adjust Medicare payment rates
5. Phase out the coverage gap ("doughnut hole") in the Part D prescription drug benefit
6. Increase resources and enhance activities to prevent fraud and abuse
7. Provide incentives to increase the quality and efficiency of care

Examples of the incentives listed in the preceding point include the creation of value-based purchasing programs for certain types of providers and measures that allow accountable care organizations that meet certain quality and efficiency standards to share in the savings. The Reconciliation Act also created a voluntary pilot program that bundles payments for physician, hospital, and post-acute care services, and it adjusted payments to hospitals for readmissions related to some potentially preventable conditions.

In the 112th and 113th Congresses, the American Taxpayer Relief Act of 2012 (ATRA; P.L. 112-240), the Continuing Appropriations Resolution of 2014 (P.L. 113-67), and the Protecting Access to Medicare Act of 2014 (PAMA; P.L. 113-93) primarily made short-term modifications to physician

(continued)

payment updates and payment adjustments for certain types of providers. PAMA also established a new value-based purchasing program for skilled nursing facilities (SNFs) and a new system for determining payments for clinical diagnostic laboratory tests. The Improving Medicare Post-Acute Care Transformation Act of 2014 (IMPACT; P.L. 113-185) required that post-acute care providers—defined in the law as long-term care hospitals (LTCHs), inpatient rehabilitation facilities, SNFs, and home health agencies—report standardized patient assessment data and data on quality measures and resource use. IMPACT also modified the annual update to the hospice aggregate payment cap and required that hospices be reviewed every three years to ensure their compliance with existing regulations on patient health, safety, and quality of care.

In the 114th Congress, the Medicare Access and CHIP Reauthorization Act of 2015 (MACRA; P.L. 114-10) repealed the sustainable growth rate formula for calculating updates to Medicare payment rates to physicians and other practitioners and established other methods for determining the annual updates. The act also introduced alternatives to the current FFS-based physician payments by creating a new, merit-based incentive payment system and setting processes for developing, evaluating, and adopting alternative payment models. Additionally, MACRA reduced updates to hospital and post-acute care provider payments, extended several expiring provider payment adjustments, adjusted income-related premiums in Parts B and D, and prohibited using Social Security numbers on beneficiaries' Medicare cards. Among other changes, the Increasing Choice, Access, and Quality in Health Care for Americans Act (Division C of the 21st Century Cures Act; P.L. 114-255) modified LTCH reimbursement and the average length-of-stay criterion; average length of stay determines whether a hospital qualifies as an LTCH. The act also delayed payment reductions and required the secretary of Health and Human Services to change how payments are determined for certain durable medical equipment, prosthetics, orthotics, and supplies. Finally, the legislation allowed beneficiaries with end-stage renal disease to enroll in MA beginning January 1, 2021.

In the 115th Congress, the Bipartisan Budget Act of 2018 (BBA 18; P.L. 115-123) made several changes to federal healthcare programs, including Medicare. BBA 18 included provisions designed to expand care for beneficiaries with chronic health conditions. For example, it promoted team-based care by providers, increased the use of telehealth services, and expanded certain MA supplemental benefits. In addition, BBA 18 extended for five years some Medicare provisions that were set to expire (or that had temporarily expired); these provisions included the Medicare dependent hospital program and add-on payments for low-volume hospitals, rural home health services, and some ambulance services. BBA 18 also specified payment updates for the Medicare physician fee schedule, SNFs, and home health services; reduced payments for non-emergency ambulance transports; and required modification of the home health prospective payment system starting in 2020. In addition, the act provided for indefinite authority for MA special needs plans, repealed limits on outpatient therapy services, and eliminated the Independent Payment Advisory Board. Starting in 2019, the act required that pharmaceutical manufacturers participating in Medicare Part D provide a larger discount on brand-name drugs purchased by enrollees in the coverage gap and created a new high-income-premium category under Parts B and D.

Source: Adapted from Davis et al. (2019).

Modification is a ubiquitous component of the overall policymaking process, as the chronology of modifications to Medicare clearly exemplifies. In Medicare and in many other areas of health policy, the likelihood that prior decisions will be revisited and changed is a readily recognizable feature of public policymaking in the United States. The propensity for modification makes policymaking distinctly cyclical and dynamic.

Another important feature of modification is *incrementalism*, the strong preference by people involved in policymaking to make relatively small changes to a policy and to do it slowly. The ramifications of incrementalism are discussed in the next section.

Incrementalism in Policymaking

Not only are most public policies modifications of previously established policies, but historically, most modifications also reflect only modest changes (Anderson 2014). As Lindblom (1969) aptly characterized it, public policymaking in the United States is an incremental process, considering how policies are continually modified in many small steps.

Of course, some policy modifications are large, but these are exceptions. Major policy shifts may occur in an atmosphere of widespread miasma or sweeping political change. Perhaps once in a generation, a policy will be a large-scale change from a previous policy. The Social Security Act of 1935—in response to the Great Depression—was a blend of both new policies (direct aid from the federal government to individual citizens) and incremental change (several grant-in-aid programs incorporated from earlier legislation). Later, the 1965 enactment of Medicare and Medicaid was certainly a large modification of the earlier Social Security Act; the 1965 legislation arose from sweeping political change and the recognition of increasing poverty among older Americans. Finally, the ACA, enacted in 2010 as an outgrowth of both political change and the recognition that the uninsured population was rising to crisis proportions, contains numerous major modifications to prior health policy.

All of these examples are the exceptions to the rule that most policy change is incremental. These major policy changes occurred for some extraordinary reasons, as responses to a crisis or to some seismic political change. Otherwise, the pattern of incrementalism is likely to continue (Gruber 2008). As evident from the rendition of federal legislation in chapter 3, modern health policy is nearly universally built on policy decisions from earlier times.

The affinity for modest, incremental policy change is not restricted to the health arena. The operation of the nation's overall political, social, and economic systems reflects preferences for modest rather than sweeping change. As we noted in chapter 2, members of the US power elite strongly prefer incremental changes in public policies. They believe that incrementalism—building on existing policies via modification in small, incremental steps—allows the economic and social systems to adjust without being unduly threatened by change. Incremental policymaking limits economic dislocation or disruption and causes minimal alteration in the social system's status quo.

The Mechanics of, and Preference for, Incrementalism

In policymaking that is characterized by incrementalism, significant departures from the existing patterns of policies occur only rarely. Most of the time, the effects of policies play out slowly and predictably. This pace suggests that policymakers in all three branches of government and stakeholders in healthcare typically have a strong preference for incrementalism in health policymaking. The stakeholders include leaders in health-related organizations and interest groups and many individuals who benefit from such policies as the Medicare and Medicaid programs, funding for biomedical research, and the subsidies to help people purchase health insurance coverage provided by the ACA.

The results of incremental decisions are more predictable and stable than are those of decisions not made incrementally. Unless a person—whether a policymaker or someone affected by policies—is unhappy with a situation and wishes an immediate and drastic change, the preference for incrementalism will almost always prevail.

Incrementalism in policymaking increases the likelihood of compromise among the diverse interests in the policy marketplace. Conversely, the political inclination toward compromise also produces incremental decision-making. The potential for compromise is an important feature of an effective and smoothly running policymaking process. Words like *incrementalism* and *compromise* used in the context of public policymaking may bring to mind compromised principles, inappropriate influence peddling, and corrupt deals made behind closed doors. However, as Paul Starr and Walter Zelman, members of President Bill Clinton's healthcare reform team, explain, "In a democracy compromise is not merely unavoidable; it is a source of creative invention, sometimes generating solutions that unexpectedly combine seemingly opposed ideas" (Starr and Zelman 1993, 8). See the following box for an example of incremental policy development.

Mental Health Parity and Incrementalism

The Mental Health Parity and Addiction Equity Act of 2008 (MHPAEA) provides an excellent example of incremental policymaking. It also shows how incrementalism can cross from one branch of government to another (legislative to executive and back to legislative) and the value of health services research to inform public policy.

The story begins with the first congressional effort to bring parity between coverage of mental health services and coverage of other health services. The Mental Health Parity Act of 1996 (MHPA) applied to large employer-sponsored group health plans for more than 50 employees. The terms of the act barred these plans from imposing higher annual or lifetime limits on mental health benefits than those applicable to medical or surgical benefits (Goodell 2014).

There were considerable limitations on this first effort. First, the law did not address treatment limits on the types of facilities covered. Likewise, it did not address the use of managed-care techniques that made mental health benefits less generous than medical or surgical coverage. For example, a plan could require a higher copayment or deductible for mental health services than it required for other health services.

Proponents of mental health parity confronted the argument that broader coverage would cause higher costs. The expansion of parity, with the directive that cost sharing, number of visits, and length of treatments be included in the Federal Employee Health Benefits program by executive order of President Clinton in 1999, had several effects. First, of course, it addressed the political and equity issue of making such benefits similar.

(continued)

But perhaps even more important, it provided an ideal health services research laboratory to compare expanded coverage and increased costs.

Thus, we have a legislative enactment; an administrative policy expanding that enactment; and subsequent research based on large-scale studies to show that mental health parity did not increase spending. Rather, consumers benefited from greater financial protection. These findings had the effect of making mental health parity more politically palatable.

Armed with that information, advocates of more complete parity for mental health services were successful in closing many of the MHPA gaps with the passage of the MHPAEA of 2008. This act added substance use disorder to covered services. It also required that a group plan offer mental health and substance use disorder (MH/SUD) benefits and that such benefits be no more restricted than those for medical and surgical benefits. The act further stipulated that there be no separate cost-sharing requirements and that if the plan included out-of-network coverage for medical and surgical benefits then it must also cover out-of-network MH/SUD services. Finally, the law required that any reason for denial of coverage must be disclosed on request (CMS 2016).

Subsequently, the ACA made the MHPAEA applicable to insurers in the individual market as well as to individual plans offered through an exchange. While the MHPAEA includes an exemption for small employers, rules implementing the ACA bring small employers into the fold of those to whom the MHPAEA applies. The ACA included MH/SUD treatment as one of the ten essential health benefits set forth in the act. Regulations adopted by Centers for Medicare & Medicaid Services (CMS) clarified that a carve-out managed behavioral health care (MBHC) plan cannot have different deductibles and out-of-pockets limits than those in the plans offered by a large employer. (Because large employers may have several health plans from which their employees choose and because the companies may "carve out" MH/SUD services to a separate MBHC, the ACA needed to ensure equity between the two, which is what the regulation clarifies.)

In short, the practice of incrementalism has been applied to this subset of health issues. Gaps in coverage existed in the initial law (the MHPA). An administrative action (Clinton's executive order) expanded those benefits to federal employees. This expansion provided the opportunity for a large-scale study of cost (health services research), and the results ultimately informed a policy that addressed gaps in the initial law through passage of the MHPAEA.

The policymaking process provides abundant opportunities for people's experiences with, and opinions about, public laws to influence future iterations of formulation and to change some of the decisions and activities that guide policy implementation as well. Two important facts overarch the mechanics of policy modification.

The most basic fact about the mechanics of modification is that participants in all three branches of government can play active roles in policy modification. Everyone who can make the authoritative decisions that constitute public policy can also participate in modifying prior decisions.

The second vital mechanistic fact about policy modification, as illustrated by the feedback arrows in exhibit 9.1, is that policies can be modified at multiple points in the policymaking process: in agenda setting and legislation development in the formulation phase and in the designing, rulemaking, operating, and evaluating in the implementation phase. These two important aspects of policy modification are discussed in the following sections, beginning with how participants in each branch of government are involved in policy modification.

Legislative, Executive, and Judicial Roles in Modification

Participants from each branch of government are involved in policy modification, although their roles differ. *Legislators* have significant responsibilities to make laws and to decide when to modify them. They also oversee the implementation of enacted laws and can direct changes in the implementation phase. Legislators stimulate modification during policy formulation and implementation. *Chief executives* (presidents, governors, or mayors, depending on the level of government) and their top appointees monitor implementation and can point out when modifications are needed. *Courts* can also determine when modifications are needed, such as when the results of one policy infringe on, or conflict with, the desired results of other policies. The roles of each branch are described more fully in the next sections.

Legislative Branch

In the case of Congress, and with parallels in state legislatures, the core activity is making and amending laws. Through committees and subcommittees, legislative bodies also have specific oversight responsibilities in the implementation phase. The purpose of oversight in a legislative context is to assess and evaluate the execution and effectiveness of laws administered by the executive branch. This oversight includes determining if there are areas in which new legislation or an amendment of existing legislation is needed. The legislative branch is aided in its evaluation and assessment of policy performance by agencies such as the Government Accountability Office, the Congressional Budget Office, and the Congressional Research Service, as was discussed at length in chapter 7.

While any congressional committee with jurisdiction can hold oversight hearings, the House and Senate appropriations committees (www.appropriations.house.gov and www.appropriations.senate.gov, respectively) have especially important oversight responsibilities in their annual reviews of the budgets of implementing organizations and agencies. Legislators seeking to influence implementation decisions routinely use the budget review mechanism.

The first or strongest indications of the need for new or amended legislation in a particular area often emerge from oversight hearings. For example, appendix 4.1 contains the opening statement of the chair of the House of Representatives Subcommittee on Oversight and Investigation of the Committee on Energy and Commerce. Representative Tim Murphy delivered the statement at the beginning of a hearing titled "Where Have All the Patients Gone? Examining the Psychiatric Bed Shortage." As the declaration suggests, a panel with diverse experience in services for individuals who are seriously mentally ill will offer perspective "on the far-reaching implications of the current psychiatric bed shortage and . . . some creative approaches to address it."

In addition to the highly formalized aspects of making and modifying policy through legislation and oversight, members of the legislative branch have other ways of modifying policy. For example, members of Congress commonly correspond directly with administrative officials in response to a particular concern. See the following box, which reprints a letter signed by 23 senators and addressed to the secretary of the Department of Health and Human Services, the acting director of the Food and Drug Administration, and the director of the Centers for Disease Control and Prevention. The letter concerns e-cigarettes, whose impact started to become a high-profile political and policy issue in 2019.

United States Senate
Washington, DC 20510
September 11, 2019

The Honorable Alex M. Azar II
Secretary, U.S. Department of Health and Human Services
200 Independence Avenue SW, Washington, DC 20201

The Honorable Norman E. "Ned" Sharpless, M.D.
Acting Commissioner, U.S. Food and Drug Administration
10903 New Hampshire Ave., Silver Spring, MD 20993

The Honorable Robert Redfield, M.D.
Director, Centers for Disease Control and Prevention
1600 Clifton Road, Atlanta, GA 30333

Dear Secretary Azar, Acting Commissioner Sharpless, and Director Redfield:

We write with significant alarm about the increase in reports of severe pulmonary disease across multiple states associated with the use of e-cigarette products (devices, liquids, refill pods, and/or cartridges). Six individuals in Kansas, California, Illinois, Indiana, Minnesota, and Oregon have already lost their lives to severe lung disease associated with vaping. E-cigarette use has sickened over 450 people across 33 states, including many adolescents and young adults, with the median age of patients diagnosed with severe pulmonary disease at 19 years.

For years, we have written to you and your predecessors about the dangers of youth use of e-cigarettes, but public health agencies—particularly the Food and Drug Administration (FDA)—have failed to act swiftly and comprehensively to address the epidemic of youth use of addictive e-cigarette products.

FDA's failure to fully implement and enforce the Family Smoking Prevention and Tobacco Control Act (TCA) and require Premarket Tobacco Applications (PMTA) for all e-cigarette products has allowed e-cigarette companies to flood the market with e-cigarette products that use nicotine salts to deliver high levels of nicotine; products are often accompanied with kid-friendly flavors. By delaying its public health review of products that were on the market as of August 8, 2016, and not rigorously enforcing the public health review requirement for products that entered the market after that date, FDA has permitted thousands of e-cigarettes to enter and remain on the market with no assessment of their health risks, addictiveness, or appeal to youth.

While the cause of the outbreak of severe pulmonary disease is still unknown, FDA's failure to adequately regulate e-cigarette products on the market has created an environment where dangerous products have flourished and put children's health at risk. FDA has the authority to regulate all e-cigarette products and components—regardless of the substances and chemicals included or added to them, where and how the products are purchased, and/or whether or not the products are modified. FDA must use this power going forward and play a leadership role in ending this epidemic.

Although your agencies have launched public health awareness campaigns, sent warning letters to some manufacturers whose products have violated the FDA's 2016 "deeming rule," released a recent health advisory, and taken other moderate steps, we believe the spike of more than 450 cases of severe lung disease in adolescents and young adults is a public health crisis that warrants more aggressive and immediate action. This action should include the following: a strong, clear message to the public about what is currently known about the dangers of e-cigarette use; immediate removal from the market of e-cigarette products that have been linked or could be linked to the pulmonary illnesses and deaths; and FDA's immediate enforcement of the required public health review of

(continued)

e-cigarette products with the authority granted to FDA under the Tobacco Control Act. FDA should also immediately take action to remove flavored products from the market, until or unless they have undergone FDA review that shows they are of benefit to the public health.

We stand ready to support your efforts to address this public health crisis, and request your responses to the following no later than Friday, September 20, 2019:

1. Please provide descriptions of all products and samples that FDA is currently analyzing in connection with the severe pulmonary disease, including the type of product and what substances they contain.
2. What is the estimated timeline for completing the investigation and determining if a specific product or substance is linked to pulmonary illness, including the deaths in Kansas, California, Illinois, Indiana, Minnesota, and Oregon?
3. Will e-cigarette products that are linked, or could be linked, to the cases of pulmonary illnesses and deaths be publicly identified and pulled from the market? Why or why not?
4. How are FDA and CDC [Centers for Disease Control and Prevention] coordinating with state health departments to address pulmonary illnesses associated with e-cigarettes?
5. What current efforts and considerations are being given to immediately begin enforcing product review requirements or setting more stringent conditions for allowing products to remain on the market prior to a public health review by FDA given the current outbreak of pulmonary illnesses?
6. Will FDA, CDC, and HHS [Department of Health and Human Services] provide weekly teleconference updates to Congressional staff as the investigation continues?

Sincerely,

Jeffrey A. Merkley
United States Senator

Edward J. Markey
United States Senator

Patty Murray
United States Senator

Richard J. Durbin
United States Senator

Chris Van Hollen
United States Senator

Richard Blumenthal
United States Senator

Sherrod Brown
United States Senator

Brian Schatz
United States Senator

Tom Udall
United States Senator

Dianne Feinstein
United States Senator

Jack Reed United States Senator	Ron Wyden United States Senator
Margaret Wood Hassan United States Senator	Robert Menendez United States Senator
Patrick Leahy United States Senator	Jeanne Shaheen United States Senator
Robert P. Casey, Jr. United States Senator	Sheldon Whitehouse United States Senator
Kamala Harris United States Senator	Kirsten Gillibrand United States Senator
Elizabeth Warren United States Senator	Mazie K. Hirono United States Senator
Cory A. Booker United States Senator	

Source: Merkley et al. (2019).

As the senatorial letter aptly shows, policy modification may well be triggered by communication between participants in the legislative and executive branches. Indeed, direct correspondence is but one of several avenues participants in the legislative branch can use to modify existing policy.

Executive Branch

Chief executives (presidents, governors, or mayors) oversee and manage the implementation phase of policymaking. They can also help set the policy agenda, which often includes the modification of existing laws through amendments. Their influence provides them with unique opportunities to initiate changes in policy. Chief executives are supported in their oversight activity by staff in the executive office and various department and agency staff who are responsible to the chief executive. As discussed in chapter 7, the Agency for Healthcare Research and Quality and the much newer CMS Innovation Center play important roles in helping modify policies. In particular, the federal Office of Management and Budget, also described in chapter 7, plays a substantial role in policy modification by managing many aspects of policy implementation carried out in the executive branch.

One powerful mechanism the executive branch has for modifying policy is executive orders. These directives issued by presidents and governors have the force and effect of law. For example, President Obama issued an executive order to direct specific actions in response to scientific advances in the treatment of human immunodeficiency virus (HIV) (Obama 2013). The following box presents the executive order in its entirety.

Executive Order 13649 of July 15, 2013

Accelerating Improvements in HIV Prevention and Care in the United States Through the HIV Care Continuum Initiative

By the authority vested in me as President by the Constitution and the laws of the United States of America, and in order to further strengthen the capacity of the Federal Government to effectively respond to the ongoing domestic HIV epidemic, it is hereby ordered as follows:

Section 1. *Policy.* Addressing the domestic HIV epidemic is a priority of my Administration. In 2010, the White House released the first comprehensive National HIV/AIDS Strategy (Strategy), setting quantitative goals for reducing new HIV infections, improving health outcomes for people living with HIV, and reducing HIV-related health disparities. The Strategy will continue to serve as the blueprint for our national response to the domestic epidemic. It has increased coordination, collaboration, and accountability across executive departments and agencies (agencies) with regard to addressing the epidemic. It has also focused our Nation's collective efforts on increasing the use of evidence-based approaches to prevention and care among populations and in regions where HIV is most concentrated.

Since the release of the Strategy, additional scientific discoveries have greatly enhanced our understanding of how to prevent and treat HIV. Accordingly, further Federal action is appropriate in response to these new developments. For example, a breakthrough research trial supported by the National Institutes of Health showed that initiating HIV treatment when the immune system was relatively healthy reduced HIV transmission by 96 percent. In addition, evidence suggests that early treatment may reduce HIV-related complications. These findings highlight the importance of prompt HIV diagnosis, and because of recent advances in HIV testing technology, HIV can be detected sooner and more rapidly than ever before.

Based on these and other data, recommendations for HIV testing and treatment have changed. The U.S. Preventive Services Task Force now recommends that clinicians screen all individuals ages 15 to 65 years for HIV, and the Department of Health and Human Services Guidelines for Use of Antiretroviral Agents now recommends offering treatment to all adolescents and adults diagnosed with HIV.

Furthermore, ongoing implementation of the Affordable Care Act provides a historic opportunity for Americans to access affordable, quality health care. The Act is expanding access to recommended preventive services with no out-of-pocket costs, including HIV testing, and, beginning in 2014, insurance companies will not be able to deny coverage based on pre-existing conditions, including HIV. Starting October 1, 2013, Americans can select the coverage that best suits them through the new Health Insurance Marketplace, and coverage will begin January 1, 2014.

Despite progress in combating HIV, important work remains. Since the publication of the Strategy, data released by the Centers for Disease Control and Prevention show that there are significant gaps along the HIV care continuum—the sequential stages of care from being diagnosed to receiving optimal treatment. Nearly one-fifth of the estimated 1.1 million people living with HIV in the United States are undiagnosed; one-third are not linked to medical care; nearly two-thirds are not engaged in ongoing care; and only one-quarter have the virus effectively controlled, which is necessary to maintain long-term health and reduce risk of transmission to others.

In light of these data, we must further clarify and focus our national efforts to prevent and treat HIV infection. It is the policy of my Administration that agencies implementing the Strategy prioritize addressing the continuum of HIV care, including by accelerating efforts to increase HIV testing, services, and treatment along the continuum. This acceleration will enable us to meet the goals of the Strategy and move closer to an AIDS-free generation.

Sec. 2. *Establishment of the HIV Care Continuum Initiative.* There is established the HIV Care Continuum Initiative (Initiative), to be overseen by the Director of the Office of National AIDS Policy. The Initiative will mobilize and coordinate Federal efforts in response to recent advances regarding how to prevent and treat HIV infection. The Initiative will support further integration of HIV prevention and care efforts; promote expansion of successful HIV testing and service delivery models; encourage innovative approaches to addressing barriers to accessing testing and treatment; and ensure that Federal resources are appropriately focused on implementing evidence-based interventions that improve outcomes along the HIV care continuum.

Sec. 3. *Establishment of the HIV Care Continuum Working Group.* There is established the HIV Care Continuum Working Group (Working Group) to support the Initiative. The Working Group shall coordinate Federal efforts to improve outcomes nationally across the HIV care continuum.

(a) *Membership.* The Working Group shall be co-chaired by the Director of the Office of National AIDS Policy and the Secretary of Health and

(continued)

Human Services or designee (Co-Chairs). In addition to the Co-Chairs, the Working Group shall consist of representatives from:

(i) the Department of Justice;
(ii) the Department of Labor;
(iii) the Department of Health and Human Services;
(iv) the Department of Housing and Urban Development;
(v) the Department of Veterans Affairs;
(vi) the Office of Management and Budget; and
(vii) other agencies and offices, as designated by the Co-Chairs.

(b) *Consultation.* The Working Group shall consult with the Presidential Advisory Council on HIV/AIDS, as appropriate.

(c) *Functions.* As part of the Initiative, the Working Group shall:

(i) request and review information from agencies describing efforts to improve testing, care, and treatment outcomes, and determine if there is appropriate emphasis on addressing the HIV care continuum in relation to other work concerning the domestic epidemic;
(ii) review research on improving outcomes along the HIV care continuum;
(iii) obtain input from Federal grantees, affected communities, and other stakeholders to inform strategies to improve outcomes along the HIV care continuum;
(iv) identify potential impediments to improving outcomes along the HIV care continuum, including for populations at greatest risk for HIV infection, based on the efforts undertaken pursuant to paragraphs (i), (ii), and (iii) of this subsection;
(v) identify opportunities to address issues identified pursuant to paragraph (iv) of this subsection, and thereby improve outcomes along the HIV care continuum;
(vi) recommend ways to integrate efforts to improve outcomes along the HIV care continuum with other evidence-based strategies to combat HIV; and
(vii) specify how to better align and coordinate Federal efforts, both within and across agencies, to improve outcomes along the HIV care continuum.

(d) *Reporting.*

(i) Within 180 days of the date of this order, the Working Group shall provide recommendations to the President on actions that agencies can take to improve outcomes along the HIV care continuum.

(ii) Thereafter, the Director of the Office of National AIDS Policy shall include, as part of the annual report to the President pursuant to section 1(b) of my memorandum of July 13, 2010 (Implementation of the National HIV/AIDS Strategy), a report prepared by the Working Group on Government-wide progress in implementing this order. This report shall include a quantification of progress made in improving outcomes along the HIV care continuum.

Sec. 4. *General Provisions.* (a) Nothing in this order shall be construed to impair or otherwise affect:

(i) the authority granted by law to an executive department, agency, or the head thereof; or

(ii) the functions of the Director of the Office of Management and Budget relating to budgetary, administrative, or legislative proposals.

(iii) This order shall be implemented consistent with applicable law and subject to the availability of appropriations.

(iv) This order is not intended to, and does not, create any right or benefit, substantive or procedural, enforceable at law or in equity by any party against the United States, its departments, agencies, or entities, its officers, employees, or agents, or any other person.

Barack Obama
THE WHITE HOUSE,
July 15, 2013.

Source: Obama (2013).

Judicial Branch

As discussed in chapter 8, the courts play vital roles in health policymaking, particularly in modifying health policy. The federal courts have responsibilities for how laws are interpreted and enforced. State courts are involved in interpreting and enforcing state laws and other policies in their jurisdictions. Teitelbaum and Wilensky (2013, 5) observe that the courts' focus in the healthcare domain is on individuals' access to care, the quality of that care, and the financing of the care. In their view, the courts focus "on why and how the government regulates private individuals and corporations in the name of protecting the health, safety, and welfare of the general public."

One important area of health policy that courts—particularly the federal court system and the US Supreme Court—influence is the wake of the ACA.

As discussed earlier in the book, the ACA was the product of a highly partisan legislative process. The resulting environment has created often-expressed legislative ambivalence toward the act. Likewise, states and some individuals have taken to the courts to attack the ACA on multiple issues. We expect more pages of history to be written about this ongoing saga.

In this section, we consider four loosely related but important elements in the ACA story—three of them judicial in character, one legislative. Two of the three court cases are discussed in the policy snapshots in parts 1 and 3. Those two cases, together with a legislative development and the third court case, may, in the final analysis, trace the beginning—and the effective end—of the ACA.

In one of the court cases, *National Federation of Independent Business (NFIB) v. Sebelius*, the Supreme Court upheld the constitutionality of the ACA by modifying—limiting—Congress's expansion of Medicaid and applying its own rationale to the underlying penalty for failure to comply with the individual mandate. Under the individual-mandate provision of the ACA, every individual was required to obtain health insurance or remit the "shared responsibility payment" to the federal government, specifically, the Internal Revenue Service.

As described earlier, there were two key elements in the *NFIB* decision. First, it declared the *mandatory* expansion of Medicaid unconstitutional. The Court said the federal government could not merely order the states to expand their Medicaid programs. The Court further said, however, that the federal incentive to expand Medicaid—funding 100 percent of the expansion costs for three years and then 90 percent of the subsequent expansion costs—could remain in place, making the Medicaid expansion decision by the states voluntary.

Second, the Court found that the individual mandate, structured as an effort to regulate interstate commerce under the Commerce Clause of the US Constitution, was impermissible because rather than regulating commerce, the act was, in effect, creating a new form of commerce. Of critical importance, however, the Court opined that the "shared responsibility payment" had all the characteristics of a tax. For example, collection of the payment was tied to the federal income tax, and the amount to be paid was partly based on the individual's income. What's more, its reporting was made a part of the annual income tax return filed by taxpayers, and the payment produced revenue. In these various ways, the mandate had all the elements of a tax. For those reasons, the Court concluded that the "shared responsibility payment" was a tax within the taxing powers of the federal government and that, on this rationale, the individual mandate was constitutional.

With these partial victories, the Obama administration proceeded to tackle the implementation of the ACA, which had multifaceted implementation challenges. The results of implementing the ACA were a noticeable increase in the number of Americans with health insurance coverage (Collins, Bhupal, and Doty 2019). Likewise, the disparity between white and black Americans in access to healthcare began to diminish (McMorrow et al. 2015).

However, as has been described here and elsewhere, the ACA was under continual political and legal attack from its opponents. Multiple unsuccessful efforts to repeal it consumed the House of Representatives. And as we have seen, the constitutionality of the ACA was challenged, literally, on the day it was signed into law in the *NFIB v. Sebelius* litigation.

The second important legal challenge, also discussed earlier in the book, is *King v. Burwell.* The plaintiffs in that case challenged the implementation of the ACA, saying that the Internal Revenue Service incorrectly interpreted the statute by equating a federal insurance exchange with a state insurance exchange to determine an individual's eligibility for tax credits that subsidize the purchase of insurance. This consideration was critically important, as it determined the plaintiffs' eligibility for the tax credits and thus whether the requirement that they purchase insurance applied to them. In *King*, the court found that because the Internal Revenue Service had correctly interpreted the statute, the plaintiffs were eligible for tax credits and would therefore be required to purchase insurance coverage pursuant to the ACA or remit the "shared responsibility payment." Not every initiative or opportunity to modify a policy concludes with a modification; sometimes, the status quo results.

By 2020, the ACA had been modified by the Court on the issues of Medicaid and the individual mandate but withstood multiple legislative challenges and a critical legal challenge. Not surprisingly, however, with the 2016 election of a Republican president empowered by a Republican-controlled Congress, new efforts to challenge the ACA would emerge and some of them would be successful.

One such challenge was in the Tax Cuts and Jobs Act of 2017 (P.L 115-97). As part of that legislation, the "shared responsibility payment" was repealed. In other words, the individual mandate requiring all Americans to have insurance coverage remained on the books, but there was no enforcement mechanism—nothing in place to penalize the failure of a citizen for noncompliance with the mandate.

We'll now consider the third judicial challenge to the ACA, *Texas v. United States*, heard in 2019. The plaintiffs in the case, 18 states and two individuals, claimed—and the federal district court agreed—that if there is no "shared responsibility payment" (which the Supreme Court said was a "tax" in upholding the individual mandate in *NFIB v. Sebelius*), then the individual mandate ceases to be a proper exercise of Congress's power to tax. If there is no exercise of the taxing power to enforce the mandate, then there can be no mandate, because it was held to be a function of such power to tax. Furthermore, the plaintiffs allege, and the district court agreed, that if there is no mandate, then the entire ACA should be declared unconstitutional. The government appealed the case to the Fifth Circuit US Court of Appeals in 2019. The Fifth Circuit upheld the district court determination regarding the individual mandate but remanded the case to the district court on the issue of severability—that is, whether the mandate can be "severed" as unconstitutional without declaring the entire act unconstitutional. By mid-2020, the Supreme Court had agreed to hear the case and was awaiting the filing of briefs by the parties (Constitutional Accountability Center 2020). As noted, there are pages in the history of the ACA yet to be written.

Here we see how the judiciary has modified policy in concert with the legislative branch. To be clear, the courts did *not* coordinate with Congress, but advocacy groups and litigants more than likely did so in an effort to produce this very result. As a result, several branches of the government, particularly the judicial branch, were involved in policy modifications because of challenges in the external environment.

Modification Through Policymaking Stages

As illustrated by the feedback arrows in exhibit 9.1, policies can be modified at multiple points in the policymaking process. Modification often occurs in the agenda-setting and legislation-development stages of policy formulation and in the designing, rulemaking, operating, and evaluating activities in the implementation phase.

Although modifications can be made at any point in the policymaking process, they are often introduced at certain stages. Modifications are far more likely in legislation development, where amendments to existing laws are made. Likewise, modifications are more common in rulemaking. In this activity, rules are modified for their ease of implementation. We begin our discussion of these modifications in the formulation phase.

Policy Formulation

Modification of policies in the formulation phase, which means amending existing policies, occurs in agenda setting and legislation development. As described in chapter 4, policy formulation—making the decisions that result in new or amended public laws—entails two distinct and sequential sets of activities: agenda setting and legislation development. The formulation phase of policymaking produces new public laws or, more likely, amendments to existing laws.

The ability of legislators to modify existing laws means that when a new law or an amendment is made, legislators can view this development as an opportunity to further modify the change that has just been made. When the ACA was enacted, for example, its opponents immediately began the battle to repeal, replace, or at least to amend the parts of the law they found especially offensive. Because legislative decisions are rarely unanimous, they invariably trigger legislators, lobbyists, and other stakeholders to modify an unwanted decision through new rounds of policy formulation.

As noted throughout this book, new public laws that pertain to health and their subsequent amendments stem from the interactions of (1) a diverse array of health-related problems, (2) possible solutions to those problems, and (3) dynamic political circumstances that relate to both. An entirely new legislative proposal or amendments of previously enacted public laws are created through legislation development. The only significant difference is that previously enacted legislation already has a developmental history and an implementation experience, both of which can influence its amendment.

Agenda Setting

Policy modification routinely begins at agenda setting, because problems already receiving attention through existing policies become more sharply defined and better understood in light of the ongoing implementation of the related policies. Possible solutions to problems can be assessed and clarified in the same context, especially when operational experience and the results of evaluations and demonstration projects provide evidence of potential solutions' efficacy. In addition, interactions between the branches of government and health-related organizations and stakeholders interested in ongoing policies become important components of the political circumstances surrounding the formulation and reformulation of future policies. People learn from their experiences with policies, and those in a position to do so may act on what they learn.

Leaders in health-related organizations and interest groups, because they and their organizations are directly affected by health policies, have a keen interest in these policies and may be among the first to observe the need to modify a policy. They can use their experience to help policymakers better define or document problems that led to the original policy. These leaders can gather, catalog, and correlate facts that more accurately depict the actual state of a problem and can then share this information with policymakers.

Similarly, these leaders are well positioned to observe the actual consequences of a policy. Leaders can devise and assess possible new solutions or alterations to existing ones through the operational experience of the organizations and groups they lead. Finally, their experiences with ongoing policies may become a basis for their attempts to change the political circumstances of a situation. When the confluence of problems, possible solutions, and political circumstances that led to an original policy is altered, a new window of opportunity may open, this time permitting the amendment of previously enacted legislation.

Legislation Development

Health policies in the form of public laws are routinely amended, some of them repeatedly and over many years. Such amendments can reflect the emergence of new technologies, a change in federal budgetary conditions, the evolution of beneficiary demands, and other developments. These and other stimuli for change often gain the attention of policymakers through routine activities and reporting mechanisms in implementation. Pressure to modify policy through changes in existing public laws may also come from the leaders of health-related organizations and interest groups—including those that represent individuals—that feel the consequences of a policy. When legislators modify legislation during its development, they follow the same procedures applied to the original legislative proposals or bills (see chapter 6).

In some instances, the impetus to modify an existing law arises from changes in another law. For example, policies intended to reduce the federal budget deficit have typically impinged on other policies, often prompting the other policies' modification. The implementation of the Deficit Reduction Act of 1984 (P.L. 98-369) required a temporary freeze on physicians' fees paid under the Medicare program. Similarly, the implementation of the Balanced Budget and Emergency Deficit Control Act of 1985 (P.L. 99-177), also known as the Gramm-Rudman-Hollings Act, required budget cuts in defense and certain domestic programs, including some health programs. As noted earlier, the enactment of the ACA meant amendments to such existing laws as the Public Health Services Act; the Employee Retirement Income Security Act; the Internal Revenue Code; the Social Security Act; and the Medicare Prescription Drug, Improvement, and Modernization Act.

The Cyclical Relationship Between Agenda Setting and Legislation Development

As shown in exhibit 9.1, there is a feedback loop between agenda setting and the development of legislation in the policy formulation phase. This feedback loop is an important relationship in policy modification. When policies are developed, especially those that are enacted and implemented, people who opposed the legislation or preferred a different version of it can immediately take the result back into the agenda-setting activity. As noted earlier, efforts to repeal or modify the ACA started immediately after the policy's enactment and continue today. Also as mentioned, between 2011 and early 2015, there were 56 attempts in the Republican-controlled House of Representatives to completely repeal, with or without replacement, or modify specific provisions of the ACA. The targets included health insurance marketplaces, the individual mandate, taxes on medical device companies, and many others. After the 2016 elections, with a Republican president in office, the Republican-controlled House was able to effectively diminish the impact of the ACA by repealing the Shared Responsibility Payment. As discussed above, these attacks on the ACA have occurred in both the legislative and the judicial branches.

Given the complexity of public laws and their inability to always satisfy everyone, modification efforts frequently are an expected part of the process. One place where these efforts routinely begin is between legislation development and agenda setting. Parties dissatisfied with proposed legislation can try to modify the agenda so that the subject can be revisited and perhaps modified through new or amended legislation.

Policy Implementation

Policies can be modified during any part of their implementation: designing, rulemaking, operating, and evaluating. However, most substantive modifications of policies in the implementation phase involve rulemaking and operating activities. Feedback from the consequences of formulated and implemented policies routinely trigger modification of rules and operations, often in both activities concurrently. Although policy modifications can be made in any part of its implementation, we will note some of the ways it happens in each activity.

Designing

Designing involves efforts to establish the agenda of an implementing organization, plan how to address the agenda, and organize to carry out the plans. When an implementing organization is given major new responsibilities, it may need to modify the design of a policy. Such was the case for CMS and its implementation responsibilities for the ACA. As described in chapter 8, implementing the ACA requires that CMS coordinate with states to set up health insurance marketplaces, expand Medicaid, and regulate private health insurance plans. The ACA also greatly expanded the organization's role in cost containment and quality improvements in the nation's healthcare system. These modifications in the responsibilities of CMS will stimulate modification in the structure and functioning of the organization.

Designing may also be modified when a change is made in a law or in how it is to be implemented; such changes may include the timing of implementation. For example, a major provision of the ACA is the mandate for employers with more than 50 employees to provide health insurance coverage to their workers. Originally scheduled to take effect in 2014, rules written by the Treasury Department delayed the requirement until 2015. The delay was made in response to employers' concerns about the challenges of meeting the requirement. Similarly, another one-year delay in some functions of the health insurance marketplaces pertained to small businesses. Such modifications are examples of how designing implementation can be used by executive branch organizations to modify laws.

Rulemaking

As discussed in chapter 8, rulemaking is a necessary precursor to the operation and full implementation of new or amended public laws; enacted legislation is rarely explicit enough to completely guide its implementation. Newly enacted or amended policies are often vague on implementation details, usually intentionally so, and implementing organizations are left to promulgate the rules needed to guide the operation of the policies. Public policies are modified most frequently through changes in the rules or regulations used to guide their implementation.

The practice of modifying policies by updating or changing the rules for their implementation pervades policymaking. As discussed, rules that are promulgated by executive branch agencies and departments to guide the implementation of policies possess the force of law. The rules themselves are policies. As implementation occurs, rulemaking becomes a means to modify policies and their implementation over time. We saw a good example of this in chapter 3. The Trump administration has encouraged states to file waiver requests to permit the imposition of work requirements in exchange for Medicaid coverage. The underlying theory is to disqualify people who might otherwise be eligible for Medicaid to save state and federal costs. This is a new policy, established through the rulemaking and operating policies of CMS. Changed rules are modified policies. This process can be a part of the routine functioning of an agency, as discussed in the following box.

Institutionalizing and Routinizing Aspects of Policy Modification

Considering that certain policy modifications through rulemaking are recurrent, often annually, it is not surprising that the policymaking process includes features that institutionalize some routine modification activities. A good example of this routine modification can be found in the payments to service providers or other vendors for Medicare beneficiaries. As noted elsewhere, these expenditures are substantial and growing. Net Medicare spending is projected to almost double from $693 billion in FY 2019 to $1.225 trillion in 2029 (Congressional Budget Office 2019). From the outset of Medicare, payments for services have been an ongoing process of modification and one of the most dynamic areas of policy modification in the entire health policymaking process.

Congress established the Medicare Payment Advisory Commission (www.medpac.gov) in 1997 to provide advice, especially to Congress, on issues affecting Medicare. The commission's mandate includes questions of payments to private health plans participating in Medicare and to participants in Medicare's traditional FFS program. Medicare payments to providers on behalf of the beneficiaries who are enrolled in the traditional FFS Medicare program and who receive inpatient hospital care are made to more than 3,500 facilities that contract with Medicare to provide acute inpatient care and agree to accept the program's predetermined payment rates as payment in full. Payments for skilled nursing care, home health care, inpatient rehabilitation hospital care, LTCHs, inpatient psychiatric hospitals, and hospice are made under separate prospective payment systems. Much of the rulemaking for payment decisions in all these services is highly routinized.

Payments made under the acute inpatient prospective payment system (IPPS) account for about 25 percent of Medicare spending. IPPS is an example of a special mechanism to institutionalize the process and to make the ongoing modifications in payment rates to 3,500 facilities that take care of millions of Medicare beneficiaries more routine and predictable. IPPS payment rates are intended to cover the costs that reasonably efficient providers would incur in furnishing high-quality care. These rates are determined through a complex but widely known formula.

IPPS pays hospitals for discharged Medicare inpatients using two national base payment rates, one covering operating expenses and the other covering capital expenses. These rates are adjusted to take into account the patient's condition and related treatment strategy as well as market conditions in the facility's geographic location. These adjustments to the national base payment rates are made as follows (Medicare Payment Advisory Commission 2019):

> To account for the patient's needs, Medicare assigns discharges to Medicare severity diagnosis related groups (MS–DRGs), which are based on patients' clinical conditions and treatment strategies . . . Each MS–DRG has a relative weight that reflects the expected relative costliness of inpatient treatment for patients in that group. CMS annually reviews the MS–DRG definitions to ensure that each group continues to include cases with clinically similar conditions requiring comparable amounts of inpatient resources. When the review shows that subsets of clinically similar cases within an MS–DRG consume significantly different amounts of resources, CMS often reassigns them to a different MS–DRG with comparable resource use or creates a new MS–DRG.
>
> . . . Medicare's per discharge payments are derived through a series of adjustments applied to separate operating and capital base payment rates. The two base rates are updated annually and are adjusted to reflect patient conditions, market conditions, and other factors recognized under Medicare's payment system.

EXHIBIT 9.2
Medicare Reimbursement Adjustment Methodology

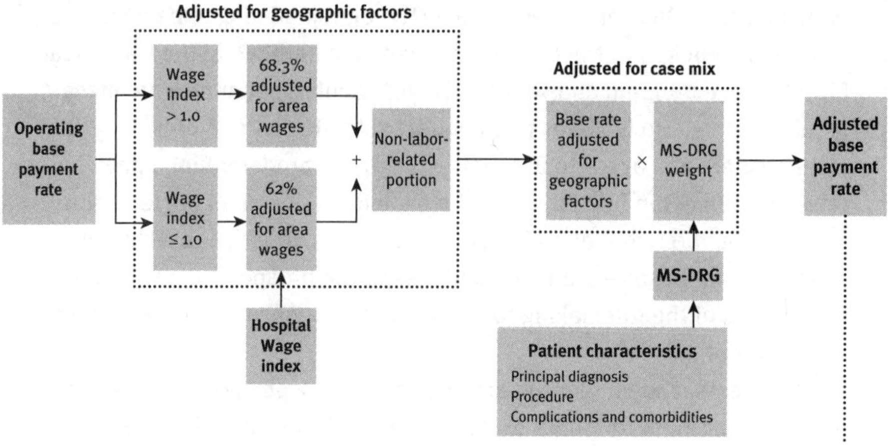

Source: Medicare Payment Advisory Commission (2019).

The formulistic approach, described in the box and shown in exhibit 9.2, for determining payment rates may not be perfect, but it does take some of the mystery out of the rulemaking process as it pertains to determining payment rates. In making the process more predictable from year to year, CMS has facilitated revenue planning for healthcare providers, in this case hospitals.

Operating

Policy operation, as discussed in chapter 7, involves the actual running of the programs embedded in public laws. The appointees and civil servants who staff the government, particularly those who manage the implementing departments and agencies, are primarily responsible for the operating activities of policymaking. The managers in charge of operating a public law have significant opportunities to modify the policy.

Policies implemented by managers who are committed to the policies' objectives and who have the talent and resources to vigorously implement the policies are qualitatively different from policies operated by managers who lack this commitment, talent, and resources. In the ongoing policymaking process, policies are routinely modified through changes in their operation.

The impetus for modification in the operation of policies comes from two principal sources, one internal and the other external. Internally, the managers responsible for operating policies can seek to control the results of operations. To accomplish this, they establish standards or operating objectives. For example, the standard might be to serve so many clients, to process so many reports, to distribute benefits to certain categories of beneficiaries, or to assess compliance with certain regulations by so many firms. Operations ensue, results are monitored, and when results do not measure up to the predetermined standards or operating objectives, changes are made in operations, objectives, or both (Longest 2015). Such routine operational modifications are part of the daily work for organizations that implement health policies.

In addition to the internal pressures to modify policy operation, there are external pressures. These pressures come from individuals and especially health-related organizations and interest groups that experience the consequences of the implemented policies. As we have noted, those who feel the effects of the policies may seek to modify them. One way to change a policy is to influence those who manage its operation.

Opportunities for policy modification arise from the sometimes-close working relationships that can develop between those responsible for implementing public policies and those directly affected by the implementers' decisions and activities. These relationships are enhanced by a prominent feature of bureaucratic careers: longevity (Gormley and Balla 2013). Elected policymakers come and go, but the bureaucracy endures. Leaders of health-related organizations and interest groups build long-standing working relationships with some of the people responsible for implementing the public policies that are of strategic importance to them.

The most solid base for these relationships is the exchange of useful information and expertise. The leader of a health-related organization or interest group, speaking from an authoritative position and imparting relevant information based on actual operational experience with the implementation of a policy, can influence the policy's further implementation. If the information supports change, especially if it is buttressed by similar information from others who are experiencing the effect of a particular policy, it may influence reasonable implementers to make some needed changes. This type of influence is especially likely if there is a well-established working relationship based on mutual respect for the roles of each party and the challenges they face in fulfilling their responsibilities.

Sometimes, those who experience the consequences of policies, usually working through their interest groups, and those responsible for implementing the policies are joined by members of the legislative committees or subcommittees with jurisdiction over the policies to form especially powerful alliances. The widely divergent interests of so many organizations have hindered the formation of such alliances in the health policy domain. Nonetheless, policy networks survive and function to modify existing policies.

An obvious and limiting problem for those who wish to modify a health policy by influencing its operation and the rulemaking that precedes it is the sheer enormity of the bureaucracy with which they might need to interact. Consider the number of components of the federal government involved in health policy rulemaking and operation. The number increases when relevant units of state and local government are added. The challenge of keeping track of where working relationships might be useful—to say nothing of actually developing and maintaining the relationships—can be enormous. Obviously, people must be selective in determining which relationships are most strategically important.

The Cyclical Relationship Between Rulemaking and Operating

An important aspect of a public law's implementation is the distinctly cyclical relationship between the rulemaking and operating activities in the process. Although rulemaking initially precedes operation, the experiences gained in operation feed directly back into rulemaking (exhibit 9.1).

This bidirectional relationship means that the experience gained with operating policies and changes in the environments where policies are operated—such as biomedical, cultural, and technological changes—can influence the modification of rules or regulations subsequently used in their operation. The FDA's efforts to further discourage cigarette smoking exemplify this cyclical nature of policymaking. Even though the percentage of cigarette smokers has fallen from 42.4 percent of US adults in 1965 (the year after the US Surgeon General's first report on the relationship of cigarettes and lung cancer) to 13.9 percent in 2017 (American Heart Association News 2018), tobacco use remains a significant public health concern. More than 34 million Americans still smoke cigarettes, and 16 million have a smoking-related illness (CDC 2019).

Regardless of this perceived success, however, the social and economic costs of smoking-related illness remain substantial, prompting the FDA to promulgate a new rule governing the warnings on cigarette packages. The new rule specifies 11 full-color graphic images accompanied by text describing several known smoking-related illnesses such as chronic obstructive pulmonary disease (COPD), head and neck cancer, other lung disease, and bladder cancer. See appendix 4.2 for a brief discussion of the rule and reproductions of the required images. Practically, the cyclical relationship between rulemaking and operating means that rules promulgated to implement policies undergo revision—which is sometimes extensive and continual—and that new rules can be adopted or existing ones changed or dropped as experience and circumstances dictate. Thus, FDA's new rule goes well beyond its previous mandates, as indicated in the following FDA summary (FDA 2020):

> In March 2020, FDA finalized the "Required Warnings for Cigarette Packages and Advertisements" rule, establishing 11 new cigarette health warnings, consisting of textual warning statements accompanied by color graphics, in the form of concordant photorealistic images, depicting the negative health consequences of cigarette smoking. These new required warnings depict some of the lesser-known, but serious health risks of smoking. The new required warnings must appear prominently on

cigarette packages and in cigarette advertisements, occupying the top 50 percent of the front and rear panels of cigarette packages and at least 20 percent of the area at the top of advertisements.

Evaluating

The evaluation of a policy brings the other activities in the implementation phase full circle. It leads to modifications primarily through its impact on the other activities in the implementation phase—that is, through its impact on designing, rulemaking, and operating activities. Evaluations and policy analyses can also help guide modification in the formulation phase of policymaking, although other factors often play stronger roles in shaping these decisions.

Large-scale experimental designs that include random assignments of individuals and control groups are the best analytical means of assessing policy impact. Randomized clinical trials, for example, are the standard in medical and scientific studies. Because of the expense and difficulty involved, studies like these are not as common in social policy research. Despite the challenges, however, some large-scale studies have been used to help guide public policy in such areas as criminal justice, education, and welfare to some extent. Large randomized-control studies are not as common in health policy, although there have been some notable successes. An early example is the health insurance experiment conducted by the RAND Corporation in the 1970s (Newhouse 1974). More recently, the Oregon health insurance experiment is producing useful guidance for policymaking (Finkelstein et al. 2012; Taubman et al. 2014).

The Oregon experiment, a randomized-control design to evaluate the impact of Medicaid, includes information about the effect of expanding public health insurance on healthcare utilization, health outcomes, and the well-being of low-income adults. Because a major feature of the ACA is Medicaid expansion, information from the Oregon study is relevant to potential modifications of the act. For example, the study has shown that having Medicaid coverage actually *increases* hospital emergency department usage (Taubman et al. 2014).

A far more common approach to evaluations in health policy has been the use of demonstration projects. The CMS Innovation Center relies heavily on demonstrations that might lead to a better understanding of what works and what doesn't for improving quality and reducing costs. The results of demonstration projects can trigger and guide modification in policies (Moran, Rein, and Goodin 2008). The most efficacious modification of policies is generally based on solid information, including that obtained through formal analysis.

Analyzing policies, especially in terms of demonstrating their outcomes, can be approached in a variety of ways. These include before-and-after comparisons, with-and-without comparisons, actual-versus-planned performance comparisons, and cost-oriented analytical approaches (Patton, Sawicki, and Clark 2012).

Analyses based on before-and-after comparisons, as the name suggests, compare conditions before a policy is implemented with conditions after it has had an opportunity to affect individuals, organizations, and groups. These *longitudinal studies* are the most widely used approach to policy analysis. A variation on this approach, known as with-and-without comparisons, involves comparing the consequences of the policy for individuals or groups with situations in which the policy does not exist. Like all studies, these comparative studies also have limitations. In this case, an inference of causation may be incorrect. Outcomes may be correlated with the policy, but the association does not demonstrate causation.

With-and-without evaluations prevail in the health policy domain because variation in the nation's states provides a natural laboratory in which such comparisons are possible. For example, the states differ in terms of seizing the opportunity the ACA affords them for federal funding to expand their Medicaid programs. By mid-2020, 36 states and the District of Columbia were expanding their programs, and 14 states were not (Kaiser Family Foundation 2020).

When some states initially try policies, the results can inform other states' or the nation's consideration of these same policies. In 2006, for example, Massachusetts undertook major health reform intended to make comprehensive health insurance coverage available and affordable for its residents (Long 2010). Many of the features of this policy found their way into the ACA.

Another useful approach to assessing policy performance, actual-versus-planned performance assessments, involves comparing policy objectives (e.g., health status improvements, dollars saved, people inoculated, tons of solid waste removed) with actual post-implementation results. The principal limitation of demonstrations is that they do not support the unassailable assignment of causation to the policies being evaluated. This limitation is a significant weakness of this approach to evaluation or assessment. Nevertheless, this approach is widely used because it tends to be easily implemented and costs relatively little. The results of demonstrations must be interpreted and used carefully.

Finally, another approach to policy analysis is based on cost-oriented assessments. This approach can be especially important in the search for policies that provide value for public dollars. Cost–benefit analysis and cost-effectiveness analysis are the two most widely used forms of cost-oriented policy evaluation (Glennerster and Takavarasha 2013). Cost–benefit analysis is based on the relationship between the benefits and the costs of a policy, where all costs and benefits are expressed in monetary terms. Such analyses can help answer the fundamental question of whether a policy's benefits are worth its costs. In cost-effectiveness analysis, a policy's performance is assessed for its ability to achieve certain objectives in the least costly way. This form of analysis compares alternative policies that might be used to achieve the same or similar objectives.

As noted at the beginning of this chapter and shown throughout this book, policymaking is an imperfect process; nor is it typically rational. As a result, policymakers must routinely review their decisions and change them as necessary.

Furthermore, health policies have huge consequences for individuals, populations, and health-related organizations and interest groups. To varying degrees, depending on their abilities and resources, these stakeholders seek to analyze and understand health policymaking and to influence it. When policies have positive consequences, such as more services, higher incomes, less pollution, or more support for biomedical research, the beneficiaries are likely to seek to maintain or increase these policies through the modification of the existing policies that affect these benefits. Similarly, those who are hurt by the policies will likely try to remedy the negative effects through modification.

Policymakers and people affected by their decisions are encouraged by the modifiability of policies and of policymaking itself. The constant modification of existing policies is an important hallmark of policymaking in the United States. Because of this continuous state of change, the results of the process can be corrected or improved over time. Of course, "improved" is in the eye of the beholder. One of the inherent characteristics of American democracy is that the right of free speech allows all sides to disagree about what constitutes an improved policy. The ability to evolve to a more "perfect union," while ever aspirational, is an important attribute, given the complexity of the world and the fallibility of human nature.

Summary

The modification phase brings policymaking full circle. Policy is modified because the performance and impact—and perceptions about performance and impact—of existing policies feed back into the formulation and implementation phases of policymaking and stimulate changes in legislation or its implementation (the bidirectional arrows between modification, formulation, and implementation in exhibit 9.1).

As depicted in exhibit 9.1, policy modification occurs in the agenda-setting and legislation-development stages of policy formulation and in the designing, rulemaking, operating, and evaluating activities of policy implementation. All three levels of government participate actively in policy modification, although in different ways.

The modification phase is extremely important to health policymaking because the ability to modify a policy in light of its results keep's the policy viable. This phase of policymaking exists because perfection cannot be achieved in the other phases and because policies are established and exist in a dynamic world.

Review Questions

1. Briefly describe the roles played by each branch of government in policy modification.
2. Discuss the distinction between policy initiation and policy modification.
3. Discuss the concept of incrementalism in public policymaking.
4. Describe modification in agenda setting.
5. Discuss how policies are modified in legislation development.
6. Discuss how they are modified in the designing, rulemaking, operating, and evaluating activities of policy implementation.
7. Discuss the interrelationship between rulemaking and operating and how it affects modification.

References

American Heart Association News. 2018. "Smoking in America: Why More Americans Are Kicking the Habit." August 30. www.heart.org/en/news/2018/08/29/smoking-in-america-why-more-americans-are-kicking-the-habit.

Anderson, J. E. 2014. *Public Policymaking*, 8th ed. Mason, OH: Cengage Learning.

Centers for Disease Control and Prevention (CDC). 2019. "Current Cigarette Smoking Among Adults in the United States." Published November 18. www.cdc.gov/tobacco/data_statistics/fact_sheets/adult_data/cig_smoking/index.htm.

Centers for Medicare & Medicaid Services (CMS). 2016. "The Mental Health Parity and Addiction Equity Act (MHPAEA)." Accessed January 5, 2020. www.cms.gov/CCIIO/Programs-and-initiatives/Other-Insurance-Protections/mhpaea_factsheet.

Collins, S. R., H. K. Bhupal, and M. M. Doty. 2019. "Healthcare Coverage Eight Years After the ACA." Commonwealth Fund. Published February 7. www.commonwealthfund.org/publications/issue-briefs/2019/feb/health-insurance-coverage-eight-years-after-aca.

Congressional Budget Office. 2019. "CBO's May 2019 Baseline." Published May 2. www.cbo.gov/system/files?file=2019-05/51302-2019-05-medicare.pdf.

Constitutional Accountability Center. 2020. "*Texas v. United States.*" Accessed June 13. www.theusconstitution.org/litigation/texas-v-united-states.

Davis, P., C. Binder, J. Hahn, S. Kirchoff, P. C. Morgan, M. Villagrana, and P. Voorhies. 2019. *Medicare Primer.* CRS Report R40425. Washington, DC: Congressional Research Service.

Finkelstein, A., S. Taubman, B. Wright, M. Bernstein, J. Gruber, J. P. Newhouse, H. Allen, K. Baicker, and the Oregon Health Study Group. 2012. "The Oregon

Health Insurance Experiment: Evidence from the First Year." *Quarterly Journal of Economics* 127 (3): 1057–105.

Glennerster, R., and K. Takavarasha. 2013. *Running Randomized Evaluations: A Practical Guide*. Princeton, NJ: Princeton University Press.

Goodell, S. 2014. "Mental Health Parity." *Health Affairs*. Published April 3. https://www.healthaffairs.org/do/10.1377/hpb20140403.871424/full/healthpolicybrief_112.pdf.

Gormley, W. T., and S. J. Balla. 2013. *Bureaucracy and Democracy: Accountability and Performance*. Thousand Oaks, CA: Sage.

Gruber, J. 2008. "Incremental Universalism for the United States: The States Move First?" *Journal of Economic Perspectives* 22 (4): 51–68.

Kaiser Family Foundation. 2020. "Status of State Action on the Medicaid Expansion Decision, 2020." Published May 29. www.kff.org/medicaid/issue-brief/status-of-state-medicaid-expansion-decisions-interactive-map.

Lindblom, C. E. 1969. "The Science of 'Muddling Through.'" In *Readings in Modern Organizations*, edited by A. Etzioni, 154–65. Englewood Cliffs, NJ: Prentice Hall.

Long, S. 2010. "What Is the Evidence on Health Reform in Massachusetts and How Might the Lessons from Massachusetts Apply to National Health Reform?" Urban Institute. Published June 24. www.urban.org/uploadedpdf/412118-massachusetts-nationalhealth-reform.pdf.

Longest, B. B., Jr. 2015. *Health Program Management: From Development Through Evaluation*. San Francisco: Jossey-Bass.

McMorrow, S., S. K. Long, G. M. Kenney, and N. Anderson. 2015. "Uninsurance Disparities Have Narrowed for Black and Hispanic Adults Under the Affordable Care Act." *Health Affairs* 34 (10): 1774–78.

Medicare Payment Advisory Commission. 2019. *Hospital Acute Inpatient Services Payment System*. Published October. www.medpac.gov/docs/default-source/payment-basics/medpac_payment_basics_19_hospital_final_v2_sec.pdf.

Merkley, J. A., R. Blumenthal, E. J. Markey, S. Brown, P. Murray, B. Schatz, R. J. Durbin, T. Udall, C. Van Hollen, D. Feinstein, J. Reed, R. Wyden, M. Wood Hassan, R. Menendez, P. Leahy, J. Shaheen, R. P. Casey, Jr., S. Whitehouse, K. D. Harris, K. Gillibrand, E. Warren, M. K. Hirono, and C. A. Booker. 2019. Letter to Alex M. Azar II, Norman E. "Ned" Sharpless, and Robert Redfield. US Senate. September 11. www.merkley.senate.gov/imo/media/doc/19.09.11%20Merkley%20E%20Cig%20LTR%20Final.pdf.

Moran, M., M. Rein, and R. E. Goodin (eds.). 2008. *The Oxford Handbook of Public Policy*. New York: Oxford University Press.

Newhouse, J. P. 1974. "A Design for a Health Insurance Experiment." *Inquiry* 11 (1): 5–27.

Obama, B. 2013. "The President, Executive Order 13649: Accelerating Improvements in HIV Prevention and Care in the United States Through the HIV

Care Continuum Initiative." *Federal Register*. Published July 18. www.gpo.gov/fdsys/pkg/FR-2013-07-18/pdf/2013-17478.pdf.

Oberlander, J. 2003. *The Political Life of Medicare*. Chicago: University of Chicago Press.

Patton, C. V., D. S. Sawicki, and J. J. Clark. 2012. *Basic Methods of Policy Analysis and Planning*, 3rd ed. Upper Saddle River, NJ: Pearson Education.

Pear, R. 2015. "House G.O.P. Again Votes to Repeal Health Care Law." *New York Times*, February 4, A16.

Starr, P. 2013. *Remedy and Reaction: The Peculiar American Struggle over Health Care Reform*, rev. ed. New Haven, CT: Yale University Press.

Starr, P., and W. A. Zelman. 1993. "Bridge to Compromise: Competition Under a Budget." *Health Affairs* 12 (suppl. 1): 7–23.

Taubman, S., H. Allen, B. Wright, K. Baicker, A. Finkelstein, and the Oregon Health Study Group. 2014. "Medicaid Increases Emergency-Department Use: Evidence from Oregon's Health Insurance Experiment." *Science* 343 (17): 263–68.

Teitelbaum, J. B., and S. E. Wilensky. 2013. *Essentials of Health Policy and Law*, 2nd ed. Burlington, MA: Jones and Bartlett Learning.

Texas v. US. 2019. 19-10011 (5th Circuit Court of Appeals, December 18).

US Food and Drug Administration (FDA). 2020. "Cigarette Labeling and Health Warning Requirements." Updated June 17. www.fda.gov/tobacco-products/labeling-and-warning-statements-tobacco-products/cigarette-labeling-and-health-warning-requirements.

CHAPTER

10

BUILDING POLICY COMPETENCE FOR HEALTH PROFESSIONALS

Learning Objectives

After reading this chapter, you should be able to

- define *policy competence* and its usefulness to health professionals;
- describe four philosophical principles that can guide ethical policymaking;
- discuss the five steps health professionals can use to influence policymaking;
- describe the relationship between social power (including sources) and influence in policymaking;
- describe the relationship between focus and influence in policymaking;
- discuss the use of a map to sharpen the focus on efforts to be influential;
- identify the health policy interests of health services provider organizations, resource providing organizations, and health-related interest groups; and
- discuss organizational design to support policy competence.

Professionals everywhere are most likely affected by public policies and, thus, should be concerned about them. The same is true for health professionals, whether their work is predominantly clinical or managerial. For that reason, health leaders should be interested in public policies and, specifically, the relationship between policies and the professionals' central goals: improved health for the individuals and populations they serve. As we have discussed, health is determined by a number of variables, all of which can be affected by public policy. These variables include the physical environments in which people live and work, their behaviors and genetics, social factors, and the type, quality, and timing of the health services they receive.

Among the social factors affecting people's health are economic circumstances; socioeconomic position; income distribution; discrimination based on factors such as race, ethnicity, gender, or sexual orientation; and the availability of social networks or social support. Thus, health professionals need a degree of working knowledge of policy and policymaking to do their core work—improving the health of those they serve—most effectively. The contemporary word for a working knowledge of something is *competence*, the subject of this chapter.

Policy Competence Defined

In any work setting, *competence* means "a cluster of related abilities, commitments, knowledge, and skills that enable a person (or an organization) to act effectively in a job or situation" (BusinessDictionary.com 2020). *Policy competence* simply means competence in relation to policy and the policymaking process. *Health policy competence*, by extension, means competence in relation to health policy and the process through which health policy is formulated, implemented, and modified over time.

This chapter will explain how health policy competence can help health professionals have a greater impact on human health. Specifically, professionals competent in health policy have more influence on policymaking decisions that contribute to improved health.

So, how much policy competence do health professionals need? Like other sorts of professional competence, policy competence comes in degrees. Some people have more; some have less. Health professionals need enough policy competence to perform their jobs well. Some will need more because of their role in policymaking. But not all health professionals have to be the most brilliant policy analysts or the most skilled lobbyists. However, they will be more effective health professionals if they understand policymaking sufficiently to exert some influence in the process toward improving human health. This idea acknowledges that a manager, physician, nurse, or another health professional can improve the lives of others through various steps. These professionals can improve access to, and the quality of, appropriate health services. They can prevent further degradation of the physical and social environments in which people live and can educate people about healthier lifestyles and choices. The professionals can also conduct or support research and can encourage participation in a host of other health-enhancing activities. In short, because health professionals routinely affect individuals' lives through health services, competence in policymaking further enables these professionals to improve the health status of populations.

The single most important way to develop policy competence is to understand public policymaking as a decision-making process that occurs in the context of policy markets. As described throughout the book, public policies, including health policies, are authoritative decisions. Policy competence requires an understanding of the context, participants, and processes of this type of decision-making. In light of the discussion of policy markets in chapter 2 and the fact that these markets are controlled by humans, an appropriate place to begin discussing how health professionals can participate in and influence the policy market is to consider the ethical questions involved.

Last but no less important, healthcare professionals need to conduct themselves ethically, at all times, including when they are engaging in advocacy for any issue or their own organization or association. Across the board, examples of unethical conduct abound in the milieu that is government, at the federal, state, and local levels. Healthcare professionals must keep in mind the core ethical precepts to which they should be dedicated. These precepts are discussed in more detail later in the chapter.

Lobbying in the Federal Government

Lobbying, discussed at length in chapters 6 and 7, is a competence that some health professionals may be called on to develop. While the First Amendment of the Constitution guarantees the right of citizens to seek redress from, or to petition, the government, there are restrictions governing the conduct of those who engage in lobbying and the appointed and elected officials with whom the lobbyists interact. (The restrictions are less limiting for elected officials.) The federal government has a variety of rules governing the conduct of its employees and, by extension, the people with whom the employees come into contact through their work.

Executive Branch

In the executive branch, the Office of Government Ethics lays out in plain language the rules governing employees' acceptance of outside gifts (OGE 2017):

> Executive branch employees are subject to restrictions on the gifts that they may solicit or accept from sources outside the Government. Unless an exception applies, executive branch employees may not solicit or accept gifts that are given because of their official positions or that come from certain interested sources ("prohibited sources").
>
> Even if an employee may accept a gift, employees should consider declining gifts when they believe that their integrity or impartiality would be questioned if they were to accept the gift. In making this judgment, employees may consider, for example, the value of the gift, the timing of the gift, whether the employee's actions could affect the donor, and whether accepting the gift would provide the donor with significantly disproportionate access.

Definition of "Prohibited Source"

A "prohibited source" is a person (or an organization made up of such persons) who:

- is seeking official action by, is doing business or seeking to do business with, or is regulated by the employee's agency; or
- has interests that may be substantially affected by performance or nonperformance of the employee's official duties.

Definition of "Gift"

A "gift" is defined to mean anything of monetary value, and specifically includes "transportation, local travel, lodgings and meals, whether provided in-kind, by purchase of a ticket, payment in advance, or reimbursement after the expense has been incurred."

For health professionals wanting to meet with a government official, then, the safest course of action is to meet with officials in their offices during normal business hours.

Working with Members of Congress

The US House of Representatives and Senate each have their own ethics committees and enforce their own rules through their own investigatory and disciplinary processes. It would be wise for health professionals to work through their professional association to avoid running afoul of any rules governing "citizen lobbyists" and their elected representatives. As a baseline matter, however, it would *never* be appropriate to suggest to a representative or senator that if the legislator voted a certain way, the official would receive a gift or even a campaign contribution. While special-interest campaign donations flow toward elected officials who support points of view held by the interested group or groups, openly soliciting in the way referenced here is clearly bribery, a felony offense. Lunches or dinners may be permissible, but expenses will need to be reported and amounts spent should not be excessive.

For a thorough discussion of this issue, including what constitutes a gift, refer to the House of Representatives Committee on Ethics website (Committee on Ethics 2020). Similarly, healthcare leaders should take care to understand the difference between lobbying (including a requirement to register with the appropriate jurisdiction) and engaging as a citizen. Your professional association should be able to assist with this issue.

Working with State and Local Officials

In the case of state or local elected officials, wise health professionals will turn to knowledgeable persons or other resources to learn what restrictions might apply. Professional associations will also typically be helpful. As a general proposition, most state governments have some permutation of an ethics commission. The National Conference on State Legislatures has provided a useful table that provides the state law citation and general jurisdiction for the ethics commission in each state (NCSL 2020).

As a practical matter, a health leader can avoid ethical difficulty in engaging public officials as a citizen or as a lobbyist by (1) never providing any material thing of value for the official and (b) meeting with the official in the person's office during normal business hours. Additionally, health leaders should become thoroughly informed about the rules and norms for their jurisdiction through their professional association or other sources such as a state ethics commission. In short, study the rules of the road carefully before engaging in lobbying activity beyond a simple letter or phone call to an official.

The Ethics of Influencing Policymaking

Because humans control policy markets and the decisions made in those markets, various mixes of altruism and self-interest influence policymaking. The operation, outcomes, and, largely, the consequences of public policymaking are directly affected by the ethics of those who participate in it.

Ethical and legal considerations shape and guide the development of new policies and the modification of existing policies by contributing to the definition of problems, the development of possible solutions, and the political circumstances that may lead to new or amended policies. The ethical behavior of all participants in the policy market should be guided by four philosophical principles. These principles, generally considered to be at the heart of ethical behavior in healthcare, are as follows: respect for the autonomy of other people, justice, beneficence, and nonmaleficence (Morrison 2020). The implications of each principle for ethical policymaking and the efforts to influence the process are discussed in the following sections.

Respect for Persons

The ethical principle of respect for persons is based on the concept that individuals have the right to their own beliefs and values and to the decisions that further these beliefs and values. This ethical principle undergirds much of the formal system of government that the nation's founders envisioned. Beauchamp and Childress (2019) point out that no fundamental inconsistency exists between the autonomy of individuals and the authority of government as long as government's authority does not exceed the limits set by those who are governed.

In the context of seeking to influence policymaking, respect for persons pertains to the rights inherent in citizenship. Specifically, it relates to the rights of individuals to self-determine how they live their lives and to their rights regarding the integrity of their bodies and minds. Respect for persons in seeking to influence health policymaking reflects issues that pertain to privacy and individual choice, including behavioral or lifestyle choices.

The principle of respect for persons includes several other elements that are important in guiding ethical policymaking behavior. One is honesty. Respect for people as autonomous beings implies honesty in relationships. Closely related to honesty is confidentiality; confidences broken in policymaking can impair the process. Fidelity, another important element of respect for persons, means doing one's duty and keeping one's word. Fidelity is often equated with keeping promises. When policymakers and those trying to influence their decisions tell the truth, honor confidences, and keep promises, they are behaving in a more ethically sound manner.

Justice

Another ethical principle of importance to public policymaking is justice. The degree of adherence to this principle directly affects the policymaking process and the policies themselves. Much of this principle's effect on policies and policymaking hinges on defining justice as fairness (Rawls and Kelly 2001). Justice also includes the ancient concept of "reap what you sow," meaning that justice is done when people receive what they deserve (Beauchamp and Childress 2019).

The principle of justice provides much of the underpinning for all health policies, whether allocative or regulatory. Gostin (2014, xiii), for example, refers to the global-health context of justice: "By global health with justice, I mean achieving the highest attainable standard of physical and mental health, fairly distributed." A just—or fair—allocative policy distributes benefits and burdens according to the provisions of a morally defensible system rather than through capricious decisions. And a just regulatory policy affects the targeted group fairly and equitably. The nation's legal system exists in part to ensure that the principle of justice is respected in the formulation and implementation of public policies and to serve as an appeals mechanism for those who believe that the process has not adequately honored this principle.

The practical implications for health policymaking are felt largely in terms of distributive justice—that is, in how fairly health-related benefits and burdens are distributed in society. Gostin and Wiley (2016, 69) argue that the principles of justice apply to public health policy:

> Public health policy conforms to the principle of social justice (it is fair) when, to the extent possible, it provides services to those in need and imposes burdens and costs on those who endanger the public health. Services provided to those without need are wasteful and, given scarce resources, may deny benefits to those with genuine need. Regulation aimed at persons or businesses where there is no danger imposes

costs and burdens without a corresponding public benefit. Ideally, services should be allocated on the basis of need and burdens imposed only where necessary to prevent a serious health risk.

The most difficult policy question related to the ethical principle of justice is, of course, what is fair? The participants in policy markets and health policymakers vary on what constitutes the fair distribution of the benefits and burdens in the pursuit of health in American society. The three most prominent perspectives on justice provide useful insight into the range of possible views on this matter.

Egalitarian Perspective

The egalitarian perspective of justice holds that everyone should have equal access to the benefits and burdens arising from the pursuit of health and that fairness requires recognition of different levels of need. The influence of the egalitarian view is evident in, for example, policies intended to remove discrimination in the provision of health services and those intended to provide more resources to people who need them most (e.g., Medicare for older individuals, Medicaid for low-income people, different subsidy levels for insurance purchased in the Affordable Care Act's [ACA's] health insurance marketplaces).

Libertarian Perspective

The libertarian perspective of fairness requires a maximum of social and economic liberty for individuals. Policies that favor unfettered markets as the means of distributing the benefits and burdens associated with the pursuit of health reflect the libertarian theory of justice. A classical libertarian would frown on programs like Medicare and Medicaid, favoring instead a completely free market system to allocate healthcare resources.

Utilitarian Perspective

The utilitarian view of fairness is best served when public utility is maximized. This view is sometimes expressed as the greatest good for the greatest number. Many health policies, including those pertaining to restricting pollution, ensuring safe workplaces, and controlling the spread of communicable diseases, have been heavily influenced by a utilitarian view.

Beneficence

In the policymaking process, beneficent participants act with charity and kindness, overtly seeking to do good. The principle of beneficence is widely reflected in policies that provide tangible benefits. Thus, it characterizes such allocative policies as Medicare and Medicaid. It plays an especially prominent role in the ACA, where so much of the policy is intended to mitigate the lack of health insurance coverage in a significant portion of the US population. The expansion of Medicaid and the subsidization of health insurance premiums are clear examples of beneficent health policy. But this principle also includes the complex concept of balancing benefits and burdens.

Stakeholders who seek to influence policymaking to obtain outcomes that benefit them or their own interests exclusively, while burdening others, violate the principle of beneficence. But stakeholders—and the policymakers themselves—who are guided by beneficence make decisions that maximize the net benefits to society as a whole and balance fairly the benefits and burdens of their decisions.

Nonmaleficence

A fourth principle with deep roots in medical ethics but also applicable to health policy is nonmaleficence. This principle is exemplified in the dictum *primum non nocere*—first, do no harm. Policymakers who are guided by the principle of nonmaleficence make decisions that minimize harm. The principles of beneficence (do good) and nonmaleficence (do no harm) are clearly reflected in health policies that seek to ensure the quality of health services and products. Similarly, policies such as those promulgated by the US Food and Drug Administration (FDA) to ensure the safety of pharmaceuticals and the policies that established and maintain the Agency for Healthcare Research and Quality are also examples of policies that reflect the principles of beneficence and nonmaleficence.

Understanding that policy competence for health professionals means the ability to influence policymaking to improve health for individuals and populations and to exert this influence ethically, we are now ready to consider the specifics of how professionals can use this ability. These specifics are the focus of the next section.

Policy Competence for Health Professionals: Influencing Policymaking

To gain policy competence, a health professional must have enough knowledge of the policy market and the policymaking process to be able to exert some influence on public policies that improve health in some way. Such competence is acquirable through formal education and other learning and experiences. For example, health professionals can use the information in this book about policy markets and the policymaking process to develop policy competence.

However health professionals acquire their policy competence, they will find a systematic approach to influencing public policy domain useful. They can take a series of steps, described in the following sections, to increase their likelihood of being influential or to improve their policy competence.

These steps are built on several key aspects of policy competence. First, a competent health professional needs sufficient knowledge of policymaking to be able to observe the process systematically and analytically (context and process were the focus of chapters 2 and 4). Armed with information from this systematic observation, health professionals can then use it to help influence health-supportive decisions.

Thus, the ability to obtain information and use it effectively enables health leaders to exercise influence on public policy. Policy competence in this way can support health professionals in their work of improving health. Perhaps the most practical way of influencing policy involves five steps:

1. *Observe* the policy market and policymaking process to identify the public policy information that might be relevant and important to your goals.
2. *Assess* the level of importance of this information.
3. *Monitor* this information.
4. *Forecast* the future direction of this important public policy information.
5. *Engage* with policymakers to influence policymaking.

Each of these steps is examined in more detail below.

Observing

Health professionals are accustomed to observing relevant developments in their professional domains. This practice simply allows them to keep up with their professional domains. They read the relevant literature, interact with knowledgeable colleagues, and participate in continuing professional education programs. This first step in developing policy competence is much like typical efforts to stay abreast with developments in a professional's domain of expertise. Like all efforts to stay current in one's professional domain, effective observation of the health policy market and policymaking provides several benefits. For professionals who want to develop policy competence, this practice helps them with several important tasks:

- Classify and organize complex information about the policy market and public policymaking, including the forces that affect this process.
- Identify current public policies that do or will affect their work and goal accomplishment.
- Identify the formulation of emerging public policies—including new laws, amendments, and changes in rules—that might eventually affect their goal accomplishment.

- Systematically speculate about potential future public policies that may be relevant.
- Link information about public policies to their professional goals and strategies and, thus, to their performance.

These potential benefits might be offset by several limitations inherent in any attempt to observe and analyze complex public policy markets and policymaking. The following limitations apply to people from all walks of life. No matter how talented they are or how well supported their endeavors, health professionals face these limitations:

- They cannot foretell the future through observation and analyses of public policy markets and policymaking; at best, they can develop informed opinions and speculate about the future.
- They cannot see every aspect of the policy market or the policymaking process; nor can they be aware of every detail of public policies that will affect them.
- They may uncover relevant public policy information but be unable to correctly interpret its effect on them or their professional goals and strategies.
- They may discern and interpret the effect of this information but find that they are unable to respond appropriately.

Despite all these limitations, the potential benefits of effective observation may justify the efforts. The abundant resources that organizations and interest groups have for this purpose is a good reason to rely on these entities for help in this observational task. Whether undertaken by individual professionals or by well-resourced organizations and interest groups, the effective observation of policy markets and policymaking is foundational to developing policy competence.

Observation properly begins with careful consideration of what one believes to be important public policy information. Health professionals need to understand that public policies are a large set of decisions shaped by many variables. Some of these decisions are codified in the statutory language of specific public laws. Others are the rules or regulations established to implement public laws or to operate government and its various programs. Still others are decisions made in the judicial branch.

Relevant public policies, however, represent only part of what should be observed. Problems, potential solutions, and political circumstances that might lead to new or modified policies must also be considered important. Thus, effective observation involves identifying relevant policies and emerging problems, possible solutions, and the political circumstances that could eventually lead to relevant policies.

Judgments about what policy information is relevant for the health professional are largely subjective. To avoid such a subjective, narrow view, more than one person should decide what should be observed. The opinions of colleagues can be helpful in this regard, particularly their take on what is relevant in the policy markets and policymaking process. Formal and informal interactions with colleagues with similar policy interests help health professionals find productive sources of information. Social media can also reveal what people in the field consider important.

Newsletter content from professional associations can reflect the collective judgment of other similarly situated people and may be helpful for this reason. Newsletters focusing on health policy may also be useful. For example, the *KHN Morning Briefing*, produced by Kaiser Health News and available online, is free to its users and offers excellent health-policy-related information.

As noted earlier, the starting point in observation is determining who or what to observe. The appropriate foci include the policymakers in federal, state, and local governments and the parties who can influence these policymakers' decisions. These parties may exert their influence by helping conceptualize problems and potential solutions or through the political circumstances that help drive the policymaking process.

In effect, health professionals should focus their observations on the suppliers of public policies and those who can have some bearing on them. As discussed in chapter 2, each branch of government promulgates policies in the policy market, although the role of each branch is different. Each should receive attention in this step. Because policies are made in all three branches of the federal government, the list of potential policymakers is lengthy, and adding those who can influence them makes it even longer. Likewise, as discussed in chapter 4, observing policy trends and influences at the state level may also be critical.

Effective observation of the policy markets and policymaking itself identifies relevant and important policies. It also identifies the emerging problems, their possible solutions, and the related political circumstances that could eventually lead to other important policies. But observing is only the first step in analyzing policy markets and the policymaking process.

Civic and Professional Engagement

As a professional of any kind, including healthcare professionals, you need to be active and engaged in your community and professional association. Keeping in mind that you serve members of the community, engaging with them keeps you informed about developments that may not appear in the larger public. Likewise, your presence serves as

(continued)

a reminder that you are a part of the community and exist to serve the needs of the population in that area. Similarly, involvement in your professional association will also help you stay informed, but it has the added benefit of providing an outlet where you can help shape the association and, by extension, the profession and perhaps even public policy. Do not underestimate the value of this kind of engagement. It is rewarding in its own right, but it also brings added value in the form of information, institutional visibility in the community, and professional stature you might not otherwise be able to attain.

Assessing

Observation may identify possibly important information in the policy market and policymaking process. Assessment determines whether the information is worthy of continuing interest. The health professional may observe much activity and acquire considerable information, but only some of it is important and relevant to the issues at hand. Determining the importance of public policy information is largely subjective and seldom easy.

One useful way to assess importance is to characterize information as an opportunity or a threat. If a piece of information clearly represents a threat or an opportunity, it probably bears continuing interest. Such assessments, however, are far from exact.

Experience with similar issues is frequently another useful basis for assessing the importance of public policy information. Like all competence, policy competence grows with experience. The experience may have been acquired firsthand, or it may come from contact with colleagues who have encountered similar public policy issues and situations and who are willing to share their experiences.

Public policies that affect the pursuit of health vary among the states; this variety can be instructive. For example, knowledge gained from the 2006 Massachusetts healthcare reform experience was useful in developing the ACA (Long 2010). Valuable lessons were also learned in the Oregon health insurance experiment discussed in chapter 9 (Finkelstein et al. 2012; Taubman et al. 2014). Similarly, professionals can draw insight from experiences in other countries. Other bases for assessments include best guesses about what some public policy information might mean and advice from well-informed and experienced others. When possible, quantification, modeling, and simulation of the potential effects of the issues being assessed can be useful, but these methods often lie beyond the realistic capabilities of the individual professional.

An appropriate assessment is rarely simple, even when all the bases we have suggested are considered. Aside from the difficulties in collecting and properly analyzing enough information to inform the assessment fully, problems sometimes derive from the personal biases of those making the assessment. Such biases can force assessments that fit some preconceived notions of importance rather than accurately reflecting a particular situation (Lindgren and Bandhold 2009).

As we have noted, many policies contain, at least implicitly, an underlying theory, rationale, or logic. They are not written as logic models, but such a model is inherent in many policies, whether they take the form of public laws, rules, regulations, other implementation decisions, or judicial decisions. Essentially, a policy's underlying theory or logic expresses how resources are meant to be used to achieve the policy's objectives. For this reason, a logic model can help health professionals assess whether a policy is important.

Any mechanism that can help better assess policies has utility. Logic models were developed in the context of program evaluation (Knowlton and Phillips 2013) and were subsequently found to be useful in managing programs more effectively, as the models depict what resources will be used in various processes to yield results. Also, logic models can show the relationships between the various results of a policy. Such models could help policymakers more carefully conceptualize policies as they are being formulated. For better or worse, these models are rarely used in this way. Policymaking is, after all, a human-driven, political process.

Consider the possible benefit when someone drafts a policy that says in clear, simple language, "These are the results I hope the policy will achieve, and these are the necessary resources that will be processed in the following ways to achieve the results." This logical thinking could certainly improve the efficaciousness of policies. If the implicit logic model of a policy can be developed, the result will probably help determine the policy's relevance and importance. The model could be useful simply because the results and the necessary resources and processes have been more clearly specified. If either the results or the resources used by a policy are relevant to the health professional's concerns, then the policy is a good candidate for continuing attention.

One way to visualize the purpose of a public policy is to think of it as a theory of how it is supposed to work. For example, one can theorize about a proposed policy as follows: If resources *a*, *b*, and *c* are assembled and then processed by doing *m*, *n*, and *o* with the resources, the results will be *x*, *y*, and *z*. For example, one element of theory inherent in the ACA was that increasing federal resources for states to use in expanding their Medicaid program enrollments by loosening eligibility requirements, modernizing and simplifying enrollment processes, and increasing outreach efforts would result in greater enrollment in the program. This theory has been realized, as the ACA has resulted in "significant coverage gains and reductions in uninsured rates among the low-income population broadly and within specific vulnerable populations" (Guth et al. 2020).

The relationships between resources, processes, and results form a policy's underlying theory, which can be used to draw a logic model of how the policy is intended to operate. Exhibit 10.1 depicts a basic logic model template for a policy.

The exhibit shows that resources are used in processes to accomplish the policy's results. The model includes feedback in the form of loops from results to resources and processes to indicate that policies can be adjusted as they are implemented. The logic model also shows that a policy exists in an external environment.

The external environment of a policy typically includes many factors that can influence operation and performance. These are illustrated in exhibit 10.1 by the top arrows that flow between the external environment and the logic model. Besides the preferences and circumstances of stakeholders, the external environment includes biological, biomedical, cultural, demographic, ecological, economic, ethical, legal, psychological, scientific, social, and technological variables.

EXHIBIT 10.1
Logic Model Template for a Policy

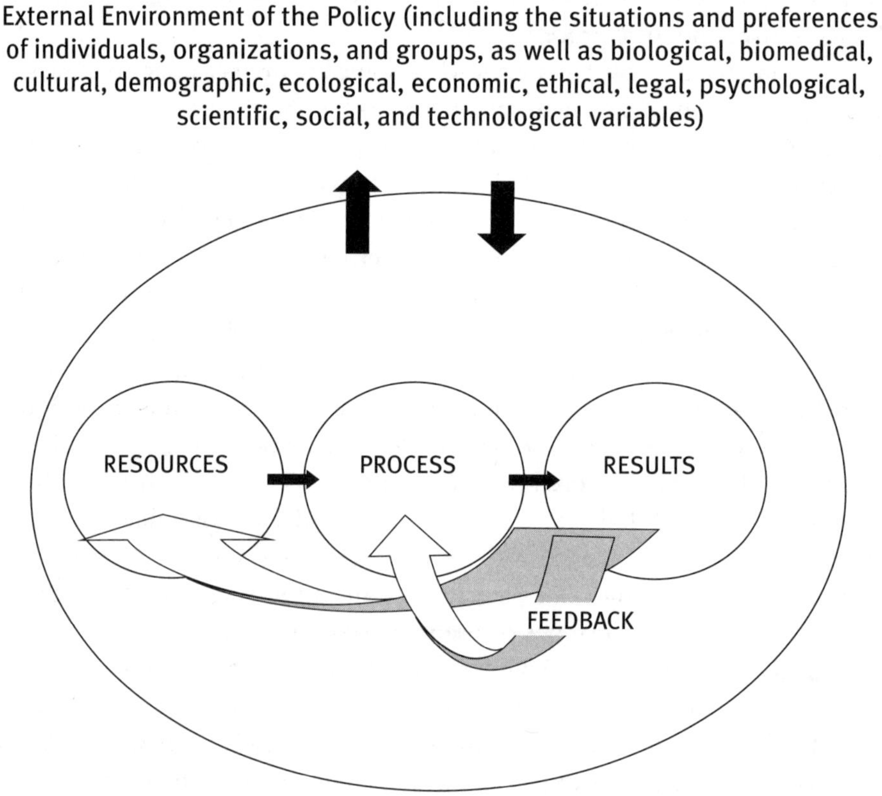

Public policies do not exist in isolation. All policies affect and are affected by their external environments. The resources needed for implementation flow from the external environment. A policy's results flow out into the external environment, where they affect individuals, organizations, groups, and such other variables as the economy and science.

When done well, observing policy information and assessing its importance will yield a set of policy-market and policymaking indicators that the health professional should then routinely monitor over time. The ability to assess the relative importance of observed sources accurately is a policy competence.

Monitoring

Health professionals should monitor, that is, track over time, the public policy information they believe to be important. Monitoring, especially when the information is complex, poorly structured, or ambiguous, permits the professional to assemble more information so that questions and uncertainties can be addressed and the importance of information can be more fully determined (Heath and Palenchar 2009).

Monitoring takes a much narrower focus than does observing (Ginter, Duncan, and Swayne 2018). The purpose of monitoring is to build a base of knowledge and insight around relevant and important public policy information identified through observation or verified through earlier monitoring. Fewer—usually far fewer—pieces of information will be monitored than will be observed in the analysis of the public policy market and the policymaking process.

The importance of public policy information can be difficult to determine. Uncertainty characterizes much of the information being observed, assessed, and monitored. Monitoring information over time will not eliminate uncertainty, but it will likely reduce it significantly as more detailed and sustained information is acquired.

As with the observing and assessing steps, multiple perspectives and expert opinions can help professionals determine what should be monitored and what the information being monitored means. Furthermore, monitoring shows that the vast majority of contemporary health policies spring from a relatively few earlier policies. In other words, public policies have histories. Many of them continually but incrementally evolve through modification. As professionals monitor these changes, they become intimately familiar with the policies' evolutionary paths. Such familiarity can serve as a background for the next step: forecasting changes.

Forecasting

Effective observation, assessment, and monitoring cannot provide all the public policy information that is relevant to health professionals. The ability to use public policy information to prepare for future changes in policy or to influence the policymaking process typically requires lead time. Observing, assessing importance, and monitoring relevant public policy information involves searching for signals, sometimes distant and faint, that may be the forerunners of important future circumstances. Forecasting or projecting involves extending the information and its impact beyond its current state.

For some public policy information (e.g., how a change in Medicaid eligibility requirements such as those included in the ACA will affect health insurance coverage for individuals and populations), professionals can make adequate forecasts by extending past trends or applying a formula. In other situations, forecasting must rely on speculation or, at the other extreme, more formal forecasting methods. However, some degree of uncertainty characterizes the results of all forecasting techniques.

Other challenges with forecasts include the complexity of important public policy information. The information never exists in a vacuum and typically involves many issues and circumstances simultaneously. Existing forecasting techniques and models do not fully account for this complexity. Nevertheless, professionals can apply some useful forecasting techniques to project the future direction of relevant public policy information they are monitoring.

Trend Extrapolation

The most widely used technique for forecasting changes in public policy information is trend extrapolation (Hanke and Wichern 2014). When properly used, this technique is relatively simple and can be remarkably effective. Trend extrapolation is simply tracking the path or trajectory of particular information to predict future changes. Public policies do not emerge de novo. Instead, they result from chains of activities that typically span many years. Understanding the history of policies and related policy information makes the results of the policymaking process easier to predict.

Even so, trend extrapolation must be handled carefully. It works best under highly stable conditions; under other conditions, it has significant limitations. When used to forecast changes in public policy information, it usually predicts some general trend—such as a directional trend in the number of people served by a program or in a funding stream—rather than small, quantifiable details.

Significant changes in policy, technology, demographics, or other variables can render the extrapolation of a trend meaningless or misleading. However, predictions based on extrapolation can be useful to health professionals as they seek to predict the paths of important policy information. For those who exercise caution in its use and who factor in the effect of major changes such as the introduction of a new or modified policy or a shift in political control of a legislative body, trend extrapolation can be useful in forecasting certain aspects of public policy information.

Scenario Development

Another technique for forecasting public policy information is the development, usually in writing, of future scenarios (Chermack 2011; Ramirez, Selsky, and van der Heijden 2010). In this context, a scenario is simply a plausible story about the future. This technique is especially appropriate for analyzing policy markets and policymaking processes because they contain many uncertainties.

In scenario development, a professional defines several alternative scenarios, or states of affairs. The professional can use the scenarios as the basis for developing contingent responses to the public policy information being analyzed; alternatively, the person can select the most likely scenario from among the scenarios and prepare accordingly.

Scenarios can pertain to a single piece of policy information (e.g., the federal government's policy regarding approval procedures for new medical technology) or to broader-based sets of policy information (e.g., the federal government's policies on regulation of health plans, funding for medical education or research, or a preventive approach to improved health). Scenarios vary considerably in scope and depth (Lindgren and Bandhold 2009).

As a general rule, forecasters will find it useful to develop several scenarios. Multiple scenarios permit the exploration of the breadth of future possibilities. After forecasters examine the full range of possibilities, they select one as the most likely. However, the most common mistake in scenario development is envisioning one scenario too early in the process and basing a response on it. Health professionals who think they know which scenario will prevail and who prepare only for that one may find that the price of guessing incorrectly can be high indeed.

Engagement

The previous steps are analytical; the health professional acquires and uses information about the public policy market and policymaking itself to help shape policymaking. In this step, the health professional actually seeks to exert influence in the policy market and policymaking to help shape decisions that contribute to health.

Mostly because of the abusive and inappropriate use of social power to shape the policy market, influence has acquired a negative connotation among some people. However, there is nothing innately wrong with a health professional's efforts to have an impact on health policymaking. After all, policy can affect the determinants of health and, ultimately, the health of individuals and populations in many ways. The health professional seeking to influence health policy to improve the health of individuals or populations is behaving appropriately. Because influencing activities can easily be tainted by self-serving purposes, however, health professionals must adhere to the ethical principles described earlier in this chapter.

Effectively exerting influence in the public policy market and the policymaking process is not a simple matter. However, a great deal is known about influence and its exercise in policymaking. Successful influence depends on two variables: (1) the possession and use of social power and (2) knowing where and when to focus efforts to exert influence. We consider both social power and focus in the following sections.

Social power is the basis of influence in public policy markets and policymaking processes. *Social power* means the degree of influence that an individual, an organization, or a group possesses. *Influence* means the capacity to have an effect on the decisions and actions of others. A health professional, or anyone else wanting to exert influence in policymaking has three sources of social power: position in society; the ability to provide or withhold rewards; and the possession of information, knowledge, or expertise. Each source can be useful to the health professional.

Positional Social Power

Health professionals may possess social power by virtue of their place or role in the larger society. They have some degree of positional social power simply because they exist as health professionals and are recognized as legitimate participants in the policy market and the policymaking process.

Policymakers entertain the opinions and preferences of health professionals, partly because the policymakers recognize these professionals as legitimate participants in the health policy domain. Positional social power is not limited to individuals. Organizations and interest groups, often through their leaders, also enjoy positional social power. This power is a good reason for individuals to associate themselves with organizations or groups that share their policy preferences as a means of increasing their ability to influence policymaking. Examples of organizations and groups with positional social power in health policymaking are Baxter International, a global healthcare company involved in medical devices, pharmaceuticals, and biotechnology; America's Health Insurance Plans, a national trade association whose members provide health insurance and supplemental benefits to more than 200 million people; and the American Hospital Association, representing the interests of the nation's nearly 5,000 hospitals and health networks.

An important aspect of using positional social power to influence policymaking is the ability of individuals and especially organizations and interest groups to bring legal actions as part of their efforts to exert influence. Positional social power alone may gain a hearing for particular views or preferences. The exertion of influence, however, usually requires social power of other kinds.

Reward-Based Social Power

Some social power is based on the capacity to reward policymakers' compliance or punish their noncompliance with preferred decisions. Such rewards include campaign contributions, votes, and the organization and mobilization of grassroots activities designed to persuade other people on particular issues. Rewards can also be withheld if policymakers' decisions are not popular with those who hold reward-based social power.

Expert Social Power

Another source of influence in policymaking is based on the possession of expertise, knowledge, or information that is valued by policymakers. In public policy markets and policymaking processes, useful information and expertise may pertain to the definition or clarification of problems or to the development of solutions. Expertise in the intricacies of the political circumstances that also help shape the public policymaking process is also valuable.

Health professionals, who can marshal the three bases of social power (expertise, knowledge, and information), and especially people who can integrate them, can be influential. The degree of influence, of course, varies. Relative influence is determined by the amount of social power a person or group has, their reputation for exerting influence ethically and effectively, and the strength of ideological convictions held by those who seek to exert influence. Whatever the bases, however, social power, as one part of the complex equation that determines influence, must be effectively used if it is to translate into influence.

Focus and Influence

In addition to marshaling enough social power to influence policymaking, health professionals must also consider the focus of their efforts. Typically, focus is guided by the identification of policies that are important or may become so and of problems, potential solutions, and political circumstances that might eventually lead to such policies. Possible foci include relevant policymakers in all three branches and all levels of government and others who have influence with these policymakers.

In addition to influencing policymakers' decisions directly, those who want to influence policymaking can help shape the conceptualizations of problems, the development of potential solutions, and the political circumstances that help drive the policymaking process. The suppliers of relevant public policies and those who can influence them form the appropriate focus for health professionals seeking to influence public policymaking.

The display of the three phases of the policymaking process in exhibit 4.1 can serve as a map of where a professional's influencing efforts can be most useful. Depending on the circumstances, the proper focus may be one or more of the three phases or the components of the phases. Influence can be exerted in the formulation of policy or, more likely, during policy modification. We can expand the map in exhibit 4.1 with the following examples of opportunities for influencing policymaking:

- Influencing policy formulation
  - At agenda setting
    - Defining and documenting problems
    - Developing and evaluating possible solutions
    - Shaping political circumstances through lobbying and the courts
  - At legislation development
    - Participating in drafting legislation
    - Testifying at legislative hearings
- Influencing policy implementation
  - At designing
    - Collaborating with policy implementers to make programs succeed
    - Serving as demonstration sites for testing new approaches
  - At rulemaking
    - Providing formal comments on proposed rules
    - Serving on, and providing input to, rulemaking advisory bodies
  - At operating
    - Interacting with, and giving feedback to, policy implementers
    - Documenting the case for modification through operational experience
  - At evaluating
    - Conducting formal evaluations and sharing results
    - Participating in evaluations conducted by others

As observed throughout this book, the vast majority of health policies result from the modification of existing policies in modest, incremental steps. Active efforts to modify policy begin when stakeholder and general public experiences with existing policies feed back into the agenda-setting and legislation development stages of the formulation phase and into the activities of the implementation phase and stimulate changes in legislation, and in the designing, rulemaking, operating, and evaluating activities of its implementation. Opportunities for health professionals and others to trigger modification of policies continually arise as those affected by the policy experience its outcomes and develop preferences for alternatives. Those who would influence policies can do so in the initial iteration of any policy, but many more chances arise during the subsequent modification of existing policies.

Influencing Policy Formulation

In the formulation of a health policy, the agenda is shaped by the interaction of problems, their possible solutions, and the relevant political circumstances. Health professionals with pertinent expertise could influence policymaking by helping define the problems being considered or by helping design possible solutions to these problems. For example, clinicians, IT specialists, or managers responsible for reimbursements in hospitals can help define financial problems in healthcare and identify possible solutions. Similarly, a senior manager with a national reputation or close relationships with powerful policymakers might influence the political circumstances around an issue. Professionals with sufficient positional or reward-based power can help shape the political circumstances necessary to convert potential solutions into actual policies, although, as is discussed in a later section, they are more likely to do so when individuals work through interest groups.

In short, health professionals' actions that shape agenda setting can also influence the policy itself. Because agenda setting involves the confluence of problems, possible solutions, and political circumstances, health professionals and others can exert their influence by making certain that problems become more sharply defined and better understood through the experiences of those affected by the policies. In fact, health professionals and others directly involved in healthcare are often excellent sources of feedback on a policy's performance, including its effects on the people and the communities they serve. Similarly, people and groups that have had experiences with particular policies can conceive of, and assess, potential new solutions to problems, especially when demonstrations and evaluations provide concrete evidence of the policies' performance and impact. Health professionals—guided by their experiences and interactions with ongoing policies—become important components of the political circumstances surrounding the modification of these policies.

Once issues take a prominent place on the policy agenda, they sometimes proceed to the next stage of the policy formulation phase: the development of legislation. At this stage, legislative proposals go through a carefully prescribed set of steps that sometimes lead to policies in the form of new legislation or amendments to previously enacted legislation (see chapter 6). Although this path is long and arduous, it is replete with opportunities to influence legislation development. Both as individuals and as members of interest groups and other organizations, health professionals can participate directly in the drafting of legislative proposals and the hearings associated with the development of legislation.

Experience with existing policies positions health professionals to identify needed modifications in policies that affect them and their patients and communities. The long evolution of Medicare legislation is a good example of this phenomenon. Over this policy's life, services have been added and deleted; premiums and copayment provisions have been changed, reimbursement mechanisms have been modified, features to ensure quality and the medical necessity of services have been added, dropped, or otherwise changed, and so on. Feedback from directly affected health professionals and others played a role in amending the original legislation, although other influences certainly contributed.

Influencing Policy Implementation

Health professionals and others can actively participate in policymaking in its implementation phase. As discussed in chapters 6 and 7, enacted legislation is rarely explicit enough to fully guide its implementation. Rather, laws and amendments are often vague on implementation details, leaving to the implementing agencies and organizations the responsibility for designing, rulemaking, operating, and evaluating activities of policy implementation. Implementation is the domain of the appointees and civil servants who staff the government and whose implementation decisions are also policies. With their relevant expertise, health professionals have abundant opportunities to influence these decisions. In fact, the implementation phase of a policy literally invites the participation of stakeholders in several ways. Some concrete examples of these ways follow.

Participating in Demonstration Projects

Many implementing organizations support demonstration projects to discover ways to improve implementation. For example, the Centers for Medicare & Medicaid Services (CMS) Innovation Center operates an extensive program of demonstration projects in which health professionals with appropriate expertise can participate. As discussed more fully in chapter 7, the CMS Innovation Center has three priorities:

1. Testing new payment and service delivery models
2. Evaluating results and advancing best practices
3. Engaging a broad range of stakeholders to develop additional models for testing

The CMS Innovation Center is running numerous demonstration projects involving many health professionals in seven categories (CMS 2014a):

1. Accountable care
2. Bundled payments for care improvement
3. Primary care transformation

4. Initiatives focused on the Medicaid and Children's Health Insurance Program population
5. Initiatives focused on Medicare–Medicaid enrollees
6. Initiatives to speed the adoption of best practices
7. Initiatives to accelerate the development and testing of new payment and service delivery models

Health professionals participating in these models have a direct impact on the shape of future health policy. The CEO of the Greater Baltimore Medical Center HealthCare System, a participant in one of the models, the Shared Savings Program, said, "We are delighted to be participating in the Shared Savings Program because of its goal to reduce costs while simultaneously increasing the quality of care and services we provide to our patients and community. The Shared Savings Program is a tangible reminder of the historic transformation taking place in our health care system and we are pleased to be a part of it" (CMS 2014c, 1).

Participating in Rulemaking

Another way that health professionals actively participate in policy implementation is through their involvement in rulemaking. Rulemaking, an important policy implementation activity discussed extensively in chapter 7, is an especially promising place for health professionals to seek to exert influence because they are literally invited to participate. With appropriate expertise, they can help shape the rules that guide policy implementation. For example, in an advance notice of federal rulemaking, published in the *Federal Register* (CMS 2014b), CMS solicited comments on its development of payment methodologies for certain durable medical equipment and enteral nutrition:

> This advance notice of proposed rulemaking (ANPRM) solicits public comments on different methodologies we may consider using with regard to applying information from the durable medical equipment, prosthetics, orthotics, and supplies (DMEPOS) competitive bidding programs to adjust Medicare fee schedule payment amounts or other Medicare payment amounts for DMEPOS items and services furnished in areas that are not included in these competitive bidding programs. In addition, we are also requesting comments on a different matter regarding ideas for potentially changing the payment methodologies used under the competitive bidding programs for certain durable medical equipment and enteral nutrition.

The federal government provides a website, www.regulations.gov, to facilitate public participation in rulemaking. Health professionals and the public can use this site to electronically submit comments on proposed rules. The website offers detailed advice for submitting effective comments (exhibit 10.2).

EXHIBIT 10.2
Guidelines for Effective Comments in the Rulemaking Process

1. Comment periods close at 11:59 ET on the date comments are due—begin work well before the deadline.
2. Attempt to fully understand each issue; if you have questions or do not understand a part of the regulatory document, you may ask for help from the agency contact listed in the document.
3. Clearly identify the issues within the regulatory action on which you are commenting. If you are commenting on a particular word, phrase or sentence, provide the page number, column, and paragraph citation from the federal register document.
    a. If you choose to comment on the comments of others, identify such comments using their comment ID's before you respond to them.
4. If a rule raises many issues, do not feel obligated to comment on every one—select those issues that concern you the most, affect you the most, and/or you understand the best.
5. Agencies often ask specific questions or raise issues in rulemaking proposals on subjects where they are actively looking for more information. While the agency will still accept comments on any part of the proposed regulation, please keep these questions and issues in mind while formulating your comment.
6. Although agencies receive and appreciate all comments, constructive comments (either positive or negative) are the most likely to have an influence.
7. If you disagree with a proposed action, suggest an alternative (including not regulating at all) and include an explanation and/or analysis of how the alternative might meet the same objective or be more effective.
8. The comment process is not a vote. The government is attempting to formulate the best policy, so when crafting a comment it is important that you adequately explain the reasoning behind your position.
9. Identify credentials and experience that may distinguish your comments from others. If you are commenting in an area in which you have relevant personal or professional experience . . . say so.
10. Agency reviewers look for sound science and reasoning in the comments they receive. When possible, support your comment with substantive data, facts, and/or expert opinions. You may also provide personal experience in your comment, as may be appropriate. By supporting your arguments well you are more likely to influence the agency decision making.
11. Consider including examples of how the proposed rule would impact you negatively or positively.
12. Comments on the economic effects of rules that include quantitative and qualitative data are especially helpful.

(continued)

EXHIBIT 10.2
Guidelines for Effective Comments in the Rulemaking Process *(continued)*

13. Include the pros and cons and trade-offs of your position and explain them. Your position could consider other points of view, and respond to them with facts and sound reasoning.
14. If you are uploading more than one attachment to the comment web form, it is recommended that you [follow the recommended file naming convention]. This standardized file naming convention will help agency reviewers distinguish your submitted attachments and aid in the comment review process.
15. Keep a copy of your comment in a separate file—this practice helps ensure that you will not lose your comment if you have a problem submitting it using the Regulations.gov web form.

Source: Regulations.gov (2020).

Participating with Policy Advisory Bodies and Commissions

Health professionals can also exert influence by serving on, or interacting with, health policy advisory bodies and commissions. The Medicare Payment Advisory Commission (MedPAC) is one such body. Operationally, MedPAC meets publicly to discuss policy issues and formulate its recommendations to Congress. During these meetings, commissioners consider the results of staff research, presentations by policy experts, and comments from such interested parties as staff from congressional committees and CMS, health services researchers, health services providers, other health providers, and beneficiary advocates. In addition to input obtained at public meetings, MedPAC invites stakeholders to comment on its deliberations on its website (www.medpac.gov/-public-meetings-).

The MedPAC commissioners include healthcare executives, clinicians, and academicians (MedPAC 2020). Although opportunities for direct service on such commissions are limited to few people, others can influence their thinking. By interacting with commission members, other health professionals can thus shape the advice that commission members ultimately provide about formulating and implementing policy.

Another implementing organization that provides extensive opportunities for health professionals to directly influence policymaking is the FDA (www.fda.gov). The agency describes its many advisory groups: "The FDA has 47 Advisory Committees, one of which, the Medical Devices Advisory Committee, has 18 panels. The committees are established to provide functions which support the FDA's mission of protecting and promoting the public health while meeting the requirements set forth in the Federal Advisory Committee Act. Committees are either mandated by statute or established at the discretion of the Department of Health and Human Services" (FDA 2020).

Likewise, CMS also uses advisory committees for a variety of policymaking purposes (CMS 2017):

- Advisory Panel on Clinical Diagnostic Laboratory Tests Past Meeting Agendas and Federal Register Notices
- Advisory Panel on Outreach and Education
- Advisory Panel on Hospital Outpatient Payment
- Advisory Panel on Clinical Diagnostic Laboratory Tests
- Medicare Economic Index Technical Advisory Panel
- APC (Advisory Payment Classification) Panel
- Practicing Physicians Advisory Council
- Advisory Board on the Demonstration of a Bundled Case-Mix Adjusted Payment System for End Stage Renal Disease (ESRD) Services
- Medicare Evidence Development & Coverage Advisory Committee

Participating Through Personal Interactions

More generally, healthcare professionals can influence policies through their personal interactions with those who have implementation responsibilities. As discussed in detail in chapter 9, opportunities to develop close working relationships between policy implementers and health professionals commonly arise. These relationships develop more often with bureaucrats, because of the relative length of their service, than with elected officials, who can change at every election cycle (Gormley and Balla 2018). A health professional providing authoritative information based on real-world experience with a policy can contribute to a positive working relationship and affect the implementation of a policy. The potential effect on policy is magnified if the information is reinforced by others with similar experiences. In well-established working relationships based on mutual respect, policy implementers may be influenced to change the existing policy.

Using Organizational Relationships to Increase Influence in Policymaking

As noted earlier, individual health professionals rarely have as much impact on policymaking as do organizations and interest groups. This relative lack of power is primarily a matter of resource availability, including the time required to engage effectively in the policy market and policymaking process. The organizational aspect of policy competence goes beyond what individuals may possess and into the realm of organizational strength. Many organizations actively participate in the nation's pursuit of health. People who are employed in these organizations, who govern them, or who independently practice their professions within them have an interest in health policies that affect the mission and purpose of these organizations, their day-to-day operations, and, ultimately, their successes and failures. In addition, individuals associated with organizations can gain synergy from these relationships in their own efforts to affect policymaking. We explore how in this section.

The individual professionals and organizations with the greatest interest in policymaking are most likely to become involved with formal interest groups to more effectively address their policy concerns and interests. As defined earlier in the book, interest groups are groups of people or organizations that have similar policy goals and that band together to pursue those goals. Thus, to assess stakeholders' utility in affecting policymaking, we should consider the policy competence of the stakeholders, whether they are health professionals, organizations that participate in the pursuit of health, or health-related interest groups to which individual professionals and organizations belong.

From the perspectives of health professionals, organizations, and interest groups, policy competence means the same thing. It means having some effect on the policymaking process. One of the ways that individual health professionals can increase this sort of competence is by joining effective organizations and groups, which typically have greater resources, in the shared pursuit of influence. Greater resources mean that organizations and groups are more likely to affect the policymaking process by using the positional power of their leaders and by using reward-based power as a source of persuasion. Many health-related organizations have strong incentives to be involved in policymaking.

Health Policy and Health-Related Organizations and Interest Groups

The performance of many organizations and interest groups is affected by health policies. Although the missions, objectives, and internal structures and resources of these organizations and groups help shape and determine how they perform, their effectiveness—whether it is measured as contribution to health outcomes for people, financial strength, reputation, growth, competitive position, scope of services provided, or some other parameter—is also heavily influenced by the opportunities and threats posed by their external environments.

The external environments that health-related organizations and interest groups face have all of the variables surrounding the policymaking process, although the variables may have different interpretations or points of emphasis. That is, external environments that policymakers must consider include the situations and preferences of individuals, organizations, and groups. They must also consider biological, biomedical, cultural, demographic, ecological, economic, ethical, legal, psychological, scientific, social, and technological variables. Health-related organizations and interest groups may look at patient satisfaction as an individual preference and consider biomedical developments from a cost–benefit perspective as opposed to a policy opportunity.

Differences between the external environments faced by policymakers and health-related organizations and groups arise, for example, because the individuals, organizations, and groups are constituents for policymakers but are also customers and perhaps even competitors for other organizations and groups. Also, for the health-related organizations and groups, policies become important variables in their external environments. Policies may determine their very existence and routinely determine their degrees of success and failure. As exhibit 10.3 illustrates, policies and the other variables in the external environment present a health-related organization or interest group with a set of opportunities and threats to which it can choose to respond.

The strategies and structures an organization or interest group creates to respond to these threats and opportunities results in its organizational performance. But these opportunities and threats are the direct result of conditions in the external environment, including the public policies that affect the organization or group.

The organizations that populate the health sector defy easy categorization, but they are all affected by, and have interests in, health policies. In

EXHIBIT 10.3 The Relationship Between a Health-Related Organization or Interest Group's External Environment and Its Performance

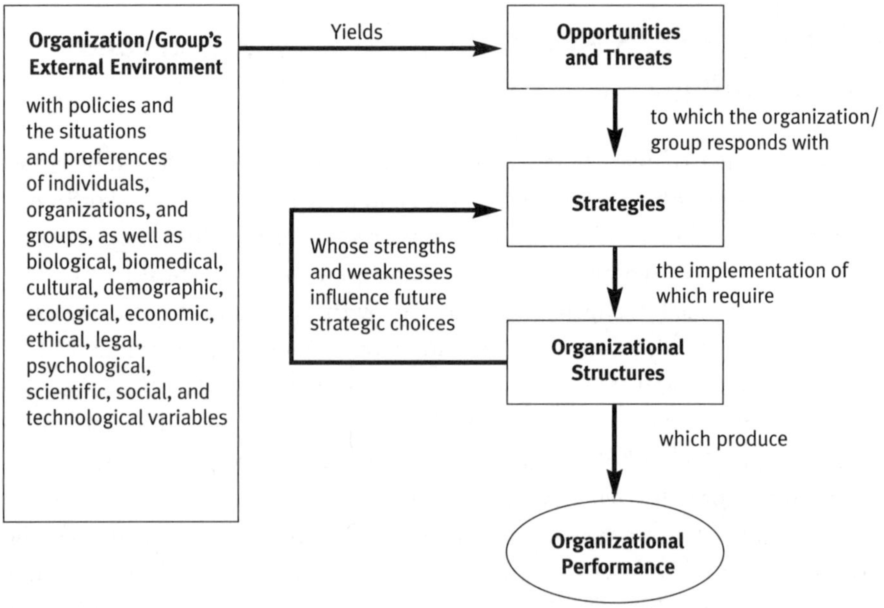
Organization/Group's External Environment
with policies and the situations and preferences of individuals, organizations, and groups, as well as biological, biomedical, cultural, demographic, ecological, economic, ethical, legal, psychological, scientific, social, and technological variables
Yields
Opportunities and Threats
to which the organization/ group responds with
Strategies
the implementation of which require
Organizational Structures
Whose strengths and weaknesses influence future strategic choices
which produce
Organizational Performance

the following discussion, we divide the organizations and groups into three categories—health services provider organizations, resource producers, and interest groups—and describe their policy interests.

Health Services Provider Organizations

Hospitals, state or county health departments, health maintenance organizations, hospices, and nursing homes are examples of health services providers whose policy interests are identifiable. These interests vary, but the leaders share certain generic concerns. Those in charge of provider organizations tend to focus, for example, on policies that might affect access to their services, the costs of those services, or their revenues from them. These executives and governing board members are also typically concerned about policies that relate to the availability of insurance coverage and the structure of the healthcare system. Other issues of concern include antitrust issues involved in mergers and consolidations; the needs of special populations; quality assurance; and ethical and legal issues related to providing access to affordable health services of an appropriate quality to all who need them.

Resource-Producing Organizations

Related to the organizations that provide health services directly are those that produce resources for providers to use in conducting their work or that otherwise facilitate this work in some way. Such organizations include educational institutions that produce the healthcare system's workforce; insurance companies and health plans that organize and facilitate payment for health services (at least the insurers and plans that are not integrated into provider systems); and such organizations as pharmaceutical, medical device, and biomedical technology companies, whose products are used in providing health services.

The policy interests of resource-producing organizations are also identifiable. Educational organizations and programs involved in producing the health workforce are interested in policies that affect the resources used in their educational missions, such as faculty, buildings, and equipment. Interest is also keen in policies that relate to licensure and practice guidelines and those that may influence the demand for their programs' graduates, including policies that affect coverage under public insurance programs. These organizations are also interested in policies that affect people's ability to pay for education.

Health plans and insurance organizations are vitally interested in policies that affect their operations and decisions. Because these organizations are licensed by the states, they are affected by federal and state policies. Similarly, pharmaceutical and biotechnology firms and medical supply companies have wide-ranging health policy interests, including specific concerns with policies that affect their markets, products, and profits.

Health-Related Interest Groups

Health services provider organizations and resource-producing organizations are not the only entities with health policy concerns. A wide variety of health-related interest groups exists because of the collective interests of their members in health policymaking and the resulting policies.

As discussed in chapter 2, a significant feature of the health policy market and policymaking process is the presence of interest groups that exist to serve the collective interests of their members. These groups analyze the policymaking process to discern policy changes that might affect their members and inform them about such changes. They also seek to influence the process to provide the group's members with some advantage. The interests of their constituent members define the health policy interests of these groups. We examine the policy interests of some of these groups next.

Interest Groups of Health Services Providers

Some interest groups have health services provider organizations or individual professionals as their members. As discussed in chapter 5, among these are the American Hospital Association (www.aha.org), the American Health Care Association (www.ahca.org), the American Association of Homes and Services for the Aging (now known as LeadingAge, www.leadingage.org), and America's Health Insurance Plans (www.ahip.org).

Other interest groups focus on individual health professionals or specialists. Physician groups include the American Medical Association (www.ama-assn.org), the American College of Surgeons (www.facs.org), and the American Academy of Pediatrics (www.aap.org). Professional groups for health professionals who are not physicians include the American College of Healthcare Executives (www.ache.org), the American Nurses Association (www.ana.org), and the American Dental Association (www.ada.org).

Interest Groups of Resource-Producing Organizations

The organizations that produce resources for health services providers have their own interest groups, such as the Association of American Medical Colleges (www.aamc.org); the Association of University Programs in Health Administration (www.aupha.org); the Biotechnology Industry Organization (www.bio.org); and Pharmaceutical Research and Manufacturers of America (www.phrma.org). These interest groups also focus particularly on policies that affect their members directly.

Indeed, all health services providers, resource-producing organizations, and health-related interest groups should be interested in health policy, if only because policy affects their performance levels. Decades ago, Mesch (1984) constructed a list of questions that senior-level managers can use to determine their relative interest in public policies. The questions, in an adapted form, are as follows:

- Do public policies influence your organization or group's capital allocation decisions or its strategic plans for services and markets?
- Have previous strategic plans been scrapped or substantially altered because of changes in public policy?
- Does the interplay of public policies and the other variables in your organization or group's external environment seem to be influencing strategic decisions?
- Are you and other senior-level managers in your organization or group displeased because of surprises resulting from changes in public policies that affected your organization or group's performance?

If the manager of a health-related organization or group, whether a health services provider, a producer of resources, or an interest group, can answer yes to even one of these questions, the manager is likely to be interested in the public policymaking process and in relevant policies. If the answer to most or all of the questions is yes, as is typical for contemporary health-related organizations and groups, they will consider interest in their public policy environment to be imperative. These organizations will make strong operational commitments to understanding and effectively responding to the threats and opportunities that public policy presents to their organization's constituents (Longest and Darr 2014). They will establish units and employ expertise devoted to influencing policymaking as described briefly in the next section.

Organization Design to Support Policy Competence

The resources of organizations and interest groups can enhance the policy competence of their individual members beyond that of individuals acting alone. As part of their organizing or structuring responsibilities, managers in these organizations and groups must establish the patterns of relationships among human resources and other resources in their domains of responsibility. These patterns are called organization designs (Longest 2015). Intentional patterns of relationships established by managers are formal organization designs. This distinction is important because existing within the bounds of formal organization designs are informal structures—relationships and interactions that lie outside the boundaries of the formal structure—that people working together invariably establish. All organization designs have formal aspects, which are developed by managers, and informal aspects, which reflect the wishes and preferences of other participants.

Management literature is replete with recommendations for creating specialized administrative units to analyze and influence the public policy market and policymaking process (Ginter, Duncan, and Swayne 2018). When a health-related organization or interest group wants to rigorously analyze and have an impact on the policy market and policymaking in general, its leaders typically establish a specialized unit—usually called the public affairs department, government affairs department, or government relations department—to do the actual work.

Some large organizations and many interest groups divide government relations into separate units in a department, one for the federal government and another for state government. The directors of such departments often report to the CEO, because CEOs have vital interests in public policy and its impact on their organizations or groups. Departments devoted to government affairs mainly serve to enhance the policy competence of an entity's senior-level managers, especially its CEO. If these units are well designed and staffed with policy-competent people, they can give an entity and its leaders the enormous advantage of lead time in dealing with the policy market and policymaking. When the leaders can anticipate policy changes months—or, better still, years—in advance, their responses can be more effective and more appropriate.

Beyond giving themselves more lead time, those who understand emerging policies or modifications in existing policies can better influence emerging policies to the advantage of their entities. They foresee the emergence of relevant public policies and the consequences on their domains of responsibility. This foresight—derived from policy competence—serves as a basis for efforts to participate in shaping policies that will affect their organizations or groups.

But how is such prescience achieved? The answer lies in the approach to policy analysis. People who look beyond specific policies to the larger public policy market and the policymaking process have a great advantage over those who merely wait until a policy is determined and then react to it. The late President John Kennedy once said: "Change is the law of life. And those who look only to the past or the present are certain to miss the future" (1963). People benefit when they focus on the policies that affect their domains, but they gain much greater advantage when they consider why and how these policies emerge and how those will factor in policy going forward. Those who focus broadly on the public policy environment of their domain increase their chances of anticipating policy changes.

This anticipatory focus—thinking about what tomorrow may bring, not simply the present moment—provides an opportunity to influence policies in their emergent states. Leaders who understand public policy environments, with all their complex interplay of actors, actions, inactions, and other variables, are better equipped to anticipate and influence policies than are their less policy-competent counterparts. The competent leaders are prepared to ask more anticipatory what-if questions.

Leadership that is based on solid predictions of future policies differs significantly from an approach that reacts to announced changes or even to soon-to-be-announced changes. Proactive thinking and attentive preparation make the opportunity to influence the ultimate shape of policies possible. After a policy changes, stakeholders can only react, typically with inadequate time for thoughtful responses. See the following box for examples of organization designs relative to public advocacy.

Examples of Organization Designs

Any group's approach to organization design is likely to be unique to its situation, as the examples in this box suggest. In each example, responsibility for influencing policymaking rests predominantly with senior-level managers and governing board members. These leaders, especially in large entities, may be assisted by specialized staff organized to fulfill these responsibilities.

1. *American Academy of Pediatrics* (www.aap.org). The academy's Department of Federal Affairs is its link to federal policymaking. Pediatricians who wish to make a difference in child and adolescent health through Congress or federal agencies receive the information and tools they need to become effective child advocates. This office prepares them to offer testimony in legislation development or to meet with representatives or senators. The academy's policy agenda includes access to healthcare for all children, immunizations, disaster preparedness, and childhood obesity and injury prevention. Its other interests include legislation and regulations involving Medicaid, the education of new physicians, the ethics of medical practice, biomedical research, and clinical laboratory testing.
2. *Wisconsin Medical Society* (www.wismed.org). The society's mission is to "improve the health of the people of Wisconsin by supporting and strengthening physicians' ability to practice high-quality patient care in a changing environment." The society's Government Relations Department is responsible for legislative affairs (lobbying), policy research and development, and WISMedPAC, the society's political action committee. Members of the lobbying team represent the society before the state and federal governments. At the state level, the WISMedPAC lobbies the legislature and a variety of government agencies. The WISMedPAC policy staff assists

(continued)

the lobbyists in seeking to affect legislation and rule changes. The society regularly submits testimony to the state legislature, and the department staff collaborates with a variety of patient advocacy organizations to strengthen mutual political agendas. In addition, the society staff communicates with other medical societies, including the American Medical Association and state and national specialty societies, to learn from related legislative activities in other states.

3. *Council on Governmental Relations* (COGR; www.cogr.edu). The council is an association of 150 leading research-intensive universities that receive a significant share of the federal funds available to higher education through contracts and grants for research and scholarship. COGR concerns itself with the influence of government regulations, policies, and practices on research conducted at colleges and universities. Its primary function is to help develop policies and practices that fairly reflect the mutual interest and separate obligations of federal agencies and universities in federal research and training. For the most part, COGR deals with policies and technical issues involved in the administration of federally sponsored programs at universities. In addition to providing advice and information to its membership, COGR makes certain that federal agencies understand academic operations and the burden their proposed regulations might impose on colleges and universities.
4. *Hospital and Healthsystem Association of Pennsylvania* (HAP; www.haponline.org). The association's mission is to "empower hospitals and health systems as the leading advocates for improving health in their communities." The Policy and Regulatory Advocacy staff, which includes a senior vice president and a senior director, is responsible for the association's policy development activities and for state and federal regulatory advocacy. The association's presence in the national and state capitals is intended to ensure that "Pennsylvania hospitals have a voice in the public policy decisions surrounding hospitals and health systems." The association's current advocacy initiatives include telehealth, medical liability, value-based care, affordable prescription drugs, and other key issues. The association maintains HAPAC (Hospital and Healthsystem Association of Pennsylvania Political Action Committee) and HAPAC-Federal as political action committees.

The Human Element in Influencing Public Policy Environments

Human control of policymaking complicates efforts to influence the process, even for those with high levels of policy competence. The diverse preferences, objectives, priorities, levels of understanding of issues, and other variables among the people in the policy market make accurate analysis or successful influence difficult. The widely divergent positions held by policymakers regarding the ACA, for example, illustrate the nature of this challenge.

The ACA and, before it, other policies such as Medicare have from their inception been the focus of contention among policymakers, including legislators responsible for formulating these policies and for the staff at CMS, who are responsible for implementation. Constant and sometimes intense pressure from organizations and groups with vested interests in such policies as the ACA, Medicare, and many others fuels the battles over the funding and operation of the policies.

Although Medicare is a simpler example than the ACA is, policymakers' perspectives on Medicare are affected by the program's massive size. Medicare expenditures were approximately $857 billion in 2020 and are projected to exceed $1.2 trillion by 2025 (CMS 2019). As they look to the continued growth in the older adult population, policymakers see a widening gap between program revenues and program expenditures (Cubanski, Neuman, and Freed 2019). This gap creates a looming government financial crisis. Policymakers, especially those who choose to seek reelection, detest difficult fiscal choices because of the political consequences such choices impose. They find themselves attempting to balance the preferences of hospitals and other providers for generous reimbursements against the understandable desires of beneficiaries for expanding benefits, all the while keeping a lid on escalating program costs and seeking new revenues. They have options in this balancing act, but there is no clear consensus on which option may be politically palatable. The variety of strongly held opinions among policy suppliers and demanders makes it more difficult to effectively analyze and anticipate the results of policymaking for Medicare or to influence the outcome.

Finally, people who engage in the policy process on behalf of their professional association should hew closely to their association's experts in governmental affairs. Titles sometimes differ—public affairs, legislative affairs—but the function is communication with governmental agencies on behalf of the profession. As a health services administration professional focused on the day-to-day activities of your organization, you should rely on professionals with experience in the nuances of communicating with all levels of government.

Summary

In any work setting, competence means "a cluster of related abilities, commitments, knowledge, and skills that enable a person or an organization to act effectively in a job or situation" (Business Dictionary.com 2020). Policy competence simply means competence in relation to policies and policymaking. Health policy competence, by extension, means competence in relation to health policy and the process through which health policy is formulated, implemented, and modified over time. Health professionals need a degree of policy competence to improve human health.

Because humans control policy markets and the policymaking process, ethical considerations are important. Four philosophical principles can help guide ethical behavior: respect for the autonomy of other people, justice, beneficence, and nonmaleficence. The implications of each principle for ethical policymaking and efforts to influence the process are discussed in the chapter.

The heart of this chapter presents a series of steps that health professionals can take to increase their likelihood of being influential—or having policy competence. These steps are built on several key aspects of policy competence. First, to develop policy competence, a professional must have sufficient knowledge of the context and process of policymaking to be able to systematically and analytically observe the process. This context and process was the focus of chapters 2 and 3. Armed with information gained by systematic observation, health professionals then need to use the information to help shape the policy decisions that contribute to health. Leaders can gather information and use it to guide, or influence, policymaking. The effective practice of influence can support health professionals in their work of improving health. The actual practice of influencing policymaking has five steps:

1. *Observe* the policy market and the policymaking process to identify potentially relevant and important public policy information.
2. *Assess* the level of importance of the identified public policy information.
3. *Monitor* the public policy information identified as important.
4. *Forecast* the future direction of this information.
5. *Engage* with policymakers.

Effective influence in the public policy market and in policymaking depends on two variables: possession and use of social power, and the knowledge of where and when to focus efforts to exert influence. Both social power, including its sources, and focus are considered in this chapter.

A health professional, or anyone else wanting to exert influence in policymaking, has three sources of social power: position in society, the ability to provide or withhold rewards, and the possession of information, knowledge, or expertise. Each source of social power is discussed.

In addition to marshaling enough social power to influence policymaking, health professionals must also know how and when to focus their efforts. Exhibit 4.1, which shows the three phases of the policymaking process, can serve as a map to direct influencing efforts to where they can be most useful.

Individual health professionals are rarely as influential in policymaking as organizations and interest groups are. This relative lack of power is primarily a matter of resource availability, including the time required to engage effectively in the policy market and the policymaking process. Individuals associated with organizations and groups can gain synergy from these relationships in their own efforts to affect policymaking. The chapter concludes with a discussion of how organizations and groups design themselves to effectively influence policymaking, and specific examples of these designs are provided.

Review Questions

1. Define *policy competence.*
2. Discuss how policy competence can help health professionals improve health in individuals and populations.
3. Discuss four philosophical principles that can guide ethical policymaking.
4. Discuss the five steps health professionals can use to influence policymaking.
5. Effectively observing the health policy market and the policymaking process provides several benefits to attentive professionals. Describe these benefits.
6. How can health professionals assess the importance of policy information they are observing? Include the role of policy theory and logic models in your response.
7. How can health professionals approach the task of forecasting policy information? Include specific forecasting techniques in your response.
8. Describe the relationship between social power (including its sources) and influence in policymaking.
9. Describe the relationship between focus and influence in policymaking. Include the use of a map to guide the focus of efforts to be influential.
10. Discuss the health policy interests of health services provider organizations, resource-producing organizations, and health-related interest groups.

References

Beauchamp, T. L., and J. F. Childress. 2019. *Principles of Biomedical Ethics*, 8th ed. New York: Oxford University Press.

BusinessDictionary.com. 2020. "Competence." Accessed June 30. www.businessdictionary.com/definition/competence.html.

Centers for Medicare & Medicaid Services (CMS). 2019. "National Health Expenditure Projections 2018–2027." Accessed February 3, 2020. www.cms.gov/Research-Statistics-Data-and-Systems/Statistics-Trends-and-Reports/NationalHealthExpendData/NationalHealthAccountsProjected.

———. 2017. "Federal Advisory Committee Act (FACA)." Updated December 22. www.cms.gov/Regulations-and-Guidance/Guidance/FACA/index.

———. 2014a. "Innovation Models." Accessed April 11. https://innovation.cms.gov/innovation-models#views=models.

———. 2014b. "Medicare Program; Methodology for Adjusting Payment Amounts for Certain Medical Equipment, Prosthetics, Orthotics, and Supplies (DMEPOS) Using Information from Competitive Bidding Programs." *Federal Register* 79 (38): 10754–60.

———. 2014c. "Medicare's Delivery System Reform Initiatives Achieve Significant Savings and Quality Improvements—Off to a Strong Start." Press release. Published January 30. www.cms.gov/newsroom/press-releases/medicares-delivery-system-reform-initiatives-achieve-significant-savings-and-quality-improvements.

Chermack, T. J. 2011. *Scenario Planning in Organizations: How to Create, Use, and Assess Scenarios.* San Francisco: Berrett-Koehler.

Committee on Ethics. 2020. "Prohibited Lobbyist Gifts." Accessed February 2. https://ethics.house.gov/gifts/prohibited-lobbyist-gifts.

Cubanski, J., T. Neuman, and M. Freed. 2019. "The Facts on Medicare Spending and Financing." Kaiser Family Foundation. Published August 20. www.kff.org/medicare/issue-brief/the-facts-on-medicare-spending-and-financing.

Finkelstein, A., S. Taubman, B. Wright, M. Bernstein, J. Gruber, J. P. Newhouse, H. Allen, K. Baicker, and the Oregon Health Study Group. 2012. "The Oregon Health Insurance Experiment: Evidence from the First Year." *Quarterly Journal of Economics* 127 (3): 1057–105.

Ginter, P. M., W. J. Duncan, and L. E. Swayne. 2018. *Strategic Management of Health Care Organizations*, 8th ed. San Francisco: Jossey-Bass.

Gormley, W. T., and S. J. Balla. 2018. *Bureaucracy and Democracy: Accountability and Performance*, 4th ed. Thousand Oaks, CA: CQ Press.

Gostin, L. O. 2014. *Global Health Law.* Cambridge, MA: Harvard University Press.

Gostin, L. O., and L. Wiley. 2016. *Public Health Law: Power, Duty, Restraint*, 3rd ed. Berkeley, CA: University of California Press/Milbank Memorial Fund.

Guth, M., R. Garfield, and R. Rudowitz. 2020. "The Effects of Medicaid Expansion Under the ACA: Updated Findings from a Literature Review." Kaiser

Family Foundation. Published March 17. www.kff.org/medicaid/issue-brief/the-effects-of-medicaid-expansion-under-the-aca-updated-findings-from-a-literature-review-march-2020.

Hanke, J. E., and D. Wichern. 2014. *Business Forecasting*, 9th ed. Essex, UK: Pearson Education Limited.

Heath, R. L., and M. J. Palenchar. 2009. *Strategic Issues Management: Organizations and Public Policy Challenges.* Thousand Oaks, CA: Sage.

Kennedy, J. 1963. "Address in the Assembly Hall at the Paulskirche, Frankfurt, 25 June 1963." June 25. John F. Kennedy Presidential Library and Museum. www.jfklibrary.org/asset-viewer/archives/JFKPOF/045/JFKPOF-045-023.

Knowlton, L. W., and C. C. Phillips. 2013. *The Logic Model Guidebook: Better Strategies for Great Results*, 2nd ed. Thousand Oaks, CA: Sage.

Lindgren, M., and H. Bandhold. 2009. *Scenario Planning: The Link Between Future and Strategy.* Basinstroke, Hampshire, UK: Palgrave Macmillan.

Long, S. 2010. "What Is the Evidence on Health Reform in Massachusetts and How Might the Lessons from Massachusetts Apply to National Health Reform?" Urban Institute. Published June 24. www.urban.org/research/publication/what-evidence-health-reform-massachusetts-and-how-might-lessons-massachusetts-apply-national-health-reform.

Longest, B. B., Jr. 2015. *Health Program Management: From Development Through Evaluation.* San Francisco: Jossey-Bass.

Longest, B. B., Jr., and K. Darr. 2014. *Managing Health Services Organizations and Systems*, 6th ed. Baltimore, MD: Health Professions Press.

Medicare Payment Advisory Commission (MedPAC). 2020. "Commission Members." Accessed June 13. www.medpac.gov/-about-medpac-/commission-members.

Mesch, A. H. 1984. "Developing an Effective Environmental Assessment Function." *Managerial Planning* 32 (1): 17–22.

Morrison, E. 2020. *Ethics in Health Administration: A Practical Approach for Decision Makers*, 4th ed. Burlington, MA: Jones & Bartlett.

National Conference on State Legislatures (NCSL). 2020. "State Ethics Commissions Jurisdiction." Published February 23. www.ncsl.org/research/ethics/50-state-chart-state-ethics-commissions-jurisdic.aspx.

Ramirez, R., J. W. Selsky, and K. van der Heijden (eds.). 2010. *Business Planning for Turbulent Times: New Methods for Applying Scenarios*, 2nd ed. New York: Routledge.

Rawls, J., and E. Kelly. 2001. *Justice as Fairness: A Restatement.* Cambridge, MA: Harvard University Press.

Regulations.gov. 2020. "Tips for Submitting Effective Comments." Accessed February 2. www.regulations.gov/docs/Tips_For_Submitting_Effective_Comments.pdf.

Taubman, S., H. Allen, B. Wright, K. Baicker, A. Finkelstein, and the Oregon Health Study Group. 2014. "Medicaid Increases Emergency-Department Use: Evidence from Oregon's Health Insurance Experiment." *Science* 343 (17): 263–68.

US Food and Drug Administration (FDA). 2020. "Learn About FDA Advisory Committees." Updated February 13. www.fda.gov/patients/learn-about-patient-affairs-staff/learn-about-fda-advisory-committees.

US Office of Government Ethics (OGE). 2017. "Gifts from Outside Sources." Published April 11. www.oge.gov/Web/OGE.nsf/Gifts%20and%20Payments/8CEAAC03A29FDE9C85257E96006364F8?opendocument.

APPENDIX

4.1

OPENING STATEMENT: HEARING ON "WHERE HAVE ALL THE PATIENTS GONE? EXAMINING THE PSYCHIATRIC BED SHORTAGE"

The Honorable Tim Murphy
Chairman, Subcommittee on Oversight and Investigations of the Energy & Commerce Committee of the US House of Representatives
March 26, 2014

Right after the December 14, 2012 elementary school shootings in Newtown, Connecticut, the Subcommittee on Oversight and Investigations began a review of federal programs and resources devoted to mental health and serious mental illness.

Recent events have shown the continuing importance of this inquiry, including the September 2013 Navy Yard shooting just a couple of miles from where we sit this morning, in Washington, D.C.

Other tragic cases, like Seung-Hui Cho, James Holmes, Jared Loughner, and Adam Lanza, all exhibited a record of untreated severe mental illness prior to their crimes. It is a reflection of the total dysfunction of our current mental health system that despite clear warning signs, these individuals failed to receive inpatient or outpatient treatment for their illnesses that might have averted these tragedies.

They all leave us wondering what would have happened if . . .

What would have happened if Aaron Alexis was not just given sleeping pills at the VA? Or if there was an available hospital bed or outpatient treatment available for others who later became violent, involved in a crime, unable to pay bills, or tossed out on the street?

Part of the problem is that our laws on involuntary commitment are in dire need of modernization—it is simply unreasonable, if not a danger to public safety, that our current system often waits until an individual is on the brink of harming himself or others, or has already done so, before any action can be taken. The scarcity of effective inpatient or outpatient treatment options in the community, as illustrated by the premature release of Gus Deeds, son of

Virginia senator Creigh Deeds, from emergency custody because of the lack of psychiatric beds, is also to blame. A sad ending that in our heart we cannot begin to imagine a parent's grief when told there is no place for your son to get help.

Nationwide, we face an alarming shortage in inpatient psychiatric beds that, if not addressed, will result in more tragic outcomes. This is part of the long-term legacy of deinstitutionalization, the emptying out of state psychiatric hospitals resulting from the financial burden for community-based care being shifted from the state to the federal government. With deinstitutionalization, the number of available inpatient psychiatric beds has fallen considerably. On the whole, the number of beds has decreased from 559,000 in the 1950s to just 43,000 today. We needed to close those old hospitals that had become asylums, lock-ups, and dumping grounds.

But where did all the patients go? They were supposed to be in community treatment—on the road to recovery—but for many that did not happen.

The result is that individuals with serious mental illness who are unable to obtain treatment through ordinary means are now homeless or entangled in the criminal justice system, including being locked up in jails and prisons.

Right now, the country's three largest jail systems—in Cook County, Illinois; Los Angeles County; and New York City—have more than 11,000 prisoners receiving treatment on any given day and are, in fact, the largest mental health treatment facilities in the country. These jails are many times larger than the largest state psychiatric hospitals.

Not surprisingly, neither living on the streets nor being confined to a high-security cellblock are known to improve the chances that an individual's serious mental illness will stabilize, let alone prepare them, where possible, for eventual reentry into the community, to find housing, jobs, and confidence for their future.

It is an unplanned, albeit entirely unacceptable consequence of deinstitutionalization that the state psychiatric asylums, dismantled out of concern for the humane treatment and care of individuals with serious mental illness, have now effectively been replaced by confinement in prisons and homeless shelters.

What can we do earlier in people's lives to get them evidence-based treatment, community support, and on the road to recovery not recidivism?

Where is the humanity in saying there are no beds to treat a person suffering from schizophrenia, delusions, and aggression so we will sedate you and restrain you to an ER bed for days?

This morning, to provide some perspective on the far-reaching implications of the current psychiatric bed shortage and to hear some creative approaches to address it, we'll be receiving testimony from individuals with a wealth of experience across the full range of public services consumed by the seriously mentally ill. These include:

- Lisa Ashley, the mother of a son with serious mental illness who has been boarded multiple times at the emergency department;
- Dr. Jeffrey Geller, a psychiatrist and co-author of a report on the trends and consequences of closing public psychiatric hospitals;
- Dr. Jon Mark Hirshon, an ER physician and Task Force Chair on a recent study of emergency care compiled by the American College of Emergency Physicians;
- Chief Mike Biasotti, Immediate Past President of the New York State Association of Chiefs of Police and parent of a daughter with serious mental illness;
- Sheriff Tom Dart, of the Cook County, IL Sheriff's Office, who oversees one of the largest single site county pre-detention facilities in the U.S.;
- The Honorable Steve Leifman, Associate Administrative Judge, Miami-Dade County Court, 11th Judicial Circuit of Florida;
- Gunther Stern, Executive Director of Georgetown Ministry Center, a shelter and clubhouse caring for Washington D.C.'s homeless;
- Hakeem Rahim, a mental health educator and advocate;
- LaMarr Edgerson, a clinical mental health counselor and Director at Large of the American Mental Health Counselors Association; and
- Dr. Arthur Evans, Jr., Commissioner of Philadelphia's Department of Behavioral Health and Intellectual Disability Services.

I thank them all for joining us this morning.

Source: Reprinted from Murphy, T. 2014. "Opening Statement of the Honorable Tim Murphy, Subcommittee on Oversight and Investigations, Hearing on 'Where Have All the Patients Gone? Examining the Psychiatric Bed Shortage.'" Published March 26, http://energycommerce.house.gov/sites/republicans.energycommerce.house.gov/files/Hearings/OI/20140326/HHRG-113-IF02-MState-M001151-20140326.pdf.

APPENDIX

4.2

EXAMPLE OF MODIFICATIONS TO RULES IN RESPONSE TO NEW INFORMATION AND OPERATIONAL CHANGES

What follows is the US Food and Drug Administration's explanation of its effort to promulgate new rules regulating the warnings on cigarette packages. As the initial statement shows, by the spring of 2020, the decision on these efforts was delayed because of the COVID-19 pandemic.

Cigarette Labeling and Health Warning Requirements

> Due to the COVID-19 pandemic and its disruptive impacts on both regulated industry and FDA, on May 8 the U.S. District Court for the Eastern District of Texas granted a joint motion in the case of *R.J. Reynolds Tobacco Co. et al. v. United States Food and Drug Administration et al.*, No. 6:20-cv-00176, to govern proceedings in that case and postpone the effective date of the "Required Warnings for Cigarette Packages and Advertisements" final rule by 120 days. FDA remains fully committed to the rule and would not agree to postpone its effective date but not for the extraordinary disruptions caused by the COVID-19 pandemic.
>
> The new effective date of the final rule is Oct. 16, 2021. Pursuant to the court order, any obligation to comply with a deadline tied to the effective date is similarly postponed. FDA strongly encourages entities to submit cigarette plans (as required by 21 CFR 1141.10(g)) as soon as possible, and in any event by Dec. 16, 2020. FDA has updated the "Required Warnings for Cigarette Packages and Advertisements" small entity compliance guide and the "Submission of Plans for Cigarette Packages and Cigarette Advertisements" guidance to include the rule's new effective date and updated timing for submission of cigarette plans. Regulated industry may contact CTP with questions about the effective date.

Required Health Warnings

The Family Smoking Prevention and Tobacco Control Act (TCA) granted FDA important new authority to regulate the manufacture, marketing, and distribution of tobacco products. The TCA also amended Section 4 of the Federal Cigarette Labeling and Advertising Act (FCLAA), directing FDA to issue regulations requiring color graphics depicting the negative health consequences of smoking to accompany new textual warning statements. The TCA amends the FCLAA to require each cigarette package and advertisement to bear one of the new required warnings.

In March 2020, FDA finalized the "Required Warnings for Cigarette Packages and Advertisements" rule, establishing 11 new cigarette health warnings, consisting of textual warning statements accompanied by color graphics, in the form of concordant photorealistic images, depicting the negative health consequences of cigarette smoking. These new required warnings depict some of the lesser-known, but serious health risks of smoking.

The new required warnings must appear prominently on cigarette packages and in cigarette advertisements, occupying the top 50 percent of the front and rear panels of cigarette packages and at least 20 percent of the area at the top of advertisements.

As explained in the final rule, each required warning must be accurately reproduced as shown in the materials contained in "Required Cigarette Health Warnings, 2020," which is incorporated by reference at 21 CFR 1141.5.

FDA recognizes that adaptations to the required warnings may be needed to avoid technical implementation issues due to the varying features, formats, and sizes of cigarette packages and advertisements. To help prevent distortion of the image and text and to minimize the need for adaptation, FDA has created electronic, layered design files, built as Encapsulated PostScript (.eps) files, in different formats and aspect ratios designed to fit packaging and advertising of various shapes and sizes. FDA is not requiring the use of these .eps files, but rather we are providing the files as a resource to assist regulated entities.

In addition to the material incorporated by reference and the .eps files, FDA is making available a technical specifications (i.e., instructions) document that includes information on how to access, select, use, and adapt the appropriate .eps files based on the size and aspect ratio of the display area where the required warning must appear.

See FDA's "Cigarette Health Warning Design Files and Technical Specifications" to download files and for further instructions.

FDA has also published the "Required Warnings for Cigarette Packages and Advertisements—Small Entity Compliance Guide" to help small businesses understand and comply with the final rule.

WARNING:
Smoking causes head and neck cancer.

WARNING:
Tobacco smoke causes fatal lung disease in nonsmokers.

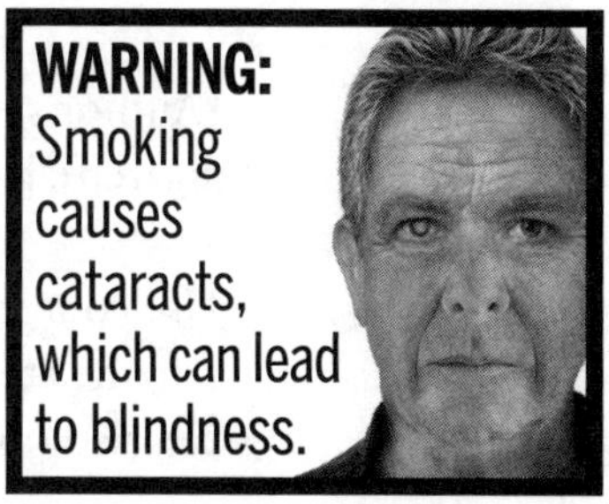
WARNING:
Smoking causes cataracts, which can lead to blindness.

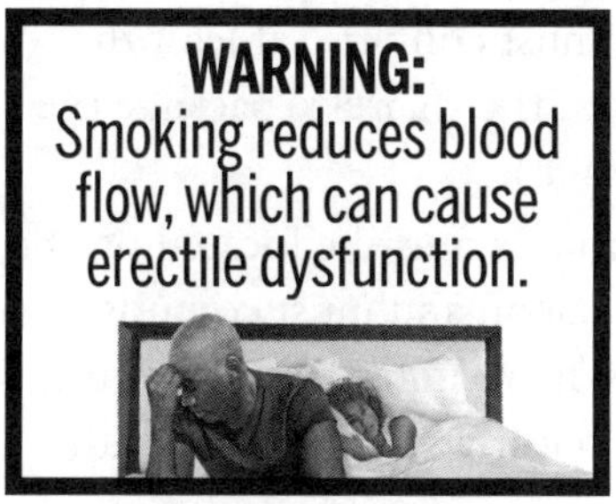
WARNING:
Smoking reduces blood flow, which can cause erectile dysfunction.

WARNING:
Tobacco smoke can harm your children.

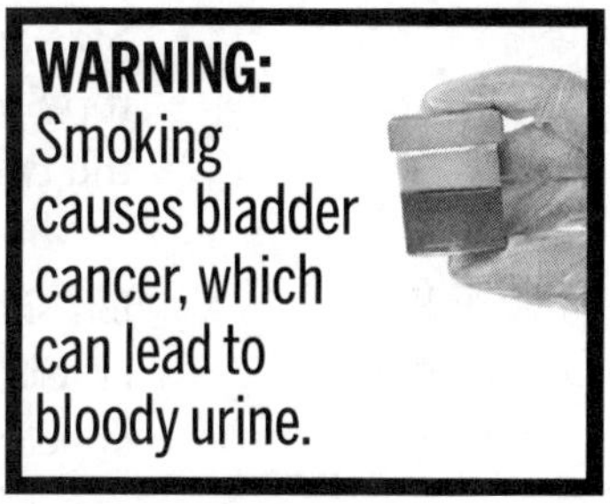
WARNING:
Smoking causes bladder cancer, which can lead to bloody urine.

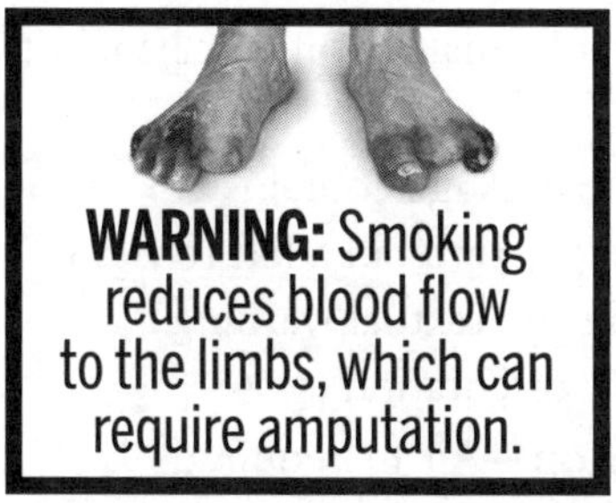
WARNING: Smoking reduces blood flow to the limbs, which can require amputation.

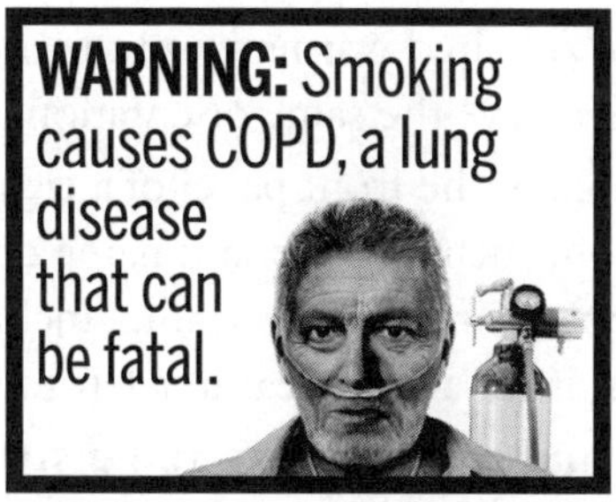
WARNING: Smoking causes COPD, a lung disease that can be fatal.

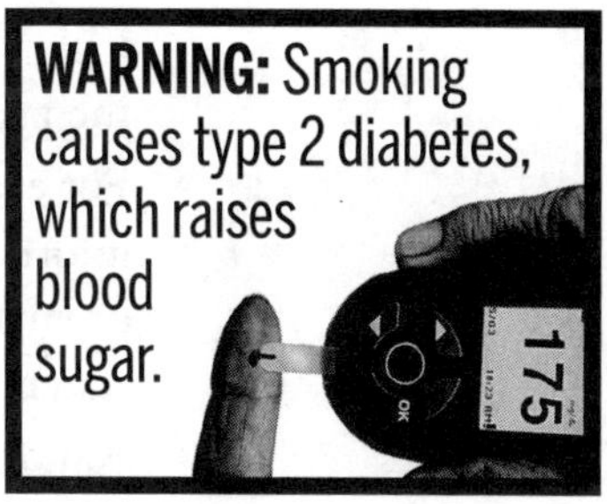
WARNING: Smoking causes type 2 diabetes, which raises blood sugar.
175

4.00 lbs.
WARNING: Smoking during pregnancy stunts fetal growth.

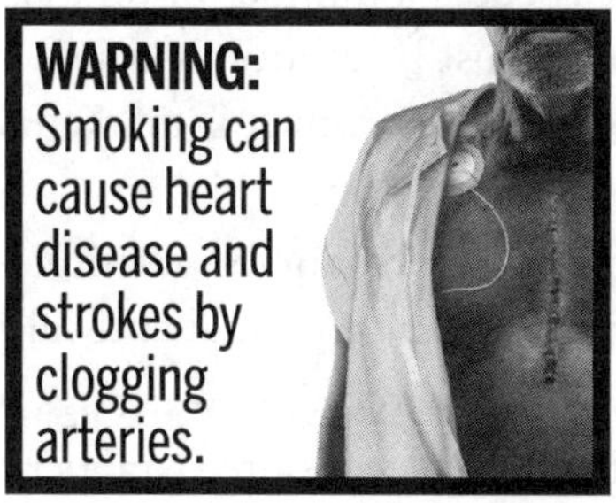
WARNING:
Smoking can cause heart disease and strokes by clogging arteries.

Interactive Cigarette Health Warning

[Author's note: Included on the website was a three-dimensional image of a cigarette pack that a user can manipulate with a mouse.]

Use your mouse to rotate this 3D image of one of FDA's new proposed cigarette health warnings to see what it would look like on a cigarette package. You can also download this interactive image, and share it on your digital space.

Cigarette Packages

- **Size and location**—The required warning must comprise at least the top 50 percent of the front and rear panels of the cigarette package (i.e., the two largest sides or surfaces of the package).

  For cigarette cartons, the required warnings must be located on the left side of the front and rear panels of the carton and must comprise at least the left 50 percent of these panels. The required warning must appear directly on the package and must be clearly visible underneath any cellophane or other clear wrapping.
- **Orientation**—The required warning must be positioned so that the text of the required warning and the other information on that panel of the package have the same orientation.
- For example, if the front panel of a cigarette package contains information, such as the brand name of the cigarette, in a left to right orientation, the required warning, including the textual warning statement, must also appear in a left to right orientation.
- **Random and equal display and distribution**—All 11 required warnings for packages must be randomly displayed in each 12-month period, in as equal a number of times as is possible on each brand of the product and must be randomly distributed in all areas of the United States in which the product is marketed, in accordance with an FDA-approved cigarette plan.
- **Irremovable or permanent warnings**—Required warnings must be indelibly printed on or permanently affixed to the cigarette package.
- For example, these required warnings must not be printed or placed on a label affixed to a clear outer wrapper that is likely to be removed to access the product within the package.

Cigarette Advertisements

- **Size and location**—For print advertisements and other advertisements with a visual component (including, for example, advertisements on signs, retail displays, Internet web pages, social media web pages, digital platforms, mobile applications, and email correspondence), the required warning must appear directly on the advertisement. Additionally, required warnings must comprise at least 20 percent of the area of the advertisement in a conspicuous and prominent format and location at the top of each advertisement within the trim area, if any.

- **Rotation**—The 11 required warnings must be rotated quarterly, in alternating sequence, in advertisements for each brand of cigarettes, in accordance with an FDA-approved cigarette plan.
- **Irremovable or permanent warnings**—Required warnings must be indelibly printed on or permanently affixed to a cigarette advertisement.

Cigarette Plans

Section 4 of the FCLAA, as amended by the TCA, and the final rule require manufacturers, distributors, and retailers of cigarettes to submit a plan for the random and equal display and distribution of required warnings on cigarettes packages and the quarterly rotation of required warnings on cigarette advertisements, and to obtain FDA approval of their plans before products required to bear such warnings enter the market.

FDA has issued the "Submission of Plans for Cigarette Packages and Cigarette Advertisements" guidance to assist those submitting cigarette plans for cigarette packages and advertisements.

The requirement for submission of cigarette plans for cigarette packages and advertisements, and the specific requirements relating to the random and equal display and distribution of the required warnings on cigarette packaging and the quarterly rotation of required warnings in cigarette advertising, appear at Section 4(c) of the FCLAA and 21 CFR 1141.10.

In addition, under Section 201(c) of the TCA and 21 CFR 1141.10(g), the agency must review and approve cigarette plans in advance of any person displaying or distributing packages or advertisements for products that are required to carry the required warnings.

FDA strongly encourages entities to submit cigarette plans as soon as possible after publication of the final rule, and in any event by Dec. 16, 2020.

Early submission of cigarette plans will facilitate timely FDA review prior to the Oct. 16, 2021 effective date of the required warnings, encourage dialogue with entities regarding any implementation concerns, and provide the ability to consider proposals from entities in a timely manner.

FDA will ensure that its review of cigarette plans will be completed no later than 6 months after receipt of an adequate plan from persons who work in good faith with FDA to complete its review (e.g., persons should work diligently with FDA and be responsive by submitting any requested information in a timely manner).

If a higher volume of submissions is received than is currently expected, FDA intends to ensure that entities who submit an adequate plan by Dec.16, 2020 and who work in good faith with FDA to complete its review are not delayed or prevented from distributing or advertising cigarette packages or advertisements due to the agency not having approved their plans by the effective date of the final rule (i.e., Oct. 16, 2021).

For efficiency of review, FDA recommends that, to the extent possible, manufacturers, distributors, and retailers submit a single cigarette plan that covers both cigarette packaging and cigarette advertising, rather than submitting each plan separately, when applicable.

For FDA to approve a cigarette plan for cigarette packaging, the plan must provide that all of the required warnings are randomly displayed during each 12-month period on each brand of the product, displayed on each brand of the product in as equal a number of times as is possible during each 12-month period, are randomly distributed in all areas of the United States in which the product is marketed, and must ensure that all of the required warnings will be displayed by the manufacturer, distributor, or retailer at the same time.

For FDA to approve a cigarette plan for cigarette advertising, the plan must provide that all of the required warnings are rotated quarterly in alternating sequence in advertisements for each brand of cigarettes.

Source: US Food and Drug Administration (FDA), 2020, "Cigarette Labeling and Health Warning Requirements," last updated June 17, www.fda.gov/tobacco-products/labeling-and-warning-statements-tobacco-products/cigarette-labeling-and-health-warning-requirements.

THE CORONAVIRUS PANDEMIC: EXECUTIVE BRANCH POLICY IMPLEMENTATION AND RAMIFICATIONS

Learning Objectives

After reading this chapter, you should be able to

- distinguish the roles of public health and the healthcare delivery system during a pandemic;
- explain containment and mitigation of disease as policy questions;
- recognize that in addition to state and local authorities, the federal government has public health responsibilities;
- discuss the appropriate roles of the federal government and state governments from the public health perspective in a time of pandemic; and
- using the pandemic of 2020 as an example, discuss how defining a problem affects its possible solution.

Introduction

> This event has broken everything.
>
> —Unidentified e-commerce analyst, *New York Times*, April 18, 2020

Indeed, everything did seem to be broken in the spring of 2020, when COVID-19 shook all aspects of American life. Parts of the health services delivery system were overwhelmed to the point of requiring the use of US Navy hospital ships and the construction of temporary army field hospitals in several locations; nurses, doctors, and other healthcare providers worked tirelessly to treat infected people while being exposed themselves because of a widespread shortage of personal protective equipment (PPE); states and hospitals desperately searched for ventilators and PPE; some hospitals were converting any available space to intensive care unit (ICU) beds; businesses both large and small were shuttered in response to stay-at-home orders from state and local authorities; millions of employees were furloughed, laid off, or terminated; children were kept home from school as most schools closed, pursuant to state-ordered mandates; universities transferred classes from the classroom to online platforms and sent students home, closing residence halls to all but a handful with nowhere else to go; educational institutions of all kinds canceled spring commencement exercises or held "drive-by" graduations; restaurants either closed or tried to survive with new takeout or curbside services; the National Basketball Association suspended the remainder of its season; and the National Collegiate Athletic Association canceled March Madness and all spring sports. And the most American institution of all, Major League Baseball, postponed the beginning of the 2020 season.

The unemployment rate soared to 14.7 percent in April (from 3.6 percent in March) amid uncertain expectations for the future (US Bureau of Labor Statistics 2020). American life as we knew it did, indeed, seem to be broken.

The outbreak of a new coronavirus, known as COVID-19 for those infected by it, in the United States (and throughout the rest of the world) in early 2020 brought about widespread death and despair. The pandemic led to a lightning-fast shrinking of the economy; stressed the American healthcare system to its absolute limits in some places; disrupted supply chains for paper products, cleaning products, and meat; and confounded policymaking and policymakers at all levels of government, among countless other consequences.

The spread of the virus from where it is widely believed to have begun, Wuhan, China, to the entire world occurred with remarkable speed and in dimensions difficult to fathom. On March 2, 2020, there were 88 confirmed cases in the United States. Just 120 days later, on July 2, there were more than 2.7 million confirmed cases. And the disease had spread from a handful of countries on March 2 to 189 nations on July 2 (Johns Hopkins University 2020). More American lives were lost—nearly 60,000—to COVID-19 in April 2020 than were lost in battle during the entire 15 years of the Vietnam War (Welna 2020). Adding to the fear was the knowledge that there were many more cases—estimates ranging from two to ten times as many—in the population that were unconfirmed (Li et al. 2020). It was, and will remain for an unknown time, a pandemic of record proportions.

A comprehensive assessment of the impact of COVID-19 on American life is not only beyond the scope of this book but also not yet feasible. As of this writing, in the summer of 2020, we are still experiencing an active pandemic. Because the outbreak came late in the production of the book, including it throughout the text as an example of various concepts or principles was impracticable. This event, however, was so devastating and created such a powerful impetus for changing how Americans lived their lives—and how Americans will live their lives in the future—that it demands inclusion in this book.

The coronavirus pandemic sharply highlights some of the health policymaking dynamics and decisions that have engaged and challenged American policymakers. This historic episode presents an opportunity to observe federal and state administrative policy processes and how they coordinated. Or didn't. We will see how the absence of an integrated, dynamic national policy to manage the outbreak produced varying responses by states, highlighting state and local public health laws and processes, and raising the discourse on the functioning of federalism, as discussed in chapter 3. As a consequence, the effort to contain the virus was a patchwork of state and local public health policies that emerged from the federal policy vacuum. In short, the absence of a comprehensive, evidence-based, public-health-centric national response created a policy void that needed to be filled by the states. The resulting multiple subnational responses arguably permitted the disease to spread farther and faster than it had spread in other countries that mounted an aggressive national response.

At the end of May 2020, the United States represented 4.25 percent of the world's population, but had 29.49 percent of the COVID-19 cases and 28.15 percent of the COVID-19 caused deaths (Johns Hopkins University 2020; Worldometer 2020). Some of this disparity can be attributed to timing—the disease is still spreading throughout the world. Some element of this disparity can be attributed to the muddled and sometimes chaotic nature of the US national response.

Caveat

There is a risk in undertaking this kind of assessment while the event is still ongoing. At this juncture, it is conceivable—even likely—that there is more to be learned about the virus and the best ways to prevent its spread. Certainly, by the time many read this book, there may well be an effective treatment for those who have COVID-19 and vaccines to prevent it. The discussion here considers what was known in late June 2020. For background on the virus and its spread, see the following box.

Background: COVID-19 and Public Health

Before we delve into a review of a complex interplay between the virus, the health services delivery system, the public health system, health policy, and politics, some background information is in order. This box discusses some details of the virus and briefly reviews the distinction

(continued)

between *public health* and the *health services delivery system*. The remainder of the chapter will focus on the substance of how the virus spread, the legal foundation for federal policy, the executive implementation of that policy, and the dynamics of federal–state relations: how the reality of federalism functioned.

A Novel Coronavirus: What It Is and How It Spreads

There are many types of human coronaviruses, including some that commonly cause mild upper respiratory tract illnesses. COVID-19 is a previously unidentified disease ("novel") that had not been seen in humans (CDC 2020c). According to Adolph et al. (2020), several characteristics distinguish SARS-CoV-2, the coronavirus that causes COVID-19:

1. it is an emergent virus to which there is no preexisting immunity, available vaccine, or proven treatment;
2. it spreads easily through human contact and airborne droplets, leading to exponential growth in cases; and
3. those affected may be contagious during a prolonged asymptomatic incubation period, and many never develop symptoms distinctive from a mild flu, making it difficult to identify and isolate the infected before they pass the virus to others.

Additionally, there is evidence that the virus can be transmitted by surface contact as well (Guo et al. 2020).

In brief, this is a highly contagious virus for which there is no existing efficacious treatment and no vaccine (as of June 2020). Furthermore, it is a *novel* (previously unidentified) virus for which there is no immunity among the population, because no one has ever been exposed to it. Such exposure typically creates antibodies that would ward off future infection from the same virus. In the case of the average flu, for example, widespread exposure creates what is called *herd immunity*. Confounding matters further, by the spring of 2020, immunity from exposure to the coronavirus was not firmly scientifically established (World Health Organization 2020).

As if the voraciousness of the contagion were not enough, its symptoms were likewise vexatious, affecting individuals in vastly different ways. Some people would remain asymptomatic for the entire duration of their "illness." Others developed flulike symptoms, such as cough, fever, shortness of breath, chills, muscle pain, and sore throat, which would devolve into a respiratory infection (CDC 2020b). Others developed extreme respiratory distress, which required assistive breathing devices—ventilators. Still others died. While ample evidence suggests that the disease was particularly dangerous to older adults and people with underlying medical conditions, there were the occasional seemingly random deaths of otherwise healthy people (Gupta 2020). One thing that seemed common to all, however, was an incubation period of five to seven days, during which time the affected individual would often be asymptomatic but be very contagious. In other words, a seemingly healthy person could attend a wedding, a funeral, or another large social gathering and unwittingly infect innumerable others (Ghandi, Yokoe, and Havlir 2020). Contact with people who are asymptomatic either in the early stages or throughout the course of their illness causes exponential spread: One person gets the disease, unaware of the infection they are carrying, and transmits it to two, five, ten, or more individuals, each of whom then in turn transmits it to still more people. See exhibit 11.1 for a real example of this phenomenon, which was documented by the Centers for Disease Control and Prevention (CDC).

Public Health and the Health Services Delivery System

This chapter focuses on executive implementation of existing legislative policy that addresses a national emergency. The administrative policymaking in this instance affects two distinct yet complementary systems of health-related services in the United States: the public health system and the health services delivery system. A brief review is in order here.

EXHIBIT 11.1 Real-Life Example of the Rapid Spread of COVID-19

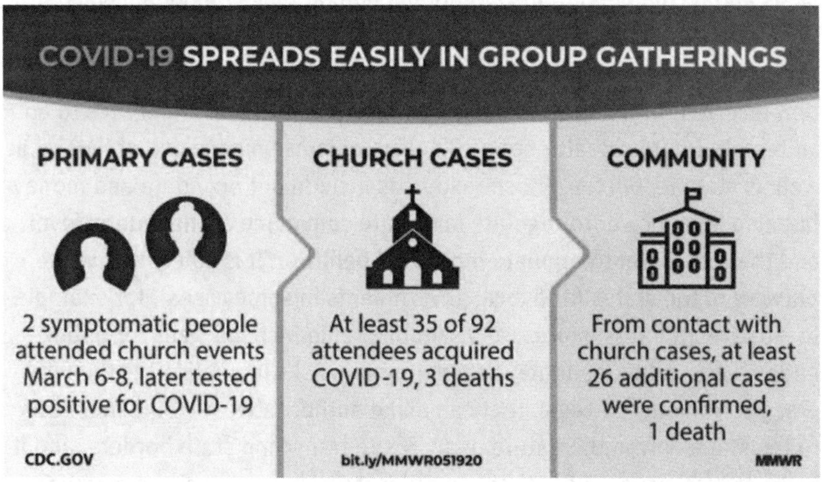

Source: James et al. (2020).

(continued)

Public health has three core functions: assessment, policy development, and assurance. Each of these functions has several domains, but we will focus on these three core functions. When we discuss warnings and the definition of the transmission of the disease, we are looking at *assessment*. The discussion about flattening the curve and other strategies such as containment or mitigation reflects *policy development*. *Assurance* takes place when authorities issue statements saying that it is safe to reopen.

The other dynamic taking place in the public health domain during this crisis, however, is the division of responsibility for *public health*. Like all health regulation at the state level, public health is an outgrowth of the Tenth Amendment to the US Constitution. As such, public health regulation is a primary function of the state, as discussed in chapter 3—within the inherent power of a state to protect the safety and welfare of its citizens. Subdivisions of the states—counties—and specially state-chartered entities, namely, cities, also have roles to play. Public health is a state function, but it comes to life at the local level, typically through county departments of public health. Some county units may have different names, as state agencies also have different names, but the function—protection of the public health—is the core mission.

The federal government, however, also has an important role derived from its power to regulate interstate commerce. As described in chapter 3, local health agencies report data to state agencies, which in turn report data to the CDC. The CDC uses the aggregated data to inform policy decisions and recommendations at national and, at times, regional levels. When this agency promulgates guidelines for mitigating the community spread of the coronavirus, those guidelines are based, in part, on information received through these reporting mechanisms. Thus, reference to an "integrated public-health-centric" policy response means use of federal as well as state resources. Those resources include not only data and money but also legal power to regulate interstate commerce at the federal level and the state level to regulate individual behavior. It is solely within the purview of the states (and local governments in some cases), for example, to close restaurants, stores, and schools; to limit crowd sizes for public gatherings; and to mandate the wearing of masks in public. It is the federal government, however, that can make authoritative recommendations to the states, given the nature of a virus to transcend state borders, and it is the federal government that can order travel bans, direct the manufacture of needed goods, and affect all things related to interstate commerce or interstate transmission of the disease.

The *health services delivery system* includes multiple components: ambulatory care and acute and post-acute organizations that deliver hands-on care. This system and public health seldom overlap, except, for example, when there is a widespread vaccination program. At times like that, public health agencies will deliver vaccines along with traditional health services delivery organizations. Again, the states have the primary power to regulate healthcare providers. The federal government, however, can also play a role in expanding the capacity of the health services delivery system by waiving certain legal requirements or providing additional resources.

In this case, however, the functions of public health and health services delivery are complementary. For example, an important reason to contain and mitigate the transmission of disease is to avoid overwhelming the health services delivery system. One challenge in this crisis was the disease's rapid spread, which, as a consequence, left the system chronically short of important supplies and equipment, straining its ability to provide necessary services. This dismal circumstance calls into question the effectiveness of the public health response to the burgeoning crisis. Testing and contact tracing were all but nonexistent. Without adequate data, public health officials were guessing at where and when to ask the public to sacrifice on behalf of the greater good. Absent effective containment and mitigation measures, the number of cases exploded. The explosion of cases overwhelmed the health services delivery system. As a result, providers reused masks that were intended for onetime use; at one point, nurses in a New York City hospital adapted large trash bags to serve as protective gowns. The key question is whether a more aggressive containment policy and more rigorous mitigation efforts would have slowed the community spread of the disease, preventing the crisis that enveloped the health services delivery system.

The health system crisis was twofold: (1) the sufficiency of the public health community (at federal, state, and local levels) to adequately answer the call against the virus and (2) the seemingly limited capability of the health services delivery system to provide necessary care safely.

Spread of the Coronavirus Timelines

A response to a national emergency in the form of a pandemic is time-sensitive. To succeed in implementing any of the legislatively mandated policies requires an awareness of when to respond, and how to do so, to best ameliorate the emergency. Policies of timely and effective intervention have been demonstrated to slow the community spread (Cowling and Aiello 2020). Thus, timelines are important tracking tools to support executive implementation of policy.

Timelines can provide several perspectives to demonstrate the spread of the disease. The most easily understood and most accessible is the daily (cumulative) total number of confirmed cases. Other measures of interest to policymakers include new cases (daily and a rolling average), new hospitalizations (daily and a rolling average), number of admissions to ICUs (daily number of patients who would require ventilators), and deaths (daily and a rolling average). Another way would be a rendition of key dates and events in the outbreak of the pandemic. Exhibit 11.2 reflects key events in the beginning stages of the outbreak, and exhibit 11.3 shows total cases and deaths at one-month intervals from the first reported case through June 21. The table reflects the exponential growth rate in cumulative cases over 120 days and a similar growth trend in COVID-related deaths.

EXHIBIT 11.2 Selected Key Events in the Early Stages of Coronavirus Pandemic, 2020

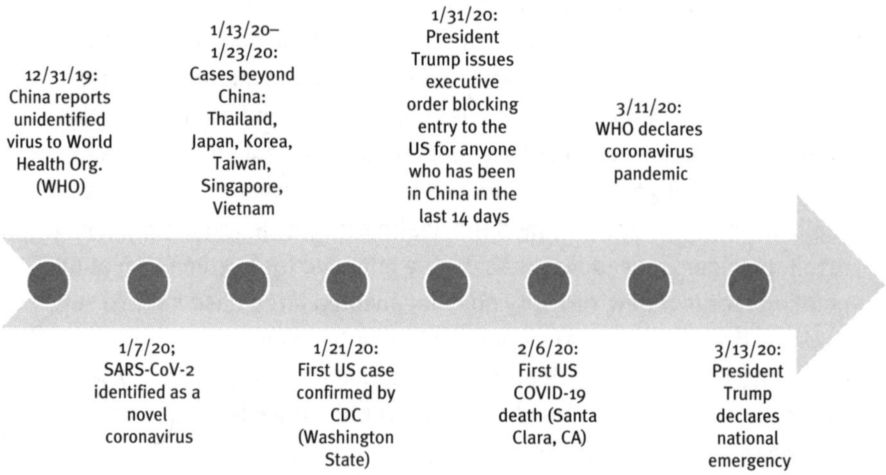

EXHIBIT 11.3 US Cumulative Case and Death Totals (one-month intervals from the first confirmed case through June 21, 2020)

	Jan 21	Feb 21	Mar 21	Apr 21	May 21	Jun 21
Cases	1	15	25,725	807,023	1,577,000	2,282,000
Deaths	0	0	260	42,539	93,439	119,868

Source: Adapted from Johns Hopkins University (2020) and Our World in Data (2020).

Testing and Timelines

Critically important in establishing an accurate count of confirmed cases is widespread testing. Two basic tests are important to consider here. (Other diagnostic tests are in development; some have received emergency approval by the US Food and Drug Administration [FDA] for use in the home or in a physician's office.) The *nasopharyngeal swab* test is used to diagnose exposure to the virus and is performed using a six-inch swab inserted into the patient's nose to obtain a material sample that is then sent to a lab for analysis. A machine reads the material to affirm a positive or negative test result. A *serology* or *antibody* test using a vial of blood determines if an individual has already been exposed to the virus. The more useful test for the purposes of projecting the location of the disease is the diagnostic swab test. Three essential components of this test are subject to the vicissitudes of a supply chain in crisis: the correct kind of swab, the reagents (chemicals) used by the machines to assay the test material, and the machines themselves.

The importance of having testing data to establish containment zones and invoke mitigation practices cannot be overstated. Consider that containment and mitigation are not only strategies for dealing with a disease but, in the public health context, also policy questions. How much should people be permitted to move about freely? Should masks be required for everyone or just those with symptoms? What is the appropriate distance people should maintain between themselves and others for safety? Where should these restrictions be imposed? For how long? Testing provides the data that make evidence-based policy decisions, answers to questions similar to those posed here, possible.

The accuracy of timelines, including cumulative number of cases or new cases, depends on widespread testing. At the outset of the pandemic, because this was a *novel* virus, there were no tests for it. Because of the limited testing capacity once tests were developed, however, their use was restricted to those with significant symptoms. Thus, new cases per day and cumulative case totals were both understated by an unknown factor.

Executive Implementation of National Emergency Policy

The COVID-19 pandemic provides a useful example of executive branch implementation of legislative policy addressing national emergencies. Note the shaded implementation phase of policymaking in exhibit 11.4. As we discussed in chapter 7, this phase requires the executive branch to design the implementation of the policy, set forth rules to enforce it, operate (or manage) the function, and evaluate the policy and how it achieves its objectives.

In this case, policy questions emanate more from the design and operating functions, so those two elements of the implementation phase will be the

EXHIBIT 11.4
Policymaking Process: Implementation Phase

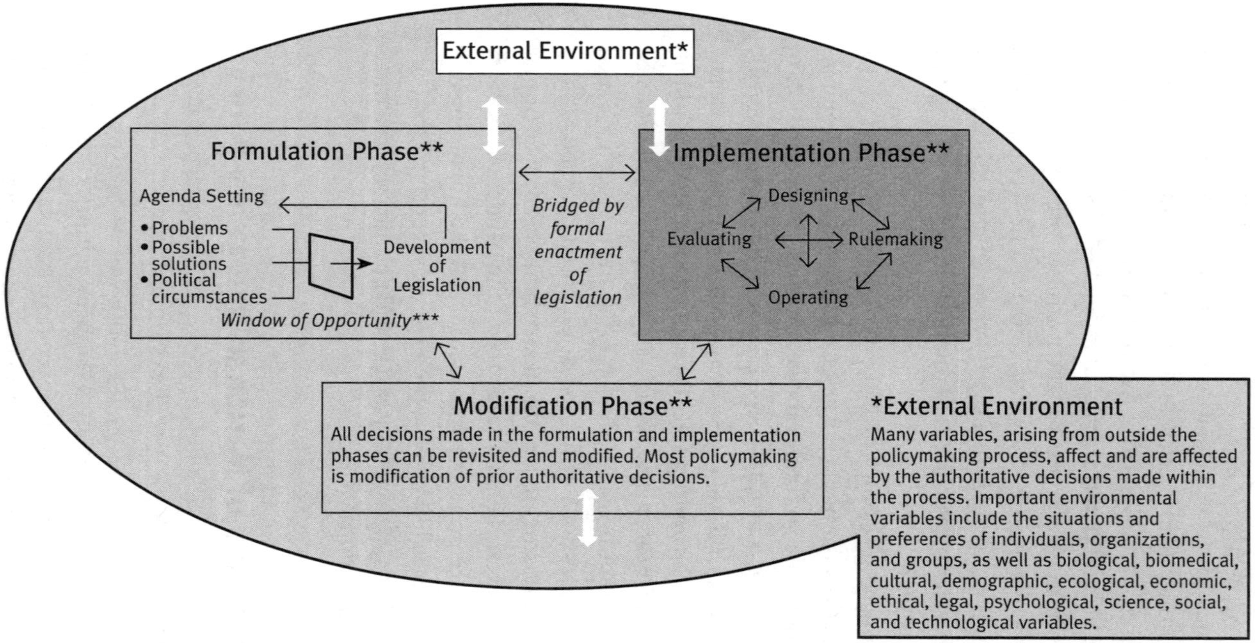
External Environment*
Formulation Phase**
Agenda Setting
• Problems
• Possible solutions
• Political circumstances
Development of Legislation
Window of Opportunity***
Bridged by formal enactment of legislation
Implementation Phase**
Designing
Evaluating
Rulemaking
Operating
Modification Phase**
All decisions made in the formulation and implementation phases can be revisited and modified. Most policymaking is modification of prior authoritative decisions.
*External Environment
Many variables, arising from outside the policymaking process, affect and are affected by the authoritative decisions made within the process. Important environmental variables include the situations and preferences of individuals, organizations, and groups, as well as biological, biomedical, cultural, demographic, ecological, economic, ethical, legal, psychological, science, social, and technological variables.

Policymakers in all three branches of government make policy in the form of position-appropriate, or authoritative, decisions. Their decisions differ in that the **legislative branch is primarily involved in formulation, the **executive branch** is primarily involved in implementation, and both are involved in modification of prior decisions or policies. The **judicial branch** interprets and assesses the legality of decisions made within all three phases of the policymaking process.

***A window of opportunity opens for possible progression of issues through formulation, enactment, implementation, and modification when there is a favorable confluence of problems, possible solutions, and political circumstances.

focus of our review. Further, because the pandemic is ongoing, it is premature to attempt conclusive evaluation of the policy.

To facilitate our review, we will examine how designing and operating the policy was affected by (1) selected legislative policies, (2) strategies for flattening the curve, and (3) the role of problem definition in policy design. And we will review how those elements shaped the federal response and federal and state relations.

This pandemic is considered a public health crisis. Legislative policy for national emergencies already exists in the form of laws, some of which contemplate a health-related crisis and others that are more general. It is necessary for the implementing agency to create an administrative policy design that is specific to the facts at hand. In other words, designing a policy aimed at widespread vaccination of the public is a non sequitur in the absence of a vaccine. The policy design would not fit the facts.

Consistent with general public health principles, in the case of the spread of coronavirus, policy design and operation should aim to *slow or prevent the community spread of the disease*. The overarching objective, of course, is to protect the public's health to the maximum extent possible. Transmission of the disease needs to be retarded, however, for three additional reasons: (1) to reduce the incidence rate of the disease, in order to (2) protect the health services delivery system from being completely overwhelmed with patients requiring acute care, and (3) to buy time for scientists to develop therapeutics to treat patients with the disease and one or more vaccines to prevent its continued transmission.

As we will see later in the chapter, scientists and public health professionals assessed the coming pandemic: They voiced their awareness of the dangers in late December 2019 and early 2020. The months of January and February provided an auspicious moment to design effective policies and strategies to stop, contain, and mitigate the coming wave of disease. Some of the continued assessment efforts were stymied by elements in the international community (Abutaleb et al. 2020), but the US government clearly had sufficient warning of this virus's potential. Later in the chapter, we will explore how the government used those two months. Reviewing the legislative policy first, however, provides the necessary context for examining executive branch implementation.

Review of Selected Legislative Policies

In implementing existing legislative policy with regard to this pandemic, the executive branch is expected to design and operate strategies for dealing with the public health crisis, effectuate one or more of those strategies, and develop an integrated response between the states and multiple agencies of the federal government. To this end, the Department of Health and Human Services (HHS), the CDC, the National Institutes of Health (NIH), the FDA, the

US Public Health Service, the Federal Emergency Management Agency, and the White House need to orchestrate a comprehensive, national response to the pandemic and engage state governments in the response. Appendix 1.3 presented a partial list of laws that speak to these agencies, along with their authority and responsibilities.

From the federal perspective, broad general legislative policy in the form of laws pertaining to national emergencies has been well established. This section will highlight three laws delegating considerable authority to the executive branch in a national emergency.

Presidential powers are broad, and in a national emergency, they are particularly broad. For the purposes of this discussion, we will examine three fundamental powers available to the president and the rest of the federal executive branch: (1) quarantine, (2) ordering production of necessary goods, and (3) the authority to waive regulatory restrictions on healthcare providers.

Quarantine

Under the terms of the Public Health Act of 1940 (as subsequently amended), the executive branch can prevent entry into the United States of anyone who is believed to have an infectious disease. Legislative policy on this question is unambiguous:

> Whenever the Surgeon General [the secretary of HHS has replaced the surgeon general for this function] determines that by reason of the existence of any communicable disease in a foreign country there is serious danger of the introduction of such disease into the United States, and that this danger is so increased by the introduction of persons or property from such country that a suspension of the right to introduce such persons and property is required in the interest of the public health, the Surgeon General, in accordance with regulations approved by the President, shall have the power to prohibit, in whole or in part, the introduction of persons and property from such countries or places as he shall designate in order to avert such danger, and for such period of time as he may deem necessary for such purpose. (July 1, 1944, ch. 373, title III, § 362, 58 Stat. 704)

Furthermore, the president apparently has the authority to impede interstate travel for individuals who might be contagious, though the authority to quarantine or bar entire populations from interstate travel is legally murky.

Defense Production Act

During times of national emergency, the president can order American companies to manufacture goods or provide services necessary to the national defense (Defense Production Act (DPA): 50 USC chapter 55; 64 Stat. 798). Since the DPA's original enactment, the concept of national defense has been expanded to include other kinds of national emergencies. The *Military Times* carries an excellent brief description of the DPA:

> The act gives the federal government broad authority to direct private companies to meet the needs of the national defense. Over the decades, the law's powers have been understood to encompass not only times of war but also domestic emergency preparedness and recovery from terrorist attacks and natural disasters.
>
> The act authorizes the president to require companies to prioritize government contracts and orders seen as necessary for the national defense, with the goal of ensuring that the private sector is producing enough goods needed to meet a war effort or other national emergency. (Tucker 2020)

Waiver of Certain Health-System-Related Restrictions

The National Emergency Act, also known as the Stafford Act (42 USC ch. 68, sec. 5121 et seq; 102 Stat. 4689) empowers the president of the United States to declare a national emergency. When the president does so, the act triggers emergency provisions in a host of other laws, including Section 1135 of the Social Security Act (ASTHO 2020; Social Security Administration 2020).

When President Trump declared a national emergency on March 13, 2020, he also issued a letter directing HHS secretary Alex Azar to use the waiver provision of Section 1135 to set aside several federal requirements pertaining to hospitals and healthcare providers (Trump 2020a). In this case, some of the limitations originate with the Centers for Medicare & Medicaid Services (CMS) as they relate to eligibility for providers to be paid under Medicare regulations. In at least one other case, the waiver related to the Stark Law (anti-kickback), or regulations related to compensation for physicians. These waivers will be discussed in greater detail later in this chapter. But suffice it to say here that some of these provisions allowed providers to practice across state lines and facilitated the use of telehealth.

These congressional policies give broad power to the executive branch to take dramatic action in the event of a national emergency with regard to both safeguarding the public health and supporting health services delivery. These three powers (to quarantine [a travel ban from other countries], to order the production of necessary goods, and to waive some provider-focused regulations) were the most prominently mentioned—and employed by the Trump administration to greater or lesser effect—in response to the COVID-19 pandemic.

Strategies to Flatten the Curve

The best strategies for dealing with the virus would be considered by public health officials and policymakers as policy options. These options play an important role in how this crisis unfolded and how they affected community spread of the disease. The question at hand is how the grants of authority in the legislation discussed previously can be used effectively to minimize the death, despair, and economic calamity associated with the pandemic.

Strategies for dealing with an outbreak, be it a small one or a pandemic like COVID-19, fall into four broad categories: containment, mitigation, treatment, and vaccination. At the beginning of the outbreak, no efficacious vaccine existed. Indeed, one reason the virus spread so rapaciously was that it was a novel coronavirus: Because it was new, no one was immune. Moreover, there was no known efficacious therapy for COVID-19 once it invaded the human body. This discussion will focus primarily on containment and mitigation in the public health domain. Part of the discussion also will focus on the acquisition of supplies and equipment needed for patient care in the health services delivery system.

In this case, not only policy choices but also the effective execution of strategies will affect population health status as reflected in the spread of the disease. In other words, tight containment and sound mitigation measures imposed earlier in the outbreak will slow the spread. A looser approach to containment, a less rigorous imposition of mitigation standards, or a slower response will accelerate the spread of the disease (Lasry et al. 2020). As explained earlier, besides protecting the public health, these strategies are also intended to avoid overloading the healthcare delivery system and to give researchers more time to develop treatment and vaccines for the disease.

The term *flattening the curve* was used frequently in the early stages of the outbreak. This referred to slowing the spread of cases by reducing the number of new cases each day—flattening the curve as it would appear on a graph—so that health systems and health services providers would not be overwhelmed. The absence of immunity in the population (for want of a vaccine) all but assures widespread transmission of the disease. Flattening the curve essentially means to distribute transmission of the disease over a longer period of time. Containment and mitigation of community spread are the two main tools to flatten the curve.

Containment is a strategy to be employed at the very beginning of an outbreak and as part of a larger mitigation strategy later in the outbreak. It is, as it sounds, an effort to restrain the spread from entering (or leaving) a location beyond its extant environs.

Travel restrictions are the most common form of containment. Whether containment is successful depends on the thoroughness with which it is deployed and its timing. To work, containment needs to be "airtight" and implemented at the very early stages of the outbreak. This strategy can be employed on multiple levels. A country, as the United States did, may order a travel ban to block or limit inbound travel. In China, the government essentially closed the city of Wuhan (to both inbound and outbound travel) at one point in an effort to contain the virus to that locale. Stay-at-home orders are a form of containment. Furthermore, long-term care facilities in the United States prohibited visits to residents in an attempt to contain the virus within their respective facilities (and to prevent it from entering). As a practical matter, containment on a local or sublocal level is often a part of a larger effort to mitigate the spread of the disease. Thus, these two strategies work both sequentially and concurrently in concert with one another. In the case of a virus with asymptomatic carriers, timing of general containment is even more critical.

Mitigation is a secondary strategy, to be undertaken once the condition has invaded the community (or country). This effort involves several measures to prevent spread once the virus has appeared. They can include *isolation* (e.g., stay-at-home orders) and the more extreme form of isolation, called *quarantine*. Understanding the virus vectors—whether the virus particle is airborne and, if so, how far it travels in the air; whether it can live on hard surfaces and, if so, for how long—is essential to undertaking effective mitigation techniques. In the case of the coronavirus, as with other viruses, mitigation involves physical separation (to prevent airborne spread), masks (to prevent inbound or outbound airborne spread), and enhanced hygiene techniques (to prevent superficial spread). (See the following box for a brief discussion of masks.) Developing and implementing containment and mitigation policies *in a timely fashion* are central to their success. One study found that if social distancing measures had been put in place one week earlier (than March 15, when CDC released its first guidelines on social distancing), deaths in the United States would have been reduced by approximately 36,000 people (Pei, Kandula, and Shaman 2020).

A Note on Masks

Not all masks are created equal. Clinicians need N95 masks, which block 95 percent of all microparticles. These masks block the virus from *entering* the wearer's body. A shortage of N95 masks was one of the early problems the health system confronted in treating the heavy inflow of patients. Cloth masks, ultimately recommended by the CDC for use by the general public, prevent the virus from *leaving* an infected person. Thus, if everyone were to wear a cloth mask, the safety of the public from the virus would be enhanced significantly. Another form of PPE is the face shield. These protect against both inbound and outbound virus droplets and also protect the eyes, which is a source of entry into the body for this virus (American Academy of Opthalmology 2020).

As discussed earlier, testing is essential to manage the disease process through the population. Mitigation techniques can be deployed most effectively when they include a comprehensive program of testing to measure the spread of the disease and *contact tracing*—tracing individuals with whom the infected person has been in contact—to identify additional potential hot spots before they occur. Testing can inform the breadth and scope of policy decisions such as stay-at-home orders and what kinds of businesses should be permitted to remain open. More specifically, testing can identify positive cases. Individuals who test positive can then be isolated or quarantined. Following that, tracing the contacts that the individual has had with others can lead to additional testing, treatment, and isolation. Applied in concert, these measures can slow the speed—mitigate the spread—of the disease in the general population.

Educating the Public

One frequently forgotten element in this part of the process is education of the public. The public is more willing to accept a stay-at-home order, for example, if there is a broad-based understanding of why. This education process is twofold: teach the public about the disease, and then inform them about containment and mitigation techniques and why these are so critical.

During the peak of the crisis in his state, New York governor Andrew Cuomo conducted daily briefings. Aided by PowerPoint slides, Cuomo showed daily statistics on cases, hospitalizations, and deaths while promoting the use of masks and social distancing. He was consistent in his message, explaining the consequences of not rigorously following mitigation techniques, and supported his message with examples and data. In short, he explained to the people of New York the *why* of the hardships that he was asking them to endure for the purpose of containment and mitigation. These hardships were not minor: loss of work, the inability to socialize in public with friends or even in large groups in private; the cancellation of community and sporting events; and the closure of all but the most essential businesses. Although New York, and New York City in particular, experienced extreme stress on their healthcare system and the economy, the population there was able to flatten the curve while other states were still anticipating the surge in their states.

See exhibit 11.5 for both a daily count of new cases and a seven-day rolling average, which also depicts the coming of a second surge of cases. The exhibit is an example of how the curve has *not* been flattened. Bear in mind that these data are for *confirmed* cases. For want of widespread testing, experts can only guess at how many cases were truly present. The exhibit also shows

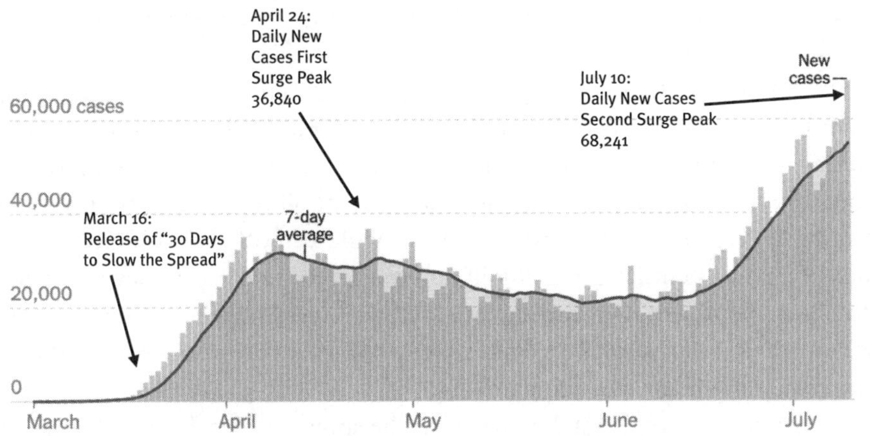

EXHIBIT 11.5
New Reported Cases by Day in the United States from March 1 through July 10, 2020

Source: Adapted from New York Times (2020).

the impact of steps taken to reopen the economies of various states before the curve was truly flattened: another surge of outbreaks reflected as a spike in, or upward turn of, the curve as June rolled into July.

Exhibit 11.5 shows the spread of the disease in the first half of 2020. The bars represent the number of new confirmed COVID-19 cases in the United States per day. As the graph shows, new cases per day grew in March and then accelerated rapidly in April, with a peak of 36,840 new cases reported on April 24. Part of the reason the number of cases continued to escalate even after the national emergency declaration on March 13 and the release of the CDC's "30 Days to Slow the Spread" guidelines on March 16 is attributable to the incubation period of the disease—as much as 14 days. The graph also depicts a second surge, with the largest number of new cases (nearly 70,000) occurring the day the chart was prepared (July 10, 2020) and no diminution in sight.

The line represents a seven-day rolling average of new cases. The curve begins to flatten, with a small decline in the number of new cases per day during the last week in April. The apparent flattening, or the approaching of that state, suggests that the mitigation techniques employed by Americans in their daily lives was working. Physical separation from others, the widespread use of masks, and good hygiene practices seemed to be having an effect.

In May, several states began to reopen their economies. They significantly relaxed many of the mitigation techniques that had proven effective: They thought the crisis had passed. Consequently, as spring ended and summer began, and as states reopened their economies, the number of cases per day again began a significant upswing. Exhibit 11.5 is evidence that relaxation of mitigation standards came too early. The failure to wear masks, maintain social distance, and take other measures are the proximate causes of the reaccelerating spread of the disease, which reached the previously mentioned peak of nearly 70,000 new confirmed cases reported.

A few other states took aggressive steps to require masks in public places, limited the number of people who could be served in stores and restaurants open to the public, and limited the size of indoor gatherings, among other things. Some states had statewide standards, some allowed local governments to impose even more stringent measures, while still others prohibited local units of government from varying in any way from state policy. Several states had phases, or stages, they implemented to try to reopen their economies. This patchwork of policies resulted from states' following their own paths without clear national guidance or standards.

There was a regional dimension to the spread of this disease. The early apparent spike of cases was predominantly in the northeast United States. Because states that were aggressive in reopening tended to be in the south and west, the focal point of the disease moved out of New York and into (at various times in the second surge) the south and Sunbelt in such states as South Carolina, Georgia, Florida, Texas, and Arizona. In response to the second surge, some state and local governments began to reconsider their reopening and took to reimposing mitigation techniques, with varying levels of rigor.

Health Disparities Magnified

As we know from the policy snapshot in part 4, health status or access to healthcare services is inequitable. Poverty and race are significant factors affecting health status. As noted earlier, it is 243 percent more likely for an African American woman to die in childbirth than it is for a white woman to die of the same cause. And African American women are 71 percent more likely to die of cervical cancer and 22 percent more likely to die of breast cancer than white women are (Hostetter and Klein 2018).

More generally, African Americans are 12 percent more likely to die from heart disease and 17.5 percent more likely to die from stroke (Hostetter and Klein 2018) than are non-Hispanic white people. Likewise, African Americans are 60 percent more likely to have diabetes (Office of Minority Health 2019a), 40 percent more likely to have elevated blood pressure (Office of Minority Health 2019b), and 20 percent more likely to have asthma (Office of Minority Health 2017), all significantly complicating factors for people with COVID-19. Moreover, in spite of advances made through implementation of the Affordable Care Act, African Americans are less likely to have a usual point of care in the healthcare system

(Riley, Hayes, and Ryan 2016). In short, both social determinants and access to care work to hinder health development in the African American population.

While viruses know no borders and, in theory, spread randomly throughout the population, those who live in poverty or at near-poverty levels bear the greater burden of infection. For COVID-19, both the number of cases and deaths as a percentage of population are disproportionately greater in African American communities than these numbers are in white neighborhoods. An early study of partial data from New York City found that the mortality rate among African Americans was 92.3 per 100,000, compared with 45.2 per 100,000 among white people (CDC 2020d). Further, national data suggests that African Americans are disproportionately represented in the number of cases, representing about 12.6 percent of the population but 26 percent of the cases (CDC 2020a).

The impact among the Hispanic community is similar. While many indicators suggest that the general health status among Hispanics is similar to that of the white population, Hispanic women are still 40 percent more likely to be diagnosed with cervical cancer and 20 percent more likely to die from it than are non-Hispanic white women (Office of Minority Health 2020). Several states reported that the Hispanic population had a disproportionate share of COVID-19 cases: Iowa, 6 percent of the population, 20 percent of the cases; Washington State, 13 percent of the population, 31 percent of the cases; and Florida, 25 percent of the population, 40 percent of the cases (Jordan and Oppel 2020). Jordan and Oppel (2020) offer an explanation for the uneven distribution of the disease:

> Public health experts say Latinos may be more vulnerable to the virus as a result of the same factors that have put [other] minorities at risk across the country. Many have low-paying service jobs that require them to work through the pandemic, interacting with the public. Others, essentially ordered to remain at work despite the absence of sufficient protective measures, were in meat-packing plants across the United States. Indeed, large clusters of cases arose in rural areas where the major (or only) large business in town was a meat-packing plant. A large number of people in populations of color also lack regular access to healthcare, which contributes to higher rates of diabetes and other conditions that can worsen infections.

COVID-19 has had a more devastating impact on communities of color because of several factors. The percentage of deaths is greater, in part, for want of access to appropriate care. It would also be attributable to the

(continued)

fact that, as a percentage of the population, African Americans have a disproportionate share of chronic conditions that increase their vulnerability to COVID-19. Finally, African Americans and Hispanics are more likely to be in service jobs that increase their exposure to the coronavirus (Wingfield 2020). These statistics underscore the inherent disparity in health status and the inequality in our healthcare delivery system for people of color. Both the statistics reflecting health status and those reflecting the delivery of care are magnified through the focused perspective of the pandemic. Exhibit 11.6 summarizes this inequality as it existed in early July 2020.

EXHIBIT 11.6
Coronavirus Cases per 10,000 People in the United States

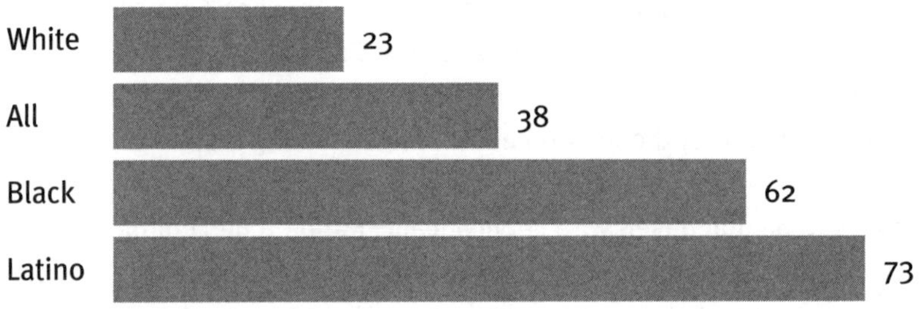

Source: Oppel et al. (2020).

The Role of Problem Definition in Policy Design

As we saw in chapter 7, the first step in executive action implementing a policy involves designing, or in more general management terms, planning and organizing. Designing a response, in this case to a burgeoning pandemic, requires a thorough cognizance of the problem. In short, an effective response requires acknowledging such elements as morbidity, mortality, degree of infectiousness, at-risk populations, and the factors affecting spread. Testing provides the data on these elements, but the perception of what the data mean provides the foundation for designing a policy response (Spradlin 2012).

The first authoritative news report of a new virus in China came on January 4, 2020 (Branswell 2020). Other significant events regarding the virus also occurred in January: the World Health Organization (WHO) confirmed cases in Japan, South Korea, and Thailand (January 20); the first confirmed case in the United States was reported (January 21); China attempted to contain the virus and "cut off" the source of the virus, the city of Wuhan (January 23); and WHO announced that the virus was a global health emergency (January 30). As exhibit 11.3 indicated, there were several warnings concerning the coming virus.

The public health function of assessment in a case such as this pandemic also implicates national security and economic development as well as healthcare agencies and stakeholders. As a result, a variety of experts, as Lipton et al. (2020) explain, were continuing their observations and evaluations behind the scenes:

> The National Security Council office responsible for tracking pandemics received intelligence reports in early January predicting the spread of the virus to the United States, and within weeks was raising options like keeping Americans home from work and shutting down cities the size of Chicago . . .
>
> . . . a Jan. 29 memo produced by his [the president's] trade adviser, Peter Navarro, laying out in striking detail the potential risks of a coronavirus pandemic: as many as half a million deaths and trillions of dollars in economic losses.
>
> The health and human services secretary, Alex M. Azar II, directly warned . . . of the possibility of a pandemic during a call on Jan. 30, the second warning he delivered . . . about the virus in two weeks.

There is corresponding evidence that the nation's military intelligence apparatus detected signs of the new virus as early as November 2019 and that accumulated data subsequently gathered and evaluated culminated in a warning included in the president's daily brief from the intelligence community in January 2020 (Margolin and Meek 2020).

Assessment of the potential risk to the public's health in this instance appeared to function as it should: CDC, HHS, NIH, and others all had been alerted, and these groups informed the requisite officials. Officials inside the federal government had timely knowledge that a pandemic was coming.

The president of the United States, however, held a different view, one that was much more optimistic than the projections of public health professionals. Here is what the president had to say about the problem on January 22: "It's one person coming in from China. We have it under control. It's going to be just fine" (Belvedere 2020).

And later, on January 24 the president also said, "We think we have it very well under control. We have very little problem in this country at this moment—five—and those people are all recuperating successfully. But we're working very closely with China and other countries, and we think it's going to have a very good ending for it. So that I can assure you" (Oprysko 2020).

Throughout the month of February, the Trump administration's public comments suggested it continued to hold an optimistic view of the pandemic, minimizing its potential danger to people in the United States, apparently in the belief that the federal government's limited containment strategy (discussed later) would work. The administration continued to define the problem as one of small dimension and limited duration. On February 10, the president said that there were only eleven cases in the United States and that the virus would "go away" in April: "We're in great shape in our country. We have 11 [cases], and the 11 are getting better. Okay?" (Trump 2020f). On February 24, the president tweeted: "The coronavirus is very much under control in the USA. We are in contact with everyone and all relevant countries. CDC & World Health have been working hard and very smart. Stock Market starting to look very good to me!" (Trump 2020e). On February 25, the president's chief economic adviser, Larry Kudlow, said the virus was "contained" (Imbert 2020). On February 26, the president said the spread of the virus was "not inevitable" (Trump 2020d). This assertion was in direct contradiction to warnings issued the previous day by the CDC, when Dr. Nancy Messionier, director of the CDC's National Center for Immunization and Respiratory Diseases, said, "It's not so much of a question of if this will happen anymore but rather more a question of exactly when this will happen. We are asking the American public to work with us to prepare in the expectation that this could be bad" (Martin 2020).

In short, throughout January and February, the president saw only minimum challenges from the coronavirus outbreak. From the first news of the emerging pandemic through the rest of February on the public record, his perception was optimistic as to the dimension, speed, and consequences of the virus. Whether the president was trying to be a cheerleader for the economy—hoping to buoy American spirits (and the US economy) by minimizing the potential risk to public health and safety—or whether he was simply unduly optimistic or held this view for some other reason has no bearing on our discussion here. The critical point is how the presidential perspective in the early stages of the pandemic shaped the federal government's policy responses to the pandemic. Those policy choices had an impact on the spread of the disease and the potential damage to the economy and challenged the states to exercise their public health and safety powers more robustly. The question is this: How does an administration design a plan to implement laws dealing with a national crisis if it does not perceive the situation to be a national crisis?

The Federal Response

As part of implementing a policy response to this pandemic, the federal government announced on February 2 a strategy of limited containment by restricting the entry into the United States by foreign nationals who had traveled to China in the previous 14 days. In taking this step, the United States joined 36 other nations restricting people's entry from China. In the case of the US restriction, however, the ban excluded the immediate families of US citizens and US permanent residents. The ban is referred to as limited containment because countries in which WHO had already confirmed cases of COVID-19—Japan,

South Korea, and Thailand—were not included. Furthermore, some 40,000 people entered the United States from China within two months after the imposition of the suspension of travel from China because they fell into one of the exceptions (Eder et al. 2020). Notably, the legislative authority for banning travel to the United States also includes the authority to ban foreign-made products from entering the country, but the federal government never employed this measure during the first half of 2020.

In designing and executing a response to a public health crisis such as this, a containment strategy is only a measure to buy time. Even the most rigorous of travel restrictions cannot guarantee complete success in evading the impact of the virus to the "containing" nation. The time gained by containing the virus should be used for further planning and organizing—policy designing and implementation, and for the development of vaccines and therapeutic treatment.

During the early weeks of the pandemic, learning more about the disease and its impact would have been useful. Data on questions such as the following could provide valuable insight on policy design:

1. How long is one asymptomatic at the onset of the disease?
2. Is the disease transmitted by air? If so, at what distance? How long does the virus remain suspended in the air?
3. Is the disease transmitted by surface contact? If so, how long does the virus remain viable on various widely used products, such as cardboard, plastic, cloth, and metal?
4. Further, how quickly does the virus transmit to another person?
5. What percentage of those infected will require acute care?
6. Does the healthcare system have the requisite capacity to handle the volume of patients who might require acute care?
7. Are some populations more at risk for a greater number of cases and a higher mortality rate?
8. Is there sufficient—fully activated—testing capability to produce reliable data regarding the number of cases and the spread of the disease? *Fully activated* means enough swabs, reagents, and necessary lab devices in place and ready to be used.

Understanding the answers to these questions can—and should, if the decision makers are creating evidence-based policy—inform what other containment and mitigation strategies should be employed. In other words, data should inform the policy design to implement the statutory authority.

Further, this information and a delay in the spread can help the health services delivery system anticipate the demand it will soon face. That understanding can then, in turn, drive decisions about preparations to bolster the ability of the healthcare system to provide appropriate care for those who need it. Keep in mind that by mid-2020, there was still no effective therapy for the virus; the best the healthcare system could provide is treatment for some of the symptoms and, in extreme cases, ventilator support for breathing. Thus, having sufficient beds, ventilators, and PPE (clinical masks, face shields, gowns, gloves) became crucial.

Some evidence in the public record shows that during the critical months of January and February 2020, an effort to design a comprehensive plan to implement the full legal authority of the government to address the crisis was being developed. On January 29, the White House announced the formation of a coronavirus task force to be chaired by HHS secretary Alex Azar (Grisham 2020). Four weeks later, on February 26, the president decided to elevate the matter by appointing Vice President Pence as chairperson and bringing on a coordinator, the State Department's global AIDS coordinator, Dr. Deborah Birx, whose office was temporarily relocated from the State Department to the White House (Santucci 2020). This task force was the entity primarily charged with policy development in implementing the national response to the COVID-19 pandemic.

By minimizing the magnitude of the problem in the early days, however, the US government foreclosed earlier mitigation, more stringent containment, and an in-depth examination of other planning and organizing activities. These activities could have included scaling up production and the development of a distribution system for allocating necessary supplies and equipment to support widespread testing and to provide sufficient PPE for healthcare workers. Healthcare providers endured unnecessary exposure for lack of proper masks, face shields, and scrubs. Public health experts were unable to project disease trends accurately because of the lack of testing capacity.

Elements of designing and organizing an effective implementation of the legal authority just discussed would have included the following:

- Widespread testing to provide transmissibility data to shape further containment and mitigation techniques (quarantine, travel limitations, mask mandates, public-gathering limits, crowd-size limits)
- Use of case origin and transmission data to consider a broad-based travel ban from outside the United States (travel ban, quarantine)
- Projecting the need for various kinds of equipment for healthcare workers (the DPA, nationalizing industries)

After having discounted the severity of the virus's spread from January to the middle of March, the Trump administration broadened its travel ban and declared a national emergency. Indeed, after his declaration of a national emergency on March 13, the president said, "Nobody knew that this would be a pandemic or epidemic of this size" (Blake 2020). That the president was still expressing some element of surprise about the coronavirus in mid-March underscores the absence of preparation during the months of January and February and at least the beginning part of March.

Perception of the outbreak is foundational to developing policy options. Understanding the morbidity and mortality potential of the disease, appreciating the speed with which it can spread and the way it spreads, comprehending the size of the population at risk—basically, understanding its severity and transmissibility—are all crucial factors to be considered in developing policy options. In short, perception is reality. Perception broadens, or restricts, the viable choices because policymakers can only respond to what they understand to be true.

The federal government eventually did impose further travel restrictions, banning entry of foreign nationals who had been in Europe, Iran, or Brazil in the last 14 days before their desired entry into the United States (US Department of State 2020). Furthermore, the CDC issued a set of mitigation guidelines on March 15, as mentioned earlier. Neither effort, however, rose to the level of a strict quarantine or a ban from travel, as envisioned by the previously mentioned Public Health Act of 1940, which gave the executive branch the power to deny US entry to anyone believed to have an infectious disease or any material thing believed to carry an infectious agent. The sufficiency—or insufficiency—of the public health infrastructure was brought into acute focus. Finally, the state development of regional partnerships ushered in a level of regional cooperation to help fill the void left by the absence of a national response.

Federal: Mitigation "Guidelines" and Containment Travel Bans

In accordance with the Public Health Act of 1940, on March 1, President Trump announced a 30-day travel ban on most of Europe, banning any alien from entering the United States if they had been in the Schengen Area of Europe within 14 days of their transit to the United States.* The United Kingdom and Ireland were not included (Trump 2020c). On March 13, when there were 1,683 confirmed cases in the United States, President Trump declared a national emergency (Trump 2020b).

Only on this declaration of a national emergency did the US government move to a second-phase strategy—mitigation of the outbreak. Concordant with that declaration on March 13, the CDC and White House released "guidelines"

*The Schengen Area constitutes the countries of Austria, Belgium, Czech Republic, Denmark, Estonia, Finland, France, Germany, Greece, Hungary, Iceland, Italy, Latvia, Liechtenstein, Lithuania, Luxembourg, Malta, Netherlands, Norway, Poland, Portugal, Slovakia, Slovenia, Spain, Sweden, and Switzerland.

on March 16 intended to inform the public about specific steps individuals could take to help mitigate the spread of the virus. The CDC, through the White House, advised the following measures:

- If you feel sick, you should stay home.
- If a child is sick, do not send them to school.
- If someone in the household tests positive, keep everyone in the household home.
- If you are an older person, stay home.
- If you have an underlying medical condition, stay home.

The guidelines further suggested that people should avoid eating and drinking in restaurants, gatherings of ten or more people, discretionary travel, and visiting nursing homes and hospitals and that they should practice good hygiene (CDC 2020e). But this document was somewhat arbitrary. Its title, "30 Days to Slow the Spread," established a deadline not driven by any data.

The federal government was, at this point, following and not leading the development of a national response to the pandemic. Indeed, a week before the president's announcement, many universities had migrated to online classes (Quintana 2020), the NCAA had canceled not only March Madness, but all spring sports (Osburn 2020), and 33 states had closed public schools (most of which adapted to an online environment) (Strauss 2020). The NBA had suspended the remainder of its season (Aschburner 2020), and other commercial enterprises like McDonald's, Starbucks, and Chick-fil-A limited their operations to drive-through only (Balu 2020). On the political and social fronts, several states delayed presidential primaries and some states had limited the size of public gatherings (Dzhanova 2020).

Between January 21 (when the United States imposed the ban on travel from China) and mid-March (when a national emergency was declared on the 13th and when the accompanying guidelines were released on the 16th), cases in the United States had climbed from one case to more than nine thousand (Johns Hopkins University 2020). During that time, the federal government could have planned for, and taken, various steps to help mitigate the spread of the virus. Its failure to do so caused the states to move ahead, some aggressively, others less so, in using their public health and safety powers to protect the populations within their respective borders.

Nationalizing Industries and the Defense Production Act

The initial reluctance of the Trump administration to take full advantage of the DPA resulted in several supply shortfalls. First, the federal government chose private-sector "partnerships" to manufacture necessary PPE, test kits, and other critical supplies. This choice may have led to overpayment for these products and certainly resulted in spotty performance, highlighted by chronic shortages (Diaz, Sands, and Alesci 2020). Second, because the government would not fully invoke the DPA and relied instead on private enterprise, critical supplies were unevenly distributed: states were forced to compete against one another for the same pools of ventilators, masks, and other supplies (Miller 2020). As a consequence, valuable state resources were consumed while an industry profited at the expense of not only those limited resources but also the states that lost the bidding competition for similar equipment.

Developing sufficient testing capability seemed to be a particularly vexatious point for the Trump administration and the states. At one point the president said, "Anyone who wants a test can get a test" (Gomez et al. 2020). That declaration turned out not to be the case. Test protocols varied from location to location because there was no national initiative toward a testing goal. In general, early in the pandemic, a patient needed to be symptomatic to get a test, and even then, it was not guaranteed. In some cases, only individuals who had traveled outside the United States *and* were symptomatic could receive a test (Meyer 2020). The federal government basically laid the problem on the states, urging the nation's governors to do more to supply test kits and the reagents (Goldberg, Ehley, and Lim 2020). And at various points in the outbreak from late January to the end of May, each element—swabs, reagents, and devices—was in short supply, more or less sequentially, meaning there were successive occlusion points on the supply chains for each component (Allen and Weyl 2020). Absent firm national leadership, reliance on private enterprise to meet these various demands cost state and local governments precious time in getting supplies into the hands of those who needed them and, as just described, left the supplies unevenly distributed nationwide.

The president was assertive in his position not to use the DPA. "Governors are supposed to be doing a lot of this work, and they are doing a lot of this work," Trump said on March 19. "The Federal government is not supposed to be out there buying vast amounts of items and then shipping. You know, we're not a shipping clerk" (Forgey 2020). This statement squarely defined the administration's position of minimizing the federal role, forcing the states to take on additional responsibility for combatting the virus, and overruling the governors' requests for an active federal response to the pandemic.

The Trump administration ultimately used the DPA in March to order 3M to produce N95 masks and to order General Motors to make ventilators, basically health services delivery system items (Watney and Stapp 2020). But it did not invoke the DPA until April to increase the production of swabs necessary for testing, a public health function. And the administration only did so after attempting to meet the demand by flying supplies into the United States from Italy (Sullivan, Smith, and Mak 2020).

Waiver of Health System-Related Laws

Part of the president's powers under the Stafford Act, which permits him to declare a national emergency, include waiving certain legal restrictions. With regard to the healthcare system, President Trump waived a number of legal restrictions placed on providers by Medicare and Medicaid regulation and the Stark legislation:

- Laws restricting telehealth to in-state use only
- Federal requirements limiting doctors' ability to provide care across state lines
- Limits on number of beds (25) and length of stay (96 hours) for critical access hospitals (CAH)
- Federal requirement for a three-day hospital stay before a patient can be admitted to a skilled nursing facility
- Federal rule limiting hospitals' ability to provide physician office space or retain physicians

During the pandemic, CMS permitted payment for physicians and nurse practitioners to provide services using telehealth. This change brought much-needed care to rural hospitals and to skilled nursing facilities (Brady 2020). At least one rural health center took advantage of its expanded CAH capacity, extended telemedicine across the state border, and used the increased flexibility to add more staff, as provided under the relaxed regulations from CMS (Cheney 2020).

Federal and State Relationships: Unwanted Deference?

Strained relationships between the federal government and the states came into focus during this time, as federal inaction forced states to expand their efforts. The absence of a comprehensive national response, giving rise to a patchwork of 50 state responses, weakened the overall response and allowed the virus to spread with even greater dispatch than it would have otherwise (Holtz et al. 2020).

This piecemeal approach yielded a kind of accidental federalism. With the federal government's ambivalence creating a vacuum, the states stepped up to fill it. Permitting states to structure their own mitigation programs further confounded comprehensive public health efforts to provide an integrated, coordinated response. Moreover, states were left to their own devices to find all kinds of necessary equipment: ventilators, swabs, testing reagents, testing machines, and masks and other PPE. While the federal government did provide some of these supplies from the federal stockpile, the amount was generally inadequate for the states whose numbers of cases were surging.

The federal government and most states did little to mitigate the spread of the virus during February; the rationale for this position was to preserve normal economic and social activity to the extent possible. By the end of February, China had 80,000 confirmed cases and Italy was observing a sharp uptick in its disease count as well. China, along with other countries during this time, began to take extreme measures to contain the spread of the disease (Reuters 2020).

By mid-March, it became clear that states would be required to exercise their public health and safety powers to keep their populations safe from this contagion. The Trump administration consistently refused to engage in matters it felt were properly left to the states. Even without legal authority to issue a national stay-at-home edict, the president did not urge uniformity among the governors with regard to starting date, standards for social distancing, or duration of such stay-at-home orders (Samuels 2020). See exhibit 11.7 for a review of these state stay-at-home orders.

Not all 50 states are represented on the exhibit. South Carolina's stay-at-home order was effective April 7, 2020. The states of Arkansas, Iowa, Nebraska, North Dakota, South Dakota, and Wyoming (as of June 2020) never issued stay-at-home orders.

Note that the time frame for state orders stretched from March 19 to April 7. Of course, states do vary in their population densities and other factors affecting disease transmission and thus might respond differently and at different times. Unfortunately, the virus does not respect state boundaries. Thus, where one state has a mitigation policy and the neighboring state (or a state connected by plane, train, or automobile) does not, the people in the state with the mitigation policy are placed at additional risk. In short, the highly mobile nature of American society increases the likelihood that the virus will spread to unsuspecting corners of the country. Accordingly, a national policy might be more effective than 50 state policies.

In the end, the Trump administration relegated the testing function—arguably the most important element in attempting to minimize the impact of the virus—to the states. While leaving the states to establish their own containment and mitigation restrictions might have been merely a missed opportunity, the failure to lead in establishing a clear and cohesive national policy and the failure to supply states with sufficient levels of materials in support of testing, appears to be a deliberate abandonment by the federal government. In a report to Congress, the Trump administration said:

> When developing testing strategies, States, territories and tribes should consider testing technologies, use cases for these technologies, and available inventory. . . . In addition, strategies should be considered living documents and adapted as needed to account for the latest information about disease transmissibility and

EXHIBIT 11.7
Effective Date of States' Stay-at-Home Orders, 2020

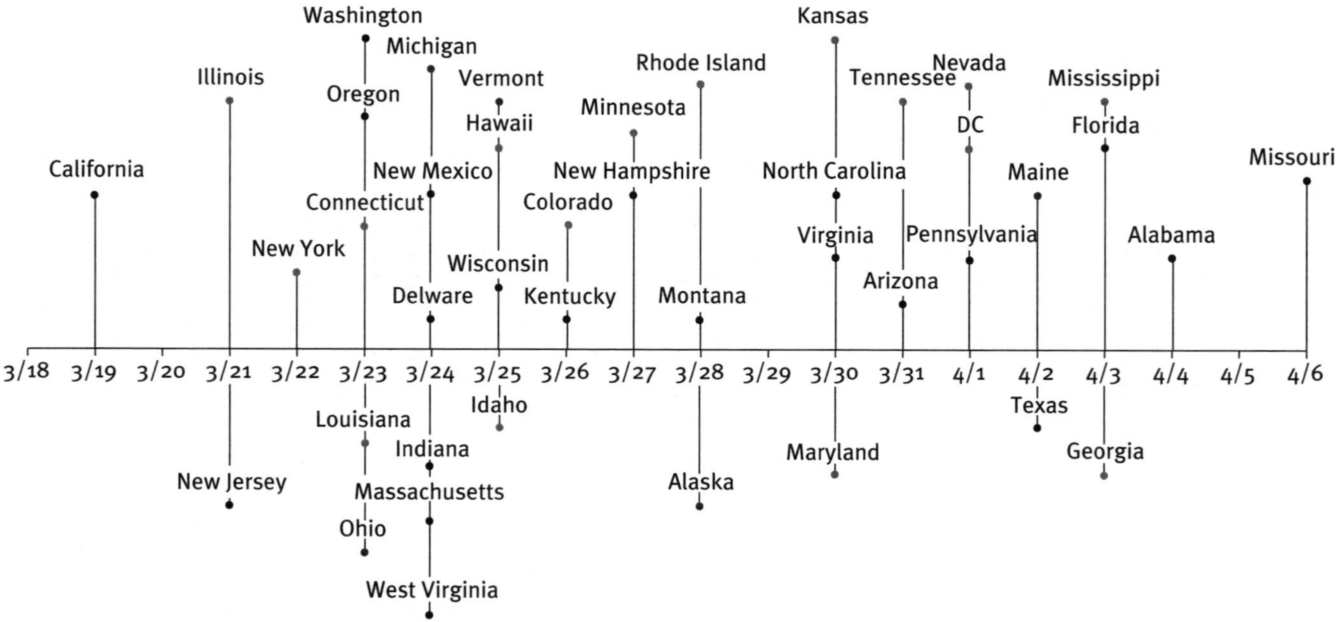

Source: Kates, Michaud, and Tolbert (2020).

immunity. Strategies should be flexible enough to incorporate new diagnostic technologies where appropriate and fit-for-purpose. At a minimum, a State's testing plan should include the following:

- How the state, territory, and tribal area will meet testing goals/targets;
- Where testing will be performed (commercial; academic; medical centers; public health labs, retail sites);
- Description of the SARS-CoV-2 testing capacity and ecosystem in the State;
- Capabilities to overcome barriers to efficient testing;
- Mechanisms to leverage the entire testing ecosystem;
- Use of new and emerging technologies, as they develop;
- A reporting structure to inform clinical care and public health decision-making;
- Mechanisms to rapidly identify any newly emergent cases or clusters of COVID-19 among symptomatic and asymptomatic individuals;
- Protocols to facilitate contact tracing and isolation strategies for newly diagnosed cases; and
- A process to ensure that underserved and high-risk populations receive adequate testing services, through the most effective means. (HHS 2020, p.7)

The question remains if this delegation of responsibility is the most effective strategy. Testing and contact tracing are costly. The robustness of each state's response to the problem will vary—as a function of resources and political ideology. Moreover, a divided state government may not be able to establish a workable consensus between the governor and the state legislature regarding testing policy. One state's lack of a robust testing effort not only leaves the residents of that state at higher risk of exposure but also leaves everyone outside the state at greater risk: Infected individuals who are not diagnosed can travel and spread the virus both within and outside state boundaries.

Our federal system is structured to permit variability among the states to accommodate the respective needs of their populations. But where is the appropriate line to be drawn for public health emergencies such as a pandemic? States do have the primary responsibility for public health and safety, but from whence should come the response to threats that transcend state (and even international) borders?

Other Significant Policy Issues to Consider for Further Exploration

Other policy issues related to the coronavirus pandemic deserve mention, but a thorough examination lies outside the scope of this book. Their brief treatment here does not suggest they lack importance. The analysis of selected issues here is primarily predicated on developments and policy questions arising from the early days of the pandemic. The ongoing nature of the pandemic limits the comprehensiveness of what can be explored at this point. Indeed, a thorough review of the pandemic as a worldwide event, or even as an intrusion on the American way of life will no doubt generate many books, journal articles, and additional debate for years to come.

For now, however, take note of a sampling of other policy questions worthy of mention and further examination over time. First, the pandemic has highlighted the role of public–private partnerships. This issue deserves further scrutiny because of its potential for abuse. Although it is too early to evaluate how these relationships functioned during the entire pandemic, we can ask key questions about them. For example, what conditions in those relationships engendered a favorable outcome for the community, and what conditions facilitated abuse? What ideological predispositions contribute to those outcomes—both good and bad? Was the product or service delivered on time, within budget, and under circumstances that engendered public trust in the transaction and the outcome? Future scholars, historians, and policy analysts will undoubtedly review what has taken place during this era.

Second, the pandemic uncovered questions about the adequacy of the public health infrastructure. As the public debate turns more to testing and contact tracing methodologies to surveil the disease and mitigate its spread, the United States clearly lacks much of what is needed to implement quickly and effectively a national policy of testing and contact tracing. Are tracing and testing an appropriate function for states in their protection of the public health and welfare? Should there be a national initiative of this undertaking, given that the virus knows no borders? What are the appropriate privacy concerns?

Moreover, the way the healthcare delivery system has adapted deserves additional study. Some existing ideas and technology, such as the use of telehealth visits to providers, have expanded during the pandemic crisis and should be considered for a more permanent restructuring of healthcare delivery. Proposals to allow providers to work across state lines will probably be answered now that the need and the benefits have been demonstrated (Schneider and Davis 2020). Telemedicine is likely to contribute both to greater access to care in general and to the provision of care across state lines.

Finally, this crisis gave new prominence to the connection of health insurance to employment. Approximately 56 percent of Americans who have health insurance obtain it through their employer (Berchick, Hood, and Barnett 2018). The pandemic brought about widespread unemployment because of mandatory business shutdowns, stay-at-home orders, and the related fears people had about going out to dinner, shopping, and so forth. Reduced revenue for business means fewer jobs for employees. Fewer people gainfully employed means higher levels of uninsured people. This downward spiral intensifies the debate about the need for other mechanisms for people to obtain health insurance.

Summary

The pandemic of 2020 will continue until such time as there is sufficient herd immunity to prevent excessive mortality in the future. Such herd immunity will come about through one or more vaccines and through a sufficient number of people developing immunity after contracting the disease. By June 2020, some experts had suggested that such worldwide immunity might not be reached until well into 2021 or even into 2022 (Moore et al. 2020).

The way COVID-19 has touched the lives of every American (not to mention countless millions worldwide) is stunning. Its effect on our lives in the future is, of course, not yet in full view. Beyond those infected and those who died, the human impact is still difficult to fathom. Countless healthcare providers and workers of all kinds have faced overwhelming challenges for days and weeks on end while the wave of infections was near its apex both upward and downward. People normally invisible to most Americans suddenly became identified as essential: grocery store employees, delivery personnel of all kinds, and building custodians, among others. Taken for granted until they were lost to many Americans, food service personnel, small retailers, neighborhood restaurants, and local businesses were suddenly missed.

By July 2020, it appeared that the surveillance (assessment) of the public health system had worked in the early days of the event. What seemed more problematic was the policy development function, which apparently fell victim to an overly optimistic view of the circumstances, a denial of what was happening, and an absence of belief in the science that demonstrated the infectiousness and transmissibility of the disease. As a consequence, the resulting policy to address the pandemic consists of multiple state and federal voices whose messages frequently were not aligned.

The implementation of established legislative policies—under emergency conditions—is difficult enough. But implementing them when political leadership challenges the very existence of a crisis is nearly impossible.

Healthcare professionals can learn priceless lessons from this ordeal. They are uniquely positioned to help shape changes to American culture. Looking back to the call to action in the policy snapshot of part 4, what can we do to prepare for the next pandemic? (Yes, there will surely be one; it's only a matter of time.) Can we help persuade our political leadership to listen to the science of public health? Or will we fall victim to the whims of those who reject data, science, and fact as mere inconveniences? What can we do on the local, state, or national level to ensure America's preparedness going forward? The challenge is broad. It includes understanding the etiology of disease, recognizing the importance of the community of nations and the value of connectedness in our own communities, and managing the stockpile of PPE and other important equipment the next time this happens.

The pandemic of 2020 (and beyond?) has, indeed, broken much of American life. It is up to leaders in the healthcare community to help repair it. Only one thing is for certain: the way Americans work and play will never again be the same. But it will only be better if we make it so.

Review Questions

1. In response to the coronavirus pandemic of 2020, the Trump administration
   - imposed a partial ban on travel from China;
   - imposed a ban on travel from Europe;
   - used the DPA to produce masks, ventilators, and testing swabs; and
   - waived several regulatory restrictions for healthcare providers to facilitate delivery of care.

   In your opinion, were these interventions well timed, or should they have been done earlier? Were they sufficient in scope, or should more have been done? Why, or why not?
2. In a national public health crisis, what role does a predisposition toward optimism play? What role does an ideological predilection for undervaluing scientific contributions play?
3. Had the federal government been more active in developing national policy aimed at forestalling the pandemic, how would that approach have changed the role of the states?
4. From a policy perspective, what is the appropriate role for the federal government with regard to the following?
   - Containment
   - Mitigation
   - Testing
5. Is there something different about a pandemic that should cause the federal government to adhere more closely to a states' rights doctrine? Or should the federal government play a larger role in regulating individual behavior in such a circumstance?
6. What would your recommendations to a president have been in the case of the COVID-19 pandemic?

References

Abutaleb, Y., J. Dawsey, E. Nakashima, and G. Miller. 2020. "The U.S. Was Beset by Denial and Dysfunction As the Coronavirus Raged." *Washington Post.* Published May 25. www.washingtonpost.com/national-security/2020/04/04/coronavirus-government-dysfunction/?arc404=true.

Adolph, C., K. Amano, B. Bang-Jensen, N. Fullman, and J. Wilkerson. 2020. "Pandemic Politics: Timing State-Level Social Distancing Responses to COVID-19." *MedRxIV* preprint. Published March 28. www.medrxiv.org/content/10.1101/2020.03.30.20046326v1.

Allen, D., and G. Weyl. 2020. "The Mechanics of the COVID-19 Testing Supply Chain." White paper. Edmond J. Safra Center for Ethics, Harvard University. Published April 16. https://ethics.harvard.edu/files/center-for-ethics/files/white_paper_9_mechanics_of_the_testing_supply_chain_0.pdf.

American Academy of Ophthalmology. 2020. "Coronavirus and Your Eyes." Published March 20. www.med.unc.edu/ophth/files/2020/03/CoronaVirusandYourVision.pdf.

Aschburner, S. 2020. "Coronavirus Pandemic Causes NBA to Suspend Season After Player Tests Positive." National Basketball Association. Published March 12. www.nba.com/article/2020/03/11/coronavirus-pandemic-causes-nba-suspend-season.

ASTHO. 2020. "Social Security Act Section 1135: Waiver Authority in National Emergencies." Association of State and Territorial Health Officials. Accessed May 21. www.astho.org/Programs/Preparedness/Public-Health-Emergency-Law/Emergency-Authority-and-Immunity-Toolkit/Social-Security-Act,-Section-1135-Waiver-Authority-in-National-Emergencies-Fact-Sheet.

Balu, N. 2020. "McDonald's, Starbucks Limit Dine-in Service in U.S. to Slow Coronavirus." Reuters. Published March 16. www.reuters.com/article/us-health-coronavirus-starbucks/mcdonalds-starbucks-limit-dine-in-service-in-u-s-to-slow-coronavirus-idUSKBN2131RC.

Belvedere, M. J. 2020. "Trump Says He Trusts China's Xi on Coronavirus and the US Has It 'Totally Under Control.'" CNBC. Published January 22. www.cnbc.com/2020/01/22/trump-on-coronavirus-from-china-we-have-it-totally-under-control.html.

Berchick, E. R., E. Hood, and J. C. Barnett. 2018. "Health Insurance Coverage in the United States: 2017." US Census Bureau. Published September 12. www.census.gov/library/publications/2018/demo/p60-264.html.

Blake, A. 2020. "Trump Keep Saying 'Nobody' Could Have Foreseen Coronavirus. We Keep Finding Out About New Warning Signs." *Washington Post.* Published March 20. www.washingtonpost.com/politics/2020/03/19/trump-keeps-saying-nobody-could-have-foreseen-coronavirus-we-keep-finding-out-about-new-warning-signs.

Brady, M. 2020. "CMS to Allow Providers to Practice at Top of License, Across States." *Modern Healthcare.* Published April 9. www.modernhealthcare.com/government/cms-allow-providers-practice-top-license-across-states.

Branswell, H. 2020. "Experts Search for Answers in Limited Information About Mystery Pneumonia Outbreak in China." *Stat.* Published January 4. www.statnews.com/2020/01/04/mystery-pneumonia-outbreak-china.

Centers for Disease Control and Prevention (CDC). 2020a. "Cases in the US." Published June 1. www.cdc.gov/coronavirus/2019-ncov/cases-updates/cases-in-us.html.

———. 2020b. "Symptoms of Coronavirus." Published May 13. www.cdc.gov/coronavirus/2019-ncov/symptoms-testing/symptoms.html.

———. 2020c. "Coronavirus Disease 2019 Basics." Accessed May 13. www.cdc.gov/coronavirus/2019-ncov/faq.html#Coronavirus-Disease-2019-Basics.

———. 2020d. "COVID-19 in Racial and Ethnic Minority Groups." Published April 22. www.cdc.gov/coronavirus/2019-ncov/need-extra-precautions/racial-ethnic-minorities.html.

———. 2020e. "30 Days to Slow the Spread." Published March 13.www.whitehouse.gov/wp-content/uploads/2020/03/03.16.20_coronavirus-guidance_8.5x11_315PM.pdf.

Cheney, C. 2020. "6 Steps for Rural Hospitals to Rise to the Coronavirus Challenge." *HealthLeaders.* Published May 6. www.healthleadersmedia.com/clinical-care/6-steps-rural-hospitals-rise-coronavirus-challenge.

Cowling, B. J., and A. E. Aiello. 2020. "Public Health Measures to Slow Community Spread of Coronavirus Disease 2019." *Journal of Infectious Disease* 221 (11): 1749–51. https://doi.org/10.1093/infidis/jaa123.

Diaz, D., G. Sands, and C. Alesci. 2020. "Protective Equipment Costs Increase over 1,000% amid Competition and Surge in Demand." *CNN.* Published April 16. www.cnn.com/2020/04/16/politics/ppe-price-costs-rising-economy-personal-protective-equipment/index.html.

Dzhanova, Y. 2020. "Coronavirus Is Disrupting the 2020 Election: Here Are the States That Have Adjusted Their Primaries." *CNBC.* Published March 24. www.cnbc.com/2020/03/24/coronavirus-update-states-that-have-postponed-2020-primaries.html.

Eder, S., H. Fountain, M. H. Keller, M. Xiao, and A. Stevenson. 2020. "430,000 People Have Traveled from China to U.S. Since Coronavirus Surfaced." *New York Times.* Published April 15. www.nytimes.com/2020/04/04/us/coronavirus-china-travel-restrictions.html.

Forgey, Q. 2020. "'We're Not a Shipping Clerk': Trump Tells Governors to Step Up Efforts to Get Medical Supplies." *Politico.* Published March 19. www.politico.com/news/2020/03/19/trump-governors-coronavirus-medical-supplies-137658.

Ghandi, M., D. S. Yokoe, and D. V. Havlir. 2020. "Asymptomatic Transmission, the Achilles' Heel of Current Strategies to Control Covid-19." *New England Journal of Medicine.* Published May 28. doi:10.1056/NEJMe2009758.

Goldberg, D., B. Ehley, and D. Lim. 2020. "States Still Waiting on Coronavirus Tests as Trump Tells Them to Do More." *Politico*. Published March 20. www.politico.com/news/2020/03/20/coronavirus-tests-states-138426.

Gomez, F., G. Segers, S. Cook, K. Watson, P. Reid, J. Chick, and V. Albert. 2020. "Trump Calls Coronavirus Test 'Perfect' and Compares It to Ukraine Phone Call." *CBS News*. Published March 6. www.cbsnews.com/news/trump-calls-coronavirus-test-perfect-and-compares-it-to-ukraine-phone-call.

Grisham, S. 2020. "Statement from the Press Secretary Regarding the President's Coronavirus Task Force." White House. Published January 29. www.whitehouse.gov/briefings-statements-press-secretary-regarding-presidents-coronavirus-task-force.

Guo, Z.-D., Z.-Y. Wang, S.-F. Zhang, X. Li, L. Li, C. Li, Y. Cui, R.-B. Fu, Y.-Z. Dong, X.-Y. Chi, M.-Y. Zhang, K. Liu, C. Cao, B. Liu, K. Zhang, Y.-W. Gao, B. Lu, and W. Che. 2020. "Emerging Infectious Diseases." *CDC* 26 (7). wwwnc.cdc.gov/eid/article/26/7/20-0885_article.

Gupta, S. 2020. "The Mystery of Why the Coronavirus Kills Some Young People." *CNN*. Published April 6. www.cnn.com/2020/04/05/health/young-people-dying-coronavirus-sanjay-gupta/index.html.

Holtz, D., M. Zhao, S. Benzell, C. Cao, A. Rahiman, J. Yang, J. Allen, A. Collis, A. Moehring, T. Sowrirajan, D. Ghosh, Y. Zhang, P. S. Dhillon, C. Nicolaides, D. Eckles, and S. Aral. 2020. "Interdependence and the Cost of Uncoordinated Responses to COVID-19." Working paper. Massachusetts Institute of Technology. Published Mary 25. http://ide.mit.edu/sites/default/files/publications/Interdependence_COVID_522.pdf.

Hostetter, M., and S. Klein. 2018. "Reducing Racial Disparities in Health Care by Confronting Racism." Commonwealth Fund. Published September 27. www.commonwealthfund.org/publications/newsletter-article/2018/sep/focus-reducing-racial-disparities-health-care-confronting.

Imbert, F. 2020. "Larry Kudlow Says US Has Contained the Coronavirus and the Economy Is Holding Up Nicely." *CNBC*. Published February 25. www.cnbc.com/2020/02/25/larry-kudlow-says-us-has-contained-the-coronavirus-and-the-economy-is-holding-up-nicely.html.

James, A., L. Eagle, C. Phillips, S. Hedges, C. Bodenhamer, R. Brown, J. G. Wheeler, and H. Kirking. 2020. "High COVID-19 Attack Rate Among Attendees at Events at a Church—Arkansas, March 2020." CDC. Published May 19. www.cdc.gov/mmwr/volumes/69/wr/mm6920e2.htm?s_cid=mm6920e2_w.

Johns Hopkins University. 2020. "COVID-19 Dashboard by the Center for Systems Science and Engineering (CSSE) at Johns Hopkins University." Accessed May 14. www.arcgis.com/apps/opsdashboard/index.html?fbclid=IwAR1iEfNDuArOdlxL65AlVdi51diqysbRmBo67YpyDfCoHcc5l9gBPJyl2AU#/bda7594740fd40299423467b48e9ecf6.

Jordan, M., and J. R. Oppel. 2020. "For Latinos and COVID-19, Doctors Are Seeing an Alarming Disparity." *New York Times*. Published May 7. www.nytimes.com/2020/05/07/us/coronavirus-latinos-disparity.html.

Kates, J., J. Michaud, and J. Tolbert. 2020. "Stay-At-Home Orders to Fight COVID-19 in the United States: The Risks of a Scattershot Approach." Kaiser Family Foundation. Published April 6. www.kff.org/wp-content/uploads/2020/04/Figure-State-Actions-by-Date.png.

Lasry, A., D. Kidder, M. Hast, J. Poovey, G. Sunshine, K. Winglee, N. Zviedrite, F. Ahmed, and K. A. Ethier. 2020. "Timing of Community Mitigation and Changes in Reported COVID-19 and Community Mobility—Four US Metropolitan Areas, February 26–April 1, 2020." *CDC Morbidity and Mortality Weekly Report* 69 (15): 451–57. www.cdc.gov/mmwr/volumes/69/wr/mm6915e2.htm.

Li, R., S. Pei, B. Chen, Y. Song, T. Zhang, W. Yang, and J. Shaman. 2020. "Substantial Undocumented Infection Facilitates the Rapid Dissemination of Novel Coronavirus (SARS-CoV-2)." *Science* 368 (6490): 489–93.

Lipton, E., D. Sanger, M. Haberman, M. Shear, M. Mazzati, and J. Barnes. 2020. "He Could Have Seen What Was Coming: Behind Trump's Failure on the Virus." *New York Times*. Published May 4. www.nytimes.com/2020/04/11/us/politics/coronavirus-trump-response.html.

Margolin, J., and J. G. Meek. 2020. "Intelligence Report Warned of Coronavirus Crisis as Early as November." *ABC News*. Published April 8. https://abcnews.go.com/Politics/intelligence-report-warned-coronavirus-crisis-early-november-sources/story?id=70031273.

Martin, J. 2020. "Trump Contradicts CDC Warning of 'Inevitable' Coronavirus Spread in U.S., Says He Doesn't 'Think It's Inevitable.'" *Newsweek*. Published February 26. www.newsweek.com/trump-contradicts-cdc-warning-inevitable-coronavirus-spread-us-says-he-doesnt-think-its-1489351.

Meyer, R. 2020. "America Isn't Testing for the Most Alarming Coronavirus Cases." *Atlantic*. Published March 13. www.theatlantic.com/science/archive/2020/03/who-gets-tested-coronavirus/607999.

Miller, H. 2020. "Governors Across the Nation Slam Federal Coronavirus Response: 'We Didn't Take This Seriously.'" *CNBC*. Published March 22. www.cnbc.com/2020/03/22/governors-say-they-are-not-getting-supplies-they-need-for-coronavirus.html.

Moore, K. A., M. Lipsitch, J. M. Barry, and M. T. Osterholm. 2020. "COVID-19: The CIDRAP Viewpoint." Center for Infectious Disease Research and Policy, University of Minnesota. Published April 30. www.cidrap.umn.edu/sites/default/files/public/downloads/cidrap-covid19-viewpoint-part1_0.pdf.

New York Times. 2020. "Coronavirus in the U.S.: Latest Map and Case Count." Published May 21. www.nytimes.com/interactive/2020/us/coronavirus-us-cases.html.

Oppel, J. R., R. Gebeloff, K. Lai, W. Wright, and M. Smith. 2020. "The Fullest Look Yet at the Racial Inequity of Coronavirus." *New York Times*. Published July 5. www.nytimes.com/interactive/2020/07/05/us/coronavirus-latinos-african-americans-cdc-data.html?utm_campaign=KHN%3A%20Daily%20Health%20

Policy%20Report&utm_medium=email&_hsmi=90822791&_hsenc=p2ANqtz-_11kCg4v3ugPFYbGJT793MSG-1WEUOMYoIsuyengiFx-v16L16J.
Oprysko, C. 2020. "Trump: Coronavirus Will Have 'a Very Good Ending for Us.'" *Politico*. Published January 30. www.politico.com/news/2020/01/30/trump-close-cooperation-china-coronavirus-109701.
Osburn, S. 2020. "NCAA Cancels Remaining Winter and Spring Championships." NCAA. Published March 12. www.ncaa.org/about/resources/media-center/news/ncaa-cancels-remaining-winter-and-spring-championships.
Our World in Data. 2020. "Daily Confirmed COVID-19 Deaths." Accessed May 29. https://ourworldindata.org/coronavirus/country/united-states?country=~USA#what-is-the-daily-number-of-confirmed-deaths.
Pei, S., S. Kandula, and J. Shaman. 2020. "Differential Effects of Intervention Timing on COVID-19 Spread in the United States." *MedRxIV*. Published May 29. www.medrxiv.org/content/10.1101/2020.05.15.20103655v1.
Quintana, C. 2020. "US Colleges Scrambled to React to the Coronavirus Pandemic. Now Their Very Existence Is in Jeopardy." *USA Today*. Published March 25. www.usatoday.com/story/news/education/2020/03/20/coronavirus-college-students-online-class-graduation-commencement-refund/2876589001.
Reuters. 2020. "Wuhan Lockdown 'Unprecedented,' Shows Commitment to Contain Virus: WHO Representative in China." Published January 23. www.reuters.com/article/us-china-health-who-idUSKBN1ZM1G9.
Riley, P., S. Hayes, and J. Ryan. 2016. "Closing the Equity Gap in Health Care for Black Americans." Commonwealth Fund. Published July 15. www.commonwealthfund.org/blog/2016/closing-equity-gap-health-care-black-americans.
Samuels, B. 2020. "Trump Resists Pressure to Issue a Nationwide Stay-at-Home Order." *The Hill*. Published April 1. https://thehill.com/homenews/administration/490666-trump-resists-pressure-to-declare-nationwide-stay-at-home-order.
Santucci, J. 2020. "What We Know About the White House Coronavirus Task Force Now That Mike Pence Is in Charge." *USA Today*. Published February 27. www.usatoday.com/story/news/politics/2020/02/27/coronavirus-what-we-know-mike-pence-and-task-force/4891905002.
Schneider, K. P., and N. Davis. 2020. "Pandemic Proves Urgent Need for National Practitioner Licensing System." *Modern Healthcare*. Published April 13.
Social Security Administration. 2020. "Authority to Waive Requirements During National Emergencies." Accessed May 21. www.cms.gov/Medicare/Provider-Enrollment-and-Certification/SurveyCertEmergPrep/Downloads/1135-Waivers-Authority.pdf.
Spradlin, D. 2012. "Are You Solving the Right Problem?" *Harvard Business Review*. Published September. https://hbr.org/2012/09/are-you-solving-the-right-problem.
Strauss, V. 2020. "Millions of Students Could Be Home the Rest of the Academic Year." *Washington Post*. Published March 16. www.washingtonpost.com/

education/2020/03/16/millions-students-could-be-home-rest-academic-year-because-coronavirus-officials-warn.

Sullivan, L., G. Smith, and T. Mak. 2020. "Despite Early Warnings, U.S. Took Months to Expand Swab Production for COVID-19 Test." *NPR*. Published May 12. www.npr.org/2020/05/12/853930147/despite-early-warnings-u-s-took-months-to-expand-swab-production-for-covid-19-te.

Trump, D. J. 2020a. "Remarks by President Trump, Vice President Pence, and Members of the Coronavirus Task Force in Press Conference." White House. Published March 13. www.whitehouse.gov/briefings-statements/remarks-president-trump-vice-president-pence-members-coronavirus-task-force-press-conference-3.

———. 2020b. "Proclamation on Declaring a National Emergency Concerning the Novel Coronavirus Disease (COVID-19) Outbreak." White House. Published March 13. www.whitehouse.gov/presidential-actions/proclamation-declaring-national-emergency-concerning-novel-coronavirus-disease-covid-19-outbreak.

———. 2020c. "Proclamation—Suspension of Entry as Immigrants and Nonimmigrants of Certain Additional Persons Who Pose a Risk of Transmitting 2019 Novel Coronavirus." White House. Published March 11. www.whitehouse.gov/presidential-actions/proclamation-suspension-entry-immigrants-nonimmigrants-certain-additional-persons-pose-risk-transmitting-2019-novel-coronavirus.

———. 2020d. "Remarks by President Trump, Vice President Pence, and Members of the Coronavirus Task Force in Press Conference." White House. Published February 26. www.whitehouse.gov/briefings-statements/remarks-president-trump-vice-president-pence-members-coronavirus-task-force-press-conference.

———. 2020e. Twitter tweet by @realDonaldTrump. Published February 24. https://twitter.com/realDonaldTrump.

———. 2020f. "Remarks by President Trump at the White House Business Session with Our Nation's Governors." White House. Published February 10. www.whitehouse.gov/briefings-statements/remarks-president-trump-white-house-business-session-nations-governors.

Tucker, E. 2020. "What Exactly Is the Defense Production Act?" *Military Times*. Published March 19. www.militarytimes.com/news/your-military/2020/03/19/what-exactly-is-the-defense-production-act.

US Bureau of Labor Statistics. 2020. "The Employment Situation—June 2020." News release. Published July 2. www.bls.gov/news.release/pdf/empsit.pdf.

US Department of State. 2020. "Presidential Proclamation: Travel from Brazil and Europe." Updated May 27. https://travel.state.gov/content/travel/en/traveladvisories/presidential-proclamation--travel-from-europe.html.

US Health and Human Services (HHS). 2020. *Report to Congress: COVID-19 Strategic Testing Plan*. Published May 24. https://delauro.house.gov/sites/delauro.house.gov/files/HHS_COVID_Testing_Report.pdf.

US Health and Human Services, Office of Minority Health (Office of Minority Health). 2020. "Cancer and Hispanic Americans." Published February 21. https://minorityhealth.hhs.gov/omh/browse.aspx?lvl=4&lvlid=61.

———. 2019a. "Diabetes and African Americans." Published December 5. https://minorityhealth.hhs.gov/omh/browse.aspx?lvl=4&lvlid=18.

———. 2019b. "Heart Disease and African Americans." Published December 5. https://minorityhealth.hhs.gov/omh/browse.aspx?lvl=4&lvlid=19.

———. 2017. "Asthma Disease and African Americans." Accessed June 2, 2020. https://minorityhealth.hhs.gov/omh/browse.aspx?lvl=4&lvlid=15.

Watney, C., and A. Stapp. 2020. "Trump Is Using the Defense Production Act All Wrong." *Politico.* Published April 9. www.politico.com/news/agenda/2020/04/09/trump-defense-production-act-175920.

Welna, D. 2020. "Coronavirus Has Now Killed More Americans than Vietnam War." NPR. Published April 28. www.npr.org/sections/coronavirus-live-updates/2020/04/28/846701304/pandemic-death-toll-in-u-s-now-exceeds-vietnam-wars-u-s-fatalities.

Wingfield, A. H. 2020. "The Disproportionate Impact of Covid-19 on Black Health Care Workers in the U.S." Harvard Business Review. Published May 14. https://hbr.org/2020/05/the-disproportionate-impact-of-covid-19-on-black-health-care-workers-in-the-u-s.

World Health Organization. 2020. "'Immunity Passports' in the Context of Covid-19." Published April 24. www.who.int/news-room/commentaries/detail/immunity-passports-in-the-context-of-covid-19.

Worldometer. 2020. "United States Population." Accessed May 28. www.worldometers.info/world-population/us-population.

INDEX

ABOUT THE AUTHOR

Public service has been at the core of Michael R. Meacham's career and has enabled him to make a positive difference in the lives of others and for the benefit of the greater good. After graduating from Wichita State University with a degree in political science, Meacham was elected to the Kansas House of Representatives at the age of 23—while still enrolled in law school—and he served the people of Kansas for eight years. His law practice focused on environmental and telecommunications matters and, later, on lobbying efforts to improve healthcare services for the Medicaid population in the region. This experience inspired him to earn his MPH from Wichita State University/Kansas University Medical Center. His passion for strengthening health services delivery then took him to the state of Connecticut's Office of Health Care Access, where he spearheaded an overhaul of the state's Certificate of Need process as Director of Health System Development. He next turned his career to a practitioner role in health administration, joining the executive team at the Eastern Connecticut Health Network (ECHN) as Vice President for Integrated Health Services. As a change agent, he was responsible for operations external to the hospital, led implementation of a hospitalist program, and enabled the administrative team to be more collaborative in its work on behalf of patients, physicians, and other healthcare providers.

Taking the lessons learned from legislative, legal, regulatory, managerial, and health services delivery perspectives, Mr. Meacham first joined academia in 1999—initially as an adjunct and then a full-time professor and guest lecturer—in a tenure that lasted more than 17 years. As a longtime student of political science as well as healthcare, he continues to teach, advise, and mentor former and current undergraduate, MHA, and DHA students in health administration preparation programs presently at East Carolina University and, previously, at the Medical University of South Carolina, The Pennsylvania State University (where he directed the MHA program), and the University of Connecticut. With a reputation as a visionary leader and student-centered educator, Mr. Meacham has been a consultant, presenter, and guest lecturer on numerous healthcare and leadership topics for healthcare organizations, at numerous conferences and professional meetings, and on campuses across the country. He served on the Board and Executive Committee for AUPHA and was a Fellow and Site Visitor for the Commission on Accreditation of Healthcare